THE OXFORD HANDBOOK OF

NEW CULTURAL
HISTORY OF MUSIC

THE OXFORD HANDBOOK OF THE

NEW CULTURAL
HISTORY OF MUSIC

Edited by

JANE F. FULCHER

OXFORD
UNIVERSITY PRESS

OXFORD
UNIVERSITY PRESS

Oxford University Press is a department of the University of Oxford.
It furthers the University's objective of excellence in research, scholarship,
and education by publishing worldwide.

Oxford   New York
Auckland   Cape Town   Dar es Salaam   Hong Kong   Karachi
Kuala Lumpur   Madrid   Melbourne   Mexico City   Nairobi
New Delhi   Shanghai   Taipei   Toronto

With offices in
Argentina   Austria   Brazil   Chile   Czech Republic   France   Greece
Guatemala   Hungary   Italy   Japan   Poland   Portugal   Singapore
South Korea   Switzerland   Thailand   Turkey   Ukraine   Vietnam

Oxford is a registered trade mark of Oxford University Press
in the UK and certain other countries.

Published in the United States of America by
Oxford University Press
198 Madison Avenue, New York, NY 10016

Library of Congress Cataloging-in-Publication Data
The Oxford handbook of the new cultural history of music.
     p.   cm.
Includes index.
ISBN 978–0–19–534186–7 (hardcover); 978–0–19–935409-2 (paperback)
1. Musicology.   2. Music—Philosophy and aesthetics.
I. Fulcher, Jane F.
ML55.O97 2011
306.4'842—dc22   2010021716

9 8 7 6 5 4 3 2 1

Printed in the United States of America
on acid-free paper

For My Husband,
Robert Muchembled

ACKNOWLEDGMENTS

This volume was truly a collective and collegial enterprise, and I would like to thank not only all of the contributors to it but also the Executive music editor at Oxford University Press, Suzanne Ryan, without whose constant advice and encouragement it would not have been possible. I am also very grateful to Michael Mauskapf, who served as my technical assistant for the volume and whose conscientious and assiduous organization, as well as positive and helpful spirit, was essential in helping to realize this endeavor. In addition, I want to express my deep gratitude to the editorial board members of the Oxford New Cultural History of Music Series, Celia Applegate, Philip Bohlman, Kate van Orden, and Michael Steinberg. Not only have their advice and participation been essential, but their scholarship, integrity, and professionalism have been a constant inspiration and example. Finally, I would like to thank my husband, historian Robert Muchembled, whose inspiration, constant support, and patience throughout this enterprise have meant more than I could possibly express.

Contents

Politics, Aesthetics, and Transmission

Contributors

Celia Applegate is professor of history at the University of Rochester in New York and teaches European and German history. Her publications include *Bach in Berlin: Nation and Culture in Mendelssohn's Revival of the St. Matthew Passion* (2005), *Music and German National Identity*, coedited with Pamela Potter (2002), and "How German Is It? Nationalism and the Origins of Serious Music in Early Nineteenth-century Germany," in *19th-Century Music* (Spring 1998). She is currently working on a major study of the musical culture of modern Germany from the eighteenth century to the present.

Michael Beckerman is professor of music at New York University, having previously taught at Washington University in St. Louis, Missouri, and the University of California–Santa Barbara. His research has focused on Czech music, and his published works include *Dvorak and His World* and *Janacek and His World*. He received the Janacek Medal from the Czech Republic and is a laureate of the Czech Music Council. Beckerman also writes regularly for the *New York Times*.

Philip Bohlman serves as Mary Werkman Distinguished Service Professor of Music and the Humanities at the University of Chicago, where he also serves on the Jewish studies faculty. His published works include *Jewish Music and Modernity* (2008), *The Music of European Nationalism: Cultural Identity and Modern History* (2d ed., 2009), and *World Music: A Very Short Introduction* (2002). A pianist, he is also the artistic director of the New Budapest Orpheum Society, a Jewish cabaret ensemble in Chicago.

Leon Botstein has been the president of Bard College since 1975. As a conductor, he serves as the music director of both the American Symphony Orchestra and the Jerusalem Symphony Orchestra. He is the author of *Jefferson's Children: Education and the Promise of American Culture*, editor of the *Musical Quarterly*, coeditor of *Jews and the City of Vienna, 1870–1938*, and editor of *The Complete Brahms*. He has been the recipient of the Carnegie Corporation Academic Leadership Award, the Award for Distinguished Service to the Arts from the American Academy of Arts and Letters, Harvard University's Centennial Award, and the Austrian Cross of Honour for Science and Art.

James Borders is the Glenn McGeoch Collegiate Professor of Music and chair of the Musicology Department at the University of Michigan–Ann Arbor. He is former associate dean of graduate studies in music, theater, and dance, and former director of the Stearns Collection of Musical Instruments. He has held fellowships from the National Endowment for the Humanities and the National Endowment for the Arts, was a CIC Leadership Fellow in 1996–1997, and was nominated for an Amoco Teaching Award in 1998. He has published on a variety of topics from plainchant to the music of Frank Zappa in journals, including the *Journal of Musicological Research* and *Perspectives on New Music*.

Julie Brown is a reader in the Music Department at Royal Holloway, University of London. Among her publications are *Bartók and the Grotesque* (2007) and the edited collection *Western Music and Race* (2007), which was awarded the Ruth A. Solie Award by the American Musicological Society. She is currently working on a book on silent film sound in 1920s' Britain.

Andreas Dorschel is head of the Institute of Music Aesthetics at the University of Arts Graz (Austria). He was visiting professor at Emory University (1995) and at Stanford University (2006). His most recent publication is a history of the idea of metamorphosis: *Verwandlung: Mythologische Ansichten, technologische Absichten* (Neue Studien zur Philosophie, ed. Konrad Cramer, Jürgen Stolzenberg, and Reiner Wiehl, vol. 22, 2009).

Andy Fry joined the faculty of King's College, London, in 2007, having previously taught at the University of California–San Diego and, as a visiting professor, at Berkeley. His principal research areas are jazz (particularly pre-1950, race, gender, and historiography) and music in twentieth-century France. His publications include "Re-thinking the Revue nègre: Black Musical Theatre in Interwar Paris," in *Western Music and Race*, ed. Julie Brown (2007). He is completing a monograph on African American music and musicians in Paris up to 1960.

Jane F. Fulcher is the general editor of the Oxford New Cultural History of Music series. She received her MA and PhD from Columbia University and is professor of musicology at the University of Michigan. Her books include *The Nation's Image: French Grand Opera as Politics and Politicized Art, French Cultural Politics, and Music from the Dreyfus Affair to the First World War* (1999), and *The Composer as Intellectual: Music and Ideology in France 1914–1940* (2005). In addition, she is editor of (and contributor to) *Debussy and his* World (2001) and co-editor of (and contributor to) *Opera and Society in Italy and France from Monteverdi to* Bourdieu (2007). She has received research awards and grants form the ACLS, the National Endowment for the Humanities, the National Humanities Center, the Wissenschaftkolleg zu Berlin, the Centre national de la recherche scientifique (Paris), the Institute for Advanced Study, Princeton, New Jersey, and has three times been visiting professor at the École des hautes études en sciences sociales in Paris.

Charles Hiroshi Garrett is associate professor of musicology at the University of Michigan School of Music, Theatre, and Dance. His graduate work at the

University of California–Los Angeles was supported by an AMS Howard Mayer Brown Fellowship, as well as an AMS-50 Fellowship, and his dissertation received the Wiley Housewright Award from the Society for American Music. His book, *Struggling to Define a Nation: American Music and the Twentieth Century* (2008), was awarded the Irving Lowens Memorial Book Award by the Society for American Music. He now serves as editor in chief of *The Grove Dictionary of American Music* (2d ed.).

James Hepokoski has taught at Oberlin College Conservatory (1978–1988), at the University of Minnesota–Twin Cities (1988–1999), and is currently professor of musicology at Yale University. He was the coeditor of the musicological journal *19-Century Music* from 1992 to 2005. His publications include "Beyond the Sonata Principle," *Journal of the American Musicological Society* 55 (2002) and *Elements of Sonata Theory* (2006), which was the recipient of the Society for Music Theory's 2008 Wallace Berry Award.

Joseph S. C. Lam is interim director of the Confucius Institute at the University of Michigan and professor of music (musicology) at the School of Music, Theatre, and Dance at the University of Michigan–Ann Arbor. He is a former (1997–2009) director of the Stearns Collection of Musical Instruments (University of Michigan) and is the author of *State Sacrifices and Music in Ming China* (SUNY Press). Lam has also published extensively in academic journals and monographs, including the titles "Chinese Music and Its Globalized Past and Present" (*Macalester International* 2008) and "Imperial Music Agency in Ming (1368–1644) Music Culture," in *Culture, Courtiers, and Competition: The Ming Court* (2008).

Richard Leppert is Regents Professor and Morse Alumni Distinguished Teaching Professor in the Department of Cultural Studies and Comparative Literature at the University of Minnesota. The most recent of his ten books are *Beyond the Soundtrack: Representing Music in Cinema*, coedited with Daniel Goldmark and Lawrence Kramer, published by the University of California Press; and *Sound Judgment*, for the Ashgate series Contemporary Thinkers on Critical Musicology.

Edward Muir is the Clarence L. Ver Steeg Professor in the Arts and Sciences and holds a Charles Deering McCormick Professorship of Teaching Excellence at Northwestern University. Besides receiving Guggenheim and NEH fellowships, he has been a fellow at the Harvard University Center for Italian Renaissance Studies at Villa I Tatti, the Institute for Advanced Study, and the National Humanities Center. He is a general editor of the book series Palgrave Early Modern History: Culture and Society and the series editor for the I Tatti Italian Renaissance History monograph series with Harvard University Press. He is the author of *Civic Ritual in Renaissance Venice*, which won the Adams and Marraro prizes, and *Mad Blood Stirring: Vendetta in Renaissance Italy*, which also won the Marraro Prize.

Leon Plantinga served on the Yale faculty from 1963 until his retirement in 2005. For six years in the 1990s he was the director of the Division of the Humanities. After retirement, Plantinga spent a year at the Princeton Institute for Advanced Study and is currently interim director of the Yale Collection of Musical Instruments. He has written widely on music of the later eighteenth and the nineteenth centuries, including *Beethoven's Concertos: History, Style, Performance* (1999) and the text book *Romantic Music* (1984).

Carlotta Sorba is associate professor of contemporary history and cultural history at the University of Padua (Italy). She has worked intensively in theater, music, and society in nineteenth-century Europe. She is the author of *Teatri. L'Italia del melodramma nell'età del Risorgimento* (Bologna 2001) and the editor of *Il secolo del teatro. Spettacoli e spettacolarità nell'Ottocento europeo, Memoria e ricerca* 29 (2008).

Michael P. Steinberg is director of the Cogut Center for the Humanities and professor of history and music at Brown University. He also serves as associate editor of the *Musical Quarterly* and the *Opera Quarterly* and was a member of the Cornell University Department of History between 1988 and 2005. He has received fellowships from the American Council of Learned Societies, the National Endowment for the Humanities, and the John Simon Guggenheim Memorial Foundation and was awarded the Berlin Prize from the American Academy, Berlin, in 2003. He has published *Austria as Theater and Ideology: The Meaning of the Salzburg Festival* (2000) and *Listening to Reason: Culture, Subjectivity, and 19th-century Music* (2004).

Philipp Ther received his PhD in history at the Free University in Berlin (1997) and is Professor of Central European Hisotry at the University of Vienna Among his publications is *In der Mitte der Gesellschaft. Operntheater in Zentraleuropa 1815–1914* (2006). A revised English version of the book is forthcoming in 2010 under the title *Under the Spell of Nations: Opera Theatres in Central Europe* by Oxford University Press. He has received numerous awards, such as the John F. Kennedy Fellowship at Harvard University (1997–1998) and at the EHESS in Paris. He was also a fellow of the Alexander von Humboldt Foundation.

John Toews is professor of history and director of the Comparative History of Ideas Program at the University of Washington. He has been the recipient of the MacArthur "Genius Grant," and his most recent book, *Becoming Historical: Cultural Reformation and Public Memory in Early Nineteenth-century Berlin* (2004), won the Hans Rosenberg Prize of the American Historical Association for the best book in German and Central European history.

Kate van Orden is professor of music at the University of California–Berkeley and has served as editor in chief of the *Journal of the American Musicological Society*.

She has held fellowships from the Warburg Institute in London and the Columbia Society of Fellows in the Humanities and serves on the editorial boards of *Acta Musicologica* and the New Cultural History of Music series (Oxford University Press). Her recent book, *Music, Discipline, and Arms in Early Modern France* (2005), won the Lewis Lockwood Award from the American Musicological Society.

Jacqueline Waeber studied at the Université de Genève in France and is currently associate professor of music at Duke University. Her publications include *Musique et geste en France de Lully à la Révolution: Études sur la musique, le théâtre, et la danse* (2009) and "Jean-Jacques Rousseau's 'unité de mélodie,'" in the *Journal of the American Musicological Society* 62(1) (2009).

William Weber, professor emeritus at California State University–Long Beach, wrote *Music and the Middle Class* (1975/2003), *The Rise of Musical Classics in 18th-century England* (1992), and *The Great Transformation of Musical Taste: Concert Programming from Haydn to Brahms* (2008). He has arranged conferences for UCLA's William Andrews Clark Memorial Library.

Michael Mauskapf (technical assistant) is currently pursuing a PhD in musicology at the University of Michigan, where his research investigates the intersections between musical and organizational practices in America, with a particular emphasis on the symphony orchestra. A graduate of the University of Pennsylvania, he has presented his research at the national meetings of the American Musicological Society and the Society for American Music, and his work has been published in various peer-reviewed journals.

THE OXFORD HANDBOOK OF THE

NEW CULTURAL HISTORY OF MUSIC

INTRODUCTION: DEFINING THE NEW CULTURAL HISTORY OF MUSIC, ITS ORIGINS, METHODOLOGIES, AND LINES OF INQUIRY

JANE F. FULCHER

I. THE NEW THEORETICAL SYNTHESIS IN TWO CONVERGING DISCIPLINES

In recent years it has become increasingly evident that cultural history, in a distinctive new form, has been undergoing a revival not only in history but in the discipline of musicology as well. Indeed, it is difficult to ignore the fact that, as a result of discernibly converging perspectives, historians and musicologists are engaging in similar inquiries and employing a common range of theoretical concepts. They are doing so, moreover, as the result of a shared commitment to return to the goal of cultural history—of grasping meaning, understanding, and experience and learning how such experience is constructed and communicated through cultural objects and cultural practice. What distinguishes it, however, is the bracing new synthesis of theoretical perspectives and methodologies drawn from the "new cultural history" and "new musicology" of the 1980s, together with recent social, sociological, and anthropological theories. This synthesis has, in part, been propelled by a sense of crisis within the field of history provoked by charges of "perspectivism" and the focus on discursive constructions of the social world independent of "objective" or social verification. The French historian Roger Chartier registered these concerns in his *On the Edge of the Cliff: History, Language, and Practices* in 1997, as did American historians Joyce Appleby, Lynn Hunt, and Margaret Jacob even earlier in their *Telling the Truth about History*, published in 1994.

It is evident that both fields are now increasingly aware of the necessity of understanding the often complex interaction of social, political, and artistic phenomena in our analysis of the symbolic realm. Just as historians attempt to grasp the construction and transmission of meaning, so musicologists are turning their inquiries not only to cultural representations but also to social dynamics and to music's distinctive "register" of communication as an abstract and performing art.[1] For many musicologists the most fruitful aspect of recent historical directions has been the turn to the question of how patterns of cultural meaning are intertwined with the encompassing world of social and political significance.[2] Historians in turn have drawn attention to the fact that such cultural significations are manipulated and refracted in the act of enunciation inherent in each art's means of communication, as well as by the changing material modes of inscription of a given work. Both fields, moreover, are increasingly aware that individuals and groups make use of or appropriate symbols within the larger field of social power and representation—that symbols can become destabilized or contested and a symbolic battle or negotiation may thus ensue.

Indeed, there has been a new awareness of "representations" and their constructions ever since the launching of the interdisciplinary journal by that name at the University of California at Berkeley in 1983. Musicologists, of course, have long been sensitive to the ways in which power may employ the theater and particularly opera to represent either the authority and social order that sustains it or that it aspires eventually to ensconce. However, they have more recently recognized that opera is neither transparent in its agenda nor ever entirely instrumental, for it is a composite form of representation, one that is both unique and in continual dialogue with the social and discursive world that surrounds it. Moreover, musicology has learned to be aware of what Louis Marin has described (with reference to painting) as "the gap between the visible—what is shown, figured, represented, staged—and the legible—what can be said, enunciated, declared."[3] As we now recognize, each mode of communication embodies a different register of representation, and although they intersect with and respond to each other as in opera, which may create a uniquely complex enunciation, they never entirely merge.

The new theoretical synthesis, of course, has built in important ways upon the dual contributions of the "new musicology" and the "new cultural history" of the past three decades. The former drew necessary attention to the questions of meaning, reception, and interpretation or "criticism," as well as to politics, ideology, and gender, and in doing so discovered or rediscovered the significance of theorists, including Jacques Derrida, Theodor Adorno, Wolgang Iser, and Clifford Geertz.[4] Simultaneously, the "new cultural history," as well as the "cultural studies" movement in several adjacent fields, felt the impact of the "linguistic turn" in the humanities, or the focus on the semiotic functions of language and the cultural construction and transmission of meaning.[5]

The new cultural history, as codified in a volume of that title, edited by Lynn Hunt and published in 1989, distinguished itself not only from social history but also from the older intellectual history. Here the focus was not on ideas or systems of thought but instead on encompassing patterns of meaning, symbols, assumptions, and feelings, and the contributors drew heavily on cultural theory, including the anthropological, the philosophical, and the literary. Of particular importance were feminist theorists such as Julia Kristeva, Luce Iragary, and Joan Scott, as well as literary theorists, including Mikhail Bakhtin and the poststructuralist Jacques Derrida, with their insights into "difference," marginalized communities, perspective or "construction," and the instability of meaning. The influence of figures such as these also helped expand the territory, as well as the sources, of historical inquiry to include the body, the senses, fiction and reading, images, and a wide range of social and cultural practices.[6]

In both the new musicology and the new cultural history, symbolic anthropology (in particular the work of Clifford Geertz) proved influential in furthering the shift from the empiricist, or the literal and "positivist," toward interpretation and a new sensitivity to the symbolic realm. Beginning in the 1980s innovative historians and musicologists thus sought to approach culture as a "text" to be deciphered—as neither a simple reflection of an economic substructure, as in older Marxist interpretations, nor an element of an encompassing idealist "Zeitgeist."[7] Significantly, however, in a seminal essay the French cultural historian Roger Chartier attacked the uncritical application of Geertzian symbolic anthropology to history. His admonitions center on two points: first, that the historian must rely not on empirical observations or fieldwork but on texts, and second, that the latter should be approached not in the literal but in the broader metaphorical sense.[8]

We must, then, as Chartier adjures, consider a source's "textuality" and perceive those larger patterns of meaning that are intertwined with the encompassing "social world of significance." For these meanings are necessarily manipulated and refracted in the rhetorical or aesthetic act of enunciation inherent in each mode, each "register" of cultural or artistic communication."[9] Second, Chartier asks, how stable are symbols, particularly in the context of advanced Western cultures—are they "shared like the air we breathe" (to quote Geertz), or are they rather mobile, polysemous, and equivocal? Is there a common symbolic universe of replicated meanings interacting within a "web" in a developed modern culture, or are symbols more characteristically diverted, subverted, and contested? Semantic investment in symbols is unquestionably central to all cultures, but in the modern world so, too, is subsequent "disinvestment" and multiple reinvestment of meaning.[10]

Indeed, Chartier was not alone in his concerns: In the course of the 1990s other scholars began to critique the overemphasis on cultural construction and the concomitant "retreat from verification" in the interest of theory and interpretation. As early as his seminal essay on "thick description" (1973), Geertz himself pointed out the limits of such textual or purely cultural analysis and observed the danger that it may "lose touch with the hard surfaces of life" such as economic and political structures.[11] By the end of the decade historians had widely begun to question what many now perceived as an overly exclusive emphasis on cultural systems and on language, or "the displacement of the social in favor of culture," as evidenced in the collection edited by Victoria Bonnel and Lynn Hunt, *Beyond the Cultural Turn*, published in 1999.[12]

One immediate response was to reexamine the implications of figures who focus primarily on the analysis of social forces and particularly of power— how it is exercised, as well as contested or undermined. These included not only the French philosopher Michel Foucault and the sociologist Pierre Bourdieu but also major figures in German sociology such as Norbert Elias and Jürgen Habermas. Foucault's examination of the social and political role of "discourse" now became increasingly influential, and the term prominently entered the vocabulary of disciplines not only in the social sciences but also in the humanities. Few today would dispute Michel Foucault's intellectually seismic assertion that discourse defines or "authorizes" knowledge: It renders visible; it "produces" what we see. As he so incisively demonstrated, discourse not only furnishes those conceptual categories through which we conceive reality within a period but also shapes or articulates and legitimizes all of our subsequent discoveries. Foucault, of course, is frequently grouped with postmodernists because of his questioning of the possibility of objective knowledge, but his insights into means of social control through discourse still impart a social dimension or grounding to his analysis.[13]

If Foucault revealed the extent to which social power is insinuated in discourse, his colleague at the Collège de France, sociologist Pierre Bourdieu, did the same with symbols and language, thus reembedding cultural analysis within the social. Perhaps the most forceful vector of Bourdieu's work for historical study has been his insight into the way in which relations of power are imminent or embodied in all realms of symbolic exchange.[14] Particularly resonant in the humanities has been Bourdieu's concept of "symbolic domination"—the attempt to constitute or reproduce social hierarchies through the definition of "symbolic legitimacy" and "symbolic capital." His concomitant concept of "symbolic violence" refers to the invisibility of this imposition, which maintains the existing order but without recourse to physical violence.[15]

As Bourdieu has shown, symbolic violence may occur not only within a colonial context and in class relations but also in the relations between the sexes, as he demonstrated so tellingly in *La domination masculine*. It also occurs politically, for groups in power impose representations or symbols that provoke a wide range of responses across a broad spectrum from domination, or acquiescence, to contestation.[16] Before feeling the full impact of Bourdieu musicology, like history, was locked in either a narrow and literal or a philosophical conception of the political; it was his work, together with Foucault's, that allowed us to identify political power in systems of representation, as well as in challenges to them. Moreover, Bourdieu, in particular, has now taught us to perceive how the symbols that authority has inculcated for political ends—in many possible forms or styles—is a prerequisite to both interpreting culture and deciphering politics.

We have hence grown increasingly aware that culture is neither extraneous to politics nor devoid of authentic political content but may rather be a fundamental symbolic expression or articulation of the political. Scholars in several fields have thus sought to unlock the language of symbolic domination and the idioms through which social actors, on various levels and in different sectors, respond. From this dialogic perspective styles or symbols we have previously considered apolitical must necessarily be reconsidered or the structure of symbolic opposition revealed.[17] Musicology, however, long neglected Bourdieu or slighted his insights into power and its deployment of symbols in favor of the social, symbolic analysis of Adorno and Geertz. Only recently has the field attempted to expand its notions of how to cast the relation between music and ideology or politics to include other approaches, those that go beyond the literal, the textual, and the philosophical or metaphoric.

As several chapters in this volume demonstrate, musicologists have begun to ask why those symbolic exchanges and the power relations that they embody, as Bourdieu has made visible, have not been identified or analyzed systematically in their field. Indeed, the issue of why musicology has skirted Bourdieu's social and political grounding of symbols has compelled the discipline to recognize premises that have long persisted without reflection, buttressing the predominance of other paradigms and in particular Adorno's.[18] One tangible example is the case of neoclassicism: From Adorno's philosophical perspective it is monolithic—a crystallized social formation and, like all traditions, inherently inimical to freedom and to the critical spirit. Within his essentialist manner of associating ideological orientations with aesthetic values and styles, contestation within neoclassicism is invisible, a theoretical impossibility.

Adorno's framework for the perception of contestation in music or of resistance to domination as he construes it is not empirical, relational, or contextual, as it is in Bourdieu. For Adorno, unlike Bourdieu, is not refuting structuralism or Sartrean existentialism but rather Hegel and the tradition of glorifying the "sublation of the individual . . . in the comprehensive other." Thus, although, like Bourdieu, he associates domination with a closed, repressive social structure, one perpetuated by a reified tradition, his answer is cast philosophically or metaphorically. Adorno, then, and those influenced primarily by him sought not to recognize semiotic strategies within a social field of power but to focus on the way in which the individual seeks "freedom" or is able to preserve an unfixed identity.[19]

Within this "negative dialectic," repressive classic forms and the rational reconciliation that they embody must be dissolved through innovation in processes that oppose authority, totality, or "structure." His paradigm, then, is the artist's new organization and working through of the material itself: This, as in Schoenberg, is what he identifies with the advanced, autonomous artwork. Given Adorno's focus on the dialectic of technique and material, the destruction of "fixed meaning" or emancipation from false resolution cannot occur within a formal tradition.[20] Yet, other scholars and I have identified a quest for freedom, for contestation of domination and repression within wartime and postwar classicism, in my case from the perspective of Bourdieu's theoretical insights. For they allow us to perceive that, historically, contestation can occur through traditional genres, forms, and styles, the logic of which can be challenged by strategies that open up or disrupt the language.[21]

The focus on strategies and "practices" is another important new historical direction, one begun by practitioners of the new cultural history and then expanded under the impetus of more recent theoretical insights. Initially the work of Mikhail Bakhtin drew attention to the ways in which popular culture could subvert, manipulate, or penetrate high culture, specifically with reference to the work of Rabelais.[22] Scholars soon combined his influence with that of theorists such as Michel de Certeau, who stressed the importance of cultural "practice" or uses as opposed to a more passive consumption of culture. As he observed, cultural products may be creatively employed, manipulated, or "appropriated" through specific strategies and often on the part of those groups who are politically or socially dominated. It is within this context that more recent historians have done important work on reading practices, which has had a palpable influence on musicology as well. Musicologists such as Kate van Orden, for example, have stressed the importance of approaching music in the early modern period within the context not only of "print culture" but also of reading practices and of actual usages. Just as influential have been recent anthropological developments in "performance theory," or the study of the ways in which performance is socially framed and how this necessarily impacts the work's enunciation, as anthropologist Victor Turner has shown.[23]

Equally important in the sphere of "practice" has been the work of the German historical sociologist Norbert Elias, who analyzed the larger social and political dynamics of cultural practice in the early modern period. Elias's book of 1939, *The Civilizing Process*, has only recently been rediscovered, now from the perspective of his study of court behavior, its gradual development, and the way in which it imposed control over the self, including both manners and the emotions.[24] More recently, historians such as Alain Corbin have focused on the history of the senses, or of perception, as shaped by changing modes of experience and by means of social control. Corbin was also a pioneer in what is now generally referred to in both musicology and ethnomusicology as the "soundscape," or the larger cultural and political context of hearing. His *Village Bells* (1994) was concerned with the way bells were heard and experienced in the past and specifically how they were closely associated with both piety and parochialism, or with a sense of place.[25] In his contribution to this volume ethnomusicologist Joseph Lam is similarly interested in the issues of both soundscape and practice with regard not only to power but also to those who were dominated in twelfth- and thirteenth-century China.

Public meaning and experience, as well as public memory, have served as another flourishing path of research not only within recent historical studies but also in the field of musicology. Initially sociologists such as the German Jürgen Habermas drew attention to what he termed "the public sphere," or the domains of public life as they developed in the course of the later eighteenth century. Habermas connected this phenomenon with the rise of what we now generally call "public opinion," which is associated with an implicit sense of responsibility and rights on the part of those governed within a political system.[26] Linked to this concept has been that of public memory, as well as of a sense of both community and traditions, as embodied in the work of figures such as Pierre Nora, Benedict Anderson, and Eric Hobsbawm.

The monumental collection of essays that Nora edited between 1984 and 1993, titled *Les lieux de mémoire*, concerns major sites of social, political, and cultural collective memory. The history of shared memory has also been developed within the context of manipulations or inventions on the part of political power, as demonstrated by the collection of essays coedited by Eric Hobsbawm and Terence Ranger, *The Invention of Tradition*. The complementary concept of the invention or "imagination" of communities was also developed by Benedict Anderson, whose *Imagined Communities* (1983) has had an ostensibly broad impact.[27] Significantly, several of the essays in this volume, written by both musicologists and historians, concern collective memory, invented traditions, and imagined communities, particularly those of historian Philipp Ther and musicologist James Hepokoski.

Just as important as the study of the cultural definition or symbolic distinction of communities has been that of their development of a sense of the "other," including their cultural encounters, or points of contact and interaction. Ever since Edward Said's seminal literary study of the way in which cultures represent, distort, or construct each other, his *Orientalism* (1978), historians and musicologists have become interested not only in the construction of cultural boundaries but also more recently with points of interpenetration and mutual discovery.[28] This we may see in historian Celia Applegate's chapter in this volume, in which she examines the cultural "symbiosis" and often the interaction of musicians through their professionally necessary international travels in the eighteenth and nineteenth centuries. Cultural "translation," or the appropriation of elements of one culture by another, has similarly become a major point of interest for ethnomusicologists, as we may see from Philip Bohlman's contribution on Herder's cultural translations in this volume.

In sum, it is evident that both historians and musicologists are now striving not only to return to the goal of capturing the texture and the complexity of experience, understanding, and communication in the past but also to do so by means of a theoretically sophisticated approach that combines a semiotic, cultural analysis with a deeper understanding of surrounding social forces and their dynamics. They are equally conscious of how their questions are framed in order to yield the most insight on both of these levels and hence attempt to define the most appropriate contexts through which to explore the cultural object and its multifaceted significance.

II. EMERGING APPROACHES, LINES OF INQUIRY, AND THE NEW AGENDA

Not only is it revealing that historians and musicologists are now asking similar kinds of questions about past cultures and employing a new synthesis of methodologies, but both fields are identifying music as a privileged point of entry into these inquiries, and thus are engaging in a sustained collaboration. It is difficult to ignore the fact that, recently, leading journals in history, such as the *Journal of Modern History* and the *American Historical Review*, now regularly review those books by musicologists that attempt to achieve these goals. Moreover, it has become an inescapable phenomenon that more and more historians are turning to music despite the difficulties of mastering the analytic dimension and the technical specificities of the musical language.[29] They are similarly aware of the necessity of understanding the "champ" or field, to use Bourdieu's term, or the specific domain of culture, with its own degree of autonomy, workings, and conventions that can, like a prism, at specific moments approach or open up to other such fields.[30]

Most striking, perhaps, is that scholars in both areas are now exploring music under similar historical rubrics, those emerging from the recent synthesis of theoretical perspectives on society and culture that we have seen. As this volume vividly demonstrates, these include questions of cultural identity and its expression, or its constructions, representations, and exchanges, into which music provides a significant mode of access. The scholars who work in these areas are concerned with those cultural sites of the construction or attempted control of identity, as well as its interrogation through active agency on a social and an individual level, which embraces subjectivity and its relation to the larger cultural unit. This line of inquiry includes the study of how new perceptions or awareness may be realized or enunciated through musical language; it also embraces investigation of the development of new modes of understanding in or around music, as well as of the way in which such meaning is produced or communicated even in the midst of social or political attempts to control it.

Here we may see attempts on the part of both historians and musicologists to engage with the new ways of perceiving the articulation of music, ideology, and politics opened up by figures such as Foucault, Bourdieu, Elias, and Habermas. For their study of meaning and symbols is both relational and contextual as they strive to unlock the idioms not only of social or political power but also of the strategies of contestation or refusal. They are similarly interested in identity as defined within the public sphere and the ways in which such public or national identity may be questioned through specific practices or the experience of cultural encounters.

Part I of this volume accordingly comprises sections devoted to *Constructions or Representations of the Body, Gender, Sexuality, and Race; Subjectivity and the Shaping of the Self in Society; Nationalism, Cosmopolitanism, and Transnationalism,* and *Popular and Elite Cultural Intersections or Exchanges.* The historians and musicologists working in these areas approach music as a cultural form that communicates diverse kinds of discourses, including ideology or political rhetoric, while realizing that the material or cultural forms that carry such discourse cannot be reduced to the discourses they were intended to carry.[31] Moreover, they are aware of what the artwork can do to the discourse or to a text either consciously on the part of the artist, or on a subconscious level, or as a result of music's unique register of representation and its specific dynamics as a performing art. As some of the chapters demonstrate, because of music's abstraction and its physical nature it can more easily transmit certain aspects of identity or experience than others, while inherently altering them in the very act of representation.

Other scholars represented in this volume are particularly interested in cultural practice, collective memory, transmission, and evaluation as they are both forged and then negotiated, as influenced by figures such as de Certeau, Corbin, Chartier, and Nora. Hence, part II of this collection is devoted to cultural experience, practice, and appropriations, grouping together those cultural arenas in which music both illuminates and is further illuminated, technically and aesthetically, by a study of its uses, collective practices, modes of inscription, and evaluation or reception. These include *Urban, Aural, and Print Culture; Symbols, Icons, and Sites of Collective Memory or Ritual*, and *Aesthetics, Politics, and Transmission*. Scholars working in these areas have become concerned with how cultural or social experience may shape creative or professional decisions and with the manner in which the public comes to appropriate or to know and use a specific artistic work.

The approaches taken here demonstrate an awareness of the fact that the manner in which a work is diffused or transmitted becomes an integral part of how, historically, it assumes a cultural "sense." The contributors to this section, both historians and musicologists, are apprised of all the dimensions that may affect the construction of signification, including specific material inscriptions and the symbolic potential of the artistic language. Hence, here we see a concern with how the forms assumed by texts become an essential element in the creation of their meaning since different groups encounter, "possess," and experience a work in various ways and within the context of different aural and visual cultures, as Leon Botstein's chapter so aptly demonstrates.

Indeed, in the computer age, when the same text may be apprehended through variable mediums of representation and reproduction, we are more cognizant of how the material means through which texts are communicated help to determine their signification or cultural sense. This has also stimulated study of how networks or communities of both creation and reception come into being within or across national boundaries and concomitantly of the role of cultural exchanges and new technologies. Scholars seeking to study the realms of cultural experience, practice, and appropriation are equally aware of how artistic works or emerging artistic languages may foster or articulate new experience, as I illustrate in my own chapter in this volume. Moreover, they perceive that truly innovative works can help to develop new modes of reception and hence of thought within different "sound cultures," both drawing on and acting back upon the social and cultural world.[32]

The new lines of inquiry, theoretical synthesis, or the agenda characteristic of the new cultural history of music—all vividly illustrated here—must, of course, be sustained through a continuing collaboration between those historians and musicologists who are centrally concerned with culture. Musicologists need to apprise themselves of the most recent and relevant historical literature and remain aware that, if they are to pose historical questions relating music to ideology and politics, they must do so with a complete knowledge not only of the musical field but also of others that, at specific moments, impinged upon it. They must similarly remain cognizant of the relevant surrounding discourses that interacted in historically specific manners with those of the musical field—how they helped to shape terminology, approaches, and central concepts.

Historians, in turn, if they seek to employ music as a significant mode of access to cultural experience, practice, and understanding in the past, must familiarize themselves with those musicological sources that illuminate essential elements of the musical language and the musical culture. Finally, both disciplines, if they wish to understand the historical and musicological significance of theatrical works (particularly of opera), must recognize the complexity of its enunciation and its close relation to its specific modes of inscription, experience, and reception, as Edward Muir's contribution to this volume tellingly illustrates. For the message of an opera historically cannot be equated simply with the supposed intent of the composer, the librettist, or the institution producing it but rather must be approached in terms of a tense negotiation or a semiotically complex interaction at temporally, socially, and culturally specific moments.

The new cultural history of music seeks to investigate precisely such arenas in which a close musical analysis must interact with a sophisticated understanding of the semiotic or linguistic dimension while maintaining a comprehensive grasp of the relevant social, cultural, and political dynamics. There are many such avenues of research, as the scholars in this volume demonstrate, all of which compel us to employ the emerging theoretical or methodological composite discussed in the beginning of this Introduction. Music examined from the perspective of areas such as print culture, aural experience, or "soundscapes" and their relation to political power, national memory, or cultural icons demands that we remain open to this resonant theoretical synthesis while seeking out the most historically relevant contexts. Such an approach will also allow us to perceive new aspects of the musical language, its meaning, and evolution, as well as how it "spoke" or communicated historically within the landscapes of now distant or foreign cultures.

Finally, as this volume demonstrates, the new cultural history of music requires that musicologists take history seriously and remain apprised of its most fruitful new directions and that historians work closely with musicologists, consulting the relevant musicological sources. To this end, departments training scholars in both fields must in turn encourage students to develop the requisite skills, historical, theoretical, and musicological in innovative new programs that cross the boundaries of the once separate disciplines. Only by doing so can we continue to recast the questions that both fields are asking, thus bringing them closer and developing the new cultural history of music in an ever more resonant, mutually fruitful synthesis.

NOTES

1. See Roger Chartier, *On the Edge of the Cliff: History, Language, and Practices*, trans. Lydia G. Cochrane (Baltimore: Johns Hopkins University Press, 1997), and Joyce Appleby, Lynn Hunt, and Margaret Jacob, eds., *Telling the Truth about History* (Berkeley: University of California Press, 1994).

2. I have focused on this interaction in several books that trace the tight imbrication of politics and ideology with French culture and music, including *The Nation's Image:*

French Grand Opera as Politics and Politicized Art (New York: Cambridge University Press, 1987), *French Cultural Politics and Music from the Dreyfus Affair to the First World War* (New York: Oxford University Press, 1999), and *The Composer as Intellectual: Music and Ideology in France 1914–1940* (New York: Oxford University Press, 2005).

3. See Charter, *On the Edge of the Cliff*, 90–103.

4. For example, see Joseph Kerman, *Contemplating Music* (Cambridge, Mass.: Harvard University Press, 1985); D. Kern Holoman and Claude V. Palisca, *Musicology in the 1980s: Methods, Goals, Opportunities* (New York: Da Capo, 1982); Rose Rosengard Subotnik, "The Role of Ideology in the Study of Western Music," *Journal of Musicology* 2(1) (Winter 1983): 1–12; Susan McClary, *Feminine Endings: Music, Gender, and Sexuality* (Minneapolis: University of Minnesota Press, 2002); Richard Leppert and Susan McClary, eds., *Music and Society: The Politics of Composition, Performance, and Reception* (New York: Cambridge University Press, 1987); Gary Tomlinson, "The Web of Culture: A Context for Musicology," *19-Century Music* 7(3) (1984): 350–62; and Carolyn Abbate, *Unsung Voices: Opera and Musical Narrative in the Nineteenth Century* (Princeton, N.J.: Princeton University Press, 1991).

5. On the "linguistic turn" in both history and the humanities see John E. Toews, "Intellectual History after the Linguistic Turn: The Autonomy of Meaning and the Irreducibility of Experience," *American Historical Review* 92(4) (1987): 879–907. Also see Lynn Hunt, ed., *The New Cultural History* (Berkeley: University of California Press, 1989). On the "cultural studies" movement as it originated in Great Britain see Peter Burke, *What Is Cultural History?* (Malden, Mass.: Polity, 2008), 140–41.

6. See Hunt, *New Cultural History*, 1–22, and Burke, *What Is Cultural History?* 51–53, 79, 116.

7. See Clifford Geertz, *The Interpretation of Cultures* (New York: Basic Books, 1973), and Tomlinson, "Web of Culture."

8. Roger Chartier, "Texts, Symbols, and Frenchness," *Journal of Modern History* 57(4) (Dec. 1985): 682–95.

9. Chartier, "Texts, Symbols, and Frenchness," 683–84. On the concept of different "registers" of communication see Chartier's discussion of the work of Louis Marin in *On the Edge of the Cliff*, 9–103.

10. Chartier, "Texts, Symbols, and Frenchness," 691.

11. Burke, *What Is Cultural History?* 115.

12. Victoria E. Bonnel and Lynn Hunt, eds., *Beyond the Cultural Turn: New Directions in the Study of Society and Culture* (Berkeley: University of California Press, 1999). See the introduction by Bonnel and Hunt, 9.

13. On the concept of discourse see Michel Foucault, *L'ordre du discours* (Paris: Gallimard, 1971), as well as his *Les mots et les choses: Une archéologie des sciences humaines* (Paris: Gallimard, 1966). Also see the introduction by Bonnel and Hunt to the collection they coedited, *Beyond the Cultural Turn*, 3, 9.

14. I have developed this point in my chapter, "Symbolic Domination and Contestation in French Music: Shifting the Paradigm from Adorno to Bourdieu," in *Opera and Society in Italy and France from Monteverdi to Bourdieu*, ed. Victoria Johnson, Jane F. Fulcher, and Thomas Ertman (New York: Cambridge University Press, 2007), 312–29.

15. For a detailed discussion of Bourdieu's concept of symbolic violence see Niilo Kauppi, *The Politics of Embodiment: Habits, Power, and Pierre Bourdieu's Theory* (New York: Lang, 2000), 6 ff.

16. Pierre Bourdieu, *La domination masculine* (Paris: Seuil, 1998).

17. See Pierre Bourdieu, "Penser la politique," *Actes de recherches en sciences sociales* (March 1988): 2–3. Also see David Swartz, *Culture and Power: the Sociology of Pierre Bourdieu* (Chicago: University of Chicago Press, 1995), p. 7.

18. Fulcher, "Symbolic Domination and Contestation," 312.

19. See Hauke Brunkhorst, "Irreconcilable Modernity: Adorno's Experimentalism and the Transgression Theorem," in *The Actuality of Adorno: Critical Essays on Adorno and the Postmodern*, ed. Max Pensky (Albany: State University of New York Press, 1997), 47–49. Also see Eric L. Krakauer, *The Disposition of the Subject: Reading Adorno's Dialectic of Technology* (Evanston, Ill.: Northwestern University Press, 1998), 139, 143.

20. See Peter U. Hohendahl, *Prismatic Thought: Theodor Adorno* (Lincoln: University of Nebraska Press, 1995), 200. Also see Theodor Adorno, *Philosophy of Modern Music*, trans. Anne G. Mitchell and Wesley V. Bloomster (London: Sheed and Ward, 1973), 165–67.

21. See Fulcher, *Composer as Intellectual*, 172–95, and Glenn Watkins, *Proof through the Night: Music and the Great War* (Berkeley: University of California Press, 2003).

22. See Burke, *What Is Cultural History?* 53–54, and Mikhail Bakhtin, *Rabelais and His World*, trans. Hélène Iswolsky (Bloomington: Indiana University Press, 1984). Significantly, as Burke points out, the book was first translated into both French and English in 1965.

23. Burke, *What Is Cultural History?* 79–80. Also see Michel de Certeau, *L'invention du quotidien* (Paris: Gallimard, 1990). On reading practices as related to the history of the book, see Roger Chartier, *Publishing Drama in Early Modern Europe* (Panizzi Lectures) (London: British Library, 1999). On the relevance of the study of print culture and reading for musicology see Kate van Orden, ed., *Music and the Cultures of Print* (New York: Garland, 2000). Also see Richard Bauman, *Story, Performance, and Event: Contextual Studies of Oral Narrative* (New York: Cambridge University Press, 1986), and Victor Turner, *The Anthropology of Performance* (New York: PAJ, 1986).

24. See Chartier, *On the Edge of the Cliff*, 124–31, and Norbert Elias, *The Civilizing Process*, trans. Edmund Jephcott (Cambridge, Mass.: Blackwell, 1994).

25. Alain Corbin, *Village Bells: Sound and Meaning in the Nineteenth-century French Countryside*, trans. Martin Thom (New York: Columbia University Press, 1998), and Burke, *What Is Cultural History?* 112.

26. See William Weber, "Opera and the Cultural Authority of the Capital City," in Johnson, Fulcher, and Ertman, *Opera and Society in Italy and France*, 167–68, and Craig Calhoun, ed., *Habermas and the Public Sphere* (Cambridge, Mass.: Harvard University Press, 1992).

27. See Pierre Nora's multivolume *Les lieux de mémoire* (Paris: Gallimard, 1984–1993). Also see Eric Hobsbawm and Terence Ranger, *The Invention of Tradition* (New York: Cambridge University Press, 1992), and Benedict Anderson, *Imagined Communities: Reflections on the Origin and Spread of Nationalism* (New York: Verso, 2006).

28. Edward W. Said, *Orientalism* (New York: Vintage, 1978), and Burke, *What Is Cultural History?* 121.

29. See, for example, Michael P. Steinberg, *Listening to Reason: Culture, Subjectivity, and Nineteenth-century Music* (Princeton, N.J.: Princeton University Press, 2004); William Weber, *Music and the Middle Class: The Social Structure of Concert Life in London, Paris, and Vienna* (London: Croom Helm, 1975); James Johnson, *Listening in Paris: A Cultural History* (Berkeley: University of California Press, 1995); and the final chapter of Carl E. Schorske's classic *Fin-de-siècle Vienna: Politics and Culture* (New York: Knopf, 1980).

30. See Burke, *What Is Cultural History?* 58, and my discussion of the implications of Johan Huizinga's related concept of historical shift in the "cultural landscape" in Fulcher, *French Cultural Politics and Music*, 12.

31. See Chartier, *On the Edge of the Cliff*, 94.

32. The concept of the interaction of text and its reception was initially developed by German scholars such as Wolfgang Iser. See, for example, his *Der Akt des Lesens* (Munich: Fink, 1976).

PART I

CULTURAL IDENTITY AND ITS EXPRESSION: CONSTRUCTIONS, REPRESENTATIONS, AND EXCHANGES

CHAPTER 1

GENDER, PERFORMATIVITY, AND ALLUSION IN MEDIEVAL SERVICES FOR THE CONSECRATION OF VIRGINS

JAMES BORDERS

MUSICOLOGISTS claiming familiarity with their field's historiography would doubtless recognize the impact Leo Treitler's work has had on chant research. It was Treitler who in the mid-1970s revolutionized the study of chant transmission by applying Milman Parry and Albert Lord's theory of oral-formulaic composition to Gregorian melodies.[1] Over the next two decades many chant specialists added their voices to the debate over Treitler's ideas.[2] Some delved into the historical record,[3] others developed linguistic models,[4] and still others looked for parallels between the musical procedures and ethnographies of contemporary and medieval singers, much as Parry and Lord themselves had done.

Preeminent among the ethnographically inclined scholars, Peter Jeffery advanced an ambitious program of cross-cultural and cross-temporal comparisons.[5] Through no lack of expertise and effort on his part, however, the kind of comparative study he envisioned over a decade and a half ago has not prospered. Not only does it still take years for students to acquire "the highly specialized skills... to investigate the ancient [chant] manuscripts and notation, the history of ancient... theoretical concepts, and the intricacies of the liturgy and its theological rationale,"[6] but few scholars of Western chant have also cultivated comparable knowledge of traditional sacred musical cultures. Moreover, chant specialists who consult recent ethnomusicological literature encounter a changed field, particularly as regards its theoretical sophistication. Informing disciplines of anthropology, linguistics, and history have also changed, as have the ways such scholarship connects with new subfields.

If the cultural study of plainchant that Treitler inaugurated and Jeffery and others enriched is to advance, scholars must forge new interdisciplinary connections to developing fields of human-centered knowledge. In this chapter I propose an appeal to ritual studies, which at its most basic seeks to explain the meaning of cultural phenomena through interpretation.[7] In the formulation of anthropologist Clifford Geertz, ritual dramatizes, enacts, or performs systems of symbols.[8] If Gregorian chants may be broadly considered as sacred, often scriptural texts sung in Christian rituals, one might ask what role the chants played in the rhetorical strategy used to create and maintain a religious worldview in the Middle Ages.[9] How did they serve as elements of medieval religious and literary discourses, not merely part of a superstructure but actually productive of power? What did the chants mean to those who sang them, and how was that meaning created?

As a step toward addressing these questions and to cast this endeavor in sharp relief against prior analyses of the Mass and office, I invite you to examine tenth- and eleventh-century rituals for consecrating virgins. These are described in pontificals, liturgical books with prayers, chants, and rubrics for services over which a bishop and sometimes an abbot presided.[10] Besides the consecration of virgins, pontificals include accounts of clerical ordination, monastic profession, church dedication, the blessing of an altar and other cult objects, and the consecration of a cemetery. These are replete with potent combinations of Christian symbolism, liturgical action, and sacred song. Pontifical services also differed from place to place and continued to develop throughout the Middle Ages, further enhancing their value for cultural historians. While preparing a music edition of medieval pontifical chants, I observed that services for the consecration of virgins were more variable than comparable ones for clerical ordination. They also included more chants, the selection of which differed greatly with location and over time.[11]

From the perspective of ritual studies, the consecration of virgins was a rite of passage in which a mature woman was inducted permanently as a nun into a female religious establishment.[12] A bishop presided; the nuns of the monastery also participated. The efficacy of the consecration depended in part on prescribed actions by the bishop, consecrands, and other participants, but equally essential were the written texts sung in the course of the ritual. These included short chants called antiphons, which were assigned to the consecrands. In this chapter I develop the thesis that the meaning that such texts imparted had an influence not just on their placement and function in the ritual but also on their language and allusions to other similarly meaningful texts within a culture-specific nexus of referents. I also consider the extent to which some of these meanings were gendered.[13] My examination focuses on the earliest accounts of the ritual but could be extended to later ones and other rituals.

The first type of pontifical to furnish texts and directions for performance, known as rubrics, sufficient to allow reconstruction is the so-called Romano-Germanic pontifical, abbreviated RGP. This widely transmitted pontifical type was compiled in the mid-tenth century, probably at the Benedictine monastery of St. Albans in Mainz. Table 1.1 outlines the RGP consecration numbered according to Cyrille Vogel and Reinhard Elze's text-critical edition.[14] The ceremony had two unequal parts. Item 1 describes a brief presentation ceremony that happened before Mass; items 3 through 28 outline a longer church ritual that took place at Mass between the introit and the gospel on certain feasts. Two eleventh-century manuscripts from Bamberg and Eichstätt, to which Vogel and Elze assigned the sigla B and G, offer a somewhat different arrangement, on which I also comment.[15]

The bishop proffered four symbols of consecrated virginity to the candidate in the main service: the religious habit (item 10), the veil (16), the ring (23), and the crown (24). Space does not permit a full examination of the religious and historical significance of these symbols. Suffice it to observe that the veil, ring, and crown were all connected with nuptial ceremonies going back to Roman antiquity. Their use in the consecration of virgins, fully documented for the first time in the RGP, became widespread in the later Middle Ages.[16] Besides these symbols, lighted candles also figure in the account in Mss B and G (item 10). The consecrand held a candle in each hand as she returned to the bishop dressed in her new religious habit. As we will see, this use of candles related to the parable of the Wise and Foolish Virgins (Matt. 25:1–13). The Wise Virgins filled their lamps with oil and lit them so as to exit the darkness and greet the bridegroom; the Foolish were unprepared, left in the dark so to speak.

Other features of the consecration of virgins suggest a marriage ritual. The candidate's father and mother (*parentes*) offered her to the bishop before Mass (item 1) even though she may have lived for some time as a novice in the monastery prior to her consecration.[17] In the main service (4), a trusted male (*astipulator*) conducted her to the church's sanctuary "and in public" (*palamque*) assented to her consecration, thereby also attesting to her intact virginity. This practice contrasted with ordinations, in which the leader of the clerical institution presented the male candidate to the bishop in church.[18] For these men, moreover, virginity was not at issue.[19] Comparison of RGP rubrics thus reveals something of the unique gendering of medieval religious women as virgins and brides of Christ, both very much on display in the ritual.

One might expect an examination of music in the consecration of virgins to begin with the antiphons. (Their incipits are printed in italics and identified as antiphons in table 1.1.) Let us, however, take the unusual step of first considering the bishop's prayers, sung on a recitation formula or *tonus*, a monotone inflected by simple melodic formulae at the beginnings and ends of phrases.[20] The bishop sang the prayers solo and in a vocal range an octave lower than that of the nuns, who sang in a group. The bishop's voice was especially prominent in the ritual since he was the celebrant. His prayers were more numerous and longer, if less musically interesting, than the antiphons. We also now know that the prayers were older than the antiphons. All but two come down to us in Roman or mixed Gallo-Roman sacramentaries, books of prayers for liturgical celebrants copied as many as three centuries before the compilation of the RGP.[21]

Table 1.1. Outline of the Ritual for the Consecration of Virgins, Romano-Germanic Pontifical (RGP), Mainz, ca. 950

Presentation

1. Before Mass, the candidate's family pXesents her to the bishop, along with the oblation. The bishop accepts her hand, which is covered with an altar cloth. The candidate and nuns standing nearby sing the antiphon *Ipsi sum desponsata…diando cum astantibus antiphona Ipsi sum…*.

Mass

3. The bishop and attending clergy conduct Mass up to the gospel (according to Mss B and G, however, the service should take place after the gospel).

4. The one [male] who gives assent [*astipulator*] and the virgin proceed publicly to the altar; he consents to the consecration. [*Tunc veniat illa que consecranda est ante altare coram ecclesia palamque in conventu cum astipulatore suo, cuius licentia religionis habitum est susceptura.*]

5. The religious habit and veil are given to the bishop to be blessed.

6. The bishop blesses the habit and veil: *Deus aeternorum bonorum fidelissime promissor…*

7. Another prayer [*Alia*]: *Domine Deus, bonarum virtutum dator…*

8. Another prayer [*Alia*]: *Exaudi, domine, preces nostras et hanc vestem…*

9. A prayer for the blessing of the veil: *Caput omnium fidelium Deus…hoc operimentum velaminis…*

10. The consecrand accepts the blessed religious **habit**, but not the veil, from the bishop. She retires to the sacristy, where she changes into the habit. (In Mss B and G, a liturgical formula accompanies the giving of the habit; according to these Mss, when the consecrand returns she carries lighted **candles**, one in each hand.)

11. Returning to the choir, the consecrand prostrates herself, saying Ps. 118:116 three times: *Suscipe me, domine, secundum eloquium tuum et vivam et non confundas me ab expectatione mea* [Sustain me, O Lord, as you have promised, that I may live, and do not disappoint me in my hope].

12. Litany (except Mss B and G).

13. The bishop blesses the consecrand, who has risen to her feet, head bowed.

14. Bishop's prayer: *Respice, domine, propitius super hanc famulam tuam…*

15. Bishop's prayer, sung in the manner of the preface at Mass: *Deus castorum corporum…*

16. The bishop may examine the candidate to ascertain her appreciation for the estate the veil symbolizes (except Mss B and G). The bishop places the **veil** on her head with the formula: *Accipe velum sacrum, puella, quod perferas sine macula ante tribunal domini nostri Iesu Christi, cui flectitur omne genu caelestium, terrestrium, et infernorum, in saecula saeculorum.*

17. The candidate intones the antiphon *Induit me dominus ciclade…* and the nuns standing around her continue it. [*Tunc ipsa velata incipit antiphonam Induit me…ceteris sanctimonialibus quae circumstant prosequentibus.*]

18. Bishop's prayer after the consecrand accepts the veil: *Famulam tuam, domine, tuae custodia muniat pietatis…*

19. Antiphon *Ipsi sum desponsata*.

20. Bishop's prayer: *Da, quaesumus, omnipotens Deus, ut haec famula tua que pro spe…*

21. Antiphon *Posuit signum in faciem*.

22. Bishop's blessing: *Deus plasmator corporum, afflator animarum…*

23. Bishop places a **ring** on the candidate's finger with the formula: *Accipe anulum fidei…*

24. The bishop fastens on the consecrand's head a **crown** or garland with the formula: *Accipe signum Christi in capite, ut uxor eius efficiaris et si in eo permanseris, in perpetuum coroneris.*

25. Meanwhile, the Antiphon *Annulo suo subarravit me* is sung [*Interim dicatur antiphona Annulo suo…*].

26. Bishop's blessing: *Benedicat te conditor caeli et terrae…*

27. Bishop pronounces the anathema and gives the nun over to the protection of the faithful.

28. The gospel is read and Mass continues. (In Mss B and G the gospel is read before the consecration. The consecrand sets aside her candles and offers the oblation. Taking back her candles, she stands with her head bowed until she takes communion and Mass is finished.)

Examples 1.1 and 1.2 give Latin texts and English translations of two of the bishop's shorter prayers. The first, transmitted in sacramentaries predating the RGP, is old and unquestionably Roman;[22] the second, which is not found in earlier sources, is later and Frankish. The first of two observations to be made about these prayers seeks to distinguish the kinds of expressions used, thereby highlighting key differences between Roman and Frankish approaches to liturgical composition. The Roman prayer in example 1.1 is sober and succinct, and in these (as in other respects) it is typical of many others.[23] It lacks scriptural allusions or references to the saints, although some Roman consecratory prayers do appeal to the Virgin Mary for her assistance.[24] By the early ninth century (if not before), prayers such as this were associated with Roman pontiffs like Leo I (d. 461) and Gregory the Great (d. 604).[25] For the Franks, who received them in several waves of transmission before the tenth century, the authority of such prayers was a function of their *Romanitas* with respect both to pedigree and the spare, at times legalistic, use of language.[26]

The Frankish prayer for the blessing of the veil in example 1.2 is more discursive and incorporates more florid expressions than the Roman. For example, God is identified as "head of all the faithful and savior of the whole body" rather than simply as "Lord." Assuming such differences of verbal style were as immediately perceptible then as now, one might speculate that it was not imitation of Roman bluntness that lent authority to written prayers like this but an affiliation to Scripture, here the parable of the Wise and Foolish Virgins in the closing lines. Allusions to this parable are found in other consecratory prayers in circulation among the Franks before the RGP. The meaningfulness of this parable to the estate of consecrated virginity, as

Example 1.1. A Prayer for the Consecration of Virgins, RGP, XX.14

Respice, domine, propitius super hanc famulam tuam N.,
ut virginitatis sanctae propositum,
quod te inspirante suscipit,
te gubernante custodiat. Per.

Look kindly, O Lord, upon this your servant, N., that she may keep the vow of holy virginity, which she embraces with your inspiration and guidance. Through [our Lord] …

Example 1.2. A Prayer for the Blessing of the Veil, Consecration of Virgins, RGP, XX.9

Caput omnium fidelium deus,
et totius corporis salvator,
hoc operimentum velaminis,
quod famula tua propter tuum tuaeque genitricis beatissimae
scilicet semper virginis Mariae amorem,
suo capite est impositura,
tua dextera sanctifica
et hoc quod per illum mistice datur intellegi,
tua semper custodia corpore pariter et animo incontaminata custodiat,
ut quando perpetuam sanctorum remunerationem venerit,
cum prudentibus et ipsa virginibus preparata, perducente,
ad perpetuae felicitatis nuptias intrare mereatur.

O God, head of all the faithful and savior of the whole body, sanctify with your right hand this covering of a veil, which is about to be placed on your servant's head for love of you and your blessed mother, namely the ever Virgin Mary, along with that which is rendered perceptible by this ritual. Under your protection may she always remain uncontaminated in body and equally in soul, so that when she shall have come to the eternal reward of the saints, having been found ready with the prudent virgins, and she herself having been made ready, may she be worthy to enter, leading, into the nuptials of eternal happiness. (References in last two lines, beginning with *preparata*, are from the latter part of the Parable of the Wise and Foolish Virgins, Matt. 25:10.)

well as its connection to the consecration ritual, are indicated by more than repeated reference. What literate observer of the procession with lighted candles, which took place immediately after this prayer (in Mss B and G), would not have appreciated the intended symbolism? The candles would have been viewed, somewhat uncharacteristically, in a matrimonial context. Yet unlike the veil, ring, and crown, they alluded to an allegorical marriage between Christ and his church, a theme developed in numerous gospel commentaries.[27]

My second observation entails a different theoretical frame. Although we have considered but two examples, it is evident in both cases that the bishop's words *did* something. They called upon God's grace and begged for his assistance, incorporating active imperative verbs: "look kindly" (*respice*) in example 1.1, "sanctify" (*sanctifica*) in example 1.2.[28] In all respects these texts are classic examples of performative utterances as defined in J. L. Austin's theory.[29] By this I mean that the bishop's prayers, together with his actions, were instrumental to a specific religious and social transaction, namely the woman's permanent induction into the monastic community as a nun.

Compared with the bishop's many performative speech acts, the consecrand's were fewer and more stereotypical. According to item 11, she prostrated herself and thrice spoke Psalm 118:116: "Sustain me, O Lord, as you have promised, that I may live; and do not disappoint me in my hope." Note the active imperative, *suscipe*. In item 12, the consecrand likely added her voice to a litany calling upon the saints, martyrs, and patriarchs for prayers and mercy: "Pray for us, have mercy on us" (*ora pro nobis, miserere nobis*). The words of the Psalm and litany clearly did something, but such texts were common to many medieval Christian rituals, including RGP services.[30] They were chiefly associated not with celebrants but other participants in these liturgies. Because the Psalms furnished many texts for the Divine Office and Mass, Psalm singing could be described as a ritually enacted hermeneutics based on Christian tradition and biblical commentary. Psalms and other Old Testament texts were understood as prophesying the events of Christ's ministry and even the lives of the saints. Nearly all the Mass chants for the principal female virgin-martyrs, for instance, are psalmodic. (See table 1.2, appendix.) Stereotypy and Psalm quotation thus detracted from the directness and immediacy of the consecrand's speech acts.

Yet in assigning even these performative utterances to a woman in ways that suggested rituals for male religious, the authors of the RGP skirted a boundary that separated female and male vocations. When the RGP was compiled in the mid-tenth century, the status of religious women was in flux. By the eleventh century, anxiety over the comparability of the sexes in religious life led the compilers of Mss B and G to rework the ritual. In a prefatory comment summarized in table 1.1, item 3, they directed that it take place after, not before, the gospel since, they argued, it was fitting that the gospel be preached *to* women, not *by* them. Male monastic profession and ordination services retained their placements before the gospel. The B and G compilers also eliminated the litany, which remained a staple of male ordinations and monastic profession. They expunged a rubric (16) that suggested the consecrand might have had some limited agency in declaring her own willingness to be consecrated in a private exchange with the bishop. Finally, the candlelit procession they interpolated into the ritual could be seen as enhancing the imagery of spiritual marriage. Yet, by linking this action so closely to the gospel parable to which the preceding prayer referred, they transformed the consecrand into little more than a *dramatis persona* in a liturgical drama, objectifying and distancing her all the more from the imagined fulfillment of marriage. She may even have held the candles through the rest of the service: Item 28 instructed her to put them aside when she offered the oblation at the Mass, which continued after the consecration.

The crude differentiation of the sexes in Mss B and G should not overshadow the subtler gendering in the more widely transmitted RGP ritual. The most distinguished historian of the consecration of virgins, René Metz, lamented the lack of harmony and balance in this service, including the four antiphons, to which I now turn.[31] Yet, the antiphon texts and their sequence in the service were well suited to the ritual's design, purpose, and symbolism. As we shall see, the texts allude to objects used in the service in the order proffered: the habit (in *Induit me*), the veil (in *Posuit signum*), and the ring and crown (in *Annulo suo*). All have nuptial themes: betrothal, gift exchange, and love of Christ as spouse. They also have similar seventh-mode melodies, as shown in example 1.3.[32] (The transcriptions are based on a notated source later than, but related to, the RGP.)[33] The RGP compilers appear to have consciously unified the consecration by using a recurring melody type in all four antiphons. They forged similar musical links in the church dedication ritual.[34]

Example 1.3. Antiphons for the RGP Consecration of Virgins

Yet the antiphons, which were the consecrand's primary speech acts, were not performative in the sense Austin intended. Performativity designates words that enact rather than those that have symbolic or other meanings.[35] Instead, while occupying the liminal space between the secular and the sacred, the consecrand sang texts that recalled the earthly fate and heavenly triumph of a virgin-martyr, St. Agnes, in the first-person singular. (See example 1.4.) The consecrand likely appreciated these chants' connection to Agnes since all were sung in her office.[36] Moreover, the texts stem from her widely transmitted legend or *passio*, the author of which was thought to have been St. Ambrose of Milan. Indeed, they quote a speech in which the thirteen-year-old Roman patrician girl declared her love for a spouse far worthier than her would-be suitor, the pagan son of the prefect. This declaration set in motion events that led to her execution. Following her trial and torture and after a sword drained her life's blood, so the *passio* concludes, "Christ consecrated [Agnes]

Example 1.4. Texts of the Four Antiphons for the RGP Consecration of Virgins and Their Connections to St. Agnes's Hagiography

> *Ipsi sum desponsata cui angeli serviunt, cuius pulchritudinem sol et luna mirantur. (CAO* 3407 [St Agnes]) ("I am betrothed to Him whom the angels serve, whose beauty the sun and the moon admire."), *cf.* Mombritius, *Sanctuarium,* vol. 1, p. 41, lines 9–12: *Iam mel et lac ex eius ore suscepi . . . cui angeli serviunt, cuius pulchritudinem sol et luna mirantur. . . .*

> *Induit me dominus cyclade auro texta, et immensis monilibus ornavit me. (CAO* 3328 [St Agnes]) ("The Lord vests me in robes woven of gold, and adorns me with boundless necklaces."), *cf.* Mombritius, *Sanctuarium,* vol. 1, p. 41, line 3: *. . . induit me cyclade auro texta et immensis monilibus ornavit me.*

> *Posuit signum in faciem meam, ut nullum praeter eum amatorem admittam. (CAO* 4346 [St Agnes]) ("He placed a sign on my face, that I may receive no lover but Him."), *cf.* Mombritius, *Sanctuarium,* vol. 1, p. 41, lines 2–3: *Posuit signum suum in faciem meam: ut nullum praeter ipsum amatorem admittam.*

> *Annulo suo subarrhavit me dominus meus Jesus Christus, et tanquam sponsam decoravit me corona. (CAO* 1426 [St. Agnes]; cf. *CAO* 5101) ("With His ring my Lord, Jesus Christ, has betrothed me, and like a spouse He has adorned me with a crown."), cf. Mombritius, *Sanctuarium,* vol. 1, p. 40, lines 52–53: *. . . annulo fidei suae subarravit me.*

to the rank of spouse and martyr" (*Christus sibi et sponsam et martyrem consecrauit*).[37] In the RGP ritual, the consecrand received symbols of consecrated virginity from the bishop and sang antiphons that alluded to them. They also simultaneously gave voice to an impassioned declaration thought to have been that of the famous virgin-martyr, whose name was included in the canon of the Roman Mass.

The affect of the consecrand's embodiment of Agnes in liturgical song was, I would argue, categorically different from the bishop's performative speech acts. The texts of these antiphons also differed from more common psalmodic and scriptural chants, which evoked a cooler hermeneutic response. The Agnes antiphons constituted a self-standing narrative of devotion, declaration, earthly trial, and spiritual union with Christ in heaven. Mimetic representation of these texts in the consecration ritual occurred within a deep and richly textured cultural context, which included the Divine Office, hagiographical literature, art, and Christian iconography. These strongly reinforced the narrative, as did the singing of all the texts to the same model melody, which itself was connected with virgin-martyrs.[38]

To learn what more these antiphons may have signified for tenth- and eleventh-century Frankish monastics, we must examine the texts in further detail. As we will see, the redactors incorporated not just Agnes's *passio* but also Scripture in ways comparable to the Frankish prayer in example 1.2.[39] Of particular significance was Isaiah 61:10, to which two of the antiphons refer.[40] This passage reads in English translation: "I will greatly rejoice in the Lord, my whole being shall exult in my God; for he has clothed me with the garments of salvation, and covered me with the robe of righteousness, as a bridegroom decks himself with a garland, adorned with a crown,

Example 1.5. Connections among the Antiphon *Induit me* (*CAO* 3328), the *Passio Agnetis*,
and Isa. 61:10 (shared texts underlined)

Ant. *Induit me dominus cyclade auro texta, et immensis monilibus ornavit me.*

Passio: … *induit me cyclade auro texta et immensis monilibus ornavit me.*
(Mombritius, *Sanctuarium*, 1: 41, line 3)

Isa. 61:10: … *quia induit me vestimentis salutis … et quasi sponsam ornatam
monilibus suis.*

like a bride bedecked with her jewels (*monilibus*)." Long before they adopted the
Roman liturgy, the Franks had associated this text with consecrating virgins. The
seventh-century Gallican Lectionary of Luxeuil assigns it as the Old Testament
reading at the Mass for consecrating virgins.[41] Comparable Roman Masses had no
such reading, only epistles and gospels; where Isa. 61:10 was assigned in the Rome
liturgy, it had no connection with the consecration of virgins or monasticism.[42]

As seen in example 1.4, *Induit me* and *Posuit signum* rely heavily on Agnes's *passio*, as does the second half of *Ipsi sum desponsata* and the opening of *Annulo suo*.
Such additions and changes are typical[43] of the kinds made when written texts were
reworked into chant librettos.[44] However, both the text redactor and the writer of
Agnes's *passio* borrowed from Scripture. As example 1.5 shows, Isa. 61:10 was incorporated into *Induit me.* The dative plural of the noun *monile* ('jewel'), *monilibus*,
appears in the Bible only in this verse, suggesting that both sound and sense were
important.[45]

The opening of *Ipsi sum desponsata* is not found in Agnes's speech. The perfect
passive participle *desponsata* does, however, occur three times in the Bible, always in
connection with Mary's betrothal to Joseph.[46] By its rarity, this word might have
been intended to liken Agnes's spiritual marriage to this earthly one. Indeed, a
Marian subplot winds its way through the prior history of the Frankish consecration of virgins. In this context, a small change in a sixth- or seventh-century Frankish
prayer for consecrating virgins, found first in the *Missale Francorum*, achieves a
large effect. In the early Frankish version, the bishop begs that the virgin be deemed
worthy to elect "after the fashion" of Mary (*ad instar*), implying that God had singled
her out as he had the Blessed Virgin. As the prayer comes down to us in later Roman
sacramentaries and the RGP, however, the nun could at best aspire to join Mary's
company.[47] Around the time the *Missale Francorum* was copied, moreover, a
Magnificat antiphon, *Spiritus sanctus in te descendet Maria* (Luke 1:35), was sung in
connection with the consecration of virgins in the Celtic liturgy, which may have
had some impact on continental Europe.[48] This antiphon and its consecratory use
both evidently fell out of favor after the Frankish adoption of the Roman rite and
with it a new understanding of Mary's unique virginity.

The most complicated and provocative use of Scripture among the four antiphons is encountered in *Annulo suo*. As example 1.6 shows, a distinctive noun-verb

Example 1.6. Connections among the Antiphon *Annulo suo* (*CAO* 1426), the *Passio Agnetis*, Isa. 61:10, and Ps. 18:6 (shared texts underlined)

Ant. *Annulo suo subarrhavit me dominus meus Jesus Christus, et tanquam sponsam decoravit me corona.*

Passio: … *annulo fidei suae subarravit me* … (Mombritius, *Sanctuarium*, 1: 40, lines 52–53)

Isa. 61.10: … *Quasi sponsum decoratum corona, et quasi sponsam ornatam monilibus suis.*

Ps. 18:6: *Et ipse tanquam sponsus procedens de thalamo suo.…*

combination from the *passio* was retained in the antecedent phrase, with new words substituted or added.[49] The consequent, however, *et tanquam sponsam decoravit me corona*, conflates two Old Testament passages, both alluding to spouses and one to a crown. A crown does not figure in Agnes's *passio*, yet the antiphon redactor evidently needed one. Again an early Frankish consecratory prayer from the *Missale Francorum* suggests why. In it the bishop begged God to help the consecrand preserve her determination and guard her purity so that she "may deserve to receive the crown of [her] virginity."[50] For the necessary text the antiphon redactor returned to Isa. 61:10, which he conflated with Ps. 18:6. Yet the "spouse adorned with a crown" in Isaiah is male, *sponsum*, who in exegetical literature and the medieval Christian liturgy was identified with Christ.[51] The crowned spouse in *Annulo suo* is female, *sponsam*.

That Agnes was identified as Christ's *sponsa* at the end of the *passio* may begin to explain such gender bending, but it hardly required the redactor to upend the well-established image of Christ as bridegroom for her office alone.[52] Could these and the other factors, including connections with the *Missale Francorum*, mean that *Annulo suo* was intended, perhaps from the beginning, for both the consecration of virgins and the office? I hasten to add here that this antiphon could not have been Gallican, that is, part of a repertory that predated the dissemination of Gregorian Chant among the Franks. Rather, it and perhaps other Agnes antiphons and responsories were later eighth- or ninth-century Frankish-Gregorian creations.

That the author of *Annulo suo* was more likely Frankish than Roman has three general arguments in its favor. First, it has long been suspected that chants for virginmartyrs were among the last added to the office repertory before it was first copied into antiphoners.[53] Second, although Agnes was a Roman saint, her *passio* circulated among the Franks before the eighth century, that is, prior to the composition of the Agnes office. Information about her martyrdom arrived in Frankish territory with the spread of the so-called Hieronymian martyrology, compiled in northern Italy in the later fifth century.[54] Agnes's feast and its octave, which had long been observed in Rome, was probably celebrated in Frisia and elsewhere in the Kingdom of the Franks in the early eighth century, thanks to Anglo-Saxon missionary efforts.[55]

Third, as we've seen, *Annulo suo* and the other Agnes antiphons quote her *passio* extensively. The Franks had long incorporated such legends into their liturgy. According to E. Catherine Dunn, Frankish monastics read the lives of saints in the Gallican office as an extension of a still older tradition of dramatic recitation.[56] The Gallican Mass could include hagiography in place of the Old Testament lection,[57] and the seventh-century Lectionary of Luxeuil contains *passiones* easily as fanciful as Agnes's.[58] The Franks adapted the practice of reading hagiography to the Roman liturgy just as they had amalgamated Gallican and Roman prayers.[59] Indeed, northern European recensions of *Ordo romanus* XIV from the second half of the seventh century explicitly mention the reading of *passiones martyrum et vitae patrum catholicorum.*

For their part the Romans had long been excessively scrupulous about liturgical authorization for saints' legends. Hagiographical texts were not read in early eighth-century Roman offices according to the primitive *Ordo romanus* XIV, confirmed by the later eighth-century *Ordo romanus* XIIIA for the Lateran.[60] *Ordo romanus* XII indicates that such restrictions were relaxed under Pope Hadrian, but he reigned during a time when the antiphons under consideration might already have been composed, namely the last quarter of the eighth century (772–795).[61] It is reasonable, then, that northerners composed chants based on saints' *passiones*, which the Romans had for so long deemed spurious. Like many chants in the "Old" Roman repertory, antiphons and responsories for St. Agnes could have entered the Roman rite by way of the Franks. As for *Annulo suo*, the Romans likely considered it inappropriate; it had no place in the "Old" Roman office for St. Agnes.

To assert the special significance for the Franks of *Annulo suo* and other Agnes chants that quote Isa. 61:10, one might inquire how many other antiphons and responsories quote and rework both a saint's legend and Scripture?[62] Of some 240 *CAO* antiphons and responsories for virgin-martyrs with texts drawn from *passiones*, only two, both for St. Cecilia, incorporate biblical passages quoted in her *passio*. Neither involved Isa. 61:10, and both differ considerably from how the Agnes antiphon incorporates borrowed texts.[63]

Broadening the search to include chants for virgin-martyrs with scriptural texts but without any borrowings from *passiones* yields a larger sample. Predominating among these are chants assigned to the Common of Virgins and secondarily to virgin-martyrs that quote Ps. 44, a nuptial ode, and Matthew's parable of the Wise and Foolish Virgins.[64] Psalm 44 is also prominent among Mass chants (see table 1.2, appendix); Matt. 25 was the gospel pericope for St. Agnes in early Roman books.[65] Given Roman sanctions against liturgical use of saints' legends, one might wonder whether these two passages of Scripture might have reflected early medieval Roman, as opposed to the Frankish, sensibilities.

Investigating Roman offices before the earliest Frankish-influenced antiphoners is like walking on thin ice over deep water. Fortunately, Claire Maître's comparison of matins psalmody and antiphon texts for virgin-martyrs and the Blessed Virgin provides a firm footing from which to depart. In brief and at the risk of oversimplifying her research, Maître observed a lack of uniformity in the selection of matins psalms for virgin-martyrs.[66] Correspondences between some of these lists and more uniform ones for matins for the Virgin Mary and the Common of Martyrs suggest the chronological priority of the latter two. Roman matins for virgin-martyrs thus appear to have derived from these offices. As regards matins psalmody for the Common of Virgins, it relates to and probably derived from the Common of Martyrs.[67]

Maître's findings permit us to begin zeroing in on connections the Romans may have made between virgin-martyrs and Scripture, but the thirty-seven psalms treated in her study are too numerous to offer specific guidance. Fortunately, she also lists chants employing psalmodic and other scriptural texts, and by analyzing these we may ascertain which were the most prominent.[68] It turns out that only three were assigned to Marian feasts, the Common of Virgins, and virgin-martyrs. The first, *Adiuvabit eam* on Ps. 45:6, is an antiphon (*CAO* 1282) and a responsory (*CAO* 6042), but the latter was restricted to the monastic *cursus*. The second, *O quam pulchra est casta generatio* (*CAO* 4069), from the Book of Wisdom (Sap. 4:10), is an antiphon only. The third, *Specie tua*, on Ps. 44:5, was, however, very widely used in both the monastic and the secular *cursus*. Its text served as an antiphon, a respon-sory, and a responsory verse in offices for Marian feasts (the Assumption in Rome), virgin-martyrs, and the Common of Virgins.[69]

In this still admittedly small number of early chants for all virgins and virgin-martyrs, the prominence of Ps. 44 is suggestive. Different and more varied scrip-tural texts were assigned—presumably first in Rome—to Marian feasts and the Common of Virgins but not to virgin-martyrs. Passages from the Song of Songs were the most frequently adapted.

Thus, in Rome, particular scriptural texts defined the qualities of female virgin-ity in the official public sphere of worship. We should not overlook Rome's impor-tance as a center for theology and doctrine in the medieval West. Psalm 44 was in its literal sense a nuptial ode. Its text had been among the most hotly debated in patristic literature, but by the seventh and eighth centuries its Christological meaning was well established. Likewise, the virgin bride and accompanying virgins, to which the latter half of the psalm alludes, submitted to a standard metaphorical interpretation. It would be reasonable, then, for the Roman clergy, conscious of this exegetical tradi-tion, to have incorporated Ps. 44 into the widest possible range of offices for virgins.

Exegesis of the Canticle of Canticles dealt less ambiguously with the nature of the relationship between Christ and his spouse, the church. It had nothing literal to do with the text's famous amorous imagery. In chants of the Roman office, this scriptural text was strongly associated with the Virgin Mary, who served as a symbol of the church. Matthew's parable of the Wise and Foolish Virgins was more ambiva-lent and could be assigned to virgin-martyrs and the Common of Virgins but not normally to Mary, probably due to the text's literal meaning.

Compared with these constellations of Roman chants, those that stem from Isa. 61:10 seem like distant stars at first. The passage was adapted in but a handful of Frankish-Gregorian chants for St. Agnes. Yet some of these took on added signifi-cance in monastic circles in their connection to the earliest recoverable ritual for the consecration of virgins. Given the distinctive ways the Agnes legend and Scripture were reworked in these chants, as well as their connections to the traditional Gallican-Frankish traditions of worship, their cultural significance for tenth- and eleventh-century Frankish nuns, including the consecrands, could not be clearer.

Table 1.2. Mass Propers for the Four Principal Virgin-Martyrs in Liturgical Order with the Sources of the Chant Texts

Type	Incipit	Source	Assignmt.
Int	*Dilexisti justitiam et odisti*	Ps. 44:8	Lucia
IntPs	*Eructavit*	Ps. 44:2	Lucia
InPsV	*Specie tua et pulchritudine*	Ps. 44:5	Lucia
Gr	*Dilexisti justitiam et odisti*	Ps. 44:8	Lucia
GrV	*Propterea unxit te Deus oleo laetitiae*	Ps. 44:8	Lucia
AllV	*Specie tua et pulchritudine*	Ps. 44:5	Lucia
AllV	*Diffusa est gratia in labiis tuis*	Ps. 44:3	Lucia
Off	*Offerentur regi virgines post eam*	Ps. 44:15–16	Lucia
OffV	*Eructavit cor meum verbum bonum*	Ps. 44:2	Lucia
OffV	*Specie tua et pulchritudine*	Ps. 44:5	Lucia
Com	*Simile est regnum caelorum homini*	Matt. 3:45	Lucia
ComPs	*Eructavit*	Ps. 44:2	Lucia
Int	*Me expectaverunt peccatores ut perderent*	Ps. 118:95–96	Agnes I
IntPs	*Beati immaculati*	Ps. 118:1	Agnes I
IntPsV	*Tu mandasti*	Ps. 118:4	Agnes I
Gr	*Specie tua et pulchritudine*	Ps. 44:5	Agnes I
GrV	*Audi filia et vide*	Ps. 44:11	Agnes I
AllV	*Ingressa Agnes turpitudinis locum*	Passio	Agnes I
Tr	*Adducentur regi virgines proximae*	Ps. 44:15–16	Agnes I
Off	*Offerentur regi virgines post eam*	Ps. 44:15–16	Agnes I
OffV	*Eructavit cor meum verbum bonum*	Ps. 44:2	Agnes I
OffV	*Specie tua et pulchritudine*	Ps. 44:5	Agnes I
Com	*Quinque prudentes virgines acceperunt*	Matt. 25:4–6	Agnes I
ComPs	*Eructavit*	Ps. 44:2	Agnes I
Int	*Cognovi Domine quia aequitas judicia*	Ps. 118:75, 120	Agnes II
IntPs	*Beati immaculati*	Ps. 118:1	Agnes II
IntPsV	*In mandatis*	Ps. 118:15	Agnes II
Gr	*Audi filia et vide*	Ps. 44:11	Agnes II
GrV	*Specie tua et pulchritudine*	Ps. 44:5	Agnes II
AllV	*Specie tua et pulchritudine*	Ps. 44:5	Agnes II
Off	*Offerentur regi virgines post eam*	Ps. 44:15–16	Agnes II
OffV	*Eructavit cor meum verbum bonum*	Ps. 44:2	Agnes II
OffV	*Specie tua et pulchritudine*	Ps. 44:5	Agnes II

Com	*Simile est regnum caelorum homini*	Matt. 13:45	Agnes II
ComPs	*Eructavit*	Ps. 44:2	Agnes II
Int	*Gaudeamus omnes…Agathae*	N.A.	Agatha
IntPs	*Eructavit*	Ps. 44:2	Agatha
InPsV	*Specie tua et pulchritudine*	Ps. 44:5	Agatha
Gr	*Adjuvabit eam Deus vultu suo*	Ps. 45:6	Agatha
GrV	*Fluminis impetus letificat civitatem*	Ps. 45:5	Agatha
Tr	*Qui seminant in lacrimis in gaudio*	Ps. 125:5–6	Agatha
Off	*Diem festum virginis sacrum hodie*	—	Agatha
Com	*Qui me dignatus est ab omni plaga*	*Passio*	Agatha
ComPs	*Eructavit*	Ps. 44:2	Agatha
Int	*Loquebar de testimoniis*	Ps. 118:46–47	Cecilia
IntPs	*Beati immaculati*	Ps. 118:1	Cecilia
InPsV	*Justificationes*	Ps. 118:8	Cecilia
Gr	*Audi filia et vide*	Ps. 44:11	Cecilia
GrV	*Specie tua et pulchritudine*	Ps. 44:5	Cecilia
AllV	*Specie tua et pulchritudine*	Ps. 44:5	Cecilia
Off	*Offerentur regi virgines post eam*	Ps. 44:15–16	Cecilia
Com	*Confundantur superbi quia iniuste*	Ps. 118:78, 80	Cecilia

Source: René-Jean Hesbert, ed., *Antiphonale Missarum Sextuplex* (Brussels: Vromant, 1935).

NOTES

Prior versions of this chapter were read at the Eighteenth International Congress of the International Musicological Society, Zürich, Switzerland, July 12, 2007, and the Midwest Chapter meeting of the American Musicological Society, Kalamazoo, Michigan, April 26, 2008.

1. Albert Lord, *The Singer of Tales*, Harvard Studies in Comparative Literature, vol. 24 (Cambridge, Mass.: Harvard University Press, 1960). Treitler's most influential essays on chant are found in *With Voice and Pen: Coming to Know Medieval Song and How It Was Made* (New York: Oxford University Press, 2003). For a view sympathetic to Treitler's, see Helmut Hucke, "Toward a New Historical View of Gregorian Chant," *Journal of the American Musicological Society* (hereinafter *JAMS*) 33 (1980): 437–67; and Hucke, "Gregorianische Fragen," *Die Musikforschung* 41 (1988): 304–30.

2. The most outspoken and erudite critic of Leo Treitler's thesis is Kenneth Levy, whose essays are collected in *Gregorian Chant and the Carolingians* (Princeton, N.J.: Princeton University Press, 1998). To gain a sense of the nature of the debate, see Communications from Treitler, Levy, and David Hughes in *JAMS* 41 (1988): 566–79. See also Communication from Treitler, Hendrik van der Werf, and Levy in *JAMS* 44 (1991): 513–25.

3. James McKinnon, *The Advent Project: The Later-Seventh-Century Creation of the Mass Proper* (Berkeley: University of California Press, 2000), is arguably the most controversial. See Peter Jeffery's review in *JAMS* 56 (2003): 169–79. McKinnon's bibliography includes many, less contentious historical studies.

4. Edward Nowacki, "Studies on the Office Antiphons of the Old Roman Manuscripts," PhD diss., Brandeis University, 1980; and Nowacki, "The Gregorian Office Antiphons and the Comparative Method," *Journal of Musicology* 4 (1985): 243–75.

5. *Re-Envisioning Past Musical Cultures: Ethnomusicology in the Study of Gregorian Chant* (Chicago: University of Chicago Press, 1992). Jeffery and ethnomusicologist Kay Kaufman Shelemay edited and examined the contemporary liturgical monophony of Ethiopian Christians. See their *Ethiopian Christian Liturgical Chant: An Anthology*, 3 vols., Recent Researches in the Oral Traditions of Music, 1–3 (Madison, Wisc.: A-R Editions, 1993–1997).

6. Jeffery, *Re-Envisioning*, 2.

7. Clifford Geertz, *The Interpretation of Cultures: Selected Essays* (New York: Basic Books, 1973), 89.

8. For a lucid summary of Geertz's approach and responses to it, see Catherine Bell, *Ritual Theory, Ritual Practice* (New York: Oxford University Press, 1992), 25–35.

9. For model approaches of this kind, see David G. Hunter, "The Virgin, the Bride, and the Church: Reading Psalm 45 in Ambrose, Jerome, and Augustine," *Church History* 69 (2000): 281–303. See also C. Clifford Flanigan, Kathleen Ashley, and Pamela Sheingorn, "Liturgy as Social Performance: Expanding the Definitions," in *The Liturgy of the Medieval Church*, ed. Thomas J. Heffernan and E. Ann Matter (Kalamazoo: Medieval Institute Publications, Western Michigan University, 2001), 695–714. A broader but nonetheless relevant study is Aaron Gurevich, *Historical Anthropology of the Middle Ages*, ed. Jana Howlett (Chicago: University of Chicago Press, 1992). Given that plainchant was a public and official representation of the church's authority, it is surprisingly little studied from the perspective of contemporary theory.

10. For an introduction to medieval pontificals, see Cyrille Vogel, *Medieval Liturgy: An Introduction to the Sources*, rev. and trans. William G. Storey and Niels Krogh Rasmussen, O.P. (Washington, D.C.: Pastoral Press, 1986), 225–55. On the symbols from which medieval bishops drew, see Eric Palazzo, *L'évêque et son image: L'illustration du pontifical au moyen âge* (Turnhout: Brepols, 1999). For a brief overview, see Palazzo, "The Image of the Bishop in the Middle Ages," in *The Bishop Reformed: Studies of Episcopal Power and Culture in the Central Middle Ages*, ed. John S. Ott and Anna Trumbore Jones (Burlington, Vt.: Ashgate, 2007), 86–91.

11. James Borders, "Distribution of Chants for the Consecration of Virgins," *Papers Read at the Thirteenth Meeting of the IMS Study Group Cantus Planus, Niederaltaich, Germany, 2006* (Budapest: Institute for Musicology of the Hungarian Academy of Sciences, 2009), 85–103.

12. Arnold van Gennep, *The Rites of Passage*, trans. M. B. Vizedom and G. L. Caffee (Chicago: University of Chicago Press, 1960), is the classic anthropological study. Van Gennep's concepts are applied to profession rituals for monks and nuns in Douglas Davies, "Christianity," in *Rites of Passage*, ed. Jean Holm with John Bowker (New York: Pinter, 1994), 60–61.

13. Gisela Muschiol, "Men, Women, and Liturgical Practice in the Early Medieval West," in *Gender in the Early Medieval World: East and West, 300–900*, ed. Leslie Brubaker and Julia M. H. Smith (New York: Cambridge University Press, 2004), 198–216, examines gendering of the Frankish liturgy in times before the period under consideration here.

14. Cyrille Vogel and Reinhard Elze, *Le pontifical romano-germanique du dixième siècle*, 3 vols., Studi e Testi, 226, 227, 269 (Vatican City: Biblioteca Apostolica Vaticana, 1963–1972). On the dating of the RGP, see vol. 1, xvi–xvii.

15. Ms B is the siglum for Bamberg, Staatsbibliothek, cod. lit. 53 (olim Ed. III, 12) from eleventh-century Bamberg. Ms G is Eichstätt, Bishop's Archive, Pontifical of Bishop Gondekar II, 1057–1075.

16. René Metz, *La consécration des vierges dans l'église romaine: Étude d'histoire de la liturgie* (Paris: Presses universitaires de France, 1954), 206–10. Victor Leroquais, *Les pontificaux manuscrits des bibliothèques publiques de France*, 3 vols. (Paris: Macon, Protat frères, 1937), reports on the use of the ring and crown in consecration services.

17. For a discussion of a comparable, if somewhat bizarre, symbolic marriage between the bishop of Florence and an abbess, see Sharon T. Strocchia, "When the Bishop Married the Abbess: Masculinity and Power in Florentine Episcopal Entry Rites, 1300–1600," *Gender and History* 19(2) (2007): 346–68. The secondary literature on medieval female monasticism is extensive, but for an overview see Jo Ann Kay McNamara, *Sisters in Arms: Catholic Nuns through Two Millennia* (Cambridge, Mass.: Harvard University Press, 1996).

18. RGP XV. 2–4, XV. 20, XVI. 1 (Ms A). Vogel and Elze, *Le pontifical romano-germanique*, vol. 1, 14, 17–18, 20.

19. For a discussion of the different treatments of women and men in the literature of monastic formation, see Barbara Newman, *From Virile Woman to Woman Christ: Studies in Medieval Religion and Literature* (Philadelphia: University of Pennsylvania Press, 1995), 28–34.

20. For a discussion of recitation formulas for prayers, see David Hiley, *Western Plainchant: A Handbook* (New York: Oxford University Press, 1993), 47–54. See also Willi Apel, *Gregorian Chant* (Bloomington: University of Indiana Press, 1958), 201–208. Two prayer *toni* were used in the RGP consecration, one simple, the other more elaborate. *Deus castorum corporum* (item 15) was performed in the more complex manner of the Preface at Mass.

21. RGP XX.9 and XX.20 were apparently new. Vogel and Elze, *Le pontifical romano-germanique*, vol. 1, 40–41, 44. On medieval sacramentaries, see Vogel, *Medieval Liturgy*, 31–134. See also Eric Palazzo, *A History of Liturgical Books from the Beginning to the Thirteenth Century*, trans. Madeleine Beaumont (Collegeville, Minn.: Pueblo/Liturgical Press, 1998), 38–55.

22. It is found in the earliest extant prayer book for the Roman rite, called *Veronensis* (no. 1103), copied in Verona from a Roman model in the first quarter of the seventh century. It was also transmitted in the Old Gelasian Sacramentary (no. 787), the Sacramentary of Gellona (no. 2607), and the supplement to the Gregorian Sacramentary (no. 1253).

23. For development of this theme, see Enrico Mazza, *The Eucharistic Prayers of the Roman Rite* (New York: Pueblo, 1986), 111.

24. *Exaudi domine preces nostras et hanc vestem quam famula tua*...(RGP XX.8) appears to be an exception since Aaron is mentioned in the text. This item did not originate in the service for the consecration of virgins, however, but was borrowed from the ordination of deaconesses (RGP XXIV.7), a quasi-clerical rank that fell out of favor in later Carolingian times. Vogel and Elze, *Le pontifical romano-germanique*, vol. 1, 40, 55.

25. Yitzhak Hen, *The Royal Patronage of Liturgy in Frankish Gaul: To the Death of Charles the Bald (877)*, Henry Bradshaw Society, Subsidia, 3 (London: Boydell, 2001), 15.

26. Yitzhak Hen aggressively develops the thesis that the Franks accepted the Roman rite and its texts over time. See *Royal Patronage*, 42–89. See also Hen, *Culture and Religion in Merovingian Gaul, A.D. 481–751*, Cultures, Beliefs and Traditions: Medieval and Early Modern Peoples, vol. 1 (New York: Brill, 1995).

27. See, for example, St. Augustine's Sermon XCIII. http://www.newadvent.org/fathers/160343.htm and http://www.catholicculture.org/culture/library/fathers/view.cfm?recnum=3403 (accessed Nov. 10, 2009).

28. For a discussion of other such expressions, see O. G. Harrison, "The Formulas *Ad virgines sacras:* A Study of the Sources," *Ephemerides liturgicae* 66 (1952): 256–69.

29. J. L. Austin, *How to Do Things with Words*, 2d ed., ed. J. O. Ormson and Marina Sbisà (Cambridge, Mass.: Harvard University Press, 1975).

30. Litanies were sung, for example, in connection with the profession of monks (RGP XXVIII.1) and clerical ordinations (RGP XV.5, XVI.21). Vogel and Elze, *Le pontifical romano-germanique*, vol. 1, 14, 28, 70. For the use of the same Psalm verse in connection with monastic profession, see RGP XXVIII.7. Vogel and Elze, *Le pontifical romano-germanique*, vol. 1, 71.

31. "L'agencement de cette partie du ritual manque d'harmonie et d'équilibre…" Metz, *Consécration*, 206–207n157. With respect to the antiphons, Metz may have had in mind the different circumstances in which the antiphons were sung in the ritual. During the brief presentation before Mass, the candidate and nuns standing nearby sang *Ipsi sum desponsata* in the presence of the bishop and family members. Later at Mass (table 1, item 17), the consecrand began *Induit me*, which her sister nuns completed; this may have been repeated depending on the number of women to be consecrated. *Ipsi sum desponsata* (19) and *Posuit signum* (21) were not connected to liturgical actions. The *ordo* merely indicates their having been sung after *Induit me* and between the bishop's blessings. Finally, *Annulo suo* (25) was sung as the ring and crown were received. The rubrics do not specify the consecrand as the singer of the latter three antiphons, but she probably was, given the nature of the texts and evidence from later pontificals stemming from the RGP. Whether the other nuns joined the singing is uncertain.

32. François Auguste Gevaert, *La mélopée antique dans la chant de l'église latine* (1895; reprint, Osnabrück: Zeller, 1967), 305–309, identified this model melody as *thème* 22.

33. Namely, I-Rvat Borghes. lat. 49, one of the sources of the so-called Roman pontificals of the twelfth century. See Michel Andrieu, *Le pontificale romain au moyen âge*, vol. 1, Studi e Testi, 86 (Vatican City: Biblioteca Apostolica Vaticana, 1938). For a description see pp. 71–77.

34. These are discussed in Thomas Kozachek, "The Repertory of Chant for Dedicating Churches in the Middle Ages: Music, Liturgy, and Ritual," PhD diss., Harvard University, 1995, 160–63. The seventh-mode type melody was already old and venerable when it was adapted to the Agnes antiphons. They are listed, for example, in two ninth-century tonaries of Metz and Reichenau. See Walther Lipphardt, *Der karolingische Tonar von Metz*, Liturgiewissenschaftliche Quellen und Forschungen, 43 (Münster: Aschendorffsche Verlagsbuchhandlung, 1965).

35. For a discussion of how Austin's theory of the performative has been extended to other kinds of utterances, see Catherine Bell, *Ritual Perspectives and Dimensions* (New York: Oxford University Press, 1997), 68–76.

36. For the texts and assignments of antiphons and responsories of the office, see René-Jean Metz, *Corpus antiphonalium officii* (hereinafter *CAO*), 6 vols., Rerum ecclesiasticarum documenta, Series maior, Fontes, 7–12 (Rome: Herder, 1963–1979).

37. The conclusion reads as follows: "…*in gutur eius Gladius gladium mergi praecepit: atque hoc exitu roseo sui sanguinis rubore perfusam Christus sibi et sponsam et martyrem consecrauit.*" Boninus Mombritius, *Sanctuarium seu vitae sanctorum*, 2 vols. (Paris: Fontemoing, 1910), vol. 1, 43, lines 29–30.

38. Gevaert, *Mélopée antique*, 306.

39. Cf. Alexander Joseph Denomy, who many years ago characterized such scriptural borrowings as a "jumbled heap of descriptive phrases." *The Old French Lives of Saint Agnes and Other Vernacular Versions of the Middle Ages* (Cambridge, Mass.: Harvard University Press, 1938), 122.

40. A further responsory with verses in the St. Agnes office, *Induit me Dominus vestimento* (*CAO* 6955), stems from the same nexus of hagiographical and scriptural texts. The responsory is a minor reworking of Isa. 61:10. *CAO* verse C quotes Isaiah verbatim; verse A has the same text as the antiphon, *Induit me*; and the remaining verse, B, stems from the *passio* without evident scriptural allusions. I'm uncertain how this chant fits in with the four consecratory antiphons, but the dependence of its text on Isa. 61:10 is unquestionable. Also see notes 46 and 53.

41. The full reading comprised Isa. 61:10–11 through 62:1–7. Pierre Salmon, ed., *Le lectionnaire de Luxeuil* (Paris, ms. Lat. 9427), Collectanea Biblica Latina, 7 (Rome: Abbaye Saint-Jérome/Libreria Vaticana, 1944), 210–11. Cf. RGP XXI, 2 (note); Vogel and Elze, *Le pontifical romano-germanique*, vol. 1, 47.

42. In Rome (*Ordo romanus XIIIA*), Isa. 61:10 was the third reading for the Office of the Epiphany and its octave. Michel Andrieu, *Les Ordines romani du Haut Moyen Âge*, 5 vols., Spicilegium sacrum lovanienses, études et documents, 11, 23–24, 28–29 (Louvain: Spicilegium sacrum lovaniense bureaux, 1931–1961), vol. 2, 487.

43. For example, compare the Agnes antiphons *Ingressa Agnes turpitudinis* (*CAO* 3337) and *Congaudete mecum* (*CAO* 1886) with Mombritius, *Sanctuarium*, vol. 1, 42, lines 16–17 and 43, lines 54–55, respectively. The texts of two other office antiphons, *Dextram meam* (*CAO* 2186) and *Ipsi soli servo* (*CAO* 3406), also quote the *passio* verbatim.

44. I am here extending Kenneth Levy's term to chants in the office. See his "Toledo, Rome, and the Legacy of Gaul," *Early Music History* 4 (1984): 49–99, reprinted in Levy, *Gregorian Chant and the Carolingians*, 31–81. In some Agnes antiphons, the process of adapting the *passio* was apparently similar to the one Levy observed in offertories. For example, the phrases of the antiphons *Discede a me, pabulum mortis, quia iam ab alio amatore praeventa sum* (*CAO* 2251); *Mel et lac ex eius ore suscepi, et sanguis eius ornavit genas meas* (*CAO* 3734); and *Cuius pulchritudinem sol et luna mirantur, ipsi soli servo fidem* (*CAO* 1968) are separated by intervening texts. See Mombritius, *Sanctuarium*, vol. 1, 40, lines 50–52; 41, lines 9–11, 12–14, respectively.

45. The dative plural also figures in the responsory *CAO* 7340, *Ornatam in monilibus filiam Jerusalem*, which combines Isa. 61:10 and Ps. 44:12. The noun *monile* occurs in *CAO* 4197, which perhaps was adapted from the *CAO* 7340, which conflates Isa. 61:10 and Cant. 1:2.

46. Matt. 1.18; Luke 1.27, 2.5. The added words, *Ipsi sum*, mimic a passage (*ipsi me tota devotione committo*) further along in Agnes's speech. See Mombritius, *Sanctuarium*, vol. 1, 41, line 14. The text redactor incorporated this passage into the Agnes antiphon text, *Ipsi soli servo* (*CAO* 3406).

47. *Missale Francorum* (49): "[Q]*ui te eligere dignatus est ad instar sanctæ Mariæ matris domini nostri Iesu Christi.*" RGP XX. 26: "[Q]*ui te eligere dignatur ad sanctae matris domini nostri Iesu Christi consortium.*" Compare Cunibert Mohlberg, ed., *Missale Francorum* (Cod. Vat. Reg. Lat. 257), Rerum ecclesiasticarum documenta, series major, 2 (Rome: Herder, 1957), and Vogel and Elze, *Le pontifical romano-germanique*, vol. 1, 46. On the place of the *Missale Francorum* in the history of the Gallican Frankish liturgy, see Hen, *Culture and Religion in Merovingian Gaul*, 46.

48. This antiphon is preserved in an eighth-century fragment from the Celtic liturgy, Colmar 144. See Louis Brou, "Le fragment liturgique Colmar 144 reste d'un pontifical

Irlandais du VIIIe siècle," *Bulletin de litterature ecclésiastique* 56 (1955): 65–71. See also Enzo Lodi, *Enchiridion euchologicum fontium liturgicorum*, Bibliotheca "Ephemerides Liturgicae" Subsidia (Rome: C.L.V. Edizioni Liturgiche, 1979), 1110, nos. 2600–2606. The full text is as follows (added text is given in angled brackets; resolved abbreviations are in square brackets): *Sp[iritu]s s[an]c[tu]s s<u>p[er]veniet in te et virtus altissimi obu<m->brabit <tibi> <quod enim ex te nascitur sanctum vo>canitur* (read *vocabitur*) *<Filius Dei>.* A shorter but similar chant text assigned to the Annunciation is found in modern Solesmes chant books. See Carolus Marbach, *Carmina scriptuarum* (Strassburg, 1907; reprint, Hildesheim: Olms, 1963), 427. The Colmar Magnificat is not in the *Corpus antiphonalium officii* and is shorter than its next medieval appearance in Piacenza, Biblioteca Capitolare C. 65, a twelfth-century chant book.

49. The origin of the expression *subarrare (subarrhare) anulo* in late antique Roman betrothals is discussed in Metz, *Consécration*, 211–12, 369–70.

50. *Idcirco serva propositum, serva castitatem per patientiam, ut coronam virginitatis tuæ accipere merearis* (Mohlberg, *Missale Francorum* [prayer no. 49]).

51. This is certain, for instance, in the Christmas matins antiphon *Tanquam sponsus dominus procedens de thalamo suo* ("Like a spouse the Lord goes forth from his bridal chamber" [*CAO* 5101]). The wider nexus of texts in which *Annulo suo* and consecrated virginity were embedded includes the male *sponsus* in the parable of the Wise and Foolish Virgins, as well as Christ as *sponsus* in a Roman consecratory preface, *Deus castorum corporum*, which is found in the earliest collection of Roman prayers, Veronensis (no. 1104).

52. A responsory in the Agnes office, *Induit me Dominus vestimento* (*CAO* 6955), also assigned in some places to the Common of Virgins, stems from the same nexus of scriptural and hagiographical texts. It is a minor reworking of Isa. 61:10 and a verse used in two centers. Verse C (*Quasi sponsum decoratum coronam*) quotes it verbatim. Verse A (*Induit me Dominus cyclade auro texta*) shares text with the antiphon, *Induit me*. Verse B (*Tradidit auribus meis*) stems from the *passio* without any evident scriptural allusions. I'm uncertain how the responsory fits with the four consecratory antiphons, but the dependence of its text on Isa. 61:10 is unquestionable.

53. It is, for instance, the basis of the methodology employed in Gevaert, *Mélopée antique*, 159–70.

54. For information on this and other medieval martyrologies, see Jacques Dubois, *Les martyrologes du moyen âge latin*, Typologie des sources du moyen âge occidental, 26 (Turnhout: Brepols, 1978), 16, 29–37. See also *Hagiographie cultures et sociétés IVe–XIIe siècles: Actes du colloque organisé à Nanterre et à Paris (2–5 mai 1979)*, Centre de Recherches sur l'Antiquité tardive et le Haut Moyen Âge, Université de Paris, 10 (Paris: Études Augustiniennes, 1981).

55. These feasts were listed in the so-called calendar of St. Willibrord, minister to Peppin of Heristall, completed before 721. Henry A. Wilson, *The Calendar of St. Willibrord: From MS. Paris. Lat. 10837*, Henry Bradshaw Society, 55 (London: Harrison and Sons, 1918), ix–xix. This calendar may have been intended for personal, not liturgical, use, and its historical impact on the continent is uncertain. Nonetheless, both feasts of St. Agnes are found in English calendars before the twelfth century. See Francis Wormald, *English Calendars before A.D. 1100*, vol. 1, *Texts*, Henry Bradshaw Society, 72 (London: Harrison and Sons Ltd., 1934).

56. E. Catherine Dunn, *The Gallican Saint's Life and the Late Roman Dramatic Tradition* (Washington, D.C.: Catholic University of America Press, 1989), 83–85. Moreover, according to Andrieu, *Ordines romani*, vol. 3, 29–30: "Sur ce point, comme en bien d'autres cas analogues, un propagateur avisé de la liturgie romain pouvait estimer plus sage, pour le

succès même de sa cause, de transiger avec les traditions locales. C'est le que fit l'auteur de notre recension β." For additional information about Frankish practices of reading hagiography, see Hen, *Culture and Religion in Merovingian Gaul*, 27; A. G. Martimort, *Les lectures liturgiques et leurs livres*, Typologie des sources du moyen âge occidental, 64 (Turnhout: Brepols, 1992), 97–102; Marc van Uytfanghe, "L'hagiographe et son publique à l'époque mérovingienne," *Studia Patristica* 16 (1985): 55; Baudouin de Gaiffier, "De l'usage de la lecture du martyrologie: Témoinages antérieurs au XIe siècle," *Analecta Bollandiana* 79 (1961): 40–59; de Gaiffier, "Martyrologes d'Auxerre: Note bibliographique," *Analecta Bollandiana* 93 (1975): 249–59.

57. Caesarius of Arles (d. 542) mentioned in passing the substitution of *passiones* for the Old Testament reading in the Mass of the catechumens. See Baudouin de Gaiffier, "La lecture des actes des martyrs dans la prière liturgique en Occident: À propos du passion-naire hispanique," *Analecta Bollandiana* 17 (1954): 146.

58. Consider, for instance, the legend of married virgins, Julian and Basilissa, which was read on the Gallican vigil of Epiphany, and Julian's *passio*. Both appear in full in the Lectionary of Luxeuil (Salmon, *Lectionnaire de Luxeuil*, 181–82, 27–57). Forced into marriage by his family, Julian convinced his wife to preserve her virginity, after which she founded a convent and he a monastery. Julian later died a martyr.

59. Hen, *Royal Patronage*, 78.

60. The oldest (*primitif*) text of *Ordo romanus* XIV, I-Rvat Palat. lat. 277, which describes the usage of St. Peter's, specifies that Office lessons were to come from Scripture and the writings of the Church Fathers (*in sancti Hieronimi, Ambrosii, ceterorum patrum*). Beginning in the eighth century, however, Frankish sources of *Ordo romanus* XIV admit *passiones matryrum et vitae patrum catholicorum*. Andrieu, *Ordines romani*, vol. 3, 29–30, 41. See also Vogel, *Medieval Liturgy*, 167–68.

61. Andrieu, *Ordines romani*, vol. 2, 478, 485–86 (*OR* XII A, no. 14). Also see Andrieu's discussion of *OR* XII in *Ordines romani*, vol. 2, 454–55, and Vogel, *Medieval Liturgy*, 166–67.

62. As far as hagiographical scholarship is concerned, surprisingly little work has been published on scriptural quotation. For an overview of literary and historical research on saints' legends, see John Kitchen, *Saints' Lives and the Rhetoric of Gender: Male and Female in Merovingian Hagiography* (New York: Oxford University Press, 1998), 3–22.

63. In the first, *Cantantibus organis*, the text of which was adapted to both an anti-phon and a responsory, Cecilia consciously quoted from Ps. 118:80 (*CAO* 1761. *Cantantibus organis, Caecilia Domino decantabat, dicens: Fiat cor meum immaculatum, ut non confundar. CAO* 6267. *Cantantibus organis, Caecilia virgo in corde suo soli Domino decantabat dicens: Fiat, Domine, cor meum et corpus meum immaculatum, ut non confundar*). In the second, likewise both an antiphon and responsory, Cecilia exhorted soldiers by quoting an epistle (Rom. 13:12): "The night is nearly over; the day is almost here. So let us put aside the deeds of darkness and put on the armor of light" (*CAO* 2437. *Dum aurora finem daret, beata Caecilia dixit: Eia, milites Christi, abiicite opera tenebrarum, et induimini arma lucis. CAO* 6531. *Dum aurora finem daret, Caecilia dixit: Eia, milites Christi, abiicite opera tenebrarum, et induimini arma lucis*).

64. In English translation (from the New Revised Standard Version), the relevant passage of Ps. 44 (45):10–15 reads: "Hear, O daughter, consider and incline your ear; forget your people and your father's house, and the king will desire your beauty. Since he is your lord, bow to him; the people of Tyre will seek your favor with gifts, the richest of the people with all kinds of wealth. The princess is decked in her chamber with gold-woven robes; in many-colored robes she is led to the king; behind her the virgins, her companions, follow. With joy and gladness they are led along as they enter the palace of the king."

65. Antoine Chavasse, *La liturgie de la ville de Rome du Ve au VIIIe siècle: Une liturgie conditionnée par l'organisation de la vie in urbe et extra muros*, Studia Anselmiana 112, Analecta liturgica, 18 (Rome: Pontificio Ateneo S. Anselmo, 1993), 123–24.

66. Claire Maître, "Du culte marial à la célébration des vierges: À propos de la psalmodie de matines," in *Marie: Le culte de la vierge dans la société médiévale. Études réunies par Dominique Iogna-Prat, Éric Palazzo, Daniel Russo* (Paris: Beauchesne, 1996), 58. I wish to thank the author for bringing this contribution to my attention.

67. Maître, "Du culte marial," 56–57.

68. Maître, "Du culte marial," 59–62.

69. *CAO* 4987 Ant. *Specie tua et pulchritudine tua* (Ps. 44:5) for Agnes, Agatha, Cecilia, Mary Magdalene (in Rome), Assumption and other Marian feasts, and the Common of Virgins. *CAO* 7679 Resp. *Specie tua et pulchritudine tua* for the Common of Virgins, Lucy, Agnes, Agatha, and Cecilia; *CAO* 7680 Resp. *Specie tua et pulchritudine tua intende* and its verse, *Diffusa est gratia* (*CAO* 7680). See also the following responsory verses: *CAO* 7452 for Agnes; *CAO* 7441 (Ps. 44:3) for the Common of Virgins, Agatha, and Cecilia; *CAO* 7826 (Ps. 44:12) for the Common of Virgins, Agnes, and Assumption in Rome; *CAO* 6308 (Ps. 44:12) for the Common of Virgins, the Nativity of the Virgin Mary, and Cecilia; *CAO* 6446 (Ps. 44:3) for Assumption, the Common of Virgins, Agnes, Agatha, and Cecilia.

CHAPTER 2

MUSIC, VIOLENCE, AND THE STAKES OF LISTENING

RICHARD LEPPERT

Perspectives must be fashioned that displace and estrange the world, reveal it to be, with its rifts and crevices, as indigent and distorted as it will appear one day in the messianic light.

—Theodor W. Adorno,
Minima Moralia: Reflections from Damaged Life

Scars have the strange power to remind us that our past is real.
—Cormac McCarthy, *All the Pretty Horses*

ANCIENT WORLD: SETTING THE STAGE

Apollo shouldered the burden of representing the forces and accomplishments of civilization. His attribute was the kithara, otherwise the lyre,[1] which served as the visual label for his claims to the establishment of cosmic order or, to aestheticize the matter, to cosmic harmony and thus to invoke the world of sound. Musical sound is an articulation of life: someone to make it, and someone to hear it. What is heard has stakes attached. The entire history of Western civilization is marked by acute concern with what is available to be heard, particularly as regards the intentional and self-reflexive sounds of music. Plato's musings on this score, channeling Socrates, provide perhaps the best-known social theory of music in the ancient world. Pretty much every student of music history has read some of the relevant prose in *The Republic*, though Plato's concerns with music are not confined to this treatise.[2] Long antedating Plato, the relation of music to the state of the social fabric is anchored in mythic accounts of two musicians, one a high-status deity, Apollo, a principal subject of this chapter, and one a high-status human being, Orpheus, concerning whom I have less to say. Regarding the deity, here is the gist of his considerable pedigree:

> [Apollo] was the god of music, poetry, and the dance, and in classical times came to be regarded also as god of the plastic arts and of science and philosophy, the god of intellect and the enemy of barbarism. He was the protector of flocks and herds.... He was the god of healing.... He was the god of prophecy. Above all, he was the god of light: of the physical light that dispels darkness, of the light of spring and summer that puts the winter to flight, and of the spiritual and moral light that dispels the darkness and ignorance from men's minds and evil from their hearts.

And here is the payoff: "The worship of Apollo was one of the most potent of the forces that brought Greek civilization to full flower."[3]

Apollo was a nice enough guy, we are told, except when something else was called for, and then he could be brutal. In particular, brutality emerged when his authority was challenged. Apollo regulated the order—better, the *harmony*—defining the unequal relation of gods to humans. Here music enters, and music was something Apollo took seriously, though perhaps less as an acoustic event as such and more for what it signaled about the general state of things.

The platonic metaphor of cosmic harmony, marked as the inaudible but real music of the heavenly spheres, following in the wake of Pythagorean mathematics, clarifies the stakes of Apollo's musicianship.[4] If the universe holds together *musically*, so to speak, then the musician-deity himself, reasonably enough, has heavy responsibilities as a kind of intermediary between heaven and earth, macrocosm and microcosm. In brief, Apollo was in charge of what we might call a sonoric ecology.

Given his status as one of the twelve Olympian deities, Apollo was understandably earnest about his place atop the musical-aesthetic pyramid. Challenge to his acoustic authority, in essence, was a challenge to the order of things generally, and nothing seems to have irritated him more than challenges from below. Enter poor Marsyas, the satyr, who learned the lesson of *hybris* from Apollo the hard way.[5] Apollo did not actually mind so much engaging in a contest with a lesser since the occasion permitted him an opportunity to remind the minions just who he was.[6] That said, he did not like to lose. Marsyas, no mean performer, nearly beat Apollo in a musical two-out-of-three; indeed, had the god not stacked the deck for the final round, Marsyas might actually have carried the day.

By most accounts, Marsyas's instrument, the aulos,[7] was invented by Pallas Athena (Minerva), who was much taken with it. However, when she performed for the other gods, they laughed at how silly she looked with puffed-out cheeks.[8] Thus embarrassed, she discarded the instrument and for good measure laid a curse on it.[9] Marsyas found the aulos and developed impressive skills playing it, such that he bragged that he was a better musician than even Apollo. This news got around to the god, who promptly challenged Marsyas to a musical dual, a kind of battle of the one-man bands, though with higher stakes than we have come to expect from such events. The contestants agreed that the winner could exact whatever penalty he desired on the loser. The Muses, Apollo's friends every one of them and deities to boot, judged the affair.[10] Accordingly, Marsyas should have known better.

Here is the play-by-play of what was a reasonably straightforward sporting event, replete with cheating. In the initial round, Apollo started things off with a kithara number, but the Muses, on hearing Marsyas's impressive performance, judged in his favor. In the second round, Apollo made his first effort to stack the deck: He both played and sang, a feat impossible for Marsyas; hence, Apollo won. Marsyas, furious, accused Apollo of cheating since the contest revolved around instruments, not voice. Apollo countered that he had done no more than Marsyas, namely, used both his hands and mouth to make music. To settle the matter a third round was required. As with other aspects of the story, sources differ on the details, but there is agreement that the god craftily tricked Marsyas such that Apollo's winning was guaranteed. One account or another says that Apollo either played his kithara turned around or, better, inverted; he then challenged Marsyas to do the same, which was, of course, impossible.[11] For good measure, not coincidentally, Apollo also sang the praises of Olympus and Helicon, a bit of flattery that produced the intended effect on the Muses.

Here is Ovid's brief account in *Metamorphoses*. What is especially noteworthy is that he has almost nothing to say about what got Marsyas into the fix with Apollo; instead he focuses on the Marsyas's punishment for his musical transgression:

> So that story
> Was ended; somebody began another,
> About that satyr whom Latona's son
> Surpassed at playing the flute [i.e., aulos], and punished, sorely,
> Flaying him,[12] so the skin all left his body,
> So he was one great wound, with the blood flowing,
> The nerves exposed, veins with no cover of skin
> Over their beating surface, lungs and entrails
> Visible as they functioned. The country people,
> The woodland gods, the fauns, his brother satyrs,
> The nymphs, and even Olympus, whom he loved
> Through all his agony, all wept for him
> With every shepherd looking after his flocks
> Along those mountainsides. The fruitful earth

Drank in those tears, and turned them into water,
And sent them forth to air again, a rill,
A stream, the clearest of all the running Phrygian rivers,
Named Marsyas, for the victim.[13]

Greek art, unlike Roman art, on the whole downplayed the violence enacted upon Marsyas, as on a fourth-century BCE relief on the base of a statue to Artemis, where the event is reduced to the most minimal facets of the story. Apollo, relaxed, sits with his kithara and listens to Marsyas playing a double aulos. Marsyas strikes a defiant pose; his tensed muscles make emphatic his hubristic arrogance, just as his athletic physique lays visual-metaphorical claim to his status as a worthy challenger to the nearly delicate, even feminine, and fully robed Apollo. The stakes of the outcome are specified by the man standing between the contestants, hand on hip, weight shifted to one leg, head appropriately inclined toward Marsyas in midtune. His right hand holds a prominently visible knife, as he awaits Apollo's orders (figure 2.1).

A second-century marble Roman sarcophagus frieze tells more of the story. With Minerva looking on at the left, the nude Marsyas performs, while Apollo, likewise nude and sporting an ephebelike body, stands at the ready with his kithara. The outcome, the flaying scene, is at the extreme right (figure 2.2).[14]

Figure 2.1. Praxiteles Workshop, *Musical Contest between Apollo and Marsyas* (ca. 350 BCE). Marble base for statue of Artemis. Athens, National Archaeological Museum. Photo credit: Scala/Art Resource, New York (ART352565).

Figure 2.2. *Sarcophagus of the Muses [Musical Contest between Apollo and Marsyas]* (2nd century CE). Roman. Marble, 220 x 105 cm. Paris, Louvre. Photo credit: Réunion des Musées Nationaux/Art Resource, New York (ART370412).

NEW WORLD: BLOOD SPORT

My principal interest in this story involves its significance in history closer to our own. In the late *quattrocento*, Apollo reemerged as a general stand-in for cultural accomplishment, a function he continued to perform into the early modernity of the seventeenth century and even later in various parts of Europe.[15] More to my concern, after long centuries of hiatus, the contest between Apollo and Marsyas reemerged as well, especially during the baroque, and this time with special emphasis given to the torture-execution—better, martyrdom—of Marsyas.[16] The trope was particularly popular in Italy, Spain, and the Low Countries, sites of highly politicized Catholic orthodoxy in the case of Italy and Spain (and opposition to Spain), marked by the Inquisition in the case of the Low Countries.

Pietro Perugino's late fifteenth-century representation of the musical contest presents the event as one involving two near equals, though Apollo, higher in the cosmic hierarchy, is physically larger; he also stands in the foreground nearest the picture plane, whereas Marsyas sits and is stationed in slight recess. Apollo listens passively, and Marsyas appears nearly as relaxed. Indeed, the event is markedly calm, governed by a kind of *politesse*, though several references to the bad outcome for Marsyas are referenced by means of sky-borne falcons diving toward prey; by anemones blooming at Marsyas's feet, conventional symbols of sorrow and death; and by deadly nightshade, also a symbol of death, growing near the rock where the satyr is seated (figure 2.3).[17]

Figure 2.3. Pietro Perugino (1448–1523), *Musical Contest between Apollo and Marsyas* (1495–1500); oil on poplar, 39 x 29 cm. Paris, Louvre. Photo: Christian Jean. Photo credit: Réunion des Musées Nationaux/Art Resource, New York (ART333377).

Over the course of the next century, Italian and Spanish painters and printmakers lavished attention on the Apollo-Marsyas contest, emphasizing the flaying and all but ignoring the musical contest that preceded the punishment. Perhaps the best known is by Titian, a gigantic painting, strikingly bloody, with life-size figures.[18] Titian takes care to draw the viewer's attention to the story's heartless violence. Thus, Marsyas is worked over by two knife-wielding men (as if one were not sufficient), and he adds for good measure a satyr with a bucket of water, presumably to help clean up the gore. Making emphatic Marsyas's suffering, as well as his degradation, Titian paints in a small dog inelegantly lapping at a puddle of the satyr's blood. King Midas, here borrowed from the Apollo-Pan musical contest, pensively looks on (figure 2.4).[19]

Titian's empathy is with the victim, highly unusual among period representations. Accordingly, he pushes Apollo off to one side, against the very edge of the frame. At first glance, Apollo seems nearly an afterthought, almost an embarrassment. Seemingly uninvolved in the proceedings, he busies himself by playing his lira da braccio,[20] the contemporary high-caste Renaissance bowed string instrument that in paintings of the period often replaces the kithara or lyre.

He looks to the heavens, posed godlike, and maintains his metaphorical distance. Apollo is not an obviously sympathetic character in Titian's rendering—nor

Figure 2.4. Titian [Tiziano Vecellio] (ca. 1488–1576), *The Flaying of Marsyas* (1570–1575); oil on canvas, 212 x 207 cm. Kromeriz, Czech Republic, Archbishop's Palace. Photo credit: Erich Lessing/Art Resource, New York (ART146689).

for good measure is he much to look at by contrast with Marsyas. Indeed, were it not for the light catching his face, together with the relative brightness of the clouds above him, Apollo would hardly be noticeable. But precisely this light draws our eyes back and forth between the two protagonists, encouraging contemplation of the difference they encode. In this regard, it is worth noting that Titian produced the painting very near the end of his long life; further, so far as is known, it was not a commissioned piece. He very likely chose the subject and decided on its unusual treatment without outside direction.[21]

Titian in fact incorporates two canines into the painting, neither of which is authorized by the myth, perhaps employing them to mirror the protagonists in a way that reinforces the reversal of our sympathies, exchanging Apollo for Marsyas. Titian diminishes Apollo's apparent moral character. One dog, the almost absurdly small one, enjoys the nectar of the martyrdom; the other dog, much larger and possessing a kind of elegant reserve, holds himself back, mirroring Marsyas's reserve while being butchered. Tiny Apollo; large Marsyas.[22]

In many Renaissance and later paintings, Marsyas plays the syrinx (panpipes) rather than the aulos. Titian hangs this instrument from a tree branch and near the neck of Apollo's lira da braccio. Compositionally speaking, the low-caste panpipes are positioned above the high-caste lira, the neck of which points directly at the syrinx, as if to draw attention to the reversal of the musical hierarchy and thus further to amplify the ambiguity of the painting's semiotics.[23]

Whereas ancient representations of Marsyas commonly afforded him the body of a man, Renaissance and later representations usually assigned him the physical attributes of a hybrid: half man, half goat. In other words, in early-modern imagery, Marsyas was demoted in the natural hierarchy; in short, he was othered, as is the case with Titian.[24] In moral-ethical terms, it is one thing to flay a man, quite another to flay a hybrid; the two are not moral equivalents.[25]

Though set within conventional parameters for representing Marsyas, Titian's remarkable painting is otherwise anything but conventional. Period paintings, Titian's included, ordinarily focused attention on Marsyas—Titian positions the satyr so that his navel marks the precise center of the composition. However, in virtually every other way, the painting stands out from others of its kind. What is particularly different with Titian is the *quiet* evident throughout the scene. The two butchers work with almost delicate care on their victim, especially the one in the foreground; concomitantly, Marsyas hardly reacts to what must be his unspeakable suffering. This detail is significant since his placid demeanor precisely replicates long-established conventions for representing the martyrdom of Christian saints. Marsyas looks out at us not as if to ask for succor but to create an empathetic bond. Titian, as it were, has visually canonized him.

Echoing Foucault,[26] Marsyas's execution reasserts the established, yet ever fragile, cultural order and social hierarchy of the mythological world. As a metaphor, it assumes the same task for the real world in early modernity. Accordingly, given the visual spectacle of the torture, we might be inclined to dismiss the musical aspects of the drama as little more than the pretext for what follows from it. However, in fact, music lies at the heart of the matter and in a number of overdetermined ways, though to get at them I have to wander away from the mythological musical contest itself. I begin by considering the relationships that tie together power, music, and, however oddly, sex.

The stakes and indeed the pleasures of Apollo's butchery are noteworthy in a homoerotic painting of the flaying attributed to Guido Reni, ca. 1625. Apollo in this instance is provided the soft face of teenaged boy; the rest of his body, somewhat outsized for the torso, is fundamentally feminine, the hips in particular. Having made the first cut, Apollo withdraws the knife to gaze weirdly upon his victim, himself a young adult with a distinctly masculine physique, his well-muscled arms outstretched in the unmistakable gesture associated with crucifixion. A distinct contrast is evident between the essentially passive face of Apollo, pausing to take in the impact of his butchery, and that of Marsyas, whose visage is profoundly distorted by his helpless scream. The difference helps to amplify the erotic tension underscored by other details (figure 2.5).

Reni treats the execution as a symbolic rape, positioning Apollo's left leg, phalliclike and duly well lighted, between the splayed (read: feminized) and darker legs of Marsyas. More to my point, the flaying starts at an odd place on Marsyas's body, the armpit. Apollo begins by cutting into a body cavity of sorts. Except for the implicit sexual implication of the choice, this makes little sense. Indeed, most representations of the flaying start with an arm or, more commonly, a leg, in which case Marsyas is suspended head down. Reni's choice of the armpit ratchets up the punishment by means of the metaphoric castration, hence effeminization, of his victim. The knife, profoundly phallic, is held as though to replicate an erection; Reni draws our attention to this detail by reflecting light off its edge. With his free hand, Apollo folds back the flesh of the armpit so that it resembles a bloodied vagina. In sum, he delivers an insult that robs the satyr of the sign of his Dionysian sexual potency,[27] *and* he makes him into a woman.[28] Marsyas is first humiliated, then murdered. And for Apollo's troubles, for getting his hands bloody, part of the payoff comes in the form of sex-tinged sadism, the pleasure evident in the look on the god's face.

The aulos in ancient Greek culture was long associated with sexual potency and Dionysian excess. Thus, vase paintings very commonly represent naked aulos players sporting notably exaggerated erections.[29] Marsyas's cousin, the satyr Pan, who also challenged Apollo to a contest, plays multiple pipes: panpipes, *all pipes*, and he usually wears one pipe more for good measure, via his private parts on prominent tumescent display, as a sort of genital exclamation point for his claims to agency. Similarly, Marsyas's aulos is a double pipe instrument: Its phallicism is compounded, *and* Marsyas knows how to use it, even to the point of wowing the ladies. The Muses, after all, initially gave him the first round of the contest, much to Apollo's consternation, thereby inducing the god quickly to adopt desperate measures. Thus, Reni's symbolic castration of Marsyas smartly reads the stakes of winning and losing by stating the matter in metaphors of sex, no matter what the degree to which he exceeds the ancient sources.[30]

Figure 2.5. Guido Reni (1575–1642), attr., *Apollo Flaying Marsyas* (ca. 1625); oil on canvas.
Turin, Galleria Sabauda. Photo credit: Scala/Art Resource, New York (ART24469).

One of the most noteworthy visual aspects of Italian iterations of the Apollo-
Marsyas trope is the gigantic size of most—though not all—of these paintings. For
example, the version, painted in 1637, by Jusepe de Ribera (1591–1652), a Spanish painter
long active in Naples,[31] is well more than two meters in length. The painting dominates
space. Something like an outsized billboard, it aggressively proclaims the dialectical
relationship of order and chaos and makes its choice between them. Like nearly all of
such images it does so by means of an aestheticization of politics. Repeatedly, period
representations emphasize Marsyas's extreme agony by giving us plenty to imagine
with regard to the method of his killing and do so—Titian notwithstanding—with no
particular regard for Marsyas's suffering, as if to proclaim a just punishment. In Ribera's

picture, Apollo has his hand in the bloody cut on the satyr's leg, the wound replicating the vaginal shape evident in Reni's version of the subject; its stark and bloody redness made emphatic by the light that seems to emanate from its depths, all the more evident against a very dark surrounding background (figure 2.6).

Common to these paintings, Marsyas's body is dramatically foreshortened; it also lies at an acute angle to the rectangular frame. Marsyas looks out from the picture plane, upside down, and calls out to us as if in the absurd hope that we might rescue him. Satyrs in back at the right look on helplessly. They cannot and will not interfere with Apollo's imposition of order. The god's voluminous drapery puffs out behind him in homage not only to his status as a deity but also to the apparent energy at his disposal. Could the musical contest ever have been in doubt? Ribera assures us that the outcome was never in question—exactly what authority wants its minions to believe. Apollo's lavish, indeed excessive, drapery hides alternative possibilities, and Marsyas, being disrobed of his suit of skin, reaffirms as much.[32]

Marsyas's flaying resonated not only with mythology but also with reality. As a form of torture execution, flaying was an ancient practice whose long history in Europe extended into early modernity.[33] It was also part and parcel of anatomical education not only for medical students but also for artists—Leonardo and Michelangelo, for

Figure 2.6. Jusepe de Ribera (1591–1652), *Apollo Flaying Marsyas* (1637); oil on canvas, 182 x 32 cm. Naples, Museo Nazionale di Capodimonte. Photo credit: Scala/Ministero per i Beni e te Attività culturali/Art Resource, New York (ART189440).

example, both worked on flayed cadavers.[34] The figure of the *écorché*, a body whose skin was removed so as to expose the muscles and sinews, was commonly illustrated in anatomical studies (figure 2.7) throughout the period.[35] Moreover, the cadavers used in anatomical education were often those available as the result of executions. No surprise, then, that the *écorché* is referenced in numerous period representations of the Apollo and Marsyas story (figure 2.8). This subject and the horrors associated with it, culturally speaking, were highly overdetermined.

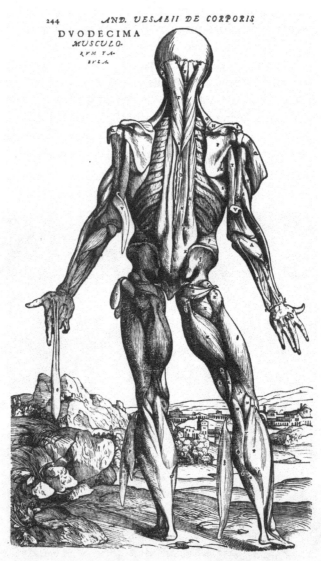

Figure 2.7. Andreas Vesalius (1514–1564), *Écorché Surveying an Italianate Landscape* (from *De humani corporis fabrica*, 2d ed., rev. 1555, 244); woodblock engraving, 39.3 x 26 cm. Minneapolis, Owen H. Wangensteen Historical Library of Biology and Medicine, University of Minnesota.

Figure 2.8. Filippo Lauri (1623–1694), *The Punishment of Marsyas* (1637); oil on copper, 17 x 22 cm. Paris, Musée du Louvre, inv. no. 337. Photo credit: Erich Lessing/Art Resource, New York (ART158123).

Modern World: The Aesthetics of Order

Southern and northern Europe alike were sites of Counter-Reformation attempts to stem the tide of the Protestant revolt. The efforts to maintain the hegemony of Catholicism were not, of course, solely the work of the Roman Church; the European states set to the task as well, Spain especially. The Catholic Low Countries were managed at the time, often violently, by local administrators on behalf of Spain and its rabidly Catholic king, Philip II (1527–1598), whose policies toward the region produced open revolt by the midpoint of the sixteenth century.[36] By 1576, following a period of terror carried out by Philip's local commander, the despised Duke of Alva, much of the countryside, as well as towns and cities, had been laid waste. Mass executions were common, sanctioned by the so-named Council of Trouble, popularly known as the Council of Blood.

By late in Philip's reign, the northern Low Countries, what became Protestant Holland, were already lost to him. Shortly before his death, he assigned rule of the Spanish Netherlands, the southern part of the territories, to his favorite daughter, Isabella, as a dowry on the occasion of her marriage to her cousin, Albert of Austria who, not coincidentally, was a cardinal in the Catholic Church when Philip II appointed him archduke (he eventually received a dispensation to marry). The region was still at war when Isabella and Albert assumed their administrative responsibilities. They inherited a devastated landscape. In 1609, however, they successfully engineered a twelve-year truce, temporarily ending the violence. The truce ended in

1621, the same year that Albert died, after which hostilities again broke out against the larger backdrop of the Thirty Years' War (1618–1648). The second half of the seventeenth century did not offer much relief. The territory was fought over, variously, by Spain, France, Holland, and even England. Finally, with the Peace of Utrecht in 1713 and the Peace of Rastatt in 1714, the Spanish Netherlands was ceded to Austria.

In the midst of the ideological, political, economic, and military conflicts afflicting the Spanish Netherlands in the late sixteenth and seventeenth centuries, Apollo was again called on, sometimes via his contest with Marsyas but also via his musical duel with Pan. Just as often and at least as important, he performed with a consort of Muses. For good measure, Orpheus also made his appearance, charming the animals in metaphorical reference to a would-be peaceable kingdom, though one made peaceful by his seemingly endless agency to get the world to do his bidding, as it were, just like Apollo. So powerfully affecting was the music of Orpheus that fauna lay down at his feet in a harmony that suspended interspecies violence; so arresting was his music that even the trees bent toward him and rocks softened.[37] Little wonder that this trope was popular at the time in the region. Like Busby Berkeley movies during the Great Depression, the Orpheus story helped to satisfy the needs of both the rulers and the ruled, serving as the metaphor of wise and peaceful government for the former, while providing the diverting fantasy of a perfect world for the latter.[38]

Busby Berkeley provided comic relief, marked by spectacle, to the troubles of the 1930s. In the northern European seventeenth century, the musical contest between Apollo and Pan accomplished something similar.[39] Pan, a minor deity, sported the legs, ears, and horns of a goat, together ample iteration of his perpetually randy state. Indeed, in Renaissance art Pan was a stand-in for the cardinal sin of lust. He had a way with ladies; his music charmed the maenads, who in turn rewarded him carnally. However, he pushed his luck with Apollo, who was not nearly as impressed. The deity Tmolus judged the contest and had the good sense to favor Apollo; King Midas, also present for the show, contrarily argued forcefully that Pan's performance was better. Apollo promptly assigned him the ears of an ass. Pan seems to have gotten off lightly for his affront, but then he was a god, whereas Midas was merely human (figure 2.9).[40]

Apollo in early modern culture is the standard bearer for *mesure*, that intangible quality of merit ascribed to order—or perhaps more fitting for the time—regulation. Nietzsche once put this nicely: "Apollo wants to grant repose to individual beings precisely by drawing boundaries between them and by again and again calling these to mind as the most sacred laws of the world, with his demands for self-knowledge and measure."[41] In terms of music, the principal and distinctly popular visual assertion of this trope was Apollo in ensemble performance with the Muses. In this instance, Apollo, gone modern, has updated his instrumentarium. Having left aside the Renaissance lira da braccio, he has taken up the violin. The Muses have updated as well; their instruments, all in use at the time, include flute, harp, lute, and an early-version violoncello, thick necked and deep ribbed. Other instruments, together with some open music books, lie on the ground: cittern, trombone (or sackbut), and two recorders, probably soprano and alto.[42] A musical updating of this sort is neither

Figure 2.9. Hendrik de Clerck (1570–1629), *The Musical Contest between Apollo and Pan*
(1600–1629); oil on copper, 43 x 62 cm. Amsterdam, Rijksmuseum, inv. no. SK-A-621.
Photo credit: Amsterdam, Rijksmuseum.

accidental nor semiotically void. To employ the very instruments that Flemings
would have readily known—and at least in principal have heard—is to purport the
rightness of Apollo's rule via the assertion of an idealized world order of the here and
now. It is up to his putative modern subjects to listen up (figure 2.10).

Apollo rests at the literal apex of an acoustic pyramid; his head, appropriately,
is aglow with a surrounding nimbus. He and his companions sit atop Parnassus; the
world, all of it markedly fecund and orderly, spreads out beneath them: quiet, lovely,
peaceful, perfect. No compositional accident, a pretty village is evident in the lower
left foreground, untouched by contemporaneous war. The sounds of the consort's
harmonies attract beautiful birds; some roost in the trees, another prominently
glides in for a better hearing. But none of it is real; not least, there is, after all, no
such landscape in the Low Countries. What can be seen is what might be wished.
The painting offers hope, though at what cost is masked. Masking in this instance is
another word for the aestheticization of politics.

The most accomplished builders of virginals and harpsichords in the region
during this period were the several members of the Ruckers family. Their splendid
instruments are well known not least for their decoration, especially the employment of Latin mottoes, block-printed on paper, glued onto the case. For the most
part, the mottoes that the Ruckers (and other builders) employed were benign, of
the sort: "I was once an ordinary tree, although living I was silent; now, though
dead, if I am well played, I sound sweetly."[43] Still, there are exceptions. Some

Figure 2.10. Johannes Tilens (1589–1630), *Apollo and the Muses*; oil. Whereabouts
unknown. Photo credit: IRPA-KIK-Brussels.

instruments carry warnings that tend toward threat. Two surviving Ruckers instruments, for example, declare the following imperative: "*Audi vide et tace / Si vis
vivere in pace*"; that is, "Listen, watch, and be silent if you wish to live in peace."[44]
The motto can be read in several ways, and its very ambiguity may well be a determining factor in its use. At a minimum, the message invites vigilance, and in a
language of privilege, Latin—not the vernacular but the language of ancient
Roman authority (Pax Romana) and the modern Roman Church. *Official* language. The motto's insistence on vigilance is anchored in consequence. Without
vigilance, peace is supplanted by its presumed opposite, war. The motto invokes
hearing and looking, but its real advice is to listen and indeed to spy. As a general
order during fraught times, the motto assertively offers strategic advice. In the end,
the radical ambiguity of the text helps to establish its overriding point. That is,
precisely because the world is so unstable, threat might come from anywhere. Only
uncertainty is certain, so take care.

　　Why the advice to remain quiet? The imperative asserts the importance of
close listening: That is, keep your mouth shut and your ears open. Sounds have
meaning, the motto suggests. Sounds have consequences. Sounds require hermeneutics. But why all this on a musical instrument? Perhaps because *all* sounds are
meaningful, even, so to speak, songs without words. Put differently, the aesthetic
has agency in the social and cultural realm of order, though in whose interest is
without guarantee.

Figure 2.11. *Double Manual Harpsichord* (17th century), Flemish, formerly attributed to Hans (Joannes) Ruckers (1578–1642). Brussels, Musée des Instruments de Musique, inv. no. 2510. Photo credit: IRPA-KIK-Brussels.

The decoration of harpsichords with Latin texts is often supplemented with case paintings, many featuring Apollo, often in the company of the Muses. Sometimes on a single instrument he makes a second appearance in a different musical story, such as his contest with Pan, as on a large double-manual Flemish instrument, formerly attributed to Hans Ruckers,[45] or even, if more rarely, his contest with Marsyas and featuring the flaying scene, a subject that by modern standards would seem distinctly inappropriate for a domestic instrument, though this was hardly the case in early modernity (figure 2.11).[46]

TABLEAU VIVANT

In 1615, in the elegant spatial enclosure of the Brussels Grand Place and surrounding streets, there was staged a highly elaborate public parade known as an *ommegang*, an annual and centuries-old affair common to many towns throughout the region. Music of various sorts was central to the *ommegang*, some of it furnished by the professional musicians of the town wind band, typically involving shawms and sackbut, and sometimes with other wind instruments as well. The Brussels *ommegang* was especially important. It was very large, having the flavor of the Macy's Thanksgiving Day parade. There were decorated wagons, of which more presently, as well as outsized figures such as giants and dragons. The many members of the fifty-four Brussels guilds marched in procession, including twenty-eight fife and drum players from the military guilds, as well as clergy and city magistrates.[47] Isabella commissioned Denis van Alsloot (before 1573–1625/1626) to produce six large paintings of the event, of which four survive. The climax of the 1615 *ommegang* was the spectacular, multipart Triumph of Isabella, represented by the fifth painting in the series (figure 2.12).

This critical portion of the parade was organized by the College of Jesuits in Brussels—the religious order was a well-established and powerful arm of the Counter-Reformation in the Spanish Netherlands. Church and state came together for what mattered most in this celebratory metaphor of the rightness of the status quo marked by court dominance. The purported context of court and civic unity organizing the *ommegang*, however, was more asserted than real and anything but permanent.[48]

In all, the Triumph of Isabella involved ten large parade wagons, preceded by men riding horses, as well as camels, animals whose exoticness helped to confirm the globalized power of Spain. Each wagon held costumed actors staging a *tableau vivant*, some representing New Testament stories, others paying direct homage to Isabella as a wise ruler. Reference was readily asserted as to the bond shared by church, state, and citizenry. Several cars represented subjects drawn from mythology, one of which, the fourth car—the object of my interest—were Apollo and the Muses. Apollo, wearing a flame-studded nimbus, is seated on a throne stationed above the Muses; the Olympian landscape is referenced by shrubbery at the front and back of the wagon. A small placard on the side of the decorated wagon references Isabella's skill with the crossbow at an important annual civic event held two weeks

Figure 2.12. Denis van Alsloot (before 1573–1625/26), *Ommegang at Brussels, 31 May 1615: The Triumph of Archduchess Isabella* (1616) (no. 5 in a series of 6 paintings); oil on canvas, 116.8 x 378.4 cm. London: Victoria and Albert Museum, inv. no. 5928-1859. Photo credit: Victoria and Albert Museum, London/Art Resource, New York (ART73738).

before the *ommegang* ("*Cedoes voster arc*"),[49] and another underscores the praise thus due her ("*Nous chantons une belle victoire*") (figure 2.13).

Apollo plays harp; the Muses play pocket fiddle, cittern, harp, lutes, perhaps lira da braccio, large five-string violoncello or perhaps bass viol, transverse flute, triangle with jingle rings, and tambourine. The instruments are modern, such that they would likely have been borrowed from a private inventory, whether intended merely as props or to be played. The ensemble is plausible for the time, and though the sounds of the stringed instruments would hardly carry far amid the din of the

Figure 2.13. Denis van Alsloot (before 1573–1625/26), *Parade Wagon with Apollo and the Muses*; detail of *Ommegang at Brussels, 31 May 1615: The Triumph of Archduchess Isabella* (1616) Photo credit: Victoria and Albert Museum, London/Art Resource, New York (ART73323).

setting, the percussion instruments would at a minimum have some chance of alert-
ing notice. What matters far more than their sound, to be sure, is the sight they offer,
though one perhaps not more dramatic than the wagon of Diana the huntress,
accompanied by eight nymphs, in mythological homage to the crossbow skills that
Isabella had demonstrated.

Apollo and the Muses visually constitute a tranquil peace. Torture-execution,
whether by Apollo or the unlamented Duke of Alba, is absent. The means by which
order was restored, prerequisite to Isabella's celebration, has no place in the event,
which is to say that the Triumph of Isabella is as much about forgetting as commemorating. The display is an elaborate disguise employed to help secure an uncertain status quo. The role of aesthetics in this ruse is paramount to the success of the
distracting claims asserted by the parade.

Near the end of the seventeenth century, painter Adam Frans van der Meulen
(1632–1690), a specialist of battle scenes,[50] decorated the case of a large double-
manual French harpsichord formerly ascribed to Hans Ruckers.[51] In this instance,
war and putative peace reside together in a forced relation of profound visual dissonance that asserts a bond between the art of music and the art of war (figure 2.14).

Figure 2.14. Adam Frans van der Meulen (1632–1690), *Landscape with Louis XIV and
Mounted Entourage* (lid); *Military Siege of Fortified Towns* (case); *Double Manual
Harpsichord*, portions of soundboard from a virginal; internal workings principally by
Pascal Taskin (1774). Brussels, Musée des Instruments de Musique, inv. no. M. 3848,
acquired in 1960. Photo credit: IRPA-KIK-Brussels.

The main scene, on the inside of the harpsichord's lid, shows a mounted entourage with a king riding at the head and tossing a coin to a beggar at the lower left in demonstration of his benevolence. He is Louis XIV (1638–1715), the Sun King, the monarch whose self-chosen emblem was the young Apollo as the face of the flaming sun. A walled town appears in the background. Though no battle is in actual progress, the effect of one is created,[52] especially by the repeated inclusion of galloping horses, their tails stretched out behind to indicate speed and the insistence with which they move—always like a text, from left to right, and out of the frame following a path paralleling the picture plane. On the instrument's sides similar scenes are replicated, but the viewpoint is raised somewhat, approximating the bird's-eye level typical of period siege pictures. In one of these panels, a town is under attack.[53]

In this extraordinary visual conceit, force and imputed violence become the agents of art. A panorama of unremitting maleness, the scenes together literally frame and direct the sonorities produced by the harpsichord. Violence and art music visually and sonorically answer to the cause of mutual justification.[54] Stated otherwise, order may be aesthetically realized; order may also be socially imposed. But in the end, it is order that counts.[55]

The insistence on order, relayed through aesthetic representation, helps explain the otherwise grotesque, virtually comic use of gigantic ears in an engraving purportedly representing hearing when what is at stake is less hearing and more what is heard. The print claims to illustrate a human sense—a trope very popular in the visual arts of the time[56]—but its real subject is listening (figure 2.15).

What these ears presumably hear (and what we see) is an ensemble at art music, peaceful, orderly, and familial, involving elegant women and worldly, cultivated men—their worldliness signaled by their hats. The scene inscribes harmony, contentment, and happiness, all of it the by-product of something else that is at once acknowledged and disguised. The foreground musical scene is set against a jarring background, tapestries with scenes of war and conquest, activities sonorically marked by the noise of the aristocratic cavalry trumpet. These images-within-the-image assert a claim that culture is the result of violent struggle, which the peaceful main scene in turn justifies.

The refinement of the chamber-music scene is sanctioned not only by armed combat but also by the redundancy of a key signifier, a fortress-château replicated three times in the print: on each of the tapestries and as a distant view through the central window directly behind the musicians. The multiple iteration of the castle makes emphatic the site and sight of ultimate authority. Look at the musicians, imagine the harmony they make; look also and acknowledge the hub from which still greater harmony ensues.

Two textual glosses, both wordy, together reiterate the alibi for the struggle upon which the music depends. The languages are Latin and French, one ancient, the other modern, across whose histories marched civilization from the classical world to the early-seventeenth-century present. The Latin text reads: "The lyre plucked by my nimble fingers delights me wonderfully, and the nightingale enraptures me with its sweet songs. But to me no harmony is ever more pleasing than the one which sings my praises with skillful art." The French text reads: "Considering

Figure 2.15. Abraham Bosse (1602–1676), *Hearing* (ca. 1635); engraving. Paris,
Bibliothèque Nationale. Photo credit: Bibliothèque Nationale, Paris.

the infinite sweetness of musical sounds and their various harmonies, it is not without reason said that the harmony of the spheres sustains the universe."[57] Apollo
himself might have uttered either remark. The ancient metaphor of a cosmos
defined by the harmony of mathematical relationships is invoked, overlaid with an
imagined frosting, the sweetness of sonorities that reaffirm the classical fantasy of
an ideal social ecology. The Latin text builds to an acknowledgment of personal
glory via nature imagery, while the language itself confirms the authority of the
secular ancients and the Catholic moderns. The French verse, linguistically current,
reiterates culture around the Platonic ideal. The two worlds, seemingly interchangeable, articulate the pleasures congruent with *mesure,* a peace defined explicitly by
power, privilege, and control—a peace not universally enjoyed.[58]

In the end, all of the invocations of order that I have discussed, ancient and early modern alike, are properly understood as exercises in structural listening—to borrow and
slightly distort a phrase from Adorno.[59] The structure I have in mind is one of forms:
cosmological, worldly, cultural, social, and in the end personal. Ultimately, all of them
are *to be* ordered if they are to be at all and, so it seems, at whatever cost necessary.
Attali put this well: "Listening to music is listening to all noise, realizing that its appropriation and control is a reflection of power, that it is essentially political."[60]

Attali aptly noted that music "reflects a fluid reality."[61] Music, like society, is always in process. Process is anxiety ridden not least because its outcome is uncertain. Listening to the world is fundamentally a listening *for*. In the terms I have explored, the ears of authority are perked up so as to decipher transgression, that which dependably walks beside authority every step of the way. Barthes noted that listening "is a mode of defense against surprise" and that it is linked to hermeneutics. Sounds must be deciphered because they tell us about the future.[62] A modern Apollo, if we can imagine him, might seek to meet his acoustic challenges with the understanding—here borrowing Attali's remarkable insight—that music is prophetic. What a modern Apollo is given to hear from a modern Marsyas, we might say, is what the sounds of the old satyr's aulos insist on, namely, that things might be otherwise. Marsyas's tune is a provocative *supplément* to the grand concept of order, which, when all is said and done, does not deliver on everything promised. The perennial conflict between high and low in its myriad forms—spiritual, somatic, experiential, and so on—is founded on the reality and the worth of *différence*.

The role that music plays in the aestheticization of politics hardly defines the only parameters within which music functions as a social practice. The recent and remarkable research by Suzanne G. Cusick[63] on the uses to which music has been put by the Bush administration as a tool employed against detainees in Guantánamo and other detention centers in Afghanistan, Iraq, and elsewhere as part of the "global war on terror" makes clear that music by no means invariably serves the interests of any form of aesthetics at all. In opposition to aesthetics, it can all too easily function as a form of unwilling listening inflicted as a form of punishment and worse, in full circle back to Apollo and his insistence on maintaining order at all costs, always, of course, in the name of civilization.

NOTES

1. Post antiquity, other stringed instruments were also assigned to him, including lira da braccio, violin, and harp.

2. In *The Republic*, for example, see books III and IV. See further Eva Brann, with Peter Kalkavage and Eric Salem, *The Music of the Republic: Essays on Socrates' Conversations and Plato's Writings* (Philadelphia: Dry, 2004); Edward A. Lippman, *Musical Thought in Ancient Greece* (New York: Columbia University Press, 1964); and Warren D. Anderson, *Music and Musicians in Ancient Greece* (Ithaca: Cornell University Press, 1994).

3. "Apollo," in *The New Century Classical Handbook*, ed. Catherine B. Avery (New York: Appleton-Century-Crofts, 1962), 124. The Apollo-Marsyas myth exists in a number of versions replete with varying details and differing casts of secondary players. For an impressively rich and nuanced account of the narrative in Greek and Latin texts, see Maria Rika Maniates, "Marsyas Agonistes," *Current Musicology* 69 (Spring 2000): 118–62; for a list of the classical sources of the story, see 150–54.

4. See James Haar, "Music of the Spheres," in *The New Grove Dictionary of Music and Musicians*, ed. Stanley Sadie (London: Macmillan, 2001), vol. 17, 487–88. On the Greek

concept of harmony, see Lippman, *Musical Thought in Ancient Greece*, 1–44; and Edith Wyss, *The Myth of Apollo and Marsyas in the Art of the Italian Renaissance: An Inquiry into the Meaning of Images* (Newark, N.J.: University of Delaware Press, 1996), 27–29.

5. Concerning the seriousness with which *hybris* was treated in ancient Greek culture, see Maniates, "Marsyas Agonistes," 139–40.

6. Some sources describe Marsyas as a human, though they are in the distinct minority. See Maniates, "Marsyas Agonistes," 132–33.

7. For a detailed account of the history, construction, performance history, and different types of aulos, see Annie Bélis, "Aulos," in Sadie, *New Grove Dictionary of Music and Musicians*, vol. 2, 178–84.

8. Other narratives simply indicate that, while performing, she looked at her reflection in water and disliked how the playing distorted her looks. See Maniates, "Marsyas Agonistes," 134. On the invention of the aulos in classical mythology, see 144–49.

9. Aristotle, *Politics*, trans. Benjamin Jowett; http://classics.mit.edu/Aristotle/politics. html (accessed Dec. 12, 2008), book 8, part VI:

> There is a meaning also in the myth of the ancients, which tells how Athene invented the flute [i.e., aulos] and then threw it away. It was not a bad idea of theirs, that the Goddess disliked the instrument because it made the face ugly; but with still more reason may we say that she rejected it because the acquirement of flute- [i.e., aulos] playing contributes nothing to the mind, since to Athene we ascribe both knowledge and art.

10. In both textual and visual narratives, the Muses were most often indicated as the judges of the contest; some sources, however, name other referees. See Maniates, "Marsyas Agonistes," 124–25.

11. For other versions of the final contest, see Maniates, "Marsyas Agonistes," 126.

12. Some sources suggest instead that he was whipped to death. See Maniates, "Marsyas Agonistes," 126.

13. Ovid, *Metamorphoses*, trans. Rolfe Humphries (Bloomington: Indiana University Press, 1955), vol. VI: 382–400, pp. 141–42. Well prior to Ovid, the Greek writer Philostratus the Younger, in *Imagines* (descriptions of pictures he had seen), likewise skips over the musical details to focus on the punishment. In particular, he emphasizes the preparations for the flaying undertaken by one of Apollo's handymen:

> He [Marsyas] glances furtively at the barbarian yonder who is whetting the edge of the knife to be applied to him; for you see, I am sure, that the man's hands are on the whetstone and the iron, but that he looks up at Marsyas with glaring eyes, his wild and squalid hair all bristling. The red on his cheek betokens, I think, a man thirsty for blood, and his eyebrow overhands the eye, all contracted as it faces the light and giving a certain stamp to his anger; nay, he grins, too, a savage grin in anticipation of what he is about to do—I am not sure whether because he is glad or because his mind swells in pride as he looks forward to the slaughter.

Apollo, looking on, meanwhile keeps his own hands clean:

> But Apollo is painted as resting upon a rock; the lyre which lies on his left arm is still being struck by his left hand in gentle fashion, as though playing a tune. You see the relaxed form of the god and the smile lighting up his face; his right hand rests on his lap, gently grasping the plectrum, relaxed because of his joy in the victory. (Philostratus the Younger, *Imagines*, trans. Arthur Fairbanks [Loeb Classical Library]; http://www.theoi.com/Text/PhilostratusYounger.html#2 [accessed Dec. 10, 2008], 2)

14. Cf. *The Punishment of Marsyas* (Paris, Louvre), Roman copy of a third-century BCE Hellenistic marble original, representing the satyr, arms tied over his head, suspended from a tree, awaiting his demise; http://www.artres.com, image ref. no. ART105089. See also Piers B. Rawson, *The Myth of Marsyas in the Roman Visual Arts: An Iconographic Study* (Oxford: B. A. R., 1987).

15. See Wyss, *Myth of Apollo and Marsyas.*

16. Emanuel Winternitz, "The Curse of Pallas Athena," in *Musical Instruments and Their Symbolism in Western Art* (London: Faber and Faber, 1967), 153–55. The earliest representations of Marsyas empathetically treated as the suffering victim of torture-execution appeared already in Hellenistic art; see 151.

17. Concerning anemones, see George Ferguson, *Signs and Symbols in Christian Art* (New York: Oxford University Press, 1961), 27.

18. See the detailed discussion of this painting in Wyss, *Myth of Apollo and Marsyas,* 133–41.

19. Other examples of note include (1) a seventeenth-century Emilian School *Flaying of Marsyas,* a crude painting on a glass panel, and an extraordinarily vicious representation (Imola, Italy, Pinacoteca), accessible online at http://www.frick.org, Frick Art Reference Library negative no. 24338; (2) Giovanni Francesco Guercino (1591–1666), dated 1618 (Florence, Galleria Palatina Pitti), accessible online at http://www.artres.com, image ref. no. ART304735; and (3) Johann Liss (ca. 1597–1629), dated ca. 1627 (Venice, Accademia), accessible online at http://www.artres.com, image ref. no. ART163306.

20. Regarding the lira da braccio in Renaissance representations of both Apollo and Orpheus, see Emanuel Winternitz, "The Lira da Braccio" and "Musical Archaeology of the Renaissance in Raphael's *Parnassus,*" in Winternitz, *Musical Instruments and Their Symbolism,* 86–98 and 185–201, respectively. In Renaissance Italian, *lira* can refer to the ancient lyre, the instrument associated most commonly with Orpheus, as well as Apollo, and sometimes to the lira da braccio (Winternitz, "Curse of Pallas Athena," 155).

21. See further Wyss, *Myth of Apollo and Marsyas,* 133.

22. For a somewhat different reading of the dog motif, see Wyss, *Myth of Apollo and Marsyas,* 136–37.

23. My reading differs in specifics, though it reaches a conclusion similar to that of Wyss, *Myth of Apollo and Marsyas,* q.v., 137–38, 141. Wyss, 120–32, discusses a few earlier Counter-Reformation images of the Apollo and Marsyas story that empathize with the satyr's fate, allegorically contrasting Apollo, as a vengeful pagan deity, with the merciful Christ, who sacrificed himself on behalf of humanity.

24. Perugino's earlier painting (figure 2.3) by contrast reflects the ancient tradition.

25. Precisely this moral issue crops up repeatedly in the sci-fi television series, *Battlestar Galactica* which revolves around the conflict between humans, survivors of a nuclear holocaust, and Cylons, robotic machines created by the humans to serve their needs. The Cylons evolve and violently rebel. There are two classes of Cylons: the seemingly numberless robot types—whom the humans refer to derisively as "toasters" and destroy with impunity—and human look-alikes, fundamentally indistinguishable from the real thing. The moral dilemma emerges over whether the humanlike Cylons are simply "toasters" or hybrid humans, thus having legal and ethical rights similar to those of people.

26. Michel Foucault, *Discipline and Punish: The Birth of the Prison,* trans. Alan Sheridan (New York: Vintage, 1979).

27. Satyrs in medieval and Renaissance allegory personify lust. See James Hall, *Dictionary of Signs and Symbols in Art* (New York: Harper and Row, 1974), 273. The association of reed instruments with sexuality and sometimes sexual license extends from

the ancient world to the modern; see Emanuel Winternitz, "The Knowledge of Musical Instruments as an Aid to the Art Historian," in Winternitz, *Musical Instruments and Their Symbolism*, 48–49. Winternitz, "Curse of Pallas Athena," 156n3: "In Greek writers [*sic*] the aulos is the instrument of passion, urges, instincts—in short, of what orthodox psychoanalysts would call the Id"; see further 152–53.

28. Reni was the dominant painter in seventeenth-century Italy; he spent most of his career in Bologna. He was likely homosexual; further, apart from his mother, he actively avoided contact with women. Richard E. Spear, "Reni, Guido," *Grove Art Online*.

29. Regarding Marsyas, however, the matter is less clear in the ancient sources; see Maniates, "Marsyas Agonistes," 138.

30. Another and nearly identical version by Reni of *Apollo Flaying Marsyas* (oil on canvas, 220 × 167 cm.) is in Toulouse, Musée des Augustins, inv. no. D 1805 4.

Noteworthy among the other gigantic iterations of the trope is a painting by Luca Giordano (1634–1705), ca. 1650s (oil on canvas, 205 × 259 cm.) in Naples, Museo Nazionale di Capodimonte, inv. no. Q 799, accessible online at http://www.artres.com, image ref. no. ART215217.

31. Naples was under the often repressive and tyrannical control of Spain from the beginning of the sixteenth century through the seventeenth. Ribera's principal patrons were the church and the nobility, including the viceroys, from whom he received numerous commissions and, during the popular uprising of 1647, physical protection.

32. Another, even larger version (1637) by Ribera of the flaying, compositionally very close to the painting in Naples, is in Brussels, Musées Royaux des Beaux-Arts.

33. See Lionello Puppi, *Torment in Art: Pain, Violence, and Martyrdom*, trans. Jeremy Scott (New York: Rizzoli, 1991), who treats the subject from the twelfth to the nineteenth century; and Edward Peters, *Torture* (Oxford: Blackwell, 1985). The torture execution of the would-be assassin of King Louis XV in 1757, Father Robert-François Damiens, recounted at the beginning of Foucault's *Discipline and Punish*, 3–4, is a late example of the practice in which heated pinchers were used to tear away pieces of his flesh as part of the ritual.

34. James Elkins, "Michelangelo and the Human Form: His Knowledge and Use of Anatomy," *Art History* 7 (1984): 176–86.

35. Jusepe de Ribera's well-known *Martyrdom of Saint Bartholomew* (ca. 1640–50), Osuna (Seville), Spain, Museo Parroquial de la Collegiata, similarly represents the saint's arm entirely flayed; the image is accessible online at http://www.artres.com, image ref. no. ART213824. A 1536 engraving by the monogrammist M. F. represents Marsyas's body as entirely flayed; Apollo holds up the skin from his body, face included, as though it were a suit of clothing. The image is accessible online at ArtStor.

36. For a detailed accounts of the period, see Pieter Geyl, *The Revolt of the Netherlands: 1555–1609*, 2d ed. (London: Benn, 1958); and by the same author, *The Netherlands in the Seventeenth Century, Part One: 1609–1648*, 2d ed. (London: Benn, 1961); *Part Two: 1648–1715* (London: Benn, 1964); and Adrien de Meeüs, *History of the Belgians*, trans. G. Gordon (New York: Praeger, 1962).

37. Ovid, *Metamorphoses*, X:86–105, 237.

38. Arthur K. Wheelock, ed., *Aelbert Cuyp* (exhibition catalogue) (Washington, D.C.: National Gallery of Art, 2001), 90.

39. Ovid, *Metamorphoses*, XI:146–93, 263–65.

40. In Hendrik de Clerk's painting, Minerva stands next to Apollo; apparently some of the Muses are also present for good measure, teaming up, as it were, for a contest that seems somewhat confused with the Apollo-Marsyas competition.

41. Friedrich Nietzsche, *The Birth of Tragedy, and the Case of Wagner*, trans. Walter Kaufmann (New York: Vintage, 1967), 72, from *The Birth of Tragedy* (1886 ed.).

42. For other representations of this subject, see Richard Leppert, *The Theme of Music in Flemish Paintings of the Seventeenth Century*, 2 vols. (Munich: Katzbichler, 1977), vol. 1, 105–107; Albert Pomme de Mirimonde, "Les concerts des muses chez les maîtres du nord," *Gazette des Beaux-Arts*, ser. 6, 63 (1964), 129–58; and by the same author, "L'Hélicon ou la visite de Minerve aux Muses," *Jaarboek van het Koninklijk Museum voor Schone Kunsten* (Antwerp: n.p., 1961), 141–50.

43. "*Arbor eram vilis quondam sed viva tacebam / Nunc bene si tangor mortua dulce solo.*" Quoted in Thomas McGeary, "Harpsichord Mottoes," *Journal of the American Musical Instrument Society* 7 (1981): 19, motto no. 4. For variants, see 21, no. 15; and 34, no. 73. None of these is a Ruckers instrument.

This study provides a detailed list of harpsichord mottoes on surviving instruments and those preserved in paintings with musical subjects that include harpsichords. See also by the same author "Harpsichord Decoration—A Reflection of Renaissance Ideas about Music," *Explorations in Renaissance Culture* 6 (1980): 1–27; Grant O'Brien, *Ruckers: A Harpsichord and Virginal Building Tradition* (New York: Cambridge University Press, 1990), 128–71; Sheridan Germann, "Regional Schools of Harpsichord Decoration," *Journal of the American Musical Instrument Society* 4 (1978): 64–74, concerning Flemish instruments; and by the same author, "Harpsichord Decoration: A Conspectus," in Howard Schott, ed., *The Historical Harpsichord*, vol. 4, *Harpsichord Decoration and the Yale Taskin* (Hillsdale, N.Y.: Pendragon, 2002), 1–213; regarding mottoes on Flemish instruments, see 21–23, and on lid paintings, 33–34.

44. McGeary, "Harpsichord Mottoes," 20, motto no. 8.

45. Painted cases—especially lids—held special value among owners. See Jeannine Lambrechts-Douillez, "Documents Dealing with the Ruckers Family and Antwerp Harpsichord Building," in *Keyboard Instruments: Studies in Keyboard Organology*, ed. Edwin M. Ripin (Edinburgh: Edinburgh University Press, 1971), 37–41. For more on this instrument, see Victor-Charles Mahillon, *Catalogue descriptif et analytique du Musée instrumental du Conservatoire royal de Musique de Bruxelles*, 2d ed., 5 vols. (Ghent: Ad. Hoste, 1893–1912 [vols. 1–4], vol. 4, 317–20; and Brussels: Lombaerts, 1922 [vol. 5]); O'Brien, *Ruckers*, 32–33, 277; Donald H. Boalch, *Makers of the Harpsichord and Clavichord, 1440–1840*, 2d ed. (Oxford: Clarendon, 1974), 25; and John Koster, "A Remarkable Early Flemish Transposing Harpsichord," *Galpin Society Journal* 35 (1982): 45–53.

46. See a panel (1531–1532) painted by Angelo Bronzino, thought to have been originally the front part of a hinged harpsichord lid, though it is painted on canvas, now in the Hermitage in St. Petersburg, illustrated and discussed in Wyss, *Myth of Apollo and Marsyas*, 108–12, and accessible on the Hermitage website. Wyss suggests (108) that Bronzino "visualized the flaying of Marsyas as scientific surgery and cast Apollo in the role of *Apollo medicus*." This makes sense, not least in light of the fact that mottoes on harpsichords and virginals sometimes make reference to music as a "medicine," as in "*Musica laetitiae comes medicina dolorum*" ("Music is the companion of joy, the medicine of sorrows"). Another Apollo-Marsyas flaying scene is painted on the lid of an Italian harpsichord by Joseph Salodiensis (1559), now in the Kunsthistorisches Museum, Vienna, and reproduced in McGeary, "Harpsichord Decoration," 16; also in the *Katalog der Sammlung alter Musikinstrumente I. Saitenklaviere* (Vienna: Kunsthistorisches Museum, 1966), cat. no. 9, pp. 12–13, and plate 3.

47. See James Laver, *Isabella's Triumph (May 31st, 1615) [by] Denis van Alsloot* (London: Faber and Faber, 1947); and Vincent Bastien, "L'Ommeganck de Bruxelles en 1615, d'après les tableaux de Denis van Alsloot," *Précis historique mélanges religieux, littéraires, et scientifique* 38 (1889), 5–19, 49–70, 193–218, 337–61, 437–56, 533–53; and 39 (1890), 153–76; Eric Larsen, "Denis van Alsloot peintre de la fôret de Soignes," *Gazette des Beaux-Arts*, ser. 6, 34

(1948), 331–54; A. J. Wauters, "*Denis van Alsloot peintre des Archiducs Albert et Isabelle* (Brussels: Weissenbruch, 1899); Leo van Puyvelde, *L'Ommegang de 1615 à Bruxelles* (Brussels: Éditions du Marais S. A., 1960); and especially Margit Thøfner, "The Court in the City, the City in the Court: Denis van Alsloot's Depictions of the 1615 Brussels *Ommegang*," *Nederlands Kunsthistorisch Jaarboek* 49 (1998), 184–207. Thøfner convincingly suggests the multiple ways that the paintings articulate the interests of the court in its relations with the civic municipality and its traditional rights; Thøfner considers the compositional organization of the paintings—more than mere straightforward documents of the event—and the site where the paintings were ultimately displayed, in a long gallery in the ducal palace at Tervuren, which she reads (196) as "a symbolic incorporation of the civic into the courtly." See also Leppert, *Theme of Music*, vol. 1, 160–73, 220–22.

48. The region was in fact a virtual Jesuit empire and the center of the Society of Jesus in all of northern Europe. The Jesuits maintained many schools in the region. See Geyl, *Revolt of the Netherlands*, 231–32.

49. See Laver, *Isabella's Triumph*, 2–3.

50. See Christoph Rueger, *Musical Instruments and Their Decoration: Historical Gems of European Culture*, trans. Peter Underwood (Cincinnati: Seven Hills, 1986), 58. Rueger incorrectly ascribes the instrument to Hans Ruckers the Elder.

51. The instrument is listed in Boalch, *Makers of the Harpsichord and Clavichord*, 133, no. 17. Boalch points out that the instrument is French but apparently built around a Flemish virginal soundboard. Boalch does not remark on the case painting. O'Brien, *Ruckers* (278) concurs with Boalch and alludes to its soundboard as a composite, some of which was taken from a virginal. O'Brien further suggests that the instrument may be the sole responsibility of Pascal Taskin, whose name, with a date of 1774, is on the instrument. However, this seems impossible to the extent that the case paintings were by an artist who died in 1690.

52. For examples of then popular paintings of battles and sieges, see F.-C. Legrand, *Les peintres flamands de genre au XVIIe siècle* (Brussels: Éditions Meddens, 1963), 189–226; and Walther Bernt, *The Netherlandish Painters of the Seventeenth Century*, trans. P. S. Falla from the 3d German ed., 3 vols. (New York: Phaidon, 1970), passim.

53. This instrument is not listed in Mahillon, *Catalogue descriptif et analytique*, since it was acquired by the museum only in 1960. However, vol. I, p. 485, cat. no. 559, the surviving lid of a French harpsichord, has the painted scene of Louis XIV as Apollo accompanied by the nine Muses.

54. The aesthetics of violence continues in history beyond the ancien régime, as, for example, in the musical fantasies of the Futurists and the poet F. T. Marinetti in particular; see the discussion in Richard Leppert, *The Sight of Sound: Music, Representation, and the History of the Body* (Berkeley: University of California Press, 1993), 127–31, q.v. for other images of this harpsichord—the instrument is incorrectly ascribed to Hans Ruckers the Elder.

55. The specifically musico-political metaphor of order that plays out on the old harpsichord's case enjoys ancient lineage. Thus, Cicero, in *De re publica*, on the ideal politician and his impact on the state, via a notably extended metaphor structured around music, says this:

> He must be a very choice and distinguished individual, for the task I set him comprises all others. He must never cease from cultivating and studying himself, that he may excite others to imitate him, and become, through the splendor of his talents and enterprizes, a living mirror to his countrymen. For even in flutes and

harps [*in fidibus aut tibias*], and in all vocal performances, a certain consent and harmony must be preserved amid the distinctive tones, which cannot be broken or violated without offending practical ears; and this concord and delicious harmony is produced by the exact gradation and modulation of dissimilar notes. Even so, from the just apportionment of the highest, middle, and lower classes, the state is maintained in concord and peace by the harmonic subordination of its discordant elements. And thus, that which is by musicians called harmony in song [*quae harmonia a musicus dicitur in cantu*], answers and corresponds to what we call concord in the state:—Concord, the strongest and loveliest bond of security in every Commonwealth, being always accompanied by Justice and Equity." From Marcus Tullius Cicero, *De re publica* [*Treatise on the Commonwealth*], in *The Political Works of Marcus Tullius Cicero*, trans. Francis Barham, 2 vols. (London: Spettigue, 1841–1842), vol. 1, book II.42; http://oll. libertyfund.org/?option=com_staticxt&staticfile=show.php%3Ftitle=546&chapter=83299&layout=html&Itemid=27 (accessed Dec. 23, 2008)

56. See Richard Leppert, *Art and the Committed Eye: The Cultural Functions of Imagery* (Boulder, Colo.: Westview/HarperCollins, 1996), 103–12.

57. The Latin: "*Pulsa placet digitis mire mihi Lyra pertitis. / Cantibus et miris me philomela rapit: / At mihi concentus numquam jucundior ullus. / Qu'am laudes docta qui canit arte meas.*" The French: "*A bien considerer la douceur infinie / Des tons de la Musique et leurs accords divers, / Ce n'est pas sans raison qu'on dict que l'Harmonie / Du mouvement des Cieux entretient l'Univers.*"

58. See further the discussion of paintings that represent the sense of hearing in Leppert, *Sight of Sound*, 52–60; the bulk of the foregoing remarks about Bosse's engraving are drawn from pp. 47–50. See also Richard Leppert, "*Concert in a House:* Musical Iconography and Musical Thought," *Early Music* 7(1) (January 1979): 15–17.

59. Essentially all of Adorno's writings on music are grounded in his concept of structural listening. On what he meant by the phrase, see, for example, *Introduction to the Sociology of Music*, trans. E. B. Ashton (New York: Continuum, 1988), 1–20; and "The Radio Symphony," in Theodor W. Adorno, *Essays on Music*, ed. Richard Leppert (Berkeley: University of California Press, 2002), 251–70. For one of the most insightful critiques of the concept, see Rose Rosengard Subotnik, "Toward a Deconstruction of Structural Listening: A Critique of Schoenberg, Adorno, and Stravinsky," in *Deconstructive Variations: Music and Reason in Western Society* (Minneapolis: University of Minnesota Press, 1996), 148–76, 245–52. See also Andrew Dell'Antonio, *Beyond Structural Listening?: Postmodern Modes of Hearing* (Berkeley: University of California Press, 2004).

60. Jacques Attali, *Noise: The Political Economy of Music*, trans. Brian Massumi (Minneapolis: University of Minnesota Press, 1985), 6.

61. Attali, *Noise*, 9.

62. Roland Barthes, "Listening," in *The Responsibility of Forms*, trans. Richard Howard (Berkeley: University of California Press, 1991), 247; cf. 250: "What is it that listening, then, seeks to decipher? Essentially, it would appear, two things: the future (insofar as it belongs to the gods) or transgression (insofar as transgression is engendered by God's gaze."

63. Suzanne G. Cusick, " 'You Are in a Place That Is out of the World…': Music in the Detention Camps of the 'Global War on Terror,' " *Journal of the Society for American Music* 2(1) (2008): 1–26.

CHAPTER 3

MUSIC AND PAIN

ANDREAS DORSCHEL

Der menschliche Körper ist das beste Bild der menschlichen Seele.

—Wittgenstein, *Philosophische Untersuchungen*

1. MYTH

The myth of Marsyas, one of European music's seminal narratives, culminates in an excess of pain. His competitor's suffering marks Apollo's triumph as the god of supreme music. Marsyas, a demon from Kelainai in Phrygia—only latter-day mythology transformed him into a silenus—had picked up the flutes that Athena invented. (The goddess had thrown them away since playing such wind instruments, she had determined, distorted the lineaments of her face.[1]) In the musical contest that follows, which sets the lyre against the flute, Apollo's sovereign detachment opposes the expressive primacy of the body. Nothing pushes the body more vehemently to its limits than a delirium of pain; Marsyas is being skinned while alive.[2] As Ovid's *Metamorphoses*[3] say of the flayed figure: "[N]ec quicquam nisi vulnus erat," he was nothing but a wound.

Art is meant to be beautiful—and pain, it seems, can never be beautiful. Or can it? Western art has never been destitute of representations of tortured bodies. There is, however, something inappropriately placid about images of the body in pain. They put the dynamic phenomenon to rest and turn it into an object of contemplation. The image makes us observe pain (*via* pain behavior). Yet pain observed is virtually the opposite of pain felt. Contact would arouse feeling; observation implies distance. Perhaps pictures cannot succeed in making pain itself visible—or if they can, then the very process of making pain visible may turn it into something else entirely. At the same time, however, images can be eminently instructive in locating pain. Jusepe de Ribera's 1637 representation of Marsyas's death stands out as a monumental artistic landmark of the Counter-Reformation's violent culture. The picture places Apollo and Marsyas within a hierarchy congenial to the ancient myth: as befits an art of design, within a spatial hierarchy.[4] Apollo is keeping his head up, while Marsyas's is hanging downward—it is, in the original sense of the word, perverted, turned upside down. Pain is not merely a fact of living nature; it concerns a norm.

Wherever there is pain, something has gone wrong: Pain reveals wrongness. De Ribera thus updates Ovid for the age of the Holy Inquisition. Through the punishment inflicted by Apollo, Marsyas's flute playing turned into a shrilling scream of pain (inaudible, though, within the visual medium)—and one of those who had relished Marsyas's music before is now (near the right margin of de Ribera's painting) found plugging his ears. Pain and screaming preclude music; at the same time, the penance executed demonstrates that Marsyas's music had too closely resembled a scream to start with: It had been steeped in bodily expression. Blowing through a wind instrument had distorted his face; accordingly, the chastisement Apollo imposed on Marsyas makes pain distort his face. Marsyas is not undergoing torture but rather torment: a painful, humiliating ordeal the quality and intensity of which are deemed adequate retribution for the deed done by the tormented.

Pain is "the most powerful device of mnemotechnics."[5] Whatever hurts gets remembered. Its end achieved, the device can be abandoned. Pain passes. Yet having suffered does not pass. We have reason to pause and reflect on how such a thing is possible, for pain lacks intentionality. When I experience pain, I do not feel, nor am I disposed to feel pain *about* anything (in the way I am, e.g., sad *about* something). In pain, I do not turn toward an intentional object, of which there is none, but rather look out for its (immediate and/or mediate) cause(s). Moral and legal mnemotechnics attempts to establish causal chains between sin and pain. In physical punishment, the desire to quench one's thirst for revenge becomes aligned with the intention to create a particular recollection in those who are punished or among those who see and hear them. The sanction backs the norm in such a way that it will never be forgotten. One can argue against charges, but one cannot argue against pain. Pain, apparently, can only be cried out—beyond the borders in which one can silently endure.

In contrast to unhappiness, pain is localized. Yet it is not merely connected to that part of the body from which it stems. It concerns the individual human being. It is not just that my head is in pain. *I* have a headache. It hurts *me*. Correspondingly, local symptoms aside, the reaction to pain is an utterance of the individual. A scream is strong pain's natural expression. The noun "woe," an old-fashioned synonym for pain, originally corresponded to a shout of someone in pain. The screamer utters pain and makes it known to others, begging for help. At the same time, screaming seems to lessen pain by way of turning something inward into something outward and by wholly occupying us—not unlike gnashing one's teeth or clenching one's fist.

People whimper and whine in pain; they moan and groan, howl and bawl: All this becomes audible as music becomes audible, yet it is a far cry from music. When pain is articulated in music, it ceases to be just pain. To the extent that it has been stylized into melody, pain has been conquered. Music would, of course, be unbearable if it could ever plainly manifest pain. To attract listening, music has to have remedies against pain within itself. Still, pain can be alive in music; indeed, music (permitting such personification of a medium for the moment) might discern more in pain than a scream does, as music registers its qualities more discretely, more delicately, and more subtly.

Ancient mythology reflected this capacity whenever it understood music as the sublimation of pain. In the myth of Marsyas, pain stirred up in the body follows a music that is bound up within the body, allegedly nonsublimated. Yet in the tales of Orpheus and Philomela, the opposite occurs, with song growing from pain. Acting on Marsyas, Apollo lowers music—as he purports, the lesser music—to pain; Orpheus, by way of contrast, raises pain to music. Philomela, whom her brother-in-law raped and—so that she would not be able to articulate his crime—silenced by cutting out her tongue, is turned into a nightingale:[6] Her pain becomes sublimated into singing so beautiful that it seems supernatural, yet is part of nature. Might this beauty justify the pain—and if it does, would it justify the rape and consequent deprivation of speech? The poet does not comment on this horrible thought. Unlike the hurtful making of *castrati* or the painful exercising techniques imposed on child prodigies—those martyrs of music—the woe inflicted on Orpheus and Philomela was no means to an artistic end. Rather, music is this pain's unintended by-product. Their relation is contingent and necessary at the same time. The pain was not aiming for art as its end, let alone its necessary consequence. Yet the former is supposed to be a necessary condition of the latter: Without pain, art cannot exist. Such is the idea of pain's sublimation into music—from ancient legends to modern times, embracing Heinrich Heine's "From my great pain / I make my little songs."[7] Philomela's art remains within what is not art: nature. However, Orpheus and his successors, up to Heine and beyond, suggest what might constitute more than a necessary condition: There has to be pain, there has to be skill, and, against all odds, there has to be an attempt to reflectively penetrate one's own pain.

Sublimation thus sets up spiritual meaning where, otherwise, effects of matter alone would prevail. While such elevation might originally be linked to artistic production, it turns out to be germane to the reception of art as well, not least to the topic of music in its relation to pain. Sounds can hurt, quite literally so. The pain caused by a very strong—piercing or excessively loud (beyond 90–110 dB)—tone is immediate and physical. It is caused by a cramp of the inner aural muscles or by excess pressure exerted on the eardrum. But does listening to music expressing pain have to be painful? Those who believe in sublimation deny that query's suggestion: Art changes the medium; it is received not by the body alone but by the mind as well. There is, of course, no pain without the body, and certainly music is related to the body, both in performance and in listening. Yet you cannot touch music as you can touch a body (or even a statue or painting). Music dematerializes whatever it relates to itself. It makes—so the story of sublimation ends—pain disappear through beauty. The birth pangs, then, might be attributed to the artist, not to the work of art.[8]

2. Philosophy

Friedrich Nietzsche, in his *Birth of Tragedy*, proposes an aesthetics of music rooted in pain,[9] or "primeval pain" (*Urschmerz*).[10] In doing so, however, he does not suggest a sequence of screams as an ideal music. To be sure, the way Nietzsche fancies the "demonic popular chant" (*dämonischen Volksgesang*) of the bacchanal (Dionysusfeier) partakes of the "piercing scream" (*durchdringende* [...] *Schrei*).[11] Yet Nietzsche himself argues that the "hard-to-grasp primeval phenomenon of Dionysian art" (*schwer zu fassende Urphänomen der dionysischen Kunst*) becomes intelligible only "within the marvelous meaning of *musical dissonance*" (*in der wunderbaren Bedeutung der musikalischen Dissonanz*).[12] Pain is disharmony: My body is not in tune with my self. Strong pain penetrates: It descends far down into the bowels, and harmony—the vertical dimension of music—must become its medium.

On a historical note, Nietzsche's reference to dissonance may have little or nothing to do with how Dionysiac festivals sounded. Rather, his reference has more to do with modern Western music history from the Italian renaissance madrigal to the mature style of Richard Wagner. Still, Nietzsche renews an ancient notion that linked insight into pain with the theory of harmony. This same notion connects musical relations to the body, conceiving the latter as an instrument on which the world may play. According to Plato (though Nietzsche denies him proper Dionysiac expertise), living beings know neither pain nor pleasure as long as there is physical harmony. Pain emerges, Plato points out, only as harmony is dissolved; the re-creation of harmony, rather than its original existence, is pleasure.[13] Dissonance participates in pain, but not in pain alone. It also evokes pleasure. Much tonal music alternates between tension and resolution. To convince us of the delights of dissonance, the dullness of strictly consonant music may suffice. Nietzsche, projecting late cultural achievements onto mythical beginnings, talks of a "primeval relish taken even in pain" (*selbst am Schmerz percipirten Urlust*).[14] Pleasure may be found in pain, even in something as domesticated as sympathy, the emotion of being touched and moved by the predicaments of others.[15]

It is not, however, the intertwinement of pleasure and pain that distinguishes dissonance from screaming. Screaming may reassure living beings of their vital powers, which pain calls into question. It can thus act to relieve some pain—a feeling that at least borders on pleasure. The difference, then, must be found elsewhere. A scream is inarticulate:[16] an outbreak—something beyond the order that linguistic conventions impose on vocal utterances. "I am in pain" markedly differs from "Ouch" in that it presupposes a whole ontology: A self is posited vis-à-vis a social world, distinct from yet relating to it; that first person undergoes changing states such as pain but remains the same self throughout the ordeal. Screams precede language; some animals cry, too, as they experience intense pain. Dissonant chords, by way of contrast, do not predate music; they emerge from its center. A dissonance is just as much a structured entity as a consonance is. To correspond to simpler or to more complex ratios is a difference that does not coincide with the opposition of what is formed to what is amorphous. When a chord contains a second or a seventh, it has not been overwhelmed by something inarticulate. The dissonant chord has its intervallic order, too—it simply differs from a consonant chord's intervallic order. Either thrives within the domain of artistry. To cherish and foster the powers of dissonance, both formal and expressive, has long been a crucial component of a composer's artistry. (To express pain by dissonance is quite different from, say, linking it with the brute force of volume, though a *fortissimo* dynamic is not inherently more disorderly than a *piano*.)

As it affects physiognomy, aches distort: The face twists in pain. The same can be said for the scream, matching pain as its expression: The voice breaks. However, dissonance relates to screaming as imagination relates to reality. It is crafted, not given. In this sense, it revokes distortion. Dissonances as such are not twisted consonances. A seventh cannot be construed as a buckled sixth or a compressed octave. It is an interval in its own right and can serve as a different, but equally legitimate, element of a chord. Composers can indeed construct deformation by means of dissonant intervals. Thus in Wagner's *Ring* we perceive the "woe motif" (*Wehemotiv*), characterized by the descending minor second, as distorting the initial "Rhinegold motif" (*Rheingoldmotiv*), with its descending major second. However, this is due to context rather than to the interval itself. A minor second elsewhere might not be heard as distorting anything at all.

Through its structure, dissonance (to borrow a phrase from Jane Fulcher) refracts pain like a prism rather than just reflecting it like a mirror. Yet imagery provides only weak pointers to musical phenomena. Where precisely is dissonance, that musical articulation of pain? Is it pinned down on the paper that the composer used to notate the work? Or does dissonance come about only in the listener's ear? In the *Birth of Tragedy* Nietzsche attempts to render an account of how Greek art, for later European audiences, had been transformed into classical beauty: into floating grace, "noble simplicity" (*edle Einfalt*), "calm greatness" (*stille Größe*). Johann Joachim Winckelmann, responding to as well as shaping eighteenth-century aesthetic debate, had introduced these formulae within the context of an argument about adequate expression (*Ausdruck*) of pain (*Schmertz*) in sculpture and painting. This argument concerned the issue of balance between soul (*Seele*) and body (*Cörper*) in art as well.[17] The modern theory of Greek tragedy characterizes the chorus as guarantor of collectedness and discretion: the authority that, level headed as it is, controls and restrains pain. Nietzsche disputes this classicist view, which portrays the Greek tragic chorus as distant observer and deliberate commentator on the action. Instead, the chorus voices exultation and pain—only modern audiences have unlearned to perceive them, in part because exultation and pain were later eroded by the tragic genre itself.

Expression of pain may get overlooked if what we really expect is the exhibition of pain. Yet ostentation of pain hardly provides an index of its intensity. Dorabella's "Smanie implacabili" (*Così fan tutte*, I.3) is ostentatious to the extent that her pain is (still) shallow. It does not need to be soothed at this early stage—the show does not silence pain but rather the lady's guilty conscience about how she might act in due course. The more such exhibition invokes tragedy, the more comic it becomes. We watch it, it interests us, yet it does not touch us and is not meant to do so here and now. Mozart knew as well as any artist about the reverse notion's power to move: veiled pain. Beauty can be one of its veils. In truth, beyond the simple opposition of beauty and pain (section 1), they may enter a dialectic. There can be pain vis-à-vis the unearthly beautiful in art: pain experienced by the viewers or listeners because they do not relate. Such pain, by implication, is the twin of shame. Certain passages in Mozart and Schubert are experienced thus: painfully beautiful.

3. MUSIC

Nietzsche's tie between pain and dissonance (section 2) is interwoven with the ways that people deal with that which hurts them—outside of art, in so-called real life. There is, of course, pain that comes on suddenly, without warning. However, even this is then placed within a person's life history: as a consequence of previous incaution, as a warning of future collapse, as deserved or undeserved punishment, as a test of bravery, or as proof of doctors' incompetence. Such interpretations place pain in contexts of temporal succession (when? before or after which other event?), of causality (from which source or influence?), and of purpose or meaning (what for?). Correspondingly, dissonance is not just any noise, free from context. It has a place and a role within the system of relationships we call tonality. Only after dissonance's irritation can consonance unfold its potential for conviction, affirmation, and finality upon listeners. Mirrored by the tonal context of dissonance, pain is something that validates the very order it disturbs.

Within modern Europe's dissonance-ridden music of pain, tonality has ensured such a relationship, at least in a general way. Yet this circumstance has not released composers from the claim to elaborate on this relationship specifically through their art. Rather, it has exposed them to such a claim to the extent that they laid claims on themselves. Claudio Monteverdi is eminently a case in point. In his madrigal for five voices, "Sfogava con le stelle," after Ottavio Rinuccini, from the *Quarto Libro* of 1603, the composer sets the words *il suo dolore* (bars 7–10) to a minor seventh by extending subdominant harmony in the lower voices. This same passage is first heard a few bars earlier against a stepwise descent in the *Canto* with the words *d'amore* (bars 4–5). Here, however, the characteristic dissonance is absent. It is very much the similarity of what we listen to, then, that makes pain stick out. *Dolore* is the reverse of *amore*. Whoever knows pleasure also knows pain and vice versa. Pressure exemplifies their continuity: What might start as a pleasant touch changes at some point, gradually increasing to the threshold of pain and beyond. Contrary to both pleasure and pain is apathy: the numbness of the body. Freedom from pain can be reached through loss of feeling—by renouncing the vitality that Rinuccini and Monteverdi designate as love. Pain emerges from life's energy, or it does not emerge at all. It is sensual—indeed, one of the intensest sense experiences human beings experience. (Sadists and masochists have discovered a peculiar erotic appeal in such negative sensuality. Their discovery may well constitute a chapter in the psychopathology of sexuality, yet it is instructive beyond the realm of mental illness.) Intense sensual episodes seize a living being in its entirety. Contra Augustine's influential doctrine,[18] pain cannot be split up between body and soul, just as music cannot.

Pain's relationship to an organism's entirety, though, must not be taken for granted. Rather, it is precarious. In a functional sense, it is beyond doubt: Disease and injury that cause pain pose threats to an organism; aches are impulses of self-preservation, localized, felt in specific body parts, yet are related to the entire living being.[19] That pain "hurts cannot be the issue since it is its essence."[20] Vehement aching, however, does not admit of any other thought or recollection. It keeps us within ourselves and the sensation of here and now. In this way, pain can make structures of existence disintegrate. We experience life, then, from one episode to the next, from one harrowing assault to another. Excruciating pain undermines identity. It wears down and spreads anarchy. Whatever provides life with regularity is dispersed by such affliction: the structure of the day, togetherness based on reliable appointments, projects and promises, deliberations and their well-considered expressions. For pain, even syntax seems to present too strict a sense of order. "Howl, howl, howl, howl!" King Lear exclaims at the starkest point of his woe.[21] It is truly ineffable.

Thus, when experiencing excruciating pain, we are no longer ourselves. Wagner was aware of this; in *Tristan and Isolde* he makes the audience's experience more bearable by suggesting that loss of identity is in fact desirable. Yet *Parsifal* presents this desolate insight without the consolatory suggestion. Amfortas does not just feel pain; he *is* pain. Consistently, no leitmotif throughout the drama is more volatile than his.[22] When compared to Amfortas's motif, that of Klingsor[23]—whose role is to inflict pain rather than to feel it—proves to be constancy itself.

Agonizing pain seems to affect crucially even God, who became human; the teleology of his life history appears shattered: "About the ninth hour Jesus cried out in a loud voice: 'Eloi, Eloi, lama sabachthani?'—which means 'My God, my God, why have you forsaken me?'" (Matthew 27:46). Perhaps no composer has opposed the anarchic force of such pain with more determination than Johann Sebastian Bach, whose music of suffering (in the cantatas and passions) presents miracles of order. In the "Crucifixus" from Bach's Mass in B Minor, flutes, violins, and voices express pain in halting sighs (*suspirationes*). Within this central section of the "Symbolum Nicenum," only the continuo remains uninterrupted by rest.

Twelve times Bach presents it identically. In this way, pain refers to a fixed order. Strict repetition endows music, that ever mobile medium, with an element of immobility. Since we experience pain as movement—as dragging, pulling, shooting, stabbing, piercing, throbbing, or raging—immobility bounds pain. It does not eliminate it but holds it in check. Order, in its consistency, thus presents itself as equal to pain or indeed superior to it. And, just as it establishes itself as the equal of pain, order assigns meaning to pain. It is because of such meaning that pain is endured. Yet the chaconne's strict order is not simply imposed upon pain, that potential threat to order and identity. By virtue of its descending chromaticism, the ground bass's order itself contains pain. At the same time, the *passus duriusculus* is part of a stylized, rhetorically codified musical language that—within the historical space and time it belonged to—made its conventions public. Intelligibility, if achieved, may soften pain.

The lamento bass of the "Crucifixus" in Bach's B Minor Mass provides a precedent for the piano part of Schubert's "Doppelgänger." Schubert, too, builds his music of pain on a four-bar ostinato. Yet nothing else remains the same.

In Schubert's song, pain is perceived as gesture: *Und ringt die Hände vor Schmerzensgewalt* [And is wringing his hands out of violent pain] (bars 29–33). This pain resides in the middle of the ternary composition.[24] What is it that happens at the song's midpoint? *Ringen* [here: wringing; otherwise: wrestling] evokes the realm of fight. This fight is violent (*–gewalt*); with a triple *forte* (bar 31), followed by a *forzando* accent (bar 32), its force breaks through undisguised. When in pain, the body is at odds or even at war with itself or, some might say, with the ego; this interpretation corresponds with the opposition of self and doppelgänger. Vis-à-vis his doppelgänger, the self experiences what has been familiar—pain—as foreign or alien. Paradoxically, pain is universal *and* bound up with the individual. On the one hand, it is common to all humans—even to all high-functioning living beings (that's why animal trainers brandish a whip). On the other hand, pain is a radically private experience that casts the individual inward. Hence, two axioms pointing in opposite directions hold true simultaneously: Everybody is (sometimes) in pain, and nobody can feel my (or anyone else's) pain. Others can try to imagine how I feel, thus empathizing with me. In doing so, they may even recall pain that they once experienced. Yet remembering pain is not the same as experiencing it. Hence, it is not pain per se but remembrance of pain. This marks a limit to empathy. Such moderation is pertinent to the "imitation of Christ," as in the "Crucifixus" of Bach's Mass. (The exceptional character of stigmata is founded precisely in the limited connection between empathy and pain; the miraculous crossing of these borders makes stigmata signs of holiness.)

Imitating pain is also what Heine's and Schubert's doppelgänger does. Yet his imitation debases: "Why do you ape (mimic) my pain of love?" (*Was äffst du nach mein Liebesleid?*) (bars 46–48). It is not apes who imitate suffering. Human beings—specifically, doppelgänger of other human beings—do. This is why imitation debases: There could be a more human (i.e., a more humane) response to pain. Hence, the doppelgänger's imitation does not relieve suffering. That pain is here viewed as both alien and one's own makes it uncanny. In the figure of the doppelgänger, pain becomes an object of observation. In normal cases, observation provides safe distance. Music, unlike image (section 1), does not force us to observe pain. The unexpected downward alteration of the dominant seventh chord's fifth (F♯–A♯–C–E instead of F♯–A♯–C♯–E) on the word *Schmerzensgewalt* (bar 32) embodies the eerie ambiguity of being alienated by what is one's own. This is manifested musically as the alien C returns on "eigne Gestalt" ("own figure") (bars 40–42); the postlude reprises this connection (bar 59).

In Schubert's "Doppelgänger," the repetition of the bass motif does not represent meaningful order. It enacts compulsion. The lyrical self's return to a place of loss, as well as his repetition in the form of the doppelgänger, are the sources of pain—albeit a pain that is expressed through nonrepetition (i.e., the alteration of C♯ to C, which infringes harmonic grammar). What this offense produces remains essentially unintelligible. "Nobody understands the pain of the other, and nobody understands the joy of the other! We always believe that we are coming together, and we always just walk past the other. O torment to become aware of this!"[25] Incomprehension of pain begets more pain. Yet Schubert's music reaches farther than the rather conventional entry in his diary. It is not just the others' pain that remains unintelligible. In the end, Schubert's doppelgänger suggests, one does not even understand one's own.

4. MEDICINE

Do we even wish to understand our own pain? Do we not instead wish to silence it? If modern European culture was once interested in how music could express pain, present preoccupations seem to have shifted toward ways in which music might numb pain.

In 1921 psychologist Esther Gatewood tried to explain music's potential analgesic effect by referencing the selectivity of the central nervous system. From the prolonged spinal marrow (*medulla oblongata*) to the structures of the interbrain (*thalamencephalon*) extends a core area called the *formatio reticularis*. This area receives information about sensations from all sensory organs via their respective channels. Depending on the relevance an organism attributes to each sensation, this area is activated (i.e., the sensory threshold is crossed). To put it nontechnically, we pay attention. A strong musical stimulus, Gatewood maintained, may make us pay attention to such an extent that subsequent—otherwise painful—stimuli might be repressed, or a preexistent painful stimulus could be diminished.[26] Although initially claimed on a theoretical basis, Gatewood's principle of counterirritation has subsequently been confirmed by mounting empirical evidence.

Virtually anything could distract us. Music, however, does so in a unique way. A sound is not a sound *about* anything. Since it is nonreferential, music seems to constitute a self-contained fabric of sounds. While words and images, via their referentiality, connect us with the world, that manifold source of pain, music does not. Sound technology perfects that state. A headset shuts the listeners' ears to the world while feeding them music. Music, particularly in recorded form, is an eminent medium of escape.

To escape from pain, no route is to be spurned. Music therapists dispense with any privileged relationship of the mind to music. Sounds that lessen pain, they have noted, are perceived all over the body via the skin. If this is true, the flaying of Marsyas can be seen in retrospect as a procedure meant to deprive him of music altogether. Since Marsyas's music had appealed not to the mind but to the body as a whole, his terminal chastisement had to do so as well.

As we perceive sounds through our skin, recent music therapy has been treating sounds as water rather than air. Norwegian therapist Olav Skille has suggested "the music bath"—a kind of massage performed through sounds.[27] Music therapy consistently disconnects music's relationship to pain from artistic merit—that European obsession that can be traced from Marsyas's mythical contest with Apollo to the disputed aesthetics of expression found in Romanticism and Modernism. This disconnect is cogent, for the physiological effect of sound remains independent of whether a work of art is composed of these sounds. If a sine tone soothes pain most efficiently, then it ostensibly becomes the music of choice (i.e., something not to be called music at all).

In its beginnings, the art of producing sound was intertwined with magic.[28] As pain was believed to be inflicted by demons, music had to pacify them. The relief music offered was thus indirect rather than direct. Modern music therapy, by way of contrast, directly turns to the sufferer, not to the pain-inducing agents. Thus, cultural history does not repeat itself. Or, at least it takes care to change the names, replacing demons with more acceptable entities.

NOTES

I am grateful to Klaus Aringer, Federico Celestini, Jane Fulcher, William Kinderman, Michael Mauskapf, Peter Revers, and Katherine Syer for their topical suggestions.

1. Ovid, *Fasti* [AD 13–18], 6.695–710, ed. E. H. Alton, D. E. W. Wormell, and E. Courtney (Leipzig: Teubner, 1988), 159–60.

2. Herodotus, *Historiae* [ca. 430 BC], 7.26, ed. Heinrich Stein, vol. 4 (Berlin: Weidmann, 1988), 39–41; Xenophon, *Expeditio Cyri* [ca. 375 BC], 1.2.8, ed. C. Hude and J. Peters, 2d ed. (Leipzig: Teubner, 1972), 5–6.

3. Ovid, *Metamorphoses* [ca. AD 1–8], 6.388, ed. William S. Anderson (Stuttgart: Teubner, 1996), 136.

4. Reproduced in Lionello Puppi, *Torment in Art: Pain, Violence, and Martyrdom* (New York: Rizzoli, 1991), 146–47. The painting is now in the Museo di San Martino in Naples.

5. Friedrich Nietzsche, *Zur Genealogie der Moral* [1887], in *Sämtliche Werke, Kritische Studienausgabe*, ed. Giorgio Colli and Mazzino Montinari, vol. 5 (New York: de Gruyter, 1980), 245–412, 295: "das mächtigste Hülfsmittel der Mnemonik."

6. Ovid, *Metamorphoses* (note 3), 6.441–670, 137–45.

7. Heinrich Heine, *Tragödien, nebst einem lyrischen Intermezzo* [1823], *Sämtliche Gedichte in zeitlicher Folge*, ed. Klaus Briegleb (Frankfurt: Insel, 1993), 150–63, 156: "Aus meinen großen Schmerzen / Mach ich die kleinen Lieder."

8. Georg Wilhelm Friedrich Hegel, *Enzyklopädie der philosophischen Wissenschaften* [1817], §462, *Sämtliche Werke, Jubiläumsausgabe*, ed. Hermann Glockner, 2d ed. (Stuttgart: Frommann, 1938), vol. 6, 304.

9. Friedrich Nietzsche, *Die Geburt der Tragödie aus dem Geiste der Musik* [1872/1886], in Colli and Montinari, *Sämtliche Werke, Kritische Studienausgabe*, vol. 1, 9–156, 43: "Schmerz."

10. Nietzsche, *Die Geburt der Tragödie*, 44.

11. Nietzsche, *Die Geburt der Tragödie*, 40–41. On scream and music cf. Richard Wagner, *Beethoven* [1870], *Gesammelte Schriften und Dichtungen*, vol. 9, 4th ed. (Leipzig: Siegel [Linnemann], 1907), 61–126, 71.

12. Nietzsche, *Die Geburt der Tragödie* (note 9), 152. Cf. Georg Wilhelm Friedrich Hegel, *Ästhetik* [1820–1829], ed. Friedrich Bassenge (Berlin: Aufbau, 1955), 840.

13. *Philebus*, 31d–33b; *Timaeus*, 81a; *Laws*, 732e–733d.

14. Nietzsche, *Die Geburt der Tragödie* (note 9), 152, cf. 41.

15. Cf. Friedrich Schiller, "Über den Grund des Vergnügens an tragischen Gegenständen" [1792], *Werke, Nationalausgabe*, vol. 20, ed. Helmut Koopman and Benno von Wiese (Weimar: Böhlau, 2001), 133–47, 137–38; Hegel, *Ästhetik* (note 12), 522.

16. Cf. Jean-Jacques Rousseau, "Essai sur l'origine des langues" [1755], ch. IV, *Oeuvres complètes*, ed. Bernard Gagnebin and Marcel Raymond, vol. 5 (Paris: Gallimard, 1995), 371–429, 382.

17. Johann Joachim Winckelmann, "Gedancken über die Nachahmung der Griechischen Wercke in der Mahlerey und Bildhauer-Kunst" [1755/1756], *Kleine Schriften, Vorreden, Entwürfe*, ed. Walther Rehm, 2d ed. (New York: de Gruyter, 2002), 27–89, 43.

18. Aurelius Augustinus, *De civitate Dei* [413–426], l. XXI, c. 3, 2 vols., ed. Bernhard Dombart (Leipzig: Teubner, 1877), vol. II, 490: "Animae est enim dolere, non corporis."

19. Cf. Immanuel Kant, *Anthropologie in pragmatischer Hinsicht* (Königsberg: Nicolovius, 1798), 170.

20. Friedrich Nietzsche, *Die fröhliche Wissenschaft* [1882/1887], §318, in Colli and Montinari, *Sämtliche Werke, Kritische Studienausgabe*, vol. 3, 343–651, 550: "[Daß] er weh thut, ist kein Argument gegen ihn, es ist sein Wesen."

21. William Shakespeare, *The Tragedy of King Lear* [1610], 5.3, *The Complete Works*, ed. Stanley Wells and Gary Taylor, 2d ed. (Oxford: Clarendon, 2005), 1153–84, 1183.

22. First appearance: act 1, bars 151–53, as Gurnemanz says: "Zeit ist's, des Königs dort zu harren."

23. First appearance: act 1, bars 627–33, as Gurnemanz says: "Jenseits im Tale war er eingesiedelt; darüber hin liegt üpp'ges Heidenland."

24. A: bars 1–24; A′: bars 25–42; B: bars 43–63.

25. Franz Schubert's diary, Mar. 27, 1824 (as copied by Bauernfeld), in *Schubert, Die Dokumente seines Lebens*, ed. Otto Erich Deutsch (Paris: Breitkopf and Härtel, 1996), 232: "Keiner, der den Schmerz des Andern, und keiner, der die Freude des Andern versteht! Man glaubt immer, zu einander zu gehen, und man geht immer nur neben einander. O Qual für den, der dieß erkennt!"

26. Cf. Esther L. Gatewood, "The Psychology of Music in Relation to Anesthesia," *American Journal of Surgery*, Anesthesia Suppl. no. 35 (1921): 47–50.

27. Olav Skille, "The Music Bath—Possible Use as an Anxiolytic," in *Angst, Schmerz, und Musik in der Anästhesie*, ed. Roland Droh and Ralph Spintge (Basel: Edition Roche, 1983), 111–14; Olav Skille, "Low-frequency Sound Massage—The Music Bath—A Follow-up Report," in *Musik in der Medizin*, ed. Ralph Spintge and Roland Droh (Basel: Edition Roche, 1985), 253–56.

28. Cf. Jules Combarieu, *La musique et la magie: Étude sur les origines populaires de l'art musical, son influence et sa fonction dans les sociétés* [1909] (Geneva: Minkoff, 1978).

CHAPTER 4

"THE ROAD INTO THE OPEN": FROM NARRATIVE CLOSURE TO THE ENDLESS PERFORMANCE OF SUBJECTIVITY IN MAHLER AND FREUD AT THE TURN OF THE CENTURY

JOHN E. TOEWS

I. INTRODUCTION: THE 1910 MEETING

In late August 1910 Gustav Mahler left his summer home in Toblach in the Austrian Tyrol and traveled to the Belgian city of Leiden for a consultation with Sigmund Freud about a crisis in his marriage that threatened his creative self-confidence and artistic identity. Freud interrupted his family vacation on the North Sea coast to meet with the world-famous conductor and composer. For four hours on August 26 they strolled through the streets of the city engaged in an intense conversation that has gained legendary status as a peripatetic psychoanalytic session, or "walking cure." Documentary evidence about what actually transpired in this consultation is meager. Mahler appeared to feel that the discussion had clarified and in some sense resolved his inner torments. On the train back to Munich the next day he sent his wife a poem that began this way: "The nightmare's dispelled by the force of persuasion, / Dispersed are the torments of self-contemplation."[1] A week later he wrote this to her: "Freud is quite right; this utter dependence on you has always been latent in me, you have always been my light and the center of my universe." Freud had persuaded him that the power of Eros, the "master of men and gods," would sustain their relationship.[2]

In 1925 Freud briefly discussed the Mahler consultation with Marie Bonaparte and indicated that he had been told that the brief clinical exchange had made Mahler more confident about the foundations of his marriage. He also noted that Mahler "demonstrated an intuitive understanding of analysis. He didn't know much about me and had not had analysis before, but right away he was in his element."[3] Ten years later Freud responded to an inquiry from Theodor Reik, who was investigating what he construed as elements of an obsessional neurosis in Mahler's personality: "In highly interesting expeditions through his life history, we discovered the personal conditions for his love (*Liebesbedingungen*), especially his Holy Mary complex (mother fixation); I had plenty of opportunity to admire the capability for psychological understanding of this man of genius (*genialen Verständnisfähigkeit*)."[4]

Freud's comments about the meeting with Mahler have encouraged the development of a series of studies that attempt to extend and complicate Freud's assessment but continue to frame the relationship as a clinical exchange between analyst and patient. In this chapter, however, I proceed from a different kind of implication that might be drawn from Freud's comments—that he and Mahler quickly recognized in each other a common understanding of the conditions and processes involved in the formation of subjective identity. It was this intellectual and emotional convergence that allowed Mahler to hear Freud's words as telling him what he already knew. This chapter examines selected works of Mahler and Freud as performing or enacting the history of subjectivity as a problematic narrative of the construction and deconstruction of identity. In other words I treat Freud's and Mahler's cultural productions, their "works," as historically parallel exemplars of a particular way of imagining human subjectivity as a reflective activity working through the dilemmas and possibilities created by the tensions between autonomy and belonging, between individuation and cultural integration. This parallelism was not grounded in mutual influence. In 1910 Freud and Mahler were unfamiliar with each other's works. Although they certainly knew of each other and lived in the same city during an important stage of their intellectual formation as students in the late 1870s and early 1880s, as well as during a critical decade of creative productivity and intellectual transformation between 1897 and 1907, they had never met before 1910, and their circles of acquaintances after their student years touched at only a few peripheral points. However, as a number of scholars, most notably historians William McGrath and Carl Schorske, have suggested, Mahler and Freud produced their works within cultural worlds that overlapped in many areas. The given historical possibilities of self-representation and identification (in the spheres of religion, ethnicity/race, nationality, and gender) available to them as they enacted their narratives of the thinking, feeling subject, fashioning and refashioning itself in relation to already constructed worlds of meaning, were shared in many, often significant, ways. Yet their experiential starting points within the general culture of fin-de-siècle Vienna and Central Europe more generally and thus their specific perspectives on the available historical possibilities available to them also frequently diverged. My aim is to open up the general question of whether both Mahler and Freud reimagined the relations between subjectivity and all forms of cultural identification (and thus the issue of identity per se) in homologous ways at a particular historical moment. Put more specifically (and crudely), Did Freud's abandonment in 1896–1897 of the narrative model of the "seduction theory" and the metapsychological assumptions in which it made sense, as well as Mahler's abandonment in 1901 of the narrative model of the *Wunderhorn* symphonies and the metamusical assumptions that framed it, represent similar, parallel turns in their perspectives on the formation of individual and collective identities? Do Freud's narratives of self-formation after *The Interpretation of Dreams* and Mahler's symphonic narratives initiated with the composition of the Rückert lieder and the Fifth Symphony mark the emergence of a shared shift toward what Arthur Schnitzler (a Viennese contemporary whom they both admired and who in turn admired—and recognized himself in—both Freud's and Mahler's works) called *Der Weg ins Freie* [The Road into the Open] and toward a resolution of the struggle for identity in a process without resolution?[5] Did both Mahler and Freud articulate a narrative of subject formation after 1900 that reimagined the individual self's quest for immanent integration or transcendent redemption as a constant struggle to sustain a move "beyond identity"?

My examination of the parallel turns in Freud's and Mahler's perspectives on subjectivity and identity around 1900 is grounded on two important assumptions. First, it proceeds on the assumption that Mahler's tonal structures and Freud's textual productions can both be read and listened to as discourses of subjectivity organized in narrative form. This first assumption also implies that these musical and textual forms have an "I" with consciousness and agency, a fictional subject that acts and speaks in the first person and in real present time. In addition, it implies that, when we speak about what the score/text does or says, we are not simply referring to the authorial subject or to an external subject represented programmatically within the work but to a musical and/or textual subject that is formed dialogically in the interchange between what we hear/read and what we bring as interpretative agents to our listening and reading. The narrative subject in a Mahler symphony or Freudian case study is not Freud or Mahler per se; its story is not a representation of the biographical experiences of its creator, nor is it a representation of a story enacted outside of the work—of the mythical hero or the patient, for example. What we experience as we read a Freudian text or listen to a Mahler symphony is the fictional voice of the narrating "I" acting out its story through encounter, dialogue, and reflection within the constantly shifting horizons of memory and expectation. In some sense, therefore, both the music and the text are autonomous subjectivities that interact with the reader/listener, not representations of the author's intentions or the realities of a world outside of themselves.[6]

II. Mahler and Freud in the 1890s: Identity as Assimilation

There is widespread (though certainly not universal) agreement within the historical scholarship on both Mahler and Freud that an important shift occurred in the organizing principles of their cultural productions in the years surrounding 1900. In Freud's case this change has been conventionally stylized as a move from the seduction theory to the Oedipal theory of psychic formation, a shift articulated in the *Interpretation of Dreams* and the classic psychoanalytic case studies beginning with "Fragment of an Analysis of a case of Hysteria" or "Dora" (written in 1901, published in 1905). In Mahler's case, scholars have generally acknowledged a significant change in the framing assumptions of his musical compositions between the Fourth Symphony (1899–1900) and the Fifth Symphony (1901–1902). This move has traditionally been indirectly designated by a change in the textual foundations of Mahler's lieder composition—from the (alleged) folk poetry of the early nineteenth-century Romantic anthology *Des Knaben Wunderhorn* to the lyrical poems of Friedrich Rückert (1788–1866)—that provided such a pervasive generative and shaping influence on Mahler's symphonic work. The first stage in my inquiry is an examination of the possibility that the musical logic and development of the *Wunderhorn* symphonies and the scientific logic and development of the investigations of neurotic dysfunction that culminated in the construction of the seduction theory shared a number of critical assumptions about the way individual selves are situated and shaped in the worlds of nature and historical culture.

In early August 1900, just after completing the composition of his Fourth Symphony, Mahler commented to his friend and musical confidante, Natalie Bauer-Lechner, that the completion of the Fourth was also the conclusion in both "content and structure" of his three earlier symphonies, producing a "clearly self-contained tetralogy (*durchaus in sich geschlossene Tetralogie*)."[7] In further discussion with Bauer-Lechner Mahler elaborated on this claim in a number of ways. First, he noted that the orchestrated song "Das himmlische Leben," which constituted the final movement of the Fourth, had originally been composed in early 1892 in Hamburg as the first of a series of *Wunderhorn* lieder that marked an outburst of creative energy after a period of stagnation. Anticipatory fragments of the concluding lied not only tied together the four movements of the Fourth but also referred specifically to a number of movements in the Third Symphony, making these two symphonies almost like twins emerging from a shared process of gestation and birth. When Mahler talked about the ways in which "Das himmlische Leben" provided a unifying thread in the evolution of musical substance from the Second to the Fourth

Symphony and especially about the ways it integrated the Third and Fourth symphonies, he sometime referred to his symphonic corpus before 1900 in spatial terms—as an "edifice" (*Bau*) in which the finale of the Fourth functioned as the "tapering spire" (*verjüngende Spitze*).[8] The belief that his symphonic work during the 1890s was structured like a Gothic cathedral was also evident in Mahler's descriptions of the emotional tone of parts of the Fourth Symphony as analogous to the beatific smiles of departed saints on Gothic sarcophagi or the two-dimensionality of medieval paintings that represented a world outside of the framing categories of earthly time and three-dimensional space.[9]

The idea of a tetralogy conjures up stages in a temporal narrative more than layers of a spatial edifice, and the Gothic cathedral model of a cosmic structure rising from the darkness of inert matter to the spiritualized point of a spire penetrated by light seems to pertain mainly to the interrelated structures of the Third and Fourth symphonies. Why Mahler might retrospectively grasp all four symphonies as a self-contained tetralogy becomes clearer, however, when one notes the relations he drew between the First and Second symphonies, on one hand, and between the Third and Fourth on the other. In 1893 he suggested that his first two symphonies gave musical embodiment to the experience of a representative individual subject— the mythic hero—moving through a set of transformations from nonreflective merger with the creative energies of Dionysian life forces, through a tortured journey of individuation and concluding in redemption through the aesthetic spiritualization of individual existence. The resolution was enacted as a moment of mystical enlightenment whose musical symbolism drew on the whole panoply of European religious traditions. However, the achievement of redemptive integration did not so much dissolve the sufferings and longings of individuated existence as provide it with affirming consolations of ultimate meaning experienced as virtually present within the aesthetic domain of the musical performance. Mahler connected this narrative of the musical subject quite specifically to his own experience. "My symphonies," he said, "contain the inner aspect of my whole life: I have written into them everything I have experienced and endured."[10] His music did not claim to represent the phenomenal reality of his life experiences but enacted the experiential process of moving from alienation to integration.[11]

As Mahler was composing the first movement of his Third Symphony, however, he indicated that he had progressed from aesthetic performance of the individual subject's redemptive narrative to a musical embodiment of the cosmic powers and structure that made that journey of individual redemption possible. In his first two symphonies, he suggested, in 1896, he had struggled with "human" questions like "Why do we exist?" and "Will we continue to exist for ever?" Such questions had been displaced in the Third and Fourth symphonies by a struggle to embody in tones the cosmic, metaphysical structures that made any redemptive narrative of individual human existence psychologically believable and sustainable. His music was driven by the desire to perform the progressive revelation of "the all," he claimed in 1896, "in which everything lives, must live and will live" (*wo alles lebt und leben muss und wird*).[12] The narrative of individuation was overwhelmed in the Third

Symphony by the attempt to give musical form to the prereflective and postreflective conditions of all narratives of individual emergence, becoming, and transfiguration and to embody the encompassing reality of being, which preceded the world of existing beings in space and time. As he worked on the Third Symphony Mahler often seemed overcome by the burden of giving birth to an aesthetic representation of the totality of life itself. He described himself as seized by nature's mystic power, drawn into "the All itself, into whose depths you sink, through whose eternal spaces you soar, so that earth and human destiny shrink behind you into an indiscernibly tiny point and then disappear."[13] This sense that, in the act of musical composition, his individual subjectivity was absorbed into and swept away by cosmic powers accessible only through his unconscious "second self (*zweiten Ich*)"[14] and that his own composing was in fact a "being composed"[15] by powers much greater than the individual ego persisted through the completion of the Fourth Symphony in the summer of 1900. Mahler continued to insist that his musical compositions emerged from, gave shape to, and in some sense actually constituted his experience. By the mid-1890s, however, he tended to perceive his own experience within the act of composition as a kind of conduit for an experience that soared beyond the confines of individualized perceptions and confidently claimed that his music actually led him and those in whom it "resonated" into an encounter with the reality of the forces of life, the unconscious powers of nature.

Music historians, analysts, and critics, beginning in Mahler's own time and continuing into the present, have elaborated in great detail on the various ways in which Mahler's attempts to articulate his compositional process and describe its products were based on a specific aesthetic philosophy that he encountered in the artistic and intellectual circles of Vienna during the late 1870s and early 1880s. This philosophical worldview, or perhaps more accurately "cultural ideology," was constructed by members of Mahler's generational cohort from works by Richard Wagner and the young Friedrich Nietzsche that had mobilized Schopenhauer's metaphysics of unconscious will and ethic of denial and transcendence for purposes of historical transformation and cultural renewal. There is abundant evidence not only that Mahler developed a deep and lasting attachment to the works of Wagner and Nietzsche during his student days but also that he chose his closest friends—like Siegfried Lipiner, Albert and Nana Spiegler, and Natalie Bauer-Lechner—from among the young artists and intellectuals who shaped their cultural identities within the conceptual frame provided by Wagner and Nietzsche. At the beginning of the 1890s, during the period of his transition from a position at Budapest to one in Hamburg, Mahler renewed some of the intensity of his youthful discipleship, and the works of Wagner and Nietzsche remained influential in his attempts to find the right phrases and metaphors in constructing verbal listening guides ("programs") for friends, music critics, and the general audiences, who were finally able to hear some of his work performed in the mid-1890s.[16] However, it would be wrong to see Mahler's compositions as nothing more than musical representations of an aesthetic philosophy derived from his own and his friends' readings of Schopenhauer, Nietzsche, and Wagner. The way in which Mahler shaped and imagined the purpose of his musical creativity was certainly influenced by his immersion in the cultural ideology of his generational cohort. Still, this ideology provided him with a way to frame a question he was convinced could be worked through and answered within the experiential compositional process of his music alone. In fact, Mahler was convinced that questions about historical and cultural identity could be answered at their profoundest and most inclusive level only through the experiential revelations embodied in the composition and reception of music.

Mahler's particular stance within the generation of aesthetic reformers inspired by Wagner and Nietzsche is perhaps most clearly articulated in his choice of the *Wunderhorn* texts as foundational "bricks" (*Bausteine*) for his musical edifice, as the "fruitful seeds" of his rhizomatic, organically proliferating musical networks, or as the "blocks of marble" whose potentially infinite meanings were made explicit by acts of the musical sculptor.[17] In each of these metaphors that Mahler used to describe his relationship to the *Wunderhorn* poems the texts themselves were defined as raw material for art rather than as artworks in their own right. Mahler believed that the *Wunderhorn* texts were direct, unreflective, naïve representations of life or nature, something altogether separate from poetry constructed by a self-conscious individual subject. It was also noteworthy that this natural ground for cultural mediation was not nationally, ethnically, or racially defined for Mahler. Unlike Wagner and many members of his own generation, Mahler was not seeking the foundations of a specifically ethnic or racial mythology. For Mahler, the founding moment of the emergence of culture from nature was universal and defined by the general humanity of the individuated lives that formed themselves into differentiated cultural communities. In a 1905 retrospective on his aesthetic choices during the 1890s, Mahler noted that during the whole decade he had devoted himself to this collection of folk poetry in full consciousness of its distinctive character and tone as an unmediated expression of life rather than a self-consciously constructed artifact.[18]

Mahler's interpretation of the character of the *Wunderhorn* poems was almost certainly influenced by Nietzsche's description of them in *The Birth of Tragedy* as folk lyrics whose primordial strophic melodies were the primitive connecting link between the Apollonian forms of cultural order and the Dionysian formlessness of the surging unconscious will of nature.[19] For Nietzsche and Mahler these songs did not represent the surface appearances of the natural world as experienced by a reflecting subject but emerged from its unmediated essence, from the formless flow of the unconscious will. Much like dreams or bacchanalian rituals, the folk poetry of the *Wunderhorn* collection opened a window into the world beyond or prior to representation. Their juxtaposed images did not conform to the law of cause and effect, and their represented objects and events did not obey the order of spatial separation and temporal sequence, which defined the world as experienced by the conscious individual subject. The variety of images and events displayed no moral order, perspectival focus, or evaluative hierarchy. This was a world beyond or at least prior to good and evil. Folk poetry imagined as such an unmediated emanation from a primal unity was pervaded by a tone of mysterious incomprehensibility. Acts of violent destruction, creative expansion, erotic merger, or triumphant conquest were set side by side or end to end without any specific rational or logical order to make them comprehensible to the conscious subject. On the one hand they appeared as expressions of absurdist, carnivalesque humor that undermined all self-conscious attempts to give rational coherence to the world. On the other hand they appeared full of mysterious philosophical and religious depths that provided momentary revelations of a world beyond the pathologies of individual striving. Popular folk poetry was a marvelous musical instrument for questioning liberal assumptions about individual autonomy and the possibility of ethical community among rational subjects. For more than a decade Mahler was able to integrate the perspective (as he interpreted it) of the *Wunderhorn* songs into a musical cosmos in which it could ally itself with the sounds of the prereflective at every level—the pure sounds of the nonhuman natural world, the confusing, fragmentary, apparently formless babble of popular musical culture from military marching rhythms to folk dance tunes, the sounds of childhood rhymes and funeral dirges, the gentle lilting of maternal lullabies.

The dreamlike, prereflective voice of the *Wunderhorn* songs revealed the ephemeral nature of human individuation, but at the same time it opened a window at least a crack into a quasi-mystical, posthuman world, a world "without gravity" and of "eternal recurrence" inhabited by Nietzschean "Overmen." From the beginning Mahler referred to his compositions of *Wunderhorn* texts as "humoresques." This was in part because of the absurd nature of their perspective when viewed from a position that assumed the absolute validity of a world of individuated subjects and objects in space and time. However, the "humor" of the *Wunderhorn* songs also referred to their ability to dissolve the reality of the phenomenal world—to make it seem absurd and pointless, to provide a context in which all individual striving for autonomy and integration seemed like an idiot's dream and individual death appeared as an entry into the "real" world.

Mahler's Fourth Symphony was composed as a kind of extended symphonization of a *Wunderhorn* song he had first composed in 1892 as one of his first five humoresques. The musical worldview that Mahler appeared to abandon when he suddenly exchanged his *Wunderhorn* "dreams" for the lyric poetry of Rückert in 1901 is exemplified in the structure of this work. After completing the Third Symphony, Mahler planned to take on the less-taxing task of composing an orchestral humoresque, a simple symphonic poem that would expand on the "fruitful seed" of the *Wunderhorn* song that he was somehow unable to fit into the cosmos of the Third Symphony despite his original intentions. Instead, Mahler chose to complete both his experiential journey of redemption and the musical representation of its cosmic context with an inclusive affirmation of aesthetically transfigured individuated being in the embrace of the universal, eternal power of (maternal) Eros and the spirit-filled community traditionally represented by the harmoniously integrated voices and decisive chords of the communal hymn, or chorale. For Mahler, it was not so much a paternal god that "spoke" to him of the ultimate triumph of the masculine will over earthly conflicts but the voice of a maternal Eros that overcame the pain of alienation and connected every creature into a community in which the wounds of individuation were both recognized and healed and where the power of death was reimagined as the enabler, the partner of love. This redemptive conclusion of the journey—"What Love {or God} tells me" in Mahler's various unofficial "programs" or concert guides—however, was originally to be followed by an orchestrated interpretation of "Das himmlische Leben" that would display individual existence, transfigured through its immersion in the power of cosmic and communal love, as a newborn, innocent child able to contemplate its previously earthly life from the standpoint of eternity and ready to remake the world as an object of its aesthetic imagination.

Mahler's dilemma in choosing among alternative resolutions of the quest for identity and closure can be usefully related to Nietzsche's famous parable of "The Three Metamorphoses of the Spirit" in *Thus Spake Zarathustra*, a work that Mahler read during his creative revivification in the early 1890s, continued to study throughout the decade, and perceived as a musical text or textual symphony in its own right.[20] In Nietzsche's fable the suffering of the camel, who is burdened by knowledge of the suffering of historical individuation, is redeemed by the defiant and conquering "no" of the masculine lion, who in turn clears the ground for the emergence of the child, who represents "innocence and forgetting, a new beginning, a game, a self-propelled wheel, a first movement, a Sacred Yes."[21] For Nietzsche, the birth of this child marked the emergent reality, which Mahler, following Goethe's *Faust*, referred to on a number of occasions as humanity reborn in the shape of a chrysalis or cocoon (*Puppenstand*) and as an embryonic reality waiting to emerge as the "Overman."[22] It is noteworthy that Nietzsche described the final metamorphosis of the spirit into the child not as a conclusion but as a beginning: "The spirit now wills his own will, and he who had been lost to the world now conquers his own world." In Mahler's Third and Fourth symphonies the question remains open as to whether or not the conclusion of the journey of redemption signals an elevation to a transcendent sphere from which earthly existence appears as the object of a peaceful, resigned, and cheerful contemplation or as a decisive, revelatory moment of self-recognition that makes possible a creative reengagement with earthly life and its fateful web of space, time, and causality. Did Mahler believe that the ascent into a sphere beyond reflection— the sphere of the dream and of a second, spiritual childhood innocence—constituted a positive conclusion to the narrative of human existence in time and space? In Mahler's Third Symphony the suffering of the historical individual is ultimately redeemed by the love of the maternal godhead, who provides the energizing erotic power for the mutual embrace of the community. However, what of the new birth that emerged from the womb of this maternal identification? "Das himmlische Leben" was to function in some of Mahler's original early "programs" for the Third Symphony as an articulation of "what the child tells me." What kind of existence would succeed the emergence of the redeemed child in its chrysalis state?

The chiming, rhythmic motif of flutes and winds, which initiates the Fourth Symphony, like the drawing back of a curtain at the opening of a dreamlike play and which continually returns throughout the symphony as a transitional bridge, boundary theme, and reminder that what we are witnessing is, after all, only a play or a dream, was described by Mahler as a musical representation of the bells of a jester's cap, thus suggesting that he meant to alert the listener that to enter the symphony was to enter a world turned upside down, a world in which causality had no validity.[23] However, it was also an obvious marking of time—a warning that this was a world in which our clocks were no longer operating and the normal developmental progression driven by the individual's longing and struggle for integration and peace was at least temporarily on hold. One way of listening to this work, which has always struck listeners as both disconcertingly clear (because it seemed too simplistic, too conventional in a formal musical sense) and oddly mysterious or uncanny, is to see it as an attempt by Mahler to organize a musical universe that is structured by the naïve, dreamlike, prereflective perspective of the child. The concluding song describing heavenly life was composed for a child's voice, and Mahler specifically indicated that it should be sung with childlike sincerity and without parody. The musical fragments of the song pervade all of the movements of the symphony not as promises of the achievement of some future goal in which they will all come together in a climactic resolution but as a indicators of a mood that has been set in advance by the perspective fully revealed in the finale.

Mahler was convinced that even his closest friends and musical confidants would have difficulty comprehending what he was trying to do in the Fourth Symphony. "What I had in mind here," he told Natalie Bauer-Lechner immediately after completing the first draft, "was incredibly difficult to do. Imagine the uniform blue of the skies, which is more difficult to paint than all changing and contrasting shades. This is the fundamental mood of the whole."[24] In later comments he described the experiential perspective of the symphony as cheerful detachment from the suffering and longings of individuated existence. At the same time Mahler noted that the stance of transcendent detachment produced an eerie, uncanny atmosphere throughout parts of the work. The calm indifference toward individuated existence of a subject transposed into a world flooded with light and under the canopy of a never-changing blue sky was also a stance in which the dissolution of particularized individuality into transparent sameness induced feelings of "panic and fear."[25] To transcend the world and to attain a perspective from which the normal, everyday world of individual experience seemed "other" was also to experience oneself as floating in a space without boundaries and without the weight of self-identity, to experience oneself as empty, rootless, and homeless.

The first three movements of Mahler's Fourth reimagine the conventional dramatic and narrative forms of symphonic composition from a position outside of the categories that structured the fate of individuated lives. The opening sonata allegro sets the stage of a world of difference open to constant variation and rearrangement but in terms of a contiguity and simultaneity that avoids the radical polar tensions and dramatic contrasts of traditional sonata musical form and thus also the driving impetus toward some goal in which the pain of difference might be overcome. When hints of forward striving energy emerge, they are ultimately unveiled as pointless and relax into tensionless silence. All differences appear as simultaneous, as equally justified, and as equally indifferent forms of life.

In the scherzo of the second movement Mahler reimagined the dance of life as a dance of death, as a whirl in which the musical subject is seduced away from the pain of separation and horror of death and willingly follows the fiddlers of death into the beyond. In this movement the painful emotions of surrender and leave taking and of the consciousness of what must be left behind come closest to breaking through the general mood of aesthetic indifference that defines the emotional tone of the symphony. However, as in the first movement, the contrast here is not so much between opposing forces engaged in a battle for resolution as between an achieved standpoint of aesthetic indifference and the muttering memories of a former life in which difference still seemed to matter. The internal dynamics or struggles of this symphony, if we could call them that, might be defined as a persistent effort to maintain the discipline of aesthetic detachment over the incessant striving of embodied, individuated life within earthly time. The eerie qualities of the piece are tied to its implicit questioning of not only the efficacy but also the value of this kind of serene detachment in the face of suffering.

The adagio of the third movement, which we might see as a retrospective reimagining of the finale of the Third Symphony, comes closest to confronting this dilemma. Composed as a set of double variations, the movement entangles and merges both the positive cheerfulness of detachment from and the brooding melancholy of the loss of the world of individuated existence that aesthetic transcendence seems to entail. Without the dramatic struggle that organized the finale of the Third, Mahler here moves toward a merging of the variations in which working through the memories of earthly life gives way to the calm joy of aesthetic detachment. Introduced by a jubilant E-major fanfare, the concluding bars of the movement articulate a resonating and gradually fading major chord that Mahler likened to the "music of the spheres" or the interior space of a Gothic cathedral. After this apparent affirmation, the orchestration of the *Wunderhorn* song "Das himmlische Leben," which constitutes the finale, suggests a revelation of the point of view from which the whole symphony was written. The words of a child describing a world beyond the categories of individuated life help the listener retrospectively frame and grasp what has been experienced in the previous movements.[26]

Listening carefully, one can perhaps discern doubts about the fulfillment achieved within the detached transcendent perspective of the heavenly sphere (of art? of childhood? of mystical faith?). The rhythmic chimes that mark the transition between the strophes of the final song might sound to some ears (mine included) as somewhat overly insistent in reminding us so loudly and firmly that what we have heard and are hearing is after all only a dream, that we will eventually have to wake up, and that the child must inevitably leave the innocent, pure potentiality of the chrysalis stage. Nonetheless, the song ends in the fading harmonies of a lullaby, a return to sleep, perhaps death, which is musically realized in affirmative tones. Mahler's stance as he completed the Fourth Symphony seems to have been dominated by the confidence that he had found a way of providing a musical realization of a narrative pattern and a metanarrative framework of human experience that confirmed the truth of the potential transformation of individuated existence into participatory membership in a transparent spiritual unity, the being that preceded and transcended all beings. The Fourth Symphony also seemed to display Mahler the composer in complete control of his art. Considering the Third and Fourth symphonies together, we find Mahler in 1900 apparently at a point where he saw his submergence in his musical composition as an identification with a world of "objective," impersonal truth, an immersion in the "all" that contextualized the world of individuated striving within an all-encompassing cosmic order.

During the mid-1890s, while Mahler was constructing the musical world of the Third and Fourth symphonies as both a paradigmatic narrative of subjective redemption and a totalizing representation of the cosmic context of all redemptive narratives, Sigmund Freud was approaching a similar breakthrough in his own quest to provide full and objective knowledge of the trajectory of individual psychic formation that led to the split, alienated selves caught in the suffering of hysterical and obsessional neurosis. Freud's persistent attempts since the late 1880s to find the pathways by which symptoms of psychic dysfunction, the impairment of human autonomy, and the loss of integration and coherence within the self were connected to the history of psychic formation may seem a much more instrumentally focused and limited quest than Mahler's ambitious desire to become the conduit for an aesthetic re-creation of the structure of *das All* and the meaning of individual existence within it. However, Freud's search for a cause of and cure for the neuroses always contained a broader agenda of self- and world understanding. One could say that the symptomatic material that Freud gathered from his patients during the 1890s, from the physical acts and conditions that seemed to ignore the rules of normal physical functioning to the plethora of mental images and verbal structures collected in dreams, fantasies, and random, free associations, all of which seemed to evade rational structures of temporal and spatial organization, operated in his intellectual search much like the texts of the *Wunderhorn* poems did in Mahler's. Working at first in collaboration with his mentor, Joseph Breuer, Freud had by 1895 become convinced that he would eventually be able to trace the origins of contemporary symptoms of psychological distress in his adult patients by reconstructing the complex network of connections (more like a genealogical tree than a chain of pearls) back to their roots in the memory traces of childhood experience.

By the time Freud composed the concluding chapter, "The Psychotherapy of Hysteria," of his collaborative volume with Breuer, *Studies on Hysteria*, in 1895, he had already begun to drift away from his mentor and partner and to present a distinctively Freudian position in a number of areas. First, he diverged from Breuer's model of therapy as psychological surgery, which was based on the assumption that the originating memory operated like a toxic substance in the psyche, a memory "tumor" that could be removed along with the affect attached to it by pursuing the particular memory chain that led to it, exposing it to the light of conscious attention, and releasing its strangulated affect through verbal expression. Instead of this eliminative model, Freud tended to see the path of association leading from the current symptom to the originating memory as both broadly entangled in rhizomatic networks and jagged in its course, a narrative that connected to other sets of associations and wandered in and out of the domain of unconscious psychic processes. Using his favored archaeological metaphor, Freud imagined the symptom as a kind of potsherd whose meaning or significance was finally revealed only with the excavation of the whole city in which it had come into being.[27] The implication of this metaphor was that curing a memory of its toxic affect occurred not through erasure by hypnotic suggestion but by bringing it back to its rightful place within the complex of mental associations accessible to consciousness that constituted the life of the healthy, integrated psyche.

Tied to this divergence from Breuer was another. Freud rejected the theory that experiences became toxic memories that operate from an unconscious split-off part of the psyche because they entered the psyche during a traumatized, or "hypnoid," state. The memory of the experience from which the current symptoms originated was pushed into unconsciousness, Freud argued, through an act of defense (*Abwehr*) by a threatened ego for whom the memory seemed incompatible with its own structural and temporal self-coherence. Memories of certain experiences were disconnected from normal associative links in acts of denial and splitting that seemed necessary for survival, acts that produced gaps in conscious memory and created a nucleus of disassociated memory traces that ultimately, if they were energized by new experiences, could burst into consciousness in enigmatic symptomatic form. By 1895 Freud had become increasingly certain that the types of experiences that produced memory traces that could not be integrated and accepted as a part of the story the conscious subject told about itself were sexual in nature. The process of defense against incompatible memories began in response to memories of childhood sexual experiences. Since Freud did not, in 1895–1896, imagine infants and young children as sexual subjects or actors, such sexual experiences took the form of sexual abuse—of rape or "seduction" (*Verführung*).[28]

In late April 1896 Freud synthesized his divergences from Breuer into an independent theory (the seduction theory), which he presented in a lecture titled "The Aetiology of Hysteria" to the Viennese Psychiatric and Neurological Association as the long-awaited solution to the "thousand-year-old problem"[29] of the origin, nature, and cure of psychoneurotic illnesses. In his description of the case of Elisabeth von R. in *Studies on Hysteria*, Freud had noted with some puzzlement that his case histories read like fictional narratives composed by an imaginative writer. He had insisted that this narrative form did not imply that his stories were fictional but was produced by his subject matter. The truth he was unveiling was a narrative of the intimate connection between the "story of a patient's sufferings and the symptoms of the illness."[30] In his 1896 lecture Freud aggressively defended the scientific objectivity of his explanation of neuroses. It was not just that the laborious procedure of memory reconstruction with every one of his patients had led back to memories of childhood sexual experiences; he was also convinced that the narrative logic in these reconstructions could not have been influenced by the conscious will of either the patient or the therapist. The associative links revealed by the patient's dreams, symptoms, and free associations were objective precisely because they were unconscious. The "logical structure of the neurotic manifestation" even overrode the patient's explicit denials. The originating sexual memory was required or demanded by the power of the associative network that functioned outside of the conscious control of the participants in the process. It was like finding the final piece of a jigsaw puzzle, Freud insisted, "whose insertion makes the course of development evident for the first time or, even, as we might often say, self-evident."[31]

By discovering the "source of the Nile (*caput Nili*)"[32] of neuropathology, Freud also believed he had found the secret of human psychic formation. As his confidence soared during the winter of 1895–1896, Freud twice wrote to his friend and confidant Wilhelm Fliess that his investigation into the psychopathology of the neuroses had been a detour that had brought him back to what he had originally imagined as the purpose of his life's work—philosophical knowledge.[33] As Freud confidently announced that his method of memory reconstruction could cure individuals of their psychic conflicts and bring them to a state of total transparency and internal coherence in which everything they had experienced would be seamlessly inserted into a self-consciously affirmed, unbroken narrative, he also worked feverishly to construct the grand edifice of scientific truth, a representation of the structure of psychophysical reality that would join together in one dynamic synthesis the physical foundations and the self-conscious spiritual transparency of life, a picture of the living cosmos that would provide the appropriate context for his clinical descriptions of individual lives moving from determinism by unconscious forces to the full autonomy of self-conscious knowledge. Freud sent drafts and outlines of various parts of his synthetic and speculative metapsychology or psychophysical philosophy to Wilhelm Fliess, culminating in the early fall of 1895 in three lengthy notebooks that synthesized most of this material. It would be a bit of a stretch to draw too close an analogy between Freud's metapsychological project and Mahler's Third Symphony. Although Freud humorously subtitled one of the last revisions that he sent to Fliess (on January 1, 1896) a "Christmas Fairy Tale,"[34] he was furious when the moderator (the well-known sexologist Richard von Krafft-Ebing) at his public lecture referred to his seduction theory as a "scientific fairy tale."[35] Freud clearly did have moments of ironic self-distancing as he labored on his metapsychological synthesis and could at times refer to his theoretical constructions as speculative "fantasies," but when he began working on his project in earnest in April 1895, he confessed to Fliess that he was totally consumed by it and that he had never previously "experienced such a high degree of preoccupation."[36] It was as if his thinking and writing were finally bringing to fruition what had somehow been his "distant beckoning goal."[37] In August he felt that his project had drawn him almost against his will into explaining "something from the very core of nature."[38] As late as October he described a visionary moment in which everything became totally clear:

> The barriers suddenly lifted, the veils dropped, and everything became transparent—from the details of the neuroses to the determinants of consciousness. Everything seemed to fall into place, the cogs meshed, I had the impression that the thing now really was a machine that shortly would function on its own.[39]

The draft of a "Psychology for Neurologists" that Freud sent to Fliess in October 1895 began with the assertion that his project was meant "to furnish a psychology which shall be a natural science; its aim, that is, is to represent psychical processes as quantitatively determinate states of specifiable material particles, thus making those processes perspicuous and free from contradiction."[40] The "reality" to which the statements of Freud's text referred, therefore, was not the flow of phenomena presented to consciousness but a hidden, deeper reality not accessible to the sensory, conscious experience of individuated beings in space and time, a reality that could be inferred only as the necessary ground or framework for experienced phenomena. Freud's model did not logically differentiate experience of external physical phenomena and internal psychological phenomena or between the essential realities of objects and subjects, physical bodies and spiritual "souls" (psyches) that were the necessary conditions of experienced phenomena. Science was universal knowledge of reality per se, a representation, we might say, of the "being" that sustained all possible "beings." The "reality" posited by Freud as that which made our world(s) possible comprised units or "material" particles called neurons, which could organize themselves into various networks under the pressure of pure formless quantitative energy (or "Q") according to the law of energy inertia or equilibrium. Psychic and physical "life" was thus a "mechanism" for energy processing that evolved from the simplest, repetitive primary processes of stimulus/response to the complex secondary processes of inhibition, attention, and memory, which provided life with its individuated forms. Consciousness emerged only at a later stage or in a more advanced stratum (in evolutionary terms) of this process or system, at the point at which qualitative sensory perception and the distinction between memory and present perception were demanded by the exigencies of life. The actual processes of psychic formation, Freud insisted, existed independently of consciousness and were to be inferred "like other natural things."[41] One could imagine where this dynamic structure would culminate—in the scientific representation of itself, in a general self-consciousness in which "life" became the object of its own perception. According to the model, "scientific knowledge" would thus have taken on some of the characteristics of Mahler's musical representation of "life" or "the All" in the Third Symphony. But Freud's ambitions never arrived at that goal. The state of a completely transparent consciousness of life, the transformation of unconscious processes into consciously known processes, remained a fantasy, a "fairy tale," which he gradually recognized as a hypothetical model rather than a representation of "reality."

Some general similarities between Freud's and Mahler's visions of identity and of full assimilation of the individual into the "all" in 1895–1896 should be noted. They both imagined a cosmic order in which pure formless energy (a version of Schopenhauer's will?) evolved from the repetitiously uniform relations of primitive matter into the complex organism of systems of particles that gradually developed into individuated forms in order to sustain and re-create the life process until it finally reached the state of self-conscious timeless knowledge or, in Mahler's terms, "eternal light." Both of their representations or "models" of the "totality" that made

individual existence possible and meaningful were imagined in terms of overlapping conceptions of a stratified edifice or structural layers and an evolutionary
process of sequential stages that moved from the formless, repetitive motion of
energy and matter to the emergence of unconscious life processes that shaped individuated forms and culminated in a higher, light-filled, "transparent" integration of
the system in which life made itself the object of its own thought activity. Both positions were essentially monistic in that they fused physical nature and spiritual nature
within the systematic and dynamically evolving totality of "life."

These admittedly general analogies between positions taken in the different
theoretical discourses, conventional practices, and cultural communities of science
and art should, for a historian at least, not be that surprising. A great deal of historical research in recent years has revealed the extent to which the theoretical and
cultural discourses that Freud and Mahler assimilated during their formative years
at the University of Vienna and during their first years in musical and scientific
practice overlapped in extensive ways. The frameworks within which they tried to
formulate projects of personal, professional, and cultural identity often derived
from similar sources and were mediated through intellectual companions and
teachers who were members of common cultural networks. Mahler's closest friend
and intellectual interlocutor, Siegfried Lipiner, was an intimate friend of Freud's
closest college friend, Josef Paneth. Both Paneth and Lipiner played critical roles in
presenting the historical/cultural implications of the philosophies of Schopenhauer
and the young Friedrich Nietzsche to their generational cohort in Vienna.[42] Through
shared friends and teachers and through common readings, Freud and Mahler also
came into productive contact with arguments about empirical analysis of the nature
and actions of the "soul" (as presented in Franz Brentano's university lectures and
seminars) or about the integration of the physical and psychical dimensions of living beings in a monistic life concept (as developed in Gustav Theodor Fechner's
popular texts). Both the speculative syntheses of the Third Symphony (including its
finale in the Fourth) and Freud's "Draft for a Scientific Psychology," as well as the
interpreted meanings of the preconscious *Wunderhorn* texts and the interpreted
meanings of the unconsciously produced texts of neurotic patients in the *Studies on
Hysteria*, were produced at a time when their authors were not only working out
their relationship to the intellectual heritage presented to them as the normative
framework of activity in the cultural institutions in which they sought meaningful
career and professional homes but also returning for inspiration to the texts of
Nietzsche and Fechner and seeking to revive the energies and commitments of their
youth in a new form.

More significant than simply the cultural availability of a common archive of
intellectual discourses, philosophical and artistic texts, and historical/cultural ideologies was the fact that Mahler and Freud engaged this context or set of contexts
with common questions that emerged from their shared experience as members of
the second generation of emancipated Jews in central Europe, who were deeply
committed to the universal ideal of individual liberation from the imposed historical prisons of particularized cultural identities and determined to define their

assimilation into their historical cultures as full participation in the inclusive collective identity of a universal humanity represented by the ideals of secular humanism in the Classical and Enlightenment traditions. Both Mahler and Freud later described their peculiar cultural perspective within their inherited historical worlds as the perspective of homeless outsiders, ultimately excluded from full participation in the ethnic, national, or religious identities so easily inhabited by their gentile contemporaries. Their specific interpretation and selective assimilation of their aesthetic and scientific inheritances, as well as their tendency to engage cultural mentors like Darwin or Wagner in ways that avoided the implications, pursued by so many of their contemporaries, of the ethnic or racial foundations of all authentic historical homes, expressed their intensive personal search for the universal essence embedded in the particularities of the historical cultures into which the modernizing processes of emancipation and assimilation had thrown them.

During the mid- and late 1890s the quest to define their journey of liberation and integration as a representation of the truth embedded in the inherited meaning of their cultural context reached a point of culmination and then of crisis and doubt. In the winter of 1896–1897 Mahler attended Roman Catholic catechism classes in Hamburg and was baptized, together with his sisters, in February. Although he clearly experienced this step as problematic, it was not a purely instrumental or hypocritical act to clear the way for the much-coveted appointment as director of the Vienna Opera. He really did feel, as his works from the 1890s demonstrate, that it was possible to expand and universalize the Catholic traditions that dominated Austrian culture and its musical heritage with a secular humanistic content and to make Nietzsche sing in a Gothic cathedral. Freud's scientific ambitions to actualize the full possibilities of the European scientific tradition and to discover the *caput Nili* of psychology by pursuing the premises of secular, humanist science to its logical conclusions were matched by an intense drive toward acceptance within the academic institutions of the University of Vienna.[43] In the mid- and late 1890s both Mahler and Freud produced works that presented the possibility of living a personal narrative that would culminate in the achievement of an assimilation without hypocrisy or denial and sustain entry into a home that recognized them as full citizens of the human community, a home in which both autonomy and integration were affirmed. Both Mahler and Freud tried to construct a representation of the truth of "life" or of "being" that would sustain such closure. They experienced their own cultural production as an activity that gave embodiment to a truth that was relayed to them by the world outside of their individual egos and by what the world "told" them, to use Mahler's repeated phrase in naming the stages of revelation contained in the successive movements of his Third Symphony. For both Mahler and Freud, however, the utopia of personal closure and immersion into a totality as a truth in which one could live rather than a fantasy into which one might escape had, by the turn of the century, turned into an illusion in its own right, and this experience pushed them to construct a meaningful frame for an existence characterized by interminable self-making in a world whose deeper truth was not accessible to the finite consciousness of existing human beings.

III. The "Turn" toward Subjectivity

In June 1901 Mahler returned to his vacation property at Maiernigg on the Wörther See in Carinthia ready to occupy the newly constructed luxurious villa that embodied his recently attained stature within the institutions of high culture and to begin the composition of his Fifth Symphony. As he struggled with the difficulty of sketching the contours of two of the movements of this projected work, however, he quickly recognized that his creative activity was being redefined by a shift in the assumptions that framed his historical and cultural consciousness. As in 1892, when he had struggled to break out of a period of creative stagnation with an outburst of lied composition that clarified a new direction for his work as a whole, so, in 1901, the clarification of his personal transformation was marked by the composition of eight new orchestral songs, all composed within the span of a few weeks in July and August. Only one of these songs—"Tamboursg'sell" [The Drummer Boy]—returned to the texts of the *Wunderhorn* anthology for inspiration. Moreover, this song is clearly a song of farewell, in which a young soldier who has lost his communal identity and become an outcast among his fellow soldiers awaits his execution and expresses an excruciatingly sad farewell (articulated in repeated "good nights") to the natural and social worlds he must leave behind as he is swallowed up in the darkness of death. In retrospect it is difficult not to hear this song as Mahler's own farewell to the *Wunderhorn* world of childhood dreams and utopian fantasies, in which the painful division between the individuated self and a world of subjective and objective others had not yet emerged into consciousness. Moreover, it seems clear from Mahler's contemporary comments that the melody and orchestration of this farewell to innocence were composed, at least in his mind, before he suddenly remembered the text that seemed to fit them so perfectly.[44] Thus, this last *Wunderhorn* song was not so much "a fruitful seed" for future compositional work as an expression of the struggle to find appropriate musical form and instrumental expression for the farewell to innocence in the "Trauermarsch" [Mourning March] of the opening movement of his new symphony. More striking than the tone of this song, however, was that the seven other songs Mahler composed in the summer of 1901 were based not on the *Wunderhorn* texts at all but on the self-consciously subjective lyrical poetry of Friedrich Rückert. Four years later Mahler noted that "After *Des Knaben Wunderhorn* I could not compose anything but Rückert—this is lyric poetry from the source. All else is lyric poetry of a derivative sort,"[45] suggesting that the ground or foundation of his post-*Wunderhorn* work was individuated difference rather than prereflective identity.

All of Mahler's compositions on Rückert texts examine the anxieties, longings, fears, and hopes of a musical subject positioned as a self-reflective, individuated "I," a subject that articulates its relation to a world clearly defined as "other" to itself. These are not songs of the unconscious will revealing the essential meaning of the life processes that constitute the "all" but of the individuated subject confronting a world in which it seeks to create a meaningful place and story for itself in relation to various others.[46] Moreover, as Mahler turned to Rückert for the texts of his lied compositions, he also changed the relationship between vocal texts and instrumental orchestration in his symphonies. None of the three symphonies of his so-called middle period (nos. 5–7, 1901–1907) contain song movements or even instrumental "songs without words" that echo his lied compositions. Short motifs and theme fragments from the Rückert lieder appear in these works, but they are clearly subordinated to the control of the symphonic voice. The "I" articulating itself in these symphonies does not require words or musical representations of external realities to supplement the message of its tones but "speaks" for itself, and Mahler became especially adamant in his rejection of any verbal guidelines or "programs" for his symphonies after 1901. The orchestration of the Rückert lieder also moves away from the full orchestra accompaniments of the *Wunderhorn* songs to a much more intimate chamber music style that emphasizes fluid sonority, textural clarity, polyphony, and a delicacy and precision that allow individual voices to find precise articulation and to interact with each other.[47]

Two of the most substantial and complex Rückert lieder composed in the summer of 1901 are particularly focused on giving musical shape not only to Mahler's new creative stance but also to the shift between the old and the new as they refer so clearly to themes of the just-completed tetralogy of the *Wunderhorn* years. "Um Mitternacht" [At the Midnight Hour] explores the fears and longings that sustain dreams of redemption through surrender to the beneficent power of some "other" being, the desire for absorption in a dazzling transcendent light that emerges in the individual at moments of absolute isolation and darkness. For four stanzas Mahler's song expresses intensifying feelings of emptiness, hopelessness, and panic in a world that appears both opaque and overpowering. It is one of his most powerful musical embodiments of anxiety and fear of abandonment. However, the fifth stanza breaks out of this mood with a startling surrender into the hands of a "Lord" who has the power to control life and death, a surrender articulated with the musical accompaniment of an intrusive, overwhelming orchestral chorale that finally completely drowns out the individual voice. In the conclusion to "Um Mitternacht," Mahler "psychologized" or internalized the redemption narrative that his earlier works had embedded in the foundational structures and evolutionary process of life. Here the sudden emergence of the eschatological moment of redemption produced by a power beyond the self arises as the effect of momentary despair and weakness and has the potentiality to destroy the self altogether. The song thus not only personalized the redemption narrative by re-creating it from the longings of the isolated individual ego surrounded by a world of darkness but also introduced a noticeable element of ambivalence into the redemptive process itself, representing the achievement of identity less as an actualization than as a destruction of the individual soul.

In "Ich bin der Welt abhanden gekommen" [I Have Become Lost to the World], the song that concluded Mahler's lieder composition in the summer of 1901, he reexamined the aesthetic transcendence of his Fourth Symphony from the standpoint of the individual psyche engaging in a process of aesthetic withdrawal from the world. He even suggested that the song articulated his very personal experience of emotional self-discipline and resistance to any new "external" experiences during the act of aesthetic self-absorption and creativity. In the song he allowed his feelings to rise up to his "lips" but not "beyond." "It is my very self!" he claimed.[48] In this stunningly accomplished lied the instrumental textures that Mahler had used to create a vision of the world as seen from the heavenly perspective of transcendent objectivity in the Fourth Symphony were applied to produce a narrative of the self's relation to the world, beginning with the world's indifference to the claims of the self, developing through the subject's increasing ability to become indifferent to the world's indifference, and culminating in the achievement of an aesthetic transformation of the relationship between self and world that left the artistic subject self-sufficient and serene within the "heavenly life" or "inner paradise" of its art. In this formulation, aesthetic withdrawal did not provide a perspective from which to transform or resolve the conflicts of the world but marked a retreat to a refuge where the poetic and musical persona could exist "alone," "in my heaven, in my love and in my art." Mahler's songs composed to Rückert texts in the summer of 1901 thus psychologized the perspective of the musical subject and created an emotional world built on the experiential perspective of an individual "I" that related to the world from a position of difference and produced a music of shifting moods in response to representations and impulses received from various "others."

Mahler's first composition of a text from Rückert's "Kindertotenlieder" [Songs of the Death of Children] during the same weeks presented a similar stance but with the addition of ambivalent emotions hardly evident in the serene fluidity of "Ich bin der Welt abhanden gekommen." The arc of this song moves from an experience of the world's indifference to the anguish of loss (the death of a child) experienced by the individual subject, to an assertion that the darkness of melancholy should not be folded within (verschrenkt) the self but immersed in light, to a tentative, anguished plea that the extinguished lamp that had lit up the subject's own personal tent might be transformed into an eternal component of "the radiant light of the world (dem Freudenlicht der Welt)," to the hope that individual death might be grasped as the condition of a more general affirmation of life itself.

Mahler's symphonic compositions did not simply repeat and affirm such experiences of subjective withdrawal from and aesthetic transformation of the world. The symphonies that followed the Fourth took the reality of difference between self and world as their thematic starting point and performed the musical subject's struggle to overcome this difference without aesthetic withdrawal or abject surrender to an externally imposed "fate." The new symphony that Mahler began in the summer of 1901 initiated a project of refashioning the difference of self and other within a reconstituted narrative of struggle, defeat, and potential triumph. The aim was not to reveal a transcendent dimension that guaranteed ultimate integration and freedom but to articulate the existential condition of the individual subjective agent, the individual "soul" situated in a world of opaque others, and to find a way to affirm the meaningfulness of individuated life without a pseudoredemptive act of self-dissolution. In this context it is important to point out that Mahler did not experience the changes in his compositional perspective in 1901 as a pessimistic disillusionment with his musical calling or as a defeat of his creative powers but more as a change in task and outlook that revitalized his creative energies and increased his self-knowledge. In early August 1901 he commented to Bauer-Lechner that he felt as though he had reached his full maturity as man and artist. Even if the heights of enthusiasm (*Begeisterung*) he had felt in earlier phases of his life were no longer available to him, such feelings of functioning as an instrument of higher powers had been replaced by a personal feeling of "complete power" and more inclusive knowledge. "I feel that I am capable of everything," he claimed, "and that my means (*meine Mittel*) now consistently listen to me and obey me."[49]

Although Mahler's self-confident knowledge and mastery of his "means" were plainly evident in his outburst of lied composition in the summer of 1901, he felt severely tested by work on the scherzo movement of the new symphony, which he began to compose at the same time and which he described in conversations with Natalie Bauer-Lechner as "entirely different from anything he had written up to this point":

> The movement is enormously difficult to work out because of its structure," he claimed, "and because of the utmost artistic skill demanded by the complex interrelationship of all of its details. The apparent confusion must, as in a Gothic cathedral, be resolved into the highest order and harmony. . . . You can't imagine how hard I am finding it, and how endless it seems because of the obstacles and problems I am faced with.[50]

A decade later, as he was once more revising the orchestration for a new performance, Mahler was amazed how he had been forced to work like "the merest beginner" in 1901 and 1902 as he tried to construct a "new technique" for a "completely new style."[51] An important part of this new technique was an intense focus on mastering old techniques like the contrapuntal and polyphonic techniques of Bach, whose work he studied assiduously during the composition of the Fifth Symphony, in order to develop his ability to control the interaction of a multitude of voices within the musical structure.

During the process of composition, however, Mahler was already convinced that his efforts at making a new beginning had produced impressive results. The scherzo, he claimed as early as July 1901, was "kneaded through and through (*durchgeknetet*) until not one grain of the mixture remains unmixed and unchanged. Every note is charged with life and everything cycles in a whirling dance (*dreht sich im Wirbeltanz*)." Unlike his previous two symphonic works, this new composition "had nothing Romantic or Mystical about it, it was simply an expression of incredible power (*unerhörter Kraft*). It is the human being in the full light of day," he continued, "at the apex of his life." Moreover, Mahler was convinced that he had found a form of symphonic expression that had no need of words: "The human voice would be absolutely out of place here; there is no need for words, everything is expressed in a purely musical fashion."[52]

After the symphony was completed, Mahler sensed that the work on which he had labored to achieve mastery of his musical language and to express his "message" with a disciplined precision that demanded no supplemental aid from written texts or the human voice would also isolate him from his contemporary listeners. In 1904, after a rehearsal of the Fifth in Köln, he wrote to his wife that the scherzo was an "accursed movement" that was destined for a long history of misrepresentation and misunderstanding. For at least the next half century, he predicted, conductors would play the movement too quickly and "make nonsense of it." The public, moreover, would not know "how to react to this chaos, which is constantly giving birth to new worlds and promptly destroying them again . . . to these primeval noises, this rushing, roaring, raging sea, these dancing stars, these ebbing, shimmering, gleaming waves."[53]

It is noteworthy that Mahler's comments on the Fifth Symphony constantly refer to the scherzo as its defining movement. Conductors and audiences would not only be alienated by his new style; they would also be disoriented by a symphony whose narrative structure was defined by a middle movement, as well as a movement form (the scherzo or dance movement) that normally played a subordinate role within a symphonic narrative framed by a first-movement presentation of a problem or question and a final-movement resolution. In Mahler's Fifth, the scherzo was the radiating source or nucleus from which the first two movements (part I) and the last two movements (part III) gained their narrative significance. It was not just an episode in the middle of the story but the structural frame for the story as a whole.

In the scherzo of the Fourth Symphony Mahler had used the solo violin (tuned up a tone for demonic effect) to lead a dance of death that would lure individuated humans into the transcendent world of heavenly life. However, the Fifth Symphony operated in a world without transcendence, and the scherzo was structured around concerto-like relations between a solo horn (the individual subject) and a cycle of dances of life based on waltz melodies in which the individual sought coherence, integration, and affirmation. Most musicological analyses of this movement have focused on Mahler's construction of the serially arranged dance sequences, pursuing the suggestive implications of his own metaphor, which compared the movement to a series of waves or constantly re-created self-sufficient forms that emerged from the chaos of the sea and then collapsed into individual droplets and ebbed back into the ocean. In his fascinating, detailed analysis of the musical architecture of these waves, David Greene has revealed an interesting pattern of development in the scherzo movement as a whole.[54] Mahler's first sequence of waves emerge as self-sufficient musical segments without a history or any evident cause to drive them forward and without dynamic relations to each other. Each of these tonal "waves," moreover, ends in a clear cadence that leaves no questions or impulses for future development. Greene suggests that such waves express submission to a series of life forms in which the innocent self receives its identity from the collective "other" and assimilates to an order given by the traditions of customary form. The dancer finds her identity by dissolving into the dance. Such meanings are too simple and empty to satisfy the specific longings of individuated existence, and as the musical subject tries to possess them in more personal and dynamic ways and connect them to each other, as in the second series of waves, they tend to disintegrate, to end in aimlessness or silence, and to open up visions of the abyss of meaninglessness, which underlies available, historically constructed, customary meanings. Attempts at individual self-actualization end in disarray, just as surrender to given forms of meaning reveal the hollowness of those forms. The affirming waltz of life thus threatens, in a brief episode initiated by the disturbed, melancholy questioning of the solo horn and marked by a dip of the waltz into a minor key and the intrusive sound of wooden clappers and glockenspiel, to collapse into a dance of death (bars 429–89).[55]

However, in Mahler's Fifth there is no transcendent solution available. The fear of death cannot be overcome by a love of death that leads to transcendence, and the soul cannot be fiddled up to heaven but must move forward in a renewed vigor to assert the will of the self and to affirm individual life and create a new dance of life in spite of the absence of metaphysically sustained historical or natural supports. At the end of the movement, the musical subject, embodied in the horn, returns to the call to join the dance of life that inaugurated the scherzo, but this time, one imagines, it is armed with self-reflective knowledge of the incapacity of inherited collective forms or natural teleology to fulfill its longings for redemption. In a "world without gravity" (one of Mahler's possible, Nietzsche-derived, verbal descriptions of the scherzo),[56] the self needs to create its own weight.

The musical meanings of the narrative structures of parts 1 and 3 of the Fifth Symphony, each composed of two closely related movements, can be at least partially illuminated by setting them within the framework, presented in the scherzo, of an immanent process of self-affirmation in a world without objective meanings. Both parts constitute minisymphonies in their own right and follow, on the surface at least, patterns of narrative development that are familiar from Mahler's earlier works. In part I, the pains and frustrated longings of life as a fateful "march of sorrow" toward inevitable extinction produces and is countered by a storm of bitter anger and violent defiance. Within the turbulence of this rebellion of the will against the irreversible fate of individual death there suddenly emerges, like a sun breaking through dark clouds, a vision of radiant triumph and integration, a brilliant brass chorale in D major with its associations of spiritual affirmation and spirit-filled community. However, this momentary paradisiacal vision is followed by a rapid movement back into chaos and collapse in the climactic conclusion of the second movement. Mahler thus makes clear, through the musical context of this vision of integration, that the triumphant affirmation of the individual will as an autonomous member in a radiantly integrated community of wills does not emerge from the actual symphonic resolution of the sorrows and conflicts that have wracked the musical subject and propelled it forward in anger and defiance. The chorale is not the conclusion of an objective process of historical evolution or natural teleology but a subjective utopian vision that sustains individual existence in the context of objective chaos, lack of meaning, and the irreconcilable opposition between self and other. The possibility raised here by Mahler is that fulfillment is subjective—that it occurs in the recollection and affirmation of the unconscious memories that define who we are, shape our past, and explain our longings. It does not reveal a possibility of a redemptive transcendence through integration into a state of being beyond our selves.

The concluding two movements evolve in a recognizably similar pattern. Mahler's famous "Adagietto," a song of aching love and desire, of yearning for integration and immersion in a maternal totality, introduces a rondo finale that seems to provide, in contrast to part I, a more carefully prepared, musically embedded, integrated, and convincing development toward a brass chorale in the tonic major that could represent a resolution of the conflicts that had emerged in the previous movements of the symphony. Many listeners, however, have found the apparently joyous, life-affirming conclusion to the symphony somewhat less than convincing. It is often experienced either as a naïve wish fulfillment or as a willful denial and repression of the realities of finite existence in a world that has not been convincingly portrayed as ultimately amenable to the individual subject's desires for integration. However, we could also interpret the finale in terms of Mahler's new post-1901 perspective as the culmination of a narrative of self-knowledge and a journey toward the self-reflective comprehension of finite existence as existence in a world that is shaped by unconscious desires for aggressive, "masculine," "paternal" control and erotic "feminine" integration. From this perspective the concluding chorale appears as a recollection and reflective understanding of the chorale in the second movement of the symphony. In that movement the chorale appeared like a symptom of unconscious conflicts—as a dream of fulfillment that had burst into consciousness in an uncontrolled, "symptomatic" fashion. It was falsely perceived as an objective historical reality and suffered almost immediate shipwreck as a consequence. In the last movement, the chorale returns, but now it is integrated into the developmental narrative of a subject that has moved toward greater self-conscious knowledge through the previous four movements of the symphony. In this sense the chorale is not a confident willful assertion or a naïve, wish-fulfilling fantasy that the future will bring about a final resolution to the struggle for identity but emerges as an emblem of the laboriously achieved knowledge that human striving and suffering are shaped by unreflective surrender to such dreams and willful denials. The true fulfillment in the joyous conclusion of the symphony comes from the self-transparency of the subject that now recognizes its own history as framed by its own unconscious memories and desires. The affirmation is one of individuated existence with full knowledge that the world does not conform to our wishes and that to affirm and accept individual mortality is not to affirm death as a transition to a transcendent realm beyond space and time but rather to affirm this immanent, individuated existence within space and time as our only existence. Of course, this process of constructing a self-identity through a recovery of the memories of the unconscious desires that have shaped the self is not one that could possibly end in a single culminating moment of self-transparent recollection, a final and complete working through of unconscious memory. Those listeners who detect a certain uncertainty, a lack of completely convincing affirmation, and who note the presence of still not fully integrated representations of unconscious memory and psychic conflict in Mahler's concluding chorale are surely right. This remaining aura of incomplete or tentative resolution, however, was not due to Mahler's surrender to naïve hopes or to a willful denial of reality. It marked, rather, a clear-eyed recognition of the always incomplete process of transforming unconscious desire and its mnemic objects into the transparent structure of a coherent self. Mahler did not finally come to know himself and his relation to the world in the Fifth Symphony. He did, however, embark on a new path in his search, one that eschewed surrender to the objective truth of nature or any overarching, eschatological metanarratives of human history and focused instead on the situation in which a finite self, guided by its unconscious desires, was seduced into subordinating itself to "illusory" representations of identity and opened up new vistas of a form of liberation and integration that might be imagined within the immanent domain of that situation.

Can the shift in the guiding assumptions of Mahler's musical composition in the transition from his Fourth to his Fifth symphony help us to think along with Freud as he abandoned the seduction theory along with its framing scientific and metaphysical assumptions in the years immediately following his self-confident assertion that he had discovered the "truth" about life in the spring of 1896? As Freud began to express doubts about the validity of his theory and the procedures that he had used to construct it, it became evident that he was facing not simply an adjustment of the theory in the light of new evidence but also a need to revise the general framework in which he had posed his problems and read the evidence his patients presented to him. As he noted in a retrospective account more than a decade later, he had found himself in a situation in which his work had lost its "foundation in reality (*Boden der Realität*)."[57] Freud's letters to his confidant Wilhelm Fliess during the years of this crisis, however, reveal that his disorientation was not experienced as despair and loss but as a mysterious opening into a path that might lead to a deeper level of understanding and the discovery of a new world. In a long confessional letter in which he listed all of the factors that forced him to admit that "I no longer believe in my *neurotica*," he also noted that "I have a feeling more of triumph than defeat (which cannot be right)."[58] Within a few weeks of this admission his letters began to formulate some of the foundational assumptions of what would become the distinctive positions of a new "psychoanalytic" perspective on the formation of psychic conflict and to adumbrate the contours of the newly discovered "reality" of unconscious psychic activity on which this perspective was grounded. In a letter dated October 15, he outlined for the first time the structural and temporal relations of the story of King Oedipus as the narrative model that would displace the seduction theory in his understanding of human psychic formation.[59] This "revelation" was matched by reformulations of the motivating energy within psychic reality as the activity of sexual desire, or "libido." Other now familiar psychoanalytic conceptualizations followed in rapid order and assembled with startling speed into an overall theory of psychic formation presented in a series of theoretically innovative works, beginning with the *Interpretation of Dreams*, written and/or published around the turn of the century.

The epochal nature of Freud's shift in perspective from 1897 to 1900 has often been obscured by a number of deceptive continuities in his work. His attentiveness to the importance of unconscious memories repressed by the defensive acts of the conscious ego, as well as to fantasies and dreams that slipped bits of disguised revelatory information past the ego's defenses, was integral to the development of the seduction theory in 1895 and 1896. Before 1897, however, Freud had read this evidence as distorted, fragmented representations within a network of connected processes and events that could be scientifically reconstructed by any objective observer, a truth external to the representation itself. In early 1897 he was especially concerned with fantasies and apparently fictional accounts provided by his patients—but he continued to read them as "embellishments" of the historical facts that revealed the origin and development of the patient's psychic conflicts. In an obvious and immediate sense the collapse of the seduction theory was a consequence of his growing inability to differentiate fact and fiction, representation and fantasy in the evidence presented by his patients, as well as of his recognition that in unconscious mental life such a distinction could simply not be made. This collapse became a triumph, however, when Freud learned to read his evidentiary materials in a new way, as signs of unconscious psychic intentionality and as acts of the subject that produced them rather than as representations of forgotten events to which they referred. Freud had recognized the realm of the psychic unconscious before 1897. What was new after 1897 was that the unconscious "realm" was now constructed as a space of subjective activity and not just a reservoir of psychic objects and processes. The contorted, disorienting nature of the evidence presented by patients in dreams and fantasies was not so much a hindrance to getting at the real truth as evidence of a special kind of truth that spoke according to a different set of rules, the language or voice of unconscious subjectivity. Most obviously, the material presented by analysands did not reveal the repressed and forgotten story of an objectively discernable series of events, of what had happened to them, but the repressed and forgotten story of their own psychosexual desires. The textual evidence needed to be read as meaningful signs that both revealed and hid the intentionality that had produced it. To come to know the truth was also to come to recognize the truth as one's own truth, as the truth of oneself.

The shift in Freud's perspective is made obvious in the difference between his construction and presentation of the case narratives in *Studies on Hysteria* (1895) and the first truly "psychoanalytic" case study (that is, outside of the fragments, largely autobiographical, Freud used in *The Interpretation of Dreams*)—"Fragment of an Analysis of a Case of Hysteria" or "Dora" (completed in 1900, written in 1901, published in 1905). In "Elisabeth von R.," for example, Freud assumed an essential, stable identity defined by rational autonomy in his patient and analyzed psychic dysfunction as due to an injury or traumatic event that produced suffering, conflict, and failure of autonomy and self-coherence The story that re-created Elisabeth's coherent identity was constructed from archaeologically excavated evidence of the sequence of events that led from the originating experience to the present symptoms. In "Dora" Freud interpreted the signs provided by the patient to produce a story of the formation of her current identity by reconstructing the fluid and conflicted sexual desires of her unconscious psyche, which emerged from her original infantile attachments to and identifications with parental figures and their surrogates. In Dora's case the narrative model, which assumed present conflict and suffering as a product of a causal sequence of external events, was condemned by Freud as itself a symptom of defensive denial and repression, a sign of the conscious ego's refusal to take possession of its own history and of its resistance to transforming the unconscious memories of libidinal desire into conscious memories. Although Freud never denied the factual accuracy of Dora's story of the "seduction" she had suffered due to the acts of others, he insisted that it was the psychic conflict produced by her own unconscious subjectivity that lay at the root of her illness. Defining oneself as a victim of events or external fate ultimately implied an unwillingness to come to terms with and work through one's own complicity in that fate.[60]

The implication of Freud's Oedipal theory of the psychic formation of self-identity was clearly that one could not find a cure or "salvation" for the soul and achieve a state of integration, transparency, and peace through submission to the external determinations of natural or historical fate. Although the transformation of unconscious psychic desire into a self-conscious ethical identity certainly was framed by the conditions of biological nature and limitations on satisfaction and power enforced by the reality of other subjects organized in historical/social structures, the complex individuated identities of self-conscious human beings were not determined by them. The Oedipal transformation of universal natural energy into psychic desire and cultural identity was not imagined as an actualization of natural essence or simple submission to external social forces but as an immanent process of individuation. Human subjective agency, or the "soul," was shaped and constructed within the world of nature and culture and could not be "redeemed" though an act that removed it from that world. Like Mahler, Freud reconceived the story of the human subject as a complex, multilayered story of the immanent production of individual identity within the conditions of space and time and construed "salvation" or "cure" as a "remembering" of this process in an act of self-possession and self-affirmation.

It took Freud more than a decade to fully develop the complexities and wide-ranging implications of the Oedipal theory of psychic formation and individuation.[61] It wasn't until 1913 that he would confidently assert that "the beginning of religion, morals and society and art all converge on the Oedipus Complex."[62] The implications of the new theory for his conceptions of narrative closure, however, were already evident in "Dora." The objective coherence of closed narratives based on the determinism of external causes or transcendent authority were clearly "illusions" that could not withstand honest confrontation with the conflicts of life as lived by individual human beings and threatened to dissolve into the experiential fragments from which they had been composed. The breakdown of the illusions of purely formal or external coherence, the coherence passed on by the authority of tradition, created a situation of agonizing but honest incoherence of fragments in search of a theory or vision that might reconnect them into some more convincing narrative structure. In "Dora" Freud also suggested that there might be a norm of narrative coherence and of transparent self-integration in which no differences were denied or repressed, a norm that could guide and ensure our finite and never quite successful attempts to bring all repressed memories into consciousness and fully appropriate the new order of association they presented to us. This would constitute what Freud referred to as a "radical cure" for psychic dysfunction, a state of complete self-transparency. The dominant narrative structure of Freud's case histories after 1900, however, was the story of a struggle for narrative coherence under conditions in which closure was never fully attainable. This struggle, moreover, was shaped by the need to experience the truth of any story through a mutual affirmation of subjective truths by both patient and analyst and thus expressed within both a framework of theoretical assumptions and a common "language" that both could affirm. The struggles and conflicts that drive the narrative of Freud's case studies are thus also the struggles and conflicts that arise from the need to define and control the conditions and terms of authentic narrative coherence. This struggle for a coherence that accepted the lack of closure and affirmed individuated human existence as an interminable process of identity formation was difficult to affirm because it seemed to leave the self in an impossible situation of psychic isolation and fluidity. Existing in an interminable flow of self-construction and self-reflection was really possible only through mutual recognition within a community of those who were similarly emancipated from the traditional politics of identity formation.

Bruno Walter, one of Mahler's followers who considered himself a comrade, as well as a disciple, expressed this dilemma of interminable self-formation best, perhaps, in his comment on Mahler's "inconstancy":

> For such was his nature that, because of its inconstancy, he was unable to hold conquered spiritual positions. His life and activity were spent on impulses, and so he was forced again and again to renew his fight for spiritual possessions. It was for this reason that life, art and personal relations seemed new to him from day to day, while the advantages of systematic progress and complete mastery and use of any gain were denied him. Every day he had to begin all over again, and every day he had to waste himself anew in struggle and surrender.[63]

Although Mahler made some determined efforts to educate contemporary critics and his musical audience so that the reception of his music might be shaped by the same theoretical and experiential assumptions that accompanied its composition, he continued to feel misunderstood and isolated in his musical production until his death. Freud, of course, made a much more concerted effort to create a movement around him within which his works would resonate and his language would find comprehension and to control the ways in which his works were appropriated, but he also often seemed condescending toward disciples' interpretations of his work and maintained the position that he shaped his views against others in a context of difference rather than with others in a context of community. Both Freud and Mahler constantly struggled to keep the process of reflective self-refashioning open as they watched their followers cling to positions they had already transcended.

The significant barriers and spaces that separated the subcultural worlds of musical performance and composition on the one hand and biomedical science and therapeutic practice on the other should make us cautious in asserting overlap and analogy in the shifts that marked the productive lives of Mahler and Freud in the years immediately surrounding 1900. This chapter simply suggests a significant "formal" analogy in these historically parallel, contemporaneous turns an analogy that cuts across the many differences in the specific contents of cultural positioning, historical experience, and discursive framework even within the relatively enclosed cultural networks of fin-de-siècle Vienna. For both Mahler and Freud the "Old Regime" from which they disengaged themselves after 1900 had similar characteristics in its cultural definition of acceptable processes of individual and collective identity formation and in the ways it framed the question of the meaning of individual "life" in a world of subjective and objective "others." Within Freud's biomedical universe of natural scientific discourse, the realm of individual experience could be grasped and integrated into the larger, all-encompassing truths of objective processes by conceiving the experience of difference as emerging from an original state of undifferentiated energy and repetitive motion, the endless cycling of primary process among identical atomistic particles. Individual forms, from the most elementary modes of plant and animal life to the sophisticated networks of self-conscious human existence, were understood by integrating them into the general laws that organized the dynamic relations of matter and energy, which eventually came to self-consciousness in a scientific representation of the whole. Individual human beings could experience themselves as at home in the world because their capability for self-consciousness implied a consciousness of the workings of the cosmic system, of which they were a part. Individual life was thus "redeemed" or "cured" of the suffering produced by separation, differentiation, or individuation when it fully grasped, made its own, the process that had created it. Despite its theoretical sophistication and scientific vocabulary, this late nineteenth-century psychophysical monism retained the redemptive patterns of an older structure of salvational knowledge in which the prereflective Eden was eventually, after the long journey of suffering produced by individuation, transformed into the totally transparent heavenly community of a New Jerusalem. The neo-Kantian dualism, from which such scientific monism had emerged in the late nineteenth century, had also embodied such a pattern even though its resolutions had ultimately been dependent on the controlling agency of the transcendent authority, represented by the "divine" reason of the transcendental subject rather than the self-sufficient immanent transformative processes of nature. What Freud could find within the general historical project of Enlightenment science and its nineteenth-century developmental offshoots like Darwinian evolutionary biology or in the psychophysics of Fechner and Helmholtz Mahler could discover in the post-Enlightenment European traditions of the fine arts and especially of art music, from the self-contained formal structures of dramatic opposition and resolution in the classicism of Mozart and Beethoven to the redemptive metamusical narratives of Wagner, Brahms, and Bruckner. As we have seen, both Mahler and Freud distanced themselves from these inherited patterns of identification-through-integration when they were unable to find a convincing resolution of the realities of their own existential conflict in the current historical forms of scientific and musical tradition. Out of this crisis of the collapsing power of cultural tradition they both constructed a new starting point from which to examine the process of individuation, the longing for a home, and the possibility of affirming individual existence within a situation of homelessness. The new starting point was the foundational difference between the individualized subject and the world of others, as well as the accompanying recognition that worldly or immanent "redemption" must occur within the context of a world defined at its very foundations by difference. In this context the goal of seamless and "eternal" integration became a dream or a recovered childhood memory that defined how we became who we are and situated our current condition. Their creative productions after 1900 unveiled maternal and/or paternal identification as a remembered historical moment in individuation, not a reality in which we could or should immerse our subjective agency and responsibility as finite individuals in a world of infinite difference.

This shift did not mean that either Freud or Mahler abandoned the language of the traditions in which they first formulated their narratives of self-formation and collective identity. Mahler's shift in perspective increased the intensity with which he studied the effectiveness of historical musical forms from Bach to Wagner as instruments for defining ever more precisely the dynamic relations between the musical subject and its world of others. Similarly, Freud became even more insistent after 1900 about the need for scientific objectivity, detachment, and distance and for a formal "scientific" language that transcended particularized identities of ethnicity, nationality, class, and gender. Mahler's Fifth symphony was, as many scholars have noted, more "classical" or "traditional" in its emphasis on historical forms than the symphonies of the *Wunderhorn* period. Disciplined use of inherited musical forms, whether Baroque counterpoint, classical sonata form, or romantic narratives of self-actualization, helped the musical subject speak its message and effectively control its relationship to this-worldly others without the external aid of vocal texts or extended thematic citations. For both Freud and Mahler, inherited forms had become an extension of the power of the subject as it oriented itself in a world of difference rather than representations of transcendent or cosmic powers that demanded the subject's submission.

Thinking along with Freud and Mahler in ways that recognize common patterns in their differences also opens up a path toward thinking through the historical conditions of that similarity. What experiential situation would help us make sense of the shared dimensions of their turns in 1900, particularly their parallel opposition to all patterns of self-identification that involved assimilation of the individuated self to a collective form of life, an immersion of the "I" in a "we," and the positive construction of new ways of thinking of the formation of selfhood based on the reality of difference as the foundational structure of "life"? Both Mahler and Freud are famously known for describing their personal and historical situation as defined by a cultural homelessness that universalized their marginalization as

Jews in an anti-Semitic environment. Mahler apparently often commented to his wife, Alma, that he was "thrice homeless, as a native of Bohemia in Austria, as an Austrian among Germans, as a Jew throughout the world; always an intruder, never welcome."[64] When Freud looked back on the emergence of his intellectual perspective on a number of occasions during the 1920s he also singled out the determining factor of his double alienation from both the traditional culture of his faith and ancestors and the world into which his emancipation from this culture had propelled him. His oppositional relation to the "compact majority," which defined the parameters of culture as a home, he claimed, had provided him with a disabused, critical perspective of the unconscious assumptions, repressions, and denials that went undetected by participants in the ruling consensus.[65]

The double alienation that characterized the situation of Mahler and Freud as emancipated secular Jews in central Europe in the decades after the 1870s provides a starting point for framing the historical determinants of their shared perspectives, but it is also a very general situation that ties them to many Jewish intellectuals whose perspectives were formed in Germany and Austria in the pre-Fascist era, as well as many non-Jewish intellectuals who experienced the modernizing process that tore them out of traditional communities and defined assimilation into a broader community of the emancipated in ways that denied difference for the sake of unity. The self-consciousness of the drive for assimilation, as well as the brutality of its denial, of course, made this pattern particularly intense and personal for secular Jewish intellectuals like Freud and Mahler—and helped shape their roles as archetypal or paradigmatic cultural representatives of the transition to a form of modernism that aimed to transcend the cultural politics of identity.

A more pointed question for the historian is why the shifts in their perspectives occurred at this particular moment (1896–1902) and in this particular place (Vienna). In both cases biographers have tended to focus on specific personal crises as instigating the change. According to Freud's own testimony,[66] the death of his father in October 1896 initiated the intense self-analysis that ultimately unveiled the repressed dynamics of unconscious infantile desire that had fueled his persistent relations of submission and defiance vis-à-vis masculine figures representing paternal authority (most recently Josef Breuer) or fraternal solidarity (most recently Wilhelm Fliess). The personal crisis that initiated Mahler's period of rethinking and transformation and culminated in the compositions of the summer of 1901 seem rather different, at least on the surface. His crisis of self-examination and transformation was inaugurated by a life-threatening medical crisis in late February 1901. His period of convalescence forced him to take a pause from his frenetic activity as the conductor of both the Vienna Opera and the Philharmonic Orchestra and examine the ultimate purpose and cost of his intense and endless striving for integration. The prospect of imminent death seems to have unveiled repressed feelings of guilt about the human suffering inflicted on others by his ambitious drive for status, fortune, and immortal artistic renown, and in the immediate aftermath of his medical crisis he imagined an obituary notice that proclaimed that he had "finally met the fate he deserved for his many misdeeds." The self-analysis and refashioning that followed this event also involved at least some consideration of memories and dreams from childhood and his conflicted relation to his all-suffering mother and deceased younger brother.[67] Just as Freud responded to his personal crisis by repudiating an unconscious "feminine," "homosexual" tendency to sustain his identity through submission to powerful, "transcendent" father figures by becoming the self-conscious "father" of a fraternity of enlightened sons (the psychoanalytic movement) and an autonomous participant in the historical vanguard of the culturally disinherited (the secular marginalized Jews of B'nai B'rith), so Mahler responded to the recognition of his own unconscious desire for merger with the various mother figures of his fantasies by courting and marrying a woman whose middle name—Maria—was the same as his suffering mother and who was young enough to embark on the creation of a new family.

Highlighting the individually specific nature of the psychological crises and personal responses in Mahler's and Freud's transformational moments at the turn of the century, however, obscures what was common to both. Psychologization of the shifts in perspective needs to be expanded through historicization in order to reveal how a cultural politics of identity was transformed into an ethics that affirmed the primacy of difference and imagined community and universality as a constantly expanding, open-ended process of recognizing the other in oneself and oneself in the other.

Any historicization that aims to expand the cultural resonance of the personal problematic of self-identity addressed by Mahler and Freud in 1900 would need to include two associated dimensions. First, it would need to provide appropriate contextual depth for the intensity of the drive for assimilation and the way it became welded to traditions of universal secular humanism within the European tradition and appropriated specific cultural forms and traditions by highlighting their universal dimensions. Within this perspective the convergence of different narratives of identification is obviously critical. The entanglement of the quest for a new or expanded version of self-integration in terms of gender, class, status, power, ethnicity, nationality, sexuality, and so on was central to the recognition that what was at stake, finally, was the general paradigm that had organized the quest in the first place. Mahler and Freud developed and stretched the cultural forms that had been made available to them as they searched for collective identities that would be both transparent and inclusive, as well as for a system of principles that could sustain a world of inclusive transparency. Freud's 1896 project for a unifying scientific representation of "life" and Mahler's similar ambitions in the Third Symphony articulate the intensity of their ambitions and hopes. The disintegration of this paradigm and the collapse of the belief that the totalities into which humans seek to insert themselves are anything other than illusions based on unconscious memories of childhood desire opened up their innovative examination of and search for a new kind of community for the emancipated, a home for strangers. The appropriation of the old ideologies of representation as tools for self-discipline and guides for ordering our actions in relation to others transformed apparent collapse into a triumph of self-affirmation and set new tasks for organizing the association of individuated existences and for constructing rather than discovering patterns of sound and word that articulate the passions, sufferings, and joys of human meaning after the emancipation from identity. This "turn" was not a withdrawal from the world into the interior spaces of self-reflection and narcissistic aesthetic contemplation, in which memories excavated from our unconscious and self-contained aesthetic constructions simply displaced belief in a world in which individuals could find meanings and fulfillment. Mahler, Freud, and their modernist contemporaries did not choose to live in their selves and in their songs but found a new way to imagine the relations among individuals in ways that avoided both the mystical fusion and the repressive domination of difference and created a vision of the transition from the discovery of identity to the assertion of the responsibilities of ethical action that remains as relevant as ever.

NOTES

1. Gustav Mahler to Alma, on the train, Aug. 27, 1910, in *Gustav Mahler: Letters to His Wife*, ed. Henry-Louis La Grange and Günther Weiss, rev. and trans. Anthony Beaumont (Ithaca: Cornell University Press, 2004), 381.

2. Mahler to Alma, on the train, Aug. 27, 1910, in La Grange and Weiss, *Gustav Mahler*, 387.

3. Marie Bonaparte, unpublished diary manuscript, cited in Stuart Feder, *Gustav Mahler: A Life in Crisis* (New Haven, Conn.: Yale University Press, 2004), 229.

4. Letter from Freud to Theodor Reik, Jan. 4, 1935, printed in both original German and English translation in Theodor Reik, *The Haunting Melody: Psychoanalytic Experiences in Life and Music* (New York: Grove, 1953), 342–43.

5. *Der Weg ins Freie* was the title of a novel about cultural identity issues that Schnitzler published in 1908. I have discussed the relationship between Schnitzler's novel and Freud's "Dr. Schreber" case study in Toews, "Refashioning the Masculine Subject in Early Modernism: Narratives of Self-dissolution and Self-construction in Psychoanalysis and Literature, 1900–1914," *Modernism/Modernity* 4(1) (1997): 31–67. Schnitzler's relationship to Mahler is discussed in Marc A. Weiner, *Arthur Schnitzler and the Crisis of Musical Culture* (Heidelberg: Winter, 1986), 30ff.

6. My perspective has been shaped by Michael P. Steinberg's *Listening to Reason: Culture, Subjectivity, and Nineteenth-century Music* (Princeton: Princeton University Press, 2004), especially 1–17.

7. Herbert Killian, ed., *Gustav Mahler in den Erinnerungen von Natalie Bauer-Lechner*, rev. ed. (Hamburg: Verlag der Musikalienbuchhandlung Karl Dieter Wagner, 1984), 164; *Recollections of Gustav Mahler by Natalie Bauer-Lechner*, ed. Peter Franklin and trans. Dika Newlin (New York: Cambridge University Press, 1980), 154. The German edition contains a number of passages missing from the English edition. Citations from the English edition in the text have been checked against and sometimes revised in relation to the German text.

8. Killian, *Erinnerungen*, 162; Franklin, *Recollections*, 151.

9. Alma Mahler, *Mein Leben* (Frankfurt: Fischer, 1960), 32 (comment, Mar. 9, 1902). See also Killian, *Erinnerungen*, 184.

10. Killian, *Erinnerungen*, 26; Franklin, *Recollections*, 30.

11. "Only when I experience something do I compose, only when composing do I experience," Mahler wrote to Arthur Seidl on Feb. 17, 1897, in *Gustav Mahler Briefe*, ed. Herta Blaukopf (Vienna: Zsolnay, 1982), 200.

12. Killian, *Erinnerungen*, 59; Franklin, *Recollections*, 62.

13. Killian, *Erinnerungen*, 59; Franklin, *Recollections*, 62.

14. Killian, *Erinnerungen*, 161–62; Franklin, *Recollections*, 150–51.

15. In July 1896 he wrote to his lover, Anna von Mildenburg, that, when his creative powers were at work, he became "an instrument played by the whole universe," in which "Nature herself acquired a voice." *Selected Letters of Gustav Mahler*, enlarged ed., ed. Knud Martner (Boston: Faber, 1979), 190.

16. The foundational work on this topic remains William McGrath's *Dionysian Art and Populist Politics in Austria* (New Haven, Conn.: Yale University Press, 1974). The claim that Mahler remained a Nietzschean in very fundamental ways throughout the various stages of his musical career is argued in Eveline Nikkels, *"O Mensch! Gib Acht!" Friedrich Nietzsche's Bedeutung für Gustav Mahler* (Amsterdam: Rodopi, 1989). Stephen Hefling is a prominent contemporary musicologist who has used Mahler's attraction to the Schopenhauer/Wagner/Nietzsche aesthetic to interpret specific works. See, for example, the first chapter of his *Mahler: Das Lied von der Erde* [The Song of the Earth] (New York: Cambridge University Press, 2000) and extended passages in many of his other essays. Peter Franklin also emphasizes this dimension in his musical analysis of Mahler's Third Symphony in his *Mahler: Symphony no. 3* (New York: Cambridge University Press, 1991). The claim that all of Mahler's compositions represent a philosophical-religious worldview is most forcefully argued in the scholarship of Constantin Floros. See especially his *Gustav Mahler*, vol. 1, *Die geistige Welt Gustav Mahlers in systematischer Darstellung* (Wiesbaden: Breitkopf and Haertel, 1977).

17. "Fruitful seeds" is from a conversation with Bauer-Lechner in fall 1900; Killian, *Erinnerungen*, 172 (not included in Franklin, *Recollections*). "Marble blocks" is a phrase he used in a conversation with Alma. See Alma Mahler, *Gustav Mahler: Memories and Letters*, ed. Donald Mitchell (New York: Viking, 1969), 93.

18. Mahler to Ludwig Karpath, Mar. 2, 1905, in *Gustav Mahler Briefe*, ed. Herta Blaukopf (Vienna: Zsolnay, 1982), 299.

19. Friedrich Nietzsche, *The Birth of Tragedy out of the Spirit of Music* (1872), section VI (New York: Penguin Classics, 1993), 33.

20. In a conversation with B. Scharlitt in 1906, published in 1920 and cited in Nikkels, *"O Mensch! Gib Acht!"* 51–52, Mahler claims that Nietzsche's Zarathustra was "born completely from the spirit of music, actually constructed in a symphonic fashion" [*Sein Zarathustra ist ganz aus den Geist der Musik geboren, ja geradezu symphonisch aufgebaut*].

21. Friedrich Nietzsche, *Thus Spake Zarathustra*, part I: Zarathustra's Speeches: "Of the Three Metamorphoses," cited in *The Portable Nietzsche*, trans. Walter Kaufmann (New York: Viking Penguin, 1954), 139.

22. In a letter to Annie Mincieux dated early November 1896, Mahler specifically referred to the "highest level of the structure" in the finale of the Third Symphony as the position of the "Overman." See *Mahler's Unknown Letters*, ed. Herta Blaukopf and trans. Richard Stokes (Boston: Northeastern University Press, 1987), 122–23. Mahler used the term *Puppenstand* in a conversation with Natalie Bauer-Lechner (Killian, *Erinnerungen*, 198).

23. Killian, *Erinnerungen*, 185 (not in Franklin, *Recollections*).

24. Killian, *Erinnerungen*, 162; Franklin, *Recollections*, 151–52.

25. Killian, *Erinnerungen*, 162; Franklin, *Recollections*, 151–52.

26. Killian, *Erinnerungen*, 198; Franklin, *Recollections*, 178.

27. Freud, "The Aetiology of Hysteria," in *The Standard Edition of the Complete Psychological Works of Sigmund Freud*, ed. James Strachey, 24 vols. (London: 1953–1974), vol. 3, 192 (hereafter cited as *SE*).

28. Although the various parts of the seduction theory that marked Freud's divergence from Breuer were already evident in a number of essays published in 1894 and 1895, in letters to his friend Wilhelm Fliess and in the concluding chapter of *Studies on Hysteria* they were first forcefully presented as components of a distinctive position in his lecture "The Aetiology of Hysteria" (1896); Sigmund Freud, *Gesammelte Werke*, 19 vols. (London: 1940–1987), vol. 1, 425–59 (hereafter cited as *GW*).

29. This was the phrase Freud used in a letter to Fliess on Apr. 26/28, 1896, in *The Complete Letters of Sigmund Freud to Wilhelm Fliess, 1887–1894*, trans. Jeffrey Masson (Cambridge, Mass.: Harvard University Press, 1985), 184 (hereafter cited as *Freud/Fliess*).

30. *Studies on Hysteria*, in *SE*, vol. 2, 160–61.

31. "Aetiology of Hysteria," in *SE*, vol. 3, 205 (*GW*, vol. 1, 441–42).

32. "Aetiology of Hysteria," in *SE*, vol. 3, 203 (*GW*, vol. 1, 439).

33. *Freud/Fliess*, 159, 180.

34. *Freud/Fliess*, 162.

35. *Freud/Fliess*, 184.

36. *Freud/Fliess*, 127.

37. *Freud/Fliess*, 129.

38. *Freud/Fliess*, 136.

39. *Freud/Fliess*, 146.

40. "Project for a Scientific Psychology" (editor's title), *SE*, vol. 1, 295.

41. "Project for a Scientific Psychology," *SE*, vol. 1, 308.

42. For the network of intellectual friendships that connected Mahler, Freud, Lipiner, and Paneth with each other and with intellectual mentors like Nietzsche and Schopenhauer, see Carl Niekirk, "Mahler contra Wagner: The Philosophical Legacy of Romanticism in Gustav Mahler's Third and Fourth Symphonies," *German Quarterly* 77 (Spring 2004): 188ff; and William McGrath, "Mahler and the Vienna Nietzsche Society," in *Nietzsche and Jewish Culture*, ed. Jacob Golomb, 218–331 (New York: Routledge, 1997). For the ties to Fechner see Michael Heidelberger, *Nature from Within: Gustav Theodor Fechner and His Psychophysical Worldview*, trans. Cynthia Klohr (Pittsburgh: University of Pittsburgh Press, 2004), 63ff; and Wilhelm Hemecker, *Vor Freud: Philosophie geschichtliche Voraussetzungen der Psychoanalysis* (Munich: Philosophia, 1991), 65ff.

43. The personal conflicts that emerged within Freud's crisis of institutional assimilation is beautifully recounted in Carl Schorske's famous essay "Politics and Patricide in Freud's Interpretation of Dreams," in Schorske, *Fin-de-siècle Vienna: Politics and Culture* (New York: Knopf, 1980), 181–207. The ambiguities embedded in Mahler's conversion are discussed in Michael P. Steinberg, *Austria as Theater and Ideology: The Meaning of the Salzburg Festival* (Ithaca: Cornell University Press, 1990), 169–72, 186–92.

44. Killian, *Erinnerungen*, 193; Franklin, *Recollections*, 173.

45. Conversation with Anton von Webern recorded in Webern's diaries and printed in Hans Moldenhauer and Rosaleen Moldenhauer, *Anton von Webern: A Chronicle of His Life and Work* (New York: Knopf, 1979), 75.

46. This epochal shift after 1901 in the way Mahler positioned the musical subject in his compositions was first clearly recognized in the classic study by Paul Bekker, *Gustav Mahler's Sinfonien* (Berlin: Schuster and Loeffler, 1921; reprint, Tutzing: Schneider, 1969), 173–75. It was developed further in relation to Romantic theories of subjectivity in Reinhard Gerlach, *Strophen von Leben, Traum, und Tod. Ein Essay ueber Rückert-Lieder von*

Gustav Mahler (Wilhelmshaven: Heinrichshofen, 1982) and has been fairly widely appropriated though not extensively developed by modern Mahler scholars. See especially the many historical essays and musical commentaries by Stephen E. Hefling, such as "The Rueckert Lieder," in *The Mahler Companion*, ed. Donald Mitchell and Andrew Nicholson, 338–65 (New York: Oxford University Press), or "Song and Symphony (II): From Wunderhorn to Rückert and the Middle-period Symphonies: Vocal and Instrumental Works for a New Century," in *The Cambridge Companion to Mahler*, ed. Jeremy Barham, 108–27 (New York: Cambridge University Press, 2007). This analysis of Mahler's shift should be distinguished from the claim that after 1900 Mahler engaged in a movement of aesthetic withdrawal from engagement with the world, that is, toward a decadent aestheticism that no longer participated in the public sphere of social and political interaction, an interpretation that has been suggested by both Carl Schorske and William McGrath. Aesthetic withdrawal was one possible variation of Mahler's rethinking of the relationship between self and world but not the only one, and it was certainly not synonymous with the shift itself. See Schorske, "Gustav Mahler: Formation and Transformation," in Carl E. Schorske, *Thinking with History: Explorations in the Passage to Modernism*, 172–90 (Princeton: Princeton University Press, 1998), and William McGrath, "Mahler and Freud: The Dream of a Stately House," in *Gustav Mahler Kolloquium 1979: Beitraege der Oesterreichischen Gesellschaft für Musik* 2, ed. Rudolf Klein, 40–51 (Kassel: Baerenreiter, 1981).

47. On this shift toward a chamber-music style in the orchestration of the Rückert lieder see Donald Mitchell, "Mahler's 'Kammermusikton,'" in Mitchell and Nicholson, *Mahler Companion*, 217–35.

48. Killian, *Erinnerungen*, 194: "Das ist die Empfindung bis in die Lippen hinauf, die sie aber nicht übertritt! Und das bin ich selbst!"; Franklin, *Recollections*, 174.

49. Aug. 4, 1901, in Killian, *Erinnerungen*, 192; not in the English edition.

50. Aug. 5, 1901, in Killian, *Erinnerungen*, 192; Franklin, *Recollections*, 172.

51. Letter to Georg Goehler, Feb. 8, 1911, *Gustav Mahler Briefe*, 403–404.

52. July 25, 1901, in Killian, *Erinnerungen*, 193; Franklin, *Recollections*, 173.

53. Mahler to Alma, Oct. 14, 1904, *Gustav Mahler: Letters to His Wife*, 179. This was after the first rehearsal for the premiere of the symphony.

54. David B. Greene, *Mahler, Consciousness, and Temporality* (New York: Gordon and Breach, 1984), 74–103.

55. There is a brief mention of this episode in Donald Mitchell's analysis of the Fifth in his "Eternity or Nothingness? Mahler's Fifth Symphony," in Mitchell and Nicholson, *Mahler Companion*, 302. The importance of the solo horn in defining the structure of the scherzo as a relationship between a searching, questioning subject and a world composed of waves of ephemeral meaning and order has been highlighted by Vladimir Karbusicky in his *Gustav Mahler und seine Umwelt* (Darmstadt: Wissenschaftliche Buchgesellschaft, 1978), 5–21.

56. Mitchell, "Eternity or Nothingness?" 301.

57. Freud, "Zur Geschichte der psychoanalytische Bewegung," *GW*, vol. 10, 55.

58. *Freud/Fliess*, 264–65.

59. *Freud/Fliess*, 272.

60. For an expanded explication of the claims of this paragraph, see John Toews, "Fashioning the Self in the Story of the 'Other': The Transformation of Freud's Masculine Identity between 'Elisabeth von R.' and 'Dora,'" in *Proof and Persuasion: Essays on Authority, Objectivity, and Evidence*, ed. Suzanne Marchand and Elizabeth Lunbeck, 196–218 (Amsterdam: Brepols, 1996).

61. I have discussed this transformation at some length in "Having and Being: The Evolution of Freud's Oedipus Theory as a Moral Fable," in *Freud: Conflict and Culture*, ed. Michael S. Roth, 65–79 (New York: Knopf, 1998).

62. "Totem and Taboo" (1913), *SE*, vol. 13, 156.

63. Bruno Walter, *Gustav Mahler*, trans. James Galston (New York: Greystone, 1941), 129–30.

64. Alma Mahler, *Gustav Mahler*, 109.

65. "An Autobiographical Study" (1924), *SE*, vol. 19, 222; "Resistances to Psychoanalysis" (1925), *SE*, vol. 19, 222; letter to members of the B'nai B'rith lodge, May 6, 1926, *Letters of Sigmund Freud*, ed. Ernst L. Freud (New York: McGraw Hill, 1964), 366–67.

66. *Die Traumdeutung*, *GW*, vols. 2–3, x; *The Interpretation of Dreams*, *SE*, vols. 4–5, xxvi. This is from the preface to the second edition (1908).

67. The textual evidence concerning Mahler's near-death crisis is most fully presented in Henry-Louis La Grange, *Gustav Mahler*, vol. 2, *Vienna: The Years of Challenge* (New York: Oxford University Press, 1995), 334–38, and subjected to psychoanalytic interpretation in Stuart Feder, *Gustav Mahler: A Life in Crisis* (New Haven, Conn.: Yale University Press, 2004), 60–74.

CHAPTER 5

....

UNDERSTANDING
SCHOENBERG AS CHRIST

....

JULIE BROWN

A surprising aspect of late Schoenberg is the presence of Christ as a model of spiritual leadership—surprising because, having converted to Lutheranism in 1898, he began a process of return to Judaism in about 1926, which was symbolically formalized in 1933. Schoenberg was careful to note the significance of the Christian phase of his life in two biographical sketches. Both in 1932 and 1944 "How I Became a Christian" figured in brief outline structures for a biography—with "How I Became a Jew Again" added to the 1944 sketch.[1] Particularly unexpectedly, the figure of Christ haunts the end of his 1927 *Tendenzstück* [political play] *Der biblische Weg*, which was prompted, it seems, by Schoenberg's invitation in 1924 to contribute to a Zionist brochure (*Pro Zion!*) and served as preliminary thoughts for the later (incomplete) opera *Moses und Aron*.[2] *Der biblische Weg* imagines an industrialized and militarized totalitarian Jewish state with a dictator, Max Aruns, leading it. Aruns seems modeled on both Moses (who led his people from slavery) and Christ (who was rejected by his own people). At the end Aruns dies at the hands of the people because he betrayed the spiritually persuasive idea in favor of a destructive mechanical weapon as a way of saving them. In his death scene, with strong echoes of the Passion story, he asks forgiveness of the people: "Lord, only now do I recognize it and implore you: accept my blood as expiation…Lord, my God, save them! Give them a sign that you are castigating only me for my sins against the spirit but that you will not let the Idea die with me."[3] Even at the end of his life, long after returning to Judaism and after a huge amount of work on behalf of Judaism in the 1930s, Schoenberg produced a set of psalms that bear witness to a continuing idealization of Christ. Drafted between September 1950 and February 1951, the ninth and longest text is titled "Jesus," whom Schoenberg presents as "the purest, the most innocent, unselfish, and idealist being" but one who was nevertheless unrecognized by Jewish historiography.

    Moshe Lazar wonders whether Schoenberg draws on the Christ model in *Der biblische Weg* unconsciously since in the midtwenties he was more familiar with the Passion of Christ and Easter than with Moses or the Jewish traditions.[4] Although Schoenberg's reflections upon Christ in that play are not especially pointed, his representation of Christ in the psalm seems more so and might even be distressing for those who wish to emphasize the growing importance of Judaism in Schoenberg's thinking. Jesus is presented as "the king of the Jews and the son of God," a second Moses who wanted to lead his people "to the true faith in the One, Everlasting and Omnipotent" God.[5] If the implication of *Der biblische Weg* is that the partly Christlike Aruns was not idealistic enough, this psalm stresses the explanation: Christ was "the purest, the most innocent, unselfish, and idealist being."

    How are we to understand Schoenberg's return to Christ in his late work? I would like to approach this question via the construction of Schoenberg's priest-like leader role by his Vienna circle around 1909, at the time he renounced tonality; the cultural contexts for reading this and the perspective Schoenberg might have had on it all from his position as persecuted Jew under the Nazis and exile in postwar North America are both critical. The fact that Schoenberg's students adopted a subservient relationship with him and frequently addressed him in a cultish language has long been known. Yet the precise nature of the language, its written contexts, and its discursive meanings have been subjected to surprisingly little scrutiny, even among recent writings about what Dahlhaus called Schoenberg's "aesthetic theology."[6] The language and mode of interaction within the Schoenberg circle at that time reflected a species of utopian thinking and yearning for salvation by a strong leader that provides us with potential footholds onto Schoenberg's later returns to the figure of Christ—especially given the radical political thinking he articulated in *Der biblische Weg*. Indeed, I suggest that it provides insights into various aspects of Schoenberg's activities from the 1920s on.

    Yet this topic presents the historian with challenges. The Schoenberg circle's views predate a historical catastrophe that was itself the outcome of radical utopianism in social and political spheres; misleading though it would be to draw exact parallels, it would be equally wrong entirely to divorce these early constructions of Schoenberg both from his own concepts of strong visionary leadership and from the devastating impact similar ideas had had in social and political spheres in the interim. When we attempt to make sense of Schoenberg's postwar activities and writings, we therefore do well to bear in mind Dominick LaCapra's observations about approaching post-Holocaust discourses. LaCapra argues that the Holocaust was so traumatic for survivor and bystander alike that it resulted in a shattering of meaning that inevitably affects accounts of it both by the historical actors themselves and by historians.[7] The Holocaust is not just the zero point of artistic representation, as Adorno has argued[8]; it is an opaque, fragmented, and, for the historian, ethically fraught moment in terms of historical representation. Schoenberg's case may serve as an exemplification of some of these issues for the cultural history of twentieth-century music. It is clear that in 1933 Schoenberg suffered a severe shock when, as a Jew, he was effectively forced out of his position at the Akademie der Künste in Berlin and went into exile, first in Paris and then in the United States. Much of his activity from this time reflects a strong need to reprocess his past in the light of sudden recent changes. He reconverted to Judaism, expressed his rejection of the Occident, and then temporarily dropped composition and embarked on a campaign to mobilize prominent people to rescue European Jewry and transfer them to an (imagined) militant Jewish state where he himself would be leader.[9] Nothing came of these efforts, and as the documents were not published at the time they must be read as Schoenberg's *private* reaction to the shock of being deprived of his German identity.[10]

Yet from 1921 on, when he was rudely awakened to the increasing prevalence of racial anti-Semitism, but above all beginning around 1933, it is also possible to detect both a reorientation in his writings and an amazing prescience about how political events might unfold. It is therefore possible to see Schoenberg's reaction to Hitler's rise to power and to the fate of his beloved Germany as including both profound shock and trauma and quite an amazing ability to predict. The idea that Schoenberg had the power of prophecy[11] implies superhuman abilities to see into the future. In this chapter I suggest, however, that Schoenberg's early prescience was as human as his later need to return to and reprocess the symbols of his earliest developments in composition.

Students' Discourse

The Schoenberg correspondence from around 1909 to 1912 involves a language that is strongly inflected with Christian mysticality, in which "discipleship" seems to have had a genuinely Christian dimension for at least some of Schoenberg's students. Some communications construct Schoenberg as a poet-priest performing a redemptive role. Of course, an extremely deferential tone toward Schoenberg on the part of his students would certainly have been expected in Vienna at this time even though Schoenberg was not much older than either Berg (eleven years) or Webern (nine years): The Berg-Adorno correspondence reveals that Adorno (eighteen years younger than Berg) adopted a highly deferential tone when writing to his teacher, for instance.[12] However, even in this context the fervor of the devotion that Webern and Berg showed toward Schoenberg is quite extraordinary.

Reading these letters alongside Schoenberg's creative activities and other beliefs is the challenge. For Adorno, for instance, Berg's reference to Schoenberg as a "holy person" is "a sign of the ultimate authenticity of the Circle's music: the relentless purification of their compositional language results in a music into which 'no social function falls—indeed, which even severs the last communication with the listener.' "[13] Dahlhaus has long read Schoenberg's religious language as self-consciously legitimizing; the tone of these letters, Dahlhaus argues, lent his radical act of 1908 particular authority and served to legitimize a musical moment whose "substance consisted in an act of decisionism and not in a systematic web of argument or historical derivation."[14] Yet to read the students' markedly Christian-mystical language in this way underplays its cultural significance, I would argue.

The published Berg-Schoenberg correspondence, between whom correspondence proper began only in spring 1911, has provided us with most of our examples of this language.[15] Berg's epistolary styling is self-conscious, circumlocutionary, and literary—so much so that his occasional use of religiously inflected language scarcely seems out of the ordinary. Earlier letters survive from Webern to Schoenberg, as do letters between Berg and Webern.[16] Frustratingly, little of the Webern-Schoenberg correspondence is published,[17] but more frustrating still, virtually no letters from Schoenberg to Webern survive from before 1926.[18] The context and tone of the letters within the circle start to become a little clearer once we can read a series of letters together. My analysis is based on a selection of published and unpublished items dating from 1909 to 1912 (see appendix to this chapter): excerpts from certain letters to Schoenberg from his students (particularly from Berg and Webern), excerpts from a few letters between Webern and Berg themselves, plus a couple of other contextual excerpts from various essays contemporaneously produced within the circle.[19] It is important to stress that these excerpts are taken from longer letters, the bulk of which tend to be devoted to more mundane matters and of course tell us nothing about what they said to each other face to face; they also represent only a fraction of the total correspondence from that period and therefore concentrate the rhetoric and considerably heighten its impact. Nevertheless, they may help to illuminate the dynamic that operated then within the Schoenberg circle.

Quite striking is the extent to which both Berg and Webern exert an influence on Schoenberg while their tone remains extremely deferential. Webern brought books and ideas to Schoenberg's attention—everything from philosophy to poetry—while periodically articulating ways in which he conceived of Schoenberg in relation to contemporaries or immediate precursors: Wagner, Mahler, Weininger, Kraus, Kokoschka, and so on.[20] Indeed, there are suggestions that Berg and Webern introduced Schoenberg to certain key works of literature and sets of ideas. For instance, Balzac's mystical novels, *Seraphita* and *Louis Lambert*, key ingredients of his "aesthetic theology," were introduced to him by Webern on March 9, 1911.[21] *Seraphita* provided Schoenberg with a poetic context within which to conceive the twelve-note method, having inspired a massive symphony by the same name, which eventually mutated into *Die Jakobsleiter*.[22]

Schoenberg's letters to Berg were typically short and factual and involved one letter to two or three from Berg. Although Webern's letters suggest that there was more exchange of ideas between him and Schoenberg, it is difficult to judge how much and of what sort. It is also apparent that Mahler's death on May 18, 1911, triggered a special desire on Webern's and Berg's parts to reassure Schoenberg of their spiritual devotion and marked a heightening of quasi-religious language. Up to that point Webern referred to Mahler in these Christian-mystical terms as much as, if not more than, to Schoenberg (see excerpts from mid-1910). On May 24 Webern even used the capitalized "Sein" and "Ihn" when referring to Mahler, either as a telling typo (of which there are many in Webern's letters) or in order to sacralize Mahler, as in English ("the impression that His work was fully completed" and "we grieve for Him"). It also becomes apparent that other students used variations of this sort, with the two framing essays in the 1912 Festschrift repeating this language in a public document. Crucially, we can see that Webern and Berg employed such language about Schoenberg even in communication between themselves, not just in deference to Schoenberg.

Notwithstanding Schoenberg's roots in and later return to Judaism, the rhetoric of his circle is messianic in a markedly Christian sense. Webern's expressed aim of experiencing and creating the "non-material aspect to a work of art," a "more spiritual, more enraptured content," as he puts it in his letter of July 6, 1910, is manifest both in his works and in Schoenberg's.[23] The language via which he and Berg and ultimately Schoenberg negotiate this move toward the spiritual is Christian in orientation, traversing a range of almost exclusively Christian parallels for both Schoenberg's role as creator and leader and their roles as followers. Reacting to Mahler's death, Berg and Webern both strongly rely upon Christian, often Roman Catholic, imagery. Berg (August 3, 1911) described Schoenberg's newly completed *Harmonielehre*, "written in the service of the deity," as having become, with its "divine" foreword and dedication, a type of Christian holy book: The foreword and dedication effected the book's "consecration," such that one needed "to cross oneself" before it. A week later (August 11, 1911) Webern was equally explicit: "I believe that the disciples of Jesus Christ could not have felt more deeply for their Lord than we for you." A week later (August 16, 1911) Webern wished for a supernatural, even Godlike power that could give Schoenberg everything he wanted; he then imagined himself as priest to Schoenberg's God, suggesting that the act of gathering money to help Schoenberg was like making an offering. Numerous references to Schoenberg's suffering also allude to this particular construction of Schoenberg as Christ figure.

In addition to the sacerdotal aspect are several constructions of Schoenberg and his work as part of a redemptive program. This discussion goes beyond the broad question of *Kulturkritik* by bringing Schoenberg's musical project into connection with vivid Christian imagery. Berg wrote to Schoenberg (September 26–27, 1911) about the "great and holy cause" for which Schoenberg was fighting in the outside world; Webern wrote to Berg (November 23, 1911) that composition, Christian redemption, and Mahler's and Schoenberg's lives of "repentance and yearning" were all connected: "To reach into the heart, filth [*Treck*] out!" Webern mentions *Treck* in several further letters. On July 16, 1910, the riffraff of society seem to be the filth that needs to be destroyed, an image that takes on a religious hue when, somewhat oddly, Webern suggests that such an idea might be consecrated by God overnight. He also connects this with the ideas of Otto Weininger, notorious Viennese theorist of ethical subjectivity: Man should cast off the animal part of himself and dissolve his material substance, a set of choices that would lead to the highest peaks of morality and ultimately to God.[24] On January 11, 1912, "filth" is the aspect of the world against which both Schoenberg and his *Harmonielehre* stand. The documentation leaves open the questions of who initiated and how Schoenberg reacted to this cultish language; it is possible that for whatever reason it might have emerged voluntarily from the students, unprompted by Schoenberg. Schoenberg's couple of documented expressions of modesty also leave open the possibility that he was not entirely comfortable with (August 18, 1911, Berlin Diary excerpt) it.

Wagner's Poet-Priest

To try to understand this language we need to consider the cultural meanings that attached to it in turn-of-the-century Vienna. The Christian-mystical aspect appears to rule out reading the priestly posture as an early manifestation of a prophetic bearing that links to Schoenberg's overtly Jewish ethical self-projections from the late twenties, of the sort proposed by Alexander Ringer. The specifically Roman Catholic element of Berg's and Webern's Christian constructions have a local Viennese import inasmuch as they were in line not only with their own confessions (broadly defined, as neither was devout) but also with Vienna's religious establishment of the time. Not only was Catholicism the religion of the Habsburgs; from 1897 to 1910 Karl Lueger was mayor of Vienna, and the efforts of his Christian Socialist Party to reestablish Catholic values within Viennese society were both inspired by and helped to reinforce the Catholic revival at the end of Josephist rule and the Congress of Vienna as well. It also ran in notorious parallel with increased intolerance of Jews.[25]

Schoenberg's and his students' own spiritual outlooks between 1908 and 1912 are difficult to reconstruct in detail. We know that Schoenberg was not religiously devout either as a Christian after converting from Judaism to the Lutheran confession as a young man or as a Jew after reconverting in 1933. In 1934, as a new exile from Hitler's Germany, he even wrote to Peter Gradenwitz as follows: "I have never been convinced by Protestantism; but I had, like most of the artists in my time, a Catholic period; but, please, this is strictly confidential!!!"[26] Given that 1911 ended for Schoenberg in personal and artistic crisis, genuine self-doubt, it may also be wrong to assume that this phase coincided with the spirituality he described to Richard Dehmel two years later. On December 13, 1912, he famously wrote that he wanted to compose an oratorio about an individual struggling to know God: "[M]odern man, having passed through materialism, socialism, and anarchy and, despite having been an atheist, still having in him some residue of ancient faith (in the form of superstition), wrestles with God (see also Strindberg's *Jacob Wrestling*) and finally succeeds in finding God and becoming religious. Learning to pray!"[27] Webern had already given expression to this central notion of "wrestling with God" in a letter to Schoenberg on August 10, 1910 (see appendix). That Schoenberg was interested in some form of mystical belief is also well-enough documented, especially in connection with artistic creation. He had recourse to the ancient discourse of artist-as-divine-vessel in a published aphorism of 1909: "So utterly full of meaning is God's greatest creation: the work of art brought forth by man."[28] His painting titled "Christus-Vision (Kopf)" is officially undated; it is said to date from "before October 1910," but this remains inconclusive evidence as to whether Schoenberg painted it before or after his students started using his and Christ's names in the same sentence—though equally it may have nothing to do with the messianist and sacerdotal discourses within the circle.[29] We find him describing composers via descriptions of strong faith, images of sainthood, and parallels with Christ in his commemorative essays on Liszt (published October 20, 1911) and Mahler (published

March 1, 1912), specifically referring to Mahler as a saint (*ein Heilige*), which clearly echoes Webern's and Berg's earlier descriptions of both him and Mahler as saints.[30] His choice of text for the String Quartet op. 10, *Herzgewächse*, and the projected *Séraphita* symphony also reflect these mystical interests, the *Séraphita* text drawing on the theosophy of Swedenberg following his engagement with Balzac,[31] which we now know was also prompted by Webern (see appendix, March 9, 1911).

In his essay on Schoenberg's aesthetic theology, Dahlhaus samples writings over the course of Schoenberg's life and points out that by the end of the nineteenth century the very conflation of art and religion had a complex genealogy. For him the strictly religious part of Schoenberg's ideas elided significantly with his psychological notion of "instinctive life," and he concludes that Schoenberg essentially adopted Freud's psychology of the instincts via Schopenhauer's metaphysics of the will and Wackenroder's emotional devotion.[32] John Covach and others have also pointed to the additional theosophical elements that flowed from his encounter with Balzac's novels.[33] Julian Johnson continues this line with a turn to the musical texts. However, Johnson is only partly right when he claims that to talk of concrete personal and intellectual influences "is always superficial." For him, "simultaneity of interest in the metaphysical and occult testifies to the manifestation of a cultural, rather than merely personal idea."[34] It is hard to disagree. However, for Johnson that "cultural idea" was "the working out of tensions in the modern European mind. Specifically,…it represents a critical development of German Idealism in the context of the modern world." What Johnson ignores is that, at this time, metaphysical longing was often deeply entwined with ideologies of cultural renewal. Moreover, Dahlhaus's decision ultimately to explain Schoenberg's aesthetic theology as a type of rhetorical flourish, glossing a moment of remarkable aesthetic and technical "decisionism" with an opportunistic and highly recognizable rhetoric of authority, seems inadequate to explain the strongly Christian claims of salvation (from filthy humanity, etc.) that we find in Webern's letters, as well as the extent to which others around Schoenberg also used this language.

The idea of artistic creation as *imitatio dei* is an old one, of course, but to couple it with genuinely religious overtones, both a concept of the creator as priest and a redemptive agenda were more recent moves. At least three potential bodies of thought about poet-priests suggest themselves as possible sources: those of Richard Wagner, Stefan George, and Otto Weininger. Chief among these was the first. Wagner's late writings on art religion ("Religion and Art" and its supplements: "What Use Is This Knowledge?" "Know Thyself," "Heroism and Christianity," "On the Feminine in the Human," and "Metaphysics. Art and Religion. Morality. Christianity"), combining Schopenhauerian philosophy, ethical aesthetics, and Christian mysticism, are intimately entwined with his theories of cultural regeneration. In "Religion and Art," which recapitulated ideas that he had already articulated elsewhere and first appeared in the *Bayreuther Blätter* in 1880, Wagner argues that artistic allegories should replace the worn-out allegories of religion, claiming that true Christianity is reborn in art, a work of redemption that achieves perfection in music, the "only art that corresponds fully to Christian faith." The poet-priest is the "artistic teller of the great World-tragedy," "the only one who never lied, [who] was ever sent to humankind at epochs of its direst error, as mediating friend."[35] It is the poet-priest who might effect regeneration. In these writings and particularly in the supplements (all of which belong to what Wagner calls the field of "ethical aesthetics"),[36] Wagner also expands the anti-Semitic attacks he first made in "Judaism in Music" (1850) and restated in his "Explanations" of 1869.[37]

His theory of cultural regeneration in these late writings, which included a program of temperance, vegetarianism, and female emancipation,[38] becomes a form of Christian mysticism. Wagner permits a gap to emerge between his view of the supposed natural superiority of white races compared to others, particularly Jews, and his commitment to Christianity as a transracial idea characterized by the capacity for suffering. He supposed white races to have the greatest capacity and made them the prime movers in a historical process that would lead humankind to a state of redemption when the inequality of races is removed. Yet, he also claimed that up to now white races have founded only a thoroughly immoral world. For these reasons, he portrayed "true Christianity" in ideal terms: as something that transcends racial differences. ("The blood of the Saviour, the issue from his head, his wounds upon the cross,—who impiously would ask its race, if white or other? Divine we call it, and its source might dimly be approached in what we termed the human species' bond of union, its aptitude for Conscious Suffering.")[39] Christ's greatest gift was his awareness of the essential unity of being and his having turned the individual will on itself by denying the will to live (pace Schopenhauer).

The Bayreuth circle, which emerged in the mid-1870s, resembled a religious sect and consolidated itself even more once the *Bayreuther Blätter* was established under Hans von Wolzogen's editorship in 1878. After Wagner's death the group became increasingly sectlike, with a core of devotees (Cosima, Wolzogen, Stein, Glasenapp, and others). "The worship of [Wagner's] person and his works increased to the level of a cult," as one observer described it: "[H]is books appeared to be confessional writings, symbolic books of the aesthetics of a new belief."[40] The circle separated itself from the rest of society in the sure belief of its status as an elite group in possession of the doctrine of regeneration. In addition, although the master-disciple model was purely secular, its use of the biblical idea of discipleship took on devotional ambiguity by virtue of its coexistence with the circle's stress on the regeneration writings and their relationship with Christianity. In other words, while Wagnerian art religion was supposed to supplant outmoded beliefs, the Bayreuth circle also used *Parsifal* virtually to reinstate a form of Christianity and a doctrine of salvation.[41]

There is plenty of evidence that Schoenberg was aware of the ideological side of Wagner's legacy and followed some of it. In 1935, just exiled from Germany, he spoke to the Jewish musical group Mailamm about the extent to which nobody could be a true Wagnerian "if you did not believe in his philosophy."[42] In that speech he characterized that philosophy with reference to "Erlösung durch Liebe" (salvation through love), *Deutschtum* (Germanness), and Wagner's anti-Semitic beliefs about Judaism in music. As if to distinguish Wagner's notion that Jewishness was a characteristic to overcome rather than a fixed racial characteristic (as under National

Socialism, from which he had just fled) and therefore that true Christianity was an ideal that transcended racial differences, Schoenberg claimed in his Mailamm lecture that "Wagner gave Jewry a chance": "out of the ghettos!"

Nonetheless, Schoenberg seems never to have made the pilgrimage to Bayreuth undertaken by many young turn-of-the-century Viennese artists and intellectuals. Was it because of his precarious financial position or because he considered acts of pilgrimage to be the lot of disciples, when he was a new leader? Webern and Berg certainly went: Webern in 1902, immediately after completing his Gymnasium studies and before attending the university, and Berg in 1909. Their accounts manifest the sort of quasi-religious devotion described earlier. Webern's diary of his "first Bayreuth pilgrimage" displays the "Liebesmahlspruch" from *Parsifal* as its heading and includes an ecstatic account of the *Parsifal* he heard: "To find words for such impressions is an impossibility! In the face of such magnificence, one can only sink to one's knees and pray in silent devotion."[43] He compares the religiosity and gravity with which he listened to the opera with some other people's apparent pleasure in it—manifest in applause, laughter, idle chatter, and the inspection of one another's wardrobe.[44] Berg in 1909 wrote to Helene Nahowski ecstatically, though less overtly religiously, of the "stirring, uplifting experience" and how "magnificent [and] overwhelming" it was. "Words cannot give you anywhere near the tremendous impression, shattering yet life-enhancing, which this work made on me. Futile trying to describe music like that, and all I can say is that I miss you now more than ever."[45]

We know that Wagner's life and sufferings and indeed letter writing were brought to Schoenberg's attention during the period when his students were addressing him as a poet-priest. At Christmas of 1909 Berg and Jalowetz gave Schoenberg his own copy of Wagner's complete writings and received a letter of thanks suggesting that they were a particularly timely gift. ("I was very pleased. Particularly because you guessed what I would have asked for.")[46] In several letters to Schoenberg in 1911 Berg draws comparisons between Schoenberg's and Wagner's lives. These letters are important because Berg's constant comparisons between Wagner's and Schoenberg's suffering and his portrayal of the inevitability of it all were given to be part and parcel of the "holy cause" they were fighting.[47]

More interesting are several letters written in December 1911, by which time Schoenberg was becoming depressed about the indifferent, if not negative, reception of his latest works. The comparisons Berg draws between Wagner and Schoenberg seem expressly designed to keep Schoenberg's spirits up and the "cause" on track. On December 4 Schoenberg wrote to Berg expressing his regret that theorizing—evidently his preparation of the *Harmonielehre* for publication—was taking him away from composing. Berg responded on December 7, saying that Wagner had similar complaints during the period after *Lohengrin*. He continued: "To take this analogy further, what cause for our rejoicing when you create your *Ring*, your *Tristan*, *Meistersinger*, your *Parsifal*."[48] Webern's letter to Berg dated December 8 about the newly published *Harmonielehre* indicates that Webern also considered some sort of spiritual affinity between Wagner's and Schoenberg's projects: He claimed that nothing like the *Harmonielehre* had been written in German since Wagner (see earlier). Schoenberg wrote to Berg on December 21, saying that he was "unusually depressed" because of the reception from Vienna, so much so that he had lost all interest in his works.[49] His letter crossed in the mail with Berg's Christmas gift of Wagner's *Mein Leben*, which Berg said had given him solace and enlightenment; "[G]reatness is inseparable from suffering...We who are fortunate enough to take part in your life need such comfort and enlightenment. But to you this book and its inner meaning will be nothing new."[50] Berg wrote again after receiving Schoenberg's depressed letter and amplified the comparison:

> What you say about your divine works is dreadful! Oh, believe me, Herr Schoenberg, you can no longer judge what they signify, they are already too far removed from you; something magnificent is growing within you, your gaze is so fixed on the future that you can no longer see the past, indeed, perhaps no longer the present...I am actually glad I was able to give you Wagner's Life...[T]he solace and enlightenment that we receive through our reverential understanding will do your anxious heart and your doubts good by way of comparison. Even if only for the moment; for I know only too well that your depression is just a matter of time and must soon give way to a more sublime, a most sublime confidence.
>
> However, if the descriptions of Wagner's struggles and myriad sufferings, and his never pure, always clouded joys raises [*sic*] even a momentary spark of confidence in you, if our unswerving worship of you is able to contribute to that, then that would be the greatest happiness this Christmas could bring me.[51]

Berg's comparisons between Schoenberg and Wagner taper off in 1912, along with their very obvious religious inflections. Whether this was under the pressure of preparing for the first performance of Schoenberg's most Wagnerian work, *Gurrelieder*, is uncertain. Meanwhile, however, Schoenberg thanked him for his intention in presenting him with Wagner's autobiography. However, he added that "This is an inner matter I have to deal with—or not—by myself...It's a kind of persecution complex; an insight can persecute one too."[52] I return to this response later. When Schoenberg wrote to Berg in mid-January about his reading of *Mein Leben*, it is evident that he was hoping to find such "insights" into Wagner's source of creativity but hadn't. He is nonetheless understanding as to Wagner's "obvious" reasons for mentioning only "external events."[53] Schoenberg clearly assumed that "inner experiences" that *could* have been told in an autobiography would somehow have found their way into Wagner's works.

STEFAN GEORGE AS POET-PRIEST

The Munich-based circle of Stefan George, whose poetry Schoenberg turned to around 1906, provides another model for the quasi-religious sect around Schoenberg at this time.[54] For Albrecht Dümling, Berg's and Webern's language and constructions of Schoenberg as a poet-priest are intimately linked with Schoenberg's turn to George's poetry, especially for those works that mark his renunciation of tonality—notably "Ich darf nicht dankend" from *Zwei Lieder*, op. 14, *Das Buch der hängenden Gärten*, op. 15, and the Second String Quartet, op. 10, whose third and fourth movements set "Litanei" and "Entrückung" from George's *Der siebente Ring* to music. Indeed, both Berg and Webern also drew on George at this time: Berg for *Der Wein* (George's translation of Baudelaire's poem), Webern for *Fünf Lieder aus "Der siebente Ring,"* op. 3, *Funf Lieder*, op. 4, four further George songs without opus number, and *Entflieht auf leichten Kähnen* for the chorus. George was certainly known in Vienna, having spent some time there and cultivated a close relationship with Hugo von Hofmannsthal (until it crumbled in 1906), but Schoenberg probably came into contact with his poetry through Vienna's Ansorge Verein (an art and culture society run by Conrad Ansorge), whose purpose was the promotion of the connection between modern music and modern poetry. Songs from Schoenberg's op. 2 and op. 3 collections were played at the society as early as February 11, 1904.

According to Dümling, Schoenberg turned to George's poetry at the time he relinquished tonality because of the usefulness of his lyric poetry for fashioning a public posture of the isolated artist, a posture that marked a step away from naturalism and was thus deeply modernist. By 1907 Schoenberg had reached a crisis, a deep isolation, and George's poetry served as "a model of the isolated artist creating the future and no longer caring for a contemporary audience."[55] In the shorter version of his account, published in English in *Schönberg and Kandinsky: An Historic Encounter*, Dümling focuses on Mathilde Schoenberg's infidelity and suggests that a parallel exists between this and George's and Richard Dehmel's encounter with Ida Coblenz. Schoenberg turned from Dehmel's freer, more sensuous poetry toward the stricter prosody and aloof masterly posture of George, which for Dümling stood in parallel to George's discovery that Coblenz had rejected him in favor of Dehmel. Through George's lyrical voice Schoenberg developed a belief in himself, which was then transferred to his students. At this time of personal crisis, the search for great men, for worthy authorities, for a patriarchal *Über-Ich* replaced love for Schoenberg. He worked himself up to a religious fervor because greatness and loneliness were identical to him in this situation.[56]

In the longer, book-length version, Dümling carves out more of a position for George's poetry and cultish circle. Here lyric poetry is key. Social isolation and loneliness were also consequences of shifts in the poet's position in culture, he suggests.[57] The fact that turn-of-the-century artists were so taken with lyric forms stemmed in part from their antibourgeois positions. George's turn toward the lyric was connected with his struggle against a culture that he experienced as reflecting broader social problems. Echoing both Nietzsche's *Birth of Tragedy* and Wagner's *Opera and Drama*, George considered drama and tragedy unavailable to artists of his generation owing to the cultural disunity caused by contemporary "spiritual" issues. Arguing not from the perspective of his personal creative position but from that of the recipient, George suggested that lyric poetry and the novel were the only possible art forms.[58] The artist experiences in an extreme form what was also true for the public: a crisis of value and worldview, of meaning and perception.

According to a 1910 essay by Margarete Susman, a writer in the outer George circle, the creation of an artistic "I" in poetry and consequently in music is to be understood as a resistance to the real situation of the person in society. It is a transcendental "I." Indeed, the lyric poetry could also be a substitute for religion: "The form in which modern humanity saved the contents of religion for itself and in the most perfect way is art…But of all the arts, none has courted religion so intensely and lived in it as did lyrical poetry: it is only by bearing in mind these roots that it can be conceived in its importance for life in our new era."[59] With its proximity to religion, the lyric achieved the greatest possible distance from naturalism. George's "I" became a type of law. Shortly before his break with Hofmannsthal, George had written to him: "I was firmly convinced that by means of our writings, we, you and I, might have been able to exercise a very salutary dictatorship lasting for years."[60]

Beginning in the 1890s but above all from around 1904 on, the George circle strongly reflected these ideas. The circle had a hierarchical nature, with George as the "master" and members of the circle as "disciples,"[61] although Michael Winkler has argued that it is perhaps more correct to refer to multiple George circles inasmuch as there was "a shifting constellation of small groups of friends…[that] constituted the core of the artistic-intellectual circles whose charismatic focus was George."[62] The always formal and detached George might have adopted this self-styling after visiting Paris and experiencing Mallarmé's circle (*le maître et le cénacle*), which had struck him as the ideal community of poets.[63] Yet various other potential sources fed into it. Although George hated Wagner's music, he would have been aware of the structures of the Bayreuth circle and Wagnerian art religion.[64] However, he also found historical vindication in Dante, who positioned Virgil, representative of antiquity, as his forerunner.[65] George's idea of the artist as an *Übermensch* was also influenced by Nietzsche: The latter's ideal became a reality in George, according to Susman.[66]

If Schoenberg and his circle's priest-disciple styling was influenced by that of the George circle, it could have come about via anecdote (from the Ansorge Verein or the Vienna coffeehouses) or via a book or an article. The image of George as a kind of *Urgeist*, a "poet priest presiding over the dawning of a new era, as a spiritual mediator standing between the sordid reality of nineteenth-century bourgeois culture and the higher reaches of a transcendent order yet to be revealed," had been presented by disciple Ludwig Klages in a 1902 book.[67] Again in 1909, shortly before the Schoenberg circle adopted a similar styling, another George disciple, Friedrich Wolters, published a short book titled *Herrschaft und Dienst* [Sovereignty and Service or Lordship and Servitude].[68] This bizarre metaphysical tract, almost a manifesto, proceeds in always highly cryptic sentences, most of which are half a page in length, and was printed with highly decorative opening pages using black and white designs that illuminate the first letters of each section in a medieval style. Its three sections are "Das Reich," which refers to the utopian "geistige Reich" [spiritual kingdom] toward which they were striving;[69] "Der Herrscher," which describes the power or dominance or lordship capable of fulfilling the "geistige Tat" (spiritual/intellectual deed) of bringing this new Reich into being; and "Der Dienst," the principle of servitude required toward the new sovereign power in bringing about the new kingdom. Excerpts from the first two chapters also appeared in a separate 1909 publication by the George circle (see figures 5.1 and 5.2).[70]

DAS·REICH

ie über den familien des blutes und der blutvermischung die familien des geistes und der geistvermischung stehen, deren geschichte noch so lange ungeschrieben bleibt, als die menschen in den grob sichtbaren erscheinungen selbst das wesen des weltgeschehens zu erkennen glauben und, statt mit innerem auge und innerem finger den formen folgend zu den ausströmenden kernen zu gelangen, an den zufälligkeiten des stoffes und des ortes die zugehörigkeit der werke und der taten mit lupe und zirkel abzumessen wähnen, so steht auch über den reichen der rassen- und der wirtschaftsgrenzen, unbeengt von berg und zoll, im freien raum der selbstgeschaffenen atmosphäre das Geistige Reich. Da der körper dieses Reiches nirgends sichtbar wird als an den spiegelungen der natürlichen dinge und ihrer seelischen bewegung, so nennen wir die Natur, mit welchem worte wir den inbegriff des ganzen sinnlich erkennbaren alls umfassen, und die Seele, mit welchem worte wir die

Figure 5.1. Friedrich Wolters, *Herrschaft und Dienst.*

DER HERRSCHER

ie schöpfung einer welt ist die bildwerdung des blutes durch den
geist. Indem wir uns vor tieferer
deutung bescheiden und in die
worte Blut und Geist wie in zwei
dunkle brunnen schauen, deren
spiegel wir nur irrend schimmern
sehen, an deren einheitlich ver-
schmolzenen grund sich kaum
die ahnung wagt, versuchen wir
an sichtbar werdenden gebilden
den sinn zu schärfen und was
an oberflächen von verborgen
brennenden geheimnissen noch
farbig zittert, durstig zu erfassen.
Wie der stoff das mittel zum werke,
das werk das mittel zum bilde ist,
so ist das mittel zur bildwerdung
des blutes durch den geist: die
Geistige Tat. Die Geistige Tat ist
der inhalt der Herrschaft, durch
welche der Herrscher, gleichgültig ob er ein überkommenes gut
zu verwalten oder ein unerhör-
tes zu errichten hat, gleichgültig
an welchen versuchten oder un-
versuchten stoffen er sein feuer
übt, sei es glaube oder ton, staat
oder stein, sprache oder zahl, mit

Figure 5.2. Friedrich Wolters, *Herrschaft und Dienst.*

It is conceivable that some of this literature had come to the attention of
Schoenberg or a member of his circle by 1910. Interestingly, the vestments of the
quasi-medieval figure that decorates the opening "D" of "Der Herrscher" are
trimmed with a line from George's poem "Entrückung" [Transport] from *Der siebente Ring* (which begins with "I feel the air of another planet"), which Schoenberg

used in the second movement of his pivotal Second String Quartet, op. 10—"Ich bin ein funke nur vom heiligen feuer / Ich bin ein dröhnen"—which continues in the poem: "nur der heiligen stimme" (I am only a spark of the holy fire / I am only a roaring [of the holy voice]).

The Schoenberg circle and the George circle nevertheless manifested a number of notable differences. The clarity of Christian mystical language used by Berg and Webern, which had been part of the later Bayreuth version of art religion, is less typical of the George Kreis; the younger men in Munich tended to look up to George as a divinely inspired prophet, but slightly odd rituals would sometimes obtain, such as when George appeared in black attire like a priest and conducted severe initiation ceremonies that involved the reading aloud of his poetry.[71] In the "Dienst" chapter of *Herrschaft und Dienst* Jesus Christ is mentioned as a model of redeeming man become God, but he stands alongside Krishna, Buddha, and Herakles in the same (labyrinthine and all-but-untranslatable) sentence.[72] While several students thought of George as a kind of divinity, George himself was searching for his own deity to worship in the form of a young male acolyte—and for a while found him in a fourteen-year-old Munich youth, Maximilian Kronberger, whom he elevated to the cult figure Maximin until the youth's tragic death at sixteen years of age.[73] In 1943 Max Scheler lauded the circle as an "erotic-religious high-aristocratic Gnostic sect" that was born "out of the spirit of the sharpest opposition to the loss of individuality in life."[74]

OTTO WEININGER'S CHARACTEROLOGY OF "PRIESTS"

The third potential model of priestly discourse comes via Otto Weininger, who, with Austrian writer and poet Siegfried Lipiner and his Pernerstorfer circle, was a prominent Viennese mediator of Wagner's art religious ideas and notions of the poet-priest. From around 1878 on, the Pernerstorfer circle functioned as a reading society of Viennese artists and intellectuals, including Mahler, who grouped around Lipiner and embraced a brand of art religion that drew, somewhat paradoxically, on both Wagner and Nietzsche.[75] By 1881, however, the circle had split between those who still held to a belief in political activism and those who chose to pursue more closely Wagner's plan for cultural regeneration through the aesthetic-religious path. The latter, which included Mahler, became the Saga Society. Schoenberg is not known to have been involved in the Pernerstorfer circle or the Saga Society, but he became a dedicated Mahler follower around 1904, when Mahler started taking an interest in him and he in turn changed his previously poor opinion of Mahler.[76] Perhaps a more direct source was Weininger, another theorist of aesthetic and cultural utopias linked with "priestly" ideas.

Weininger described "priest" in the chapter "On Characterology" of his posthumously published collection of essays, *Über die letzten Dinge* [On Last Things], a section also published as a free-standing essay titled "Sucher und Priester" [Seekers and Priests] in *Die Fackel*, a satirical journal edited by Karl Kraus and read by Schoenberg and his circle.[77] Weininger set up a paradigmatic dualism similar to the type M (man)/type W (woman), which underpins his theory of ethical subjectivity in *Geschlecht und Charakter* [*Sex and Character*]:

> The seeker searches, the priest informs. The seeker searches above all himself, the priest reveals himself above all to others. The seeker searches his whole life long for himself, for his own soul; the priest's ego is given from the outset as a presupposition of everything else. The seeker is always accompanied by a feeling of imperfection; the priest is convinced of the existence of perfection...Of course, seeker and priest are extremes; the greatest people are both, most often seekers at first, so that they then can transform themselves into priests when they have found the source, have lived to see their self.[78]

Weininger continues that the priest is not simply a type disconnected from real priestly attributes, for "the priest has revelation behind him...The priest already stands in league with the deity; only he knows mystical experiences." His lot is not easy: "For the priest must not be a peaceful, idyllic man; he has meaning only as a fighter for victory, not for the effort of the struggle, not for fear before defeat." Classic seekers were, for Weininger, Rousseau, Calderon, Sophocles, Mozart, and the Beethoven of *Fidelio* (although he becomes a priest in the *Waldstein* Sonata, whose final movement is the highest summit of Apollonian art). Schiller is a failed priest, incapable of tragedy or of recognizing the struggle between human grandeur and pettiness: "Schiller hardly seems to have known the enemy in one's own breast, loneliness and its terrors, human fate."[79] He is really just a journalist—a characterization that Kraus may have found especially interesting, given his ongoing campaign against Viennese journalism. By contrast, Richard Wagner started out as a seeker with *The Flying Dutchman, Tannhäuser* ("the Pilgrims' Chorus gives a wonderful representation of seeking"), and *Tristan* but ended as a great priest with *Siegfried* and *Parsifal*.

Weininger does not elaborate on "priest" in much detail, but his conceptualization might be linked to the theory in *Geschlecht und Charakter*.[80] Despite the fact that much recent scholarship, especially musical scholarship, has tended to reduce Weininger to a source of misogynist turn-of-the-century formulations about woman's endemic sexual, immoral, and uncreative nature, *Geschlecht und Charakter* was in fact a lengthy tract about ethical subjectivity that made use of man and woman as opposing ideal types, with the Jew as a mediating third type. It is undeniably misogynistic and anti-Semitic, but it is more than that. All ethical, creative, and intellectual values are attributed to type M, the only intelligible, autonomous subject, while a collection of misogynist stereotypes constitute type W, the amoral, all-sexual, all-irrational, feminine principle, the antithesis of the values associated with type M. Though Weininger's Jew is in many ways identical to type W, it stands as the principle of the consciously unethical. Woman and Jew were not autonomous subjects but mere bundles of sensations; however, unlike W, Weininger's Jew is capable of moral autonomy: He has simply not chosen it. While every real person is a mix of all these characteristics, Weininger's ideal types betray his fundamental view that ethical human subjectivity belongs to the Aryan male. According to the categorical imperative, man must cease to have sex with woman and overcome his Jewishness if he is to be truly ethical. The extreme asceticism underpinning this recuperation of the autonomous ethical self would logically mean the end of the human race, albeit signaling the beginnings of man's immortality.

For Weininger, Christ was the paradigmatic ethical human being: According to the logic of his theory, Christ's defining act, his "world-historical role," was his redemption of humankind from Jewishness, his overcoming of his own racial origin. Astonishingly, Richard Wagner was only a small step behind Christ: Weininger felt that Wagner achieved the same feat for German culture.[81] For this reason, Weininger felt free to attribute a little of type Jew to Wagner, arguing that Wagner's special status as creative genius enabled him to put his accretion of Jewishness to "ethical" use—namely, by creating its opposite, *Deutschtum*, at the highest peak of artistic expression. As I have discussed in some detail elsewhere, Weininger's writings are imbued with musical and particularly Wagnerian significance[82] not only by virtue of his recourse to Wagnerian source material in order to illustrate many points but also because his overall theory amounts, at least at some level, to what Nike Wagner has described as a "retranslation of *Parsifal* into the language of speculative metaphysics."[83]

Although today Weininger's ideas seem binaristic in the extreme and his views on woman and Jew are obviously as offensive as they are absurd, he was widely read in artistic and intellectual circles at the time. He was a *cause célèbre* in Vienna of the early 1900s not only because of the notoriety of *Geschlecht und Charakter* but also because of the author's own performative death by suicide (in a room in the house in Schwarzpanier Straße in which Beethoven had died), undertaken, it would appear, partly as a logical extension of the ideas in the book. Karl Kraus immediately championed Weininger's posthumous cause, although many judged his suicide to have been the act of a madman. Indeed, on October 29, 1903, immediately after his death, it was the essay "Seekers and Priests" that Kraus published in *Die Fackel* (months before its publication in *Über die letzten Dinge*). Some of the most famous writers and thinkers of the time were serious Weininger readers.[84] Among musicians, Schoenberg, Berg, Webern, Alexander Zemlinsky, Franz Schreker, and Hans Pfitzner at the very least were also enthusiastic Weininger readers.

Berg closely engaged with Weininger from the year *Geschlecht und Charakter* first appeared. He kept scrapbooks of ideas and quotations and devoted one to Weininger: He cut out two Weininger quotations from "Sucher und Priester" when it was printed in *Die Fackel*, plus a collection of ideas from *Geschlecht und Charakter* (revolving, according to Susanne Rode, around his gendered typologies of the two basic categories, "individual" and "genius," but also intellect, morality, and sexuality) published in *Die Fackel* in October 1904 under the title "Psychologies des Volkstribuns. Aktuelle Gedanken aus Otto Weiningers 'Geschlecht und Charakter.'"[85] He then received a copy of what was already the sixth edition of *Geschlecht und Charakter* from his brother Charly in summer 1905.[86]

Webern specifically brought Weininger back to Schoenberg's attention while the latter was preparing his *Harmonielehre*—and just before he and Berg started addressing Schoenberg in priestly terms. In one letter Webern admires Weininger's "intellectual rigour" and says that he is thinking of Schoenberg alongside Weininger because both of them had "superb intellects" with "the red glow of emotion" (June 23, 1910; see appendix). In another he notes Weininger's point that woman is "essentially different from man" (August 4, 1910). In another (July 16, 1910) Webern goes to the heart of *Geschlecht und Charakter:* He says that in order to reach the peak of morality, one has to cast off the qualities of "animal" man and strive for a metaphysical ideal. Interestingly, Webern even tackles head-on the logical objections to Weininger's utopian ideas, namely that to do as Weininger theorized meant "there won't be any human beings left." For Webern, this is probably "exactly what is meant, away with them": "[T]his path leads directly to God." Of course, with only Webern's side of the correspondence we don't know how Schoenberg responded to this. However, we know that in 1910 Webern was bringing Weininger *back* into Schoenberg's mind ("I have *re*-read Weininger"), which suggests that they were both already familiar with him—highly likely given his notoriety. The slippage in Webern's and Berg's letters between priest and deity as designations for Schoenberg is certainly consistent with Weininger's typology of the priest. ("The priest already stands in league with the deity; only he knows mystical experiences.")

Schoenberg's own view of Weininger is more difficult to pin down. Although he owned copies of both volumes, the 1908 edition of *Geschlecht und Charakter* and the 1907 edition of *Über die letzten Dinge*, as well as Weininger's *Taschenbuch und Briefe an einen Freund* (1919),[87] all are clean of marginalia, and Schoenberg's only overt mention of Weininger comes in the preface to the *Harmonielehre*. At the end of a paragraph in which he points out the absurdity of subscribing to a philosophy or *Weltanschauung* that addresses moral issues if one contemplates only what is pleasant and comfortable and takes no heed of the rest, he considers Weininger to be among those who "have thought earnestly" on the topic. It is worth applying some interpretative pressure to this thought.

Problems of Interpretation

How do these three potential contexts for understanding Schoenberg's early construction as poet-priest with messianic powers contribute to our understanding of Schoenberg's late activities? It is hard to avoid the fact that all three not only carry strong implications of cultural redemption, or *Kulturkritik*, as discussed in connection with Karl Kraus's approach to language and Adolf Loos's attitude about architecture (both of which were also models for Schoenberg), but all three are also wedded to concepts of German cultural purity, *Deutschtum*, and, in the case of both Wagner and Weininger, a form of Christian mysticism linked with notions of Jewish self-overcoming.

One way of understanding this last element is to consider the idea that between 1909 and 1911 Schoenberg, then a Jew converted to Protestant Christianity, saw himself and was seen by several of those in his immediate circle as a self-redeeming Jew in the Wagnerian sense—seen by Berg, Webern, and Linke at least, but not by his brother-in-law Zemlinsky. We have already seen that in his 1935 Mailamm lecture he confessed to having believed the message in Wagner's "Judaism in Music," and we would have little problem in assuming that Berg and Webern did as well, given their devotion to Wagner. Perhaps Schoenberg was recognizing that inevitably he was one of the Jews Wagner wrote about when, in 1911, he thanked Berg for presenting him with Wagner's autobiography, referring to the persecution that "an insight" can bring to one.

Weininger's metaphysical theory of ethical subjectivity, what Nike Wagner has called a "retranslation of *Parsifal* into speculative metaphysics," certainly proves a telling discourse to bring to bear on Schoenberg's renunciation of tonality. It is worth reflecting further on Schoenberg's mention of Weininger in his introduction to the *Harmonielehre*. The context is a series of gestures toward the "new laws of morality." Here and throughout the preface Schoenberg stresses the importance of searching and explicitly brings into question the wisdom of posing as a "demigod." When Schoenberg wrote the introduction at the end of the writing process, he was clearly feeling more like a seeker than a priest, as is consistent with what we know of his mood in mid-1911, when he would have been writing.[88] This followed a series of personal and professional setbacks. Nevertheless, perhaps the *Harmonielehre* served for Schoenberg as a musical equivalent of Weininger's *Geschlecht und Charakter*. Consider his broad construction of the state of tonality in *Harmonielehre* and also the gendering evident in his move from his very first, freely atonal works through to the emergence of the twelve-note method. There is, for example, a theoretical parallel between *Harmonielehre* and *Geschlecht und Charakter* in the way Schoenberg describes the dissonances as ultimately pulling the tonal system apart. He describes them in *Harmonielehre* in terms of erotics; dissonance is thought by Schoenberg to be protectively wrapped so that the "excitement" and "desire" it generates (to borrow Susan McClary's characterization) cause no damage.[89] He also describes chromatic harmonies as *Harmoniefremdentöne* (nonharmonic tones; literally, "tones alien to harmony") and a matter of "vagrancy" (I have suggested elsewhere that Schoenberg wished to signal that rampant chromaticism was a type of degenerate [Jewish?] element within music).[90] Crucially, he *also* describes dissonances in mystical terms as higher/remote overtones that might become floating (*schwebende*) tonality, a gender-free, asexual harmony, if the otherwise erotic chromatic elements are set adrift and sublated (*aufgehobene*). It is as if he theorizes a type of redemption of tonality as a system by allowing for the cutting free—"emancipation" as he later described it—of these bearers of tonality's eroticism and vagrancy. Although for a progressive composer this will mean the end of functional harmony, the way Schoenberg figures it promises a new and fascinating future with metaphysical implications. The erotic chromatic element, once loosened from the main system, can have a higher, transfigured incarnation first as *schwebende tonalität* and then as a new harmony of the future that even in the *Harmonielehre* Schoenberg likens to that of the angels: asexual. This construction shares obvious similarities with *Geschlecht und Charakter*, where ethical subjectivity is achieved by man's resisting woman and possibly also by overcoming his Jewishness. Although Weininger's construct leads to the end of the human race, it is at the same time the beginning of a new metaphysical future, as Webern noted (letter to Schoenberg, July 16, 1910). Likewise, although Schoenberg's theory imagines a new metaphysical future for music, it leaves tonality in one piece: The erotic and vagrant elements are separated and sublated to something higher. As we know, Schoenberg came to his twelve-note method through his work on the angelic *Seraphita* symphony and was quite overt in his descriptions of the new tonal space opened up by the twelve-note method as being like Swedenborg's heaven (which he encountered via Balzac). It is even possible to understand the distinctly unmystical *Erwartung* as a work of symbolic Parsifalian wandering. Both woman and newly freed dissonance go through a period of wandering before being reimagined in a big metaphysical work.

If we take Schoenberg at his later word—that he was among those Austrian Jews who believed both in *Deutschtum* and in Wagner's anti-Semitic beliefs about "Judaism in Music"[91]—we need to ask what implications this might have had in practice. Schoenberg had a famously robust ego; on the surface he appeared not to have been damaged by such critical claims about what he, a Jew, might have been "responsible for" according to Wagner's theory and some contemporary reception. While his dominance may have masked a great deal of insecurity, one way to understand his sense of rightness and strength is to contemplate the idea that he considered himself to be the one who acted, the exception. To take the sort of musical "action" I have suggested in my reading above of the *Harmonielehre* would have been entirely consistent with the relationship between theory and self in the case of Otto Weininger himself, who famously committed suicide shortly after theorizing his own Jewishness as the unethical element in human subjectivity. That, at least, is how his performative suicide—itself strongly inscribed with musical significance—was widely read at the time.[92] As I have argued elsewhere, the connections Weininger forged between his theories and Wagner's thought, coupled with his own performative suicide in the specially rented room in the Schwarzpanierhaus, in which Beethoven died, forced his own "case" into broader musical discourse.

However, even if we choose to feel that Schoenberg was immune to the negative projections about Jewish German composers inherent in Wagner's theories, and even if one does not accept the terms of my interpretation and parallels with the sensational case of Otto Weininger, it should not be surprising that later events would lead to some fundamental reorientations on Schoenberg's part. It is hardly surprising, for instance, that Schoenberg was especially shocked on experiencing exclusionary anti-Semitism for the first time in 1921 and to have felt infinitely more under threat as a Jewish German on Hitler's coming to power in 1933.

The sort of disorientation that Schoenberg experienced and the extent to which his worldview as integrated, if not also "self-redeeming" German Jew shattered, might be described as traumalike. The idea that a psychoanalytic concept such as trauma might be useful in elucidating the relationship between the present and the past not only as a matter of self-construction but also as one of historical construction is Dominick LaCapra's and stems from his work on representations of the Holocaust.[93] For LaCapra, certain issues associated with Holocaust studies—the rhetoric of the unspeakable, levels of historical repression, and what he identifies as the return of the repressed—might have broader historiographical import. While I am in no way suggesting that a qualitative correspondence exists between trauma-like features in Schoenbergian discourse and the traumas of survivors of the death camps, I *would* suggest that LaCapra's thinking might provide some useful lessons for approaching Schoenberg. For LaCapra the central trauma is the Holocaust, the fate of Jewry under the Nazis. For Schoenberg, the central trauma is the moment he was forced to confront his Jewishness—to realize that many fellow Austro-Germans considered his conversion to Christianity an insufficient way to assimilate into German society and *Kultur*. This was the immediate prehistory of the Holocaust and, from the postwar perspective of a survivor, indelibly linked to it; for someone committed to *Deutschtum*, it must have been deeply traumatic. As Reinhold Brinkmann points out, "for Jewish citizens the dis-integration of life began in many cases very early, with the 'exile before the exiling.'"[94] However Schoenberg must surely also have been subject to a second trauma in the wake of post-War revelations of the Holocaust itself, of the atrocities committed in political and human spheres in the name of a German ideology of racial purification.

If trauma can often lead to withdrawal and total silence, in Schoenberg's case the first trauma led to amazing insight: an attempt to take political action on the one hand and a reconfiguring and reinscribing of the shards of his previous world-view on the other. It is possible to read Schoenberg's efforts in the 1920s and 30s in light of earlier events, that is, as working through aspects, in some cases troubling aspects, of his *own* identity, ideas, and earlier activities. This starts with his gradual return to Judaism in the 1920s, about which much has been written.[95] It is also traceable in *Der biblische Weg*. He also sketched a large number of essays that reflected on his earlier activities and acquaintances: These include writings about a range of Jewish topics, including those on his own identity ("We Young Austrian Jews"), a small number of spleen-filled essays (*Denkmäler*) about various individuals, including Webern (essays he invariably returned to and expressed regret over), sketches or marginalia about Wagner's anti-Semitic writings and possible Jewish identity, and notably a conceptualization of music via the idea of the *Musikalische Gedanke*. After the end of the war we find him writing essays titled "Human Rights," "My Attitude Toward Politics," and pieces on numerous others topics (many fragmentary jottings) in musical biography, history, and psychology.

I cannot examine all of these here, but it is worth briefly considering some of Schoenberg's anxious unpublished writings about Wagner dating from around 1931–1933, several of which suggest that he recognized common ground between Wagner's anti-Semitism and theories of cultural regeneration (though he does not refer to the latter directly) and increasingly anti-Semitic, National-Socialist Germany.

Anxiety about Wagner's attitude toward Jews bubbles up in a couple of occasionally incoherent unpublished essays dated December 2, 1931.[96] In "Geyers-Sohn, Geyers-Enkel, Geyers-Enkels-Witwe" [Geyer's Son, Geyer's Grandson, Geyer's Grandson's Widow], Schoenberg takes up the question of Wagner's paternity, expressing annoyance with the way in which Wagner flirts with the idea that the Jewish Geyer might be his father but ultimately leaves it up to the reader. Like Nietzsche, Schoenberg feels quite sure here that Wagner was, in the end, completely convinced of his Jewish lineage but was simply embarrassed because it did not fit in with "all that German rubbish." He also has the idea that Wagner included the equivocal passage at the beginning of *Mein Leben* partly as a sop to Cosima, whom Schoenberg thinks had a Jewish mother: He "offers her encouragement with a wink of the eye." Schoenberg wants to read this positively: The thought about Cosima "speaks in favor of his having had Jewish blood." Indeed, he wants to read it as a confessional document: Since Wagner intended that his autobiography should not appear until thirty years after his death—"by which time he had perhaps 'anticipated' cultural conditions superior to those he himself had furthered"—it was a question of "fear that it could be found out too early; yet the desire that one day it would be known". In the end, what we find is a mixture of fascination with the question of Wagner's possible Jewish parentage, recognition of the potential significance of Siegfried and Winifred's alignments with "the pogromist Hitler" (this being only 1931), and a desire to keep Bayreuth spiritually "clean": untainted by commercialism in order that the "sacred" intentions of the works themselves would become evident. Schoenberg's decision to write about Brahms in 1933, an important anniversary year for both Brahms and Wagner, may likewise be connected with this manifest anxiety about the connection between Wagner's theories and rising National Socialism.

Schoenberg also seems to return to and in some cases to rewrite elements of his earlier Messiah- and Christlike construction within his Vienna circle. For instance, coinciding with the beginning of his return to Judaism, the reference to Christ at the end of *Der biblische Weg* may be more conscious than Moshe Lazar would have it. The end of the play seems a forgiving critique of false Messiahs. Aruns dies with the words "Lord, my God, I have been vanquished, smitten, castigated. I am dying, but I feel that you will allow the Idea to survive. And I shall die in peace, for I know that you will always provide our nation with men ready to offer their lives for this concept of the one and only, eternal, invisible and unimaginable God." In earlier drafts Aruns is called a "false Messiah," although Schoenberg removed this statement from the final version. "Forgive Collaborators," an essay in which Schoenberg says to forgive silly artists who express political views because they don't know what they are doing is in a similar vein. In the late psalm mentioned at the start of this chapter, Schoenberg's construction of Christ as "the purest, the most innocent, unselfish, and idealist being" is uncannily like that of Otto Weininger. Is the psalm a kind of confessional? Schoenberg's "cause" in 1910 was described by his students in sacrificial and redemptive terms, with Schoenberg the Christlike figure. In the psalm, Schoenberg's text says that Jesus's martyrdom was not represented truthfully; he did not want to divide the Jewish nation but rather "to restore the religion in its purest form." Schoenberg's rhetoric of returning to "a pure musical idea" after 1933 stood in stark contrast to his earlier claims to be performing an ethical, creative act. By 1933 those "ethics," above all Weininger's "ethics," might have looked very different to Schoenberg. Was Schoenberg anxiously reflecting upon and trying to rewrite his own earlier, Christlike messianism?

Running in parallel with this, however, are the insights and attempted political action. Two particular moments bear witness to Schoenberg's remarkable ability to anticipate the seriousness of the situation for European Jewry long before almost everyone else. The first is his famous letter to Kandinsky of May 23, 1923, written two years after he had been expelled from Mattsee, a holiday area that had declared itself closed to Jews. In that long letter Schoenberg names Hitler and recognizes him as someone with an approach to Jews altogether different from that of those who would consider him and others to be completely German; he also connects these observations with Trotsky's and Lenin's willingness to spill "rivers of blood in order to turn a theory—false it goes without saying...—into reality... [W]hat is anti-Semitism to lead to if not to acts of violence?"[97] All of this was six months before Hitler's 1923 *Putsch* and ten years before he came to power. When that time came and Schoenberg and other Jews found themselves hounded out of their jobs, he almost immediately left the country and started his campaign to save all other European Jews. Notwithstanding his disturbing vision of the new Jewish state, by anyone's reckoning these two fundamental insights were for their time astonishing.

An attempt at political action began with Schoenberg's efforts to work "for the salvation of the Jews" soon after he arrived in Paris at the beginning of his exile, when he started a letter-writing campaign to form an international network of prominent Jews capable of solving the Jewish question.[98] His letters and plans reveal that he imagined these efforts in militant terms that resemble the modus operandi of totalitarian leaders and proposed himself as the future leader of the fledgling Jewish nation. He even referred to his earlier experience in such a role: He wrote to Rabbi Wise, "I could point out that...I founded an artistic group of which I was a dictator, in full consciousness of the value of such a symbol (I called myself then the first dictator of Europe!)."[99] It seems counterintuitive that Schoenberg, a Jew fleeing from oppression, would choose such a model. His self-image as a potential *Führer* rescuing Jews from Europe and then leading them in their new Zionist land seemed to serve as a necessary counterweight to Hitler. It was as if he were able immediately to recognize Hitler's potential to make ideas political reality. His frantic efforts on behalf of this project reflect not only the shock of finding himself an exile from his beloved country but perhaps also the trauma of recognizing certain similarities between Hitler's and his and others' earlier, more "purely artistic" aims. Although this is speculation, it is consistent with Schoenberg's comment to Kandinsky about the rivers of blood that Trotsky and Lenin had spilled in order to turn theory into reality. Recognizing not simply a dictator-like mentality and ideologies of German supremicism and cultural purity but also real aspirations to racial purity is perhaps why he was able so presciently to predict real potential for acts of violence in the type of racial anti-Semitism he experienced in the early 1920s.

One of the interesting things about reading Schoenberg in this way is that he becomes the historical actor whose case seems to raise the question, why didn't others see the same thing? As Michael André Bernstein has pointed out, there is a tendency in the writing of history to indulge in "backshadowing, a kind of retroactive foreshadowing in which the shared knowledge of the outcome of a series of events by narrator and listener is used to judge the participants in those events as though they too should have known what was to come."[100] In this case, our knowledge of the Holocaust is sometimes used, he suggests, to expose the "blindness" and "self-deception" of Austro-German Jewry, their imagined unwillingness to save themselves from a doom that supposedly was clear to see—namely, that Hitler's social (and racist) utopianism might lead to unimaginable horrors. This is entirely unreasonable, as Bernstein also points out: How could we expect anyone at the time to have foreseen acts that even now many find incomprehensible. Yet Schoenberg did have moments of astonishing insight: He was at least willing to see the worst, perhaps because he recognized the underlying racially inflected utopianism. Having engaged with such theories in the artistic sphere, Schoenberg had good grounds for predicting a catastrophic outcome of political developments in his beloved Germany.

The epistolary style of Berg and Webern raises fascinating questions about the moment when Schoenberg renounced tonality and its immediate aftermath. The parallels between cultural milieu and music now seem so well rehearsed (affinities with Kraus, Loos, Altenberg, Wittgenstein, etc.) that ten years ago a volume on the music of the Second Viennese School declared the need only to provide an outline of the prevailing cultural set of conditions: "[A]nalogies with the musical modernism of the Second Viennese School...will be obvious."[101] These letters make it clear just how unfamiliar the thinking of the period is to us now and in doing so raise awkward questions. Writing about ideological contexts of the turn of the century that, with the hindsight of subsequent events, may link with subsequent events is not easy when the subject of discussion is the very stuff of musical modernism, and the events are the atrocities of the Holocaust. In the first two decades of the century utopianism, posing as a solution to cultural decline, often drove modernist approaches to art; in the 1930s a utopian political ideology posing as a solution to cultural decline brutally attempted to control music and society as a whole. Although the urge to interpret the latter as the culmination of the former is tempting, the interpretative stakes are very high: The latter was also closely associated with an ideology that led to the extermination of millions—Jews, Gypsies, homosexuals, political dissidents, and those who were elderly, physically, and mentally vulnerable. How can we approach music that we believe to be connected to events in such ways? Need it necessarily affect our relation to the music? Art at either end of the aesthetic spectrum was deemed by different people at different times to manifest cultural decline or, conversely, cultural renewal. Moreover, although music is a product of culture and history, it can also be reappropriated for other times. We learned that lesson long ago with Wagner. I have no easy answers about how to negotiate this ethically fraught terrain as cultural history. Is it acceptable for historians to ignore an important chapter in Europe's history as a point of reference because to so use it is fraught with interpretative and ethical difficulties? Is it acceptable to admit of interpretative playfulness or multiple simultaneous readings that resist any claims to truth? Dominick LaCapra has pointed out that the creation of certain distinctions can be immensely important.[102] The ethical and ideological positions we might imply by the words we choose, even unwittingly or unconsciously, are also brought into especially sharp focus when we talk, even by association, about a historical catastrophe with such profound emotional, cultural, and ethical investments as the Holocaust. Being aware of the potential trauma and historical sensibilities at the center of it all is surely a beginning. The legacies of German Jews such as Schoenberg whose personal histories encompassed much of the troubled modern history of European Jewry—from emancipation to destruction and beyond to diaspora existence and Zionism—are more complex than most.[103] Schoenberg's beginning and end-of-life identifications with Christ offer windows to understanding, but windows that are smeared with the traces of ideologies embraced and later reconsidered. The utopian aspirations of both modernism and the Schoenberg circle resist easy rewriting.

APPENDIX

Excerpts from Letters

December 8, 1908: Webern to Schoenberg[104,105]

With humble greetings and full of gratitude for you—but you are against thanks, how should I say it? Can it be said? Who has ever received as many acts of charity as I have from you?

August 30, 1909: Webern to Schoenberg[106]

[The letter is quite defensive about Schoenberg's apparently having believed that Webern failed with a job at Koblenz.]

Believe me, Herr Schoenberg, I always strive for one thing only: to keep a distance, respect, nothing is taken for granted. Respect—

For me it is a blessing to know you, and everything—just the way you treat me—

December 24, 1909: Webern to Schoenberg[107]

Dear Herr Schönberg,

Permit me to give you Plato's "Phaidon" for Christmas this time. It is so remarkable that all the important men that ever lived have sacrificed their lives, either directly or indirectly, for the idea of the immortality of the soul. Socrates, Jesus Christ; and Beethoven, Strindberg?

Should that be the meaning of this life?

It's always the same story:

There is more than you can perceive with your physical senses.

But what is the outcome of this?

All this is a riddle to me.

And that the words of Socrates or Plato are today as true as they were 2000 years ago, that just proves again that there is something that persists over time and that works through selected men.

Selected by whom?

If the spiritual, mysterious stands above the material, how does it come in this particular potency into this person?

Can the spiritual even be bred? By whom?

Which power is exerting its force here and—why?

June 23, 1910: Webern to Schoenberg[108]

At the moment I'm re-reading Weininger (Über die letzten Dinge). I find it quite wonderful. He also sees things from the other side and in context. And above all that intellectual rigor.

Tell me, can one really describe thinking and feeling as totally different matters?

I cannot imagine any superb intellect without the red glow of emotion.

With Weininger this is certainly the case, and [surely also] with Strindberg, Plato, Kant, Kraus?

It just flows out of the human being, directly.

That's what is so superb with Weininger. It is also the reason it is written in such a wonderful manner.

At the moment I am always thinking of the following men: you, Kokoschka, Mahler, Kraus, Weininger.

July 6, 1910: Webern to Schoenberg[109]

Mahler really is something magnificent; it is not at all art—aestheticism; perhaps if one did [not?] know his life, one could reconstruct it from his symphonies. They really must be most closely connected with his inner experiences.

I also see a development: from the most intense worship of nature to an ever more spiritual, more enraptured content. This is, again and again, my compelling impression. I couldn't care less whether it is right....

It is so wonderful—radiating from the most high.

July 16, 1910: Webern to Schoenberg[110]

[Refers to Herr Stefan's having written about Strauss being "one of our highest hopes."]

I do know one thing—you have to be as hard as possible against the rabble— they still believe you depend on their mercy.

A kick up their backsides.—

If an insight just grows within the heart—overnight—so, in the morning, is the dewdrop in the rose consecrated directly by God, that is what is so beautiful.

From childhood on, one has to go through the dung heap of education wearing blinders so that not a whiff of pestilence penetrates the heart.

I think significant people receive this gift; some kind of rampart grows around them. I would like to become a robber-chief and annihilate this human scum. But how many people would remain?

I believe more and more that Weininger was right: In the end the man who casts off, one after the other, the qualities of lower forms of life also has to refrain from that which reproduces humankind in the animal sense. That, then, is a path: from the animal to the dissolution of material substance as such.

I grasp that completely clearly.

The utmost peak of morality, the earthly shell falls.

If there is any development, then it can only be this: Out of the animal-man a living being gradually grows that comes to realize that it does not need life on this earth. Thus the human being disappears again, the physical one.

This path leads directly to God.

This eliminates the objection that someone might say: If everybody follows this insight, there won't be any human beings left, but probably that's exactly what is meant, away with them.

I am writing this to you, Herr Schoenberg, because I would like to discuss this with you. I would like to know your opinion of this.

August 4, 1910: Webern to Schoenberg[111]

He [Rilke] makes, for instance, the distinction between fate and life, connecting the man with the former and the woman with the latter.[112]

The saint refuses destiny and chooses life "opposite God." Then it is said: "But the fact that woman, in accordance with her nature, must make the same choice in relation to man—this is what causes the doomed quality of all love relationships: resolute and fateless, like an eternal being, she stands beside the one who transforms himself.

The woman who loves always surpasses the man she loves because life is greater than fate. Her self-surrender wants to be infinite: This is her happiness. But the nameless suffering of her love has always been that she is required to limit this self-surrender."[113]

That is the essence of the point of view of Strindberg, of Weininger: that woman is, so to speak, nature itself, something essentially different from man, totally without relationships. But it can be put more beautifully than Rilke does?

...I'll give you the book as a present, for I really want you to read it.

August 10, 1910: Webern to Schoenberg[114]

What you have told me about your book is tremendous.[115]

You know, when I read the letter I felt as if I were in a surging sea or in the knowledge or perhaps only in the premonition of a torrent, a gigantic flood.

Oh, it is immense.

How can you think that I am somehow holding back from you....

I am going to climb the Triglav...Maybe you will find it ridiculous that I do things like that, but:

The strange thing I find when on the mountain peaks, this delicacy and purity: that attracts me time and again....

The solitude and the wrestling with God.

Wiping off all filth.

When I thought of my works, I started feeling better.

I have come to realize that they are good.

November 9, 1910: Webern to Schoenberg[116]

I remain completely under the impression of your wonderful work. Apart from Beethoven and Mahler, I don't know anything that moves me so much as your music.

Probably also Wagner; but that is something else. Just in these last few days, while we were rehearsing and performing the *Meistersinger* here, I've had quite a number of ideas...

In Berlin I saw the van Gogh exhibition....

For me there are only three painters: they are you, van Gogh and Kokoschka.

March 9, 1911: Webern to Schoenberg[117]

I am reading a book at the moment that is not written out of the spirit of man: *Seraphita* by Balzac. Seraphita is a being beyond gender, an angel.

March 21, 1911: Webern to Schoenberg[118]

I'm still reading *Seraphita*.

Every sentence in it is a miracle....

Every word in the book does nothing but serve the truth that belief is the highest [good]. Did you read about Claudel in the latest "Fackel"? It is probably true: All really outstanding men reached a total belief in God. In any case, Balzac is certainly one of the greatest and most amazing human beings.

* May 18, 1911: Mahler dies

May 24, 1911: Webern to Schoenberg[119]

Mahler's death makes me sadder every day. It is becoming increasingly inconceivable to me that it has happened. Mahler is dead....

After all, you too said yourself that you had the impression that His [sic] work was fully completed....

I have the feeling that Mahler knows how much we grieve for Him [sic]....

Rest assured, Herr Schoenberg, that each of us clings to you with his whole heart. The planned book [i.e., the 1912 Festschrift] will grant you an insight that will confirm to you the truth of these words.

The past days in Vienna are of immense significance to me: Mahler's death and the certainty that I possess your friendship forever. Gustav Mahler and you.

There I see my course quite distinctly. I will not deviate.

God's blessing on you.

[End of July 1911]: Berg to Webern[120]

[Berg has just explained why he failed to visit Schoenberg when he arrived in Vienna, something that had annoyed Schoenberg.]

And I can only implore you, too, my dear friend, by the sacredness of our art…that, despite my curious action, there was *not a spark* of lovelessness, lack of interest, let alone indifference in me for Schoenberg; rather that through the sorrow, *in advance*, I could make him embittered through my *apparent* neglect, and not *be able* to avoid his rage,—that I—as already said—through this suffering in advance, that is before Schoenberg told me directly that he was angry,—already felt,—that there is no greater way to confirm so holy and *unchanging* a love as this one which we feel for him, *than with this suffering.*

August 3, 1911: Berg to Schoenberg[121]

I have now received the conclusion of the *Harmonielehre*, as well as the beginning: the divine [*gottvolle*] foreword—and the dedication. This wonderful book has now received its final consecration [*Weihe*]: Before entering the sanctuary [*Heiligtum*] one kneels devoutly [*andachstvoll*] and crosses oneself in profoundest humility. The appropriate words of composure, a heartfelt sigh from a believer's breast before commencement of the holy service [*Gottesdienstes*].

And that this work was written in the service of the deity [*im Dienste der Gottheit*] becomes ever clearer and more certain to me, the more I read it, the deeper I delve into it. And that we poor mortals may partake of it—that is our highest joy.

August 11, 1911: Webern to Schoenberg[122]

[Webern is referring here to an unpleasant series of interactions between Schoenberg and his neighbor.[123]]

Be assured, we will help you.…

Dear Herr Schönberg, just trust in us. May what I say now not appear ridiculous to you: I believe that the disciples of Christ cannot have felt more deeply for their Lord than we for you. God protect you, my dear Herr Schönberg.

August 13, 1911: Berg to Schoenberg[124]

…I've just heard from Webern of your sudden departure…Last night I received the dreadful news. But is it really news? When you, esteemed Herr Schönberg, had anticipated and feared it for months? Is it not rather the fulfillment of the fate of genius? Regardless whether manifested negatively, in the incomprehension of a thousand "sensible" people, or positively, in the hatred of a madman! I only know that this hatred, this diabolical madness, which ordinarily lies concealed, was revealed on this occasion in a crime against your holy person [*an Ihrer heiligen Person*]—of course the details are unknown to me—but I do know (—with the sublime conviction born of unerring hope and expectation—) that the world, which heretofore passed by your deeds with a "shrug of the shoulders"—must pause before the misdeed of a fiend—if only to come to its senses. At this moment of reflection—which beneficently intervenes in the lives of all great men—has surely interceded now in your distress—or in any event cannot be long in coming, for it is high time.——

But!! What meaning can time or things temporal have for you, dearest Herr Schönberg— even sublime moments of suffering—since you have been granted the "deep deep eternity of all joy"?![125]

We mortals can only bow before your destiny, must realize that even our most fervent hopes are insignificant: Somewhere there must be a sublime Judgment, a divine Will. And surely that is infallible—even if it appears all too enigmatic to us.—

August 16, 1911: Webern to Schoenberg[126]

[The letter begins with Webern saying that he is collecting money from the other students to assist Schoenberg.]

I don't know whether you see what I was trying to hint at here?

I would like to be an invisible power that can give you everything you would wish for. Or to put it another way:

One makes an offering to God; not an offering in the sense of a gift which is difficult to give for one reason or other; the priest who reads the mass; a prayer.

I really can't express it.

To me it was such a holy act, doing this.

You will surely understand me.

As for Berg and all the others: I know that they love you without bounds.

August 18, 1911: Schoenberg to Berg[127]

[Thanks him for his warmth. Reassures him that what had come between them is now forgotten. After the following excerpt, he reveals that Webern has sent him one thousand Kronen and that he suspects Berg was one of the contributors.]

One thing, though: I fear being overrated! Try not to do it. It weighs upon me a little. And perhaps it is partly the fear of being overrated that makes me so suspicious. Perhaps because I fear: the impending backlash, the moment I am no longer overrated, perhaps because I continually fear the inevitable moment when people will actually begin to underrate me, perhaps that's why I detect a hint of defection in the slightest negligence…

August 19, 1911: Webern to Schoenberg[128]

Here at Berg's place I have read your wonderful introduction to the *Harmonielehre*. It is so overwhelming and so indescribably touching.

Dear Herr Schoenberg, you thank us?!

What I am, everything, everything is through you; I only began to live through you.

That you could use us to confirm yourself was our boundless luck, a boundless blessing for us. If only I could possess this wonderful book already.

August 21, 1911: Webern to Schoenberg[129]
[re: Harmonielehre]

At this moment in time I would like to set aside the factor that you are our music teacher in order to make this as clear as possible:

The effect of your words, considered in the context of morals, and your ethical power.

And already I sense that I should not have made this distinction: it flows into one. And the most factual instruction in musical things is rooted in your heart. That's the very thing that moves me so much about your book: this purity, holiness, when you discuss these things.

Your knowledge blossoms precisely out of this moral force.

Even if it is only at this very moment of your confession that your self-examination shines in the most marvelous radiance, for me it had already been a model for a very long time.

That is my aspiration: to approach, like you, to illuminate oneself to the inner-most; watching over one's most secret thoughts every second.

And behind this terrible constraint I sense something really delicate and quiet.

August 21, 1911: Berg to Schoenberg[130]
[Berg refers here to Schoenberg's forgiveness of his failure to visit him, as mentioned earlier.]

And with your forgiveness I feel reborn, purified, and today, 2 days after receiving your letter, your anger seems to lie far, far away...

The fact that you yourself, Herr Schönberg, believe you won't ever need to withhold that goodwill from me again, that is the crowning glory of your letter.

August 23, 1911: Webern to Schoenberg[131]
I'm really happy that you're reading *Seraphita* and *Louis Lambert*.

September 8, 1911: Webern to Schoenberg[132]
But I have less and less to do with all these people [Strauss, Pfitzner, Debussy, and Reger, whom he had just mentioned].

I know only two things:

your works and Mahler's.

September 8, 1911: Webern to Berg[133]
I saw the death mask of the saint [i.e., Mahler] in a volume of *Die Musik*.

My dear friend, there is only one thing [to do]: to strive with all one's might for a life here that is completely dedicated to ideals and that is already touched by a breath from this distant, other life. [He seems to mean Schoenberg.]

September 25, 1911: Berg to Schoenberg[134]

[Asked by Schoenberg to be his substitute teacher, Berg says how deeply honored he is by the idea.]

For there is something so wonderful in being the chosen one [*der Berufene*], the champion and comrade-in-arms for your ideas, your ideals, your artistic intentions—even if it is only in this God-forsaken city. May my joy over this priestly function [*Priester-Amt*] (for so I should like to call it) be your guarantee, dear esteemed Herr Schönberg, that I will administer it to the best of my ability. Perhaps I shall even succeed in accomplishing something in this very restricted sphere of activity for the great and holy cause [*heilige Sache*] for which you, surrounded by an ever-growing body of followers, will be fighting in the world outside.

October 6, 1911: Josef Polnauer to Schoenberg[135]

[This letter is dominated by details about Polnauer's packing Schoenberg's personal possessions to move to Berlin. He goes on to say his good-byes, acknowledging that he doesn't feel he was part of the inner circle.]

I don't know whom I owe the more: the teacher or the man Schoenberg. But in the end it doesn't matter because with you the one cannot be separated from the other…You didn't remain merely a teacher to any of your students; you always became the "model."… [T]here is now one more man [i.e., Polnauer] who loves you with all his heart, who wants to hold on to the memory of the encounter with you as a holy good and who will always want to remain thankful to you in small and very small ways—I don't think I can do otherwise—if you would only provide the opportunity.

October 20, 1911: Schoenberg, "Franz Liszts Werk und Wesen"[136]

Liszt's importance lies in the one place where great men's importance can lie: in faith. Fanatical faith, of the kind that creates a radical distinction between normal men and those it impels…

He believed in himself, he believed in One Who was greater than himself, he believed in progress, in culture, in beauty, in morality, in humanity. And he believed in God!…

Altogether his effect has perhaps been greater, through the many stimuli he left behind for his successors, than Wagner's has been—Wagner, who provided a work too perfect for anyone coming later to be able to add anything to it. But there is certainly no need to think of him only this way. One need think merely of his *Christus* to know a work whose effect has still to dawn. Perhaps the day has almost come when contact will be re-established with its tone, its intentions, for our time is again seeking its God; this search characterizes it better than do the most outstanding technical achievements…

Great men's effect, if any, on life is infinitely slight. If one observes what Plato, Christ, Kant, Swedenborg, Schopenhauer, Balzac and others thought and compares it with what people now believe and the way people now conduct their lives;…then one doubts whether progress exists.

November 23, 1911: Webern to Berg[137]

[Talking about playing Das Lied von der Erde *to Schoenberg.]*

But this is possible: to strive toward deserving it. To reach into the heart, filth out! Upward! "Sursum corda" [Lift up your hearts] says the Christian religion.

Thus Mahler lived, thus Schoenberg.

There is repentance and there is yearning.

December 8, 1911: Webern to Berg[138]

The *Harmonielehre* has appeared!!!...

At last the work is there. I believe it will be sold in masses. Hertzka need only arrange for it to appear in all the shop windows. Now the work has taken its place in the world. I am eager to know what will happen. I have a feeling that everyone who reads it will put his hand to his head; "Ah, it must be so."

The whole world must put its hand to its head; a sign of the astonishment of the whole of nature must become apparent. Since Wagner nothing like it has been written in the German language.

Perhaps even since Schopenhauer. I can hardly wait to read the book as a whole at last. You know the whole thing already, yes?

December 26, 1911: Erwin Stein to Schoenberg[139]

I must thank you for your *Harmonielehre*. Even though I already knew much of it, everything is a new revelation to me now that I read it as a coherent book. That a theory of harmony can be such a humane book. And that wonderful foreword. I nearly feel ashamed that my name also appears in such a context. I have a guilty conscience about you: that I could not be involved in things that should have made life easier for you. I could not do that and therefore, for a long while did not dare write to you.

January 11, 1912: Webern to Berg[140]

Have you heard anything about the *Harmonielehre*? Please, [tell] Schoenberg only half-way favorable judgments.

It is all so dreadful. That is why our book must turn out to be really special...

After all, people used to abuse Beethoven and still do abuse Mahler, but it is dreadful, appalling to have to go through this at such proximity.

I hope that the words of our book will have great power.

It must be effective.

I want to perish for rage and fury. Do write something more for the book, something really beautiful.

Let's all write something more. ~~Let's raise this man up.~~ (ah no), let's tear the clouds and fog asunder with our ardor so that this light will finally be made visible to this miserable earth.

How beautiful this *Harmonielehre* is.

All events in nature and art, they are God's wonders, are secrets for us; they are here, are eternal.

Measured against that, our book is nothing, but with regard to the filth of this world it can be something.

Schoenberg doesn't need us.

But we can worship; we must do so.

We need him.

March 1, 1912: Schoenberg, "Gustav Mahler"[141]

"Gustav Mahler was a saint...

To Gustav Mahler's work!

Into its pure air!

Here is the faith that raises us on high. Here is someone believing, in his immortal works, in an eternal soul..."

June 9, 1912: Webern to Schoenberg[142]

This, our relationship to you as our guide, our leader, is something deeply blissful for me.

You are the bond, the insoluble bond that unites us. We all live for you. Believe me.

Excerpt from Schoenberg's Berlin Diary

February 25, 1912 (written March 11)[143]

Evening, large party at the Zemlinsky's...Alex [Zemlinsky] is not quite as nice. Above all he denies me any word of praise almost out of principle. He seems to think that I am too highly praised within my circle and obviously wants to prevent me from behaving like a megalomaniac....I feel I am being talked about in really much too effusive a way. I am too young for this kind of praise, have accomplished too little, and too little that is perfect. My present accomplishment, I can still only regard as a hope for the future, as a promise that I may keep; but not as anything more. And I have to say, were I not spoiling the joy of my students by doing so, I might possibly have rejected the book. On the other hand, however, I was so overwhelmed by the great love which shows in all this, that I really had been happy, insofar as something like this can provide happiness. And I was proud as well: I find everything, almost everything, written so well and with such beautiful words, that I really should have a high opinion of a group of human beings like these. Above all, of course, Webern! He is a wonderful human being. How moved he was when he handed the book to me. Solemn and yet so unpretentious. Almost like a school boy; but like one who only prepared something so as not to be overwhelmed. I have resolved to drink brotherhood[144] with him at the first opportunity. Then Berg, then Linke and Jalowetz. Yes, even Horwitz. And: Kandinsky. A magnificent essay!

But I was embarrassed in front of Alex. He is somewhat skeptical. I know he does not like to believe. And though he thinks much of me—I almost feel he would like it best if he alone thought highly of me! Strangely enough, he does not trust or believe in the enthusiasm of others. Despite the fact that he himself is capable of so much genuine enthusiasm! Why?

NOTES

1. In Joseph Auner, *A Schoenberg Reader: Documents of a Life* (New Haven, Conn.: Yale University Press, 2003), 8.

2. On this play see both Moshe Lazar, "Schoenberg and His Doubles: A Psychodramatic Journey to His Roots," *Journal of the Arnold Schoenberg Institute* 17(1–2) (June and November 1994): 9–150, and Klára Móricz, *Jewish Identities: Nationalism, Racism, and Utopianism in Twentieth-century Music* (Berkeley: University of California Press, 2008).

3. Arnold Schoenberg, *The Biblical Way*, in *Journal of the Arnold Schoenberg Institute* 17(1–2) (June and November 1994): 162–329 (319).

4. Lazar, "Schoenberg and His Doubles," 89.

5. Móricz makes this point in *Jewish Identities*, 325.

6. Carl Dahlhaus, "Schoenberg's Aesthetic Theology," in *Schoenberg and the New Music*, trans. Derrick Puffett and Alfred Clayton, 81–93 (New York: Cambridge University Press, 1987).

7. The question of whether to use the word "Holocaust" or "Shoah" has been subject to discussion among historians, with some such as Michael André Bernstein (*Foregone Conclusions: Against Apocalyptic History* [Los Angeles: University of California Press, 1994]) preferring the Hebrew word "Shoah" because it does not carry the unwelcome theological implications of a divinely sanctioned sacrifice of "Holocaust." For further discussion of the question see, for instance, Dominick LaCapra, *Representing the Holocaust: History, Theory, Trauma* (Ithaca: Cornell University Press, 1994), 85.

8. See Theodor Adorno, "Commitment," in *Notes to Literature*, vol. 2, trans. Shierry Weber Nicholsen (New York: Columbia University Press, 1992), 76–94.

9. For an account of these efforts see Móricz, *Jewish Identities*, 201–21.

10. As Móricz notes in *Jewish Identities*, 204.

11. Principal among these is Alexander L. Ringer, *Arnold Schoenberg: The Composer as Jew* (Oxford: Clarendon, 1990), esp. 23–34. In some respects I reverse the chronological direction of the gaze that Móricz casts upon Schoenberg's strivings toward a leadership role around 1933.

12. Henri Lonitz, ed., and Wieland Hoban, trans., *Theodor W. Adorno and Alban Berg: Correspondence 1925–1935* (Cambridge: Polity, 2005).

13. Joseph Auner seems to agree with this in "The Second Viennese School as a Historical Concept," in Bryan R. Simms, ed., *Schoenberg, Berg, and Webern: A Companion to the Second Viennese School*, 26 (Westport, Conn.: Greenwood, 1999).

14. Dahlhaus, "Schoenberg's Aesthetic Theology," 90.

15. Whether there was significant communication before then is uncertain, as the editors note in Juliane Brand, Christopher Hailey, and Donald Harris, eds., *The Berg-Schoenberg Correspondence: Selected Letters*, 1 (London: Macmillan, 1987). This correspondence has now been published in full in German: Juliane Brand, Christopher Hailey, und Andreas Meyer, eds., *Briefwechsel Arnold Schönberg–Alban Berg*, 2 vols. (Briefwechsel der Wiener Schule, hrsg. von Thomas Ertelt, Bd. 3) (Mainz: Schott, 2007).

16. The Berg-Webern series is being prepared for publication as I write (early 2009).

17. The only published run of letters between the two consists of the eighteen from 1926 to 1939. See Arnold Schönberg, "Arnold Schönberg an Anton Webern: Eine Auswahl unbekannter Briefe," in Ernst Hilmar, ed., *Arnold Schönberg Gedenkausstellung*, 44–67 (Vienna: Universal Edition, 1974). For references of published letters to Roberto Gerhard,

Hildegard Jone, Josef Humplik, Hanns Eisler, Willi Reich, Erwin Schulhoff, and others see Zoltan Roman, *Anton von Webern: An Annotated Bibliography* (Detroit: Information Coordinators, 1983). Excerpts from some of the earlier letters are nevertheless found in Hans Moldenhauer, *Anton von Webern: A Chronicle of His Life and Work* (London: Gollancz, 1978), 49–52. Regina Busch has begun work on an edition of this correspondence.

18. A rough typescript of much of the Berg-Webern and Webern-Schoenberg correspondence has long been available for inspection at the Wiener Stadt- und Landesbibliothek; however, many of the originals are now digitally reproduced on the website of the Arnold Schönberg Center, Vienna. For the best available account of the extant Schoenberg correspondence see "Preliminary Inventory of Schoenberg Correspondence," *Journal of the Arnold Schoenberg Institute* 17(1–2) (June and November 1995) and 19(1–2) (June and November 1996).

19. The first and last entries in the 1912 Festschrift presented to Schoenberg by his students are also relevant but are not reproduced here. See *Arnold Schönberg: In höchster Verehrung* (Munich: Piper, 1912); trans. Barbara Z. Schoenberg in *Schoenberg and His World*, ed. Walter Frisch, 198–261 (Princeton: Princeton University Press, 1999).

20. In another letter to Berg (Dec. 12, 1911) not quoted here, he gives Berg a collection of Kant's letters for Christmas, drawing parallels between Kant and Beethoven and between Schopenhauer and Wagner. He then says, "And Strindberg and Mahler? Maeterlinck and Schönberg? Also Strindberg and Schönberg! Rays of God." Full letter quoted in *Die Reihe*, vol. 2 (Bryn Mawr, Penn.: Presser, 1958), 16.

21. This was well before Schoenberg mentions Balzac and Swedenborg in his published Liszt essay of Oct. 20, 1911, "Franz Liszts Werk und Wesen," translated as "Franz Liszt's Work and Being" in Leonard Stein, ed., and Leo Black, trans., *Style and Idea: Selected Writings of Arnold Schoenberg* (Berkeley: University of California Press, 1975), 446.

22. For full details on the genesis of this work see Jennifer Robin Shaw, "Schoenberg's Choral Symphony, Die Jakobsleiter, and Other Wartime Fragments," PhD diss., State University of New York at Stony Brook (December 2002). Shaw nevertheless does not identify Webern as the source of Schoenberg's knowledge of Balzac and hence *Séraphita*.

23. See, for instance, Susanne Rode-Breymann (trans. Mary Whittall), "...Gathering the Divine from the Earthly ...": Ferdinand Avenarius and His Significance for Anton Webern's Early Settings of Lyric Poetry," in *Webern Studies*, ed. Kathryn Bailey, 1–31 (New York: Cambridge University Press, 1996).

24. I return to Weininger later.

25. On Lüger's Vienna see, for instance, Richard S. Geehr, *Karl Lueger: Mayor of Fin de Siècle Vienna* (Detroit: Wayne State University Press, 1990).

26. Quoted in Lazar, "Arnold Schoenberg and His Doubles," 110.

27. *Arnold Schoenberg Letters*, ed. Erwin Stein (London: Faber, 1987), 35. Dehmel did not write this text for him.

28. *Die Musik* 9/4 (21) (1909): 160.

29. Arnold Schönberg, *Catalogue raisonné*, 2 vols., ed. Christian Meyer and Therese Muxeneder, item 78, 160 (Vienna: Arnold Schönberg Center, 2005).

30. Schoenberg, "Franz Liszt's Work and Being" and "Gustav Mahler: In Memoriam," in Stein, *Style and Idea*, 442–47, 447–48. He also wrote a lecture about Mahler (dated Oct. 13, 1912) that was revised in 1948 for Dika Newlin's *Style and Idea*, in Stein, *Style and Idea*, 449–72. Peter Franklin suggests that the later essay is conceived to some extent "as an example of how he would best have liked his own adherents and acolytes to write about himself"; of course, they already had in their letters and in *Arnold Schönberg: In höchster Verehrung*. See Franklin, *The Idea of Music: Schoenberg and Others* (London: Macmillan, 1985), 77–90 (82).

31. See John Covach, "The Sources of Schoenberg's 'Aesthetic Theology,'" *19th-century Music* 19(3) (Spring 1996): 252–62.

32. Dahlhaus, "Schoenberg's Aesthetic Theology."

33. Covach, "Sources of Schoenberg's 'Aesthetic Theology'"; Covach, "Schoenberg and the Occult: Some Reflections on the Musical Idea," *Theory and Practice* 17 (1992): 103–18.

34. Julian Johnson, "Schoenberg, Modernism, and Metaphysics," in Jennifer Shaw and Joseph Auner, eds., *The Cambridge Companion to Schoenberg* (New York: Cambridge University Press, 2010), 108–119.

35. "Religion and Art," in Richard Wagner, *Religion and Art*, trans. William Ashton Ellis (London: Kegan Paul, Trench, Trübner, 1897). Reprint, Lincoln: University of Nebraska Press, 1994, 247.

36. "Know Thyself," in Wagner, "Religion and Art," 265.

37. See Richard Wagner, *Judaism in Music and Other Essays*, trans. William Ashton Ellis (London: Kegan Paul, Trench, Trübner, 1894). Reprint, Lincoln: University of Nebraska Press, 1995, 75–122.

38. Wagner, *Judaism in Music and Other Essays* (there titled "On the Womanly in the Human Race"), 335.

39. "Heroism and Christianity," in Wagner, *Judaism in Music and Other Essays* (there titled "Hero-dom and Christendom"), 280.

40. Wilhelm Heinrich Riehl, quoted in Winfried Schüler, *Der Bayreuther Kreis: Wagnerkult und Kulturreform im Geiste völkischer Weltanschauung* (Munster: Aschendorff, 1971), 53, in Mary A. Cicora, *"Parsifal" Reception in the Bayreuther Blätter* (New York: Lang, 1987), 20–21.

41. On the Bayreuth circle see Cicora, *"Parsifal" Reception*, and Ernst Hanisch, "The Political Influence and Appropriation of Wagner," in Ulrich Müller and Peter Wapnewski, eds., *Wagner Handbook*, 191–95 (Cambridge, Mass.: Harvard University Press, 1992).

42. Lecture given on Mar. 29, 1935, to the Jewish Mailamm group members who were helping the Hebrew University to build and maintain a music department. In Stein, *Style and Idea*, 502–503.

43. See quotations in Moldenhauer, *Anton von Webern*, 49–52.

44. Hardly has the crowd left the temple when laughing and idle chatter start again, when each one inspects the other's wardrobe and behaves as if he had not experienced at all something that transports our kind out of this world. And then! There was, on top of it, applause! If people start to applaud after the end of *Parsifal* it cannot be anything but a display of the greatest rudeness. Do they wish to prove, perhaps, that they have most graciously taken pleasure in the performance? This is really ridiculous to a gigantic extent. But, away with these thoughts! (Moldenhauer, *Anton von Webern*, 51)

45. Aug. 8, 1909: *Alban Berg, Letters to His Wife*, ed., trans, and annotated by Bernard Grun (London: Faber, 1971), 83.

46. Letter to Jalowetz, Jan. 6, 1910: *Arnold Schoenberg Letters*, 24.

47. See, for instance, his letter of June 16, 1911, about a month after Mahler's death:

One bright spot during these sad days has been reading Wagner's autobiography, which we bought in Graz. Out of the completely straightforward, unadorned enumeration of experiences there emerges a monument to the most unbelievable artistic suffering, which in its simplicity and intensity often reminds me of Strindberg (indeed, some things could have been written by him)—which is, I believe, unprecedented; here one individual is writing for all, and that should be a warning, a lesson for all centuries to come! But critics, publishers, theater directors and actors, and various other "artists" continue undisturbed in their destructive work and the true artists must suffer and suffer until they can suffer no more. Oh, dear Herr Schönberg, while reading this I have to think repeatedly and often of you and of—Mahler. (*Berg-Schoenberg Correspondence*, 3–4)

48. *Berg-Schoenberg Correspondence*, 53.
49. *Berg-Schoenberg Correspondence*, 60.
50. *Berg-Schoenberg Correspondence*, 60.
51. *Berg-Schoenberg Correspondence*, 61.
52. *Berg-Schoenberg Correspondence*, 62.
53. Jan. 13, 1912, *Berg-Schoenberg Correspondence*, 65.
54. Albrecht Dümling, *Die fremden Klänge der hängenden Gärten: Die öffentliche Einsamkeit der neuen Musik am Beispiel von Arnold Schönberg und Stefan George* (Munich: Kindler, 1981), 177. For a shorter version of the key argument of this book in connection with Schoenberg's *Das Buch der hängenden Gärten*, see Albrecht Dümling, "Public Loneliness: Atonality and the Crisis of Subjectivity in Schönberg's Opus 15," in *Schönberg and Kandinsky: An Historic Encounter*, ed. Konrad Boehmer, 101–38 (Amsterdam: Harwood, 1997).
55. Dümling, "Public Loneliness," 111–12.
56. Dümling, *Die fremden Klänge*, 177.
57. Dümling, *Die fremden Klänge*, 25.
58. Dümling, *Die fremden Klänge*, 29.
59. Quoted in Dümling, *Die fremden Klänge*, 25.
60. Quoted in Dümling, *Die fremden Klänge*, 48.
61. According to Stefan Breuer, cited in Paul Bishop, "Stefan George and the Munich Cosmologists," in Jens Rieckmann, ed., *A Companion to the Works of Stefan George* (Rochester, NY: Camden House, 2005), 172.
62. Michael Winkler, "Master and Disciples: The George Circle," in Rieckmann, *Companion to the Works of Stefan George*, 149. The other key grouping was the Munich-based "cosmic circle," which formed around Ludwig Klages and Alfred Schuler, out of which the George circle grew, though it did not operate on the same master-disciple basis. See Paul Bishop, "Stefan George and the Munich Cosmologists," in Rieckmann, *Companion to the Works of Stefan George*, 161–187.
63. See Jens Rieckmann, "Introduction," in *Companion to the Works of Stefan George*, 8. Also Bishop, "Stefan George and the Munich Cosmologists."
64. In the first volume of *Blätter für die Kunst*, founded by George, Carl August Klein contributed an essay about Stefan George that stated that his new art did not look abroad for influences; its mainstays were Richard Wagner the composer, Friedrich Nietzsche the orator, Arnold Böcklin the painter, and Max Klinger the drawer (*Zeichner*).
65. Winkler, "Master and Disciples," 146.
66. Quoted in Dümling, *Die fremden Klänge*, 41. Friedrich Wolters, an even more intimate member of the circle, said the same thing a bit later: Wolters, *Stefan George und die Blätter für die Kunst: Deutsche Geistesgeschichten seit 1890* (Berlin: Bondi, 1930), 543.
67. Robert E. Norton, *Secret Germany: Stefan George and His Circle* (Ithaca: Cornell University Press, 2002), 326. See Ludwig Klages, *Stefan George* (Berlin: Bondi, 1902).
68. Friedrich Wolters, *Herrschaft und Dienst* (Berlin: Einhorn-Presse im Vorlag Otto von Holten, 1909). Wolters may have sought to draw a connection with Hegel's "Herrschaft und Knechtschaft" in his title. On Hegel's master-slave dialectic see Frederick Neuhouser, "Desire, Recognition, and the Relation between Bondsman and Lord," in Kenneth R. Westphal, ed., *The Blackwell Guide to Hegel's Phenomenology of Spirit*, 37–54 (Oxford: Wiley Blackwell, 2009).

69. "Das geistige Reich" can be translated as "spiritual empire," "realm," or "state," and "geistige" retains connotations of "intellectual," as well as "spiritual." "Das geistige Reich" was the utopian successor to "das schöne Leben" [beautiful life], which George had written of in "Der Besuch," in *Sämtliche Werke*, vol. 5, *Der Teppich des Lebens und die Lieder von Traum und Tod* (with a prologue) (Stuttgart: Klett-Cotta Verlag, 1984), 10.

70. *Blätter für die Kunst: Eine Auslese aus den Jahren 1904–1909* (Berlin: Bondi, 1909).

71. See Ritchie Robertson, *The "Jewish Question" in German Literature, 1749–1939: Emancipation and Its Discontents* (New York: Oxford University Press, 1999), 370.

72. See Wolters, *Herrschaft und Dienst*, 64.

73. On the Maximin cult see, for instance, Rieckmann, "Introduction," 13, and Norton, *Secret Germany*, 326–44. George's homoerotic interests are well documented and were apparently well known. As early as 1914 an article by Peter Hamecher titled "Der männliche Eros im Werke Stefan Georges" appeared in sexologist Magnus Hirschfeld's *Jahrbuch für sexuelle Zwischenstufen* 14(1) (1914): 10–23), edited since 1899 on behalf of the "Wissenschaftlichhumanitäres Komitee," the first organization of the gay emancipation movement, founded in 1897. I take this information from Marita Keilson-Lauritz, "Stefan George's Concept of Love and the Gay Emancipation Movement," in Rieckmann, *Companion to the Works of Stefan George*, 207.

74. Quoted in Max Rychner, "Stefan George" in *Zur europäischen Literatur* (Zurich: Atlantis, 1943), 79.

75. William McGrath, *Dionysian Art and Populist Politics in Austria* (New Haven, Conn.: Yale University Press, 1974), esp. 85–164.

76. Julie Hubbert, "Mahler and Schoenberg: Levels of Influence," PhD diss., Yale University, 1996, 61. As Hubbert points out, it is unclear whether Schoenberg reversed his opinion of Mahler because of his personal contact with this powerful Viennese music figure or "because of the persuasive power of the Third Symphony."

77. See Susanne Rode, *Alban Berg und Karl Kraus: Zur geistligen Biographie des Komponisten der "Lulu"* (Frankfurt am Main: Lang, 1988), and Julian Johnson, "Karl Kraus and the Schönberg School," *Journal of the Arnold Schönberg Center (Arnold Schönberg's Viennese Circle, Report of the Symposium 12–15 September 1999)* 2 (Vienna, 2000): 179–89.

78. *A Translation of Weininger's "Über die letzten Dinge" (1904/1907)/On Last Things*, trans. and with an introduction by Steven Burns (Lewiston, N.Y.: Mellen, 2001), 68–69.

79. As Steven Burns points out, quoting *On Last Things* (71), in "Sex and Solipsism: Weininger's *On Last Things*," in David G. Stern and Béla Szabados, eds., *Wittgenstein Reads Weininger* (New York: Cambridge University Press, 2004), 95.

80. A new translation has recently appeared from the first edition: *Sex and Character: An Investigation of Fundamental Principles*, trans. Ladislaus Löb, ed. Daniel Steuer with Laura Marcus, intro. by Daniel Steuer (Indianapolis: Indiana University Press, 2005).

81. Of Wagner he writes, "one still greater than Wagner first had to overcome the Jewishness within him before he found his special mission," in Steuer, *Sex and Character*, 276.

82. See Julie Brown, "Otto Weininger and Musical Discourse in Turn-of-the-century Vienna," in *Western Music and Race*, ed. Julie Brown, 84–101 (New York: Cambridge University Press, 2007).

83. Nike Wagner, "*Parsifal* et l'antisémitism juif à Vienne, dans les anneés 1900," *L'Infini* 3 (Summer 1983): 22–32. See also Nike Wagner, *The Wagners: The Dramas of a Musical Dynasty*, trans. Ewald Osers and Michael Downes (London: Weidenfeld and Nicolson, 2000), 118–30.

84. See Nancy A. Harrowitz and Barbara Hyams, eds., *Jews and Gender: Responses to Otto Weininger* (Philadelphia: Temple University Press, 1995).

85. Rode, *Alban Berg und Karl Kraus*, esp. 106–13.

86. Wolfgang Gratzer also suggests that the mystical ideas articulated by Weininger in *Über die letzten Dinge* probably contributed to Berg's broader mystical and superstitious outlook: *Zur "wunderlichen Mystik" Alban Bergs: Eine Studie* (Vienna: Böhlau, 1993), esp. 93–101. Within the broader Schoenberg circle Georg C. Klaren identified Schreker as a likely Weininger reader as early as 1924: See Klaren, *Otto Weininger: Der Mensch, sein Werk, und sein Leben* (Vienna: Braumüller, 1924), 229 ("Schreker, der gewaltigste lebende Komponist, hat sogar die Weiningerschen Geschlechtsprobleme vertont, auf seine Bücher wenigstens haben sie stark abgefärbt"). It is also tempting to read Schreker's sketch of July 20, 1909, *Der neue Parsifal*, in Weininger's wake. Schreker presents Parsifal not only as a figure of redemption but also as a metaphor for the creative artist, glossing aspects of Parsifal with the myth of the Blaue Blume, while hinting at the pantomime plot for which he had already composed music, Oscar Wilde's "The Birthday of the Infanta," and an opera libretto he was yet to write, *Die Gezeichneten*. Lyrical and operatic constructions of women and of the relations between the sexes by several other composers, notably Strauss and Pfitzner, have been made with reference to Weininger's characterology of woman. See Gabriele Busch-Salmen, " 'Menschenliebe im allerhochsten Sinne': Zu den Frauenrollen in Hans Pfitzners Buhnenwerken" ["Brotherly Love in Its Highest Sense": The Female Roles in Hans Pfitzner's Stage Works], in *Frauengestalten in der Oper des 19. und 20. Jahrhunderts*, ed. Carmen Ottner (Vienna: Doblinger, 2003), 116–34.

87. Vienna: Tal, 1919.

88. This paragraph could even be read as alluding to Weininger's suicide: Weininger formulated new "laws of morality" but could not, according to contemporary accounts of his suicide, "live with guilt."

89. Arnold Schoenberg, *Theory of Harmony*, trans. Roy E. Carter (London: Faber, 1978), 96. This aspect of Schoenberg's construction of harmony is discussed by Susan McClary in *Feminine Endings: Music, Gender, and Sexuality* (Minnesota: University of Minnesota Press, 1991), 107.

90. Julie Brown, "Schoenberg's Early Wagnerisms: Atonality and the Redemption of Ahasuerus," *Cambridge Opera Journal* 6(1) (1994): 51–80.

91. As he put it in his Mailamm speech in Los Angeles on Mar. 29, 1934: Stein, *Style and Idea*, 502–503.

92. On this see Julie Brown, "Otto Weininger and Musical Discourse in Turn-of-the-century Vienna."

93. LaCapra, *Representing the Holocaust*.

94. Brinkmann, "Reading a Letter," in Reinhold Brinkmann and Christoph Wolff, eds., *Driven into Paradise: The Musical Migration from Nazi Germany to the United States*, 3–20 (8) (Berkeley: University of California Press, 1999).

95. On this topic see, for instance, Michael Mäckelmann, *Arnold Schönberg und das Judentum: Der Komponist und sein religiöses, nationales, und politisches Selbstverständnis nach 1921* (Hamburg: Wagner, 1984), and Móricz, *Jewish Identities*; Hartmut Zelinsky, "Arnold Schönberg—der Wagner Gottes: Anmerkung zum Lebensweg eines deutschen Juden aus Wien," *Neue Zeitschrift für Musik* 4 (1986): 7–19. Zelinsky examines the relationship between Schoenberg's earlier and later dictator-like postures and his Wagnerism but comes to rather different conclusions than I do.

96. Arnold Schönberg Center, Vienna, T5–28.TRL: "Was man nicht vergessen sollte" [What Should Never Be Forgotten] (Denk 203a) and "Geyers-Sohn, Geyers-Enkel, Geyers-Enkels-Witwe" (Denk 203b). In the former, Schoenberg remarks ironically that, "following the principle that what is bad is Jewish, and what is Jewish is bad," Wagner referred to Brahms as a "Jewish balladeer," an accusation subsequently repeated by Wagner's followers, along with the naming of Brahms's triplets as "Jewish triplets."

97. Arnold Schoenberg, *Wassily Kandinsky: Letters, Pictures, and Documents*, ed. Jelena Hahl-Koch, trans. John C. Crawford, 78–82 (London: Faber, 1984).

98. Móricz (*Jewish Identities*, 208–12) shows that allusions to his far-reaching plans in Jewish affairs started in 1933.

99. Quoted in Móricz, *Jewish Identities*, 210.

100. Bernstein, *Foregone Conclusions*, 16.

101. This is the opening proposition of Dagmar Barnouw's "*Wiener Moderne* and the Tensions of Modernism," in Simms, *Schoenberg, Berg, and Webern*, 73–127. "So important is the legacy of the Wiener Moderne that I turn in this chapter away from music per se in order to analyze the phenomenon in its own right and to describe the highly complex set of conditions under which it thrived. Analogies with the musical modernism of the Second Viennese School, described in other chapters of this book, will be obvious."

102. La Capra, *Representing the Holocaust*; see, for instance, 9–11.

103. Steven J. Cahn usefully sums up the German Jewish trajectory: "On the Representation of Jewish Identity and Historical Consciousness in Schönberg's Religious Thought," *Journal of the Arnold Schönberg Center (Arnold Schönberg and His God, Bericht zum Symposium 26–29 June 2002)* 5 (Vienna, 2003): 93–107.

104. [SUGGEST MERGING fn 104 and 105. See below.]

105. "Mit ergebenem Gruß und voll Dank für Sie—aber Sie sind gegen den Dank, wie soll ich es sagen? Kann man es sagen? Wer aber hat jemals so viel Wohlthaten erhalten, wie ich von Ihnen?" This and all other letters from Webern to Schoenberg quoted here are digitally reproduced on the website of the Arnold Schönberg Center, Vienna; http://www.schoenberg.at/index.php?option=com_content&view=article&id=365&Itemid=696&lang=de. I am grateful to Dr. Regina Busch for her generous assistance in correcting the transcriptions from the Webern-Schoenberg correspondence and to Dr. Simone Hohmaier for confirming transcriptions from the Berg-Webern correspondence. I have maintained Webern's spelling except where changes were necessary for clarity's sake. I am also grateful to Eric Graebner and especially Irene Auerbach for their assistance with the English translations. Excerpts from Webern letters by kind permission of Peter Halbich.

106. "Glauben Sie mir Herr Schönberg, dies eine bemüh' ich mich immer: Distanz halten, Achtung, nichts ist selbstverständlich. Ehrerbietung—

Mir ist es ein Glück, Sie zu kennen und alles—so wie Sie halt zu mir sind—"

107. "Lieber Herr Schönberg,

Erlauben Sie, dass ich Ihnen diesmal zu Weihnachten Platons "Phaidon" schenke.

Es ist so merkwürdig, dass alle bedeutenden Männer, die je gelebt haben, ihr Leben entweder direkt oder indirekt für die Idee der Unsterblichkeit der Seele geopfert haben. Sokrates, Jesus Christus; und Beethoven, Strindberg?

Sollte das der Sinn dieses Lebens sein?

Immer wieder dieselbe Geschichte:

es gibt noch was anderes als man mit den leiblichen Sinnen aufnimmt.

Aber was kommt dabei heraus?

Mir ist das alles ein Rätsel.

Und dass die Worte Sokrates oder Platons heute so wahr sind wie vor 2000 Jahren, das beweist nur wieder dass es etwas gibt was über der Zeit steht und das in auserlesenen Männern wirkt.

Von wem auserlesen?

Wenn das geistige, rätselvolle über dem materiellen steht, wieso kommt es gerade in dieser Potenz in diese Person? Kann denn das geistige [*sic*] auch gezüchtet werden? Von wem?

Welche Macht wirkt hier und—warum?"

108. "Ich lese jetzt wieder Weininger (Über die letzten Dinge). Ich finde das ganz wunderbar. Der sieht auch die Dinge von der anderen Seite und was herum ist. Und überhaupt diese Stärke des Gedankens.

Sagen Sie, kann man überhaupt Denken und Fühlen als etwas gänzlich verschiedenes bezeichnen?

Ich kann mir keinen großartigen Intellekt ohne die Glut der Empfindung vorstellen. Bei Weininger ist doch das gewiss so, und bei Strindberg, Plato, Kant, Kraus?

Das kommt halt aus dem Menschen heraus, unmittelbar.

Das ist bei Weininger so großartig. Es ist auch darum wunderbar geschrieben.

Ich denke jetzt immer an folgende Männer: Sie, Kokoschka, Mahler, Kraus, Weininger."

109. This is the second letter of July 6, 1910. "Mahler ist ja wahrhaftig was großartiges; das ist so gar nicht Kunst—ästethisches [*sic*]; vielleicht, wenn man sein Leben ["nicht"? missing in original] wüßte, man könnte es aus den Symphonien reconstruieren [*sic*]. Sie müssen doch im engsten Zusammenhang stehen mit seinen inneren Erlebnissen.

Ich sehe auch eine Entwicklung: von höchster Naturverehrung zu immer geistigeren [*sic*], entrückteren [*sic*] Inhalt. Das drängt sich mir immer wieder auf. Ganz wurst, ob's stimmt....

Es ist so wunderbar—Ausstrahlung des allerhöchsten."

110. "Drum ich weiß ja—so hart als möglich muß man gegen das Pack sein—sie glauben ja noch immer, man ist auf ihre Gnade angewiesen.

Einen Fußtritt in den Hintern.—

Wenn eine Erkenntnis so im Herzen entsteht—über Nacht—so wie am Morgen in der Rose der Tautropfen—unmittelbar, von Gott geweiht, das ist das schöne.

Man muß von Kindheit an mit Scheuklappen durch den Mist der Bildung gehn, dass kein Pesthauch ins Herz dringt.

Ich glaube bedeutende Menschen bekommen jene geschenkt, irgend ein Wall entsteht um sie.

Ich möchte Räuberhauptmann werden und diesen Treck der Menschheit vernichten[.] Aber wie viel blieben da übrig.

Ich glaube immer mehr dass Weininger Recht hat: der Mensch der die Eigenschaften niederer Lebewesen eine nach der anderen abstreift muß zuletzt auch dasjenige unterlassen, was die Menschheit im tierischen Sinne fortpflanzt. Das ist dann ein Weg: vom Tier zur Auflösung der materiellen Substanz überhaupt.

Ich begreife das vollkommen klar.

Der höchste Gipfel der Sittlichkeit, die irdische Hülle fällt.

Wenn es eine Entwicklung gibt dann kann es nur die sein: aus dem Tiermenschen entsteht allmählich ein Lebewesen, das zur Erkenntnis kommt, es bedarf des Lebens auf dieser Erde nicht. So verschwindet der Mensch wieder, der leibliche.

Dieser Weg führt direkt zu Gott.

Damit entfällt der Einwand, dass jemand sagt, wenn alle dieser Erkenntnis folgen gibts keine Menschen mehr, eben das ist wohl der Sinn, fort mit ihnen[.]

Ich schreibe Ihnen das, Herr Schönberg, weil ich gerne mit Ihnen darüber reden möchte. Ihre Meinung dazu möchte ich wissen."

111. "Er [Rilke] macht, z.B. die Unterscheidung zwischen Schi[c]ksal und Leben und verbindet den Mann mit jenem und die Frau mit diesem[.]

Der Heilige lehnt das Schi[c]ksal ab und wählt das Leben 'Gott gegenüber,' dann heißt es[:] 'Dass aber die Frau, ihrer Natur nach, in bezug auf den Mann die gleiche Wahl treffen muß, ruft das Verhängnis aller Liebesbeziehungen herauf: entschlossen und schi[c]ksalslos, wie eine Ewige, steht sie neben ihm, der sich verwandelt.

Immer übertrifft die Liebende den Geliebten, weil das Leben größer ist als das Schi[c]ksal. Ihre Hingabe will unermeßlich sein: dies ist ihr Glück. Das namenlose Leid ihrer Liebe aber ist immer dieses gewesen: dass von ihr verlangt wird, diese Hingabe zu beschränken.'

Das ist im Wesen die Anschau[u]ng Strindbergs, Weiningers: dass die Frau gleichsam die Natur selbst ist, etwas wesentlich ganz verschiedenes vom Mann, ganz beziehung[s]los. Aber kann es schöner gesagt werden, als Rilke es thut.

…Ich werde Ihnen das Buch schenken; denn ich möchte zu gern, dass Sie es lesen."

112. Webern is referring here to Rilke's *Die Aufzeichnungen des Malte Laurids Brigge* [The Notebooks of Malte Laurids Brigge].

113. Translation of Rilke taken from Rainer Maria Rilke, *The Notebooks of Malte Laurids Brigge*, trans. Stephen Mitchell (New York: Limited Editions Club, 1987), 161.

114. "Was Sie mir von Ihrem Buche erzählt haben, ist großartig.

Wissen Sie, wie ich den Brief gelesen habe war ich wie in einer Brandung oder im Wissen oder vielleicht nur im Ahnen eines Stromes, einer riesigen Flut.

O es ist unermeßlich.

Wie können Sie glauben, dass ich irgendwie zurückhalte Ihnen ge[ge]nüber…

Ich werde den Triglav in Krain besteigen, ein sehr hoher (gegen 3000 m) Berg und ziemlich schwierig. Vielleicht finden Sie es lächerlich, dass ich so was thue, aber:

Das seltsame auf den Höhen der Berge[,] dieses zarte und reine, das zieht mich immer wieder an.…

Die Einsamkeit und das Ringen mit Gott[.]

Allen Trek abstreifen.

Wie ich an meine Werke gedacht habe, ist mir wohler geworden.

Es ist mir bewußt geworden, dass sie gut sind."

115. Schoenberg was working on the *Harmonielehre* at this time.

116. "Ich stehe noch ganz unter dem Eindruck Ihres wunderbaren Werkes. Ich weiß außer Beethoven und Mahler nichts was mich so ergreift, wie Ihre Musik.

Wohl auch Wagner; aber das ist was anderes. Ich bin gerade in den letzten Tagen, da wir hier "Meistersinger" probierten und aufführten[,] auf manche Ideen gekommen…

In Berlin habe ich mir die van Gogh-Ausstellung angesehn…

Es gibt für mich nur drei Maler; das sind Sie, van Gogh und Kokoschka."

117. "Ich lese jetzt ein Buch, das nicht von Menschengeist geschrieben ist: 'Seraphita' von Balzac. Seraphita ist ein übergeschlechtliches Wesen, ein Engel."

118. "Ich lese noch 'Seraphita.'

Jeder Satz darin ist ein Wunder.…

Jedes Wort in dem Buche dient nur der Wahrheit, dass der Glaube das höchste ist. Haben Sie das über Claudel in der letzten "Fackel" gelesen? Es ist wohl wahr: alle ganz überragenden Männer sind zum absoluten Gottesglauben gekommen. Balzac ist jedenfalls einer der allergrößten und herrlichsten Menschen."

119. "Der Tod Gustav Mahlers macht mich von Tag zu Tag trauriger. Es wird mir immer unbegreiflicher, daß das geschehn ist. Mahler ist todt.…

Sie sagen ja auch, dass Sie den Eindruck haben, Sein [sic] Werk sei völlig abgeschlossen.…

Ich habe das Gefühl, das[s] Mahler weiß, wie wir um Ihn [sic] trauern.…

Seien Sie versichert, Herr Schönberg, dass jeder von uns mit ganzer Seele an Ihnen hängt. Das geplante Buch wird Ihnen einen Einblick gewähren, der Ihnen die Wahrheit dieser Worte bestätigt.

Die vergangenen Tage in Wien sind für mich von ungeheurer Bedeutung. Mahlers Tod und die Gewissheit, dass ich für immer Ihre Freundschaft besitze. Gustav Mahler und Sie.

Da sehe ich ganz deutlich meinen Weg. Ich werde nicht abweichen.

Gottes Segen über Sie."

120. "Und ich kann auch Dich, Lieber, nur beschwören, bei der Heiligkeit unserer Kunst, beim Leben meiner Frau, daß, trotz meinem eigentümlichen ["Eigentümlichen" in original] Vorgehn, *nicht ein Funke*[u8] Lieblosigkeit, Interesselosigkeit, oder gar Gleichgültigkeit in mir für Schönberg war, ja daß ich durch das Leid, *im Vorhinein*, ihn durch meine <u>anscheinende</u> Vernachlässigung zu erbittern, und seinen Zorn nicht vermeiden zu *können*,—daß ich—wie gesagt—, durch dieses Leiden im Vorhinein, bevor mir [inserted] also Schönbg direkt sagte, daß er bös sei—schon fühlte,—daß es keine größere Art gäbe, eine so heilige, *unwandelbare* Liebe zu betätigen wie die ist, die wir für ihn fühlen,—*als dieses Leiden*."

121. Brand, Hailey, and Harris, *Berg-Schoenberg Correspondence*, 6–7. See also Brand, Hailey, and Meyer, *Briefwechsel Arnold Schönberg–Alban Berg*, vol. 1, 1906–1917, 42–43.

122. "Seien Sie versichert, wir werden Ihnen helfen....

Lieber Herr Schönberg, vertrauen Sie nur auf uns. Möchte es Ihnen nicht lächerlich erscheinen, was ich jetzt sage: ich glaube die Jünger Christi können nicht mehr mit ihrem Herrn gefühlt haben, wie wir mit Ihnen. Gott beschütze Sie, mein lieber Herr Schönberg."

123. For full details, see Brand, Hailey, and Harris, *Berg-Schoenberg Correspondence*, 11n1.

124. Brand, Hailey, and Harris, *Berg-Schoenberg Correspondence*, 7–8.

125. Quotation from Friedrich Nietzsche's "Das trunkne Lied," from *Also sprach Zarathustra*. See Brand, Hailey, and Harris, *Berg-Schoenberg Correspondence*, n. 3, 8.

126. "Ich weiß nicht, verstehen Sie, was ich da anzudeuten suchte?

Ich möchte eine unsichtbare Macht sein, die Ihnen alles geben kann, was Sie sich wünschen. Oder anders:

Man bringt Gott ein Opfer; Opfer nicht in dem Sinn einer Gabe, die einem schwer fällt, aus irgend einem Grunde; der Priester, der die Messe liest; ein Gebet.

Ich kann es wirklich nicht sagen.

Mir war das so heilig, dies zu thun.

Sie werden mich schon verstehn.

Wegen des Berg und aller anderen: ich weiß, dass die Sie grenzenlos lieben."

127. Brand, Hailey, and Harris, *Berg-Schoenberg Correspondence*, 8.

128. "Ich habe hier beim Berg Ihre wunderbare Vorrede zur Harmonielehre gelesen. Das ist ja so überwältigend und so unsäglich rührend.

Lieber Herr Schönberg, Sie danken uns?!

Was ich bin, alles, alles durch Sie; ich lebe erst durch Sie.

Dass Sie an uns sich betätigen konnten, war ja unser grenzenloses Glück, ein grenzenloser Segen für uns. Wenn ich nur schon endlich dieses wunderbare Buch besäße."

(Italicized translation in Moldenhauer, *Anton von Webern*, 146.)

129. "Ich möchte in diesem Augenblicke einmal das Moment, dass Sie unser Lehrer in der Musik sind, ganz bei Seite lassen, um nur dieses so deutlich als möglich zu machen:

Die Wirkung Ihrer Worte in moralischer Beziehung, Ihre sittliche Macht.

Und schon spüre ich, dass ich nicht hätte diese Scheidung machen sollen; das fließt in eins[.] Und die sachlichste Anweisung in musikalischen Dingen wurzelt in Ihrem Herzen. Das ist es, was mich an Ihrem Buche so ergreift: dieses Reine, Heilige, wenn Sie diese Dinge behandeln.

Ihre Erkenntnis blüht eben aus dieser sittlichen Macht.

Wenn sich auch gerade jetzt in dem Augenblicke Ihres Bekenntnisses Ihre Selbstdurchleuchtung in allerherrlichstem Glanze zeigt, so war sie doch schon seit ganz langer Zeit für mich vorbildlich.

Das ist mein Streben, dem nahe zu kommen, so wie Sie, sich ins Innerste zu leuchten; so jede Secunde [*sic*] seine geheimsten Gedanken zu überwachen.

Und hinter dieser fürchterlichen Umgrenzung spüre ich etwas ganz Zartes und Leises."

130. Brand, Hailey, and Harris, *Berg-Schoenberg Correspondence*, 9–10.

131. "Daß Sie 'Seraphita' u. 'Louis Lambert' lesen freut mich riesig."

132. "Aber ich habe immer weniger mit allen diesen Leuten zu thun.

Ich weiß nur zwei Dinge:

Ihre Werke und die Mahlers."

133. "Ich habe in einem Heft der Musik die Totenmaske des Heiligen gesehn.

Mein Lieber, es gibt nur das: mit aller Macht nach einem Leben hier zu streben, das völlig aufgeht in Idealen und das schon ein Hauch von diesem fernen, anderen Leben berührt."

134. Brand, Hailey, and Harris, *Berg-Schoenberg Correspondence*, 20.

135. "Ich weiß nicht, wem ich mehr schulde: dem Lehrer oder dem Menschen Schönberg. Das ist aber schließlich gleichgültig, denn bei Ihnen läßt sich das eine vom anderen nicht sondern…Sie sind ja keinem Ihrer Schüler bloß ein Lehrer geblieben, Sie wurden stets das 'Vorbild.'…[E]s jetzt einen Menschen mehr gibt, der Sie von ganzem Herzen lieb hat, der die Erinnerung an das Beisammensein mit Ihnen als ein heiliges Gut bei sich halten will und der Ihnen im Kleinen und Kleinsten—anders kann ich wohl nicht—immer dankbar bleiben will, wenn Sie nur die Gelegenheit geben wollten." Polnauer to Schoenberg, Oct. 6, 1911. This letter is preserved at the Library of Congress but is now digitally reproduced on the website of the Arnold Schönberg Center, Vienna.

136. "Franz Liszts Werk und Wesen," Liszt issue of *Allgemeine Musik-Zeitung*, Berlin (Oct. 20, 1911); "Franz Liszt's Work and Being," in Stein, *Style and Idea*, 442–47.

137. "Aber das gibt es, danach zu streben, dass wir es verdienen. Hineingreifen ins Herz, Trek heraus, hinauf, "sursum corda" sagt die christliche Religion.

So hat Mahler gelebt, so Schönberg.

Es gibt die Reue und gibt die Sehnsucht."

138. "Die 'Harmonielehre' ist erschienen!!!…

Endlich ist das Werk da. Ich glaube es wird in [corrected from "im"] Massen verkauft werden. Herzka muß nur sorgen, dass es in alle Auslagen kommt. Nun ist das Werk in die Welt gesetzt. Ich bin begierig was geschehn wird. Ich hab das Gefühl, ein jeder, ders liest, muß sich an den Kopf greifen; 'Ah, so muß es sein.'

Die ganze Welt muß sich an den Kopf greifen; ein Zeichen des Erstaunens der ganzen Natur muß sichtbar werden. Seit Wagner ist in der deutschen Sprache so etwas nicht geschrieben worden.

Vielleicht sogar seit Schopenhauer. Ich kann es kaum erwarten das Buch endlich im Zusammenhange ganz zu lesen. Du kennst es schon ganz, wie?"

139. "Ich muß Ihnen für Ihre Harmonielehre danken. Obwohl ich doch Vieles daraus kannte, ist mir jetzt, da ich's als Buch im Zusammenhang lese, Alles neue Offenbarung. Daß eine Harmonielehre ein so menschliches Buch sein kann. Und das wunderbare Vorwort. Es ist mir fast beschämend, daß in solchen Zusammenhängen auch meine Name steht. Ich habe Ihnen gegenüber ein schlechtes Gewissen: daß ich mich nicht an Dingen beteiligen konnte, die Ihnen das Leben erleichtern sollten. Ich konnte nicht und traute mich deshalb lange nicht, Ihnen zu schreiben." Library of Congress, but now digitally reproduced on the website of the Arnold Schönberg Center, Vienna.

140. "Hast Du was über die 'Harmonielehre' gehört? Bitte, an Schönberg nur halbwegs günstige Urteile.

Es ist alles so schrecklich. Drum muß unser Buch ganz fein werden...

Man hat ja auch Beethoven beschimpft und den Mahler beschimpft man noch, aber es ist schrecklich, entsetzlich das in solcher Nähe mitmachen zu müssen.

Ich wünsche den Worten unseres Buches eine große Kraft.

Es muß wirken.

Ich möchte vergehn vor Zorn und Wut. Schreib Du noch was fürs Buch, was ganz schönes.

Schreiben wir alle noch was. Erheben wir diesen Menschen. (ach nein), zer[r]eißen wir mit unserer Glut die Wolken, die Nebel, dass dieses Licht endlich sichtbar wird dieser armseligen Erde.

Wie schön ist diese 'Harmonielehre.'

Alle Geschehnisse der Natur und Kunst, das sind die Wunder Gottes, sind Geheimnisse für uns; sie sind da, sind ewig.

Daran gemessen ist unser Buch nichts, aber in Bezug auf den Trek dieser Welt kann es was sein.

Schönberg braucht uns nicht.

Aber wir können anbeten; wir müssen es.

Wir brauchen ihn."

141. "Gustav Mahler," *Der Merker* (Mar. 1, 1912); translated as "Gustav Mahler: In Memoriam," in Stein, *Style and Idea*, 447–48.

142. "Dieses unser Verhältnis zu Dir, als unsern Führer, Leiter hat etwas tief beseligendes für mich.

Du bist das Band, das unlösliche Band, das uns vereint. Wir alle leben für Dich. Glaube es mir."

143. Anita Luginbühl, "Attempt at a Diary," *Journal of the Arnold Schoenberg Institute* 9(1) (June 1986): 36.

144. "Brüderschaft trinken" is the act of two men deciding to call each other by their first names, which nearly always happens over a drink.

CHAPTER 6

THE STRANGE LANDSCAPE OF MIDDLES

MICHAEL BECKERMAN

THIS is the beginning of this chapter. Think of all the work that lies ahead in the next few paragraphs. I've got to set up terms and parameters, create the tone (which I have probably started to do already) and outline in some way all those things that both connect and differentiate this bit of writing from all others that have come before. I must introduce, in some sense, myself, my subject, and my method and approach. Looking ahead, the reader must decide whether to keep reading or stop (unless it is a homework assignment). These initial moments are exhausting for both reader and writer. All we can basically do is hang in there until the engine gets moving and we have some sense of where we are and where we might be going. But then we have to think about endings as well (of paragraphs, as well as articles). Nothing could be more treacherous. Concluding something is like stopping a train engine; after getting the thing in motion we have a hurtling railcar, subject to all kinds of powerful forces of inertia and gravity. We apply the brakes with a screech, somehow hoping that all the parts will miraculously stop at once, that all the energies and forces engaged can somehow be simultaneously corralled. In order for this to work, everything must be done in just the right way at precisely the correct moment.

Some things, however, begin twice. I have in mind piano concertos and operas that commence and then start again when the curtain opens or the soloist enters. This chapter now begins again with a different tone. Just imagine: The heavy lifting of beginning has been accomplished, and the weight of closure is still far in the distance. We are in the middle. We tend to have two radically different ideas about middles. The first suggests that the middle is crucial, the soul, the heart and core, and the other that the middle is somehow irrelevant. These are, for the most part, replicated in discussions about music. Considering the primacy of "sonata form" and its spinoffs, there is a tradition of considering the center as a place of great power, the "development" but at the same time, therefore, also something perpetually unstable and thematically unsettling. The second musical view, the prevalent one, looks at middles and sees basically nothing, and "nothing" in music goes by names such as "filler," "transition," and "contrasting passage," and other names we shall also encounter at the very end of this chapter.

Despite such caricatures, however, I maintain that musical middles exhibit rare properties. Indeed, when you throw the basic materials of Western sound up in the air, the parts do not come down randomly; certain kinds of things make their way to the beginning and end, and other, very different kinds of things find themselves falling into the middle. And this middle, whether in *Alice in Wonderland* or a Beethoven symphony, is quite simply somewhere else, a zone with different laws and different rules.

SOME MIDDLES NEAR THE BEGINNING

Here is "Oh! Susanna," Stephen Foster's minstrel song published in 1848 and one of the biggest hits of the nineteenth century:

Example 6.1.A.

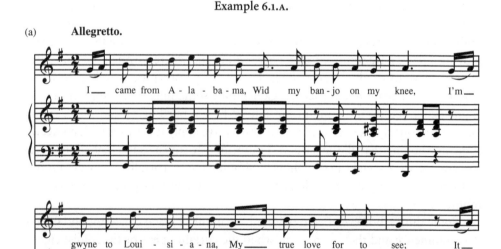

Something happens. The song "begins." And for its opening bars the tune seems to race up and down like a rubber band being stretched. The same thing happens twice, but then everything changes. The words, heretofore nonsense ("sun so hot I froze to death"), become sensible, the near manic patter disappears, and in its place is a pure cry of pathos: "Oh! Susannah," something as unexpected as it is powerful. But before we can register this utterly personal plea, this almost unacceptable bit of intimacy, we are back to the style of the beginning again, with a closing shape that has surrounded the cry of "Susannah" and barricaded it in a particularly

Example 6.1.B.

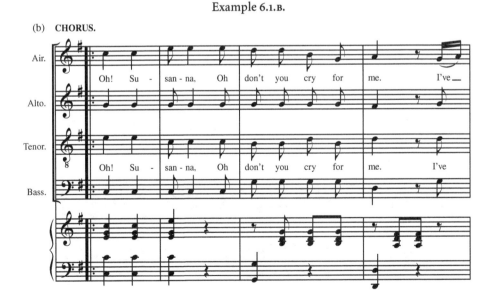

expressive prison. In fact, the name should have double quotes around it. So in this particular *aaba* it is *b* that has the special properties.

A song even more commonplace: "Happy Birthday!" We sing "Happy Birthday to you" twice, and then, the third time around, a particular name—Abdul or Jane or even Susanna—takes the place of "you," falling into that soft middle and coming almost to a complete halt after the languorous descent of the unexpected octave leap that precedes it. The engine starts. The engine runs. The engine stops. And in the middle the thing says what it has to say. It may be worth noting that, in its earliest appearances of "Happy Birthday!" in print, there is no indication that the middle should slow down and come to a pause. That would seem to have been a collective invention that came about over time—the effect of being in the middle.

Here is something a bit more complex. At the start, the Allegretto scherzando from the Cello Sonata op. 58 sounds like a somewhat conventional Mendelssohnian scherzo, rich in gestural charm and effortless counterpoint, somewhat like the elfin scherzo from *A Midsummer Night's Dream*.

Example 6.2.

Its stability and control are reinforced by a second part, marked *cantabile*, that seems to balance the opening.

Example 6.3.

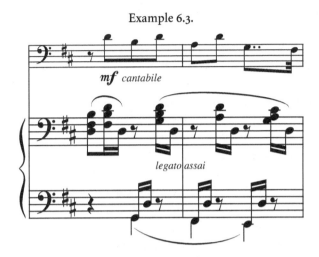

However, seemingly without any provocation something like a full-blown musical tantrum then ensues, leading to a heroic and passionate statement of the original elfin theme.

Example 6.4.

It would be foolish to maintain that these three examples serve as firm evidence of a rigorous mode of sonic storytelling that mandates that over time certain kinds of things were permitted on the outsides and certain things had to go in the center. In addition, though I offer an equation of sorts in the very middle of the chapter, it will probably not be possible to turn this subject into a fully scientific inquiry. In fact, as we try to figure out just why and how certain things tend to fall into the middle, we should also try to catalogue just what kinds of things we find there. In doing so we may have a chance to glimpse a familiar landscape from the inside out.

DEATH

The funeral march as we know it was invented around the time of the French Revolution. The previous sentence, though practically meaningless (what does "around the time" mean?) suggests that the conventional military march was decelerated and "minorized" as part of the practice of memorializing fallen heroes in the public sphere. Imagine the opening bars of a Mozart piano concerto, say the nineteenth or the twenty-first slowed to a *largo*, turned to the parallel minor, and sheared of its quicker note values, and we have the basic recipe for the funeral march. However, for the funeral march to enter the world of the symphony or the sonata, its ideal placement had to be discovered. Death, it turns out, is not usually something encountered at the outset, nor, despite its obvious finality, does it appear at the end. Death goes in the middle. This is certainly the case with Beethoven's prototypical funeral march from the *Eroica* Symphony and with Chopin's equally influential march from the Piano Sonata in B-flat Minor.

A host of followers continue the tradition: The funeral march in Schubert's Trio in E-flat, according to a recent theory, is a memorial to the fallen Beethoven. Schumann's Quintet in Eb features an inner-movement funeral march, as does Dvořák's Quintet in A major.

Another example of the way death finds the middle may be heard in the Largo from Dvořák's *New World* Symphony. The movement is based on two passages from Longfellow's *Song of Hiawatha*. After the opening chords—a musical portal marked "beginning of a legend" by the composer—the famous main theme enters, according to the composer, based on the chapter "Hiawatha's Wooing." The C♯ minor middle section, however, has slightly murkier bona fides but almost surely reflects Dvořák's setting of Minnehaha's dying, limned by a descending chromatic passage, and death itself, portrayed by the funeral march ("Then they buried Minnehaha / In the snow a grave they made her").[1]

SLOWNESS

Another creature of middles is the almost unexplored category of slowness itself, with all its associations, positive, negative, and ambiguous. Boris Asafiev, in his *Musical Form as a Process*, neatly sums up the conventional wisdom about slow movements:

> The slow (second) movement, much more concentrated than the sarabande or aria, is an expression of contemplation, contrasting with the action [of the first movement]; lyrical conditions, in their most varied stages and nuances, are concentrated with depth and force of expression with the formation of the symphonic adagio.[2]

Similar commentaries can be found in the works of theorists from Koch to A. B. Marx and in textbooks everywhere. Most recently slow movements, in particular the Adagio, were the focus of an article by Margaret Notley, which effectively summed up the qualities and the reception of the Adagio in late nineteenth-century chamber music.[3] She argues convincingly that the Adagio is tantamount to a genre, with its own conventions and expectations.

Nonetheless, surely there are some fundamental questions that remain unanswered. Asafiev uses the word expression twice in his brief discussion, and it is conventional that somehow slow movements are associated with the idea of expression. But how did slow movements get so slow, and what is slowness?

Milan Kundera is one of the few thinkers to treat this theme explicitly in his novel *Slowness*, though, as one witty reviewer noted, it is rather a quick read. The book is an artful meditation on an eighteenth-century French novel interspersed with several parallel contemporary stories (additionally, it is the only novel I know where a scholar forgets to give a paper). Central to the plot is nocturnal lovemaking in several centuries. In commenting upon the protagonist's love tryst, Kundera writes:

> By slowing the course of their night, by dividing it into different stages, each separate from the next, Madame de T. has succeeded in giving the small span of time accorded them the semblance of a marvelous little architecture, of a form. Imposing form on a period of time is what beauty demands, but so does memory. For what is formless cannot be grasped, or committed to memory. Conceiving their encounter as a form was especially precious for them, since their night was to have no tomorrow and could be repeated only through recollection. There is a secret bond between slowness and memory, between speed and forgetting...In existential mathematics that experience takes the form of two basic equations: the degree of slowness is directly proportional to the intensity of memory; the degree of speed is directly proportional to the intensity of forgetting.[4]

Thinking about multimovement structures with this in mind, we must ask how slow movements got to where they are. Was it because of some need for balance between qualities associated with "outer," such as daylight, logic, and the external, while those, like nocturnal fantasy and illogic, became related to the notion of "inner"? Or did slow movements really only become comparatively slow when they were placed in the middle?

One of the few cases I know where we can watch the process of a famous slow movement getting slower and slower in just this way is the Largo from Dvořák's *New World* Symphony. Marked "Andante" in the original sketches, it was called "Adagio" in the final manuscript (and the composer referred to it as an Adagio in the newspaper on the day of the premiere). At virtually the same time, almost certainly under the influence of the Wagnerian Anton Seidl, Dvořák crossed out "Adagio" and wrote "Larghetto" and then crossed that out to put down "Largo." Thus, the very quality irrevocably associated with the movement, lyrical nostalgia, was a collaborative effort between Dvořák and a conductor who understood the power of slowness.

While the connection between slowness and middles is obvious in the way the movement structure of the common practice period plays out, there are other ways that speed and memory connect. Dvořák's Piano Quintet in A features a scherzo in a sparkling Czech style that recalls the composer's *Carnival* Overture.

Example 6.5.

In the trio, however, something strange happens. Various slowed-down strains of the scherzo appear, interspersed with passages that sound like quotes from the slow movement of Schubert's B-flat Trio, op. 99. Dream memories, shadowy recollections populate this particular middle, suggesting that, among other things, the middle functions as a work's unconscious.

Example 6.6.

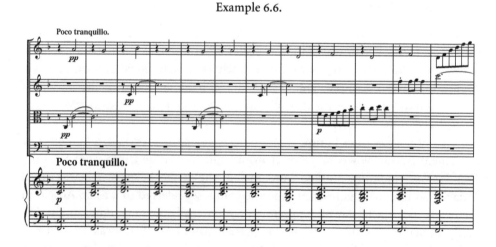

The connection between speed and narrative is taken up in another context by film critic Benjamin Halligan, who writes about the use of almost relentless "long takes" in the cinema of Tarkovsky:

> The speed of the tracking is of the utmost importance here; its slowness strips the camera movement of a narrative function, since the camera movement does not advance the narrative progression of the film in this long take. So what does this slowness do to the aesthetic? Having removed it from the context of the film's narrative, it reworks it as a meditative, perhaps hallucinatory, swell of mobile imagery.[5]

This place, which for Tarkovsky is meditative and hallucinatory and for Kundera invokes the concept of "memory," is often conjured as deeply expressive in the world of slow middles.

EXPRESSION

Nothing is more elusive than the idea of expression in music. If music is expressive, it should be expressing *something*, and if it is expressing something, we should be able to articulate what it is that is being expressed. But we have never really been able to do so.

This is somewhat frustrating because, on the surface, nothing seems more straightforward than expression. For the last several centuries, composers have peppered their scores with markings, directing performers either toward specific passages in their works or designating entire movements to be played *espressivo*. But just how do we play expressively? Should expressive style vary from composer to composer and from work to work, or are there standard agreements about what such things designate? Should composers simply use "expressive codes," even those consisting of gestures such as head movements, sighs, and grimaces? Expression may be a tautological invitation to "distort in the service of expressivity" or even a mode of stylized subjectivity and thus beyond our grasp. Yet we can still draw a few basic conclusions based on the placement of expressive markings. As a rule, they tend to appear far more in the middle than at the beginning or the end, like the *cantabile* marking in the scherzo from Mendelssohn's Cello Sonata. Looking, for example, at Beethoven's set of sonatas for violin and piano as a typical example, we see that in the ten sonatas the word root "espress-" occurs four times in movement titles, always in a middle movement; its related descriptor, *cantabile*, occurs once.

In the first twenty-four measures of the Adagio espressivo from the tenth sonata, not including the movement title, we find the terms *sotto voce*, *espress.*, and *molto dolce*, in addition to several *cresc.* markings, four sets of crescendo-diminuendo markings, and meticulous instructions for pedaling. From these things we might hazard a guess that expression for Beethoven and possibly his contemporaries meant something like "play with human nuance, with the kind of variability that mimics human behavior." And the place for this kind of behavior is essentially in the middle.

SOME THEORY IN THE MIDDLE

An understanding of the relationship between death, expression, or broad ideas of slowness does not really help explain the unpredictable Mendelssohn example at the beginning of this chapter, nor does it help us to understand how this or hundreds of other such "unprovoked" outbursts might function within the context of the larger work. For some help with this question and since we are now in the very middle of this chapter, we may turn to the work of Charles Altieri, a thinker who wrestled with issues of literary middles in an article titled "The Qualities of Action: A Theory of Middles in Literature," published in 1977. His concerns are obvious, and his conclusions straightforward and radical:

> Middle refers to a vision of the kind of authority which justifies a concern for the quality of the actions and sharply opposes itself to the authority required to support claims about beginnings and endings... [Middles are] a mode of discourse and grounds for assessing statements which are very different from those appropriate to questions of beginnings and endings. Both traditional metaphysics and science have different but related ways of proposing explanations that require a causal progression from a definable beginning to a final state somehow implicit in the beginning (what we sometimes falsely describe as "organic"). And both are essentially rational and analytic: truth depends on ascertaining a secure beginning and then testing how various abstract causal relations will determine the end of the process.[6]

So it follows for Altieri that "Discourse in the realm of middles is dramatistic, not referential or propositional, and hence it asks to be assessed in different terms than those of truth and falsity."
He also asserts that:

> Authority in the realm of middles, then, is not dependent on analytic procedures, which involve separating out discrete testable elements and laws for combining them in some kind of sequence. It is instead primarily circular: judgments of quality depend on one's cultural education and can only be justified by leading others to see the images of human value one is relying on.

Thus, by operating under different laws, by evading the rigorous approaches of logic and experimental method, middles pose a genuine challenge and also create remarkable opportunities. One way to explain Mendelssohn's move in his Cello Sonata op. 58 is to say that he does what he does in the middle... because he can.

Some of Altieri's views are echoed in a recent study by John Corbett titled "Out of Nowhere: Meditations on Deleuzian Music, Anti-cadential Strategies, and Endpoints in Improvisation":

> To make music consisting only of middle. Intermezzo. Interminable work. Work that always remains to be made. Nothing radical, only radial. No ends, mere means. No succession of segments. To subvert the formal and underlying ideological function of the cadence.[7]

For Corbett the enemy of all things is the cadence, and he brilliantly depicts the ineffable quality of middles in his peroration:

The cadence completes the musical piece, sealing it off and crushing down what appeared in its middle, reducing the vulnerable, inconclusive interiority to disposable filler. In Deleuzian terms, the cadence is territorial. Using highly codified emotional signifiers embedded in functional harmony and Western conventions of rhythm, it asserts a stratification, a hierarchical placement of elements that organizes how one should feel in response to a particular musical event. Earlier, tension is produced, chaos is introduced, but with the cadence it is resolved, warded off. The conclusion is effective. The acoustical field has been reterritorialized.

A Promised Equation

Perhaps it seems infantile to back up from Deleuzian rhizomes to something like alphabet soup, but there may be something gained by reducing our inquiry to a single dumbed-down musico-mathematic equation: $a + b + a = ?$

Most would tend to answer with something like $2a+b$. That is, the sum total of these parts is a combination of the quality of a and the quality of b, but since there is more of a, and we hear it at the beginning of the end, it is somehow more important to the identity of the thing. This is further implied by our effortless associations of a as something more valuable (see A-game, A-list, I got an A! and also B-movie, etc.).

However, there are some discussions, implied in certain textbooks, analyses, and elsewhere that suggest that a more correct answer is $3a$! In this model the function of b is to—in the words of Noel Coward—"writhe at the feet" of a in a "frenzy of self-abasement" for the purpose of calling attention to a's more notable qualities. In this model, b self-immolates and a is enshrined.

As should be obvious, we have been pursuing another solution, one that answers the equation $2b$! This implies that, contrary to our understanding, it is often the function of the outer parts to protect from the rest of reality the inner singularity that is truly valuable. In this world, which I shall promptly term *BAB*, the center represents what a composer really *wants* to do after figuring out the somewhat hefty task of beginning and ending a piece or a movement. The middle is what can be done when one can, more or less, do anything one likes and is therefore more a signal of the composer's taste and individuality than the more conventional outer parts.

The Fractal Middle and a Middle with No Middle

Before leaving the more theoretical consideration of middles we might ask an overdue question: Just how broadly can one define a middle? In a general sense I would argue that middles display the very kinds of self-similarity we find in fractals. Thus, a multimovement work has middle movements, but each of those movements has

its own middle, and each section, phrase, or utterance within a piece has a beginning, an ending, and a middle. The strong version of *BAB*, then, is to argue that any
of these middles, by the very virtue of being in the middle, by virtue of not being
obligated to begin or end, will display special properties.

Indeed, at certain moments middles behave like middles absent anything like a
middle section. On October 30, 1888, Elizabet von Herzogenberg wrote to Brahms
on the subject of his D minor violin sonata:

> I rejoiced to find the *Adagio* undisturbed by any middle part, for, as I have often
> admitted, however nice the middle parts are, I never can enthuse over them. That
> kind of contrast almost always strikes me as artificial, and my chief pleasure in an
> *Adagio* is its continuity of emotion. For that reason this compact movement, so
> expressive in its contracted form, pleases me particularly.[8]

Let us remind ourselves of the opening theme of this piece, a classic Brahms Adagio.

Example 6.7.

And from a certain formal standard she is correct, there is no specific middle
section. There is, however, something in the middle:

Example 6.8.

As much as anything we have heard, in its suddenness, its almost excessive passion, it conforms to the ideas about middles here explored.

A List with Some Reasons

Before returning to some additional kinds of musical middles, here are several possible points that help explain the special properties of middles:

1. Middles, not having the same structural obligations as beginnings and endings, are free to go where they want and may even ignore the overall structure.
2. The reader/listener/performer has become familiar with the work's parameters and is more comfortable in the middle and thus able to engage greater variety.
3. Along these lines, the room has already been built, so we are free to make changes in it, to decorate in ways that need not conform to its overall design and that do not involve structure but have a fundamental effect on experience.
4. Since the middle is a place of psychoacoustic weakness, it is an ideal position to hide those things that are again too troubling, too sexy, or too weird to touch the rest of world. Maybe no one will notice (of course they do).
5. Finally, one argument holds that the middle must be extraordinary in order to save itself from being completely obliterated by beginnings and endings, like a middle child fighting for attention. Middles are thus passionate, conspicuous, and overpacked because otherwise they cannot survive.

The Soft Underbelly of Nation

Smetana's overture to *The Bartered Bride* begins with some contrapuntal busyness recalling the beginning of Mozart's *Marriage of Figaro*.

Example 6.9.

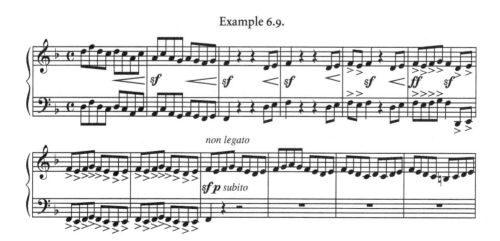

There is nothing in this particular opening to suggest that we are about to hear an opera consciously construed as "Czech." Yet after a short while we come to a bit of marked Czechness, set off with folk syncopations and accents that suggest the Czech language, at least as spoken in Prague.

Example 6.10.

While it may be revealing that the Czech bit comes second here, a more conspicuous passage may be found later in the overture. The work seems to start again, to work itself up into a frenzy only to stop dead, while a modulation separates a slow and expressive statement of the "Czech" moment, supported by a timeless drone. National essence as *memory* finds its way into the middle.

Example 6.11.

Smetana and his colleagues do this time and time again. In the fourth (and middle) work of *Má vlast*, "From Bohemia's Woods and Fields," a striking G minor opening quickly gives way to a pastoral passage. In Smetana's words, "The music moves from G minor to G major as a naïve country girl is pictured walking through the fields." This figure of the girl in national costume also appears in the middle section of Josef Suk's Fantasy in G Minor for Violin and Orchestra. The nationally charged tune was, according to the composer, "a young girl in national costume."

The hypernational middle is found not only in the Czech tradition but also in the earliest examples of consciously patriotic music. Many of Chopin's mazurkas feature a middle section in a distant tonality that clearly suggests rural music making, using either Lydian inflection, drones, unisons, or other elements.

Another example of slipping a kind of expressive nationalism into the middle occurs in Bartók's *Concerto for Orchestra*. The fourth movement is one of the only pieces of orchestral music for which the composer provided something like a program. After a dramatic opening gesture, a passage appears depicting something like "a Hungarian village." This is followed by one of the most lyrical passages in Bartók's works, a theme based on a popular Hungarian song by Zsigmond Vincze, "You Are Lovely, You Are Beautiful, Hungary."

All these pieces have in common the use of middles to create a kind of protected space where delicate and vulnerable images of national essence can appear and survive. That these images are, at least in several cases, explicitly conceived as female raises suggestive questions about gender and middles, which awaits fuller treatment.

SECRETS AND CONFESSIONS

Middles have also attracted their share of compositional attention as a place to hide things. The very psychoacoustic weakness of their placement makes them attractive.

I have already mentioned Dvořák's Quintet in A Major. Its slow movement is titled *dumka*, referring rather generally to a Ukrainian elegy—death in the middle again. While this may have been one of Dvořák's pan-Slavonic gestures, certain things in the movement go beyond nation or death. For the middle movement is based on a fragment from one of the composer's love songs. Dvořák, like many of his colleagues, was rather fond of putting such material in the center of a work, where it was simultaneously hidden and obvious. Perhaps the most famous example is the Concerto for Violoncello, intimately bound up with the illness and death of the composer's sister-in-law.

Whether one believes, as did Dvořák's biographer Otakar Šourek, that the composer had been in love with his wife's sister, Josefina, while a young man, or takes the romance-novel scenario that he was still in love with her, or decides with appropriate skepticism that none of it is provable, the middle movement and its middles prove fascinating. The movement's character is set by a kind of pastoral chorale, populated by languorous sighs. A return of the opening idea in G major is suddenly interrupted by a fragment of a funeral march in G minor.

Example 6.12.

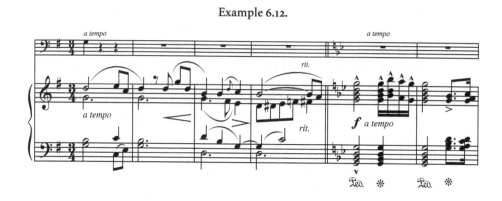

However, this interruption is interrupted by another one; this time we hear another fragment, but this time it is a passage based on the composer's "Leave Me Alone," from op. 82.

Example 6.13.

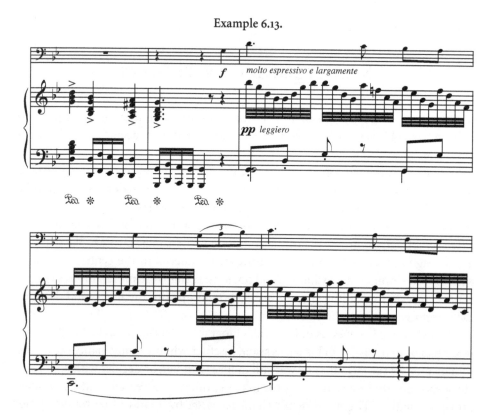

This song is itself modeled on one he had written thirty years earlier possibly for Josefina.

Political Action and the Message in the Bottle

Over the years a particular class of secrets has caught the attention of thinkers. Entertaining the notion of "writing between the lines" in his *Persecution and the Art of Writing*, Leo Strauss deals with the problems of philosophers working under repressive regimes. He notes that their writings begin and end "in the quiet, unspectacular and somewhat boring manner which would seem to be but natural." But there is something hidden: "Only when he has reached the core of the argument would he write three or four sentences in that terse and lively style which is apt to arrest the attention of young men who love to think."[9]

We may transpose this bit of writing to another time and place: Terezín in the late summer and autumn of 1944. Designed originally as a kind of "spa" for Jews too important to disappear, its identity as a garrison village made it both an ideal concentration camp and an imitation small town at the same time. The Nazis used this ingeniously by gradually transforming Terezín into a powerful propaganda vehicle. Throughout 1943 and the first part of 1944 the town was beautified, and artists, writers, performers, and composers were encouraged to create sanitized works to occupy themselves. In the spring of 1944 a Red Cross delegation was completely fooled by this charade, and by the summer the Nazis were making a propaganda film, directed by celebrity prisoner Kurt Garron, perversely using an entire soundtrack of otherwise forbidden Jewish music.

Composers like Pavel Haas, Viktor Ullmann, and Gideon Klein wrote important compositions during the months before they were transported to Auschwitz. While for obvious reasons they left no written commentary about their structural use of middles, each of them secretes material in slow movements or middles in general. Haas quotes the famous "Svatý Václave" (St. Wenceslaus) chorale in his "Far Away Is the Moon of Home," from *Four Songs from Chinese Poetry*. Ullmann waits till the middle section of the final movement of his Piano Sonata no. 7, composed in August 1944, to quote the Hussite song "Ye Who Are God's Warriors" as a patriotic move and then combines it with a German chorale and the B-A-C-H motif.

Gideon Klein's final composition, written less than two weeks before his transport and the final work written in Terezín, is a string trio of conventional appearance. The slow movement, however, is based on a Moravian folk song with a text about shooting the wild goose, a Terezín symbol of freedom. In various places it quotes works such as *Kindertotenlieder* and Suk's *Asrael* Symphony. Even more conspicuously, an interruption by the cello in the middle of the middle variation, marked *con gran espressivo, quasi improvisate senza rigore*, combines elements of the Verdi *Requiem*, a Jewish prayer, and the blues, forming a kind of ultimate personal protest.

Example 6.14.

In the Potemkin village of Terezín, compositional middles became reverse Potemkin villages, pretending to be nothing and containing everything. No works demonstrate the power and paradox of middles more than this group of compositions.

Conclusion

In the end I fall back on yet another unprovable argument and suggest, in what I hope is concordance with points made by Altieri in his article, that the very power of so many different kinds of musical pieces is an outgrowth of the irreconcilable tension between models. The first is a linear narrative argument that wishes all aspects of the endeavor to conform to the gravitational force of musical logic and design (and therefore be verifiable in some way); a parody of so-called organicism. The second is an approach that prizes expression for its own sake, refuses to move in any direction other than the one in which it wishes to go at the moment, and never feels an obligation to conform to anyone's narrative, story, or authority.

One could, of course, conclude, even after all this, that middles are actually made up of things that are not important enough to go at the beginning or the end, and some readers may continue to consider the center as a repository of secondary themes, *b* sections, transitions, fillers, and bridges. However, others may agree or eventually find that with great frequency middles conform to the delicate yet powerful singularity of the *BAB* model and, as such, represent precisely what someone wants to say—either consciously or not.

This is the end of the chapter, and as such it is no place to introduce new ideas, nor is it ultimately much of a place for mystery, for concealing or confessing. Here at the very end we must admit that there are no coherent theories for how just how these middles manage to reemerge after being obliterated by closure; in fact, I have found no cognitive, metaphysical, or psychological explanations for this at all. Nonetheless, I believe this does happen again and again and defines the ways in which we come to experience so many different kinds of music. Middles may be too disturbing, delicate, odd, or precious to touch the real world, and perhaps they must always be protected by the hard walls and edges of opening and closing gestures. Indeed, they are probably forgotten as we applaud and leave the hall. However, in my view much of the power of the musical experience depends on the way middles haunt our dreams for days, months, and years after we have seemingly forgotten them.

NOTES

1. See my *New Worlds of Dvořák* (New York: Norton, 2003). The practice of quoting one's own work to support one's comments is precisely what is so problematic about the footnote approach to documentation. It looks scientific, but is it? Anyway, the best I can say is that I have thought about this issue for more than a decade, and this is what I think.

2. Boris Asafiev. *Musical Form as a Process*. Books One and Two. Second Edition (Leningrad: Musika, 1971): 167.

3. Margaret Notley, "Late-nineteenth-century Chamber Music and the Cult of the Adagio," *19th-Century Music* 23(1) (Summer 1999): 33–61.

4. Milan Kundera, *Slowness*. New York: HarperCollins, 1996, 38–39.

5. Benjamin Halligan, "The Long Take That Kills: Tarkovsky's Rejection of Montage Technique," *Central European Review* 2(39) (November 2000). (I accessed this on the internet at: http://www.ce-review.org/00/39/kinoeye39_halligan.html)

6. Charles Altieri, "The Qualities of Action: A Theory of Middles in Literature," part 1, *Boundary* 2(5) (1977): 323–50; part 2, *Boundary* 2(5) (1977): 899–914. The earlier citations are from pp. 324–26.

7. John Corbett, "Out of Nowhere: Meditations on Deleuzian Music, Anti-cadential Strategies, and Endpoints in Improvisation, " in *The Other Side of Nowhere: Jazz, Improvisation, and Communities in Dialogue*, ed. Daniel Fischlin and Ajay Heble, 388–89 (Middletown, CT: Wesleyan University Press, 2004).

8. Available online in several places, including: http://www.archive.org/stream/johannesbrahmshoobryagoog/johannesbrahmshoobryagoog_djvu.txt.

9. Leo Strauss, *Persecution and the Art of Writing* (Glencoe, Ill.: Free Press, 1952), 24.

CHAPTER 7

THE GENRE OF NATIONAL OPERA IN A EUROPEAN COMPARATIVE PERSPECTIVE

PHILIPP THER

THE nationalization of opera in the nineteenth century encompassed many areas. One can distinguish between the nationalization of plots, of opera ensembles, and of the singing language. One can view the nationalization as a differentiation of opera in various "national schools," which would then deserve further attention and demythification in single cases, such as Michael Beckerman has demonstrated for Czech opera or Richard Taruskin for Russian opera. However, the nationalization of opera can also be interpreted as a process of convergence. The basis of this interpretation is a comparative viewpoint. The invention of German, Czech, Russian, Polish, Hungarian, and other national traditions of opera demonstrate that the nationalization of opera was in fact a European phenomenon. That said, one can ask why and how so many countries "invented" their own tradition[1] and how the very genre of national opera came into being.

A very useful tool to help us answer this question is the approach of "transferts culturels," a concept that was developed by French cultural historians in the late 1980s.[2] The empirical focus of this approach is on cultural exchanges, the agents who carry out the exchange, and the local adaptation of cultural goods and models imported from abroad. However, it also has an explanatory dimension. According to studies of cultural transfers, the exchange of cultures is not explained by an internalist perspective but by deliberately studying the possible impact of external factors or agents. This means, for example, that the development of German or Czech opera is not analyzed within the self-referential framework of the nation-state or a national culture but by taking into account influences of and exchanges with neighboring cultures. In this way, one can surpass the national framework prevalent in history and musicology well into the late twentieth century.

This chapter shows that the nationalization of opera was paradoxically the result of exponentially increasing cultural transfers. In the course of the nineteenth century, first in the German-speaking lands and then in other countries of central and eastern Europe and finally even in western Europe, opera was made thoroughly national. Yet this process of nationalization also had limits, especially when operas were produced on stage. Moreover, England and the United States are noteworthy exceptions that deserve special attention.

The term *cultural transfer* might suggest a peaceful and happy exchange of cultures. By using it one can also study conflicts and deliberate attempts to "other"—to alienate—certain cultures. The competition between various "invented" national opera traditions resulted in the musical chauvinism of the 1870s and 1880s. However, one can observe a process of convergence in the following two decades. The various "invented" opera traditions were increasingly exchanged around the turn of the century. The result of this process of convergence was a standard repertoire that was based on the one hand on various national traditions and schools and on the other hand on an international repertoire. Apart from this, there was Europeanization of opera. In the late nineteenth century cultural agents on the fringes of Europe and on the other side of the Atlantic Ocean increasingly perceived this standard repertoire and the entire genre of opera as "European."

Beneath this common denominator, opera guides and the older standard academic literature even today subdivide opera into various national schools. This chapter might shed some light on how this nationalized view of European culture and history came into existence in the late nineteenth century and how it might be amended today. This is of relevance for the history of Europe and how it is taught beyond the topic of opera.[3]

National Ideologies of Opera

Since the early nineteenth century, the social function of music has given rise to utopic notions of its social effect. In 1808 a Viennese newspaper noted the following: "The art of music (Tonkunst) effects the same miracle as love: it makes everyone equal. Be they noble or middle class, princes or their servants, chairmen or their inferiors, they all sit together at the same table as the musical harmonies allow them to forget the disharmonies of their respective positions."[4] One can regard this utopia as a social equivalent of the artistic utopia of opera as a "Gesamtkunstwerk." These unifying utopias were a reaction to the sharply increasing differentiation of cultures and societies in modern Europe. In the period from 1815 to 1848, these unifying utopias assumed a national character in Germany and Italy and soon after in central and eastern Europe. Music and singing were seen as tools of nation building. Communal singing was believed to help unite a nation.

In the vein of nationalism studies by Eric Hobsbawm or Benedict Anderson, these utopias can be deconstructed as an ideological component of nation building. Nonetheless, that would not fully explore the profound impact of this nationalization on European cultures. Music and the representative genre of opera in particular were seen at first as an expression of national cultural ambitions and then even as the very essence of the nation. From this follows the question of why audiences in various European countries interpreted opera in these ways and imbued it with a specific national meaning.

The tendency to classify music (and opera in particular) with national categories was based on the Romantic idea that every nation has a specific artistic voice. This was at the heart of the extensive collections of folksongs established since the early nineteenth century, which played a special role for nations without a nation-state. In his philosophical treatises, written in the 1830s, the Italian revolutionary Giuseppe Mazzini distinguished between the structure and depth of German music as demonstrated by Beethoven and the Italian melodiousness, which he saw as a unifying element for the Italian national movement.

In the Romantic spirit, Mazzini did not combine this distinction with a normative judgment. His idea was to merge the German and the Italian schools into a new and qualitatively better European music. A similar notion was proposed by Carl Maria von Weber, who wrote the following in his uncompleted novel, "Tonkünstlers Leben": "It should go without saying that I am referring to the opera which the Germans and the French strive for, a self-contained work of art in which related skills are applied in contributions which blend together and somehow form a new world."[5] As choirmaster at the Estates Theater in Prague and the German opera department at the Court Theater in Dresden, Weber arranged his program accordingly. He favored French opera but had it translated into German. This approach was in line with Romantic nationalism, while the translations he commissioned also fostered the position of German as a language of opera.

Adolf Bernhard Marx, one of the founders of the Berlin Conservatory of Music, changed the tone in the 1830s.[6] In his four-volume book on musical composition, which became a standard reference in the nineteenth century, he divided opera into three national schools. According to Marx, Italian opera stood for melodiousness, French for drama and musical effects, and German for authenticity and cerebral and earnest thought.[7] Hence, the normative judgment of Italian and French opera became clearly negative. As editor of the *Neue Zeitschrift für Musik*, Franz Brendel proposed a specific program for German opera based as well on these subdivisions of international opera. In a 1845 treatise, he argued for a departure from number opera, calling instead for dramatic unity and the elevation of German opera to "the level of national substance."[8] In this respect, Brendel anticipated many of Richard Wagner's writings, such as "Opera and Drama."[9] The discursive mechanism of "inventing" German opera was no longer synthesizing, as in the case of Weber, but antagonistic.

Wagner (who was especially polemical), Brendel, Marx, and other intellectuals sharply distanced German opera from Italian and French opera through the usage of national stereotypes. In abstract terms one can speak of a cultural transfer through negation because foreign musical cultures, especially grand opera, continued to influence German composers (and Wagner), although they would not acknowledge this. In recent German literature, Richard Wagner tends to be portrayed first and foremost as an opera reformer and political thinker.[10] He saw himself as well as a national activist, especially during his years in Dresden, and indeed he was an active nationalist.[11] This fact seems to have been overlooked at times in the recent international disputes over Wagner's anti-Semitism and other unpleasant features of his personality.

Wagner's national motivations and the mechanism of the creation of a national ideology of opera on stage can be effectively illustrated with reference to the cult he initiated around Carl Maria von Weber. In 1844 Wagner had the remains of the Dresden Kapellmeister shipped back to Germany from London despite his widow's doubts. Once the ship carrying the bones had docked in Dresden, the coffin was accompanied by torch bearers and an eighty-member-strong orchestra to the Catholic cemetery. Wagner composed two funeral marches with motifs from Weber's opera *Euryanthe* for the evening procession, which, according to contemporary reports, was attended by huge crowds. The church choir was made up of two rows of singers from the Court Theater dressed in black. According to Wagner's own report, the singers "wept as they silently laid laurel and immortelle wreaths on the coffin, as it was placed before them." In order to heighten the dramatic effect of the event, Wagner ordered that the coffin be buried the following day, at which time he spoke at the open grave. His speech culminated in this fulsome claim: "You were the most German musician ever to have lived!" (In German Wagner expressed himself in an awkward comparative: "Nie hat ein deutscher Musiker gelebt als Du!")[12]

Through this event Wagner created a lasting veneration of Weber, whose *Freischütz* was produced in Dresden more than five hundred times in the coming fifty years.[13] He positioned himself as the heir of the tradition of German opera, which he himself had invented. Wagner also carried out a national program as a Kapellmeister, increasing the number of German operas in the repertoire and staging imported operas in German translation only.[14]

This strict language policy was later copied by the Czech Theater in Prague, which is located only one hundred miles south of Dresden. The Provisional Theater in Prague (the precursor of the Czech National Theater) was similarly rigorous in its promotion of the Czech language. When Bedřich Smetana became Kapellmeister in 1866, he instigated the immediate creation of a purely Czech ensemble and commissioned translations of several operas into Czech. In the wake of the Russification policy after the Polish uprising of 1863, the government in St. Petersburg was eager to promote an imperial opera culture based on the Russian language. In general, translating operas became standard practice in most European countries until the end of the nineteenth century. England was a notable exception. As on the East Coast of the United States, constructing and practicing a national opera culture tended to be neglected here in favor of importing operas and hosting international guest stars.

However, the composers and Kapellmeisters who contributed to the nationalization of opera were not driven by patriotic fervor alone. They also hoped it would bring them increased public attention and material gain. Wagner, for example, called for the founding of an "association of dramatic poets and composers"[15] to monitor the opera houses' programs and serve as a national cartel that would control productions. This association did not come into being for more than fifty years because Wagner was forced to leave Dresden after the revolution of 1848 (in 1903, Richard Strauss founded the Genossenschaft Deutscher Tonsetzer). But in Prague, the Czech composers moved forward, incidentally as Wagner had proposed. In 1874 the Union of Czech Dramatic Writers and Composers was able to push through similar demands in a contract with the Provisional Theater, guaranteeing its members pivotal privileges. Two important factors for the nationalization of music were also contemporary music critics and the specific nonverbal quality of music. The meaning of music is less easily grasped than that of a book, a drama, or the visual arts. Although it may seem paradox, this is why music could be interpreted in nationalist ways (and why later audiences were able to change their ways of interpretation).

After going into exile, publisher and composer Wagner continued to refine the artistic agenda of German opera. In his Zurich treatises, he criticized French and Italian opera in stronger terms than ever.[16] His aversion to what he saw as foreign cultures peaked in his notorious essay titled "Jewishness in Music," an example of his xenophobic leanings. These have been well documented and do not need to be repeated in this chapter.[17] Nonetheless, it remains important to analyze the basic mechanism behind these discourses on opera and national culture. By contrasting various national opera traditions, Wagner attempted to draw up a specific agenda for German opera. However, his writings were characterized by a fundamental contradiction. On the one hand he discussed universal problems of opera in national categories, provoking hostility in France and Italy. On the other hand, his rejection of number opera, use of *leitmotifs*, and call for an elevation of the orchestra to a dramatic element in its own right was so radical that the response even in Germany was cautious.

In the nineteenth century, Richard Wagner's influence on public opinion in Germany was unparalleled by that of any other composer in central and eastern Europe. His generational peers, including Michail Glinka, Stanisław Moniuszko, Bedřich Smetana, and Ferenc Erkel, restricted themselves mostly to composing music. Consequently, the construction of a national opera tradition in central and eastern Europe was based more on the perception and canonization of certain works as "national operas." Stereotypes of other musical cultures also played an important role, but the invented national style was not defined in contrast to one single school of opera.[18] However, intellectual history and texts about music are not sufficient to explore the nationalization of music. The following chapter focuses on social history and musical associations.

Musical Associations and Movements

In central Europe, the nationalization of music was not merely the "invention" of a few intellectuals and composers. Associations and, increasingly, mass movements perceived music with nationalist fervor. In the 1830s, singers' associations were established at first in the German lands, a generation later also in Bohemia, Galicia, and the Baltics.[19] In the German lands, along with gymnasts, they formed the cornerstone of the national movement. Because hopes for a German nation-state were dashed in 1848, music continued to play an important role in nation building even after the revolution.

The activities of the singers' associations peaked at the 1865 Singers' Festival in Dresden. The three-day event was attended by around 200.000 people, among them at least twenty thousand outside guests, who came together to celebrate song as a force for creating national unity. Special trains arrived in Dresden from across the German Confederation, from nearby Bohemia, the German-speaking regions of Austria, and the German diaspora in Hungary. "What is the German fatherland?" asked one of the keynote speakers at the event. "It extends wherever the German language is spoken and God in heaven sings."[20] The speaker was a passionate advocate of the singers' movement's national agenda:

> If this enthusiasm for the German nationalist striving arising everywhere should, God forbid, be violently crushed to earth despite its respect for the law, then, German singers . . . let your songs give us strength to continue singing them throughout the German lands. And even if it takes time, the outcome is certain: those who oppress our national faith will be converted and slink away like the executioner of Saint Cecilia did from her holy songs. In this spirit I hail this circle of singers: "Heart and song, fresh, free, healthy! God protect you, the German singers' association"—Amen.[21]

This speech attests to the close link between music and nationalism in the nineteenth century. In its various genres ranging from popular folksong to classical music and opera, music was seen as an expression of national identity and a tool for nation building.

As in neighboring Germany, a mass musical movement gathered momentum in Bohemia. As of the 1860s, countless music and singing associations were founded and ultimately became the backbone of the national movement.[22] Singing was believed to trigger a sense of national belonging and social equality. It was also an emotionally moving collective experience. In the spirit of Romanticism, national activists believed that folksongs captured the very essence and the spirit of a nation.[23]

Music associations also flourished in Galicia, the Baltic regions, and other parts of the multinational continental empires. If they were to become mass movements, however, certain social preconditions were needed. The more extensive the middle class and the greater the level of literacy, the more people participated in these associations. These social factors explain why Germany and parts of the Habsburg

Empire were home to such a dense network of singers' associations in comparison with Italy, rural France, and the Russian heartlands. A further important factor was rivalry among national movements. In Bohemia, for example, German associations competed with Czech rivals. Similar competition occurred in other multiethnic empires of Europe.

The activities of the music and singing associations belong to the wider context of "cultural nation building,"[24] which was based on structural characteristics of the eastern half of Europe. Until well into the nineteenth century and in many cases even as late as 1918, the German, Polish, Czech, and other national movements lacked the framework of a nation-state. This meant they had to employ cultural criteria and institutions to mobilize the prospective members of the nation over large distance (horizontal mobilization) and bridging class differences (vertical mobilization).[25] However, members of the various musical associations were fully aware that their concept of national music could flourish only within an institutional framework. Intellectuals of the age were therefore eager to see national opera develop as a genre in its own right and campaigned for a national theater in which these operas could be staged.

The concept of the national theater enjoyed two heydays in central Europe. The first occurred in the late eighteenth century, when national consciousness was transformed into a political program for the first time. Friedrich Schiller called for the opening of a German national theater, which he described as an instrument of national unification. In the two decades before 1848 this idea was spread among the German public by the Schiller associations and the closely connected singers' associations, and it was widely discussed in Bohemia, Poland, and Hungary. Based on his activities as a nation builder, Richard Wagner was as well a prominent contributor to the debate on a national theater.[26]

Because of the failure of the revolution, all national movements and the various proposals for a national theater were suppressed after 1848. None of the German states pursued the idea to establish a pan-national theater. The idea then lost even more relevance once the German Reich was founded in 1871. German unity was now a matter of "blood and iron," and the nation no longer needed a theater in order to be unified.

However, the idea of the national theater remained prominent in the Habsburg Empire and among the non-Russian nationalities within the Russian Empire. Polish intellectuals described theater as "an important national institute for us." According to a Galician journal, its task was to "educate society in the saintly virtues of our forefathers and teach the masses about national civic duty. Its purpose is profoundly national."[27] National theaters were founded in Poland and Hungary even before the 1848 revolution and represented the respective national elites and their political and social aspirations.

The Czech national movement kept a close eye on such developments.[28] In 1845 a group of three hundred people formed an initiative to found a Czech national theater. In the founding manifesto they wrote: "We are filled with bitter shame to think that we Czechs, who look back at our forefathers with pride, who can rival our neighbors in all the fine arts, remain so backward in this artistic discipline. Without our own theater, we stand alone among the educated nations. We do not wish to trail behind like a barbarian in Thalia's refined arts."[29] In 1850 the Austrian government reluctantly approved the Association for the Building of a National Theater (Sbor pro zřízení českého Národního divadla v Praze).[30] The reason for this momentous decision was that the neoabsolutist regime was unable to ban every social initiative. Culture, it felt, was relatively apolitical. The association wasted no time, began official fund-raising, and bought land for the theater in 1852. The call to donate was answered not only by various patriotic aristocrats and the bourgeoisie in Prague but also by craftsmen, small businessmen, and wealthy farmers. By 1862 enough money had been raised to build and establish the Royal Bohemian Provisional Theater (Prozatímní divadlo). Its opening had major repercussions for Prague's traditional Estates Theater. The Czechs moved out of this institution, which therefore became an exclusively German-language theater. The theater was in fact the first major public institution to be divided between the two nationalities.

The next milestone in the history of the national theater was the laying of the foundation stone in May of 1868. This took place in the immediate wake of the Austro-Hungarian accord of 1867 and was the largest public manifestation in the nineteenth-century history of Bohemia. The three-day event was attended by some two hundred thousand visitors and had repercussions throughout central and eastern Europe. Following the Hungarians' example, the Czechs called for recognition as a third and equal nation-state within the Habsburg Empire.[31]

The foundation stones came from parts of the country believed to have played key roles in national history and mythology. The heaviest stone weighed two tons and was quarried at the mythical Mount Říp, twenty miles north of Prague, where, legend has it, forefather Čech had founded the Czech nation in prehistoric times. The transport of the stones was accompanied by mass rallies. Tens of thousands of people demonstrated at the Říp for national and social equality for the Czechs, singing and playing music in the cause of the nation. In Prague, a cross-section of society attended the festive parade marking the laying of the foundation stone. Craftsmen were the largest group and marched in sections organized according to profession, waving flags and banners. Bringing up the rear were the workers. They represented the largest individual contingent, followed by 2,600 singers and 1,500 gymnasts.[32] In the evening, the Provisional Theater hosted the premiere of Smetana's opera *Dalibor*, which I deal with later.

The event illustrated the close link between opera and nation building in an entirely new fashion. It was deliberately organized like a celebration of the nation. The laying of the foundation stone was a catalyst for further fund-raising. More and more sections of the population were prompted to donate, and the national theater finally opened in 1883.

The overwhelming success of the initiative did not go unnoticed by other national movements within the Habsburg Empire—and even beyond its borders. The Poles in Prussia, the Poles and Ruthenians in Galicia, Croats, Slovenes and Serbs all sent prominent representatives to the laying of the foundation stone and then the opening of the theater in Prague. Dozens of congratulatory telegrams were sent. This support for the Czechs reflected the comparable political situations of the Polish, Ukrainian, and southern Slavic national movements. Their goal was also to emancipate themselves from the cultural dominance of the respective empires and their ruling nations. Even the German speaking population in Bohemia followed the Czech example. When the success of the Czech National Theater pushed the Estates Theater into temporary bankruptcy in 1885, German industrialists and some Jewish entrepreneurs formed an initiative for a new German theater, which opened in 1888.[33] By the end of the nineteenth century, not only Czechs and the Bohemian Germans but also Poles (in all three partitions) Croats and Slovenes had established national theaters that needed to be filled with a repertoire. This was a strong impetus for, on the one hand, the creation of a genre of national opera and, on the other hand, the nationalization of imported operas by translations and by singing in the national language.

Cultural nation building and the musical mass movements were not restricted to central Europe. The opening in 1908 of the Palau de la Música Catalana in Barcelona followed a similar pattern. Funds were raised for a public institution to promote development of a representative culture for a domestic audience. Simultaneously, the goal was to gain recognition abroad.[34]

The idea of a national theater, part of the broader belief that culture could be used as a tool for national building, also gathered momentum on the fringes of the Russian empire. The Estonian National Theater opened in Tallinn on the eve of the First World War. It was also funded by public donations.[35] The Estonian case has a particular historical resonance because it repeated itself in the late twentieth century. "Singing for the nation" was a symbol of resistance to Soviet rule, hence the name "the singing revolution" (laulev revolutsioon) for the events of 1988–1991. Similar initiatives pushing for the creation of a national culture and national theater also occurred in Ukraine, Georgia, and Azerbaijan in the early twentieth century. Again, the establishment of national music institutions, often financed by social movements, was closely connected with the creation of national opera, which is the topic of the next section.

NATIONAL OPERAS IN COMPARISON

German- and English-language musicology uses the term *national opera* to describe work considered representative of the respective "invented" national opera traditions. Carl Dahlhaus has stressed that this genre is primarily defined through reception and not through stylistic characteristics.[36] Nevertheless, numerous similarities between various national operas exist in terms of plot and composition techniques. As a rule, these operas tackle subjects of national history and integrate musical elements from the countries' respective folk traditions.

Due to his explicit distance from contemporary folk music, Richard Wagner has been ignored in research on national operas. However, this exclusion is mainly due to traditions of reception that developed in Germany in the late nineteenth century and continue to influence German- and English-language musicology to this day. Breaking with this tradition, this chapter examines Wagner within the framework of national opera and other nineteenth-century opera composers and compares their respective reception by various audiences in Europe.

The influence of the national movement on Richard Wagner was already apparent in his choice of material once he was appointed Kapellmeister in Dresden. The first of his attempts to explore national myth resulted in the opera *Tannhäuser*. Wagner set the plot at the Wartburg, an important German "lieu des mémoires." The subtitle, *Der Sängerkrieg auf der Wartburg*, was a reference to the nationally encoded singers' festivals, popular when the opera was written, and referred to "German musicality." In spite of these nationalist connotations the opera failed to become a success in the first decade after its world premiere because its psychological plot proved difficult for contemporary audiences to grasp. As the critics noted, there was no hero with whom they could identify and, above all, no beguiling female character.[37] After just a few performances, *Tannhäuser* disappeared from the repertoire in Dresden in 1845 and was not staged anywhere else. Despite this failure, Wagner's interest in national mythology and history continued.

He set the plot of his next opera, *Lohengrin*, in a crucial era of Saxon and German history. The opera opens with King Henry the Fowler assembling the German tribes to fight a "threat from the East" and to expel the Hungarians from his dominions in the tenth century. The motif of the fight against foreign foes was a recurrent one in almost all central and eastern European national operas. In *Lohengrin* the main actor plays a very political and national role. Lohengrin, the potential successor to the throne, enjoys the support of the people and defends the rightful rulers against intrigue, thus preserving national unity.[38] The opera features numerous crowd scenes, in which the German nation appeared on stage as a collective unit. Moreover, national politics serves as a framework for the plot. When Lohengrin leaves the stage in the famous swan boat, he predicts a great future for the German empire.[39]

The national emphasis is reflected in the music. Wagner emphasizes the word "deutsch" by a reduction of the harmonic structure to its root in C major whenever the word is sung.[40] In short, both the subject and the music of *Lohengrin* have features that explain why contemporary audiences in Germany and in other countries perceived this work as specifically German. Given the political circumstances of the late 1840s the creation of a national opera was a good strategy for garnering a popular audience and a positive reception of his opera. However, due to Wagner's persecution as a result of the failed revolution, for many years this was no longer possible in Germany.

A crucial change in Germany's hesitant response to Wagner occurred as a result of the scandal surrounding the performance of *Tannhäuser* in Paris in 1861. After an organized audience protest, the opera was canceled. When it was performed in

Dresden, the audience applauded demonstratively.[41] One year later, Saxon king Johann I pardoned Wagner for his role during the revolution. Henceforth, his operas were staged with increasing frequency. Wagner's status as the most popular German opera composer was consolidated by *Die Meistersinger von Nürnberg*, in which he idealizes the protestant burghers as the true bearers of German culture and was hailed by contemporary audiences in Germany and especially the primarily German-speaking cities in Austria.[42]

To what extent can the *Meistersinger* be characterized as a national opera? Wagner's work features no evidence of any reference to folklore or popular dance traditions, but he did use similar structural tools. Wagner integrated historic instruments and compositional techniques, which created a distinctive tone color. In the libretto, the opera's protagonist, Hans Sachs, succinctly puts it: "It sounded so old, but it was so new."[43] The audience considered not only the plot but also this sound—and indeed Wagner's entire oeuvre—as German. The opera's reputation abroad confirmed the status of *Meistersinger* as the definitive German national opera. It was staged, for example, at the opening of the New German Theater in Prague, where it served as the equivalent to Smetana's *Libuše*, which was staged at the opening of the Czech National Theater. One can conclude that the contemporary German-speaking audiences saw and heard a specific national meaning in these works of Wagner.

In the wake of his success, other German composers also began exploring national plots and myths. Opera greatly contributed to the evolving Germanic mythology, which intensively influenced the imperial culture in literature (for example, the novel *Der Kampf um Rom*) and the arts.[44] In the two decades after the founding of the Wilhelmine empire, numerous Germanic operas were performed on Germany's stages, including *Die Folkunger, Heinrich der Löwe, Thusnelda und der Thriumphzug des Germanicus*, and *Armin*.[45]

One of the most prominent music critics of the time, Eduard Hanslick, noted that Germanic operas like *Die Folkunger* had very limited artistic value. He especially criticized the style of the songs as being taken from singing at bar tables. But the appeal of these operas was also due to their design. The sets were naturalistic down to the smallest detail. Heavily armed and clad in coarse robes, furs, and helmets, the performers looked exactly as audiences imagined the ancient Germanic people. Critics praised the meticulous "visualization of time, place and nationality"[46] and repeatedly described the protagonists as "*Deutsche.*" Germanic opera influenced the response to Wagner's *Ring des Nibelungen*, as well as the production style. In Dresden, Leipzig, Berlin, and other German cities, the cycle was staged in the "Germanic" style in the 1880s.[47] Allusions to the decline of the middle class, the folly of megalomania, and the critique of capitalism, which have dominated modern interpretations of the *Ring*[48] played no role in the late nineteenth century. Reviews show that audiences believed they were watching the nation's forebears enact a very real chapter of history. This phenomenon had a profound effect on the understanding of Wagnerian myths. Unlike today, his operas were not understood as timeless parables but rather as historical reality.[49]

All of this corresponded to Wagner's concept of "people's history," which he drew up during his years in Dresden. In his essay "The Wibelungen: World History as Told in Saga," which forms the basis of the *Ring*[50] Wagner criticized academic versions of history based on traditional archival sources. The composer believed that oral histories, myths, and sagas should be given equal due. In the course of his life, Wagner produced an oeuvre that can indeed be regarded as an alternative narrative of perennial German history, one that drew mass audiences. His operas covered a timespan from the Renaissance (*Meistersinger*) to the Middle Ages (*Lohengrin* and *Tannhäuser*) and early history (*Ring des Nibelungen*).

Toward the end of his life and after his death, Wagner became the very symbol of German opera and German arts in general. In 1887 the highly respected journal *Der Kunstwart* ran a lead article on the national significance of Richard Wagner.[51] In it he was described as a genius whose music was "the ultimate distillation of the Germanic spirit." In the last twenty years of the nineteenth century, the work of Richard Wagner made up one-third or more of the opera repertoire in Dresden and other main German cities, while the market share of German opera rose to 50 percent and higher.[52] Hence, one can speak of a nationalization of repertoires, a key component of the nationalization of opera.

This boom added to the international appeal of German opera, which was seen across Europe as an example for building a national culture. The founding of the Société nationale de musique after the French defeat in the war of 1870–1871 had the explicit goal of creating an equally well-organized and successful musical culture to rival Germany's.[53] Russia's "Moguˇcaia kuˇcka", a group of powerful composers, wanted to promote a Russian national style and musical culture.[54]

Michail Glinka (1804–1857) was championed by music critics close to the kuˇcka as the father of Russian opera. His major success was *Žyzn za tsaria* [*A Life for the Tsar*], which was set during the "Smuta", a period of unrest in early seventeenth-century Russia, when the country was divided by dynastic conflicts and Moscow was occupied by Poland. During the Soviet era, the opera was staged under its original title, *Ivan Susanin*. The main figure is a farmer who leads a marauding Polish army astray and deliberately sacrifices his life.[55] Glinka set off the plot with a nationally infused sound that deeply moved the audiences.[56] A performance in Moscow in 1866 even caused a riot, with the audience chanting "Down, down with the Poles."[57] This emotional reception has to be seen in the context of the Polish uprising of 1863, which exacerbated anti-Polish feelings in Russia.

In structural terms, Glinka's *Žyzn za tsaria* is a number opera that is based on the traditional operatic form. Folk dances and melodies can easily be integrated and specifically arranged in this structure. Stanisław Moniuszko (1819–1872) composed his two operas, *Halka* and *Strazny Dwór* [The Haunted Castle][58] in a comparable style, and they were similarly received as national operas. The first uncensored production of *Straszny Dwór* in the Polish city of Lwów is very telling for other cases of reception of national operas. When the opera was staged in the capital of the Austrian partition of Poland in 1877, it was received like a national anthem. Parts of the audience started to cheer and to cry in specific scenes that alluded to Poland's glorious past. Tears were especially shed during an aria in which one of the noble protagonists sings about a clock in the haunted castle that had stopped running, much like Poland's history as an independent state as a result of the partitions of the late eighteenth century. In the song and the orchestral accompaniment this very special clock started to tick again, like Poland's pulse of national cultural life in Galicia. One of the journalists in the audience touchingly wrote: This is not an old watch, but the genius of our fatherland. Although bereft of its physical power, it shouts loudly to all the world in the works of great poets, painters, and musicians. Poland is not lost yet."[59]

The strong emotional reactions to national opera can be attributed to several closely related factors. One of them is the expectation of the audience.[60] Contemporary music critics had advocated *Žyzn za tsaria* and *Straszny Dwór* as national operas even before the two aforementioned productions. Hence, people were already attending the opera with a certain enthusiasm. The visual elements of production played an important role as well because the common historical plots were produced so that they could be understood as a part of present-day history (Vergegenwärtigung). However, just as important was the music itself, which, according to many reports, struck a chord with the audiences and aroused their emotions even in repeated performances. Last but not least, all of these elements of opera—the drama, the visual effects, and the music—culminated in one specific event: the opera evening.

Another case of the invention of a national music tradition was Bohemia. The Czech case is especially interesting because it shows the contradictions and conflicts that often accompanied the creation of a canon of national opera. In the period from 1815 to 1848, music developed a special status among the Czech national movement because language and literature were relatively undeveloped. National activists strongly believed that the Czechs were a particularly musical people. They also pointed to the fact that its regular emphasis on the first syllable made Czech a particularly suitable language for opera.[61] Bedřich Smetana (1824–1884) came to be seen the pivotal Czech composer. In his first opera, *Brandenburgers in Bohemia* (Braniboři v Čechach), the plot is again based on a fight against foreign foes. The "good" Czechs are fighting the "evil" Brandenburgers, who symbolize the Habsburgs. The pivotal point of this opera, which premiered in 1866, is the eighth scene, in which the people of Prague vote to make the beggar Jira their king. This amounted to a call for a democratic legitimation of the monarchy reminiscent of *Lohengrin*. Jira is, however not a mythical figure like Wagner's creation but a member of the lower classes who symbolizes the right to equality and to participate in politics. *Brandenburgers in Bohemia* was written in the context of the upsurge of nationalism in Bohemia after the liberalization of Austria in 1860/61. Smetana's opera reflects this context in terms of both plot and music. Like many Italian and French composers of grand operas, he used a chorus to represent the nation and thus created a powerful visual image on stage.[62] Equally intense were Smetana's recurring marching rhythms, which symbolized the progress of the national movement. The composer developed a sophisticated musical dichotomy for the dramatic form of his first opera. The Brandenburgers were generally accompanied by just a few instruments—a musical expression of their social isolation. However, Jira, as king, generally enjoyed a rich accompaniment of many voices and/or the orchestra in order to show that the national movement had the people's support. Smetana consolidated his reputation as an opera composer one year later with *The Bartered Bride*.

Much less positive was the response to his opera *Dalibor*, which illustrated the contradictions inherent in the construction of national music. *Dalibor* was performed in 1868 to mark the laying of the Czech National Theater's foundation stone. An enthusiastic response was therefore to be expected. Nonetheless, music critics accused Smetana's work of bearing too close a resemblance to Wagner's dominant orchestration, recurrent use of a brass section, and *leitmotifs*. The Czech debate over Wagnerism was driven mostly by contemporary political conflicts but also by the dilemma of whether Czech national opera should follow the text-based, dramatic German example or adhere to the conventions of traditional number opera and include elements of folk music. Smetana and his followers, including the eminent musicologist Otakar Hostinský, advocated the former. Since the late 1870s they had been able to win broad public support. Wagner was no longer seen as a representative of a rival nation but as the founder of a national culture.[63] The Czech response to Wagner served as a blueprint for other, "small nations", as defined by Hroch in Europe including the Ukrainians, the Catalans, and the Poles in Galicia. In 1885 *Lohengrin* was performed for the first time in the National Theater, of course in Czech, on the grounds that the stage director and the key critics agreed it was a universal example of how to write a national opera.

Similar to Wagner's operas, Smetana's were set in temporal tableaux ranging from the myths and legends of early history to Bohemia's recent and even contemporary history—as in *The Bartered Bride*. The construction of national history in opera is a hallmark of all of the national opera traditions that emerged in central and eastern Europe in the course of the nineteenth century. Moniuszko in Poland, Erkel in Hungary, Glinka and Mussorgsky in Russia, Ivan Zajc in Croatia, and numerous other composers later deemed "national composers" imbued their countries with ancient dignity and created new figures with whom the audiences could identify. Very often historians have studied nationalism in Europe by analyzing the writings of nationalist historians like Heinrich von Treitschke, František Palacký or Mikhaylo Hruševsky. However, the national myths and history shown in opera reached a far bigger audience. Accordingly, the national composers became celebrated national heroes themselves. Smetana's symbolic status and the great success of his operas in Germany and the Habsburg Empire were important factors for raising the share of Czech operas in the repertoire of the National Theater to 50 percent. As with Wagner and German opera, the reception abroad played a key role in building up a national canon at home.

If cultural nation building can be described as a political strategy, then it was a highly successful one for the Czechs. Within just thirty years, between the opening of the provisional theater in 1862 and the success in Vienna in 1892, the Czechs elites succeeded in establishing their own institutional and artistic national culture. Given their international recognition as a cultural nation, the Czechs' disadvantaged status within the Habsburg Empire could no longer be legitimized with cultural arguments. Music therefore helped them capture a more equal status prior to World War I within the Habsburg monarchy and then independence in 1918.

Nonetheless, the lively response to Smetana's operas and Czech instrumental music in Germany had a downside.[64] At the turn of the century, Czech music was seen as exclusively national, while German critics and musicologists saw Wagner's music as universal in both content and effect. The response to Russian music followed a similar pattern, exerting a defining influence also on English-language literature. National harnessing of east European cultures, as well as the presumable universality of Wagner and German music traditions, served as a basis for the unfounded decision of Carl Dahlhaus and other German musicologists not to include Wagner in a study of national opera.

By comparing these processes of invention of tradition in central and eastern Europe, one can distinguish two (Weberian) ideal types: a German and an Italian type of national opera. While Smetana and to some degree Lysenko adhered to the Wagnerian concept of musical drama, Glinka, Moniuszko, Erkel, and Zajc preferred the traditional form of number opera.

The nationalization of opera had a deep impact on western European opera cultures. Once seen as the definitive opera, Italian opera was perceived in the late nineteenth century as just one of many national variations. Paradoxically, this was partly due to resistance to Wagner in Italy.[65] His reformist agenda was criticized primarily on nationalist grounds and unfavorably compared to Italian melodiousness. This meant that the normative assessment of Italian opera vis-à-vis German opera had changed, but this discourse was based on a comparison of national styles, as was the case in Germany.

In France, resistance to German opera was even institutionalized. The Société nationale de musique attempted to counter German opera and instrumental music with an organic French tradition. However, public curiosity eventually undermined the boycott of Wagner imposed in response to his chauvinistic comments in 1870–1871. When *Lohengrin* was staged at the Palais Garnier in 1891, it was a major posthumous triumph for the composer. Fifty performances took place in the first six months of that year alone, and they were followed by another hundred in the next two years.[66] In the beginning of the 1890s, the resistance to Wagner also faded in Milan, where public sentiment was against him for a long time. Still, Wagner operas were staged in Paris or Milan as definitive expressions of German culture. Just as in Germany, the productions employed nationalist imagery. The same is true of contemporary productions of Smetana, Mussorgsky (who replaced Glinka abroad as *the* Russian composer), Moniuszko, and other national composers.

Present-day producers and audiences usually do not ascribe a specific national meaning to these composers' operas, but in the late nineteenth and early twentieth century, both a national interpretation and appropriation were common. This "internationalism of national cultures" dominated the European opera theaters until the postwar period. Paradoxically, the national interpretation did not affect the language of productions. In continental Europe the works discussed here were performed in translation. This practice—the nationalization of the performance language—remained the norm until the postwar period.

This chapter has shown that the creation of national opera in various European countries that range from Germany to Russia was dependent on the context of the national movements, as well as their reception of music in general and opera in particular. Opera was imbued with extramusical content that greatly influenced the production on stage, the reception, and eventually also the aesthetic choices of the individual composers. These three phenomena need to be studied in both a local and a national context. Still, one should not forget the pivotal role of responses abroad.

Wagner's fame as *the* national German composer and Smetana's sacralization were also shaped by their international reception. In Wagner's case, the rejection in Paris created solidarity in Germany, which preceded his breakthrough as national composer with the premiere of the *Meistersinger* in 1868. Smetana's oeuvre was in quantitative decline in the newly opened Czech National Theater throughout the 1880s. In his case the success of the National Theater opera ensemble at the International Music and Theater Exhibition in Vienna in 1892 secured him a universal acceptance as a symbol of national culture. As in the case of Verdi, the ascension of these composers into the pantheon of national heroes was not a linear process but took place mostly toward the end of their life or even after their death.

This canonization turned out to be a straitjacket for the next generation of composers, especially in central Europe. In Germany only Richard Strauss managed to overcome the focus on national myths and plots and the musical "Wagnerism." In the Czech lands, Hungary and Poland, it took the work of musical modernists such as Leoš Janáček, Bela Bartók, and Karol Szymanowski to unmantle the national canon. They all started out eager to discover the "true" national music in rural regions, but the early ethnomusicology these modernists carried out destroyed the national canon from within. Because of their work, it became clear that the previous national style had been a contrivance. They demonstrated with their specific styles that a single national canon cannot exist and that the culture of small nations must be built upon a stylistic pluralism.

Moreover, there always was a deviation from the nationalization of opera on the western fringes of Europe. Instead of inventing their own tradition, the English opera theaters and public chose to import the most popular works, to hire the greatest stars, and to prefer the original language. In spite of demands in the press for the creation of "American music," the United States also refrained from developing its own tradition of "classical" music or opera prior to World War I. A window of opportunity for this appeared when Antonin Dvořák was invited to the East Coast of the United States in 1893 and proposed during his stay to build national American music on the rhythms and melodies of the former slaves. However, the contemporary American elites considered it inconceivable to thus elevate the "negro melodies" that Dvořák cherished.[67] The refusal of the Metropolitan Opera and of the Covent Garden opera to nationalize the opera languages and to foster an indigenous repertoire clearly distinguished them from the opera theaters in continental Europe. This cosmopolitanism had a price: Because of the competition from international opera, English and American composers found it very difficult to achieve the same status and popularity as Wagner, Glinka, or Smetana.[68]

However, should this be perceived as a deficit, as it was by contemporary American intellectuals and music critics? If music history is understood in terms of linear progress, as in much of the traditional literature,[69] then indeed the development of a national school of music might have appeared to be a pivotal stage of development. However, composers from countries that missed this "stage" went on to produce especially successful modern operas in the twentieth century. A case to be made here is that of England and Benjamin Britten, which may have happened because the opera market was not yet dominated by a traditional canon as it was in Italy and Germany. To put this speculation in more philosophical terms: Sometimes latecomers can be newcomers, and it is certainly easier to develop a new genre of opera if the market of music theater is not strongly dominated by an already existing canon. Still, these considerations require one to think in terms of temporal circles instead of linear time. This was alien to nineteenth-century agents of music, whether they were composers, critics, or musicologists. Therefore, the development of a national canon was perceived as a matter of catching up, of being among the most "civilized" nations, and of acquiring power in fields other than opera or music.

DIFFERENTIATION AND CONVERGENCE

In abstract terms, the nationalization of opera can be understood as a process of differentiation.[70] National opera traditions emerged in the course of the nineteenth century first in Germany, then in Russia, Poland, Hungary, Bohemia, Croatia, Ukraine, and eventually after the turn of century in Georgia, Azerbaijan, Turkey and other countries on the fringes of Europe. Italian opera was nationalized as well despite having been a universal genre. However, because opera was nationalized almost everywhere, this process of differentiation resulted paradoxically in a convergence in various European countries and cultures.

Even Wagner was acknowledged as part of a universal culture, and his oeuvre began to occupy a more permanent place in European and global opera repertoires. Verdi, who was a much less antagonistic figure, also held an exceptional position. Every leading opera house regularly produced at least three or four of his works. The standard repertoire around the turn of the century also contained selected grand operas, a few more recent French works such as *Faust* and *Carmen*, and a small selection of bel canto operas. Then there were two newcomers, who are often lumped together as "Slavic opera." Czech opera became a huge success in the late nineteenth century throughout central Europe and was even exported to New York. Russian opera was at first exported only to Prague but was transferred from there to various German and Austrian opera houses. Prior to the First World War, it appealed to even wider audiences in Paris, London and New York.

Along with these international genres, the continental European opera houses cultivated their respective national repertoires. In Germany, central Europe, and the Russian Empire, the share of homegrown works ranged from one-quarter to one-half, depending on the city and the period. Even though national traditions failed to surpass imported works in terms of popularity in some countries like Poland and Hungary, the respective national operas served an important representative function. Works such as *Halka* would open the opera season in Warsaw, Lemberg or Poznań, and the country's elites would gather at the event to celebrate the official national culture.

The aforementioned convergence of opera repertoires was not merely a matter of repertoire statistics. In Paris and Milan, the staging of Wagner was just as Germanic as it was in Berlin and Bayreuth. Other sets became standardized as well, showing, for example, Mediterranean landscapes with or without the sea, mountain ranges, mediaeval towns, castles, and banquet halls.[71] Even the sets of the national operas were interchangeable, as the example of Prague shows. For example, the castle and mediaeval town used for *Libuše* in the National Theater in 1883 looked very similar to the sets used for *Lohengrin* in 1885. This is remarkable because, more than any other Smetana work, *Libuše* glorified the Czech nation and was therefore used for the opening of the National Theater, whereas *Lohengrin* was seen as a symbol of German national opera.

This phenomenon attests to the aesthetic limits of nationalism. The prose works of Wagner, of the Russian composers organized in the Mogučaja kučka, and the anti-Wagnerians in Italy and France contain numerous insights into what a respective national opera culture should *not* be. However, it was far harder to implement the concept of "Germanness," of Russian "narodnost" and of "French civilization" in compositions and even more so on stage. Moreover, a comparison of the various and presumably unique national schools of music shows that supposedly specific national rhythms and harmonies can be identified in several European musical cultures. The structural similarity of these invented national traditions helps us to understand why they were increasingly exchanged after the end of the nineteenth century. Even composers who had a clear nationalist mission still used a musical language that was compatible with European stylistic conventions of opera.

A further key element in the convergence of European opera repertoires was the decline in premieres and the growing significance of a musical canon. Prior to the late nineteenth century, opera repertoires were dominated by novelties, like today's cinema. The concept of "classics"[72] (i.e., of canonized pieces of art created in earlier periods) was not universally accepted. However, around the 1880s a change took place, and again the concept of national opera schools played an important, if paradoxical, role. None of the national composers, not even

Wagner, could fulfill the great demand of the contemporary audiences for novelties. Therefore, the musical nationalists looked to the past to create a canon of
national operas.

Newspapers and journals played a major role in canonizing opera first in Europe
and then on a global level. In the period between 1815 and 1848, for example, the
Wiener Allgemeine Theaterzeitung and the *Allgemeine Musikalische Zeitung* from
Leipzig had correspondents who reported about productions in Paris, Vienna, and
Milan, as well as in smaller towns such as Lemberg and Riga. The aforementioned
journals were not aimed merely at musicians and composers but also the broader
public. Although the content of many articles was nationalist and sometimes even
xenophobic, music journals represented the nucleus of a European public sphere.[73]

The invention of mass media, railways, and steamboats greatly accelerated the
pace of cultural exchange after the mid-nineteenth century. International reception
of new operas could gain momentum within months even though the libretti were
usually translated. A good example is Richard Strauss's *Der Rosenkavalier*. The
Czech premiere in Prague took place barely six months after the world premiere in
Dresden in 1911.[74] That same year, the Italian version premiered in Milan, and the
Hungarian version in Budapest, and the following season a Polish version opened
in Lemberg. The opera premiered in the original German in London and New York,
which again confirms the different, more cosmopolitan path of music theater in
England and the United States.

Contacts between directors, singers, and musicians across Europe are too
numerous to be dealt with here in detail. Regular trips to Milan, Paris, and Vienna
were part and parcel of life for theater directors. In the late nineteenth century,
musical metropolises such as Prague or Dresden also drew opera professionals from
around Europe. Rich opera consumers increasingly traveled through Europe. Opera
tourism took off around the turn of the century, and special trips were organized to
premieres and major guest performances. Cultural exchanges were crucial for a
convergence of the ways music was enjoyed. As James Johnson has demonstrated
for Paris, people stopped drinking, eating, and chatting during performances in the
early nineteenth century and began to listen to music as present-day audiences do.
Sitting still and concentrating on the music first became the norm in Vienna and
Berlin as well. These cities later became models when it came to how a "civilized"
audience was supposed to behave.[75]

The exponentially increasing cultural exchanges transformed the mapping of
European culture. A novel geographic imagination crept especially into journals
and newspapers in eastern Europe and outside of Europe. In the 1880s, for example,
the Warsaw journal *Echo Muzyczne, Teatralne, i Artystyczne (EMTA)* began publishing a column titled "From Europe."[76] It featured news of premieres, singers, and
guest performances on the entire continent. In the United States newspapers such
as the *New York Times* came to use a similar mental mapping. Although opera was
divided into national traditions, it was perceived as a European art and thereby
essentialized as being European. Therefore, one can speak about a Europeanization
in terms of structural convergence and discourse.

Repertoires in New York were organized accordingly. In its first ten years, the Metropolitan Opera (Met) alternated between Italian and German seasons. This was less an ideological than a financial move because German singers were much cheaper at the time. After 1897 operas were generally performed in their original language because the New York audiences wanted to import the best traditions and casts Europe had to offer.[77] The Met also had the money to pay for this internationalization. At times it employed three choruses, an Italian, a German, and a French one, and it was able to pay much higher honorariums for singers than the best-known theaters in continental Europe. In London the opera business worked in similar fashion, which suggests that in fact England was more similar to the United States in terms of opera history than it was to continental Europe. For many years, the commonalities between London and New York went beyond matters of taste. Between 1897 and 1903 both Covent Garden and the Metropolitan Opera were directed by the Maurice Grau Opera Company.[78] Grau had made his fame and fortune as an impresario initially in New York, where he had codirected the Met since 1891. Hence, the opera business in New York had already influenced Europe. Apart from London, Grau and the Met controlled the opera business in the United States. The New York opera company offered extended opera seasons in Philadelphia and Boston and shorter seasons in several cities in the Midwest.

One can conclude from these examples that obviously there is not *one* European history of opera. Therefore, one also should be careful not to overgeneralize about the nationalization of opera, which affected continental Europe most intensively. The London opera theaters and the Metropolitan Opera were much more internationally oriented and hired the most expensive singers and world-famous conductors, such as Gustav Mahler and Arturo Toscanini (who played a key role in establishing a modern operatic canon in New York). It was simple enough to attract and import these stars. By the end of the nineteenth century, New York could be reached within a week by ocean liner, and the pay at the Met for the singing stars was two to four times higher than in Vienna or Milan.[79]

It still requires research to find out why opera eventually became more international in continental Europe as well. Until the 1960s, the nationalization of opera still dominated continental Europe. Operas were mostly translated and sung in the language of the country where the theater of performance was located.[80] Musicology and musical journalism were centered on the respective national traditions and supported this line. Even today, standard opera guides and academic literature are organized in national divisions like Italian, French, and German opera, at least in the sections dealing with the nineteenth century and, hence, the period that dominates the global repertoires.[81]

However, over the postwar period, a pivotal change occurred in the global opera market. From the 1960s first in western Europe and then also in central and eastern Europe, productions in the original language became more common and set artistic standards. Opera returned to its cosmopolitan roots for several reasons. First, opera stars traveled even more than before, particularly over the Atlantic. This pointed to financial reasons, especially the meager budgets of theaters in Europe after World

War II. The relative attraction of opera theaters in the United States was greater than ever before. Because of this increased international exchange, theaters on the continent found it more difficult to keep their stars at home. Second, once the international star system became dominant, it made more sense to produce operas in the language in which the soloists could sing them best. This was usually the original language and not a translated version, or could anybody have attracted Maria Callas to sing Verdi in German because his operas were staged in Berlin or Munich? The Americans and the English were looked down upon by continental Europeans, especially by German cultural elites, for a long time for not having an indigenous opera tradition.[82] However, in the postwar period the language cosmopolitanism of Covent Garden and the Met celebrated a late victory.

Last but not least, beginning in the postwar period, the canonized national operas came to be interpreted differently than before. In Germany, an important reason was the catastrophe wrought by National Socialism. Even strongholds of musical nationalism like the Festspiele in Bayreuth had to drop their traditional interpretation of Wagner. In Russia and Czechoslovakia, nationalist interpretations of operas such as *Ivan Susanin* (the renamed and rewritten version of Glinka's *Žyzn za tsaria*) and *Braniboři v Čechach* were revived during and after World War II, but the de-Stalinization put an end to the crudest interpretations. The post-nationalist interpretations of works such as the *Meistersinger* and *Boris Godunov* attracted large audiences. The nationalization of the singing language prevailed for a longer time under communism. However, in today's global opera industry, theaters that deliberately choose to sign in only one language are exceptions. In certain respects, a circle of history that we can call the age of national opera came to an end in the 1960s.

Summing up, this chapter has shown that nationalism shaped many of the features of opera history, as well as its institutional and artistic levels. One can observe a nationalization of repertoires, plots, the singing language, and in part the visual production. The share of indigenous work in the repertoires of opera theaters in continental Europe rose from a marginal position in the eighteenth century to a half in some countries (Germany and Bohemia) and to about a quarter in Poland, Hungary, and Croatia. This process of nationalization not only was a result of the context of the "age of nationalism" (Hobsbawm) but also was driven by music critics and composers. However, even in countries with a strong cultural nationalism the "original production" never reached a monopoly. Still, the nationalization of opera east of the Rhine challenged and changed the previous international genres such as Italian and French opera, which were increasingly perceived as one of many national schools.

The nationalization of opera was symbolized by the creation of national opera as a representative genre. The success of this genre and subsequently of canonized national styles can only partially be explained by an internalist perspective on single national contexts. It is important to take into account the international reception of national operas and styles. Although this at first appears to be a paradox, national operas and composers gained status through their reception abroad. While the previous German- and English-language literature has restricted the discussion of national operas for eastern Europe and left out Germany, this chapter has shown that Wagner cannot be omitted in the discussion of national opera and the nationalization of opera on other levels. Although the nationalization of opera waned after World War II, one cannot ignore its heavy impact on opera even today.

NOTES

1. For this term see E. Hobsbawm and T. Ranger, eds., *The Invention of Tradition* (New York: Cambridge University Press, 1983).

At several international conventions and conferences colleagues from history and musicology have brought the topic of the nationalization of opera up for discussion. I would like to thank the members of the "Potential for a 'Musical Turn' in the Study of Modern Eastern Europe" roundtable at the Thirty-sixth National Convention of the American Association for the Advancement of Slavic Studies (AAASS), 2004, in Boston; of the symposium "Musik in der Geschichte: Gesellschaft, Musik, und kulturelle Nationsbildung im 'langen' 19. Jahrhundert" at the International Convention of the Gesellschaft für Musikforschung on "Musik und Kulturelle Identität," 2004, in Weimar, and the panel "Geschichte als Oper: Die Konstruktion und Inszenierung von Geschichte im europäischen Musiktheater des 19. Jahrhunderts" at the Forty-sixth German Historikertag, 2006 (see a report about this panel at http://hsozkult.geschichte.hu-berlin.de/tagungsberichte/id=1177. On the basis of my own research a book with the title *In der Mitte der Gesellschaft: Operntheater in Zentraleuropa 1815–1914* (Vienna: Oldenbourg, 2006) has been published. This book also contains a chapter on the nationalization of opera.

2. An excellent overview of this approach appears in Michel Espagne, *Les transferts culturels franco-allemands* (Paris: PUF, 1999).

3. For the methodological basis of the study of cultural transfers, see the original concept developed by Michel Espagne and Michael Werner, "La construction d'une référence culturelle allemande en France: genèse et histoire (1750–1914)," in *Annales* ESC (July–Aug. 1987): 969–92; Michel Espagne *and* Michael Werner, eds., *Transferts: Les relations interculturelles dans l'espace franco-allemand (XVIII e XIX siècle)* (Paris: Editions Recherche sur les civilizations, 1988).

4. Quoted in Theophil Antonicek, "Biedermeierzeit und Vormärz," in *Musikgeschichte Österreichs*, vol. 2, ed. Rudolf Flotzinger and Gernot Gruber, 217 (Graz: Styria Verlag, 1979). For this utopia of unity see also Lothar Gall, *Bürgertum in Deutschland* (Berlin: Siedler Verlag, 1989), 201, 213; Christoph Trilse, "Eduard Devrient und die Geschichte des bürgerlichen Theaters," in Eduard Devrient, *Geschichte der deutschen Schauspielkunst*, ed. R. Kabel and C. Trilse, vol. 2, 425–63, 435 (Munich: Henschel, 1967).

5. Quoted in "'...Ein in sich abgeschlossenes Kunstwerk': Vorbemerkungen zu einer Geschichte der Dresdner Oper im 19. Jahrhundert," in *Die Dresdner Oper im 19. Jahrhundert*, ed. Michael Heinemann and Hans John, 7–12, 8 (Laaber: Laaber Verlag, 1995).

6. See Celia Applegate, "The Internationalism of Nationalism: Adolf Bernhard Marx and German Music in the Mid-nineteenth Century," in *Journal of Modern European History* 5(1) (2007): 139–59.

7. Quoted from Hans-Joachim Hinrichsen, "Johann Nikolaus Forkel und die Anfänge der Bachforschung," in *Bach und die Nachwelt*, vol. 1: 1750– 1850, ed. Michael Heinemann and Hans-Joachim Hinrichsen, 193–254, 241 (Laaber: Laaber Verlag, 1997).

8. For Brendel see Hans-Joachim Hinrichsen, "Ferdinand Hillers Dresdner Opern und Richard Wagner," in Heinemann and John, *Die Dresdner Oper*, 251–70, 253.

9. "Opera and Drama" is printed in Richard Wagner, *Sämtliche Schriften und Dichtungen* (hereafter SSD), 12 vols. (Leipzig 1912–1914), here vol. 3, 223–320, and vol. 4, 1–229. In English Wagner's prose works are accessible at the virtual Wagner library: http://users.belgacom.net/wagnerlibrary/. This article refers to the German original only.

10. See, for example, the publications by Udo Bermbach, especially *Der Wahn des Gesamtkunstwerks: Richard Wagners politisch-ästhetische Utopie* (Frankfurt/Main: Fischer Taschenbuch Verlag, 1994).

11. For Wagner's German nationalism see Hannu Salmi, *Imagined Germany: Richard Wagner's National Utopia* (Frankfurt/Main: Peter Lang, 1999).

12. Richard Wagner, "Bericht über die Heimbringung der sterblichen Überreste Karl Maria von Webers aus London nach Dresden," in SSD, vol. 2, 41–49. For the event see also a report in the Leipziger Zeitung, quoted in Eckhard Kröplin, "Wagner und Weber: Der Vorgang einer Theatralisierung," in *Carl Maria von Weber und der Gedanke der Nationaloper: Wissenschaftliche Konferenz im Rahmen der Dresdner Musikfestspiele 1986*, ed. Günter Stephan and Hans John, 336–44, 339 (Dresden: Agenda Verlag, 1987).

13. For the pompous celebration of this event see Tage-Buch des Königlich Sächsischen Hof-Theaters 1894, 89–90. (The annual "diaries" of the Court Theater in Dresden were published between 1819 and 1917 and are a great source of information on the repertoire, festive events, and everyday life.)

14. For the repertoire statistics under Wagner see Robert Prölls, *Geschichte des Hoftheaters zu Dresden: Von seinen Anfängen bis zum Jahre 1862* (Dresden, 1878), 541, 644–46.

15. See Richard Wagner, "Entwurf zur Organisation eines deutschen National-Theaters für das Königreich Sachsen (1849)," in SSD, vol. 2, 233–73, 270.

16. See "Oper und Drama," in Wagner, SSD, vol. 3, 223–320, and vol. 4, 1–229. Volume 3 also contains the essays "Kunstwerk der Zukunft" and "Die Kunst und die Revolution." Particularly interesting is also "Ein Theater in Zürich," in SSD, vol. 5, 20–52. In this essay Wagner developed an artistic program for an opera theater.

17. See Marc A. Weiner, *Richard Wagner and the Anti-Semitic Imagination* (Lincoln: University of Nebraska Press, 1995).

18. For the discourse on the practice of national styles in Europe see Helga de la Motte-Haber, Nationaler Stil und europäische Dimension in der Musik der Jahrhundertwende (Darmstadt: Wissenschaftliche Buchgesellschaft, 1991).

19. See "Die schwäbische Sängerbewegung in der Gesellschaft des 19. Jahrhunderts: Ein Beitrag zur kulturellen Nationsbildung," in Dieter Langewiesche, *Nation, Nationalismus, Nationalstaat in Deutschland und Europa* (Munich: C.H. Beck, 2000), 132–71.

20. "Was ist des Deutschen Vaterland? So weit die deutsche Zunge klingt und Gott im Himmel Lieder singt," *Dresdner Journal* (July 25, 1865), 3. The presence of so many attenders from Austria casts doubt on Dieter Langewiesche's thesis, namely, that the Austrian Germans participated only slightly in the singers' movement and hence in the German national movement.

21. Sollte—Gott wird es verhüten—noch einmal diese überall sich regende Begeisterung deutsch-nationalen Strebens, trotz seiner Achtung vor Gesetz und Recht, mit Gewalt zu Boden geworfen werden, dann, deutsche Sänger . . . laßt unsre Lieder uns dann anstimmen und fortsingen durch alle deutsche Gauen hin, und brauchts auch Zeit, ist es dennoch gewiß: die Unterdrücker unsers nationalen Glaubens werden bekehrt sich davon schleichen wie der Henker der Cäcilie einst von ihren heiligen Liedern. In diesem Sinne und Geiste rufe ich hinein in diesen großen Sängerkreis: "Herz und Lied, frisch, frei,

gesund! Wahr' dir's Gott, du deutscher Sängerbund"—Amen. (speech by Professor Fricke from Leipzig, quoted in *Dresdner Journal* (July 26, 1865): 2–3)

22. For Bohemia see Christopher Storck, *Kulturnation und Nationalkunst: Strategien und Mechanismen tschechischer Nationsbildung von 1860 bis 1914* (Cologne: Verlag Wissenschaft und Politik, 2001), 266. For Galicia see Joanna Tokarz, "Kultura muzyczna Galicji," in *Galicja i jej dziedzictwo, vol. 4* (Rzeszów: Wydawnictwo Wyższej Szkoły Pedagogicznej, 1995), 155–64.

23. For the contemporary concept of folksongs see Carl Dahlhaus, *Die Musik des 19. Jahrhunderts* (Laaber, Germany: Laaber Verlag, 19892), 87–92. As Dahlhaus points out, the so called folk (and in fact folkloristic) music was mostly an urban invention. Hence, it needs to be deconstructed like the term "nation". There also is an English version of Dahlhaus's fundamental work, which could not be consulted for this chapter.

24. For this term see Langewiesche, *Nation, Nationalismus, Nationalstaat*, 82 f.

25. For the definition of nation and nationalism used here see Benedict Anderson, *Imagined Communities: Reflections on the Origin and Spread of Nationalism*, 2d ed. (London: Verso, 1990).

26. For the discourse on national theaters in Germany see Ther, *In der Mitte*, 36–45.

27. Quoted in Jerzy Got, *Das österreichische Theater in Lemberg im 18. und 19. Jahrhundert: Aus dem Theaterleben der Vielvölkermonarchie*, vol. 2 (Vienna: Verlag der Österreichischen Akademie der Wissenschaften, 1997), 720. See also a similar article in the journal *Nowiny* (Dec. 20, 1867, Dec. 27, 1867, and Jan. 3, 1868).

28. For the importance of the theater for the Czech national movement see Vladimír Macura, *Znamení zrodu: České národní obrození jako kulturní typ* (Prague: Pražska imaginace, 1992), 191–200.

29. See the original document in F. A. Šubert, *Národní divadlo v Praze: Dějiny jeho i stavba dokončena* (Prague, 1881), 17.

30. On the foundation of the national theater see Ther, *In der Mitte*, 260–68.

31. This estimation was given by the Polish Gazeta Narodowa (May 19, 1868), 1. Some Czech papers mentioned even higher numbers but may have exaggerated.

32. See the complete overview of the procession in Storck, *Kulturnation*, 223.

33. On the New German Theater see Alena Jakubcová, Jítka Ludvová, Václav Maidl (eds)., *Deutschsprachiges Theater in Prag: Begegnungen der Sprachen und Kulturen* (Prague: Divadelni Ústav, 2001).

34. On Catalan cultural associations and the Palau de la Música Catalana see Joan-Lluís Marfany, *La cultura del catalanisme: El nationalisme catala en els seus inicis* (Barcelona: Editorial Empúries, 1995), 307–78.

35. On the Estonian singer and theater movement see Jaak Rähesoo, *Estonian Theatre*, 2d ed. (Tallinn:, Estonian Theatre Union, 2003).

36. See Dahlhaus, Musik im 19. Jahrhundert, 181–90; Wulf Konold, "Nationale Bewegungen und Nationalopern im 19. Jahrhundert," in *Der schöne Abglanz: Stationen der Operngeschichte*, ed. Udo Bermbach and Wulf Konold, 111–28 (Hamburg: Reimer Verlag: 1992).

37. For the reception of *Tannhäuser* in the 1840s see Otto Schmid, *Richard Wagners Opern und Musikdramen in Dresden* (Dresden, 1919), 22f.

38. On the national contents of Lohengrin see Udo Bermbach, Wo Macht ganz auf Verbrechen ruht. Politik und Gesellschaft in der Oper (Hamburg: Europäische Verlagsanstalt, 1997), 220.

39. See Richard Wagner, *Lohengrin: Oper in drei Akten. Klavierauszug mit Text von Felix Mottl*, Peters Edition no. 3401 (Frankfurt/Main, undated), 257.

40. See Lohengrin, Klavierauszug, erster Aufzug, bars 24, 72, and 96. Hans Mayer has observed that in the *Meistersinger* Wagner used C major again in the opera, wherever the topic was Germany and its greatness. See Hans Mayer, *Richard Wagner: Mitwelt und Nachwelt* (Stuttgart: Belser, 1978), 148.

41. On this scandal in Paris see Jane Fulcher, French Grand Opera, 191–93. On the reception of *Tannhäuser* in Dresden see Martin Gregor-Dellin, Richard Wagner: *Sein Leben, sein Werk, sein Jahrhundert* (München: Piper, 1983), 469.

42. See Thomas Grey, "*Die Meistersinger* as National Opera (1868–1945)," in *Music and German National Identity*, ed. Celia Applegate and Pamela Potter, 78–104 (Chicago: University Of Chicago Press, 2002).

43. Richard Wagner, *Die Meistersinger von Nürnberg: Klavierauszug mit Text von Gustav F. Kogel*, Peters Edition no. 3408), (Frankfurt, undated), 201.

44. On the Germanic myth see Rainer Kipper, *Der Germanenmythos im Deutschen Kaiserreich: Formen und Funktionen historischer Selbstthematisierung* (Göttingen: Vandenhoeck & Ruprecht, 2002).

45. On the *Folkunger* see Michael Heinemann, "Alternative zu Wagner? Edmund Kretschmars *Die Folkunger* in der zeitgenössischen Kritik," in Heinemann and John, *Die Dresdner Oper im 19. Jahrhundert*, 295–302.

46. Quoted from a review of the opera *Armin* in *Dresdner Journal* (Oct. 16, 1877), 1–2.

47. See the positive review of this style in *Dresdner Journal* (May 16, 1885), 1.

48. The breakthrough was made through Chereau's *Ring* in 1976. For the productions of the Ring see Udo Bermbach, "'Des Sehens ewige Lust': Einige Stationen der *Ring*-Deutungen seit 1876," in *"Alles ist nach seiner Art": Figuren in Richard Wagners "Der Ring des Nibelungen,"* ed. Udo Bermbach, 1–26, 14–15 (Stuttgart: J.B. Metzler Verlag, 2001).

49. For the relationship between mythology and history see Petra-Hildegard Wilberg, *Richard Wagners mythische Welt: Versuche wider den Historismus* (Freiburg: Rombach, 1996), 17–21, 149–80.

50. See Richard Wagner, "Die Wibelungen: Weltgeschichte aus der Sage," in *SSD*, Bd. 2, 115–65, 123.

51. *Der Kunstwart* 1 (1887): 121–25.

52. See *Opernstatistik für das Jahr 1894: Verzeichnis der vom 1. Januar bis zum 31. Dezember 1894 in Deutschland und auf den deutschen Bühnen Oesterreichs, der Schweiz, und Russlands aufgeführten Opern*, comp. M. Friedlaender (Leipzig, 1895).

53. On the société see Michael Strasser, *Ars Gallica: The Société Nationale de Musique and Its Role in French Musical Life* (Urbana: UMI, 1998); see also Michel Duchesneau, *L'avant-garde musicale et ses sociétés à Paris de 1871 à 1939* (Sprimont: Mardaga, 1997), 15–17.

54. See Helga de la Motte-Haber, *Nationaler Stil und europäische Dimension in der Musik der Jahrhundertwende* (Darmstadt: Wissenschaftliche Buchgesellschaft, 1991), 47.

55. On this opera see David Brown, *Mikhail Glinka: A Biographical and Critical Study* (London: Oxford University Press, 1974), 91–136. On the problem of national expression in music see Richard Taruskin, Defining Russia Musically: Historical and Hermeneutical Essays (Princeton: Princeton University Press, 1997).

56. For the dramatic function of elements of national style in Russian, Czech, and Polish opera see John Tyrrell, "Russian, Czech, Polish, and Hungarian Opera to 1900," in *The Oxford History of Opera*, ed. Roger Parker, 157–86, 163–74 (New York: Oxford University Press, 1996).

57. This is how Piotr Čaikovskii reported the event in a letter to his brother dated April 1866. Quoted in Siegrid Neef, Hermann Neef (eds.), *Handbuch der russischen und sowjetischen Oper* (Berlin: Henschelverlag Kunst und Gesellschaft, 1985), 193.

58. The most comprehensive biography of Moniuszko is now Rüdiger Ritter, *Musik für die Nation: Der Komponist Stanisław Moniuszko (1819–1872) in der polnischen Nationalbewegung des 19. Jahrhunderts* (Frankfurt/Main: Peter Lang, 2005). For further information on Moniuszko also see Ther, *In der Mitte*, 231–41, 396, 374.

59. See the reports of the opera and the production in *Dziennik Polski* (Jan. 20, 1877, 2, and Jan. 21, 1877, 1). The very last sentence in the review is a quotation from the national anthem, "Jeszcze Polska nie zginela."

60. For the "Rezeptionserwartung" on a theoretical level see Hans Robert Jauß, "Rückschau auf die Rezeptionstheorie: Ad usum Musicae Scientiae," in *Rezeptionsästhetik und Rezeptionsgeschichte in der Musikwissenschaft*, ed. Hermann Danuser and Friedhelm Krummacher, 13–36 (Laaber, Germany: Laaber Verlag, 1991).

61. See Vladimir Macura, *Znamení zrodu*, 197.

62. On the earlier usage and political meaning of choruses in Italian and French opera see Philip Gossett, "Becoming a Citizen: The Chorus in Risorgimento Opera," *Cambridge Opera Journal* 2 (1990): 41–64; Fulcher, French Grand Opera, 40–42. The way Smetana used his chorus dramatically and musically in *Braniboři v Čechach* brings to mind the example of Italian opera, especially Bellini's *I Puritani*. However, transfers from Italian opera in his work are much less researched than Smetena's alleged Wagnerism, which caused deep public conflicts over his work.

63. For the conflict over Smetana's presumable Wagnerism see Marta Ottlová and Milan Pospíšil, *Bedřich Smetana a jeho doba* (Prague,: Nakladatelství Lidové noviny; 1997), 96. On the conflict in English see Brian S. Locke, *Opera and Ideology in Prague: Polemics and Practice at the National Theatre 1900–1938* (Rochester. University of Rochester Press, 2006), 23–28.

64. For the reception of Smetana's music see Vlasta Reittererová and Hubert Reitterer, "*Vier Dutzend rothe Strümpfe…*": Zur Rezeptionsgeschichte der Verkauften Braut von Bedřich Smetana in Wien am Ende des 19. Jahrhunderts* (Vienna: Verlag der Österreichischen Akademie der Wissenschaften., 2004).

65. For the reception of Wagner in Italy see Ute Jung, *Die Rezeption der Kunst Richard Wagners in Italien* (Regensburg: Gustav Bosse Verlag, 1974).

66. For the repertoire statistics at the Opéra Garnier see Stephane Wolff, L'opéra au Palais Garnier (1875–1962) (Paris: Deposé au journal L'Entracte, 1962), 134–35. For the appropriation of Wagner by French composers in the late nineteenth and early twentieth centuries see Jane Fulcher, *French Cultural Politics and Music from the Dreyfus Affair to the First World War* (London: OUP, 1999), 66–71, 104–108.

67. For Dvořák's proposal and contemporary reactions see Joseph Horowitz, "Dvořák and the New World: A Concentrated Moment," in *Dvořák and His World*, ed. Michael Beckerman, (Princeton: Princeton University Press, 1993) 92–103, 96.

68. This was noted even by contemporary critics. See the (fruitless) demands for creating an American tradition of opera in "The New Plays, "*Harper's Weekly* (Dec. 30, 1905); and "Ten Million Dollars Paid to Foreign Musicians," *New York Times* (Nov. 10, 1907). See also *Metropolitan Opera Archive*' William J. Henderson Scrapbook, vol. 10, Nov. 2, 1900–Mar. 2, 1902, esp. Dec. 2, "Americanism in Music".

69. For this debate in Germany see Vladimir Karbusicky's criticism of one of the doyens of postwar musicology in West Germany, Hans Heinrich Eggebrecht. Vladimir Karbusicky, *Wie deutsch ist das Abendland? Geschichtliches Sendungsbewußtsein im Spiegel der Musik* (Hamburg: Von Bocker Verlag, 1995).

70. For this term see Niklas Luhmann, "Differentiation of Society," in *Canadian Sociological Review* 2 (1977): 29–53.

71. For the convergence of repertoires, stage sets, and directing see Peter Stachel and Philipp Ther, eds., *Wie europäisch ist die Oper?* Geschichte des Musiktheaters als Zugang zu einer kulturellen Topographie Europas (Vienna: Oldenbourg/Böhlau, 2009) See Gesa zur Nieden, Vom *Grand Spectacle* zur *Great Season*. Das Pariser Théâtre du Châtelet als Raum muskalischer Produktion und Rezeption (1862–1914), Wien: Oldenbourg/Böhlau, 2010, 284–300.

72. For the term and its evolution see the extensive article[2] *Ästhetische Grundbegriffe*, ed. Karlheinz Barck/Martin Fontius/Dieter Schlenstedt/Burkhart Steinwachs/Friedrich Wolfzettel, 7 vols. (Stuttgart: J. B. Metzler, 2000–2005), vol. 3, 289–304, and for music 292–93.

73. For the term and history of a European public see Hartmut Kaelble, Europäer über Europa: Die Entstehung des europäischen Selbstverständnisses im 19. und 20. Jahrhundert (Frankfurt/Main: Campus, 2001).

74. On the enthusiastic reception of Strauss see the Czech journal *Dalibor* 32(16–17) (Jan. 27, 1911).

75. See James H. Johnson, *Listening in Paris: A Cultural History* (Berkeley: California University Press, 1995), 228–36.

76. See EMTA, vols. 9, 10, and 18.

77. See Irving Kolodin, *The Metropolitan Opera 1883–1966: A Candid History* (New York: A. A. Knopf, 1966), 128.

78. For this period see Kolodin, *Metropolitan Opera*, 159–98.

79. See *Metropolitan Opera Archive*, Paybook 1908–1909, 116–18.

80. This cultural practice coincides with Charles Maier's periodization of European history and his age of "territorialization." See Charles S. Maier, "Consigning the Twentieth Century to History: Alternative Narratives for the Modern Era," in *American Historical Review* 105 (2000), 807–31.

81. See, for example, Roger Parker, ed., *The Oxford History of Opera* (New York: Oxford University Press, 1996).

82. One of the first major artists who refuted this stereotype was Gustav Mahler. See his positive statement about the cultural life of New York in his first extensive interview to an American newspaper in *Metropolitan Opera Archive*, vol. 10, "Gustav Mahler Amazed by New York's Interest in Art," in *American* (Jan. 21, 1908).

CHAPTER 8

....

COSMOPOLITAN, NATIONAL, AND REGIONAL IDENTITIES IN EIGHTEENTH-CENTURY EUROPEAN MUSICAL LIFE

....

WILLIAM WEBER

MUSIC historians have written a great deal about nationalism, showing how it brought powerful political movements to bear upon musical culture in many contexts. Two issues need to be raised about such discussion. In the first place, the concept of nationalism has come under increasing criticism for imposing conditions found in major states during the twentieth century upon quite different conditions elsewhere or in earlier periods. What exactly do we mean when we use the words "Germany," "Italy," or" Britain"? Benedict Anderson led the rethinking of the concept by showing the great variety of forms it can take in different regions in the same period.[1] In the second place, little has been done to analyze what nationalistic movements *opposed* within musical culture. While musicologists take for granted the primacy of international expectations over styles or repertories, few have asked how such authority was constituted in aesthetic or political terms. The concept of *cosmopolitanism* can help clarify this issue by defining the nature of international authority in musical culture. What were the geographical and musical perimeters of international influence? How did cosmopolitan, national, or other identities compete, and what kinds of compromises were reached between them? How did different types of music compare in all this?

This chapter explores how scholars have defined cosmopolitanism in contrasting ways and then suggests how the concept can be applied to musical life. In order to see how geography played out with cultural authority, I compare how composers from different regions appeared on concert programs in Leipzig, Paris, London, and Vienna during the 1780s. The texts of concert programs enable concise comparison between the repertories performed in different cities. Concerts figured centrally in opera life since overtures, arias, ensemble numbers, and choruses were found in the great majority of concerts during the eighteenth century and indeed much later.[2]

INTERDISCIPLINARY STUDY
OF COSMOPOLITANISM

The concept of cosmopolitanism has contributed in vital ways to historical discussion of either individual thinkers or social frameworks. On the one hand, Amanda Anderson has argued that Charles Dickens, George Eliot, and Oscar Wilde attempted to cultivate intellectual distance through a cosmopolitan order of thinking. Though not inherently hostile to the nation, these thinkers sought impartiality through ethnographic cosmopolitanism to achieve distance from nationally defined discourse.[3] On the other hand, Judith Walkowitz has defined our concept in broad social terms in her study of erotic dancing in London around 1900. Seeing such entertainment as a cosmopolitan "site of pleasure and danger," she shows how orientalist music, costume, and dance broke so decisively with the English theater and its gender roles that such acts were immediately labeled "cosmopolitan."[4]

Cosmopolitanism has also helped analyze long intellectual or social traditions, especially during the early modern period. Scholars and theologians had by tradition done their business on an international basis; networks of thinkers protected them from repressive tendencies locally. In his book on Nicolas-Claude Fabri de Peiresc (1580–1637), Peter Miller goes so far as to speak of a "Republic of Letters" in that period, which made possible "a welcome haven of friendship and sodality" for colleagues from Nuremburg to Rome to London.[5] Eighteenth-century philosophes then took the cosmopolitan republic into the public marketplace more as publicists than as scholars. In an early work on this concept, Thomas J. Schlereth argued that the breadth of the term *cosmopolitanism* makes it better than universalism in defining the ideal or "attitude of mind" that "attempted to transcend chauvinistic national loyalties."[6] That applied to the arts as much as to the philosophy Schlereth studied. Cosmopolitanism was fundamental to structures of authority found in the various arts even though each one defined such a framework in idiosyncratic terms. In 1785, for example, Michel-Paul de Chabanon, wrote that "In their free circulation, the arts lose all of their *indigenous* character; they transform that trait as they mingle it with *foreign* characteristics. In this regard Europe can be thought to be a mother country where all the arts are citizens."[7]

More recent thinking has identified processes of negotiation going on between the cosmopolitan and the domestic in their power relations. In a book on travel narratives and other writings, Matthew Binney argues for a major change in the nature of cosmopolitan thinking at the turn of the eighteenth century. The notion of a cosmic community dating from the ancient Greeks gave way to cosmopolitanism "that respects the foreign and necessitates the acceptance of cultural differences," bringing negotiation between the cosmopolitan and the particular. He defines the old approach as *representative* (as Jürgen Habermas saw the public sphere) and the new one as *complex* and involving *reciprocity*.[8]

Indeed, such interaction went on between cosmopolitan and local identities in musical life. Other scholars have shown how tenuous the union of the cosmopolitan and the particular could be. Adriana Craciun traces the way in which late eighteenth-century English women writers began with a radical cosmopolitan feminism (the "woman philosopher") but shifted toward a nationalistic outlook as the French Revolution heated up public opinion.[9] Anne Mellor demonstrates that an "embodied cosmopolitanism" continued to appear in plays where women married men of other races.[10]

Cosmopolitanism in Musical Culture

We are essentially thinking in a political language when we ask how conflict, negotiation, and reciprocity took place between cosmopolitan and other geographical identities in musical life. Let us be clear about key terms in this discussion. Whereas *international* is a descriptive term to denote repertories performed in multiple regions, *cosmopolitan* carries greater conceptual weight by indicating that such music exerted cultural authority. The term *universalism* is inappropriate here because, as usually employed, it does not involve the political aspect so essential to this discussion. To define geographical identities rivaling the cosmopolitan, one should in mind keep a variety of terms. Since it is problematic to speak of a *national* identity for some regions in the eighteenth century, one might also draw on words such as the *local, regional, domestic,* or, as Chabanon suggested, the *indigenous*. The *national* and the *nationalistic* need also to be differentiated. Whereas a national identity is basically internal in nature, focused on the life of a community, a nationalistic one involves conflict with a larger political or cultural force. The two tendencies could of course mingle in some contexts. National identities tend to be more deeply rooted historically than nationalistic ones but may need the ideology of the latter politically.[11]

Cosmopolitan repertory and taste played a central role in musical life throughout the Western world since at least the late Middle Ages. A region could not exist on its own musically; in choosing what to perform, a musician or a patron almost always had to take cosmopolitan practices into account. Italian opera was itself cosmopolitan since "Italian" was the educated language and different from dialects on the Italian peninsula. By 1720 opera on the Italian model had become what John

Rosselli called "a regular and foremost entertainment" within northern and central Italy and from the Iberian peninsula to London and many cities in central Europe.[12] Operas by Italian composers or set in Italian genres by composers from other countries predominated in the opera repertories of almost all of the major cities. Paris was a special exception since the Académie Royale de Musique departed from French works only in only two short periods (1729–1730 and 1752–1754) until its repertory was fundamentally transformed in the 1770s.[13]

The balance between cosmopolitan and alternate identities in a repertory varied according to the different musical genres. On a certain plane, the balance between nationalities in a repertory arose from the complex of locations where leadership in different genres was based. Whereas Italian music exerted a hegemony over vocal music as a whole from the late seventeenth century on, composers from central Europe—not just the German states—by 1780 tended to dominate instrumental genres, most of all the symphony. No single region dominated the concerto since the far-flung tours of virtuosos made styles from different regions interact with one another so closely.[14] A balance between the domestic and the foreign also usually existed in repertories of sacred music. We thus find that during the eighteenth century opera dominated with a more comprehensive hegemony than was the case with the other major genres. A quite different framework of cosmopolitan repertory emerged as older works deemed "classical" survived in repertories during the first half of the nineteenth century. Even though it was conventional to speak of the classics as German, the music spread so widely around the Western world and attained so high a cultural status that it functioned primarily as a cosmopolitan authority.[15]

Musicians themselves followed cosmopolitan careers in different ways. A composer would move as good opportunities appeared, adapting his music to the needs of a city far from his birthplace by intermingling local and foreign practices. That is how Jean-Baptiste Lully established French opera, Handel crafted the English oratorio, and Luigi Cherubini helped reshape French opera during the revolution of 1789.[16] Less notorious cases also existed. After becoming famous in Dresden, Johann Naumann went to Stockholm in 1786 to set the opera *Gustav Wasa* to a Swedish text about the country's heroic monarch of the early sixteenth century. Naumann followed the French vocal style in this work not only because the court had close relations with France politically but also because he found the style useful to his musical purposes.[17]

THE SOCIAL ASPECTS

The cosmopolitanism of eighteenth-century opera was rooted in the fabric of elite society. Opera houses served as the most important place for public socializing among the upper classes. The authority exerted by opera might indeed be compared to that of the high-quality perfumes, clothing, and spices that had long been imported from the Near East. To be sure, leading aristocratic and bourgeois families had long defined their high status by flaunting the internationalism of their culture. However, that tendency became more pronounced in the middle of the seventeenth century, as elite families began residing for a substantial part of the year in London, Paris, Madrid, and Vienna. By the 1720s the metropolis predominated over the court in upper-class social life in London and Paris. A redistribution of wealth from countryside to capital city thus came about, enabled by the state.[18]

By 1770 London and Paris were arbiters of taste within a larger European culture of consumption. This culture and its social underpinnings, often called the *beau monde* or "The World," were both bourgeois and aristocratic, involving lesser nobles, nontitled landed families, high-level lawyers, theater producers, and influential members of the female demimonde.[19] A new kind of consumer-oriented magazine kept readers informed about elite pleasures—dress, promenading, equipage, politics, theater, and a good deal of Italian opera. Germans, knowing how weak Berlin seemed compared to London or Paris, saw the change with particular clarity while reading the *Journal des Luxus und der Moden*, begun in Weimar in 1787, and the journal *London und Paris* begun in Leipzig in 1798. The latter periodical published articles only from London and Paris.

Other major cities were gradually drawn into the vortex of the two capitals to some extent. By the 1770s Vienna came under the influence of the new upper-class culture of open-ended sociability and discourse. Even though its salons followed the Parisian model as Joseph II allowed greater press freedoms, he retained tight control of the opera, limiting the role of dance as the monarchs of France and England could not think of doing.[20] In Leipzig the concert hall built in the Gewandhaus in 1781 became the social equivalent of the opera. Journalists satirized the public looking through lorgnettes at who wore what, the *haute bourgeoisie* (the women particularly) trying to act like the nobility.[21]

I compare the place of Italian opera in Leipzig, Vienna, London, and Paris by focusing on the status granted foreign and domestic composers in the main opera house. Just how non-Italian composers would function in the principal opera hall was a major issue in every city's musical life, and considerably different policies were followed in the four cities. At the major central European opera houses in Vienna, Dresden, and Berlin, non-Italians—Carl Heinrich Graun, Johann Adolf Hasse, and Christophe Willibald Gluck most of all—rose to prominence by writing Italian operas even though they were necessarily subordinate to Italians such as Domenico Cimarosa and Giovanni Paisiello.[22] A similar balance of regional origins existed in Leipzig, where the absence of a local opera company focused attention on excerpts performed at the Gewandhaus concerts. By contrast, the policies followed in London and Paris went in opposite and extreme directions. In London domestic composers had almost no access to the King's Theatre even though they commanded a public that was passionate about English opera. In Paris the Opéra offered almost exclusively French opera until a housecleaning of repertory made in the 1770s brought the house into line with European cosmopolitanism.

Concert programs illustrate vividly how music by domestic and foreign composers was represented in the four cities. The principle of miscellany dictated that a program maintain contrast and balance in its sequence of pieces. Most basic of all, a public concert had to include both vocal and instrumental pieces, and opera selections were often the center of attention. Two or more examples of the same genre could not occur back to back, and contrast was maintained among male and female singers and soloists playing on different instruments. These practices reflected a deep fascination with virtuosity in its contrasting forms. Voices and instruments had long been thought to depend upon one another in what one musicologist has called the "love duet" inherent in the long tradition of *bel canto*.[23] Around 1785 listeners would flock to concerts to hear a rondo by Domenico Cimarosa followed a violin concerto by Giovanni Viotti. Love of virtuosity made the contrasting genres succeeding one another on a program appear seamless to the attentive listener.

A program also needed to be varied with respect to the regional origins of the composers represented. As a general rule, musicians balanced domestic and foreign names according to which region tended to lead in each genre. It was unusual to put on a program made up of music just from the local region. While it seems strange to find opera selections along with symphonies and sacred pieces, note that songs—the *chanson* or *romance* in France or the lied in German-speaking regions—were not often found on concert programs.

Leipzig

1. *Subscription Concerts, Gewandhaus, Leipzig, November 14, 1782*[24]

Symphony	J. B. Vanhal
Aria, "Io crudele!"	Pasquale Anfossi
Concerto for flute (Herr Vetter)	*? Vetter*
Duet, "Al primo amor fedele," *Perseo* (London 1774)	Antonio Sacchini
—	
Symphony	Carl von Dittersdorf
Aria, "Superbo di me slesso," *Olimpiade* (Dresden 1755)	Hasse
Chorus, *L'italiana in Londra* (Milan 1780)	Cimarosa
Symphony	Antonio Rosetti

A program given at the Leipzig Gewandhaus in 1782 (example 1) was typical of that period.[25] The performance of a duet, an aria, and a chorus illustrates the variety of genres normally chosen, in all cases by leading Italian composers (Cimarosa, Antonio Sacchini, and Pasquale Anfossi). It is notable to find an aria by eighty-three-year-old Hasse from an opera he had composed twenty-seven years before. Operas by Hasse and Graun had survived in the repertory of the Berlin opera and the Gewandhaus concerts until shortly after King Frederick II died in 1786.[26] None of the three symphonies on the program were by Germans. Vanhal grew up in Bohemia but worked in Vienna. Dittersdorf was born in Vienna but had a position in the Silesian city of Jauernig (now Javorník), south of Breslau. Rosetti was Bohemian by birth but adopted an Italian name; he served in a court near Augsburg and promoted his music actively during a trip to Paris in 1781.[27] Finally, the flute concerto may have been composed by the performer, a local musician named Vetter. The Gewandhaus programs did not distinguish between composer and performer until the 1810s.[28]

Nevertheless, a program made up almost entirely of music by German or central European composers did sometimes occur at Advent, Christmas, Passiontide, or Easter. Parts of a mass or an oratorio would be inserted in the two parts of the program. At Advent in 1784 the Gewandhaus subscription concerts offered a Gloria and a Sanctus by a Bohemian, either František Brixi (1743–1771) or Viktorin Brixi (1716–1803). Such a program always had several secular works, in this case a violin concerto and symphonies by Vanhal and Carl Stamitz. Leipzig's Amateur Musical Society (Musikübende Gesellschaft) presented another such program in 1787 (see example 2), borrowing the term *concert spirituel* from the famed Parisian series, as was done widely across Europe. Zimmerman had been born in Silesia in 1741, and Schmidt presumably came from Saxony. However, the organization's programs normally resembled those of the Gewandhaus in focusing on Italian opera, symphonies, and concertos.

2. *Musikübende Gesellschaft, "Concert Spirituel," Leipzig, December 9, 1787*[29]

Symphony	†Anton Zimmermann
65. *Psalm*	Johann Reichardt
—	
Concerto for violin	Schmidt
Overture, Aria, and Chorus, "Tröstet, Tröstet mein Volk,"	†Handel
Messiah	

Pieces from German operas were also occasionally performed at the subscription concerts in Leipzig. Excerpts from operas by Ignaz Holzbauer, an Austrian who served as Kapellmeister in Mannheim, were frequently staged in the mid-1790s, *Günther von Schwarzburg* (1777) most often.[30] Numbers from stage works by Johann Peter Schulz were also presented, chiefly a setting of Racine's *Athalia*. Yet Mozart's German operas were not often performed at the Gewandhaus in the late eighteenth century. While excerpts from his Italian operas were done at least a half dozen times almost every season from 1790 on, only twice did pieces from *Die Zauberflöte* appear on a program until 1832, three decades after the "Private Concerts", a subscription series, in Birmingham offered a duet from what it called *Il flauto magico*.[31] Pieces from *Die Entführung aus dem Serail* appeared six times between 1792 and 1810 but not again until 1835. Mozart indeed puzzled some commentators. In a critical survey of productions done at the Rannstädter Theater in 1783, the author, a military officer, declared that, though fascinated with *Entführung*, he knew nothing like it and was at a loss to evaluate such musical theater.[32]

Even though the Gewandhaus programs always saved room for pieces by German composers, commentators put pressure on the directing board to offer a good deal more. The Leipzig periodical *Olla Potrida* attacked the hegemony of Italian opera in 1779:

> Lully endowed the French with their musical nature during the last century. German music has likewise been in the situation mostly of borrowing from other countries. We differentiate ourselves only by virtue of our careful craftsmanship, proper definition of pieces, and through the depth of feeling with which we endow our music.[33]

The claim made here for "depth of feeling" looks ahead to the self-consciously serious values that journalists such as Robert Schumann articulated in the critique of salon music in the 1830s. Unable to make a claim for fashion, German commentators might stress the seriousness of their region's music. The practice of performing works by German composers in holy seasons lent an intellectual and spiritual distinction to the music of that region and to the sense of a "national" music. Nevertheless, as Schumann was the first to admit, many Germans continued to favor Italian and French opera over the German for the rest of the century.

Vienna

A particularly strong tension existed between local and Italian composers in Vienna.[34] Whereas a rich tradition of learned composition existed in Austria, only a few of Vienna's leading composers had become internationally prominent by 1770. The Habsburg court was the first stop northward on the tour of a rising Italian singer or composer; royalty and aristocrats there lavished more upon musicians than almost anywhere but London. "Taste in music here is ruled by the Italians," reported a magazine in 1803.[35] A benefit concert put on by esteemed *opera buffa* baritone Stefano Mandini in 1788—who was privileged to book the Burgtheater (example 3)—illustrates how musicians were breaking from the tradition of balancing vocal and instrumental pieces on their programs:

3. *Stefano Mandini, Burgtheater, Vienna, February 5, 1788*[36]

Symphony	Mozart
Recitative/aria	Gioacchino Albertini
Scene/aria, *L'olimpiade* (1784)	Cimarosa
Aria	Paisiello
Trio, "Che vi par Dorina," *Fra i due litiganti il terzo gode* (Milan 1782)	Giuseppe Sarti
Concerto for violin	Composer unknown
Symphony	Haydn
Canon a capella, 3v	[? †Giovanni Battista] Martini
Aria, *L'impressario in angustie* (Naples 1786)	Cimarosa
Scene/rondo	Antonio Bianchi
Exit aria, *Axur re d'Ormus* (Vienna 1788)	Salieri
Trio	[?Pietro Alessandro] Guglielmi

Vienna's Society of Musicians (Tonkünstler Societät) was less significant in concert life than the Gewandhaus series was in Leipzig, offering only a fraction of the total number of events presented any season. However, the society tended to foster the interests of local composers because it enjoyed special access to the Kärntnertor Theater as the corporate body for musicians' pensions. In its first decade many programs combined an oratorio or a cantata with a concerto, a symphony, or both. However, programs of a miscellaneous nature increasingly became the main pattern of the series. A program performed with somewhat different components two days in a row in 1797 (example 4) included pieces by six Viennese composers, including Beethoven, his eminent teacher, Johann Albrechtsberger, the Burgtheater conductor Paul Wranitzky, and his brother, the violinist Anton. That Italian opera pieces predominated at the end of the concert nonetheless illustrates the centrality of that music.

4. *Tonkünstler Societät, Kärntnertor Theater, Vienna, December 22–23, 1797*[37]

Symphony	Paul Wranitzky
Chorus	†Handel
Aria, patriotic cantata *Der Retter in Gefahr*, clarinet obbligato	Franz Süssmayr
Dec. 22: Concerto for oboe	Krammer
Dec. 23: Concerto for violin and cello	Anton Wranitzky
Chorus, "Allelujah"	Johann Albrechtsberger
Aria	Cimarosa
Aria	Vincenzo Righini
Dec. 22: Chorus	Sacchini
Dec. 23: Trio and variations on "La ci darem la mano" (Mozart, *Don Giovanni*), 2 oboes, English horn (woo 38, 1795)	Beethoven
Vocal quartet and chorus	Righini

London

In no other major city were "indigenous" composers excluded so systematically from the cosmopolitan opera hall. The King's (or Queen's) Theatre held a monopoly on opera with Italian texts, and almost no works set by British-born musicians were presented there from its founding in 1708 to the first performance of *Falstaff* composed with Italian text by Michael William Balfe in 1838. The only known performances of music by British-born composers between those years were a one-night production in 1765 of *L'olimpiade* by Thomas Arne and works set in 1788 and 1792 by Stephen Storace, who was usually not regarded as British because his father was an Italian bassist.[38] Most important, there is no evidence that Arne's widely produced *Artaxerxes* (1762)—an all-sung work with an English text—was ever performed at the King's Theatre. "Soldier tir'd of war," the opera's final air, achieved canonic status, rivaling selections from Handel's oratorios among the best-known pieces performed in the early nineteenth century.

The policy of not admitting British composers to the privileged theater grew out of the search for political stability after the constitutional settlement of 1689. By 1720 the social world of the peers and related families had become almost entirely Whig, and these aristocrats attempted to extend their authority on a social and cultural basis. Just as Tories were banned from government posts under Robert Walpole, so Whigs alone were invited to be directors of the Royal Academy of Music in the 1720s. The reconstituted ruling faction wielded cultural authority by making Italian opera the symbol of its authority.[39]

5. *Salomon Subscription Concerts, Hanover Square Rooms, London, May 27, 1791*[40]

Symphony ["Overture"]	Rosetti
Italian opera aria (Theresa Negri)	
Concerto for violin	*Salomon*
Italian opera aria (Giacomo Davide)	
Concerto for flute and bassoon	*[? J. and F. Küchler]*
Intermission	
Symphony ["Overture"]	Haydn
"Cantata" [? scene, *L'anima del filosofo*, 1791]	Haydn
New string quartet	Haydn
Italian opera aria (Theresa Negri)	
Concerto for pedal harp	*Anne-Marie Krumpholtz*
Italian recitative and aria (Giacomo Davide)	
Finale [Symphony movement]	Rosetti

We can see the central role played by Italian opera in a 1785 program for the prestigious subscription concerts directed by Johann Saloman (example 5). The program amounted to an expanded version of the concert at the Gewandhaus discussed earlier—four pieces performed by Italian singers and a cantata in Italian by Haydn contrasted with two concertos, three symphonies, and a string quartet, all by three central European composers. The presence of the French harpist Anne-Marie Krumpholtz indicates the cosmopolitan nature of the concerto. However, even though a British violinist or oboist might play his own concerto there, it was otherwise unusual to hear a piece by a British composer at this series, indeed even music by Handel, which some scholars define as "domesticated." This policy extended the rigid focus on cosmopolitan repertory established at the King's Theatre. The Philharmonic Society of London, begun in 1814, had a similar though somewhat less stringent policy.

Yet British music flourished in many other types of concerts. It was conventional for songs of English opera to be performed in pleasure gardens and nonlicensed theaters; the second half of a program might involve an act from such a work. A canon of such songs was firmly established in this period: In 1780, for example, Lincoln's Inn Fields offered sections from Arne's *Artaxerxes*, Handel's *Acis and Galatea*, and Purcell's *Bonduca*.[41] During the following decades British singers put on concerts that balanced British and foreign pieces, both recent and canonic. In 1789 Samuel Harrison put on a benefit concert (example 6) that included seven pieces by British composers (two by Purcell), four opera selections by Italians (one by Pergolesi), and six central European instrumental pieces (Corelli, Haydn, Mozart, and J. C. Bach).

6. *Benefit Concert, Samuel Harrison, London, April 27, 1789*[42]

"Military" Symphony	Haydn
Air and Chorus, *King Arthur*	†Purcell
Glee, 8v.	Samuel Webbe
Song, "Poor Zelica"	†J. C. Bach
Glee	Stephen Storace and Joseph Corfe
Duet for pianoforte	†Mozart
Glee, 4v.	Webbe
Canzonet with harp	Haydn
Vocal sextet	Paisiello
Recitative and chorus, *Joshua*	†Handel
Intermission	
Concertante	Ignaz Pleyel
Glee, 5v. with harp, pf	R. S. Stevens and Thomas Greatorex
Aria	Sarti
Portuguese hymn	Greatorex
Solo for violin	†Giovanni Corelli
Sacred aria	†Giovanni Pergolesi
Song	Paisiello
Choral finale, *Bonduca*	†Purcell
God Save the King	

In this period Britain began to experience what Nicholas Temperley termed a "failure of confidence" in its composers due to their lack of international acclaim.[43] The origins of this problem reach as far back as the Reformation, when the idiosyncratic theological position of the Church of England discouraged interaction with liturgical music on the Continent and led the Chapel Royal to employ only British-born musicians. The English Civil War and a century of subsequent crises disrupted composition in sacred music and led to a canonic performing tradition with no close parallel save in Spanish America. Even though Italian sacred works remained central to the repertory of "ancient" music, Italian and German composers did not participate significantly in its development. The search for stability under the Walpole government then isolated opera from British composers as much as they themselves pursued insular careers.

Still, music by British composers continued to delight audiences at Drury Lane, Covent Garden, and many kinds of concerts. These musicians proved highly successful in producing music outside the most prestigious or learned idioms. After 1769 the glee and the catch took them into the center of aristocratic social life, most of all the Catch Club, founded in 1761.[44] Songs written for the theater or the pleasure gardens made Thomas Arne, Charles Dibdin, and William Shield among the most sought-after figures in cultural life. The failure of confidence became more serious when, around 1830, Romantic thinking was that a composer would not be taken very seriously if he did not produce good works in "higher" idioms such as the symphony or the string quartet. Such music nonetheless persisted in a variety of concert repertories for the rest of the century.

Despite the emerging problem of confidence, British musicians initiated an aggressive movement to establish avenues for the performance of their music and develop an ideology propounding its value. Indeed, I would argue that a nationalistic movement emerged earlier and in stronger form among composers in Britain than in France or Germany. Composers fought against their exclusion from key elite venues by promoting their music with an ideology linked to national politics. After King George III brought Tories back into the government, a movement grew up among radical Whigs in the 1770s that made a harsh critique of the monarchy and called for an extension of parliamentary authority. Musicians found that point of view useful in propagating the cause of their music in nationalistic terms. In 1790 the writer, composer, and theater producer Charles Dibdin published a periodical called *The Bystander*, in which he used language of the opposition Whigs to attack the Concerts of Antient Music, which were focused on Handel and offered no music less than twenty years old. Dibdin questioned why the Prince of Wales and his retinue were not welcome in the royal household: "Who forbids them? Is it the King? It were treason to suppose it." Dibdin derided the Concerts of Antient Music for being "employed in nothing but a blind and bigoted admiration of a German modern." He called for the series to pay attention to Thomas Arne to serve the "great and noble national benefit."[45]

7. *Vocal Concert, February 14, 1793*[46]

Overture, *Arianna in Creta* (1734)	†Handel
Glee (3v.) and chorus, *Glorious Apollo*	Samuel Webbe
Catch (3v.), *Come, honest friends*	†Simon Ives
Scena, "Dall' adorato bene"	Dussek
Glee (4v.), *Swiftly from the mountain's brow*	Webbe
Catch (4v.), *Would you know my Celia's charms?*	Webbe
Song, "Ye verdant plains," *Acis and Galatea*	†Handel
Glee (3v.), "Peace to the souls of the heroes," *Ossian*	John Wall Callcott
Glee (5v.) and chorus, *Blest pair of Syrens!*	John Stafford Smith
—	
Overture Concertante	Ignaz Pleyel
Glee (4v.), "Tweed-fide"	Joseph Corfe
Song, bassoon obligato, "Odi grand 'ombra'"	Paisiello
Glee (4v.) and chorus, *Since Harmony deigns with her Vot'ries to dwell*	Webbe

New Round in 3 parts, *Lads and lasses hither come*	Luffmann Atterbury
Glee (5v., double choir), *A gen'rous friendship*	Webbe
Glee (3v.) and chorus, *When Britain on her sea-girt shore*	†Arne

London musicians went significantly beyond European practice in putting on concerts devoted almost entirely to British music and indeed to vocal works. In 1791 singers Samuel Harrison and William Knyvett began a series called the Vocal Concert (example 7), a series that would appear on and off for the next four decades. Only five of the sixteen pieces were by foreign composers—by Handel, Paisiello, Jan Ladislav Dussek, and Ignaz Pleyel. The British canon was represented by Arne (typically at the end) and by Simon Ives (1600–1662), a singer at St. Paul's who seems to have taught Anne Cromwell, the first cousin of Oliver Cromwell, Lord Protector of the Commonwealth.

Samuel Webbe, the most respected composer of glees throughout the genre's history, was represented by four pieces. Most concertgoers were also familiar with glees and catches by J. W. Callcott, J. S. Smith, Joseph Corfe, and Luffman Atterbury.

Paris

Compared with Britain, cosmopolitan and domestic music held an opposite relationship in Paris. Not only did the Académie Royale de Musique offer few Italian works prior to 1770, it also enforced a monopoly dating from 1669 on performing music set to French texts in public. The Concert spirituel, begun in 1725, accordingly offered selections from the Italian operas that many listeners wanted very much to hear. Thus was a compromise forged between the court and the musical public and between indigenous and cosmopolitan music. Pieces composed by Lully, who had left Florence at age fourteen in 1647, were defined in national terms and remained in performance as late as 1779. It was novel, indeed unique, for a major court to define its opera in *national* terms; I do not have the space to speculate on just why French absolutism clung to this practice. During the 1770s the Opéra removed all the old operas and began featuring works by Italians in French translation, in so doing accepting the hegemony of cosmopolitan music found in Europe as a whole.[47] The ban on performing French opera selections nonetheless persisted until the French Revolution.

8. *Concert Spirituel, Paris, March 30, 1787*[48]

Symphony	Haydn
Ode, *Carmen seculare*	F.-A.-D. Philidor
Airs for harp (Mlle. Dorison)	?Dorison
New Italian air	Sarti
New concerto for clarinet (Wachter)	Wachter
Carmen seculare	Philidor
New concerto for violin (Mestrino)	Niccolò Mestrino
Italian air	Cimarosa

Programs given at the Concert spirituel followed neat symmetrical patterns, as we see in one given in 1784 (example 8). A French work was the focal point—*Carmen seculare* (1779), a much-admired ode to words by Horace, written for London by François-André Danican Philidor. The choice of concertos by a French harpist, a German clarinetist, and an Italian violinist typified the cosmopolitanism of the genre. However, the placement of arias by Sarti and Cimarosa at the end of each half indicates the hegemonic role that such music had assumed in Paris by that time. The arrival of Italian opera in Paris aroused a firestorm of protest in the music profession. Commentators drew upon the nationalistic rhetoric that arose in political discussion after the Seven Years' War.[49] A *Dialogue entre Lulli, Rameau, et Orphée, dans les Champs Élisées*, published in 1774, used language parallel to that expressed in Leipzig (discussed earlier):

> Today we cling to a host of prejudices: the most ridiculous of them all for our Nation is to think that our Music must cede to the dominance of that of Italy or Germany. I'm not about to say, as has been claimed, that we really have no music; that reproach, being so sweeping, has no basis whatsoever in fact.[50]

Such nationalistic slogans tended to be narrowly oriented toward the musicians' professional self-interest: they did not communicate a deep sense of the national nature of the music.

However, musical absolutism did not apply in a provincial city such as Bordeaux, where French opera selections were regularly performed in the 1780s. Every two weeks from January to September between 1783 and 1793, the Musée de Bordeaux presented a lecture or a poetry reading, followed by a concert directed by Franz Beck, a violinist born in Mannheim and trained in Italy. Musicians performed for free in the orchestra because they were thereby allowed to present benefit concerts in the museum for their own profit or loss. The Bordeaux programs included French opera numbers in a profusion of genres, as was not done in Parisian concerts until 1790.[51] A program given in 1788 included selections from a *drame lyrique* by Nicolas Dalayrac, a *lyri-comique mêlé d'ariettes* by Antonio Salieri, and *tragédies lyriques* by Niccolò Piccinni and the Alsatian Jean-Frédéric Edelmann. The program maintained a balance of pieces by composers born in France, Italy, and central Europe, as well as an emigrant from each of the latter two regions (Beck and Piccinni).

9. *Séance Publique, Musée de Bordeaux, June 6, 1788*[52]

New symphony	Haydn
Italian *ariette*	[? Giacomo Gotifredo] Ferrari
Concerto for violin	Mestrino
"Je vois briller l'aurore," *Arianne dans l'isle de Naxos* (Paris 1782)	J.-Fr. Edelmann
Symphonie concertante	G.-M. Cambini
—	
Duo, *Iphigénie en Tauride* (Paris 1781)	Piccinni
Chaconne	Franz Beck
Ariette, *Azémia et Azémir* (Paris 1787)	Nicolas Dalayrac

| Duo for piano and violin | ? Marchal |
| Duo, *Les Danaïdes* (Paris 1784) | Salieri |

Interestingly enough, the concerts during holy seasons at the Musée de Bordeaux offered significantly less sacred music than those in Leipzig and Vienna. On Christmas Day 1789, the program included six pieces by Italians and five by central Europeans but not a single sacred work or piece by a Frenchman. Still, the amateur orchestra that played there tended to offer a good deal more French music than at the main series, probably because amateurs would find the Italian style difficult to master. A program given on November 1, 1784, seems to have been entirely French save for two selections by Gluck and possibly Piccinni.[53]

In Sum

The most basic conclusion for this chapter is that we must think about cosmopolitanism in musical culture as part of a political process. Tension between the internal and the external is basic to a cultural world, and for that reason its dimensions took a variety of forms in different times and places and changed significantly over time. Matthew Binney's concept of reciprocity helps us understand how negotiation developed and how some kind of compromise was reached between cosmopolitan and rival repertories. The reciprocal political process established a balance between music with competing identities appropriate to conditions in a region. What was "domestic" or "foreign"—or perhaps "local" or "regional" or "national" or "nationalistic"—could have a different character in different places with regard to composers, performers, or musical genres. Musicians knew how to read their publics in adjusting opera or concert repertories. Cosmopolitanism took on authority with particularly strong hegemony in opera and the least with either the concerto or sacred works. We have seen how the authority of cosmopolitan—read Italian—opera was defined differently in London, Paris, Leipzig, and Vienna, and that changed significantly in some places, most of all in Paris after 1770.

The dichotomy between the English and the French cases represents the extreme points in the solutions arrived at with regard to the authority of domestic and cosmopolitan opera. In both countries the geographical focus of repertory grew out of the solution to the experience of civil war in the mid-seventeenth century. On the one hand, the unstable, open-ended political system in Britain led to an unusually exclusive order of cosmopolitan taste. On the other hand, the problematic absolutism that emerged in France led to a unique inward orientation of opera life that excluded cosmopolitanism from the stage of the Opéra—but not that of the principal concerts. Recent work by Georgia Cowart and Don Fader on French opera and ballet show how conflict between nobility and the monarchy was involved in the rivalry between French and Italian music.[54]

The compromises reached in German-speaking cities accordingly suggest a commendable diplomacy at work within the musical community. It is impressive that works by both Italian and regionally born composers such as Graun, Hasse, Gluck, and Mozart were put on stage together. That did mean, of course, that Mozart became identified in large part with Italian opera culture. In 1829 a London musician complained in *The Musical Reformer* that overpaid Italian singers chose "*toujours* Mozart, Rossini, and Meyerbeer."[55]

It is also important to see that in every country a sense of inferiority developed toward the cosmopolitan authority of Italian vocal music during the eighteenth century and that tension between educated and regional Italian persisted in Italy itself. This pattern was to continue in changing form as the cosmopolitan authority of classical music emerged. Katharine Ellis has gone so far as to say that in the nineteenth century French musical commentators had an "inferiority complex" about their musical past.[56] British musical life experienced the strongest conflict between cosmopolitan musical culture and the needs of its composers. If Charles Dibdin made British music a nationalistic issue with particular vehemence in 1790, eighty years later composer George Macfarren set up a dichotomy between what he called the "cosmopolite" and the "indigenous" in 1870: "Alas, for the *cosmopolite*, whose citizenship is so *universal* that he has no special affection for the soil that gave him birth!...It is the misfortune of Englishmen...to be indifferent to, if not to ignore, our *indigenous* capacity for music."[57]

NOTES

1. Benedict Anderson, *Imagined Communities: Reflections on the Origin and Spread of Nationalism*, rev. ed. (London: Verso, 1991).

2. William Weber, *The Great Transformation of Musical Taste: Concert Programming from Haydn to Brahms* (New York: Cambridge University Press, 2008); Mary Sue Morrow, *Concert Life in Haydn's Vienna: Aspects of a Developing Musical and Social Institution* (Stuyvesant, N.Y.: Pendragon, 1989); Simon McVeigh, *Concert Life in London from Mozart to Haydn* (New York: Cambridge University Press, 1993).

3. Amanda Anderson, *The Powers of Distance: Cosmopolitanism and the Cultivation of Detachment* (Princeton, N.J.: Princeton University Press, 2001).

4. Judith R. Walkowitz, "The 'Vision of Salome': Cosmopolitanism and Erotic Dancing in London, 1908–1918," *American Historical Review* 108 (2003): 337.

5. Peter N. Miller, *Peiresc's Europe: Learning and Virtue in the Seventeenth Century* (New Haven, Conn.: Yale University Press, 2000), 11.

6. Thomas J. Schlereth, *The Cosmopolitan Ideal in Enlightenment Thought: Its Form and Function in the Ideas of Franklin, Hume, and Voltaire, 1694–1790* (Notre Dame, Ind.: University of Notre Dame Press, 1977), xi–xii.

7. Quoted in Michel Noiray, *Vocabulaire de la musique de l'époque classique* (Paris: Minerve, 2005), thus: "...119; emphasis on foreign added."

8. Matthew Binney, *The Cosmopolitan Evolution: Travel, Travel Narratives, and the Revolution of the Eighteenth-century European Consciousness* (Lanham, Md.: University Press of America, 2006), 1.

9. Adriana Craciun, *British Women Writers and the French Revolution: Citizens of the World* (London: Palgrave-Macmillan, 2005).

10. Anne Mellor, "Embodied Cosmopolitanism and the British Romantic Woman Writer," *European Romantic Review* 17 (2006): 289–300. See also Camila Fojas, *Cosmopolitanism in the Americas* (West Lafayette, Ind.: Purdue University Press, 2005), for an interesting analysis of domestic and cosmopolitan culture.

11. Celia Applegate, *Bach in Berlin: A Cultural History of Mendelssohn's Revival of the St. Matthew Passion* (Ithaca, N.Y.: Cornell University Press, 2005); Philipp Ther, *In der Mitte der Gesellschaft: Operntheater in Zentraleuropa, 1815–1914* (Vienna: Oldenbourg, 2006).

12. John Rosselli, *Singers of Italian Opera: The History of a Profession* (New York: Cambridge University Press, 1992), 20–21.

13. On the rivalry of Italian and French opera, see Don Fader, "The 'Cabale du Dauphin,' Campra and Italian Comedy," *Music and Letters* 86 (2005): 380–413; and Georgia Cowart, *The Triumph of Pleasure: Louis XIV and the Politics of Spectacle* (Chicago: University of Chicago Press, 2009).

14. Simon McVeigh and Jehoash Hirshberg, *The Italian Solo Concerto, 1700–1760: Rhetorical Strategies and Style History* (Rochester, N.Y.: Boydell, 2004).

15. Weber, *Great Transformation of Musical Taste*, chs. 2, 3, 5, 6.

16. Michael Fend, *Cherubini's Pariser Opern (1788–1803)* (Stuttgart: Steiner, 2007).

17. A. G. Meissner, *Bruchstücke zur Biographie J. G. Naumann's*, 3 vols. (Prague, 1803).

18. David Ringrose, "Capital Cities and Urban Networks," in *Capital Cities and Their Hinterlands in Early Modern Europe*, ed. Bernard Lepetit and Peter Clark, 217–40. (New York: Cambridge University Press, 1996).

19. Hannah Grieg, "Leading the Fashion: The Material Culture of London's *Beau Monde*," in *Gender, Taste, and Material Culture in Britain and North America, 1700–1830*, ed. John Styles and Amanda Vickery, 267–92 (New Haven, Conn.: Yale Center for British Art, 2006).

20. Bruce Brown, *Gluck and the French Theatre in Vienna* (Oxford: Clarendon, 1991), 25–63.

21. "Concerte in Leipzig," *Journal des Luxus und der Moden* (July 1800): 351–53; Weber, *Great Transformation of Musical Taste*, 107.

22. John Mangum, "Apollo and the German Muses: Opera and the Articulation of Class, Politics, and Society in Prussia, 1740–1806," PhD diss., University of California, Los Angeles, 2002.

23. Rodolfo Celletti, *A History of Bel Canto*, trans. Frederick Fuller (Oxford: Clarendon, 1991), 3.

24. Abonnenten-Concerte, Stadtgeschichtliches Museum, Leipzig. An italicized name of the composer indicates that that person was also a performer at the concert. The sign † denotes a deceased composer.

25. Alfred Dörffel, *Geschichte der Gewandhausconcerte zu Leipzig vom 25. November 1781 bis 25. November 1881*, 2 vols. (Leipzig: Breitkopf and Härtel, 1881–1884); Arnold Schering and Rudolf Wustmann, *Musikgeschichte Leipzigs*, 3 vols. (Leipzig: Kistner, 1926–1941), vol., 3, 557–83; Hans-Joachim Nösselt, *Das Gewandhausorchester: Entstehung und Entwicklung eines Orchesters* (Leipzig: Köhler and Amelang, 1943).

26. Mangum, "Apollo and the German Muses."

27. "Antonio Rosetti," *Oxford Music Online* (accessed Sept. 15, 2008). Debate surrounds the claim that he was baptized as Anton Rössler.

28. See collection of the Abonnenten-Concerte in the Stadtgeschichtliches Museum, Leipzig.

29. "Musikübende Gesellschaft," Stadtgeschichtliches Museum, Leipzig.

30. Gloria Flaherty, *Opera in the Development of German Critical Thought* (Princeton, N.J.: Princeton University Press, 1978), 267; Jost Hermand, "Die erste deutsche Nationaloper," in *Revolutio germanica: Die Sehnsucht nach der "alten Freiheit" der Germanen, 1750–1820*, ed. Jost Hermand and Michael Niedermeier, 158–71 (Frankfurt: Lang, 2002).

31. Birmingham Private Concerts, Nov. 30, 1801, Birmingham Central Library.

32. [Johann Friedrich Erst von Brouve], *Raisonnirendes Theater Journal von der Leipziger Michaelmesse 1783* (Leipzig: Jacobaer, 1784), 32–33.

33. *Olla Potrida* 2(3) (Leipzig, 1779): 240. The title came from a Hungarian word for stew.

34. Morrow, *Concert Life in Haydn's Vienna*; Bruce Brown, *Gluck and the French Theatre in Vienna* (Oxford: Clarendon, 1991); Otto Biba, "Grundzüge des Konzertwesens in Wien zu Mozarts Zeit," *Mozart-Jahrbuch* 26 (1978–1979), 132–43, and "Beobachtungen zur Österreichischen Musikszene des 18. Jahrhunderts," in *Österreichische Musiks/Musik in Österreich: Theophil Antonicek zum 60. Geburtstag*, ed. Elisabeth Hilscher, 213–30 (Tutzing: Schneider, 1998).

35. Quoted in Morrow, *Concert Life in Haydn's Vienna*, 214.

36. Morrow, *Concert Life in Haydn's Vienna*, 270; "Mandini family," in *New Grove Dictionary of Music and Musicians*, 30 vols., ed. Stanley Sadie and John Tyrell, vol. 15, 736 (London: Macmillan, 2001).

37. C. F. Pohl, *Denkschrift aus Anlass des hundertjährigen Bestehens der Tonkünstler-Societät* (Vienna: Tonkünstler-Societät, 1871), 59; Bernd Edelmann, "Händel-Aufführungen in den Akademien der Wiener Tonkünstlersozietät," *Göttinger Händel-Beiträge* 1 (1984), 172–74, 178–79, 65–66; Morrow, *Concert Life in Haydn's Vienna*, 295.

38. "Stephen Storace," *Oxford Music Online* (accessed Sept. 15, 2008); "Arne," *Oxford Music Online*. The marginal role of Storace music with regard to British national self-consciousness is evident in the rarity of his pieces in the many editions of songs put out in the middle and late decades of the nineteenth century.

39. William Weber, *Rise of Musical Classics in Eighteenth-century England* (Oxford: Clarendon, 1992); Elizabeth Gibson, *Royal Academy of Music, 1719–1728: The Institution and Its Directors* (New York: Garland, 1989); and Paul Monod, "Politics of Handel's Early London Operas, 1711–1719," *Journal of Interdisciplinary History* 26 (2006): 445–72.

40. Quoted in H. C. Robbins Landon, *Haydn in England, 1791–1795*, vol. 3, *Haydn: Chronicle and Works* (Bloomington: Indiana University Press, 1976), 80–81.

41. Simon McVeigh, Calendar of London Concert Programs, 1750–1800, database, Apr. 30, 1780.

42. McVeigh, *Concert Life*, 249.

43. Nicholas Temperley, "Zenophilia in British Musical History," *Nineteenth-century British Musical Studies*, ed. Bennett Zon, 16–18 (Ashgate: Aldershot, 1999), and "Musical Nationalism in English Romantic Opera," in *Lost Chord: Essays on Victorian Music*, ed. Nicholas Temperley, 143–56 (Bloomington: Indiana University Press, 1989).

44. Brian Robins, *Catch and Glee Culture in Eighteenth-century England* (Woodbridge, UK: Boydell, 2006).

45. *The Bystander, or, Universal Weekly Expositor, by a Literary Association* (London, 1790), "Weekly Retrospect," 45, 303–304.

46. *Harrison and Knyvett's Vocal Concert*, British Library. The origins of "When Britain on her sea-girt shore" (different from "Rule, Britannia!": "When Britain first at heaven's command"), here ascribed to Arne, have not been identified. Presently no stage work is known by Dussek prior to 1798, but the program cites Dussek singing the number,

suggesting it was a work in manuscript. On the Vocal Concert, see Ian Taylor, " 'A Period of Orchestral Destitution'? Symphonic Performance in London, 1795–1813," *Nineteenth-century Music Review* 2 (2005): 139–68.

47. William Weber, "*La musique ancienne* in the Waning of the Ancien Régime," *Journal of Modern History* 56 (1984): 58–88; and "L'institution et son public: L'opéra à Paris et à Londres au XVIIIe siècle," *Annales ESC* 48(6) (1993): 1519–40; "La culture musicale d'une capitale: L'époque du beau monde à Londres, 1700–1800," *Revue d'histoire moderne et contemporaine* 49 (2002): 119–39; Michel Noiray, "Inertie sociale et dynamique de la musique de 1740 à 1770," in *La Musique: Du théorique au politique*, ed. Joël-Marie Fauquet, 211–18 (Paris: Aux Amateurs de Livres, 1991).

48. Constant Pierre, *Histoire du Concert spirituel: 1725–1790* (Paris: Société française de musicologie, 1975). 334. See Michel Brenet [Marie Bobillier], *Les concerts en France sous l'ancien régime* (1900; repr., New York: Da Capo, 1970), 320. The clarinetist Wachter seems to have been a visiting German; see David Charlton, "Classical Clarinet Technique: Documentary Approaches," *Early Music* 16 (1988): 397, 405.

49. On nationalism in France, see David A. Bell, *The Cult of the Nation in France: Inventing Nationalism, 1680–1800* (Cambridge, Mass.: Harvard University Press, 2001), 43–49; and Jay Smith, *Nobility Reimagined: The Patriotic Nation in Eighteenth-century France* (Ithaca: Cornell University Press, 2005).

50. *Dialogue entre Lulli, Rameau, et Orphée dans les Champs Élisées* (Amsterdam: Stoupe, 1774), vi; Bell, *Cult of the Nation in France*, 43–49.

51. See William Weber, "Les programmes de concerts, de Bordeaux à Boston," in *Le Musée de Bordeaux et la musique, 1783–1793*, ed. Patrick Taïeb, Natalie Morel-Borotra, and Jean Gribenski, 175–93 (Rouen: University of Rouen, 2005); and Katharine Ellis, *Interpreting the Musical Past: Early Music in Nineteenth-century France* (Oxford: Clarendon, 2005), 36–41, 62–63.

52. Taïeb, Morel-Borotra, and Gribenski, *Musée de Bordeaux et la musique*, 190.

53. Ibid., Nov. 1, 1784.

54. Fader, " 'Cabale du Dauphin' "; Cowart, *Triumph of Pleasure*.

55. T. D. Worgan, *The Musical Reformer* (London: Maunder, 1829), 25.

56. Ellis, *Interpreting the Musical Past*, 16–21.

57. George Alexander Macfarren, "The National Music of Our Native Land," *Musical Times* (July 1, 1870), 519 (emphasis added).

CHAPTER 9

....

MENDELSSOHN ON THE ROAD: MUSIC, TRAVEL, AND THE ANGLO-GERMAN SYMBIOSIS

....

CELIA APPLEGATE

In March of 1837 Felix Mendelssohn Bartholdy waited in Frankfurt am Main for the documents to arrive from Leipzig that would provide the final legal basis for his marriage to Cecile Jeanrenaud, that is, a formal letter from the city of Leipzig stating that he was both a legal resident and a bachelor.[1] Mendelssohn was not likely to strike any one of his contemporaries as a potential bigamist, and in fact his life since about age sixteen had been so scrutinized, so comparatively open to the public eye that it was hardly likely that he could have sneaked in a secret marriage somewhere along the way. However, the proof of settled domicile represents a slightly more arcane bit of paperwork, gesturing to something important about the Europe in which Mendelssohn made his living as a musician. That someone born in Hamburg and raised and educated in Berlin should have had a job and a house in Leipzig and be on the verge of marrying the daughter of a family from Frankfurt attested less to the dispersal of the descendants of Moses Mendelssohn (that is, to the lives of Jews and converts from Judaism in Germany) than to the career path of a professional musician. Indeed, that particular set of places only scratches the surface of all of Mendelssohn's musical travels by this early point in what would have been, but for untimely death, a long and travel-filled career.

This chapter focuses on certain elements of his and others' lives as musicians in order to suggest some answers to the question of what cultural work travel accomplishes. Musicians have always traveled. Evidence of the existence of musical travelers of one kind or another dates back as far as evidence of music making itself can be confirmed. In every time and place for which a history can be written, one could probably—in most cases definitely—find musicians on the move. In the modern period of travel and exploration, sooner or later European musicians traveled to all of the places that Europeans lived and colonized.[2] If we stretch the notion of travel to include that not only of musicians but also of the music they performed, then one comes quickly to the conclusion that movement represents the defining characteristic of the art form itself in Western culture and thus of its practitioners. Yet the cultural work of travel is easy to miss, given its obvious practical purpose in getting musicians to where they might find work. By looking more culturally at musicians' travels, we can perhaps illuminate one way in which national communities took shape and functioned through cultural exchange.

That musical travel of any sort, whether constant or occasional, should have anything to teach us about nationhood is not, in fact, an especially paradoxical proposition—who better to dramatize the generalized placeness of nation and national belonging than someone who moved across all parts of it and represented it elsewhere? Such observations fit well within our reigning paradigm of national constructivism, and historians and musicologists now routinely include music among the representational phenomena that have shaped a sense of the national belonging. What is trickier to explain is the relationship of travel to the formation of those social bonds that music has a uniquely powerful capacity to create and maintain. All cultures are "traveling cultures," wrote James Clifford in his essays on how "culture makes itself at home in motion," yet it might still seem something of a stretch to suggest that what works to sustain postcolonial identities in an age of globalization has antecedents, even by analogy, in an age of nation building and imperialism.[3] Music is, moreover, different from some of the more obvious markers of nation making—monuments, museums, memorials, paintings, poems, and parks. It is not so different as to make it incomparable but different enough to force us, perhaps, to abandon (as does Clifford) metaphors of buildings and edifices, which suggest solidity and permanence, and to return to Renan's daily plebiscite, which suggests the occasional, the momentary, the repetitive. Music exists in the performance of it, and even after the advent of the age of mechanical reproduction, it still involves continual production and reproduction to exist in the world. The movements of musicians in order to perform thus become a central element in any history of music in society, including those about nations. Indeed, just telling stories about nations does not make them any less stories about displacement and "tangled cultural experiences," about "impure, unruly processes of collective invention," and about continual moving among places and crossing over borders.[4] The traveling musician thus remains a key figure in our understanding of groups that formed around music making and found sources of identity in it.

The travel of musicians enabled many things: It transmitted knowledge, both practical and theoretical, which in turn made possible the development of new musical styles, instruments, and institutions, all of which themselves became part of a self-sustaining process of continual change in all of its parts—self-sustaining only because and through and with travel. The whole story of the development and spread of styles and genres—monophony, polyphony, homophony, functional harmony; plainchant, organum, motet, madrigal, mass, opera, concerto, concerto grosso—is one of explorations and elaborations of patterns in sound, which depended on the creation of a system of musical notation that could record exact pitch and time and thus provide the possibility of building on the explorations and elaborations that had come before. However, the point of musical notation is that it was portable, and so musical developments also depended fundamentally on travel among monasteries, courts, and towns and by musicians, whether monks or minstrels, saints or scoundrels, and all those in between.[5]

Musical travel also fulfilled social needs, specifically those of courts, towns, and churches, for people with a particular sort of training who could undertake particular functions—to entertain, to enhance worship, to accompany a public ceremonial of one kind or another. In the history of the musical professions, the regular employment of musicians by towns was the last kind to emerge, as towns, too, sought to create their own formal soundscape—of bells calling people to church, of trumpets announcing the arrival of people and goods at the city gates, of pipers and drums accompanying civic ceremonials. Over the centuries, these three overlapping domains of music making—church, court, and town—achieved a kind of regularization of the ways in which people wrote, performed, and heard music in Europe, one that did not exclude a certain amount of geographical mobility, though it did not encourage it, either. The result was that music making became less and less an itinerant trade, and musicians were able to settle down in towns and cities and train their children in their profession.[6] Nonetheless, they were still Johnny-come-latelies in the money and moral economy of early modern towns and cities and never able entirely to shake off the hint of disreputability that adhered to those without a fixed abode, musicians among them, who wandered around trying to pick up work where they could.[7] Musicians' guilds were the most persistent strategy to erase the stigma of disreputability, and the earliest one dates probably to the fourteenth century. Town records of localities all across Europe are filled, from then until the near total disappearance of musicians' guilds in the early nineteenth century, with evidence of endless bickering over who did and did not belong to a guild or deserve to belong to one or perform services that should be restricted to one. Those who threatened such control were usually musicians from the outside, which is to say, traveling ones.

Finally, in the modern period of nation-states or emerging nation-states, the most obvious effect of musical travel was to create a transnational space, one recognized by the end of the eighteenth century in the phrase "the musical world."[8] The musical world increasingly consisted less of courts, religious communities, and the road itself than of members of national groups. Musical practices helped to make these imagined communities into actual ones, and the traveling musician became an especially potent representative of national identities that did not correspond to nation-states. This presents us with a muted paradox. Musical interchange, within and among nations, was certainly all the more rapid and pervasive because of the

nonlinguistic nature of music—that "fatal diversity of human language," on which
Benedict Anderson put so much conceptual weight. However, the people who
engaged in it were not wordless, nor were those who listened, organized, and wrote
about performances. Thus, through multiple means, national discourses intertwined with musical practices, not necessarily to the detriment of either, indeed for
most of the long nineteenth century to the benefit of both. At the simplest level we
can say that this intertwinement illustrates a truism, that music is a social practice,
as well as a repertoire, and that as a social practice it engaged in European social and
cultural development altogether. Still, there is nothing simple about the ways in
which music engaged society and certainly nothing merely reflective about this relationship, as the rest of this chapter shows.

In 1988, in his Albert Shaw Memorial Lectures at Johns Hopkins University, Akira
Iriye asked rhetorically, "Who can deny that thinkers, artists, and musicians . . . have
contributed decisively to the making of contemporary history?" His main interest
was in those who "sought to develop an alternative community of nations and people on the basis of their cultural interchanges" by fostering "international cooperation through cultural activities across national boundaries."[9] However, his attention
to the importance of cultural interchanges, which by their very nature require movement and exchange, remains relevant to the history of national communities as well.
Nations are hardly unproblematic wholes. Their boundaries come in different varieties and rarely remain stable: Some, in Prasenjit Duara's famous formulation, are
hard and cannot be crossed without violating the integrity of the community, whereas
others are soft and easily crossed, easily blurred.[10] Among the latter one would certainly include music, and the history of how it both was and was not a boundary
among nations, how its practitioners both were and were not representatives of their
nations, promises to help clarify what nations were and perhaps are.

These ways of thinking about nations as defined as much through external relations as internal essences provide us, then, with a way to gain productive critical
distance from the kind of nineteenth-century musical idealism that saw the importance of music and indeed of musical travel in precisely its ability to tear down the
Tower of Babel and create something transcending petty divisions of language and
custom. As cultural historians, we are not in the business of labeling such notions
right or wrong, naïve or disingenuous, but in understanding their relation to actual
contexts in which musical practices developed. In that spirit, Felix Mendelssohn
provides a vivid embodiment of the capacity of musical travel to define and
strengthen national communities by traveling among them—a community building for which "internationalism" or, to rely on Iriye again, "cultural internationalism" seems the appropriate term. This is not necessarily a native category, and were
one to look for one, the term *cosmopolitanism* might seem a more obvious choice.
Plenty of people in Mendelssohn's time used the word *cosmopolitan* in reference to
the musical world but very often in derogatory terms that referred to a kind of
urbane, showy style (of music, of life), associated above all with Paris.

Take, for instance, the remarks of Ignaz Moscheles, the great Prague-born pianist, dear friend of Mendelssohn, and his main connection to (and entrée into)

London musical life. "Why is it," he wrote to a friend, lamenting the apparent inability of the Parisian public to appreciate the German violinist Ludwig Spohr, "that Spohr cannot arouse any general enthusiasm in this place? Does the French national pride not allow them to give praise to any violinists other than their own? Or could it be that he is too uncommunicative, too detached for the cosmopolitan taste of the Parisians?"[11] His words reveal the extent to which musicians were very much aware of national characteristics, especially as they affected the musicians' livelihood, that is to say, increasingly, their ability to draw in paying audiences. Moscheles here poses for us two possible reasons that a musician might appeal to the public: first, simply by being of the same nationality—this we can call the chauvinistic, or more charitably, the patriotic appeal; and second, by being a cosmopolitan, that is, for Spohr a matter of *abjuring* any national coloring whatsoever through the embrace of pure showmanship. Neither of these relationships of the musician to nationality seemed to him particularly praiseworthy, and indeed lurking behind them were two more.

The first (or rather the third, beyond the chauvinistic and the cosmopolitan) option was that musicians, traveling or otherwise, represented a kind of distilled version of their nationality—Jenny Lind, the Swedish nightingale, for instance, or more comically for Moscheles, a family of Austrians from the Zillertal who came to London in search of a little fame and some fortune, peddling their Tyroleanism. This Rainer family, who sought Moscheles's help in setting up concert dates, seems to have been a sort of Trapp Family Singers *avant la lettre*, and London society was so taken with them, their folk songs and their costumery, that Moscheles, invited to Kensington Palace to play for the then Princess Victoria, wrote in his diary, "The ladies and gentlemen took a friendly interest in my playing, but I think they enjoyed most of all my improvisation on some of the now very fashionable Tyrolean songs, since the Duchess had already invited the Tyrolean singers to her home on two occasions."[12] Moscheles seemed quite tolerant of this sort of thing, though it was certainly not his own mode of musical existence. We might call it the appeal to national character, which is itself closely related to, indeed in some sense the same thing as, musical exoticism—Spanish dancers, whirling dervishes, gypsy bands, and all the many and varied manifestations that such exoticism could take.[13] Mendelssohn, though defter than most of his contemporaries at incorporating an appeal to national character into his compositions, regarded its use as a marker of personal identity with considerable impatience. In a letter to his family in 1829 from one of the places on earth most prone to exploiting the charm of its musicality, that is to say, from Wales, his exasperation burst forth in the first line, "No more national music!" "Ten thousand devils take all this folksiness," he continued, "in every reputable tavern, a harpist can be found playing some so-called folk melody, which is to say, dreadful, vulgar, badly played junk with a hurdy-gurdy churning out more melodies in the background."[14]

However, there is a fourth possibility for the relationship of musicians to their nationality, and it is the one that Moscheles and with him his close companion in all things musical, Mendelssohn, represented and strove all their life to uphold and promote. It involved a definite consciousness of national identity, marked by recognition that one worked within a national tradition of which one was proud. Nonetheless, it also involved a fundamental acknowledgement of the value of other traditions and a commitment to working within an arena of cultural activity and interchange that was at least European in scope (and increasingly North American as well).

Now, to return more or less to where this section began, it is this relationship of music to nationality that one should label musical internationalism, given that the very word *international* acknowledges the existence of the national as the essential unit of interchange. In the majority of cases, the people for whom this term is apposite were men and women of broad training and relatively broad horizons, many of whom traveled a great deal among the nations of Europe and beyond. Nevertheless, they felt themselves to be and were perceived as being the representatives of a national tradition. Whenever a widely celebrated musical figure, like Robert Schumann or Johannes Brahms, worked within a relatively confined geographical area, this was something worthy of notice, and it did not reflect their chauvinism but something more like discomfort, dislike of travel, even existential insecurity. Mendelssohn was, in any case, not among those few but a major musical figure who traveled incessantly, exhausting himself in work and work-related travel. The work that this travel did, beyond the outpouring of performances and compositions and friendships that it certainly produced, was the double-barreled one of consolidating the German musical tradition and musical institutions at home and, just as interesting, strengthening what R. Larry Todd has called "a German-English musical axis connecting Leipzig and London" and what I call, switching from a more limited mechanical to a more all-embracing biological analogy, the Anglo-German symbiosis.[15]

One of the most striking features of European political and cultural life in the eighteenth and the first half of the nineteenth century was the ever-more extensive and dense network of ties between the German states and Great Britain. These were various, pervasive, and consequential, so much so that the question of why all of these ties eroded, allowing the two countries to drift catastrophically apart in the last decades before war in 1914, is one of the great questions over which historians have labored for more than a century.[16] In the formative period in which the institutions, practices, and repertoire of modern musical life took shape, the British and German people shared a myriad of dynastic, cultural, religious, and economic ties into which things musical were completely intertwined.

But intertwined does not necessarily mean symbiotic. A symbiotic relationship, evolutionary biologists tell us, can take three forms—mutualism, commensuralism, and parasitism. These concepts are easily abused; accusations of parasitism were, after all, an essential part of the calumnies later leveled against Mendelssohn by Richard Wagner and his followers. However, the first two less-loaded terms can be of some use in thinking about the nature of musical ties between two distinct social groups of people. It might, for instance, make sense to regard the musical relationship between the English and the Germans as a commensuralist one, in which one side benefited from the arrangement while the other was neither harmed nor helped.

If one wanted to see it that way, then one would argue that English musical life as a whole benefited enormously from a steady infusion of German musicians and German music into their collective musical life and that German musical life as a whole suffered no harm—moreover, individual Germans made out very well indeed. This trend started in the eighteenth century, when a significant number of orchestral players, together with composers, made their way to the country, sometimes permanently. In the oft-repeated words of Handel's contemporary and friend, Hamburg composer and music writer Johann Mattheson, "He who in the present time wants to make a profit out of music takes himself to England." "The Italians," he continued along the same lines, "exalt music; the French enliven it; the Germans strive after it; and the English pay for it."[17]

In the nineteenth century, the numbers of German musicians working in the British Isles also included street musicians, whom Henry Mayhew included in his famous account of London's underclass. As conditions of travel improved, so, too, did numbers of essentially itinerant musicians, ranging from the great virtuosi and celebrated conductors to the brass bandsmen who came over only for the summer.[18] Mendelssohn himself, of course, traveled to England frequently—ten trips over the course of his life, and every one of them musically significant both for him and especially for his fervent English admirers. In the roughly two decades of sojourning in England, he grew from an extraordinarily precocious and talented young man to the dominant figure in English musical life, appearing as pianist, organist, violinist, and above all conductor. He shaped musical places ranging from private salons to massive festivals, especially the Birmingham Triennial Festival, which became a key platform for the expression of his eminence and for which he wrote *Elijah* (premiered in 1847).

Counterfactuals are difficult to control and often result in what is little more than loose speculation, but that said, it is still worth wondering what would have become of the English oratorio tradition without Mendelssohn's contributions to it of *Paulus* and especially *Elijah*. The least one could say is that he gave a new lease on life to the tradition by rescuing it from endless repetition, invigorating it, giving it the incalculable effect of the new—the thrill of a premier, the frisson of his foreignness, as well as the familiarity of his earnestness, all of that. The musical public in the nineteenth century did have a tremendous and even growing appetite for tradition and historical revival, and one would be hard pressed to find evidence that the English were showing any signs at all of losing interest in singing the *Messiah* before Mendelssohn came along. Nevertheless, not only did Mendelssohn make historical revival glamorous, but he also became a key figure in transforming it from mere repetition into a living force in musical life. One of the first acts in his conducting career (and in some sense the defining act of his career) had been a revival of a major choral work. The *St. Matthew Passion* is not, strictly speaking, an oratorio; moreover, it never achieved the kind of mass popularity that the oratorios of Handel and Haydn did. Nonetheless, its revival signaled a consciousness that was as essential to the mind of the nineteenth century as was its love of the new, and that was a consciousness that the present and the future were engaged in an ongoing conversation with the past, a conversation that simultaneously limited and enriched what was possible. As the music historian Carl Dahlhaus once put it, the "century of revolutions was also the century of museums," a wonderfully paradoxical phenomenon, the sense of which is an understanding that all that is new today will eventually pass into history, where it will not be dead and gone, quite the contrary, but a guide to all those who come after.

Thus, one could argue that Mendelssohn's success in reviving the *St. Matthew Passion* in 1829 had effects well beyond the Bach revival itself, already an extraordinarily multifaceted phenomenon. It made it possible, only six years later, for Schumann to write that his musical "attitude" was "simple": "to recall the past and its music with all the energy at our disposal, to draw attention to the ways in which new artistic beauties can find sustenance at a source so pure."[19] From this perspective, Mendelssohn's composition of *Paulus* and *Elijah* (and much else, of course) made it clear that elements of the past could be incorporated into new ones, both giving the old a new life and enriching the musical idioms of the future. A contemporary German critic, G. W. Fink, in an account of *Paulus*'s London premier, wrote that "the work is so manifestly Handelian, Bachian, and Mendelssohnian that it appears as if it really exists to facilitate our contemporaries' receptivity to the profundities of these recognized tone-heroes."[20] Mendelssohn's successful blending of historical and contemporary idioms, of Baroque chorale and modern lyrical song, seemed to many reform-minded people (not least his hard-to-please father) the sort of reconciliation they envisaged as the stable yet progressive point between the calcification of restoration and the chaos of revolution.[21] Thus, when Abraham praised his son for solving "the problem of combining ancient conceptions with modern appliances" (as pithy a statement of Berliner reformist historicism as one is likely to find), he was thinking about society and political life as well.[22] *Paulus*'s resonance in English public life was of course differently shaded, but in all European countries, the challenge of reconciling tradition with modern dynamism shaped the politics of culture and the culture of politics. Mendelssohn's music, especially the oratorios, enjoyed their critical and popular success in precisely that field of significance.

Another avenue for answering this unanswerable question of what the English oratorio tradition and English musical culture *tout court* would have been without Mendelssohn's contributions to it would be to attempt to place these works in relation to all his other compositional and conducting activity in Great Britain. Here the point to emphasize is that Mendelssohn's example demonstrated that serious instrumental and choral music need not be regarded as separate domains, the latter especially relegated to a slightly lesser status as a source of pious uplift for the middle-class amateurs and their audiences. Indeed, Mendelssohn, unlike any other figure in English musical life, bound together its disparate and at time warring parts. Historians Simon McVeigh and William Weber have outlined the tensions in British musical life in the first decades of the nineteenth century, with McVeigh going so far as to call them "culture wars"—among the patricians of the Concerts of Ancient Music, the bourgeois and educationally serious Philharmonic Society for orchestral music, and the more evangelical Sacred Harmonic Society's devotion to moral uplift through oratorio singing.[23] What seems clear, though, is that Mendelssohn's arrival into this contentious scene in 1829 and his subsequent and frequent visits played a major role in calming the troubled waters and creating a remarkable consensus about the kind of music that would be played—a repertoire that ranged from chamber music that could be heard both at the somewhat snobby venue of the Musical Union and the Popular Concerts, which reached a shilling public, a symphonic repertoire that ranged from (again) the more highbrowed Philharmonic Society concerts to the gigantic undertakings of the exhibitions and the subsequent Promenade concerts, an oratorio repertoire whose performers ranged from across a spectrum of classes and religious tendencies. For most of Mendelssohn's life and for many decades after he died, British musical culture was varied but not venomous, with many venues and kinds of performance, a great deal of music criticism and reportage, all marked by a basic acceptance of the value of free markets as the context for artistic, as well as commercial (not that the two were distinct), undertakings. It is difficult to imagine this kind of overall consensus about musical value emerging without the peripatetic figure of Mendelssohn, who was traveling not just to the British Isles from a part of the world whose thought and music were already highly regarded by the British, but also around the British Isles, inscribing parts of it, both geographical and literary, into his very compositions (the *Hebrides* Overture, the *Midsummer Night's Dream* music, and so on). Few other figures in British musical life of that period had the geographical and the musical reach of Mendelssohn, and withal he remained a gentleman and a Protestant—both perhaps as essential to his mediating role as his constant movements across space and time.

The case for the Anglo-German symbiosis as a kind of commensuralist relationship might then be summed up as follows: From Handel to Haydn to Mendelssohn to Charles Hallé (aka Karl Halle of Hagen, Westphalia) to Max Bruch to Hans Richter, including also the countless forgotten jobbing musicians and street musicians among them, England's experience of both classical and, increasingly, popular music (in the form of brass bands and street musicians) was enriched and shaped by the presence of these musically talented Teutons, who often seemed to contemporaries to be compensating for some mysterious failure of the English to be sufficiently musical themselves. Moreover, in some loose sense, this is how the English and the Germans themselves tended to regard the case in the nineteenth century, as a matter of compensating symbiosis. In the words of Mendelssohn's admirer and friend Henry Chorley, delivering a series of lectures on "The National Music of the World," the English had "never produced a great instrumental composer, neither a towering player on any instrument," and a journalist in *The Musical World* suggested that "no one in his senses would think of asserting that we have produced a Bach, a Handel, or a Mozart . . . [as] our country grows no such men— they are a distinct race of beings."[24]

The English needed the Germans, in other words, and looked to them for musical leadership.

Over the course of the nineteenth century, English musicians did from time to time organize to promote their own agenda, as in the case of the founding of the Society of English Musicians in the 1830s. In such moments, English musicians made arguments that suggested that they at least thought that the relationship of Germans and all foreigners to the English musical scene was closer to one of parasitism than mutual benefit. Foreign musicians allegedly monopolized the salons and the commercial venues alike, deliberately or not, preventing English musical talent from ever receiving a fair hearing.[25] Yet no one really followed through on such complaints with any measures of musical protectionism. London in particular became the shining example of what free trade in musical talent, an open market for musical consumption, and the careful infusion of patronage and knowledgeable guidance into the whole scene could produce—that is, a vibrant, varied, innovative range of musical offerings, including the most demanding and excellent, as well as the most easily digestible. Still, as late as 1895, a music critic lamented the "almost invariable lagging behind the age on the part of our musicians," whose new works sounded as though they had been written a half-century earlier. Revealing the continuing strength of the Anglo-German symbiosis, he urged his compatriots to "let Mendelssohn's words be ever borne in mind: '... The only things that interest me are new compositions.'"[26]

Nevertheless, to see the Anglo-German symbiosis as a relationship in which all the benefit was to the English and all the travelers were German leaves out any benefit to German musical life that might have resulted from the English enthusiasm for its representatives. Even if we acknowledge that individual Germans gained enormously—in their own compositional and professional development and their financial security—from the English connection, it still remains for us to think about the implications of this relationship for German musical life as a whole, which were considerable. To call this relationship, then, one of mutualism is simply to emphasize its transnational character, that is to say, its participation in a wider process of exchanges and circulation of ideas, inventions, policies, goods, and services across and among nations in the nineteenth century. Money, in other words, was not the only thing changing hands between the English and the German musicians and musical publics.

We can see this operating on two levels, one abstract, the other more practical. To consider the practical first, the clearest case of mutual benefit is the oratorio— the oratorio understood not just as a genre and a set of musical works within that genre but also as a cultural practice. That brings us at least briefly to the figure without whom the entire Anglo-German exchange would hardly have had the weight it did—the artist originally known as Georg Friedrich Händel. The first large-scale choral performances of any sort, immediate ancestors of the immense number and variety of choral gatherings in the nineteenth century, took place not on the Continent but in England and grew out of a congeries of Anglican musical rituals that crystallized by the mid-eighteenth century around the Lenten performances of Handel's new oratorios. As early as 1784, with the enormous centenary commemoration of Handel in Westminster Abbey, the model received an early apotheosis, with choirs and choral societies traveling from all across England to sing the *Messiah*. Only in retrospect and only disingenuously could Germans try to claim that there was anything especially German about these origins—the oratorio, as genre and as practice, belonged to the English. The British developed in a short amount of time a "social and musical ritual" that, in the words of William Weber, "proved remarkably appealing and adaptable" and indeed highly portable.[27]

Two German men, at least, were deeply impressed, one famous, the other less so. The less famous one, Johann Adam Hiller, was the first director of Leipzig's Gewandhaus concerts, and bringing Handel back to the Germans formed one part of a varied career as composer, theorist, pedagogue, and impresario, working as much outside of as inside the established niches for musicians in church and court. At various times in his life, he organized concert series, established musical societies for amateurs, ran a school for singers out of his own house, and founded a short-lived but pioneering musical periodical. His treatises on singing instruction were pathbreaking and quite out of step with his time, and his collections of songs for children and for household music making reflected fresh, progressive ideas about the place of music in the German household and the enlightening sociability inherent to music making as a whole. For all this work, with its obvious legacies to nineteenth-century musical practices, Hiller remains an obscure figure, perhaps indeed because he rarely traveled.[28] In any case, Hiller's most famous act in his lifetime and after was one of importation. In 1786 he produced and directed the first full performance of the *Messiah* in German-speaking Europe, in explicit imitation of the British. It took place in the Berlin Cathedral, with an orchestra and chorus numbering in the hundreds, and he followed it up with similarly large-scale performances in Leipzig in 1786 and 1787, then in Breslau in 1788—taking it on the road, so to speak, among the leading musical centers of north-central Germany.

At around the same time, a more internationally famous musician, Joseph Haydn, had an opportunity to make two extended trips to London, where he wrote and conducted new symphonies for his enthusiastic public there. During this happy time for him, he was deeply impressed by the English fervor for Handel's oratorios, and he himself attended the last of the huge Handel Commemoration festivals in Westminster Abbey in 1791. "He found," as the great émigré musicologist Karl Geiringer interpreted him, "a whole nation aroused by compositions offered in monumental performances . . . [and] desired intensely to write as Handel had written, works meant for a whole nation."[29] This meant, among other things, composing not just for the cultivated aristocracy but also for the large and growing middle class and, geographically speaking, for a musical audience that extended beyond Vienna to every corner of the German-speaking world to which published music in the German language would reach. This meant, in short, composing for Germany. So when on his second trip he was handed a libretto in English on the subject of the creation of the world, fashioned from bits of Genesis and John Milton's *Paradise Lost*, he had it translated into German—"clothing the English poem in German garb," in the words of his translator, Baron van Swieten—and set it.[30] He then had the text, so artfully fit to the music, translated back into English—the whole procedure being both a metaphor and the actual marker of a unique process, that of the first large-scale work conceived for and written and circulated in the transnational space of Great Britain and German-speaking Europe.

The Creation was duly taken up by choral directors and their choruses and audiences in both places, and each had reason enough to see the work as peculiarly theirs. For the English, the echoes of the English of Milton and the King James Bible, even though compromised by the back-and-forth of the translation process, were enough to prove its essential Englishness quite apart from Haydn's source and site of inspiration in Westminster Abbey, ringing with the sound of Handel's *Messiah*. For their part, the Germans, whether north or south, Catholic or Protestant, regarded Haydn and all his works as their own. Carl Friedrich Zelter, the leader of the first amateur choral society in continental Europe, Berlin's Singakademie, found additional evidence of *The Creation*'s (or rather, *Die Schöpfung*'s) Germanness in Haydn's musical engagement with the legacy of the composer increasingly regarded as the greatest *German* of them all, Johann Sebastian Bach. In words that foreshadow Mendelssohn's own use of historical tradition—and indeed as his composition teacher, one would be justified in calling this a matter of influence rather than anticipation—Zelter praised Haydn for "noble and clear" fugal work throughout the piece. "The man who has left all his contemporaries behind him, with all his genius and his eternally fresh and youthful richness of invention," he wrote, "is not ashamed to adorn his works with contrapuntal beauties, and as a result, despite all the changes of time and fashion, they will remain immortal so long as music lives."[31]

The amateur choral movement in both Great Britain and Germany, into whose fledgling organizations *The Creation* stepped, as though custom made for them (which in a sense it was) was one of the principal and somewhat underappreciated sustainers of transnational exchanges in the long nineteenth century and certainly one of the major sources of reception and dissemination of the Anglo-German symbiosis. The German version of choral amateurism was among the legacies of Johann Adam Hiller, although the first such permanent society, the Berlin Singakademie, was founded not by him but by the Prussian court composer Carl Friedrich Christian Fasch. Amateur choruses in Great Britain, Germany, and elsewhere came in all shapes and sizes and genders and places, but geographically dispersed and socially diverse though these choruses were, they loosely united around a common repertoire, at the core of which was Handel, then Haydn, then Bach, and soon Mendelssohn. They also coalesced around a common set of practices, among which the most nationally significant were choral festivals. The number, sizes, and purposes of the festivals expanded enormously over the course of the nineteenth century, crowding its civic calendars with commemorative and contemporary celebrations of composers, monarchs, events, and inventions too numerous to recount. From the virtually round-the-clock oratorio performances (in a regular rotation of Handel's *Messiah*, Mendelssohn's *Elijah*, and Haydn's *Creation*) that accompanied the Great Exhibition of 1851 to the three thousand Orphéonistes who descended on London in 1860 for friendly international competition to the exhibitions of "Welsh choral prowess" displayed annually at the Eisteddfodau to the chorus of ten thousand and orchestra of one thousand that gathered in Boston for the National Peace Jubilee and Musical Festival of 1869 (and sang excerpts from Handel, Haydn, and Mendelssohn), nineteenth-century singers left behind an impression of constant motion and tireless enthusiasm.[32]

In German Europe, after Hiller's pioneering but singular festivals, the first in an enduring series of large-scale events took place in 1810 in the small Thuringian town of Frankenhausen. Its organizer, an obscure local cantor and court musician named G. F. Bischoff had been so entranced by hearing Haydn's *Creation* performed by a court orchestra and chorus in nearby Gotha, that he invited Ludwig Spohr, its conductor, to direct a larger-scale festival in his Frankenhausen, a town at the foot of the Kyffhäuser mountain, in which, as German folk legend had it, the emperor Frederick Barbarossa lay, waiting for the call to awake and unite the scattered German people. As a result, when hundreds of German musicians, both amateur and professional, did gather to perform Haydn's *Creation* and Beethoven's Fifth Symphony there, the event carried strong national overtones. Five years later, even more of them gathered again in Frankenhausen, this time to commemorate the great victory over Napoleon two years earlier at the Battle of the Nations in Leipzig. They sang Gottfried Weber's *Te Deum*, as well as Spohr's newly composed oratorio, *Das befreite Deutschland* (Germany Liberated). Three years later, in 1818, the first of what became the most musically ambitious of the German festivals, the Lower Rhine Festival, took place in Elberfeld, with a large orchestra and chorus drawn from the surrounding Prussian Rhine Province. The repertoire of that festival was from the outset dominated by Handel's oratorios, a circumstance that did not, though, shut out the performance of oratorios and smaller-scale choral works by other composers—Haydn's *Creation* and *Seasons* chief among them, as well as works by Reichardt, Beethoven, Mozart, Spohr, Weber, and Schneider, in short oratorical Germans, most of whom were following in the Handelian footsteps.

In 1836 the Lower Rhine Music Festival was the site for the premier of Mendelssohn's own *Paulus*, a work that owed more musically, perhaps, to Mendelssohn's engagement with Bach but which as cultural practice owed everything to Handel and the English. *Elijah* is, of course, even more an English work, written for the English, its libretto honed by an English speaker (in contrast to awkward translations of the *Paulus* text), its musical language less Bachian, more Handelian, but, as Todd has written, this was a "historicism blended subtly into the composer's mature style."[33] Mendelssohn was planning to direct its premier in a number of important German musical centers at the time of his death; it never really established itself after that, not to the extent it did in the Anglo-American context. Nevertheless, the English connection had by this time done its cultural work in Germany to the extent that one cannot truly speak of a German oratorical tradition at all but only of an Anglo-German one.

The oratorio and its institutions amount to a concrete example of the more abstract notion of a nation, however construed, benefiting from the engagement of its native-born musicians in a larger world. In addition, that benefit, to come back to our initial query about the work that travel did, was to consolidate what in fact it meant, musically, to be German. Germans especially, for whom a straightforward political understanding of their national identity was not available, developed a shared culture and sense of common purpose through many different registers— language, religion, economic activity, science, scholarship, art, and music. Not all these senses of Germanness were consonant with each other—language differences, construed as dialect, continued to bedevil a sense of commonality well into the nineteenth century, religious differences were a persistent and deep-rooted fault line, and music itself was diverse in its parts. However, for the German musicians who traveled abroad, their nationality seemed much less ambiguous and unclear than it did back home. Likewise for those Germans who were reading in the press about their compatriots abroad—Haydn's triumphs in London were widely reported in the German-language press—nationality became clearer from this international recognition. From his first trip to Paris through the rest of his life, Mendelssohn's letters revealed his consciousness of being German despite or even because of his ambivalence about the movement for political unification as such. In Paris, the thirteen-year-old was a young champion of Beethoven and Bach, his countrymen; in England, to state the obvious, he became the very embodiment of German musical culture. But there is more to the phenomenon than just that. The concrete results of the Anglo-German exchange worked to give shape to German national culture— and not coincidentally. After all, the Handelian commemorations in England had been, in William Weber's account of them, *national* celebrations that stabilized the relationship between state, state church, and society; the imitation of them in German-speaking Europe did not produce exactly the same kind of phenomenon— how could it have?—but it produced something like it, under the changed, more politically fragmented circumstances.[34] The festivals and musical performances, in which Mendelssohn in his lifetime played such a defining role, were in their own way national celebrations that expressed the relationship between the German musical past and its present and future and sketched out a role for music that made it, as it were, the chief negotiator in relations among localities and individual states, as well as in Catholic, Protestant, and Jewish musical life—at least for a while, because national consciousness changed and with it musical life, though perhaps less than one might think.

The Anglo-German symbiosis or the Anglo-German exchange, whatever we might want to call it, was also crucial in the creation and sustenance of something that went beyond English and German musical traditions and national traits. In writing earlier about the musician's relation to nationality, I called that of Moscheles and Mendelssohn—and to them we could add nearly every composer or performer of art music of the nineteenth century (Berlioz, Chopin, Liszt eventually, Verdi, Gade, Grieg, Sullivan, Bruch)—musical internationalism. We might also call it, citing the philosopher Kwame Anthony Appiah, "rooted cosmopolitanism." The cosmopolitan patriot is someone who can imagine a world in which a person is "attached to a home of her own with its own cultural particularities, but taking pleasure from the presence of other, different, places that are home to other, different people." Such a person would also enjoy travel while accepting the "citizen's responsibility to nurture the culture and the politics of their homes."[35] Appiah was talking about a dream of a future beyond national hostilities, but he could just as well have been describing the dominant characteristic of art musicians of the long nineteenth century. The Anglo-German symbiosis was just one relationship within a series of intersecting and interlocking relationships among composers and performers and increasingly also among people who traveled to listen to serious music and to study it at European conservatories (especially German ones). Of course, middle-brow and popular musicians and music consumers traveled extensively also but perhaps to less nationalizing effect (though this is a question to be investigated). The kind of broadly European perspective on the past and future of musical traditions and their importance to the health and vitality of European nations (including those stranded in the Americas) tended to remain the characteristic of art music, that is, music with aspirations to permanence. Among these travelers, Mendelssohn must surely be regarded, in his lifetime and in our own retrospect, as one of the greats.

NOTES

1. R. Larry Todd, *Mendelssohn: A Life in Music* (New York: Oxford University Press, 2003), 347.

2. See, for instance, Jeffrey Richards, *Imperialism and Music: Britain 1876–1953* (Manchester: Manchester University Press, 2001).

3. James Clifford, *Routes: Travel and Translation in the Late Twentieth Century* (Cambridge, Mass.: Harvard University Press, 1997), 17.

4. Clifford, *Routes*, 2–3.

5. The life of one of first composers known to us as such, Guillaume de Mauchaut (ca. 1300–1377), consisted of a travelogue of epic proportions, from his birth in Rheims to Paris, then to Luxembourg, Prague, Lithuania, and Italy, then back to Bohemia, then to Normandy, Paris, Navarre, and finally (and unexpectedly) an appointment as canon at Rheims Cathedral, where he died, back where he had begun.

6. The most famous example of this was, of course, the Bach family, of whom more than fifty members were professional musicians (for the most part in Thuringia). Johann S. Bach was himself so fascinated by this family history that he prepared a genealogy in 1735. The first generation to go "out in the world" were his sons.

7. Such people often fell into the category of the "unhonorable trades," among which were also executioners and sheep shearers. See the pioneering work of Werner Danckert, *Unehrliche Leute: Die Verfemten Berufe* (Munich: Francke, 1963). See also Kathy Stuart, *Defiled Trades and Social Outcasts: Honor and Ritual Pollution in Early Modern Germany* (New York: Cambridge University Press, 1999). For the later eighteenth century, see Carsten Küther, *Menschen auf der Strasse* (Göttingen: Vandenhoeck and Ruprecht, 1993), and Carsten Küther, *Räuber und Gauner in Deutschland*, 2d ed. (Göttingen: Vandenhoeck and Ruprecht, 1987). On traveling musicians in particular, especially in premodern times, see the definitive work of Walter Salmen, *Der fahrende Musiker im europäischen Mittelalter* (Kassel: Hinnenthal, 1960), as well as the essays in Salmen's edited collection, *The Social Status of the Professional Musician from the Middle Ages to the 19th Century*, trans. Herbert

Kaufman and Barbara Reisner (New York: Pendragon, 1983), especially those by Heinrich W. Schwab, "The Social Status of the Town Musician," and Dieter Krickeberg, "The Folk Musician in the 17th and 18th Centuries."

8. William Weber, *The Great Transformation of Musical Taste: Concert Programming from Haydn to Brahms* (New York: Cambridge University Press, 2008), 21.

9. Akira Iriye, *Cultural Internationalism and World Order* (Baltimore: Johns Hopkins University Press, 1997), 2.

10. This distinction comes from Prasenjit Duara in *Rescuing History from the Nation: Questioning Narratives of Modern China* (Chicago: University of Chicago Press, 1997), 65.

11. Charlotte Moscheles, ed., *Recent Music and Musicians, as described in the Diaries and Correspondence of Ignatz Moscheles*, trans. A. D. Coleridge (New York: Holt, 1873), 26–27.

12. Quoted in Emil F. Smidak, *Isaak-Ignaz Moscheles: The Life of the Composer and His Encounters with Beethoven, Liszt, Chopin, and Mendelssohn* (Aldershot, Hampshire: Scolar, 1989), 68–69.

13. See Jonathan Bellman, *The Exotic in Western Music* (Boston: Northeastern University Press, 1998); and Ralph Locke, *Musical Exoticism: Images and Reflections* (New York: Cambridge University Press, 2009).

14. Mendelssohn to his family in Berlin, Llangollen, Aug. 25, 1929, in *Felix Mendelssohn Bartholdy: Sämtliche Briefe*, ed. Juliete Appold and Regina Back, vol. 1, 380–81 (Kassel: Bärenreiter, 2008).

15. Todd, *Mendelssohn*, xx.

16. The classic account is Paul M. Kennedy, *The Rise of the Anglo-German Antagonism, 1860–1914* (Boston: Allen and Unwin, 1980).

17. Johann Mattheson, "Vom Unterscheid der heutigen Italiänischen / Frantzösischen / Englischen und Teutschen Music," *Das Neu-eröffnetes Orchester* (Hamburg, 1713), part III, ch. 1, http://www.koelnklavier.de/quellen/matth-orch1/_index. html; English translation by John Fuller-Maitland and William Henry Hadow, *The Oxford History of Music* (Oxford: Clarendon, 1902), 316.

18. Panikos Panayi, *German Immigrants in Britain during the 19th Century, 1815–1914* (Oxford: Berg, 1995), 126–27.

19. Schumann, opening statement of the *Neue Zeitschrift für Musik* (Jan. 2, 1835), 1.

20. G. W. Fink, "Mendelssohns Paulus," *Allgemeine musikalische Zeitung* 39 (March 1837), 209.

21. For the political and intellectual manifestations of this reformist view, see John Edward Toews, *Becoming Historical: Cultural Reformation and Public Memory in Early Nineteenth-century Berlin* (New York: Cambridge University Press, 2004).

22. Todd, *Mendelssohn*, 337.

23. Simon McVeigh, "A Free Trade in Music: London during the Long 19th Century in a European Perspective," *Journal of Modern European History* 5(1) (2007): 71.

24. Emily Auerbach, "John Bull and His 'Land ohne Musik,'" *Victorian Literature and Culture* 21 (1993): 69.

25. Simon McVeigh, "The Society of British Musicians (1834–1865) and the Campaign for Native Talent," in *Music and British Culture, 1785–1914: Essays in Honour of Cyril Ehrlich*, eds. Christina Bashford and Leanne Langley, 145–68 (New York: Oxford University Press, 2000).

26. H. Davey, "Discoveries in English Musical History," *New Quarterly Musical Review* 3(9) (May 1895): 35.

27. William Weber, *The Rise of Musical Classics in Eighteenth-century England: A Study in Canon, Ritual, and Ideology* (Oxford: Clarendon, 1992), 101.

28. In Friedrich Rochlitz's tribute to him in the *Allgemeine Musikalische Zeitung* shortly after Hiller's death in 1804, Rochlitz noted (invoking Lessing's phrase) that "some are famous, others deserve to be so." "Every epoch," he continued, "seems to begin suddenly, its preparation to take place only inwardly, and subsequent fame accrues only to those who make the epoch, not to those who prepared its way." Rochlitz, "Zum Andenken Johann Adam Hiller," *Allgemeine musikalische Zeitung* (1804), 137, 158.

29. Karl Geiringer, *Haydn: A Creative Life in Music* (New York: Norton, 1946), 318. In 1938 Geiringer had fled Vienna, where he was curator of the library and the archives of the Gesellschaft der Musikfreunde. Although a Roman Catholic himself, both his parents had been Jewish. His own desire to see Haydn and indeed all of the great Viennese composers whose papers he had curated and whose biographies he wrote speak for the German nation rather than the Germans who had forced him to flee seems palpable in these observations.

30. Quoted in Nicholas Temperley, *Haydn: The Creation* (New York: Cambridge University Press, 1991), 21.

31. Zelter, review of the published full score, *Allgemeine musikalische Zeitung* 4 (1801–1802), excerpted and translated by Nicholas Temperley in the appendix to his *Haydn*, 92. Zelter clearly regarded this as an opportunity also to pontificate a bit in his self-appointed role as guardian of the Bach legacy: "Eager young composers may have noticed that all the fugal choruses are light, supple, and free and that in all this great work there is not a single strict fugue," he wrote Zelter, but "let them be warned that such ease and freedom are possible only for someone who knows how to write a strict fugue with all its trappings."

32. Percy A. Scholes, *The Mirror of Music, 1844–1944: A Century of Musical Life in Britain as Reflected in the Pages of the* Musical Times (London: Novello, 1947), vol. 2, 642. See also the complete program of the Boston Peace Jubilee by Patrick Sarsfield Gilmore, *History of the National peace jubilee and great musical festival: Held in the city of Boston, June, 1869, to commemorate the restoration of peace throughout the land* (Boston: Lee and Shepard, 1871), 432–42.

33. Todd, *Mendelssohn*, 548.

34. Weber, *Rise of Musical Classics*, 127–41.

35. K. A. Appiah, "Against National Culture," in *Text and Nation: Cross-disciplinary Essays on Cultural and National Identities*, ed. L. Garcia-Morena and P. C. Pfeiffer (Columbia, S.C.: Camden House, 1996), 175–76.

CHAPTER 10

"SHOOTING THE KEYS": MUSICAL HORSEPLAY AND HIGH CULTURE

CHARLES HIROSHI GARRETT

In the nation, as comedy moves from a passing effervescence into the broad stream of a common possession, its bearings become singularly wide. There is scarcely an aspect of the American character to which humor is not related, few which in some sense it has not governed. It has moved into literature, not merely as an occasional touch, but as a force determining large patterns and intentions. It is a lawless element, full of surprises. It sustains its own appeal, yet its vigorous power invites absorption in that character of which it is a part.

—Constance Rourke, *American Humor: A Study of the National Character* (1931)

You're willing to pay him a thousand dollars a night just for singing? Why, you can get a phonograph record of "Minnie the Moocher" for 75 cents. And for a buck and a quarter, you can get Minnie.

—Otis B. Driftwood (Groucho Marx) on the going price of an operatic tenor in *A Night at the Opera* (1935)

During tough times, laughter represents one of the most vital and significant ways in which we cope and survive. Writing in 1934, in the midst of the worst economic challenge of the twentieth century, Martha Bensley Bruère and Mary Ritter Beard responded to what they saw as an outpouring of humor: "It may seem that in an hour of nation-wide depression, laughter is the last thing to ponder on. But wit and humor feed on failure as well as on success; their nutriment is absurdity, incongruity, and conflict, no less than satisfaction, and peace."[1] The nature and form of humor, however, have always been quite complex. Humor can provide distracting amusement from current troubles; it can offer joking or deceptively light commentary about the current situation; or it can deliver a satiric punch directed at the apparent causes of the problems at hand. This chapter examines how humor acts not only as a type of psychological comfort or comic relief but also as an avenue for cultural critique and a site of competition and interchange between popular and elite culture. I pay special attention to how musical humorists have engaged with various aspects of the world of classical music and what this engagement reveals about cultural history and the changing status of classical music in the United States.

Choosing to begin this inquiry during the era of the Great Depression reflects the wealth of humor created during this period, as well as the kinds of subjects toward which it was directed. As the epigraph from Constance Rourke's influential study suggests, humor was seen by some critical voices to have influenced nearly every aspect of American life. Furthermore, some of America's most beloved humorists established their careers in the shadow of the Great Depression. The Marx Brothers, for instance, produced the vast majority of their comic films between 1929 and 1941. On what many saw as the higher end of the cultural spectrum, classical music in America also flourished in this period. Aided by technological advances and the rapid growth of radio, film, television, mass media, and the entertainment industry, classical music increased its reach and popularity, with the rise of star conductors like Arturo Toscanini, the splashy release of Walt Disney's *Fantasia* in 1940, and the success of the Boston Pops at marketing "light" classical music. Audiences were also exposed to more American concert works once questions arose during World War II about the appropriateness of performing Austro-German repertoire.[2] According to a poll conducted by *Fortune* magazine in January 1938, "62.5 percent of all Americans liked to listen to classical music on the radio." Although this figure may be skewed to some extent by the target demographic that characterizes the readership of this money magazine, the following year *Harper's* estimated that 21.5 percent of Americans preferred "classical music" above all other musical genres, while 52.8 percent enjoyed both "classical and popular music."[3] Such figures would astound and delight any development officer working for a professional orchestra or opera company today, and they stand in sharp relief to those gathered in 1974 by Joseph Rody, who found that "only 1 percent of the American population had attended a single symphony orchestra concert."[4] Because a little success breeds imitation and because even greater success often breeds comic imitation, the popularity of classical music inspired parodies, spoofs, and send-ups, which emanated from the vaudeville stage, the movie house, the radio broadcast booth, and the concert hall.

The Marx Brothers were at the center of a great deal of this nexus of comedy and classical music, and they are responsible for the classic film *A Night at the Opera* (1935), which one music historian suggests may be "the most successful large-scale spoof on opera in the twentieth century."[5] Mocking high culture through the lens of opera came naturally for a comedy team that specialized in producing satire, as evidenced by their earlier film *Duck Soup* (1933), which lampoons the clumsy blow-hards leading a Fascist regime. Enacting class critique by musical horseplay also perfectly suited a group that included accomplished musicians whose performances often parodied classical music throughout their career on the vaudeville stage and in film. Perhaps most significantly, as outlined earlier, satirizing high culture, along with its associations of wealth and privilege, in the midst of the Great Depression held great promise for wide popular appeal. By this moment, as Lawrence Levine has documented in rich detail, cultural hierarchy in the United States had become more firm, clearly bounded, and defined. No longer were serious operatic acts freely intermingled with popular numbers or burlesque acts, as had been more common in nineteenth-century America. Instead, audiences interested in what had come to be considered elite culture—whether this involved a trip to the museum or a night at the opera house—were now accustomed "to approach the masters and their works with proper respect and proper seriousness, for aesthetic and spiritual eleva-tion rather than mere entertainment."[6] Not necessarily so, asserted the Marx Brothers.

Their night at the opera instead is all about impropriety and upheaval, as Groucho, Chico, and Harpo wield their vaudeville chops and musical expertise to achieve the greatest amount of improper disrespect. Their satire begins with the nature of the medium of film itself since *A Night at the Opera* stages this entire battle of low versus high culture on the new media terrain of film rather than stag-ing it as a competing work in the opera hall. As Lawrence Kramer points out, this choice is crucial to the satiric project carried out by the Marx Brothers in terms of how the film "takes apart the opera in order to claim both theatrical and social superiority for itself."[7] Although the film is filled with scripted chaos, this is not to say that it lacks coherence or significance—the aesthetics of humor are capable of delivering deadly serious messages—but instead reflects how heavily this satiric work relies on comic techniques, including slapstick comedy, word play, music-based comedy, exaggeration, physical humor, incongruous surprises, droll humor, parody, and much more. Much of the responsibility for verbalizing the terms of class critique in *A Night at the Opera* falls to the grifter and charlatan Otis B. Driftwood, played by Groucho Marx. As the opening epigraph suggests, it is Driftwood who expresses the film's primary concerns about popular and elite culture by offering satiric commentary about the enormous salary an operatic tenor could command in comparison to a much more affordable recording of the comic record "Minnie the Moocher" (1931) by the effervescent bandleader Cab Calloway. Spicing things up further and acting the louse, Driftwood extends the joke by salaciously claiming that Minnie herself might be for sale for the right price. Throughout the film Driftwood hurls equally satiric and off-color jokes, which range from the utterly ridiculous to the bitingly acerbic. He draws continuous attention to the stuffy elitism of the wealthy and the shallow caprice of high society, meanwhile trying to bull his way through the door. As Mark Winokur explains in his detailed examination of Hollywood film comedies from the 1930s, the "Marx Brothers' satire of the wealthy is always a satire of the pretensions of upward mobility and a denial of the existence of authentic gentility."[8] In this film Groucho achieves these goals both by exposing the foibles of the rich and by playing Driftwood, the scheming phony who wishes to join their ranks.

At the heart of this broader satire is the world of opera, which centers the film's narrative and bears the brunt of much of its humor. According to the film's narrative, the culture of opera is overrun by pretentious snobs who are too rich for their own good, so much so that they are willing to assume the massive cost of musical patronage for the sake of even higher standing. The film's self-centered opera tenor is worse: so greedy that he is unwilling to sing until a paycheck is visible, so lascivious that he corners the film's heroine with unwanted attention, so cruel that he abuses an assistant for wearing his stage costumes (in truth, Harpo probably deserves it for wearing three separate costumes on top of his own clothes). Little wonder that Driftwood asks his driver to slow down on the way to the opera house so he's not in danger of getting there on time. However, unfortunately for Driftwood and perhaps for some opera buffs, he does arrive in time to see the final staged number of Verdi's *Il Trovatore* (1853), a tragic work at the heart of the operatic canon that serves as the backdrop for the film's conclusion. Nearly everything goes wrong for Verdi in this comic spectacle, which includes several troublemakers being chased on stage by policemen and angry men in tuxedos, one getting knocked out by a frying pan and another performing a kind of gymnastics on the scenery backdrop. The stuffy tenor is kidnapped—thus making way for the triumphant New York debuts of the film's young hero and heroine—and even when he escapes and makes his way to the stage, the lout is greeted by boos and pelted with fruit. In addition to the havoc onstage, the two imps played by Chico and Harpo also raid the pit orchestra, where they experiment with new uses for the violin. Harpo attempts to make music by sliding the violin bow across the belly of a trombone, next employs it as a weapon to fence with the orchestra conductor, and finally puts the violin itself to use as a baseball bat as part of a mock ballgame staged in the pit. Driftwood can't resist contributing to the commotion, as a popular sporting pastime upends a high-class orchestra, and he stalks the theatre aisles yelling "Peanuts, Peanuts."

Leonard Bernstein was acutely aware of proper conventions in the concert hall as a result of his many years as the conductor of the New York Philharmonic, but despite or perhaps because of such intimate familiarity he was terribly amused by such foibles. Bernstein described the Marx Brothers as representing utter chaos: "It's not logical, that's all, and logic has been destroyed. That's why we've laughed for years at Laurel and Hardy and Charlie Chaplin and the Marx Brothers and the Three Stooges. Because they make a hash of logic—they destroy sense, and we laugh our heads off, just as we do at the man slipping on a banana peel."[9] Describing laughter as arising from our reaction to nonsense reflects the influence of a long-held theory that ties humor as one human response to incongruity inasmuch as it can emerge when we encounter things that don't make sense within our frame of reference. It is true that some audience members, following Bernstein, may be laughing more at the nonsensical activities of the Marx Brothers, delighting in their chaos without end. At the same time, there is more at stake in *A Night at the Opera* than can be explained by pure chaos, for the Marx Brothers are making a hash not only of logic but also of operatic high culture. As Lawrence Kramer explains, drawing on the work of Mikhail Bakhtin, *A Night at the Opera* may rely on hectic frenzy, but it ends up "flouting official culture, defying its rules and degrading its representatives."[10] We might therefore consider the nature of the Marxes' satiric humor to be closer to Plato's assertion that humor is based on expressions of superiority. We laugh when a man slips on a banana peel because we believe we are smarter than that, and we laugh *with* the Marx Brothers and *at* the targets of their jokes because the Marxes convince us that we are superior to the members of elite society as well.

Yet, even these explanations do not do full justice to what the Marx Brothers accomplish in *A Night at the Opera*, perhaps in part because competing explanations of humor have not coalesced into a single grand theory of humor. "The only factor on which commentators seem to agree," writes Miguel Mera, "is that humor is connected with expectation. Almost all humor is set up by creating a sense of anticipation that is then subverted or dislocated. For an audience to find something funny, they must be complicit in this anticipation; they must expect what you predict them to expect."[11] All parody and satire require a certain level of cultural knowledge to succeed, and there is no doubt that the Marx Brothers were brilliant at dreaming up the unexpected. Nonetheless, Mera's point about complicity is also critical for understanding the multilayered way in which the Marx Brothers attempted to reach multiple audiences. As Kramer notes, even while staging the "aggression of have-nots against haves," the film must also "depend on and yearn for the very operatic pleasures it claims to surpass."[12] To be more specific, cultural insiders like Bernstein are able to better enjoy the film, for the more one understands the conventions, practices, and repertory of opera, the greater the response the film elicits, whether one's reaction takes shape as irritation or laughter.

Musical jokes are laced throughout the film, starting with the idea of building the comic finale around what opera aficionados would recognize as one of Verdi's intensely serious, dramatic, and tragic works. The Marx Brothers further extend this subversion by including several jokes that depend on the audience's knowledge of another staple of the operatic repertoire, Ruggero Leoncavallo's opera *Pagliacci* (1892), one that similarly ends in bloodshed, even though its lead character is known for performing the role of a clown. Driftwood tells us as much when he sings a melodic fragment from its most famous aria, "*Recitar!...Vesti la giubba*" but freely substitutes some new words: "*Ridi Pagliacci*, I love you very macc-i." In a separate scene, the haughty tenor (supposedly the best since Enrico Caruso, who was acclaimed for his performance of this very aria) is confronted with a question about his clown costume: "Can you sleep on your stomach with such big buttons on your pajamas?" Finally, just when audiences think that the film's rambunctious finale has been restored to enough order that the young singers can perform the concluding numbers from Verdi's *Il Trovatore* in grand fashion, it turns out that one performs an aria from the "right" opera and the other chooses to sing an aria from *Pagliacci*. Although all audiences might laugh at the sight gag with the pajama buttons, it is likely that filmgoers without any knowledge of Caruso, Leoncavallo, or the music of *Pagliacci* would find Driftwood's brief operatic ode incongruous at best and would miss the structural irony of the final performance altogether. Like many other effective satirists, the Marx Brothers were simultaneously aiming low and aiming high, hoping to entertain audiences with varying degrees of exposure to opera.

Similarly, the film also holds greater potential to capture the attention of anyone with exposure to piano performance in Western classical music and beyond. In addition to turning instruments into props for physical comedy, the Marx Brothers overturn traditional techniques of making music, a natural outgrowth of their theatrical upbringing and comic flair. Harpo was known to choose unconventional instruments; in addition to the harp, he whistled, tooted a horn, and performed on kazoo, comb, and the piano keyboard with the lid closed. Chico Marx, whose keyboard chops led to early jobs as a barroom entertainer and accompanist, often performed flashy piano solos on stage and on screen. His talent was clear and his repertory wide—ranging from Chopin waltzes to the "Beer Barrel Polka," Delibes to "I'm Daffy over You"; in fact, before the Marx Brothers spent "a night at the opera" with Verdi's *Il Trovatore*, Chico had already performed the opera's "Anvil Chorus" as part of a medley in the film *Animal Crackers* (1930). Even more delightful for his fans and perhaps more notorious to piano pedagogues, Chico drew from a barrelful of entertaining vaudeville tricks, whether flamboyantly gliding the nail of his finger up the keyboard to perform a glissando ascent or rolling an orange quickly back and forth with his right hand to approximate a trill. In *A Night at the Opera* Chico playfully entertains a group of children with a version of "All I Do Is Dream of You" by changing dynamics with comic abruptness, surprising them with snazzy glides, flicking the keys back and forth with his index finger as if it were the arm of metronome set on the highest tempo, raising his index finger dramatically between phrases, and finishing his performance by "shooting the keys"—Chico's signature move, in which he extends his index finger and thumb as if he were a kid shooting a gun, and then hits each key with the tip of his index finger while simultaneously closing his thumb to accentuate each shot. These sorts of musical tricks and stunts not only were designed to delight these young onlookers but also came to be an expected part of Chico's musical numbers in Marx Brothers films. Just as the entire family poked fun at the broader conventions of elite musical culture, so, too, did Chico's style offer something intentionally incongruous and radically different from classical approaches to playing the piano.

By staging their cultural upheaval and poking holes in opera through the less-elevated medium of film, by tricking the elite members of the orchestra into playing a musical ode to the joys of the common sport of baseball, by shooting the piano keys instead of playing them with grace and conventional respect, the Marx Brothers wielded humor as a battering ram against the walls of high culture. Furthermore, they formed bonds with audiences who appreciated their jokes, for just as humor can serve to humiliate or mock antagonists, it can also bring together people who find the same thing funny. As Levine notes, "the Marx Brothers and a legion of other popular comedians built parodies of that meaning into the very heart of their humor: they created a rapport with their audiences that generated a sense of complicity in their common stand against the pretensions of the patrons of high culture."[13] However, just as they enforced and satirized notions of a divide between popular and elite culture, the Marx Brothers continually bridged that divide to offer more-nuanced entertainment to viewers with a deep knowledge of and admiration for opera. *A Night at the Opera* simultaneously expresses irreverence and affirmation, love and disrespect for its given subject of parody. After all, the film's young hero and heroine do not reject the genre of opera for the world of popular entertainment; instead, their triumph occurs when they perform their glorious debut as representatives of the next generation of opera stars.

Exposure to parody may also serve to draw audiences closer to the original sources, and this process can even shape the musical lives of the parodists themselves, as the experience of Harpo Marx makes clear. Born Adolph Marx in 1893, Harpo ended his formal schooling after completing second grade and eventually joined his brothers as an actor/comedian on the vaudeville circuit, becoming, in his words, "the most fortunate self-taught harpist and non-speaking actor who ever lived."[14] Although he was entirely self-taught as a harpist and learned to play by ear, that did not stop him from bringing the instrument into the brothers' act shortly after he began playing. As he liked to tell the story, Harpo was unable to sing, dance, act, or crack jokes, so playing the harp enabled him to stay in the group and prompted his stage name. He performed a few popular tunes, as well as a harp arrangement of the sextet from Gaetano Donizetti's opera *Lucia di Lammermoor* (1835), demonstrating that the incongruous juxtaposition of slapstick high jinks and musical high culture held plenty of appeal for vaudeville audiences. Harpo's cinematic persona turned to the harp sometimes for comic purposes and other times as a means of spotlighting his special virtuosity amid the onscreen chaos, but his interest in exploring classical music was by no means limited to the silver screen. Over the years he developed a special fondness for the music of Bach, Mozart, and Debussy, as well as the records of Spanish guitarist Andres Segovia, and he developed a minor obsession with Maurice Ravel's compositions for harp and ensemble. During the 1950s he released three LPs of harp music for Mercury and RCA Victor, and he was known for receiving guests at his Hollywood estate while in the midst of playing the harp. Although classical harpists have been hesitant to instruct their students to follow Harpo's technique—he tuned the harp strings incorrectly and for many years leaned the harp against the wrong shoulder—his musical peers were both fascinated and flabbergasted by his unusual technique. Harpo recalled that his first and only official harp lesson, after eight years of professional experience, was given by a harpist from the Metropolitan Opera, who seemed far more interested in mining Harpo's unconventional technique than in retraining him to play the harp in conventional fashion. More strikingly, over the years Harpo has become a beloved figure among not only the large community of Marx Brothers fans but also the smaller group of professional harpists because of his comedic charm, his obvious love for playing the harp, and his frequent and beautiful harp solos. Although Harpo's transition from a vaudeville parodist to a purveyor of high culture seems rather unusual—parodists of classical music often begin their musical careers at the conservatory—his memoirs suggest how constant exposure to classical music, by whatever means or medium, may cultivate interest in a new group of musicians and audiences alike. As much as it skewers class politics and derides elite culture, the satiric work of the Marx Brothers simultaneously works to dress down and to delight audiences of classical music today.

COMEDY IN MUSIC

A Night at the Opera represents the capstone of the Marx Brothers' satirization of opera and musical high culture. Their films continued to integrate memorable parodies of classical music, along with some more dignified performances, but such musical numbers became just one part of their comic arsenal in their larger satiric strategy. The prominence of classical music in the United States, however, presented plenty of fodder for a few performers who devoted their careers to musical parody and also inspired creative artists working in different mediums to find comedy in classical music. Animated film became a prime medium in which to express parody, satire, and love for classical music. In his book *Tunes for 'Toons* Daniel Goldmark explains how cartoons have introduced many Americans to classical music and helped make these sounds familiar and durable even as they have drawn criticism from those who believe they are cheapening or misrepresenting the classics.[15] Like the films of the Marx Brothers, comic animation often stages the struggle between high and low culture implicitly by comparing its own often-derided medium to the lofty heights of the concert hall and explicitly by pitting classical music against various adversaries. Such cultural wrangling has taken shape as a highbrow opera singer struggling against a lowly banjo-playing bunny (*Long-haired Hare*, 1948), a mythic conductor figure flummoxed by a wise-cracking audience member (*Magical Maestro*, 1952), and a virtuosic feline soloist battling a troublesome mouse living inside the piano (*The Cat Concerto*, 1946). According to its creator, Chuck Jones, the cartoon *What's Opera, Doc?* (1957) was designed to "take 14 hours of *The Ring of the Nibelungen* and reduce it to six minutes."[16] While such comic parody of Wagnerian opera led to accusations of blasphemy in some corners and perhaps calls for the development of video cassette recorders in others, Goldmark explains how such humor, like *A Night at the Opera*, represented not only cultural upheaval but also confirmation of the status quo. Cartoons such as *What's Opera, Doc?* remind us, writes Goldmark, that "classical music is high art; every time we see these cartoons, we are reminded that the object of their parody—opera—occupies a place of honor in our culture. By focusing on music and concert hall culture as worthy subjects for deflation, these cartoons more firmly set the music and spectacle in their high place."[17] Just as they tear down and undercut notions about the elite nature of classical music, so, too, do these animated works maintain the status of classical music.

We can understand the work of musical humorist Anna Russell (1911–2006) through a similar lens, for her parodies of classical music were built on deep familiarity with and love for classical music. Indeed, had her musical talents been more conventional, Anna Claudia Russell-Brown would have happily pursued a career in classical music, but as things turned out she made a career out of "finding the comical in serious music."[18] Born in London, England, to a wealthy family, Russell was "terribly serious about music and singing," and she gamely studied at the Royal College of Music: playing the piano, singing, and becoming intimately familiar with the works of Chopin, Liszt, Bach, and Beethoven.[19] Unfortunately, the self-deprecating Russell failed to make headway as an opera singer because she possessed what she later described as a ridiculous, tin voice: "In my heart of hearts I would love to have had a great voice, and to listen to mine is rather wounding to the ego."[20] Although this initial setback proved upsetting, Russell decided to write and perform musical numbers that parodied the music of Bellini, Debussy, Schubert, and other composers she admired. After moving to Toronto with her family on the eve of World War II, she began appearing as an entertainer on local radio shows and landed her first one-woman show in 1942. The prominent Canadian orchestral conductor Sir Ernest MacMillan took a liking to her brand of musical humor, which led to further concerts, increased attention, and, in 1948, her New York debut at the age of thirty-six.

From that point on, Russell became one of the world's best-known musical satirists. Russell's decision to parody classical music ironically seems to have upped her own cultural standing, and she was anointed with especially grand titles, including "the funniest woman in the world," "the clown princess of comedy," and "the queen of spoof." Ironically, it appears she was marketed as the best in the world at her craft of musical parody in part because of her engagement with high culture. Presenting comic monologues, parodies of Schubert lieder, deeply felt presentations on how to play the bagpipes, and humorous instructions on "how to write your own Gilbert and Sullivan opera," she toured internationally, from England and the United States to South Africa and Australia. She recorded numerous commercially successful albums, and *Anna Russell Sings?* (question mark intended) rode the top of the classical charts for much of 1953, a fact Russell found to be extremely ironic: "fancy being considered classical?"[21] She also appeared on the Broadway stage, performed on *The Ed Sullivan Show*, and worked in film and television. In addition to her public role as a performer, Russell composed her own material for her musical parodies and wrote several books: *The Power of Being a Positive Stinker* (1955), *The Anna Russell Songbook* (1960), and her autobiography, *I'm Not Making This Up, You Know* (1985). She continued performing into her seventies, then lived out her remaining years in New South Wales, Australia.

To a much greater extent than the Marx Brothers, Russell's rather staid performance style and deadpan delivery required the complicity of audiences who were musically knowledgeable and ready to accept such a focused style of humor. It was not surprising that most of her high-profile tours were booked into the same concert halls she sometimes mocked, providing a gentle interruption from the music she loved and roasted. This is not to say that Russell shied away from silly puns, stage props, and funny hats, but she did not aim for the kind of zany chaos favored by the Marx Brothers or Bugs Bunny. Nor was it coincidental that these comic lessons were being delivered by an entertainer who might be compared to a stereotypical British schoolmarm. Russell's droll delivery and her matronly persona prompted careful attention by audiences and made her comic exclamations and mock outrage that much more surprising. It would be unfair and positively Russellesque to compare her appearance on the classical music scene to the British invasion of popular music that took place in the United States two decades later; however, the fact that she was British and emerged shortly after World War II cannot be ignored. Russell's literate, nuanced, and sometimes understated humor could best be appreciated by English speakers—her record releases and tour stops focused mainly on the former or waning British Empire—and such sophisticated comedy was especially welcomed by fellow Brits recovering from the war, any former products of the British school system, those familiar with British musical culture (including the music of Gilbert and Sullivan), and anyone who could appreciate Russell's ability to acknowledge and defuse anxieties surrounding social class.

Along the lines of other forms of American and British cultural production during and shortly after World War II, Russell also took special delight in making fun of German culture, most obviously because of its elite standing within the musical world and perhaps less explicitly because of Germany's defeat at the hands of the Allies. By no means did Russell's droll manner affect the extent to which she went after some of the most famous composers and works in the classical canon. Her most famous set piece, "The Ring of the Nibelungs (An Analysis)," offers her personalized take on Wagner's Ring cycle, including a comic synopsis, her twisted performances of selected musical examples, and her wry reflections about the grand silliness of it all. Premiering in 1953, four years prior to *What's Opera, Doc?*, Anna Russell's Ring took a comparatively leisurely parodic route, clocking in at around twenty-five minutes, or four times the length of time devoted by Chuck Jones. Although she does not engage in similarly blatant parody throughout the entire act, Russell mixes in heavy helpings of irony and sometimes downright mockery. Toward the end of the piece, which she released as a recording and performed countless times live, she introduces Gutrune Gibich as "the only woman that Siegfried has ever come across who hasn't been his aunt," takes a deep breath, and then exclaims: "I'm not making this up, you know." This is one example of many dozens of the kind of "conditional" joke told by Russell in the sense that it "can only work with certain [knowledgeable] audiences, and typically is meant only for those audiences."[22] Although Russell's style of humor by definition could reach only so far outside her core audience of classical music aficionados, her distinctive approach enabled her to accomplish just what she always longed for as a child—a prime spot on the concert hall stage.

Even Russell's success did not match the achievements of the most successful humorist of classical music in the twentieth century, Victor Borge (1909–2000), the Danish pianist, comedian, and multifaceted entertainer who became known affectionately as "the great Dane" and "the clown prince of Denmark," monikers that highlighted his nationality while making both low- and high-culture comparisons to a breed of dog and to Shakespeare's Hamlet. Like Russell, Borge had been displaced from Europe during the upswing to World War II; unlike Russell, he had even greater reason to emigrate, for he was born into a Jewish family and had been touring as part of a European revue in which he occasionally told anti-Nazi jokes. Having studied piano at the Royal Danish Academy of Music and toured for several years as a concert pianist, Borge was an even more-accomplished performer of classical music. Even critics who were not moved by Borge's eventual mixture of comedy and music found ways to express their respect for his musical talent: "Mr. Borge plays the piano so well—even when eating a sandwich at the same time—that one cannot help wondering why he doesn't just play it, leaving the 'humor' to other times and other places."[23] According to Borge, his signature blend of piano music, stand-up jokes, and skits had its origins in the slapstick humor he found upon seeing a concert pianist accidentally fall off the piano bench. After arriving in the States, Borge continued to hone his musical humor, starting with a stint on Rudy Vallee's radio show and continuing with more radio work and small film roles. By 1946 he was so well known that NBC hired him to host his own live show, where he polished many of his trademark routines.

Equally adept at comic timing and inflection, Victor Borge drew on all types of humor, including stand-up comedy, his take on slapstick (which included a breakneck four-hand routine in which he and a fellow pianist ended up knocking each other off the piano bench), prop comedy (he used a car seatbelt to fasten himself down to the piano bench "for safety"), a grab bag of visual gags, and a steady flow of puns, double entendres, and word games. For instance, his playful skit on "inflationary language" featured Borge incrementing numbers or their homonyms (e.g., "wonderful" became "two-derful"; "tender" became "elevender"). Most famously, although perhaps not to the same relentless extent as Anna Russell, Borge included running commentary about and music-related skits based on the practices, composers, and greatest hits of Western classical music. He played with the names of beloved composers (e.g., Giuseppe Verdi became "Joe Green") and those not so well known (such as the Danish composer "Mozart…Hans Christian Mozart."). Many of his jokes were not restricted to specialists but were intended for anyone remotely familiar with the subject: For example, he described the piano as terribly boring when the instrument consisted of only one large key but noticeably more exciting after someone invented all of the cracks ("it changed everything"). Finally, Borge would pull the biggest surprise of all: In the middle of an act filled with nonsense and satire, he would sometimes interrupt his comic routine by performing classical music in a conventional, straight manner, whether choosing to play a Chopin waltz or a Mozart minuet.

Borge combined all of these crowd-pleasing elements in *Comedy in Music*, which opened in October 1953, ran for 849 performances, and became at that time the longest-running one-man show in Broadway history. Writing for the *New York Times*, Stephen Holden described it as a blend of "stand-up comedy, Marx Brothers horseplay, and unsophisticated musical humor…that very gently deflates the intimidating mystique of classical music."[24] Borge tried to pursue a number of aesthetic strategies at once. First, he attempted to establish the right balance between levity and respect: "I have a telegraph to the audience," he said, which indicates "this is serious," whereas "this is just fun."[25] Second, he explained that "I have always worked for two audiences at the same time. One is sophisticated, the other not musically oriented. I notice that the ones who laugh most are composed of professionals, as when I do my act with orchestras. But my jokes must be understood by everybody. Nobody must be bored."[26] Finally, like Anna Russell, Borge claimed (and critics generally agreed), his clowning and tomfoolery represented a labor of love: "I think that I have brought in my share of new listeners for serious music. I hope to open a window. I bring new listeners to the concert hall, and some of them go back for other concerts without the comedy. I never make fun of the music. I make fun with the music. I also think that I have helped some orchestras sustain their seasons."[27] Such claims are difficult to dispute, considering that Borge's career included upward of six thousand concerts, more than a dozen albums, hundreds of radio broadcasts, guest conducting gigs, video releases, and television appearances that ranged from *The Ed Sullivan Show* to *Sesame Street*. Stalwart fans now upload video clips of Borge's performances to YouTube, which brings selected highlights of his distinctive act to contemporary audiences.

To gauge the impact of musical humorists like Russell and Borge, it is tempting to play up the extent to which they ridiculed and roasted the object of their attention, how they figuratively pierced the walls of elitism associated with high culture. Moreover, certainly, their irreverence poked enough fun at classical music to be thought of as being oppositional to some degree. At the same time, however, both entertainers appealed to audiences who were clearly knowing collaborators and were ready and willing to accept this gentle satire. Furthermore, as Borge suggested, less-experienced audience members who enjoyed such performances could eventually turn into avid concertgoers. Consequently, this style of musical humor represented not only a challenge to classical music by certain elements of popular culture but also a multifaceted site of cultural exchange, where ideas about classical music and elite culture were variously prodded, mixed, repackaged, transformed, and refreshed.

Although their performances sometimes elicited complaints or stone silence from classical music purists, musical humorists like Anna Russell and Victor Borge posed no real threat to the cultural practices surrounding classical music. They occasionally occupied elite concert music venues, displaced other musicians in the process, and attracted the attention of potential classical music audiences, but both artists also celebrated the institution of classical music and enabled those in the know to laugh at the practices they knew so well. Just as they both started out to become classical performers, both Russell and Borge ended up enlivening the classical music scene. By the time they reached the peak of their fame, they no longer stood outside looking in but rather stood inside looking around.

Swinging the Classics

More potentially ominous humor about the prospects for American classical music was produced during the war years and beyond by musicians left outside the classical music fold, such as Hazel Scott (1920–1981) and Dorothy Donegan (1922–1998). Both Scott and Donegan were African American female pianists who initially pursued careers in classical music during an era of systematic racial segregation, which led them to turn instead to boogie-woogie and jazz. Scott learned her keyboard skills by playing church music, pounding out popular tunes, and taking private lessons from a Juilliard professor, but she found her niche while trying to compete with another lounge entertainer: "Finally, one day, I had had enough," she explained. "I said, 'I know, I'll play the Bach inventions and I'll syncopate them, really up, up tempo, and see if she does THAT in her show.' "[28] Taking the classics and "ragging" them in the ragtime era or "jazzing" them up after the birth of jazz was nothing new. Indeed, as Gary Giddins observes: "A ripe sense of humor is indigenous in jazz. It's a music quick to enlist whatever barbs can best deflate pomposity and artificiality."[29] For a number of black female pianists, however, to "boogie" the classics in midcentury offered a very different take on what it meant to parody classical music from the perspective of marginalized outsiders.

In 1940 Scott applied the bluesy syncopations of boogie-woogie to the music of de Falla, Chopin, and Liszt—whose music she had once performed straight as a child—in her first solo album, *Swinging the Classics*. In response to "From Bach to Boogie-Woogie," a recital staged at Carnegie Hall the following year, *Collier's* enthusiastically pronounced Scott's performance to be "the most impudent musical criticism since George Bernard Shaw stopped writing on the subject....It was witty, daring, modern but never irreverent. I think Liszt would have been delighted."[30] Because she took artistic inspiration from the classics and did not explicitly ridicule her source material, Scott's performance may not have struck critics as being irreverent in the same sense as a Marx Brothers sketch. However, in other respects, her performance was far more revolutionary. Scott's improvisatory attitude, her combination of incongruous genres, her near complete dismissal of Liszt's instructions on the printed page, and the appeal of her music to fans outside the classical realm well expressed the kinds of challenges to come for classical music in the United States.

We can see how this cultural transformation took shape in performance by turning to an early appearance by Dorothy Donegan, who followed Scott's footsteps as a boogie-woogie pianist and established a career that lasted for more than five decades. Donegan was outrageously talented, as well as simply outrageous. Writing for *The New Yorker*, Whitney Balliett compared her "rich, flying left hand" and her "roller-coaster lines and ten-pound chords" to one of Donegan's mentors, Art Tatum.[31] Still, not all critics were sure what to make of her idiosyncratic approach or her larger-than-life stage act, which mixed jazz standards with stylistic parodies of other jazz pianists, incongruous medleys of unrelated songs, humorous asides, and salty jokes. Leonard Feather appreciated her distinctive style but lamented that "Donegan's problem is that she has never appeared to take herself seriously."[32] One of her first triumphs involved performing at the age of nineteen in the Hollywood film *Sensations of 1945*. Wearing a stylish white dress and seated at a white grand piano, Donegan begins what at first appears to be a solo performance of Franz Liszt's *Second Hungarian Rhapsody*. She solemnly plays the opening phrases of Liszt's 1847 composition but gradually and relentlessly transforms the original melody, harmony, and tempo until Liszt's piece dissolves and up sprouts a flashy boogie-woogie number à la Hazel Scott. Donegan steams ahead, kicking her left foot to the beat, smiling at the camera, improvising on passages by Liszt, and all the while displaying her tremendous keyboard skills. Midway through, her piano begins to rotate slowly, as if to move even further away from Liszt and toward the sensation of popular culture, at which point another jazz pianist, Gene Rodgers, joins her in a boogie duet. The two engage in a friendly competition, and then Cab Calloway, the popular bandleader who made Minnie the Moocher famous, appears on screen to spur their rollicking duet to the finish.

As popular culture increasingly challenged the authority of high art during the twentieth century, there was plenty of comic potential to be realized in poking fun at a classical warhorse through a popular idiom like boogie-woogie. Indeed, Liszt's rhapsody served as fodder for numerous cartoons, including two the following year—one starring Bugs Bunny (*Rhapsody Rabbit*), the other Tom and Jerry (*The Cat Concerto*). Like the work of Russell and Borge, the humor of Donegan's musical surprise works best for someone who is familiar with the original Liszt composition. Knowing audiences realize something is quite out of order when she starts to jazz things up, and they may react with amusement or despair when Donegan later inserts brief quotations from the original composition. However, in contrast to Borge and Russell, the focus here shifts from foregrounding any reverence for classical music to the exploration of jazz improvisation, as the rhapsody melts into the propulsive drive of boogie-woogie. Liszt the composer remains present in the background as Donegan the performer firmly takes the lead. Consequently, Donegan's humor did not seek explicitly to revere or preserve classical music in the United States but instead to overturn the European classical tradition using a vernacular African American approach.

Donegan was classically trained herself, which explains in part why she often drew on classical music in her performances, and she released many boogie-woogie renditions of classical pieces such as Beethoven's Minuet in G and Grieg's Piano Concerto. Although this subgenre of concert boogie-woogie later ran into resistance from jazz critics who felt that it pandered to white middle-class audiences and reduced jazz to burlesque, for Donegan this mixture offered an appropriate personal metaphor that functioned as a creative wellspring to which she returned for the next half-century. A few years after appearing in *Sensations of 1945*, she set aside her jazz career to pursue classical music full-time, returning to jazz only after finding little opportunity to build a career as a female African American classical pianist. Playing the trickster with Liszt thus symbolized both a triumph and a disappointment for Donegan—a triumph in terms of this musical act of transformation and a disappointment in terms of what it implied about the failure of her alternate career goals. Occasionally she voiced her frustrations to interviewers about the lack of opportunity within the classical musical world, but much more often she offered musical commentary on the situation by "boogie-ing" the classics and making them her own. For performers like Donegan, there were serious reasons that "jazz took pleasure in skewering anything that made the mainstream feel safe and smug."[33] Today we may still perceive plenty of humor in her work, although our understanding and appreciation of her musical experience in America now seems tinged with some regret.

Classical Music, Why Bother?

Irreverence, incongruity, subversion, parody, satire, irony—all of these modes of humor appear in performances by the Marx Brothers, Victor Borge, Anna Russell, Hazel Scott, and Dorothy Donegan. Nevertheless, regardless of their precise aesthetic positions and whether or not each of them stood inside or outside the classical world, this handful of musical humorists did not single-handedly sway the trajectory of classical music in the United States. Certainly these artists influenced public opinion by scratching the veneer of elite culture, but some also worked to confirm the status of elite culture and, in certain cases, to spread the joys and expose the humor of classical music. Comedians Jack Benny and Danny Kaye even turned to musical humor as a means of supporting classical music more directly by combining physical comedy, jokes about classical music, and philanthropy in the form of benefit concerts that mocked the musical institutions for which they netted substantial funding.[34] From Gretchen Wheelock's work on humor in the music of Haydn, we know how individual composers and musicians are subject to the "shifting values of wit and humor" and the changes in public taste.[35] The past six decades also tell us that musical humorists are also at the mercy of their targets. For parody to thrive as a convoluted form of flattery, its source material has to be equally robust and popular. In the wake of the explosion of popular mass-mediated culture after World War II, including moments when these developments also drove the popularity of classical music in the United States to remarkable heights, the last several decades have been particularly rough on the fortunes of classical music in America despite the impact of government funding, as well as other public and private philanthropy. It is not that classical music as a whole or individual genres such as opera have disappeared but rather that this music no longer dominates national conversations and cultural debates about America's musical life. Not surprisingly, the fortunes of parodists who specialize in classical music have declined as well, notwithstanding the brilliant early work of Dudley Moore and the contributions of P.D.Q. Bach, the alter ego of Peter Schickele, whose smart and fantastically silly satires of classical music first appeared on the concert stage in 1965.

In retrospect, it seems as if the success that Moore and P.D.Q. Bach found in the late 1960s and early 1970s now represents an era when humor so reliant on a larger classical music audience also began to diminish. As Schickele explains, "most satirists make fun of what they like, not of what they don't like," and the smaller audience devoted to classical music has meant a concomitant decrease in classical music satirists.[36] The real competition for classical music in the twentieth century, after all, has involved the proliferation of new media—radio, film, television, video games, digital media, the Internet, and beyond—and the concurrent rise of popular music and popular culture. Although there have been some notable exceptions, as in 1956, when Chuck Berry celebrated rock and roll by ordering Beethoven to roll over and tell Tchaikovsky the news, American popular culture has not been overly concerned with poking fun at classical music but rather has been busy carving out its own cultural space. Strong feelings such as love, hate, passion, and anger may inspire satire and humor, but apathy indicates that not as many people are paying attention.

As a result of orchestras struggling, classical radio stations going dark, record companies cutting back, television turning its lens to other musical practices, and the challenge of cultivating new and younger audiences, chroniclers of classical music openly acknowledge the various obstacles that lie ahead. As part of his sweeping history of American music, Richard Crawford describes how the "concert hall [has begun to look] increasingly like part of a historical age that might be winding down."[37] Likewise, as made evident in the title of his book *Classical Music in America: A History of Its Rise and Fall*, Joseph Horowitz argues that the spread of postmodernism and the decline of clear distinctions between high and low culture have meant that "the history I tell has largely run its course."[38] Earnest attempts to defend the worth of classical music in print now take shape in book titles such as *Who Needs Classical Music?*, *Classical Music, Why Bother?*, and *Why Classical Musical Still Matters*.[39] Although there remain some opportunities for comic intervention—such as the cameo made by a cartoon representation of Philip Glass on the animated television series *South Park*—the decline of classical music traditions is no longer a joking matter, and the potential audience receptive to such humor has shrunk. It has become more common for contemporary parodists to resort to gallows humor, as in the episode of *The Simpsons* ("The Seven Beer Snitch") in which the town of Springfield builds its own concert hall, a replica of Frank Gehry's Walt Disney Concert Hall, which instantly goes bankrupt and ends up serving as a penitentiary. Consequently, a performer falling off a piano bench might raise far more concern than laughter. Today's most successful musical parodists, such as "Weird Al" Yankovic and The Lonely Island, have turned their attention to larger audiences of more commercially lucrative genres, such as pop music, R&B, and hip-hop. Only a few professional humorists who engage with classical music remain active today, and none have entertained nearly the number of live audience members as Borge or Russell. Two of the most successful contemporary parodists are violinist Aleksey Igudesman and pianist Richard Hyung-ki Joo, who partnered in 2004 as the musical comedy duo of Igudesman and Joo, have toured concert halls, played international festivals, and reached more than ten million Internet viewers through YouTube. While both Igudesman and Joo are quite accomplished as conventional performers in the world of classical music, the pair has found musical parody to be a lucrative and fun outlet for exploring the music they hold dear. Relying on larger-than-life stage props, slapstick humor, and a deep admiration of all things ridiculous, Igudesman and Joo carry on the Borge tradition in their stage show with the slightly askew title "A Little Nightmare Music," a play on Mozart's work that only those in the know will catch. However, even these musical parodists have adapted to the changing times by often featuring incongruous mixtures of classical music with other popular elements, whether that means moving from Rachmaninov to *Riverdance*, combining Mozart's Symphony no. 40 with the main theme from James Bond films, or performing Gloria Gaynor's disco classic "I Will Survive" as a twisted violin sonata while wearing a tuxedo jacket and shorts. It appears today that trafficking in classical music alone is not enough to sustain contemporary musical parodists. The irony, especially for those who may have been displeased by any musical humor that once went too far or cut too deep, is that the ability of musical parody to thrive also offers one of the clearest signs of a genre's health.

NOTES

1. Martha Bensley Bruère and Mary Ritter Beard, *Laughing Their Way: Women's Humor in America* (New York: Macmillan, 1934), v.

2. American performances of Austro-German works declined from around 80 percent of the complete symphonic repertoire in 1875 to around 50 percent in the World War I era, and anti-German sentiment, combined with pride in American music, caused this figure to dip to an all-time low of 46 percent during World War II. Joseph Horowitz, *Classical Music in America: A History of Its Rise and Fall* (New York: Norton, 2005), 268; Philip Hart, *Orpheus in the New World: The Symphony Orchestra as an American Cultural Institution* (New York: Norton, 1973), 407.

3. Horowitz, *Classical Music in America*, 399.

4. Joshua Fineberg, *Classical Music, Why Bother? Hearing the World of Contemporary Culture through a Composer's Ears* (New York: Routledge, 2006), 13. Fineberg cites Rody's piece in W. MacNeil Lowry, ed., *Performing Arts and American Society* (Englewood Cliffs, N.J.: Prentice Hall, 1978).

5. Daniel Goldmark, *Tunes for 'Toons: Music and the Hollywood Cartoon* (Berkeley: University of California Press, 2005), 134.

6. Lawrence W. Levine, *Highbrow/Lowbrow: The Emergence of Cultural Hierarchy in America* (Cambridge, Mass.: Harvard University Press, 1988), 146.

7. Lawrence Kramer, *Musical Meaning: Toward a Critical History* (Berkeley: University of California Press, 2002), 136.

8. Mark Winokur, *American Laughter: Immigrants, Ethnicity, and 1930s' Hollywood Film Comedy* (New York: St. Martin's, 1996), 128.

9. Leonard Bernstein, *Young People's Concert: Humor in Music,* originally broadcast Feb. 28, 1959. A transcript of this broadcast is archived at http://www.leonardbernstein.com/ypc_script_humor_in_music.htm (accessed Feb. 5, 2009).

10. Kramer, *Musical Meaning,* 139.

11. Miguel Mera, "Is Funny Music Funny? Contexts and Case Studies of Film Music Humor," *Journal of Popular Music Studies* 14 (2002): 91.

12. Kramer, *Musical Meaning,* 136–37.

13. Levine, *Highbrow/Lowbrow,* 235.

14. Harpo Marx, *Harpo Speaks!* with Rowland Barber (New York: Geis, 1961), 27. The following biographical information on Harpo derives from this source.

15. Goldmark, *Tunes for 'Toons,* 107–108, 121.

16. Cited by Goldmark, *Tunes for 'Toons,* 133.

17. Goldmark, *Tunes for 'Toons,* 159.

18. Anna Russell, *I'm Not Making This Up, You Know: The Autobiography of the Queen of Musical Parody,* ed. Janet Vickers (New York: Continuum, 1985), 1. The basic outlines of Russell's life summarized here derive primarily from this source.

19. Russell, *I'm Not Making This Up,* 1.

20. Russell, *I'm Not Making This Up,* 129.

21. Russell, *I'm Not Making This Up,* 144.

22. Ted Cohen, *Jokes: Philosophical Thoughts on Joking Matters* (Chicago: University of Chicago Press, 1999), 12.

23. R. L., "Victor Borge Makes Concert Debut Here," *New York Times* (Oct. 14, 1945), 41.

24. Stephen Holden, "Victor Borge and 'Comedy in Music,'" *New York Times* (Dec. 28, 1986), 53.

25. Ruth King, "Victor Borge, Comedy's Music Man," *Music Journal* 35(10) (1977): 7.

26. Harold C. Schonberg, "Laughter Is Still Music to Victor Borge's Ear," *New York Times* (Dec. 5, 1989), C19.

27. King, "Victor Borge," 7.

28. Karen Chilton, *Hazel Scott: The Pioneering Journey of a Jazz Pianist from Café Society to Hollywood to HUAC* (Ann Arbor: University of Michigan Press, 2008), 46.

29. Gary Giddins, *Visions of Jazz: The First Century* (New York: Oxford University Press, 1998), 143.

30. Luther Davis and John Cleveland, "Hi, Hazel!" *Collier's* (Apr. 18, 1942), 16.

31. Whitney Balliett, *Collected Works: A Journal of Jazz, 1954–2001* (New York: St. Martin's Press,), 526.

32. Leonard Feather, "Jazz," *Los Angeles Times* (Dec. 19, 1982), U84.

33. Giddins, *Visions of Jazz,* 143.

34. Kenneth H. Marcus, "The Seriousness of Comedy: The Benefit Concerts of Jack Benny and Danny Kaye," *American Music* 25(2) (2007): 137–68.

35. Gretchen A. Wheelock, *Haydn's Ingenious Jesting with Art: Contexts of Musical Wit and Humor* (New York: Schirmer, 1992), ix.

36. Donald Rosenberg, "Schickele: The Man behind P.D.Q. Bach," *Early Music America* 7(3) (Fall 2001): 22.

37. Richard Crawford, *America's Musical Life: A History* (New York: Norton, 2001), 696.

38. Horowitz, *Classical Music in America*, xv.

39. Julian Johnson, *Who Needs Classical Music? Cultural Choice and Musical Value* (New York: Oxford University Press, 2002); Fineberg, *Classical Music, Why Bother?*; Lawrence Kramer, *Why Classical Music Still Matters* (Berkeley: University of California Press, 2007).

CHAPTER 11

YVETTE GUILBERT AND THE REVALUATION OF THE *CHANSON POPULAIRE* AND *CHANSON ANCIENNE* DURING THE THIRD REPUBLIC, 1889–1914

JACQUELINE WAEBER

Guilbert's "Two Careers"

As is well known, the French *diseuse* Yvette Guilbert (1865–1944) had two careers. The fact is substantially documented not only by Guilbert's autobiographical writings[1] but also by a variety of sources, including letters and documents from her contemporaries.[2] In her first career she was known as the *diseuse fin de siècle*, a reputation that blossomed in the early 1890s in Paris during the Belle Époque. The second started in 1901, after a serious illness had forced Guilbert to retire from the stage in 1899. What made these two careers so different was a dramatic change of repertoire that had led her to abandon the *chanson moderne* of the café concert (with emblematic songs such as "Le p'tit cochon," "Je suis pocharde," "Le fiacre"[3]) for a new repertoire entirely dedicated to the celebration of the historical French *chanson*, the origins of which can be traced as far back as the Middle Ages.

In her interviews and writings, Guilbert has explained the motivations behind such a dramatic shift, which can be summarized by her attempts to "elevate" her art and to depart from the low-brow repertoire of the café concert.

> At the height of her career as a music-hall or vaudeville artist, Madame Guilbert canceled her engagements to develop her art. "I felt within me infinite possibilities for higher things; but I should have to change my surroundings first." From that time on she resurrected and re-created the songs and ballads of ancient France, the Middle Ages, and later centuries.[4]

Or at least, this is how the story goes. For this notion that Guilbert had two completely different (if not opposing) careers is undoubtedly the most enduring myth about her and is still well established today.[5] The purpose of this chapter is to pinpoint the ideological subtexts that motivated Guilbert to construct a supposedly new repertoire dedicated to the celebration of the *chanson ancienne* and the *chanson populaire*. The time period considered here, from 1889 to the eve of World War I, is crucial for understanding how Guilbert defined her conception of the "canon" of the *chanson* through its process of historicization, which was at work during the Troisième République, while being ideologically appropriated by the left and the right wings. Focusing solely on Guilbert's career up to 1914, this chapter also considers her early pedagogical career in the light of other contemporary pedagogical experiences developed in France, essentially Gustave Charpentier's Conservatoire de Mimi Pinson and Ernest Chebroux's Œuvre de la Chanson française.

Guilbert's artistic activities were led by her acute sense of propaganda and of self-promotional flair, notably through the press. The 1916 article in *Current Opinion* (see note 4), blindly following Guilbert's (auto)biography written by Simpson, is one of many instance of such propagandist manipulation, as is the following article, published in the November 1908 issue of the French monthly magazine *Musica*. The article was to provide an overview of the evolution of the chanson from the 1870s to 1908. Clearly, *Musica* held that the *chanson française* was embodied in the holy trinity of Thérésa,[6] Madame Judic,[7] and, naturally, as their sole heiress, Yvette Guilbert. Although *Musica* asked Guilbert to reflect on her art (as she had frequently been asked to do since the 1890s), she primarily gave her reasons for abandoning her first career, which had begun in the late 1880s with the café concerts, which had made her internationally famous as the *diva fin de siècle*. As she explains (referring to herself in the third person):

> We are convinced...that Yvette Guilbert, when singing for instance "Le Petit Cochon", was only being libertine. A few persons only could or were able to admit that this was only the cruel satire of the conjugal depravities...; and the satire was made under the form I have mentioned to you, through joyful couplets that didn't hide the lesson...I would have sung the virtues of my time if my time had been showing off virtues...I made do with the vices of my century, I made the work of a satirist according to the strength of my resources.[8]

In the most revealing manner, Guilbert attempts to justify her first career in the café concerts of the 1890s. It is easy to read between the lines of this article and identify Guilbert's need to reinvent herself and ideally to distance herself from the café concert, notably by abandoning the genre of the chanson moderne in favor of a historical repertoire of chansons anciennes and chansons populaires, celebrating the French genius. In retrospect it was comforting for her to find in her 1890s' repertoire the seeds of the morality she would so keenly defend during her so-called second career, which took off in the 1900s.

The nuances in the adjectives *moderne, populaire*, and *ancien* must be discussed here. Like other contemporary commentators on the French chanson, Guilbert would often refer indifferently to the chanson populaire *or* the chanson ancienne, for the notions of "ancien" and "populaire" had frequently been conflated since the last third of the nineteenth century, essentially through the Republican revaluation of the chanson undertaken by scholars such as the medievalist Gaston Paris and the musicographers/folklorists Jean-Baptiste Weckerlin and Julien Tiersot.

Guilbert was one of many who played the notions of the chanson ancienne or populaire against the chanson moderne, the latter expression being nevertheless a confused one since it could refer to "contemporary songs" (i.e., from the 1880s on), which could be part of an artistically elevated repertoire (like the songs by Aristide Bruant or Léon Xanrof, which were part of her repertoire in the 1890s[9]). However, chansons modernes could also refer to a less-dignified category, encompassing the songs of the decaying café concert of the early twentieth century, which Guilbert abhorred, and the new repertoire of the music hall, with its singing stars such as Mistinguett, Yvonne Printemps, Damia, or Marie Dubas—the last two having been the object of Guilbert's acerbic comments. After the First World War this latter repertoire would again be referred to as the chanson populaire, but here *populaire* had acquired a negative connotation, separating itself from the chanson ancienne and now conflating with the chanson moderne. In order to avoid any misleading translation (such as the English "folksong" to refer to "chanson populaire"), I use the French expressions throughout the text, especially as they appear in the sources.[10]

Guilbert's new repertoire must be considered within this typical French practice of drawing indiscriminately from both high and popular cultures and from modern and past repertoires. This is a phenomenon that Jann Pasler has recently identified as a "conscious juxtaposition of [musique] *ancienne* and [musique] *moderne*," as shown by the late nineteenth-century French programming practices in the concert hall,[11] the ideological and cultural mechanisms of which, however, are still perfectly relevant to Guilbert.

Of course, other factors explain Guilbert's desire to reinvent and distance herself from the café-concert universe: By the end of the 1890s the café concert was already perceived as a moribund genre that had imploded into several subgenres, from the *comique troupier*, illustrated by Paulin, to the *chanson réaliste*, which culminated in the careers of Damia, Fréhel, and finally Édith Piaf (a genre to which Guilbert cannot be attached), as well as the growing success of the music hall, as exemplified by the rising careers of Dranem, Fragson, and Félix Mayol—the latter often referred to as the last star of the café concert and the first star of the music hall. Guilbert was well aware of being a fin-de-siècle icon, and her paradoxical fame was to be fashionable precisely because she was embodying a genre already perceived as passé, thus perfectly suited for celebrating the growing nostalgia surrounding a century just about to end. As I discuss later, such awareness had already led her during the 1890s to search for new directions in her repertoire, a fact that has been largely neglected, notably because this chapter of Guilbert's 1890s' repertoire has been essentially assimilated into that of the low-brow café concerts.

However, more personal issues were at stake: During her convalescence in 1900–1901, Guilbert started gaining weight and never recovered her original, almost emaciated silhouette, which had made her famous. The point may seem merely anecdotal, but for an artist who had so painstakingly constructed her stage persona in accordance with a specific repertoire, the consequences were dramatic. For Guilbert deserves to be viewed as the first *popular* artist to have been fully aware of the implications and potentialities of a well-crafted artistic image, as can be shown by the abundant iconography representing her during the 1890s. Henri de Toulouse-Lautrec epitomized Guilbert's silhouette, characteristic of her career during the 1890s, in many paintings and sketches, the most famous being the 1894 portrait of the *diseuse* greeting her audience at the café concert Le Moulin Rouge: A long green arabesque evoking her lanky body in her trademark dress, punctuated by two black streaks like stylized ravens for her long gloves, a bun of red hair atop her head, and her clownesque face.[12]

Still, it took Guilbert some five years, from 1885 to 1890, to construct this remarkably stylized image. Her debuts at the Parisian café concerts were difficult: She struggled to find a repertoire that would suit her and, above all, that would make her different from other *diseuses*. Because of her emaciated appearance, by then much against the grain of the standards of feminine beauty, Guilbert was teased and even mocked during her first performances. Her early fiascos testify to her inadequacy in a repertoire that had already been largely popularized by the *chanteuses de beuglant* in the tradition of Thérésa. In November 1889 the audience of the café concert L'Eldorado laughed at her gauntness, awkwardly disguised in the traditional bouffant dress worn by *diseuses* such as Félicia Mallet, Judic, and Thérésa, as well as at her lack of voice and the stiffness of her gestures. On the whole, Guilbert's rendition of songs was considered plain and dull. However, before finding a stage appearance that suited her, Guilbert had to find a repertoire that worked for her. Three decisive events shaped the fame of the *divette fin de siècle:* The discovery of Léon Xanrof's songs, her first performance at Rodolphe de Salis's cabaret, Le Chat Noir (in 1892), and her short tenure at the Éden Concert in December 1889—following the Eldorado debacle. It was thanks to Polin,[13] Guilbert's colleague at the Eldorado, that she discovered the collection *Chansons sans gêne* by Léon Xanrof.[14] A *chansonnier* much in vogue in the Bohemian milieu of the Montmartre cabarets, Xanrof was a member of the Chat Noir circle, and it was also because of Polin that Guilbert visited the cabaret for the first time. This exposure to the more-cultivated, yet eccentric, atmosphere of the Bohème de Montparnasse greatly influenced Guilbert.

Guilbert had already discovered Xanrof's songs when she performed at the Éden Concert. Also known as *le café-concert des familles*, the Éden boasted of having a decency lacking in other Parisian café concerts. In 1885, the poet and critic Francisque Sarcey and the poet and chansonnier Ernest Chebroux[15] had launched weekly *vendredis classiques* at the Éden, consisting of *tours de chant* dedicated to the chanson ancienne, what Chebroux referred to as "la bonne et saine chanson de nos pères"[16] in the tradition of Pierre-Jean de Béranger. These *vendredis* attracted many literati of the conservative vein, such as the Parnassian poets François Coppée[17] and Sully-Prudhomme. At the Éden Guilbert was for the first time fully exposed to the repertoire of the *vieille chanson* and was immersed once more in another type of refined and literary audience, although of a more conservative nature than the one at Le Chat Noir. Although brief and moderately successful, Guilbert's tenure at the Éden must not be overlooked inasmuch as it helped her develop a strategy for constructing a new repertoire that would please two radically different types of audience: The popular and the elite, the latter encompassing the Bohemian spirit of the Montmartre cabarets, as well as a more conservative audience. If she was not permitted to sing Xanrof's songs at the Éden, Guilbert was prompt in realizing the potential that her "new" style could tap by integrating this old repertoire into a more modern one. Furthermore, Xanrof's songs had a flavor of the *ancien*—which was perfectly in tune with the neomedievalism that was characteristic of the fin de siècle and had colored many productions at and around Le Chat Noir.[18] Next to Xanrof, who had chosen a Latinized (with a twist) pen name, other chansonniers from Le Chat Noir, such as Jules Jouy, Jean Richepin, and Aristide Bruant, were frequently compared to medieval poets and troubadours if not referred to as "modern Villons"—perhaps the most famous of these being the poet Paul Verlaine, another member of the Chat Noir circle, although Bruant was also frequently compared to the author of "La Ballade des Pendus."

In 1891, an article on Guilbert's brand new fame by the American art critic and writer Theodor Child used just such a comparison. It was accompanied by a further medieval reference to Abélard, when referring to Xanrof and his song "L'hôtel du numéro 3"—in the *divette*'s repertoire since 1890:

> Xanrof is a barrister, a man who has taken his degree at the Sorbonne, who adores literature in the form of couplets. He is a sort of Villon fin de siècle, gay, cynical, without venom, sarcastic, and yet ingenuous. Nothing is more unlike the usual march and waltz music, or the stupid flouflous [*sic*] of the ordinary chauvinist or obscene café concert songs than the unconventional songs of Xanrof: Chansons sans Gêne, as he calls them. Xanrof's songs have a literary turn. His music has an Old World innocence that suggests reminiscences of the gentle airs of the pavane and the minuet. Take, for instance, "L'Hôtel du Numéro 3"... [The article gives the twenty first bars of the vocal part of the song: see next page.]
>
> The song gives an excellent and faithful picture of the hotel garni, of the furnished lodgings of the Latin quarter, of the chamber which has taken the place of the bundle of straw in a barn of the days of Abelard and the Rue de Fouare.[19]

Guilbert's first successful engagement was in 1890 at the Parisian Divan Japonais, a café concert attended by members of the working class. There she appeared in her green dress and for the first time sang Xanrof's songs, among which was "Le fiacre," already

well known at the café concert for having been one of the great successes of its dedicatee, Félicia Mallet, a pantomime artist and *diseuse* who specialized in Bruant's songs. However, Guilbert's new manner marked a radical departure from the realist style used by Mallet and other café concert artists. Guilbert's brilliant plan was to use a costume that would enhance rather than hide her physical idiosyncrasies. Reducing herself to a silhouette, almost a sketch, Guilbert created a new appearance that perfectly matched her uncluttered use of gestures, which had earlier been derided as mechanical. In so doing, Guilbert brought to the café concert a degree of stylization and an art of distance unknown until then. Her artistic ambition and efforts to elevate the art of the *diseuse* were indeed unknown among her predecessors. They also explain Guilbert's search for songs with a distinctive *literary* quality. In 1896 Guilbert had met and corresponded several times with the writer Pierre Louÿs about a project involving an *opéra-comique* composed by Camille Saint-Saëns and based on Louÿs's newly published novel, *Aphrodite: Mœurs antiques* (1896), in which she was to sing the role of Chrysis. It is obvious from the correspondence with Louÿs that Guilbert was by then definitely trying to divest herself of her image as *diseuse fin de siècle* and *diva du café concert:*

> Suppose for five minutes that I were not Yvette Guilbert, a singer of "bouffant"

she said to Louÿs.[20] The libretto would have to be written by Maurice Donnay:

> I have seen Maurice Donnay[,] he is delighted by the idea—Saint-Saëns is in Brussels[;] *I have just written him to remind him his promise to write music for me when an interesting subject will give him the opportunity*[.] You will see that him as well will tell us yes, and damn it is if with such a trinity I do not manage to make forget my turned up nose![21]

However, the project failed, Donnay and Louÿs having decided against it (in reality, the latter disliked Saint-Saëns's music).

Outside of France, Guilbert's success grew rapidly. Theodore Child's aforementioned article gives a vivid explanation of Guilbert's ascension, stressing how she was "discovered" by Bohemian poets and journalists. In other words, Yvette's pedigree was one of a true artist from Montmartre, which confirmed her credentials with the artistic and intellectual élite:

> In less than six months she has become famous. Last August [1890] she was singing in a little café at Montmartre called Le Divan Japonais, where she was discovered by some Bohemian poets and journalists. Then she passed to the joyous Moulin Rouge [where she] increased her public. She won the esteem of a score of poets and journalists, who began to talk about her in the papers. The song writer Xanrof found in her an ideal interpreter of his dry and as it were ingenious cynicism. Thus she became a celebrity, but her fame remained confined to the artistic Bohemia of Montmartre, having only a feeble echo at Tortoni's on the grand [sic] boulevards. Still, there was a rumor that Montmartre had produced a new fledging, a future artist...
>
> Then followed...in November a real début at Paris in the Concert Parisien, a small café chantant in the Faubourg St. Denis of no great reputation....[F]urthermore the Concert Parisien is close to the boulevard...Yvette made her début...Her fame spread, and *the clubmen and the swell cocottes went to the Concert Parisien, contrary to their custom*, to applaud the new diva. Curious hostesses wondered whether they could have Yvette at their soirées.[22]

As Guilbert would explain in 1893, "You see, the café concert is a special place for a special audience; the great audience, the one with education, finesse, delicacy, is only an audience of passers-by, the one on a walkabout; the great art is to attract it often."[23] At the popular café concert Le Divan Parisien she was then able to attract the audience of the "Grands boulevards" ("the clubmen and the swell cocottes"), who would experience the delicious shiver of slumming at the café concerts.

Guilbert's dazzling ascension was bluntly described in René Mazeroy's article, published in the *Gil Blas Illustré* (July 12, 1891): "She was almost an extra at the Variétés, two years ago. She earns today more than fifty thousand francs for singing songs 'fin de siècle' in the *beuglants* and the salons. Was discovered and made a star by a few literati. Panurge's flock followed."[24] Indeed, Guilbert was proud of having been the object of such recognition. Later in *Autres temps, autres chants* she recalled her 1892 invitation to perform at Le Chat Noir:

> In 1892, the Chat-noir, making an exception to its rule, honored me by an invitation to sing my songs. It was its way to thank me for having been the first to bring to the boulevards the spirit, the new laughter from the Butte [Montmartre], and for having propagated the chat-noiresque verve through the couplets by its most celebrated poets and *chansonniers*: Maurice Donnay, Jules Jouy, Rollinat, Xanrof, Bruant, Richepin.[25]

As Derek Scott puts it, "Guilbert successfully 'crossed-over,' and by the mid-1890s, had admirers in both classes."[26] Child's 1891 article not only confirms this but also pushes her successful "crossover" to an earlier date. Child's article was written only a few weeks after another highlight in Guilbert's early career, her engagement in January 1891 at the Théâtre d'application (also called La Bodinière, in reference to its founder and director, Charles Bodinier)[27] for a series of five lecture-recitals titled "L'ingénuité fin de siècle," given by journalist Hugues Le Roux with Yvette. The audience of La Bodinière counted noted members of the haute bourgeoisie and Parisian literati. In 1890 Bodinier had started organizing *matinées-causeries*, following a trend that had started at the end of the Second Empire: Among the *conférenciers* who began appearing from then on at La Bodinière were poets, playwrights, writers, and critics such as Maurice Bouchor,[28] Paul-Armand Silvestre, Ferdinand Brunetière, Anatole France, François Coppée, Maurice Donnay, and Francisque Sarcey.[29]

Yvette's success at La Bodinière was huge, especially among female audience members, who would not have dared to attend one of Guilbert's *tours de chant* in popular café concerts such as the Divan Japonais, the Nouveau Cirque, or the Concert Parisien: "Eventually Yvette arrives. She comes from Brussels. Practically no one knows her in Paris. Hugues Le Roux introduces her, and the whole [of] Paris comes to La Bodinière."[30] However, Guilbert's success also indicates a renewed interest in the chanson, which had now acquired—thanks to her—a higher form of recognition and respectability and thus began a new trend for such lectures. For after Guilbert's 1891 appearances, La Bodinière continued to program several other lecture-recitals featuring actors and singers (among which was the famous pantomime artist and singer Félicia Mallet) in what could be described as "historical recitals"—a form of recital that became Guilbert's favorite routine from the 1910s on. Such performances had much in common with the *vendredis classiques* of the Éden Concert. At La Bodinière, *la romance de nos pères* and *les chansons d'autrefois* were the quaint attributes of the chanson, now valorized as a canonic repertoire that needed to be defended by relevant erudition:

> The chanson monopolizes the morning talks [at la Bodinière]: one can hear the *chansons brutales* by Félicia Mallet, presented by Maurice Lefèvre; the *romance* of our fathers deliciously sighed by Mme Mathilde Auguez and M. Cooper; the *chansons d'autrefois*, said with a lot of wit by Mme Amel, from the Comédie-Française, presented by Georges Boyer; one can also hear Simon-Girard, Alice Lavigne and Victor Maurel... Eventually, it is yesterday that we have heard the interesting talk by M. Robert de Montesquiou on Mme Desbordes-Valmore, that was given in front of an audience of princesses and marchionesses.[31]

Guilbert's success at La Bodinière and her growing fame among the literary circles became the subject of a lengthy review published in February 1891 in *Le Mensuel* by an admirer of Guilbert, the twenty-year-old Marcel Proust. Not without causticity did Proust deconstruct the "ingenuousness" of Yvette. Apparently not fooled by her purported perversity *fin de siècle* (which was precisely what attracted the bourgeois audience), Proust saw in Guilbert one of the very last remnants of naturalism—thus, an artist already old fashioned: "As she is, in her bodily appearance—as well as in her diction—she reminds [us] of the naturalism already out of fashion, by all means so different from today's art... We admire more than anyone the talent of Mlle Yvette Guilbert. But, despite all our good will, we do not find her perverse at all."[32] What Proust bluntly reveals is no less than Guilbert's remarkable ability to maintain an ambiguous image, one that

would be differently understood by various types of audiences, from members of
the lower classes to the more prominent attendees. As Mazeroy put it, Guilbert
did sing "in the *beuglants and* the salons": Without abandoning her tours de
chant at the popular café concerts, she had managed to find an aura of respectability thanks to the chaperonage of some distinguished literary figures. In so
doing she blurred as much as possible the delimitations between high-brow and
low-brow repertoires.

Guilbert's ambivalent image was not lost on some perspicuous commentators,
whether admiring or criticizing the singer. A later review in 1896 by the poet and
playwright Maurice Lefèvre provides a radically different perspective on Guilbert by
describing her as the embodiment of the chanson moderne, this symptom of the
pourriture fin de siècle:

> Let's enter the Chanson Moderne. There she is! Long leech, sexless! She crawls,
> creeps with hissings, leaving behind the moiré trail of her drool....On both
> sides of this boneless body hang, like pitiful wrecks, tentacles in funereal gloves.
> For she will, indeed, lead the burial of our Latin race. Complete negation of our
> genius...
>
> First she was celebrated...Then came the infatuation [with her] and
> Paris-Panurge appeared. Then the true *œuvre* began...Contemplate her...
> this clown's face. Out of this powdered mask comes a dry, broken voice....Do not
> curse this modern *Chanson*...It is not its fault, it is ours. It is not it that
> decomposes us, it is born from our own rottenness, we created it, it is our vices
> that made it viable. Poor little Chanson, faithful mirror in which men reflect
> themselves, are you responsible for their hideousness?[33]

Although he did not mention her name, it is clear that the target of Lefèvre's
review is Guilbert (the dry, broken voice, the clownish face, the black gloves, the
powdered mask...as well as the caricature published on the previous page of
the article): Utilizing metonymy, Guilbert embodies the "chanson moderne,"
stigmatizing the decadence of the fin de siècle. Ironically, Lefèvre's critique
seems to announce Guilbert's 1908 article for *Musica*, in which she claimed
that she "would have sung the virtues of [her] time if [her] time had been
virtuous!"

Beyond the implicit attack on Guilbert, this statement must be viewed in a larger
context. Coming from *Le journal pour tous*, the *supplément illustré* of the conservative *Le Journal* and written by Maurice Lefèvre, an admirer of Félicia Mallet (they had
appeared together at the *matinées-causeries* at La Bodinière), the content of the article should not be a surprise. In 1893 Lefèvre had authored *À travers chants*, a book in
defense of the chanson populaire and dedicated to Mallet.[34] The book's preface, written by Jules Claretie, states that the "chanson populaire" is "back in fashion":

> Thus the chanson, like pantomime, has become once more back in fashion. But
> have we ever ceased to sing chansons, in this country of France? *Between the epic*
> Chanson de Roland *and the realist and socialist chanson of Bruant, one can say that
> this is our whole history.*[35]

Claretie's encompassing reference to the period from the Middle Ages to Bruant clearly pinpoints a revaluation of the patrimony of the French chanson, which had been at work since the early 1880s. He also provides an idealized historical landscape of the chanson, which extended over some eight centuries, which is precisely what Guilbert aimed to revive from the 1890s. Lefèvre's book also emphatically praises such historical dimension:

> To say the novel, the odyssey of the chanson, would be to make the history of peoples...Because the chanson is the interpreter of a people's soul.[36]

By integrating Bruant's "chanson réaliste et socialiste" in 1893 Claretie reconfigured a new canon for the chanson, one that was, however, still strongly rooted in the moral and educative values of the chanson populaire as established during the Second Empire and with an emphasis on the "collective" genius proper to the Republican ideals.

In Praise of "L'érudition Chansonnière"

Claretie and Lefèvre were among those who spread the fruits of the scholarly revaluation of the chanson populaire, which had been brilliantly illustrated by societies and institutions such as the Société des traditions populaires, founded in 1885 by the folklorist Paul Sébillot—of which Claretie was a member.[37] The organization had originated as an offspring of a group of French folklorists who, in 1878, had launched the scholarly journal *Mélusine*, dedicated to collecting French popular traditions and myths.[38] One main figure of this renewed interest in the chanson was the medievalist Gaston Paris, one of the founding members of the Société des traditions populaires.[39] A specialist in the chanson ancienne, in 1875 Paris had published a collection titled *Chansons du XVe siècle*, with modern transcriptions by the composer and music historian Auguste Gevaert, a noted scholar of Gregorian chant.[40] Paris had been a frequent interpreter of popular songs at least since 1885 and certainly during the 1890s within the erudite and exclusive audience of the Parisian Cercle Saint-Simon. The first of these concert-lectures had been inaugurated in 1885 by both Paris and Tiersot, with "*la première audition méthodiquement organisée de chansons populaires,*" in which they both sang some of the songs.[41] The year before, the French government, via its Institut National de France, decided that the Prix Bordin would, for 1885, be awarded to a study on

> popular melodies and on song in France, from the early 16th century up to the end of the 18th. To summarize its history, to define the characters and different forms under a musical angle, and to determine the role that they have played in religious and secular music.[42]

The award went to Tiersot's study "Histoire de la chanson populaire en France." The most important French folklorist of the Troisième République, Tiersot pub-

lished the study in 1889; this epochal book in the field of folklorist studies proposed
a common history for the chanson populaire and French medieval music by demonstrating the direct connection between medieval monody and the chanson.
Tiersot had, of course, a political agenda in tying together the different folklores of
the French provinces, sometimes stressing their common features and at other
times propounding the notion of French national unity.[43] Tiersot's series of
Mélodies populaires des provinces de France, published between 1887 and 1928,
remains the largest collection of French popular tunes. Tiersot also collaborated
with the composer Vincent d'Indy by providing him with the tunes for the two
volumes of *Chansons populaires du Vivarais*, harmonized by d'Indy and published
in 1900 and 1930.[44] Guilbert's successful "crossover" must also be viewed in the light
of these intricate ramifications between exclusive, erudite audiences and the general public of the café concert—the cases of the Éden concert and the concert-
lectures of La Bodinière offer particularly visible points of intersection. Guilbert's
ambition to expand her repertoire was also profoundly influenced by such scholarly attitudes. Among the many documents housed at the Fonds Rondel of the
Bibliothèque Nationale is a cutting from an unidentified newspaper, dated February
15, 1895,[45] that offers an unexpected portrait of the *divette*. Titled "Pourquoi Yvette
Guilbert court les bibliothèques," the article takes the form of a long letter written
by Guilbert. The article appears to be promotional in nature—an exercise in which
Guilbert excelled:

> But I go very often to the library! And not only the one on rue Richelieu, but also
> to Carnavalet, to l'Arsenal!...I have found there works more interesting than
> certain novels, and it made me regret to be a star from 1894...because I was
> afflicted not to find in the 19th century the great liberty that the chanson had in
> the 17th and the 18th centuries.
>   We used to sing the king!—the king's mistresses—the Parliament!—the
> ministers!—the courtiers, the generals, everything was set to mocking, joking
> or witty couplets. Today we must not laugh...my goodness...it would be
> expensive! The song loses something...because there would be many
> amusing things worth saying...The ones that one dares in the small intimate
> vaults, the Chat Noir, and elsewhere, that have such a huge success...First, it
> would prevent the authors to pick up disagreeable subjects, even sad
> ones...The chanson is a strength that in all times had a utility that has been
> removed today, since it is shackled like a condemned man.
>   Freedom for the chanson, please! It is the playtime of the ordinary people
> and it does not hurt anyone! On the contrary! It would oblige people to have
> some sort of morality. The fear of the chanson would make them honest.[46]

Guilbert did not even wait until 1908 (with her open letter to *Musica* quoted
earlier) to emphasize the moralizing high ground of the chanson, which "makes
people honest," and her interest in the chanson populaire (here clearly encompassing
the meaning of *ancien*) also dates from this period. In 1896 the *Los Angeles Times*
published a long article by the American journalist and famous early muckraker Ida
Tarbell, who was then living in Paris. It is to some extent reminiscent of the aforementioned article:

> Among the transient women students whom I remember to have seen in the
> Bibliothèque, was…Yvette Guilbert.…The enterprising little girl was hunting up new
> songs for her café chantant repertoire. *Having exhausted all the clever fin de siècle slang
> and vulgarities of Paris—not an easy task—she had decided to go back to the days of
> Rabelais and François Villon and their like and adapt their atrocities to modern audiences.
> For days she came regularly working over the ribald songs and rhymes of the monks and
> curés of the fifteenth and sixteenth centuries…*It is only one of many original and
> enterprising notions she has followed out to keep herself at the head of her class.[47]

Guilbert's correspondence shows that in 1902, if not earlier, she was in regular
contact with the music historian and folklorist Jean-Baptiste Weckerlin, by then
curator of the library of the Conservatoire de Musique in Paris. In a letter dated
November 1902, she explains her need to see him

> To guide me in the choice of a series of chansons anciennes![48]

We do not know which songs Weckerlin suggested, and contrary to what could
have been expected, he did not seem to have directed her toward the numerous collections he had himself published since the 1850s.[49] Except for one song, Guilbert's
repertoire of chansons anciennes, which had started appearing in several publications in 1905, does not make any use of songs edited by Weckerlin.[50] However, Yvette
was obviously satisfied with the curator's guidance:

> I'm already working on your chansons. Do not forget my minuet! Where can I
> find the turlututus,[51] I went through whole Paris trying to dig these out![52]

Thus, from 1895—if not earlier—Guilbert had started expanding her fin-de-
siècle repertoire by trying to imitate what was in her opinion the scholarly method
exemplified by the likes of Paris and Tiersot. Guilbert's health problems in 1899
could not have been, so to speak, more timely. Her comeback to the stage in 1901
had to correspond to the new career that she wanted to see as a radical departure
from her fin-de-siècle persona. However, the facts betray Guilbert's explanations.
On January 11, 1901, Guilbert reappeared at La Bodinière with her usual repertoire—
having added only songs by the *chansonnier chat-noiresque* Maurice Rollinat and
premiered "L'éternel féminin," a song on a poem by Jules Laforgue. On June 11, 1901,
Guilbert sang at the Olympia, starting a new tour in Germany, Austria, and eastern
European countries. Called "Montmartre en ballade," the tour was poorly received,[53]
and as mentioned earlier, her recent weight gain was often ironically commented
upon and created some embarrassment for her. However, she made her comeback
at the Folies-Bergère in 1904, wearing her trademark green dress with the black
gloves (and maybe she had even managed to shed some pounds):

> But this is not anymore the "too healthy" Yvette, it is really now the tall and thin
> Yvette from earlier times. We have found again the green dress and the black
> gloves, we have found again the biting elocution and the precise gesture.[54]

By 1904 Guilbert was still searching for new artistic directions, as stated by the
actress Ethel Barrymore, who had attended one of Guilbert's recitals in London:

Guilbert had become "an extraordinary beautiful singer" of the old Provencal [sic] songs. "She used to sing awful things, but still with great art," Miss Barrymore harked back. Now, clad in a black dress, she sings the "awful things" only in the first part of her entertainment; then attired in a little pompadour dress and with hair powdered, she devotes the second part to the old Provencal [sic] ballads.[55]

It is more likely that Weckerlin was behind several of the songs chosen for Guilbert's new recitals, made up of chansons anciennes and "chansons 1830" (partly presented in 1904 in London). On March 23, 1905, she premiered at the Bouffes Parisiens, dressed in an eighteenth-century costume, often referred to as "costume Pompadour."[56] Numerous photographs have popularized Guilbert wearing her "costume Pompadour," and there is no doubt that the striking visual opposition it created with her fin-de-siècle silhouette greatly helped her become comfortable with the idea that she had two careers. For an artist who had been strongly defined by the unique stylization of her silhouette, the necessity of finding a visual appearance in accordance with her repertoire was perfectly justified. The historical trend displayed by Guilbert's "recitals en costumes" was, however, hardly an invention of hers. Wearing a purportedly adequate costume is a trend that may lead back to the 1889 Exposition Universelle, with its competition for "airs populaires," dedicated to French provinces and foreign countries and displaying to the Parisian audiences a colorful series of regional attire. Aiming to expose audiences to various types of folklore and, for the French provinces, the multiplicity of traditions, the competition also emphasized the continuity between past and present.[57] Not only did the choice of the costume visually strengthen the idea of historical accuracy, but it also reinforced the notion of historicization, which by the 1900s was a major concern in the pedagogical missions defended by the Paris Conservatoire (essentially publicized through the music history lectures of composer, folklorist, and former anti-Dreyfusard Louis Bourgault-Ducoudray, who had been appointed professor of music history at the Conservatoire in 1878), and by the Schola Cantorum, both of whom, despite their diverging ideological agendas, were working for the revalorization of the French past and its traditions.

Guilbert's recitals of chansons anciennes and of "chansons 1830" were also strongly reminiscent of her tenure at the *vendredis classiques* of the Éden Concert. This sort of recital, which provided a historical overview of the chanson, had by the mid-1890s become one of the highlights of the Théâtre de la Bodinière (where Guilbert had made a sensational appearance in 1891). Georges Fragerolle, a former member of the Club des Hydropathes and pianist at the Chat Noir (a task he shared with Satie) had appeared at La Bodinière in 1894 with his own *Chansons des soldats de France* (1894), a collection of pastiches imitating

the forms and character from every [historical] period, from the King Henri's arquebus men up to the chanson d'actualité.[58]

Another important yet unacknowledged model of Guilbert's new repertoire of chansons anciennes was a *sociétaire* of the Comédie-Française, Madame Amel,[59] who had been appearing at La Bodinière since 1894. She subsequently became a frequent performer at this theater, where she specialized in the chansons anciennes. In 1897 Madame Amel published a collection of songs titled *Chansons d'aïeules*, with a preface by Jules Claretie.[60] Her recitals were mostly of the *concert-causerie* type that Guilbert would favor in 1915–1922 in New York. Madame Amel's first recitals at La Bodinière featured *chansons d'autrefois* and were performed with a speaker, Georges Boyer:

> No doubt that the sincere artist [Madame Amel], who, the first, dared to make alive again our old an poetic songs of France, will find once more with her audience, who was rushing to her at her first recital, the glowing success that she owes to the penetrating charm of her elocution.[61]

A few days later *Le Figaro* reported that

> Not willing to keep herself to the chansons from one period only, the faultless *diseuse* made us go from the barbarian or melancholic songs of the fifteenth century to the gay refrains of the eighteenth century [and to the] songs of the Restauration, with which our grandmothers have rocked our childhood.[62]

Such a broad historical survey of the "chanson de France" is exactly what Guilbert was defending in her recitals from the 1910s on. However, during the previous decade, Guilbert's repertoire had centered mainly on eighteenth- and nineteenth-century chansons (with modern arrangements), and it certainly did not mean the disappearance of her former repertoire (the 1904 recital in London described by Ethel Barrymore is an example of its persistence). The years 1905–1913 reveal an emphasis on the eighteenth century and the chanson ancienne, but a closer look also reveals that Guilbert's second career coincided with an increased interest in the repertoire of the chanson ancienne and populaire during the 1900s. There was indeed a proliferation of such songs in the 1900s, and Guilbert's interest in the chanson ancienne rose in parallel with a conception of the chanson more ideologically connected with an exaltation of the French heritage in a way that could or value the Republican ideal of French national unity or single out its regional diversities, which was what the anti-Republican and monarchist factions were aiming to do.

The first decade of the 1900s is highly revealing of the porosity between Left and Right with regard to such musical matters. Despite their divergent finalities, intersections between these opposing camps were not unusual. Thus, within the pages of the inaugural issue of *Les chansons de France*, the journal of the Société "Les chansons de France," a brainchild of Charles Bordes (one of the cofounders of the Schola Cantorum), one might encounter statements typical of the Republican cultural and pedagogical agendas, such as the following, written by Bourgault-Ducoudray:

> The revelation of the "National Soul" will create a link between the different social classes. It would be used as a binding and joining for all the French souls, allowing to give a common ground of aesthetic culture to all the French people.[63]

Five years later in *Musica*, an article by Scholiste and monarchist Déodat de Séverac, "Chansons du Languedoc et du Roussillon," while emphasizing the *regional* heritage of the "Sud-ouest," nevertheless praised Tiersot and Bourgault-Ducoudray (who was himself a contributor to *La tribune de Saint Gervais*, the journal of the Schola Cantorum):

> Today the traditional popular singing is racked by terrible enemies: the primary
> school, in which is taught the contempt for everything that is "old" [ancien], despite
> the magnificent efforts made by people such as Bourgault-Ducoudray and Tiersot.[64]

Interested in the success of Guilbert's recitals at the Bouffes Parisiens, the music publisher Alexis Rouart had in 1905 commissioned two volumes from Séverac titled *Chansons du XVIIIe siècle* (published respectively in June and October), securing the addition of the label "chantées par Yvette Guilbert". Guilbert's involvement with the "chansons populaires et anciennes" could then also be interpreted as a perfect instance of the defense of this repertoire, which was on the agenda of the monarchist wing. For the Scholistes, the preservation of the chanson populaire was seen as an essential link in reinforcing the connection with an idealized past, preserved from the outrages of the revolutionary period. Such were the goals of the Schola Cantorum and the Société "Les chansons de France" (figure 11.1).

The re-creation of such an idyllic past and the appropriation of the ancien régime are obvious in the front and back covers of Séverac's *Chansons du XVIIIe siècle*, with the male musician directly derived from Watteau's Pierrot (known as *Gilles*) and a female character, whose large skirt but simple coiffure (not the complex architecture characteristic of Louis XV's time) are also very reminiscent of the Régence period (several female characters in Watteau's paintings, notably actresses of the Théâtre-Italien, by the painter Nicolas Lancret—his *Portrait de Mlle Camargo*—could have served as models for her). The front cover perfectly suited Maurice Lefèvre's 1893 description of the chansons

> that tells us the beribonned graces of the eighteenth century, the time of the
> shepherds with crook and the elegant little abbots[65]

—precisely what became the main source of inspiration for Guilbert's chansons anciennes at the Bouffes Parisiens.

Séverac's correspondence with Rouart only briefly mentions this collaboration and incidentally discloses a not-too-unexpected cynicism not only from Séverac but also from Rouart and Guilbert herself: On September 1, 1905, Rouart informed Séverac that Guilbert found his harmonization

> way too good for a chanson to be sung in front of the gross audience! [and] it is
> obvious that because of the deplorable banality of the text, your music completely
> outshines it, something for which I can myself only congratulate you[.][66]

Guilbert sang ten of Séverac's songs in a recital she gave on December 31, 1905, at the *Figaro* with the Chanteurs de Saint Gervais, the performing group founded in 1892 by its choirmaster, Charles Bordes. Thus, the purpose of the publication of Séverac's two volumes with Guilbert's "patronage" was a clever marketing move by Rouart a few months before the December concert given in celebration of the newly founded

Figure 11.1. Front cover of the *Chansons du XVIIIe siècle*, arranged and harmonized by Déodat de Séverac (Paris: Rouart, 1905). Private collection.

Société "Les chansons de France." The Société also launched its own journal, *Les chansons de France*: Published between 1906 and 1913 by Rouart, it was mostly dedicated to the melodies and lyrics of popular songs from the French provinces (often proposing several tunes for one song).[67] The Société aimed to gather

> under the aegis of the "Schola Cantorum" a new grouping that aims to collect the scattered treasures of the chanson française whether in the memory of the people, whether in the libraries and to encourage their publication and their performance.[68]

Such a claim could not have been completely unknown to the former *divette fin de siècle*, who probably had many reminiscences of her instructive experience at the Éden Concert some fifteen years ago:

Madame Yvette Guilbert, the princess of the chansons from France, who, as we
know, has started to dedicate all her great talent to the popular French melody
and by bringing back into honor of *our fathers' old chansons,* from which so many
delightful specimens are still locked in our libraries.[69]

In 1907 Guilbert's name reappeared in another of Rouart's publications,
*Chansons de la vieille France, recueillies et chantées par Yvette Guilbert, reconstituées
et harmonisées par Maurice Duhamel.*[70] Guilbert does not seem to have sung any of
these songs in her recitals, except for the "Cloches de Nantes," mentioned in a review

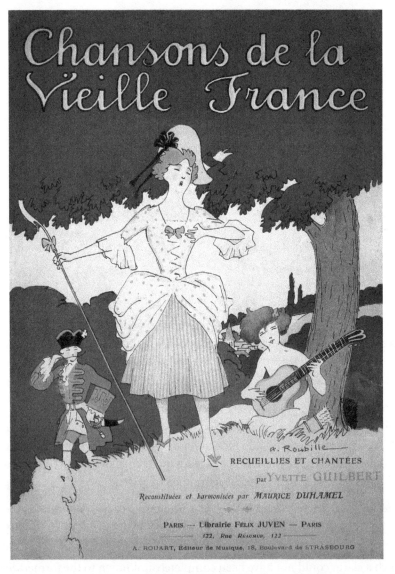

Figure 11.2. Front cover of the *Chansons de la vieille France,* "collected and sung by Yvette
Guilbert, reconstituted and harmonized by Maurice Duhamel" (Paris: Rouart, 1907).
Private collection.

published by the *New York Times* in 1909 (the title of the review speaks for itself: "Boorish Treatment of Yvette Guilbert"). By 1907 she was clearly struggling to win over her former audience, which was still expecting her to be the *diva fin de siècle*, and since her 1901 comeback she had experienced a series of less-than-stellar successes (her 1905 European and American tours), if not downright fiascos, such as her 1909 tour in the United States.

Also rooted in an imaginary re-creation of the eighteenth century, Duhamel's volume, however, slightly differs from the imagery garnered in Séverac's collection (figure 11.2). The main visual element that recalls the ancien régime is the soldier in the background, but the atmosphere of the Régence is effectively gone, and the clothing clearly refers to the very end of the century. Dressed as a *bergère* and despite the stylization of the drawing, the woman displays signs of a lesser sophistication, somewhat helped by the presence in the background of a rural setting (a village and a nude boy—or a cupid without wings?—seated next to his quiver). The whole, however, seems located in a past even more improbable than that of the Séverac collection, the cover of which at least established a clear visual stylistic reference to the Régence; here, the tone is of an idyllic and idealized re-creation of an ancien-régime era devoid of its aristocratic, courtesan atmosphere.

Guilbert's participation with *Les chansons de France* remains poorly documented: Nothing in her correspondence or any other documents, such as her writings and recollections, gives details of her collaboration with Séverac or Rouart. However, she must have found such experience worth pursuing, yet probably in a different context, one in which she would have had complete control of the situation. In 1905 she had found an obliging collaborator in the person of the Genevan pianist and composer Gustave Ferrari, who created most of the arrangements for her series of chansons anciennes for her "Collection Yvette Guilbert" in six volumes published by Schott (volumes 1 to 5 were published in 1911; volume 6 in 1914)[71] and offered a repertoire of songs from the fifteenth to the nineteenth centuries (figure 11.3).

The second and fourth volumes of the "Collection Yvette Guilbert" (respectively, "Bergers et Musettes" and "Chansons et rondes anciennes") have an imagery that evokes the ancien régime, while the fifth volume, "Les petits soupers de Versailles," establishes the connection essentially through its title. The fourth volume refers to the topical couple of young shepherds, who are often found in Boucher's paintings, while the second volume, like Séverac's cover, is a variation on a typical Régence work of art, Watteau's *L'escarpolette* (ca. 1712; not to be confused with the painting by Fragonard). The surroundings of *L'escarpolette* in Guilbert's collection are nevertheless different, for in the original the lady in the swing is accompanied only by a young man who is pushing her, while here she is accompanied by a young man playing a recorder or an oboe and another woman holding a score. However, contrary to the imagery in the "chansons de France," the "Collection Yvette Guilbert" aimed to provide a precise historical contextualization for its choice of chansons, and the first volume is exemplary of this. The choice of an engraving based on the colored woodcut of Gregor Reisch's *Margarita Philosophica* (1503), representing music as a liberal art, also resonates in terms of

Figure 11.3. Frontispieces of the six volumes of *Chansons anciennes* of the "Collection Yvette Guilbert" (Mainz: Schott) Private collection and Bibliothèque du Conservatoire de Musique de Genève.
Volume I. *Chansons du Moyen Âge à la Renaissance* (harmonisées par Gustave Ferrari) (1911).

gendering (and, if we suppose that Guilbert herself chose the images for the covers, the allegorical meaning of the *Typus Musices* was probably much less important to her than the womanly figure in the center). The allegorical figure in the center, symbolizing music, completely reverses the situation described by Jann Pasler in her comment on the cover page of *Les chansons de France* since its first issue in 1906,[72] in which the male characters (eleven minstrels) in the foreground, are musicians who are playing for six noble women who are seated in the background.

Figure 11.3. (*Continued*)
Volume II. *Bergers et musettes* (harmonisées par Gustave Ferrari) (1911).

When one examines the six volumes of the Guilbert collection in order, one notices a progressive dissolution of the central female figure, culminating in the third volume ("Chansons de tous les temps"), which shows a color photograph of Guilbert herself. Curiously, if not comically, it conflates her "costume crinoline," which she wore while performing her "chansons 1830," with two chromatic attributes of her fin-de-siècle persona, the green dress and the red hair. In the fourth volume, the female figure shares the center with her male companion, while in the fifth volume she has disappeared, and three winged cherubs have taken her place. The sixth volume, "Légendes de Noël" (published three years after the others) stands

Figure 11.3. (*Continued*)
Volume III. *Chansons de tous les temps* (harmonisées par Gustave Ferrari) (1911).

apart—and for reasons that also reflect its conception. As explained in its preface, Guilbert had "collected and reconstituted" certain episodes of Jesus's life. Most likely her inspiration came from Tiersot's *Chants de la vieille France*, a collection of songs from the thirteenth to the eighteenth centuries.[73] In his preface, Tiersot explains that the songs have been taken from "handwritten or printed sources" and

Refrains des Jeunes

Quinze Chansons

et

Rondes anciennes

Figure 11.3. (*Continued*)
Volume IV. *Chansons et rondes anciennes* (harmonisées par Gustave Ferrari) (1911).

that "all these songs have been taken from the original sources."[74] Further, he draws on Pierre Aubry, who made the modern transcription of three tunes from the thirteenth and the fourteenth centuries; Émile Blémont, who adapted the lyrics to modern French; and the authority of the published works of Gaston Paris and Gevaert. Similar to Tiersot's *Chants de la vieille France*, Guilbert's own copyright states that

> These chansons, from the collection Yvette Guilbert, have been drawn from the very sources themselves, and collated with the original scores. [They are published] here for the very first time.[75]

Volume V. *Les petits soupers de Versailles* (harmonisées par Hélène Chalot) (1911).

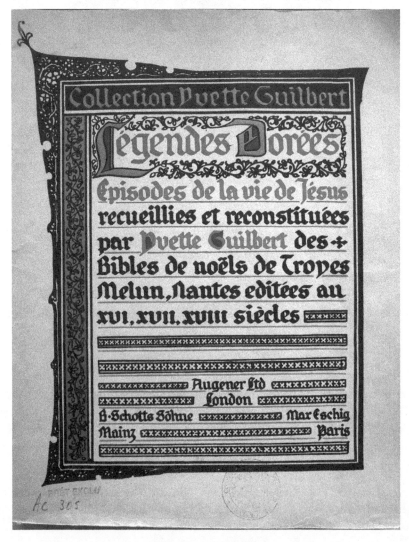

Figure 11.3. (*Continued*)
Volume VI. *Légendes dorées* (harmonisées par Gustave Ferrari) (1914).

The claim is certainly overdone. Amusingly, the German and English translations of this copyright, which appear on the same page, state that "the songs…are freely adapted from the original sources and are now published mostly for the first time." Credit for "reinventing" these songs should be attributed entirely to Gustave Ferrari (who also created the arrangements for volumes 1, 2, 3, 4, and 6; the copyright for those of volume 5 belongs to Hélène Chalot). Ferrari's autographs of these songs[76] show that the sources were largely late nineteenth-century collections of songs and essentially those published by Tiersot and Weckerlin. However, such names were a sufficient guarantee for Guilbert, who was eager to reclaim the appearance of scholarship. The point is illustrated by the following quotation, which shows that in 1911 Guilbert had not only approached France's greatest medievalist, Joseph Bédier, but also tried to compare her work with the publications of Jean Aubry and Hugo Riemann:

> I am currently studying your *Chansons des Croisades*—out of these, I made a small group of four or five—but I am slightly confused by what I read from Hugo Riemann, the German musicographer, who transcribes the music of these songs with a different rhythm than [Pierre] Aubry's. Who is right, Riemann or Aubry?? I have set the couplets that you have set *in prose* to the "Aubry" rhythm. I even managed to make up expressions [from the Old French], in many couplets, where your translation avoided them (probably to [facilitate] the reader's comprehension)…. [I] wish I could have talked to you about these beautiful things, begging you to tell me: to which forthcoming edition are you referring on page XI, I think, from your preface, introduction, in which you announce *some pious tales* with the "jeux-partis" that will be published soon, you say?
>
> With the exception of all the Christmas Bibles, are there any other works that I can draw from? Maybe you are aware, sir, that, having abandoned the music hall twelve years ago, I am *very seriously* occupied with reconstituting chansonniers that are passionately appreciated abroad? Even this last winter in Paris I have been able to pique the interest and to surprise *gens de lettres* such as messieurs Jules Lemaître, [Alphonse] Daudet, Paul Hervieu, etc., with [my] curious musical and poetic reconstructions. I am currently working on a collection of songs from the 15th to the 18th centuries, of pious legends (Christmas) and others. But maybe is there going to be another new edition? How much, sir, I would be grateful if you could give me some information about this! Maybe Mr. [Frantz] Funck-Brentano informed you of my desire to meet you? … I have decided to inconvenience you without having the honor of knowing you. Please, sir, accept my apologies for being *sans-gêne*, and understand that this is only due to my great desire to know a scholar who has a passion for *all these things I love!* [77]

The tricky question of rhythm naïvely raised by Guilbert was indeed one of the thorniest issues in recent studies on medieval monody.[78] It is not known whether Bédier ever replied to Guilbert, but their paths would nevertheless cross again after the First World War—at the Société des Anciens Textes Français, which, presided over by Bédier, elected Guilbert as one of its members in 1922.

Guilbert's Pedagogical Mission

Guilbert's revaluation of the chanson populaire had to go hand in hand with what she referred to as her pedagogical "mission" (a word she frequently used). Here as well, her ideas perfectly concur with the pedagogical values conveyed by the chanson populaire—against the perversities of the chanson moderne—as they had been defended since the 1880s. Pierre Lalo's letter, published in the inaugural issue of the journal of the Société "Les chansons de France," summarizes the entanglement between educational values and French national pride:

> An assiduous familiarity with the art of their ancestors and their race can revive in them [the children] the national sense, to bring them back to the use of their genuine language, and lead them to make music, not anymore Italian or German, but French.[79]

The chanson's moral value, as well as its historical and national relevance, would also explain Guilbert's pedagogical ambitions in the 1910s.

In October 1913, at her home on boulevard Berthier, Guilbert opened her first school, the "École de la chanson," for children from working-class families. The experience was short lived but not the idea, for Guilbert's pedagogical activities would be maintained well after the 1920s, essentially during her New York stay (1915–1922).

Although undated, the photograph in figure 11.4 must have been taken during the last semester of the year 1913 (it also resembles another photograph published in an article on Guilbert's newly opened École de la chanson in the October 1913 issue of *Musica*). The photograph provides some interesting information about Guilbert's concern for the legacy of the chanson. On the left wall, a poster carries the following inscription: "La chanson française | Une série | Causerie-Audition | Par M. G. Dumestre." No doubt it refers to Gaston Dumestre (1875–1949), a French chansonnier active at the Chat Noir in the 1890s. In 1902 Dumestre had settled in Brussels, where he served as director of the Dutch and Belgian branches of the music publisher Salabert. In 1894, with two well-known chansonniers from the Chat Noir, Xavier Privas and Pierre Trimouillat (nicknamed by Bruant "Baron Trimouillat"), Dumestre established Les soirées du Procope (every Tuesday, Friday, and Sunday) at the famous Café Procope. A short report on these new soirées published in 1894 in *La Plume* stresses that Dumestre and his colleagues were exploiting a nostalgic trend, aiming to revive the past charms of the former Chat Noir:

> it is said that the Chat Noir is in decay: is it that gaiety has left Montmartre to come on the Left Bank? The Soirées du Procope are going to remind soon the greatest successes of the famous cabaret of Rodolphe Salis, who himself became, the gentleman-cabaretier, farmer in the Poitou.[80]

Like Guilbert, Dumestre's involvement with the chanson aimed to define its proper canon. Patently naïve though it is, the poster shown on the wall of Guilbert's

Figure 11.4. "École Yvette Guilbert, Boulevard Berthier."
Yvette Guilbert at her home, boulevard Berthier, teaching a class, ca. 1913. Bibliothèque
Nationale de France, Département des Arts du Spectacle; Fonds Schiller.

salon features three concepts: the revolutionary period (a *sans-culotte*), the diversity of French regionalism (a woman in a regional dress), and national unity (symbolized by the Gallic rooster).

The right side of the photograph shows an unidentified picture partly hidden by a coat and a cloak: One is tempted to see the typical accessories of Aristide Bruant, the father of the *chanson réaliste et socialiste*—to use Claretie's expression. In 1917 Guilbert impersonated Bruant (figure 11.5) in New York in a series of recitals called "Chansons Rouges," in which she sang songs from the Chat Noir repertoire, as well as the collection also known as "Chansons Rouges" (a high point of what Claretie would have called the *chanson socialiste*), by Maurice Boukay, a chansonnier at the first Chat Noir (and also librettist of Massenet's *Panurge*). Published in 1896, the music was written by another chansonnier of the Chat Noir, Marcel Legay. In his preface, Boukay defined his songs as *chansons sociales:*

> I was listening to the great voice of the people...Do not be surprised then to
> listen here to the original, simple, familiar and sometimes brutal idiom of the
> Plowman, of the Winegrower, of the Grinder, of the Resigned, of the Rebel, of the
> Rich, of the Poor, of the Noble, of the Bourgeois...the social chanson is red...It
> is the extreme color of the tricolour flag, the one that goes straight to the heart of
> all the miseries, the one that floats in the wind of all liberties.[81]

Figure 11.5. Yvette Guilbert as Aristide Bruant. New York, 1917.
Bibliothèque Nationale de France, Département des Arts du Spectacle; Fonds Schiller.

Dumestre's poster, which alludes to the national, regional, and revolutionary heritage of the French chanson, and the sartorial signs (likely indicating Bruant) represent the progressive assimilation of the chanson into the French cultural canon, which
had started in the early nineteenth century, first by combining the ancient with the
popular, then by integrating the chanson moderne, as exemplified by the repertoire of

the Chat Noir (e.g., Bruant, Xanrof), now considered to be a historical object, as well as its most direct outgrowth, the *chanson sociale* or *chanson réaliste et socialiste*.

In 1913 Guilbert could refer to several inspirational models to build her own pedagogical program. The most important and probably the first to come to mind was Gustave Charpentier's Conservatoire populaire de Mimi Pinson, which opened in 1902. The conservatory was a successful attempt to bring art and culture to "the masses." The conservatoire offered Parisian working women a free musical education provided by professionals: For instance, the classes of chansons populaires were taught by Marcel Legay. These attempts to educate the masses must also be understood as a reaction against the elitism of the *décadence fin de siècle* and the symbolist movement. Drawing from utopian Fourierism and Michelet's social ideals, Charpentier's conservatoire was linked with the outgrowth of the *universités populaires*, which were established in 1896.

Mimi Pinson, however, had a model. Preceding Charpentier's project by only one year, the singing society known as "L'œuvre de la chanson française" was founded in 1901 by Ernest Chebroux (the cofounder [with Sarcey] of the *vendredis classiques* at the Éden concert).[82] Classes were similarly free, and the objective was to enable the female pupils to learn one song per week from professional singers.

That Charpentier had himself called "L'œuvre de Mimi Pinson" a series of related projects for the "rénovation des chants populaires" and designed to enhance attendance at theatrical performances and concerts and even on one's vacation (*voyages de vacances, excursions à prix réduits*[83]) reveals without ambiguity how the project followed in the footsteps of Chebroux's Œuvre de la chanson française. The parallel between Chebroux's Œuvre and Charpentier's Mimi Pinson may seem paradoxical, considering their different ideological positions, but Charpentier's conservatoire was nevertheless sufficiently rooted in the revaluating discourse of the chanson as a moral and educative tool to please the more conservative milieux, who supported Chebroux.[84] In any case it demonstrates Charpentier's ability to fuel his project with influences from diverse (yet somewhat overlapping) tendencies, notably the moral and nationalistic virtues of the chanson. As Jane Fulcher stresses, Charpentier "knew how to manipulate the 'official mentality,' having been dependent on both academic and official culture as a composer from a humble social background," and his activities at the Mimi Pinson conservatory reveal his mastery of a "rhetoric [that] appealed to current Republican cultural themes and to those of the Socialists, as well as of other groupings on the political Left."[85]

"L'Art pour tous," a *société de vulgarisation artistique* founded in 1901 by Louis Lumet, was another important movement that impacted on Charpentier's Mimi Pinson conservatory "at a moment of populist fervor and amid the cultural propaganda of the Right."[86] "L'Art pour tous" aimed "to make known the worth of our public and private collections, the beauty of our museums and monuments, the discoveries of our scholars, the values of our sites": a phraseology that clearly "recalls [the composer Alfred] Bruneau's *Rapport* and its attempt to define the monuments of French arts in specifically Republican terms."[87] The *Rapport* had resulted from the 1898 initiative of the Ministère de l'instruction publique to provide an official history of French music from its origins to the present in the context of the 1900 Exposition Universelle (Bruneau's *Rapport* came out in 1901). Its aim was to provide a firm basis for the construction of a French musical canon, the roots of which were to be found in the revaluation of the *populaire*, here necessarily understood as synonymous with *ancien* for Republican scholars such as Julien Tiersot. Going back to Bourgault-Ducoudray's first music history lectures at the Conservatoire (in 1878) and Julien Tiersot's 1889 *Histoire de la chanson populaire en France*, Bruneau defended Adam de la Halle as the first important figure of the "French School," and his *Jeu de Robin et Marion*, by drawing its inspiration from the "popular" (according to Bruneau), embodied the founding model of French musical specificity by integrating the trope dear to the Republicans of the *collective* genius of the "voix du peuple."[88]

If Guilbert's various collaborations, notably with the *vendredis classiques* and the Théâtre d'application in the early 1890s, later with "Les chansons de France" in the 1900s, were experiences targeted toward a conservative, right-oriented audience, she could not have ignored other tendencies that had developed since the 1890s: Her own conception of the chanson, in which its nationalistic virtues are strongly backed by their educative value, indifferently mixed values from the Right and the Left. Yet Chebroux's Œuvre remained, at the end, the greatest influence on Guilbert's pedagogical ambition, even greater than Charpentier's Mimi Pinson: In 1902 an article published in the weekly magazine *Femina* devoted two pages to Madame Amel. The article contained several photographs, one of which showed her teaching a large crowd of young working-class women at the Mairie of the fourth arrondissement in Paris.[89] As the very first lines of the article explain, Madame Amel,

> [r]ecently acclaimed *Queen of the chanson* by the "Caveau de Paris"... had proposed to revive the taste of the true chanson française, of the tender, gay, dramatic and tasteful chanson, that used to be so popular in France during the last century. This is why she founded the *Œuvre de la chanson française* and that she gives every Saturday at the town hall of the 4th arrondissement a free class, in which are invited the young female workers and employees from factories, stores, and administrations.[90]

Of course, "L'œuvre de la Chanson française" was Chebroux's creation, and Madame Amel was herself a member of Chebroux's circle—in which she was indeed most commonly referred to as the *reine de la chanson*, a title that Guilbert would have coveted more than anything.[91] Madame Amel's activities prefigure so well what Guilbert would do in the following decades that it seems impossible to imagine Guilbert having ignored the career of such a potential rival. What is more, the *Musica* article is titled "L'art de dire une chanson," and one cannot help but compare this title with that of Guilbert's small book published first in English in 1918 (*How to Sing a Song*), then republished in French in 1928 as *L'art de chanter une chanson*. In 1913 Guilbert was well aware of Chebroux, Amel, and Charpentier. Two months after the opening of her school that same year, Guilbert's views were summarized in "La chanson française," an article published by *Musica* in its Christmas issue. The chanson is celebrated according to ideals that still aligned with the conservative views illustrated by Chebroux (the chanson celebrating piousness and national pride), the milieu of the Schola, and the Société des chansons de France in the exaltation of the educative virtues of the chanson and the valorization of the past:

> Oh small and great chansons telling the past of the races... Oh dear pretty chansons exalting the faith... through beautiful legends, coloured like the precious stained glass of the high cathedrals! Beautiful reflections of French generations what are we doing of you, for you? Nothing—or so few... The chanson? This admirable, this sumptuous French richness unknown by the French themselves! Because, if we except the little publications by people such as Weckerlin and other lovers of this Beautiful Lady, who maybe are about thirty, who takes care of it? Which house, which palace shelters it as it deserves?... When then will we institute a chair, a true class on singing erudition, with people such as Funck-Brentano, Bédier, Cohen, for the splendid period of medieval literature, for instance.[92]

However, such claims also coexist under Guilbert's pen with a defense of the social implications of the chanson by Mimi Pinson (the chanson for the lower classes):

> The chanson! This comforter of the common people, the workers, of all those who struggle.[93]

A further connection to the Conservatoire de Mimi Pinson also appears in the direct allusion to the radical socialist Maurice Couyba, author of *L'art et la démocratie* (1902) and future minister of labor in 1914. In referring to Couyba the politician, Guilbert could not ignore his pen name, Maurice Boukay, the author of the *Chansons rouges* (mentioned earlier). Also, on the eve of World War I, Guilbert's claim that to ignore the chanson "c'est anti-patriotique" echoes Claretie's famous 1893 statement:

> The chanson, like the bayonet, is a French weapon... but today it is a weapon gnawed by the rust of indifference. And we do not want to be felon-soldiers.[94]

What truly indicates the originality of Guilbert's ideas in comparison with her former inspirational models is her allusion, in the form of a *captatio benevolentiae*, to the erudition of medievalists and historians, disclosing Guilbert's interest in the tradition of the chanson: Joseph Bédier, historian Frantz Funck-Brentano (already mentioned in Guilbert's letter to the former), and Gustave Cohen, one of Bédier's most talented disciples, who in the 1930s became the most influential historian of French medieval theater in the twentieth century.[95] The archivist Frantz Funck-Brentano (1862–1947), former curator of the Bibliothèque de l'Arsenal, was a renowned authority on the ancien régime and biographer of Marie-Antoinette.[96] In 1905 Funck-Brentano joined the ranks of the *ligue royaliste*, known as the Action française, founded by Charles Maurras.[97] As for Bédier, his political views were similar, although less publicly declared than Funck-Brentano's.[98] A pupil and disciple of Gaston Paris, Bédier did not share his master's opinions, as well as the Republicans' views, that the *chansons de geste* had a collective origin—as claimed by Claretie, Lefèvre, Tiersot, and others. On the contrary, Bédier dearly defended the notion of the individual creative genius—a view approved by the Action française, which was quick to rally Bédier's position.[99] Certainly such fundamental ideological nuances have been lost in Guilbert's enthusiastic praise in 1913. However, it is precisely this somewhat incoherent conflation of leftist and rightist values that makes her position highly revealing—on the very eve of World War I—of how the values of the Left and the Right eventually merged into an overtly nationalistic discourse.

Guilbert's pedagogical ambition was thus based on an assemblage of ideas and themes emanating from the different wings of the Republican Left—what was known in 1902 as the "Bloc républicain," comprising socialists, radical socialists, radicals, and anticlerical progressives ("Poincaristes"). Guilbert's pedagogical activities were based primarily on Charpentier's Mimi Pinson, and her conception of the song as a powerful educative—and ideologically oriented—tool aligned easily with Republican ideals. Yet, as we have seen, this position did not prevent her from being used as well by those who would become the main opponents of the Republican ideals and who gathered at the Schola Cantorum under the aegis of Vincent d'Indy and Charles Bordes. As for the notion of her "second career," if any, this would be better reserved for the period extending from 1915 until her death in 1944, a period that saw Guilbert taking refuge in the glories of the French Middle Ages. This later period epitomizes a form of escapism that can be described as an example *avant la lettre* of *troubadourisme*, a neologism defined in 1942 by the French *résistante* Edith Thomas in a fierce review of Marcel Carné's *Les visiteurs du soir:*

> Troubadourism is a malady of art and literature that appears in regressive periods and consists of an ingenuous sentimentalizing of an imaginary past. To make this past as imaginary as possible, it is pushed back as far as possible, to the point where public memory fades into legend. And the Middle Ages does the job very well![100]

Certainly such troubadourism could be viewed as the ultimate consequence of the fin-de-siècle revival of medievalism, popularized in circles such as the cabaret Le Chat Noir, but the trend took on increasingly ideological undertones after the First World War. This attitude led Guilbert, especially during her New York stay (1915–1921), to an aggravated isolation, to which must be added her growing mysticism, which seems to have reached almost pathological dimensions in the late 1910s.

Perceived through the political lenses of the 1900s and 1910s, Guilbert's own celebration of the historical value of the chanson as part of the French patrimony can easily be assimilated with the reinvigoration of a nationalistic impetus that had continued to grow after the Franco-Prussian War. Guilbert's "second career" must then be understood in the larger context of Jules Ferry's ideas on education and the efforts developed during the Troisième République for valorizing the French past in order to strengthen nationalistic consciousness, notably through a cultural and pedagogical reappropriation of the popular heritage of the French provinces, a plan defended by leading Republican scholars. Such is also the context against which one has to read Guilbert's pedagogical ambition, which began in the 1900s and eventually culminated during her New York stay with the Yvette Guilbert's School of Theatre (1915–1924).

A closer scrutiny of Guilbert's notion of "two careers" reveals that her "second" career certainly did not mark a break with the "first" one, to such an extent that the notion of a second career per se has to be rejected, for it was the logical outcome and continuation of the former. Guilbert did not completely reject, as she pretended, her fin-de-siècle repertoire, and in this new light, the differentiation of her two careers along the notions of "low-brow" and "high-brow" repertoires is also largely obsolete since her repertoire after 1899 maintained a large part of her chansons modernes in a skillful balance with what she referred to as chansons populaires and chansons anciennes.

Thus the legend of the two careers has to be understood as the outgrowth of a careful construction narrated not only by Guilbert herself but also by her contemporaries. Critics and commentators favored such a reading because Guilbert's "two careers" not only suited the new artistic directions aiming to depart from the fin-de-siècle decadence celebrated in the 1890s and of which Guilbert had been one of the most-celebrated icons. They also perfectly aligned with the rise of the ideological agendas, whether from the Left or the Right on the eve of First World War, and aspired to the revaluation of French patrimonial and nationalistic values.

NOTES

1. See Harold Simpson's biography of Yvette—written under her supervision, *Yvette Guilbert, Struggles and Victories of My Life* (London: Miles and Boon, 1910), as well as Guilbert's autobiographical memoirs, *La chanson de ma vie (mes mémoires)* (Paris: Grasset, 1927), and especially the chapter "Ma seconde carrière (1900–1927)," 191–200.

2. The story of Guilbert's "deux carrières" appears in innumerable texts, reviews, and essays that were published during her lifetime and well after her death. Guilbert's obituary in *Comœdia*, by Gustave Fréjaville, is titled "Yvette Guilbert et ses deux carrières," (Feb. 19, 1944), 4.

3. Respectively by Eugène Héros (lyrics) and Hubbard T. Smith (arr. Fragson), 1893; Léon Laroche and Louis Byrec, 1890; and Léon Xanrof (from his *Chansons parisiennes*, 1890).

4. Anon. "How Yvette Guilbert converts old songs into poignant Dramas," *Current Opinion* 60(2) (Feb. 1916), 100–101, 100. This article refers directly to Harold Simpson's 1910 biography, *Yvette Guilbert*.

5. Simpson's *Yvette Guilbert* and Guilbert's autobiographical texts have provided the basis for the two most recent books dedicated to Guilbert's life: Bettina Knapp and Myra Chipman, *That Was Yvette: The Biography of a Great Diseuse* (London: Muller, 1966), and Claudine Brécourt-Villars, *Yvette Guilbert, l'irrespectueuse* (Paris: Plon, 1988). Both monographs were written in the style of novelized biographies and are not always accurate or reliable; however, Brécourt-Villars provides sources and primary documents (yet with frequent sloppy or nonexistent references), as opposed to Knapp and Chipman, who take all of Yvette's words as granted. Both books also maintain a hagiographic tone with regard to Yvette, bypassing or ignoring her most conservative features, her opportunism, and her exalted Catholic mysticism.

6. Emma Valadon, 1837–1913.

7. Anne Marie-Louise Damiens, 1849–1911.

8. "Yvette Guilbert par Yvette Guilbert," *Musica* 74 (Nov. 1908), 171.

"On est persuadé…qu'Yvette Guilbert, en chantant par exemple *Le Petit Cochon*, n'a fait qu'œuvre libertine. Quelques personnes seulement voulurent ou surent s'apercevoir que ce n'était que la cruelle satire des turpitudes conjugales qui nourrissent le plus flagrant de ce qu'on appelle l'esprit parisien.…C'était à l'époque où toutes les scènes étaient occupées par les turpitudes…; et la satire en fut faite sous la forme que je vous indique, par des couplets joyeux qui ne cachaient pas la leçon…J'aurais chanté les vertus de mon époque si mon époque avait affiché des vertus…Je me suis rabattue sur les vices de mon siècle, j'ai fait œuvre de satiriste selon la force de mes moyens."

9. Furthermore, Aristide Bruant was, in the 1890s, often referred to as a *chansonnier populaire*:

"Aristide Bruant, le chansonnier populaire, titre qu'il revendique, dont il est fier, et que nul d'ailleurs ne peut réellement lui disputer…" (Horace Valbel, *Les chansonniers et les cabarets artistiques* [Paris: Dentu, 1895], 153): the same expression reappears on p. 276.

"Aristide Bruant, the popular chansonnier, title that he reivindicates, of which he is proud, and that no one else by the way could really contest him…"

10. Since this chapter deals with the chanson populaire up to ca. 1914, the conflation "populaire"/"moderne" does not yet appear.

11. Jann Pasler, "Concert Programs and Their Narratives as Emblems of Ideology," in Jann Pasler, *Writing through Music: Essays on Music, Culture, and Politics* (New York: Oxford University Press, 2008), 365–416, especially 369–72.

12. Guilbert's habit was to wear a green dress during the winter season and a white one during the summer. However, Toulouse-Lautrec was not the first to immortalize Guilbert's green costume and black gloves: Probably the very first was Ferdinand Bac, in a watercolor dated June 28, 1891. It is reproduced, along with many other portraits and photographs of Guilbert, in the exhibition catalogue *Yvette Guilbert: Diseuse fin de siècle* (Paris: Bibliothèque Nationale de France, 1994), 18. The Toulouse-Lautrec portrait is reproduced on p. 26.

13. Pierre-Paul Marsalés (1863–1927), one of the first artists of the "comique troupier" genre.

14. Alfred Fourneau (1867–1953). The pen name "Xanrof" is the reverse of "fornax," "oven" in Latin, "fourneau" in French.

15. An ardent defender of Béranger, Chebroux started his career as a chansonnier in the 1880s, notably at the conservative Lice chansonnière (founded in 1834), and he became president there in 1888. On Chebroux's career in the 1880s, see Camille Roy, "Ernest Chebroux," *Revue du Siècle, Littéraire, Artistique, et Scientifique Illustrée*, vol. 2, 1888, 610–19. In 1893 Chebroux published a special issue of the journal *La Plume*, on the "chanson classique" (no. 99, June 1, 1893).

16. See the brief report of the "Concours de la Lice Chansonnière de Paris," Ernest Chebroux presiding, in *Revue du Siècle, Littéraire, Artistique, et Scientifique Illustrée* 8 (1894), 298.

17. The archives of the Institut de France in Paris house an autograph letter from Guilbert to Coppée (shelfmark 17 AP 1). The letter is not dated, but it was most likely written after Guilbert's tenure at the Éden. In it Guilbert asks Coppée to write an article for

a charity shop (*œuvre de bienfaisance*) in an unidentified journal, possibly *La revue hebdomadaire*, with which Coppée had begun collaborating in 1898. The letter refers to Guilbert's address, avenue Villiers, which was her address during the 1890s before moving to Boulevard Berthier after her illness.

18. *Consuming the Past: The Medieval Revival in fin de siècle France*, ed. Elizabeth Emery and Laura Morowitz (Aldershot: Ashgate, 2003), provides an interesting and wide selection of essays on this topic.

19. Theodore Child, "Mlle Yvette Guilbert. In Six Months she has become famous," *Chicago Daily Tribune*, no. 1872 (Mar. 17, 1891), 9.

20. Guilbert's letter to Pierre Louÿs, dated Oct. 22, 1896 (BnF, Département des Arts du Spectacle, Mn 25/6 [2]).

"Supposez cinq minutes que je ne sois pas Yvette Guilbert, une chanteuse de bouffant,"

21. Guilbert's letter to Pierre Louÿs, dated Oct. 23 or 28 [?], 1896 (BnF, Départment des Arts du Spectacle, Mn 25/6 [3]); my emphasis.

"J'ai vu Maurice Donnay[,] il est ravi de l'idée—Saint Saëns est a Bruxelles[;] *je viens de lui écrire pour lui rappeler sa promesse de me faire de la musique quand un sujet intéressant lui en fournirait l'occasion*[.] Vous allez voir que lui aussi va nous dire oui, et du diable si avec une telle trinité je n'arrive pas à faire oublier mon nez retroussé!"

22. Child, "Mlle Yvette Guilbert," 9; my emphasis.

23. "Voyez-vous, le Café Concert est un endroit spécial à public spécial; le public extra, le public instruit, fin, délicat, n'est que le public passant, en excursion; le grand art, c'est de l'attirer souvent." Guilbert's 1893 letter (no further date) to the critic Adolphe Brisson, quoted in Romi [Robert Miquel], *Petite histoire des Cafés Concerts parisiens par Romi: Préface de Robert Beauvais* (Paris: Chitry, 1950), 25.

24. "Elle était presque une figurante aux Variétés, il y a deux ans. Gagne aujourd'hui plus de cinquante mille francs à détailler des chansons 'fin de siècle' dans les beuglants et les salons. Fut découverte et sacrée étoile par quelques littérateurs. Le troupeau de Panurge suivit." Quoted in Romi, *Petite histoire des Cafés Concerts*, 24.

25. Yvette Guilbert, *Autres temps, autres chants* (Paris: Laffont, 1946), 59.

"En 1892, le Chat-noir par exception à sa règle, me fit l'honneur de m'inviter à y faire entendre mes chansons. C'était sa façon de me remercier d'avoir, la première, fait descendre sur les boulevards l'esprit, le rire nouveau de la Butte, et propagé la verve chat-noiresque par les couplets de ses plus célèbres poètes et chansonniers: Maurice Donnay, Jules Jouy, Rollinat, Xanrof, Bruant, Richepin."

26. Derek Scott, "Music and Social Class," in *The Cambridge History of Nineteenth-century Music*, ed. Jim Samson, 544–67, 550 (Cambridge, UK, New York: Cambridge University Press, 2001).

27. A former "sociétaire" of the Comédie-Française, Bodinier opened the theater in 1888. It was originally conceived as an annex for the pupils of the Conservatoire de déclamation et d'art dramatique, in which they could perform plays.

28. Bouchor collaborated with Julien Tiersot for the *Chants populaires pour les Écoles: Poèmes de M. Bouchor, mélodies recueillies et notées par J. Tiersot* (Paris: Hachette, 1897).

29. On the history of La Bodinière, see chapter 5 of Adolphe Aderer, *Le théâtre à côté*, preface by Francisque Sarcey (Paris: Ancienne Maison Quantin, 1894), 68–83.

30. Aderer, *Le théâtre à côté*, 79. "Enfin, Yvette vient. Elle arrive de Bruxelles. Paris ne la connaît presque pas. Hugues Le Roux la présente. Elle dit ses chansons, et tout Paris vient à la Bodinière."

31. Aderer, *Le théâtre à coté*, 80–81. See also the review by Louis Gallet in *La Nouvelle Revue* (Apr. 1, 1895), 687: "À la Bodinière, Mlle Mathilde Auguez fait connaître et popularise de nouveau les *Naïves chansons*; Mme Amel y dit les *Chansons des ancêtres*."

"La chanson accapare les matinées-causeries [à la Bodinière]; on entend les *chansons brutales* avec Félicia Mallet, que présente Maurice Lefèvre; la *romance* de nos pères, que soupirent délicieusement Mme Mathilde Auguez et M. Cooper; les *chansons d'autrefois*, que dit fort spirituellement Mme Amel, de la Comédie-Française, présentée par Georges Boyer; on entend aussi Simon-Girard, Alice Lavigne et Victor Maurel... [C]'est hier enfin que nous entendions l'intéressante conférence de M. Robert de Montesquiou sur Mme Desbordes-Valmore, qui fut dite devant un parterre de princesses et de marquises."

32. "Telle, en sa corporelle apparence—ainsi qu'en sa diction—elle fait penser au naturalisme, au naturalisme déjà démodé, si différent en tous cas de l'art d'aujourd'hui.... Nous admirons plus que personne le talent de Mlle Yvette Guilbert. Mais, malgré toute notre bonne volonté, nous ne la trouvons pas perverse du tout." Marcel Proust, "Pendant le carême. À propos de l'*Ingénuité fin de siècle* et Mlle Yvette Guilbert, cinq conférences au théâtre d'Application, par M. Hugues le Roux," *Le Mensuel* 5 (February 1891), 4–5, in Marcel Proust, *Écrits de jeunesse, 1887–1895*. Textes rassemblés, établis, présentés et annotés par Anne Borel, avec la collaboration de Alberto Beretta Anguissola et al. (Illiers-Combray: Institut Marcel Proust International, 1991), 174–92, 177.

33. "Faites entrer la Chanson moderne. La voilà! longue sangsue, sans sexe! Elle rampe, elle glisse avec des sifflements, laissant derrière elle la traîne moirée de sa bave.... De chaque côté de ce corps invertébré, pendent, lamentables loques, des tentacules gantées de deuil. C'est qu'en effet elle va conduire l'enterrement de notre race latine. Négation complète de notre génie... Tout d'abord on lui fit fête.... Puis vient l'engouement et Paris-Panurge parut. Alors commença l'œuvre véritable.... contemple-la... cette face de clown. De ce masque enfariné sort une voix sèche, brisée... Ne la maudis pas cette Chanson moderne... Ce n'est point sa faute à elle, c'est la nôtre. Ce n'est pas elle qui nous décompose, c'est de notre pourriture qu'elle est née, c'est nous qui l'avons créée, ce sont nos vices qui la rendent viable. Pauvre petite Chanson, miroir fidèle en qui les hommes se reflètent, es-tu responsable de leur hideur?" (July 15, 1896). Maurice Lefèvre, "Les gestes de la chanson," in *Le journal pour tous* 29: 6.

34. Maurice Lefèvre, *À travers chants* (Paris: Ollendorff, 1893).

35. Jules Claretie, preface to Lefèvre, *À travers chants*, 11; my emphasis.

"Voilà la chanson, comme la pantomime, redevenue tout à fait à la mode. Mais a-t-on jamais cessé de chanter des chansons, en ce pays de France? *Entre l'épique chanson de Roland et la chanson de Bruant réaliste et socialiste, on pourrait dire que c'est toute notre histoire*."

36. Lefèvre, *À travers chants*, 15–17.

"Dire le roman, l'odyssée de la chanson, ce serait faire l'histoire des peuples.... Car la chanson, c'est l'interprète de l'âme d'un peuple."

37. Among its first members were Frédéric Mistral (also its honorary president) and Julien Tiersot, as well as these members of the Schola Cantorum: Vincent d'Indy and Maurice Bourgault-Ducoudray, members of Le Chat Noir circle; poet and chansonnier Jean Richepin (the list describes him as "homme de lettres"); and composer Charles de Sivry. Other members included Augusta Holmès, Jules Massenet, Maurice Sand (for the

"Traditions du Berry"), Pauline Viardot, Théodore Hersart, vicomte de la Villemarqué (and author of the famously polemical *Barzaz Breiz: Chants populaires de la Bretagne* [1839]). Ernest Chausson and Constant Pierre were among the new members who joined in 1889 (see the *Annuaire de la Société des Traditions Populaires*, t. v, 1890). On the society, see Jann Pasler, "Race and Nation: Musical Acclimatization and the *chansons populaires* in Third Republic France," in *Western Music and Race*, ed. Julie Brown, 147–67; here 151–52 (Cambridge, UK, New York: Cambridge University Press, 2007).

38. *Mélusine, recueil de mythologie, littérature populaire, traditions et usages* (Paris, 1878–1912).

39. Société des traditions populaires (1839–1903). On Paris, see Maurice Croiset, "Notice sur la vie et les travaux de Gaston Paris," *Bibliothèque de l'École des Chartes*, 65/65 (1904), 141–73, and Harry A. Senn, "Gaston Paris as Folklorist (1867–1895): The Rise and Decline of French Folklore Studies," *Journal of the Folklore Institute* 12 (1975): 47–56.

40. Gaston Paris, *Chansons du XVe siècle: Publiées d'après le manuscrit de la Bibliothèque Nationale de Paris par Gaston Paris; et accompagnées de la musique transcrite en notation moderne par Auguste Gevaert* (Paris: Firmin-Didot, 1875).

41. Tiersot's recollection is given in his *La chanson populaire et les écrivains romantiques* (Paris: Librairie Plon, 1931), 325, footnote. There is no mention of Gaston Paris singing, but *Le Ménestrel* is more explicit:

> "Le mercredi 3 juin, a eu lieu, au Cercle Saint-Simon, une audition très réussie de mélodies populaires françaises, dirigée par M. Julien Tiersot et précédée d'une intéressante causerie de M. Gaston Paris. M. Tiersot doit être triplement félicité: au point de vue du choix des chansons très variées qui figuraient sur le programme, comme auteur de plusieurs harmonisations adaptées à ces mélodies, et comme diseur incomparable...Parmi les chansons les plus applaudies de cette séance, citons les chansons bretonnes recueillies et chantées par M. Quellien, dont une, harmonisée par M. Bourgault-Ducoudray, a été bissée; la chanson Jean Renaud...chantée par M. Gaston Paris, a valu à l'éminent érudit un succès musical."

> "On Wednesday June the 3rd took place, at the Cercle Saint-Simon, a very successful audition of French popular melodies, conducted by M. Julien Tiersot and preceded by an interesting talk by M. Gaston Paris. M. Tiersot must be congratulated in three respects: because of the choice of the very diversified chansons that were part of the program, as author of several harmonizations adapted to these melodies, and as incomparable *diseur*...Among the most applauded chansons of this audition, we may cite the Breton chansons collected and sung by M. Quellien, among which one, harmonized by M. Bourgault-Ducoudray, was encored; the chanson "Jean Renaud"...sung by M. Gaston Paris, earned to the eminent erudite scholar a musical success." (*Le Ménestrel* [June 14, 1885], 223).

42. "Nouvelles littéraires: Institut National de France," *Journal des Savants* (October 1884), 590.

> "des mélodies populaires et de la chanson en France, depuis le commencement du XVIe siècle jusqu'à la fin du XVIIIe. En résumer l'histoire, en définir les caractères et les différentes formes au point de vue musical, et déterminer le rôle qu'elles ont joué dans la musique religieuse et la musique profane."

43. Jacques Cheyronnaud, "Poétique sonore de la République: Le modèle Julien Tiersot," *Ethnologie française* 225 (1995): 581–90.

44. Vincent d'Indy, *Chansons populaires du Vivarais recueillies et transcrites avec accompagnement de piano*, op. 52 [vol. 1] (Paris: Durand, 1900), and Vincent d'Indy, *Chansons populaires du Vivarais recueillies et transcrites avec accompagnement de piano*, op. 101 [vol. 2] (Paris: Durand, 1930). D'Indy also published, with Jos Jullien and Jean de la Laurencie, *Six Chansons anciennes du Vivarais* (Saint-Félicien-en-Vivarais: Au Pigeonnier, 1926).

On d'Indy's involvement with the chanson populaire, see Jann Pasler, "Deconstructing d'Indy, or the Problem of a Composer's Reputation," in Jann Pasler, *Writing through Music: Essays on Music, Culture, and Politics*, 101–39; esp. 115–22. On Tiersot's scholarly work on the chanson, see Katharine Ellis, *Interpreting the Musical Past* (New York: Oxford University Press, 2005), 163–77.

45. The date is written in pencil, so there is no certainty about its validity. The date is maintained in Brécourt-Villars's book, wheres she refers to the cutting as "coupure d'un journal non identifié, 15 février 1895, Fonds Rondel" (Brécourt-Villars, *Yvette Guilbert*, 199).

46. BnF, Départment des Arts du Spectacle, Fonds Rondel 8-RO-16088.

"Mais j'y vais très très souvent à la Bibliothèque! Et pas qu'à celle de la rue Richelieu, mais aussi à Carnavalet, à l'Arsenal!... J'y ai trouvé des ouvrages plus intéressants que certains romans, et cela m'a fait regretter d'être une étoile de 1894... [p]arce que j'étais affligée de ne pas retrouver au 19e siècle la grande liberté qu'avait la chanson au 17e et 18e.

On chansonnait le roi!—les maîtresses du roi—le Parlement!—les ministres!—les gens de la cour, les généraux, tout était mis en couplets railleurs, blagueurs ou spirituels. Faut pas rigoler de notre temps... bigre... ça coûterait cher!... La chanson y perd... car il y aurait bien des choses amusantes à dire... Celles qu'on ose dans les petits caveaux intimes, Chat Noir, et ailleurs, qui ont un succès fou.... D'abord cela empêcherait les auteurs de se rabattre sur des sujets désobligeants, parfois tristes.... [L]a chanson c'est une force qui de tout temps avait une utilité qu'on lui ôte en ce moment, qu'elle est entravée comme un condamné à mort.
La liberté pour la chanson, s.v.p.! C'est la récréation du populo et ça ne fait de mal à personne! au contraire! Ça forcerait les gens à avoir une sorte de moralité. La peur de la chanson les rendrait honnêtes."

47. Ida Tarbell, "Using a Library: Yvette Guilbert's work in the Bibliothèque Nationale," *Los Angeles Times* (July 22, 1896), 3; my emphasis.

48. F-Pmus. Signed autograph letter, dated Nov. 26, 1902.

"pour me guider dans le choix d'une série de chansons anciennes!"

49. To mention only a few: *Échos du temps passé: Recueil de chansons, noëls, madrigaux, airs à boire et à danser, menuets, chansons populaires, etc. du XIIe au XVIIIe siècles*, 2 vols. (Paris, 1853, 1857); *Chansons populaires des provinces de France, notices par Champfleury, accompagnement de piano par J. B. Weckerlin...* (Paris, 1860); *Album de la Grand'Maman: Romances[,] Mélodies et Brunettes en Vogue au Siècle dernier: Recueillies et transcrites avec accompagnement de Piano par J. B. Weckerlin* (Paris, [1883]); *Bergerettes: Romances et Chansons du XVIIIe siècle* (Paris, 1898); *Pastourelles: Romances et Chansons du XVIIIe siècle* (Paris, 1898).

50. One exception is the song "Les belles manières." Similarly, Guilbert's repertoire included almost none of the anthologies published by Tiersot except for one of Guilbert's favorite songs, "Joli mois de mai." On Weckerlin and his interpretation of the French national heritage of the chanson in comparison with Tiersot and Gaston Paris, see Annegret Fauser, "Gendering the Nations: The Ideologies of French Discourse on Music

(1870–1914)," in *Musical Constructions of Nationalism: Essays on the History and Ideology of European Musical Culture 1800–1945*, ed. Harry White and Michael Murphy, 72–103, esp. 80–81 (Cork: Cork University Press, 2001).

51. In French, *mirliton* [small reed pipe].

52. F-Pmus. Signed autograph letter, dated Jan. 5 [or 3?], 1903.

"Je travaille déjà vos chansons. N'oubliez pas mon menuet! Ou puis-je trouver les turlututus, j'ai fait tout Paris pour les dénicher!"

53. During the tour, Mévisto, one of the artists accompanying Yvette, kept several documents revealing its difficulties and financial failures (Fonds Mévisto, Bibliothèque Nationale de France, Département des Arts du Spectacle). As usual, Guilbert's recollections remain eloquently silent about the failures and difficulties of this 1901 tour.

54. "Courrier des Spectacles," *Le Gaulois* (Jan. 12, 1904), 3.

"Mais ce n'est plus l'Yvette 'trop bien portante,' c'est bel et bien l'Yvette longue et mince d'antan. On a retrouvé la robe verte et les gants noirs, on a retrouvé aussi la diction mordante et le geste précis."

55. "The Musical Side of Ethel Barrymore," *New York Times* (Feb. 19, 1905), SM7.

56. For these recitals Guilbert was accompanied by the members of the Société des concerts d'instruments anciens (Marguerite Delcourt, harpsichord and pianoforte; Henri Casadesus, viole d'amour; and Marcel Casadesus, viole de gambe), founded in 1901 by Camille Saint-Saëns. On Landowska's wrath at Marguerite Delcourt's playing harpsichord and especially the pianoforte at Guilbert's recitals, see Annegret Fauser, "Creating Madame Landowska," *Women and Music: A Journal of Gender and Culture* 10 (2006): 1–23, 14–15.

57. See Julien Tiersot, *Musiques pittoresques: Promenades à l'exposition de 1889* (Paris: Fischbacher, 1889), 26.

58. Louis Gallet, in *La nouvelle revue* (Apr. 1, 1895) (Paris: 18 Bd Montmartre, 1895), 687. The lyrics of the *Chansons des soldats de France* were written by Tiret-Bognet.

"les formes et le caractère de chaque temps, depuis la chanson des arquebusiers du roi Henri jusqu'à la chanson d'actualité. 'Avant le combat' est dans le ton du vieux Grétry."

59. Loys Amel.

60. *Chansons d'aïeules dites par Mme Amel, de la Comédie Française*. Preface by Jules Claretie (Paris: Tellier, 1897).

61. *Le Figaro* (Feb. 8, 1894), 4.

"Nul doute que la sincère artiste [Mme Amel], qui, la première, a osé faire revivre nos vieilles et poétiques chansons de France, ne retrouve auprès du public, qui se pressait autour d'elle lors de sa première séance, l'éclatant succès qu'elle doit au charme pénétrant de sa diction."

62. *Le Figaro* (Feb. 15, 1894), 4. On Mar. 1, 1894, *Le Figaro* mentions some of the authors of the songs, including Vauquelin de la Fresnaye and Rémy Belleau (sixteenth century), as well as Moncrif and Désaugiers (eighteenth century).

"Ne voulant pas s'en tenir aux chansons d'une seule époque, l'impeccable diseuse nous fait passer des chants barbares ou mélancoliques du quinzième siècle aux gais refrains du dixhuitième [et aux] chansons de la Restauration, dont nos grand'mères ont bercé notre enfance."

63. Louis Bourgault-Ducoudray, "De la nécessité de recueillir les mélodies populaires," in *Les chansons de France: Organe de la Société "Les chansons de France,"* numéro de propagande (July 1, 1906), 4 (repr., Geneva: Slatkine, 1980).

"La révélation de 'L'Âme Nationale' créerait un lien entre les différentes classes sociales. Elle servirait de reliure et de soudure à toutes les âmes françaises, en permettant de donner un fond commun de culture esthétique à tous les Français."

64. *Musica* 111 (December 1911), 241.

"Aujourd'hui, le chant populaire traditionnel est en proie à de terribles ennemis: l'école primaire, où l'on apprend le mépris de tout ce qui est 'ancien,' malgré les magnifiques efforts des Bourgault-Ducoudray et des Tiersot."

65. Lefèvre, *À travers chants*, 26.

"qui nous disent les grâces enrubannées du XVIIIe siècle, l'heure des bergers à houlette et des petits abbés papillons[.]"

66. Déodat de Séverac, *Déodat de Séverac: La musique et les lettres.* Correspondance éditée et annotée par Pierre Guillot (Sprimont: Mardaga, 2002), 234.

"beaucoup trop bien pour une chanson à chanter devant le gros public! [et] il est évident qu'étant donné la déplorable banalité du texte votre musique l'écrase complètement, ce dont je ne puis, quant à moi, que vous féliciter."

67. For instance, issue 1 (January 1907) gave seven versions of "Les répliques de Marion," also known as "Corbleu Marion" (sung by Guilbert at the Bouffes Parisiens), or "Le jaloux et la menteuse," from Tiersot's *Mélodies populaires des provinces de France*, E. Rolland's *Recueil de chants populaires*, Th. de Puymaigne's *Chants populaires du pays Messin*, and Aimé Atger's *Poésies populaires du Languedoc.*

68. [La rédaction], "La Société 'Les chansons de France,'" *Les chansons de France: Organe de la Société "Les chansons de France"* (July 1, 1906), 2 (repr., Geneva: Slatkine, 1980).

"sous les auspices de la 'Schola Cantorum,' un nouveau groupement qui se propose de recueillir les trésors épars de la chanson française soit dans la mémoire du peuple, soit dans les bibliothèques et d'en encourager la publication et l'exécution."

69. [La rédaction], "La Société 'Les chansons de France,'" *Les chansons de France: Organe de la Société "Les chansons de France"* (July 1, 1906), 2; my emphasis.

"Mme Yvette Guilbert, la princesse des chansons de France, qui, on le sait, vient de consacrer tout son grand talent à la mélodie populaire française et à la remise en honneur *des vieilles chansons de nos pères* dont tant de délicieux spécimens sont encore enfermés dans nos bibliothèques."

70. A native of Brittany, Duhamel (1884–1940) had founded Le Gringoire, a *chansonnier* cabaret, in 1905. A close friend of the Breton Paul Ladmirault, also a composer of the circle of "Les chansons de France," Duhamel later published Rouart-Lerolle's *Les chansons de France* and the *Chansons populaires du pays de Vannes*. He also played an important role in the revaluation of the Breton tradition (especially Celtic music) and participated actively in the Breton federalist movement of the 1930s.

71. The Swiss musician Gustave Ferrari (1872–1948) was introduced to Guilbert in 1905 in London and served as her accompanist until 1917; he also went with her to New York.

Until his death, Ferrari pursued his career in the United States, where he specialized in these "historical recitals," popularized by Guilbert, with different singers.

72. Jann Pasler, "The *Chanson populaire* as a Malleable Symbol in Turn-of-the-century France," in *Tradition and Its Future in Music: Report of SIMS 1990 Osaka*, ed. Y. Tokumaro, M. O. Kanazawa, O. Yamaguti, T. Tukitani, A. Takamatsu, and M. Shimosako, 203–209; here 205–206 (Tokyo: Mita, 1991).

73. *Chants de la vieille France: Vingt mélodies et chansons du XIIIe au XVIIIe siècle: Transcrites et harmonisées par Julien Tiersot* (Paris: Heugel, [1904]).

74. Tiersot, *Chants de la vieille France*, [i–ii].

"Les chants…sont pris…à des sources écrites ou imprimées…Tous ces morceaux ont été pris aux sources originales."

Note, however, that there is some ambiguity in Tiersot's use of the adjective "originales" in that he seems to imply that the "sources imprimées" he used are also original.

75. Unpaginated. This copyright appears in all of the volumes of the "Collection Yvette Guilbert."

"Ces chansons, de la collection Yvette Guilbert, ont été puisées aux sources mêmes, et collationnées sur les originaux. [Elles paraissent] ici pour la première fois."

76. Bibliothèque de Genève, Fonds Ferrari.

77. "J'ai à l'étude vos Chansons des Croisades—j'en ai formé un petit groupe de quatre ou cinq—mais je suis un peu troublée par ce que je lis de Hugo Riemann le musicographe allemand qui transcrit avec un rythme différent de celui d'Aubry les musiques de ces chansons. Lequel de Riemann ou d'Aubry est dans le vrai??— J'ai remis sur le rythme "Aubry" les couplets mis *en prose* par vous. J'ai même réussi à farder des locutions du temps, dans beaucoup de couplets, où votre traduction les évitait (sans doute pour la compréhension du lecteur)…. [J]'aurais bien voulu vous causer au sujet de ces belles choses, et vous prier aussi de me dire: De quelle édition prochaine vous parlez à la page XI je crois de votre préface, introduction où vous annoncez avec les jeux-partis *des légendes pieuses* qui paraîtront bientôt, dites-vous? En dehors de toutes les Bibles de Noëls y a-t-il d'autres ouvrages où je puisse puiser? Peut-être savez-vous, Monsieur, que depuis douze ans que j'ai abandonné le music-hall je m'occupe *fort gravement* de reconstituer des chansonniers qu'à l'Étranger on goûte passionnément? Même cet hiver à Paris j'ai pu intéresser et surprendre des gens de lettres tels que MM. Jules Lemaître, Daudet, Paul Hervieu, etc. et avec de curieuses reconstitutions poétiques et musicales. J'ai en train un chansonnier qui va du XVe au XVIIIe de légendes pieuses (Noëls) et autres. Mais peut-être y a-t-il un nouvel ouvrage réédité? Combien, Monsieur, je vous serais reconnaissante de vouloir bien me renseigner à ce sujet! Peut-être que Monsieur Funck Brentano vous a dit mon désir de vous connaître?… [J]e me décide à vous importuner sans avoir l'honneur de vous connaître. Veuillez, Monsieur, m'excuser de ce sans-gêne, et n'accusez que mon grand désir de connaître un savant qui se passionne pour *tout ce que j'aime!*" (Autograph letter from Yvette Guilbert to Joseph Bédier [undated]. Private collection of Pierre Bédier); emphasis in the original.

The letter was sent from the Hôtel de l'Europe, Bad Gastein, Austria. Before moving to New York at the end of 1915, Guilbert regularly spent her summers at Bad Gastein. The hypothetical date of 1911 is based on her mention of "depuis douze ans." My thanks to Alain Corbellari for making the content of this letter available to me.

78. See John Haines, "The First Musical Editions of the Troubadours: On Applying the Critical Method to Medieval Monophony," *Music and Letters* 83(3) (2002): 351–70.

79. *Les chansons de France*, 1 (July 1, 1906), 6.

"Une familiarité assidue avec l'art de leurs ancêtres et de leur race peut ressusciter en eux [les enfants] le sens national, leur rendre l'usage de leur langage véritable, et les conduire enfin à faire de la musique, non plus italienne ou allemande, mais française."

In this same issue, other letters, also stressing the educational high ground of the chanson, were signed by Frédéric Mistral, who criticizes "les refrains idiots [du] café-chantant" ("the stupid refrains of the café-chantant" [5]), Bourgault-Ducoudray, in which he stresses that the chansons can "créer un lien entre les différentes classes sociales... et [donneraient] un fonds commun de culture esthétique à tous les Français" ("can create a bond between the different social classes... and [would give] a common ground of aesthetic culture to all the French" [4]).

80. *La plume* 113 (Jan. 1–15, 1894), 52.

"On dit le Chat Noir en décadence: est-ce que la gaité aurait quitté Montmartre pour venir sur la Rive Gauche? Les Soirées du Procope vont rappeler bientôt les plus beaux succès du célèbre cabaret de Rodolphe Salis, devenu lui, le gentilhomme cabaretier, fermier en Poitou."

81. Maurice Boukay, *Chansons rouges, musique de Marcel Legay: Illustrations de Steinlein* (Paris: Flammarion, [1896]): v–vi.

"J'écoutais la grande voix du peuple... Ne sois donc pas surpris d'entendre ici la parole originale, simple, familière et parfois brutale du Laboureur, du Vigneron, du Rémouleur, du Résigné, du Révolté, du Riche, du Pauvre, du Noble, du Bourgeois.... La chanson sociale est rouge.... C'est la couleur extrême du drapeau tricolore, celle qui touche au cœur de toutes les misères, celle qui flotte au vent de toutes les libertés."

82. On "L'Œuvre de la Chanson française" and its possible impact on Charpentier's conservatoire, see Jane Fulcher, *French Cultural Politics and Music: From the Dreyfus Affair to the First World War* (New York: Oxford University Press, 1999): 100–101, and Mary Ellen Poole, "Gustave Charpentier and the Conservatoire Populaire de Mimi Pinson," *19th-Century Music* 20(3) (1997): 231–52.

83. For a description of "L'œuvre de Mimi Pinson," see Fulcher, *French Cultural Politics and Music*, 101, and on its origins as an "Association des ouvrières parisiennes," see Poole, "Gustave Charpentier," 239.

84. See Poole, "Gustave Charpentier," 234–35.

85. Jane Fulcher, *The Composer as Intellectual: Music and Ideology in France 1914–1940* (New York: Oxford University Press, 2005), 102.

86. From "L'Art pour tous," a text detailing its statutes, housed at the Archives Nationales, quoted in Fulcher, *French Cultural Politics and Music*, 100.

87. From "L'Art pour tous," quoted in Fulcher, *French Cultural Politics and Music*, 100.

88. The claim is repeated with more vigor in Tiersot's "Bibliographie la chanson populaire française," in which he asserts that the melodies of *Le jeu* were directly taken from "chansons et airs populaires" (*Revue musicale* [1904], 618). On Bruneau's report and its responses, see Fulcher, *French Cultural Politics and Music*, 42–48, and Ellis, *Interpreting*

the Musical Past, 252–55. Bruneau's dismissal and simplistic treatments of Gregorian chant and particularly the Renaissance period were, however, strongly criticized in anti-Republican and anti-Dreyfusard circles.

89. *Femina* 33 (June 1, 1902), 176–77.

90. *Femina* 33 (June 1, 1902), 176.

> "proclamée récemment *Reine de la chanson* par le 'Caveau de Paris'... [Madame Amel]s'est proposée de faire renaître le goût de la vraie chanson française, de la chanson tendre, gaie, dramatique et de bon ton, qui fut si populaire en France au cours du siècle dernier. C'est ainsi qu'elle a créé l'*Œuvre de la Chanson française* et qu'elle donne chaque samedi à la mairie du IVe arrondissement un cours gratuit, auquel sont conviées les jeunes ouvrières et employées des ateliers, des magasins et des administrations."

91. In 1905 Mme Amel was elected honorary president of the Caveau Lyonnais, which had been founded the same year as the Lyon branch of Chebroux's Œuvre de la chanson française (*La chanson* [Lyon: Cours la Liberté, 1905], 231).

92. *Musica* 135 (December 1913), 236.

> "O petites et grandes chansons racontant le passé des races...O chères jolies chansons exaltant la foi...en de belles légendes coloriées comme les vitraux précieux des hautes cathédrales! Beaux reflets des générations de France que fait-on de vous, pour vous? Rien—ou si peu....La chanson? Cette admirable, cette somptueuse richesse française inconnue des Français! Car, à part les petites feuilles des Weckerlin et autres amants de la Belle Dame qui sont peut-être une trentaine, qui s'occupe d'elle? Quelle maison, quel palais l'abrite comme elle le mérite?...Quand donc instituera-t-on une chaire, une vraie classe d'érudition chansonnière, avec des gens comme Funck-Brentano, Bédier, Cohen, pour la splendide époque de la literature médiévale, par exemple."

93. *Musica* 135 (December 1913), 236.

> "La chanson! Cette consolatrice des humbles, des ouvriers, de tous ceux qui peinent."

94. *Musica* 135 (December 1913), 236, 237. Claretie's quotation comes from the preface to Lefèvre's book, *À travers chants*, 11.

> "'La chanson, comme la baïonnette, est une arme française'...or aujourd'hui... [c]'est une arme rongée par la rouille de l'indifférence. Et nous ne voulons pas être des soldats félons."

95. Cohen had been acquainted with Guilbert at least since her return from New York in 1922—and perhaps earlier, although no document seems to confirm this.

96. *La cour de Louis XIV, d'après les archives de la Bastille* (Paris: Hachette, 1899). He published the widely successful *L'affaire du collier, d'après de nouveaux documents recueillis en partie par A. Bégis* and *La mort de la reine: Les suites de l'affaire du collier*, both in 1901.

97. During the two world wars, Funck-Brentano was viewed in France as arguably the most important historian of the ancien régime and one of the fiercest critics of the French Revolution: On Funck-Brentano and the Action française, see Philippe Boutry, "L'Action française, la Révolution, et la Restauration," in *L'Action française: Culture, société, politique*, ed. Michel Leymarie and Jacques Prévotat, 26–59 (Villeneuve-d'Ascq: Presses Universitaires du Septentrion, 2008).

98. Bédier was a pure product of the Republican medievalism that was popular in the 1870s, through the output of scholars such as Gaston Paris. In 1880 the *Chanson de Roland* was declared compulsory reading at the lycée (in 1882 for female students), conflating in the imagination of the younger French citizens the values of the epic and the national. On Bédier's youth (on the island of La Réunion) and the early impact of *La chanson de Roland* on his intellectual formation, see Michelle R. Warren, "'Au commencement était l'île': The Colonial Formation of Joseph Bédier's *Chanson de Roland*," in *Postcolonial Approaches to the European Middle Ages: Translating Cultures*, ed. Ananya Jahanara Kabir and Deanne Williams, 205–26 (Cambridge, UK, New York: Cambridge University Press, 2005).

99. In an article published in *L'Action française* on Sept. 19, 1938, Alphonse Daudet perfectly summarized this ideological divide:

> "Jusqu'à Bédier les chansons de geste, les grands thèmes légendaires étaient considérés comme des produits anonymes de la spontanéité populaire, comme des engendrements de l'inconscient ou du subconscient collectifs. Cette thèse, originaire d'Allemagne, comme tout ce qui touche à l'*Unbewusst*, avait été adoptée par les romantiques, en même temps que celle des deux races (l'envahissante ou franque, l'envahie ou gauloise) ayant donné par la suite les seigneurs et le prolétariat: et d'après laquelle la Révolution serait une revanche du second sur les premiers. Thèse qu'a détruite Fustel [de Coulanges] dans son grand ouvrage *Les institutions politiques de l'ancienne France*. C'est donc à la thèse de l'origine anonyme des chansons de geste et de la légende de Tristan et Iseult en particulier que s'en est pris ce grand Breton de Bédier, élevé à la Réunion." (Quoted in Paul Renard, *L'Action française et la vie littéraire (1931–1944)* [Villeneuve-d'Ascq: Presses Universitaires du Septentrion, 2003]: 51–52).

> "Until Bédier, the chansons de geste, the great legendary themes were considered as anonymous products of the popular spontaneity, like the begettings of the collective unconscious or the subconscious. This thesis, originated in Germany, as everything that deals with the *Unbewusst*, had been adopted by the Romantic, at the same time that the thesis about the two races (the invader or the Frank, the invaded or the Gallic) having given the lords and the proletariat: and after which [thesis] the Revolution would be a revenge of the latter on the former. Thesis that was destroyed by Fustel [de Coulanges] in his great work *Les institutions politiques de l'ancienne France*. It is then against the thesis of the anonymous origin of the chansons de geste and of the legend of Tristan and Isolde in particular that M. Bédier, the Great Breton, brought up in La Réunion, has been working."

100. Edith Thomas, *Pages de journal, 1939–1944: Suivies de Journal intime de Monsieur Célestin Costedet*, présenté par Dorothy Kaufmann (Paris: Hamy, 1995), 189–90:

> "Le troubadourisme est une maladie de l'art et de la littérature qui apparaît en période régressive et consiste en un attendrissement ingénu sur un passé imaginaire. Pour que ce passé soit le plus imaginaire possible, on le repousse aussi loin qu'on le peut, dans une mémoire qui se confond pour le public avec la légende: le Moyen âge fait fort bien l'affaire!"

CHAPTER 12

REMEMBRANCE OF JAZZ PAST: SIDNEY BECHET IN FRANCE

ANDY FRY

On a Negro Orchestra: Ansermet Gets Animated

Among the many tributes to the New Orleans reedman Sidney Bechet, following his death in Paris in 1959, the least likely may be the most telling: *Tintin*, "the magazine for the young, aged 7 to 77," made the great man its cover story.[1] While the iconic, tufty-haired boy and his dog peer down from atop the weekly magazine, a rosy-cheeked Bechet leads a cartoon band inspired to the point of ecstasy or even possession. In the foreground, a rack of gleaming white teeth and a bright red tongue set off a familiar "Satchmo" pose. But, standing farther back, Bechet is relaxed and composed; unlike his band mates', his eyes remain open, addressing the reader benevolently (figure 12.1).

Inside, cartoon panels of Bechet's life extend across four pages. Like Bechet's autobiography (which I discuss later), the comic begins by journeying back "a long way," to the plantations of the Old South. "After a day's hard labor," the first caption explains, "the blacks got together and sang" white hymns in their own peculiar fashion. Later, in New Orleans, "all the blacks were crazy about music," none more so than the family Bechet. Even Maman joins in their homemade band on her washboard before the children run off to hear a funeral parade. Seeing his older brother Leonard charm a sick man with music, Sidney steals away secretly with his clarinet; next, the young boy surprises everyone when he is able to fill the shoes of the renowned George Baquet (figure 12.2).

Figure 12.1. Sidney Bechet as cover story of a comic magazine. *Tintin: Le journal des jeunes de 7 à 77 ans* 11(580) (Dec. 3, 1959).

Bechet's next few years elided in the cartoon, he is soon off to Europe with the Southern Syncopated Orchestra (SSO) under Will Marion Cook. In London, classical musicians take an interest, among them Swiss conductor Ernest Ansermet. One "longhair" to another: "Have you seen what Ansermet wrote about this black musician?: 'He's an extraordinary virtuoso. He shocks by the richness of invention, force of accent, and daring of novelty.'"[2] Yet fame and fortune are not forthcoming: Despite some short-lived success, Bechet is reduced during the Depression to running a Harlem tailor shop. Not until his return to Europe—to France—after the war,

Figure 12.2. Bechet's childhood as imagined by *Tintin*.

the cartoon suggests, is his true worth again recognized and celebrated (figures 12.3 and 12.4). I want, in this chapter, to reexamine the tenor of Bechet's pictorial obituary, with its emphasis not only on youthful epiphanies but also on international recognition. Prizing apart some interlocking myths, I hope to suggest a more complex and contested, self-conscious, and, finally, more musical account of Bechet's assimilation to France, as well as that of jazz all told.

It is not a surprise to find Ansermet's well-known review recalled here, even in this least scholarly of sources. In London with the Ballets Russes, the conductor heard Cook's large band several times and quizzed the musicians about their playing; he subsequently wrote a lengthy article, "Sur un orchestre nègre" (1919), for the Swiss journal *La revue romande*. As astute as it is generous, this text has been as

Figure 12.3. Ernest Ansermet's review of Bechet's performance in London, 1919 (*Tintin*, continued).

Figure 12.4. Bechet's triumph at the Paris Jazz Festival, 1949 (*Tintin*, continued).

widely cited, discussed, and anthologized as any in the jazz literature. When Ansermet's review appeared in the 1947 book *Frontiers of Jazz*, for example, editor Ralph de Toledano chided his readers: "It cannot be too often repeated, to our shame, that Europeans realized the importance and value of jazz many years before the Americans who originated it.... Ernst-Alexandre Ansermet...was able to make mature and still-valid pronouncements of the nature of jazz in 1919."[3]

At its best, this trusty symbol of European prescience is indeed startlingly perceptive. Noting the musicians' African descent, for example, Ansermet identifies musical retentions of various orders: a nuanced rhythmic sense incorporating, in addition to syncopation, fractional delays and anticipations; a tendency to employ scale tones outside the diatonic system, particularly around the third and the seventh (i.e., "blue notes"); and unconventional instrumental and vocal techniques that allow for a wide range of attacks and great timbral variation. Collectively, he believes, such stylistic traits—still textbook material today—reflect "a racial genius."[4]

Less-often acknowledged is that Ansermet's biological determinism extends beyond such innocuous praise. Finding the SSO's harmonic language derivative despite the musicians' innovative approach to rhythm and melody, for example, he suspects that this is "an element that enters into musical evolution only at a stage that the Negro art has not yet attained."[5] And though he reserves his highest praise for Bechet, famously calling him an "artist of genius," the conclusion to which this leads him is troubling:

> When one has tried so often to rediscover in the past one of those figures to whom we owe the advent of our art...how moving it is to meet this very black, fat boy, with white teeth and a low brow, who is very glad one likes what he does, but who can say nothing of his art, save that he follows his "own way," and then one thinks that his "own way" may be the highway the world will rush along tomorrow.[6]

While he is prescient about jazz, the racial stereotypes Ansermet employs patently do not describe the light-skinned Bechet, perhaps even recalling ideas from physiognomy or craniometry (his "low brow").[7] Moreover, the notion that such "natural" musicians (read "primitives") cannot put into words—or even fully understand—what they are doing is an insidious myth of jazz criticism.[8] More than this, Ansermet seems to think that he is catching the evolutionary process in action—that he is glimpsing Europe's lost musical past. Conflating cultural and historical difference in this way, his interest in the end may be ethnological as much as it is musical.

Ansermet's bright view of jazz in any case dimmed in later years. When a reunion with Bechet was engineered in Chicago in 1948, the conductor was happy to see him again, but he displeased publicists by exclaiming that "The days of jazz are over."[9] Asked, in the 1950s, to explain his change of heart since 1919, Ansermet insisted:

> The Negro-American art has not disappointed me...But I have better understood since then that its very nature as *folklore*...limited from the beginning the development that was possible....*Historical growth* is the act of music of *culture* (that which we call "art music")...A folk practice is born, forms "types," then just lives on.[10]

Ansermet's theories about music—and about race—eventually came together in his two-volume *Les fondements de la musique dans la conscience humaine [The Foundations of Music in Human Consciousness]*, published in 1961.[11] Seeking a phenomenological approach to musical understanding, he combined elements of cognitive science, mathematics, and philosophy. But he also borrowed from "historians of civilizations" heavily marked by racial ideology, such as Oswald Spengler and Houston Stewart Chamberlain (whose French translator, Robert Godet, was Ansermet's friend and dedicatee *in memoriam* of *Fondements*).[12] The result was an all-embracing theory of musical and social development based around "three ages of man"—eras of history that were in large part racially defined. Despite its recent provenance, jazz was a remnant of an earlier age, like non-Western traditions around the world. As time in jazz was circular, not linear, repetition was its only option—a statement that applied equally to its internal form and to its prospects for evolution.

In the manner of such tomes, it is paradoxically Ansermet's global reach—his aspiration to the universal—that most clearly betrays the insularity and Eurocentricism of his thought: Enlightenment philosophy, nineteenth-century anthropology, and modern racialism form an unholy alliance, which Husserl's phenomenology (read through the lens of Sartre) does nothing to break apart. While the consequences of these ideas are too easily lost in *Fondements* among the dense theoretical prose—and logarithms—they were stated in balder form in a series of in-depth interviews on Swiss radio (subsequently published) that sought to expose his views to a wider audience. Asked about contemporary composers' use of non-Western scales in their works, for example, Ansermet replied that a "return to intervals of music of the second age" is "very far from being progress." He could explain their misjudgment: "We live at a time in which, at the United Nations, peoples of the second age are put on the same footing as those of the third age, and one is inclined to put musics of ancient civilizations and Western music on the same footing too"—a practice that, for him, overlooked the "natural" superiority of tonal music.[13]

Brazen as this is, Ansermet's prejudices may not in themselves be so remarkable. What is more surprising is that jazz history has, for generations, celebrated the text of a man who not only was fairly ambivalent about the music but whose racialized historiography and pseudoscience trapped jazz, along with those who created it, in a premodern age. Ansermet's canonization in jazz criticism notwithstanding, "primitive" jazz figured for him, as it has for many, not as a parallel tradition but rather as a foil for European art music.

A further irony: Ansermet's 1919 article remained, for almost twenty years, wholly unknown. French discourse of the 1920s and 1930s never made mention of it, though the small coterie of jazz writers frequently referenced one another's work. It was not until 1938 that his text was rediscovered and republished, with a fawning preface and parallel English translation, in the magazine *Jazz Hot*.[14] Although it had been written in London by a Swiss, French jazz critics immediately adopted Ansermet as their forerunner; his presence lent support to a growing sense of superiority among the French critics about their pioneering acumen. In this roundabout way, then, Sidney Bechet came forever to be associated with bringing jazz to a prescient and appreciative Europe, and France's youth would eventually learn about Ansermet's text in their weekly installment of *Tintin*.

BECHET'S BLUES

The rediscovery of Ansermet's text was timely. If Bechet had indeed paved the road the world would travel, he too often had been pushed aside in the rush. Not until the late 1930s did the New Orleans revival movement finally bring him the regular, sometimes even lucrative, small-group gigs and recordings in New York and Chicago that would ensure his place in jazz history. Nor was it correct to infer, as was sometimes imagined, that Bechet had been reputed in Europe throughout the intervening decades. Pig-headed, itinerant, and unlucky, he had no more triumphed there than he had in the States.

Bechet's movements in the twenties and early thirties are still somewhat difficult to piece together.[15] He played with the Southern Syncopated Orchestra or its various spin-offs and other ensembles around Europe—before being briefly imprisoned and then deported from Britain in November 1922. He returned to Europe in 1925, first to Paris with *La revue nègre* and then farther afield; 1928 found him back at several venues in the French capital. Although he was often featured as a soloist, however, Bechet did not gain great celebrity during this period. Rather, he was a gigging musician, moving somewhat itinerantly where work and fortune took him. Nor did he always receive a warm welcome. As much is shown by a newspaper report of Bechet's arrest in Paris in December 1928 after a shooting incident involving a fellow African American musician, Mike McKendrick. Wondering if Montmartre had moved to the Wild West, the author complains how many Negroes are found in this quarter; he concludes, wistfully, *"Ah! qu'il était beau mon Paris..."* ["Oh! how beautiful my Paris was..."].[16]

The last line is a pointed reference to "Mon Paris," a Lucien Boyer and Vincent Scotto song nostalgically evoking the city at a time when "Everyone spoke but one language." Bechet would have understood the tenor of it: Recounting this incident in his autobiography, he admits wrongdoing but also insists that, as a foreigner without means, his guilt was assumed, his plea of self-defense went unheeded, and even his lawyer betrayed him; the injustice of the trial, he claims, troubled him more than the next eleven months in jail.[17] On release, Bechet was required to leave the country. He spent a little more time in Europe over the next couple of years but would not return again for almost two decades.

Baffling is how, throughout this early period, Bechet moved beneath the radar of the French critics. Recognized now as a New Orleans pioneer second only to Louis Armstrong—perhaps ahead of him in France—he is more or less absent from their celebrated early histories of jazz. Bechet rates only a single, passing mention in both Robert Goffin's *Aux frontières du jazz* of 1932 and Hugues Panassié's *Le jazz hot* of 1934. Neither is sure how to spell his name; Panassié more or less admits that he is unfamiliar with his playing.[18] Ansermet's forgotten article notwithstanding, Bechet's star had thus far risen no higher in French than in foreign skies.[19]

Back in the States, the 1930s were hard for Bechet, as they were for many musicians. But he was still in work as a musician more than he was out of it, and he spent no time behind bars. His second career as tailor did not actually occupy him for long, and he never had to act on his other ideas of working as an undertaker or short-order cook. More is the point, in the last years of the decade, he entered an intensive period of performances and recordings. By the time Hugues Panassié—impresario, as well as critic—sought to record Bechet with Panassié's old friend Mezz Mezzrow in New York in 1938, he found him under contract to another label. The recordings went ahead but had to be released under the name of the trumpet player, as Tommy Ladnier and His Orchestra.[20]

Whereas the revival took off for real in America during the early forties, in France it did not gain wide influence until after the war. When it did, the adventurous French performers who sought to learn the style by imitating the new recordings of Bechet or the older ones of King Oliver were typically very young students (often not twenty) with, at the beginning, more enthusiasm than ability. Nevertheless, performers such as Claude Luter and Pierre Braslavsky quickly built up considerable support, and the *caves* (cellar bars) of theaters and restaurants in the Saint-Germain-des-Prés area on the Left Bank soon became filled with their sophomoric playing in the "new" idiom.

So, when artists such as Bechet began to consider returning to France in the late forties, there was already considerable interest in their music, a growing body of local players, and an audience of sufficient size to make such a venture commercially viable. Yet, in 1948, Panassié twice tried, unsuccessfully, to coax Bechet over: The first time, the financial terms were not satisfactory to the musician; by the second, for the Nice Jazz Festival, he was amid a long run in Chicago and sent his young student Bob Wilber instead.[21] It took a much more generous offer from Panassié's estranged colleague Charles Delaunay, for his own Paris Festival of Jazz the following year, to get Bechet on the plane: He was hardly champing at the bit.[22] Still, Bechet's decision to participate in the 1949 festival—alongside Charlie Parker, a young Miles Davis, and many others—was fortuitous. Although it was not the first time since the war that celebrated American musicians had visited, or even the first jazz festival, no previous event had approached its range, scale, or cost; the international reputation of the French jazz scene can arguably be dated from here.

The 1949 festival was also a kind of coming-out party for the Fédération des Hot Clubs Français. This new association of local chapters of the fan club had been set up by Delaunay to rival the Hot Club de France, after an acrimonious split with its director, Panassié. The causes of this dissolution were an inextricable mix of the aesthetic and the personal. Having honed his critical muscle enforcing a strict separation of what was "hot" from what was not in the 1930s, Panassié had, since the war, taken a hard line against bebop, arguing for New Orleans jazz as the only authentic style. The ensuing battle with Delaunay and some younger critics had resulted in Panassié's resignation as editor of the magazine *Jazz Hot* and the division of hot clubs across two competing organizations. Their dispute was less between traditional and modern styles per se than it was between "closed" and "open" notions of the jazz tradition; it also involved a healthy slice of professional jealousy.[23]

This context would have been at once familiar and strange to the visiting musicians. As has been well discussed, there had been long-running critical disputes in the States about styles of jazz.[24] In New York, Bechet and Parker had recently shared a stage in a mock battle between bebop and traditional jazz—one of several attempts to profit from the publicity generated by the debate.[25] But in Paris, where both men were embodying music already known on disc, it was Bechet whose stature grew most in live performance; he, rather than Parker, was the revelation of the festival. One writer, noting that Luter's and Braslavsky's bands were not up to the task of playing with Bechet, could nevertheless barely contain his excitement: "his fire, impossible to put out, even at his age…52 years old…his air of distinction…his ideas…his swing…and this fire, this fire," he spluttered.[26] Composer and critic André Hodeir, himself more inclined toward modern jazz, nevertheless agreed that "The great triumph of the festival was without any doubt Sidney Bechet, whose every appearance on stage sparked off a huge wave of enthusiasm."[27]

The closest to dissent came from the musician and writer Boris Vian, an important chronicler of jazz in France in the postwar years. Although he was delighted to see this belated recognition of Bechet's talents, Vian was baffled that the French public was "twenty-five years behind the times." Recalling that Bechet had first visited France some thirty years earlier, he feared it would take a similar period before Parker received the same attention (by which time, of course, the volatile musician, whose only visit to France this was, would long be dead).[28] In the process, Vian captured the paradox in which Bechet—and his music—were at once new and old, familiar and unfamiliar: "Listeners accustomed for several months to New Orleans music will not by any means be surprised by Bechet's style; but they will be by the spirit that animates this leader in the field, as sprightly at fifty as at the time of his first European tour, in 1919."[29] Or at least so Vian—who was not born at the time of Bechet's now-legendary visit—imagined. Thanks in large part to Ansermet, French audiences could congratulate themselves for long ago having appreciated the importance of an artist they had, in reality, only recently come to know.

Cultivating a New Audience:
Monsieur Bechet

Recognizing that Bechet had struck a chord at the 1949 festival, Delaunay hastily arranged a follow-up tour of France for him later in the year. On this second visit, Bechet lay down the first of his huge catalog of French recordings, made both with local musicians and with other visiting Americans. The big hit of these initial sessions was "Les oignons," a catchy if trivial tune based on an old Creole folksong, which, over the next ten years, came to be Bechet's signature; by the time of his death in 1959 it had sold well over a million copies.[30]

As is often the case with hit songs, the extent of "Les oignons'" popularity is, in retrospect, a little hard to fathom. Certainly, it does not place great demands on the listener—its simple tune little more than a riff repeated time and time again. On the other hand, perhaps it made the perfect introduction to traditional jazz, whose noisy polyphony can leave newcomers perplexed. "Les oignons'" tune is stated and restated before any variations on it are made; the counterpoint is of the simplest kind, mostly in rhythmic unison with the melody; and even the breaks have nothing tricky to fill them—rather, silence in anticipation of the return of the theme. When, finally, Bechet takes a solo, the same tune continues underneath; having caught our attention by soaring high, his line is itself made up of brief motifs that fit its rhythmic syntax. In short, this is a form of ragged march, reconstructing in coarse but not unappealing terms the earliest days of jazz. For French fans it had a further attraction: You could dance to it "like a bourrée."[31]

Similar numbers on French folksongs (or their ur-type) would follow, many of them becoming jukebox hits. If Bechet was far from the first to add a Gallic tinge to his repertoire—at least since the early thirties, French bands such as Ray Ventura's had swung local songs—he lent the enterprise a legitimacy that it had previously lacked: As one writer put it in 1956, he provided at once "a style of jazz more accessible to Latin ears" and an attachment to "the authentic and passionate music discovered by black Louisiana slaves."[32] Moreover, he pandered to a long-standing desire of the French to lay their hands on jazz. Describing the origins of jazz, Bechet once said: "The rhythm came from Africa, but the music, the foundation, came from right here in France."[33]

In another song recorded in the same session, "Buddy Bolden Story," Bechet went further to establish his credentials as an originator of the New Orleans style. At the beginning, he and Claude Luter engage in some light-hearted banter (in French). Bechet remarks that playing the blues takes him back to his earliest days in New Orleans. However, he laughs off Luter's suggestion that he was already performing with jazz pioneer Buddy Bolden at age six or seven, modestly insisting this was not until he was twelve or thirteen. Given that Bolden had been admitted to a psychiatric hospital by the time Bechet was ten, it is possible that he could have remembered hearing the trumpeter play but not that he had joined his band:[34] It was a tall tale designed to authenticate Bechet as a living record of the earliest jazz.

Between these two songs and others, Bechet achieved a careful balancing act: He was not only a New Orleans jazzman but also a Creole who had, in a sense, come "home" to France and was happy to play a Gallic-inflected repertoire. In a review of these recordings in *Jazz Hot* Gérard Pochonet remarked on his "delightful accent [*savoureux accent*]" speaking French and his "striking inspiration," which made these "the best souvenirs...of Bechet's visit to France."[35] What the musician (or perhaps his new manager, Delaunay) had been quick to realize was that it was not only exoticism or "authenticity" that underlay his appeal but a feigned familiarity, too. As early as October 1949 *Jazz Hot* was reporting that Bechet's renown in the jazz community was crossing over into mainstream success; the general public was falling for him despite their customary disinterest bordering on animosity about jazz.[36] The next month, André Hodeir tried to explain the broad base of Bechet's appeal:

> Sidney Bechet pulls off the miracle of enthralling at once the jazz fan, the musician and the uninitiated listener. To the first, he brings all the joys expected of jazz. He stuns the second with his mastery of the least sympathetic of instruments. Finally, the sentimental and slightly facile side of his music appeals to the last.[37]

And so it was that, over the next few years, paunchy, gray-haired Bechet became an unlikely national celebrity in France. For a while, he shipped his Cadillac back and forth with him from the States, but by 1951, when his wedding in the south of France was celebrated with a re-creation of a New Orleans Mardi Gras parade, Bechet's move had become permanent. Aside from his regular performances in St. Germain clubs (beyond both the price range and the comfort zone of many record fans) and occasional concerts, Bechet would come to play on mixed bills at the music hall. Though not a new practice among jazz musicians in France (far from it), this signaled a continued desire to reach out to audiences rather than to accept a niche appeal.

Music-hall critics commonly praised Bechet's performances even as they admitted knowing next to nothing about jazz and caring even less for its arcane wrangles. But their lack of vocabulary for the music left them grasping for metaphors, which capture an important (if troubling) aspect of Bechet's allure. His "coppery stream of black lyricism" came with "the nice, broad smile of old Uncle Tom," thought one writer.[38] For another, more extraordinarily, Bechet had succeeded in turning the hall into "a New Orleans tavern, in the same way that Vivien Leigh [in *Gone with the Wind*] took us, galloping on her horse, back to the Civil War."[39] Indeed, the musician seems to have tapped into a deep vein of nostalgia in the 1950s for simpler times (a theme to which I return later). Asked one more reviewer in 1955:

> Is it not the sun, the flowers, the water, the sky of which this Negro with white hair and a face wrinkled like a chestnut speaks to you—of Montmartre and of Montparnasse of recent times, of New Orleans of yesteryear? Is it not *joie de vivre* and love that he wishes you in the strident cry of his clarinet?[40]

Yet Bechet's success was only the most conspicuous sign of a more general change in audience patterns—and behaviors. Ludovic Tournès has traced a dramatic rise in audiences in the 1950s. From a postwar slump of just ten thousand attendances per year at jazz events in Paris from 1944 to 1946, the figures rise to an average of around four times that during 1947–1951 and peak at greater than three hundred thousand in 1954.[41] This audience was typically young and educated, often still studying, although it did extend into middle age. Broadly speaking, their tastes seem to have broken down like this:

> New Orleans jazz, by its rude spontaneity and its simple themes, appeals to the very young and...to the over fifties, who find in it a vestige of an already distant past. Modern jazz reaches the generation in between, who take pleasure in this music in which all is searching [recherche] and refinement.[42]

The ages of the audiences, as well perhaps as the style of performances, produced different behaviors. Concerts of New Orleans music were, far from historical re-creations, often riotous affairs, once described by trombonist Mowgli Jospin as "a battle between the bands and the public to find out which one could make the most noise."[43] In a bizarre but real way, the older New Orleans musicians and the young French pretenders experienced, for a while in the early to midfifties, the adulation and hysteria that would soon be reserved for "rock and roll" stars. Gate crashing, overcrowding, and a degree of hysteria were evident at Bechet's Paris concerts as early as 1950.[44] Tournès has even coined a term for the phenomenon: Bechetmania.[45]

Matters came to a head at a free concert Bechet gave at the Olympia music hall in 1955 to celebrate the sale of his millionth record. While three thousand fans overcrowded the hall, up to the same number who had not gained entry ran amuck outside. One hundred police arrived, twenty people were arrested, and two were injured. The photo story in *Paris-match* spoke of a "maladie du jazz."[46] *Jazz Hot* meanwhile congratulated Bechet heartily on his success and role in the diffusion of jazz but deplored how:

> the excessive enthusiasm—the word is insufficient—of the very young people who made up the core of the audience turned into a violent rage [espèce de furie dévastatrice] that was absolutely inexcusable....[A]fter the acts of vandalism committed at the Olympia, it is to be feared that the "general public" will get on its high horse again about "the music of savages," and that to the greatest detriment to jazz.[47]

Critics need not have worried. By the end of the decade, concerts of "rock and roll" would displace those of jazz as the venue of such displays of ebullience bordering on unrest. The spotlight went out on jazz, and, from that point forward, musicians could but wish their performances would be interrupted by clamoring young fans.

BUT IS IT AUTHENTIC? CRITICAL DISPUTES

If the public and mainstream press loved Bechet, the attitude of specialist critics during his last decade in France was much more mixed—a situation that is only partly explained by the postwar factionalization of the French jazz community.

As we have begun to see, the dynamics of jazz criticism in postwar France were complex and personal. Bechet makes an interesting case study, however, as reactions to him sometimes ran contrary to established positions, revealing what was truly at stake. Paradoxically, the "progressive" *Jazz Hot* critics were ultimately sympathetic, albeit with reservations. Bechet's more natural champion, Hugues Panassié, however, turned his back, suspicious of his very popularity, his divergence from New Orleans classics, and—perhaps particularly—his management by Delaunay.

In Panassié's record reviews of the 1950s, a pattern emerged in which reissues of Bechet's pre- and immediately postwar recordings were celebrated, while those made "after the fall" were derided. He played "dreadful baloney" [*affreux "saucissons"*] and corny old tunes [*rengaines*] that he did not swing but warbled—"as anti-jazz as possible."[48] To begin, Panassié's distaste could still be overcome by a disc in which Bechet's "magnificent inspiration" shone through or in which "on retrouve le grand Bechet."[49] As time passed, however, such occasions became increasingly rare; his most successful recordings just stank, to the critic, of commercial compromise.

In preference, Panassié turned back to one of his early informants about jazz, the Chicago clarinetist and self-proclaimed white Negro, Mezz Mezzrow, whose autobiography, *Really the Blues*, had recently done much to cement a view of black life as one of "natural" depravity. Before the war, the critic had taken great pains to win Mezzrow a chance to record with Bechet. Ten years later, he was celebrating Mezzrow's musical "authenticity" over Bechet's "corruption." *Really the Blues* was, Panassié insisted, essential reading: "the finest, truest book that has ever been written on our music" and a "message of life and of hope...to all men, white or black, jazz fans or not."[50] His playing, too. Panassié had "scarcely heard jazz, even in the United States, that swung as intensely"; Mezz's was "true jazz, jazz in its pure state."[51]

Finally, the two men's records began going head to head in Panassié's criticism. Mezzrow's recording of "Black and Blue" was the only one worth hearing after Louis Armstrong's and "far superior to Sidney Bechet's."[52] A few months later, Panassié complained that Bechet's recordings were becoming "less and less good." He proposed to his readers an experiment:

> After having heard all these [new] performances by Bechet, listen straight away to those by Mezz...with the same band of [Claude] Luter. It's like night and day. There's as much life, swing and jazz atmosphere in the new recordings of Mezz-Luter as there is little of it in the new Bechet. Not to say anything about Mezz's inspiration, so superior to that of Bechet.[53]

Mezzrow, whose last dealings with Bechet had ended with the latter pulling a knife on him to retrieve some disputed money, was doubtless happy to agree about Bechet's "corruption." But by insisting that musicians reproduce old styles and repertoire exactly, Mezzrow and Panassié had arrived in a place similar to Ernest Ansermet's, if by a different route: Regarding jazz as the folk music of a deprived minority, they considered its transformation as its degeneration and an abandonment of its cultural roots. In other words, they tried to tell African American musicians how to be black.

At the same time, Panassié was goading the *Jazz Hot* critics, whose "incompetence" he never hesitated to advertise, into a response: "Zazotteux," as he called the offending writers (combining *Jazz Hot* with *zazou*, a wartime term for swing fans now implying youthful foolishness) were under strict instructions to be "béchetolâtre" (Bechet-ites).[54] Having refused to spend column inches debating with Panassié, the *Jazz Hot* critics finally hit back in a one-off issue of a supposed new journal, *La revue du jazz*, in July 1952. Designed to resemble Panassié's *Bulletin du Hot Club de France*, its rhetoric was no subtler than his, stating up front that its purpose was to counteract his "sometimes dangerous" writings.[55] Aside from predictable complaints about the critic's exclusion of modern jazz, his tastes in the traditional music and their motivations came under attack: Panassié had organized a huge "press campaign" for (his charge) Mezzrow, but he had maintained a "veritable conspiracy of silence" about (Delaunay's client) Bechet.[56] The pièce de résistance of the team's special magazine was a copy of a letter from Bechet to Panassié complaining that his dispute with Delaunay was making musicians' lives difficult and bemoaning in particular his mention in print of Bechet's earlier expulsion from France: "I wouldn't have treated a dog like that."[57]

Nevertheless, in the face of the *Bulletin*'s critical onslaught, affirmations of Bechet in *Jazz Hot* sometimes sounded a little defensive; over time, the writers became more circumspect. In 1955 a group of them even got together to discuss "Le cas Sidney Bechet" without, however, reaching any firm conclusions. One, René Urtreger, thought his appeal lay in his extraordinary presence: "[H]e looks like a grandfather and he plays like crazy [*comme un fou*]."[58] Still, this did not explain why André Hodeir's mother, "who doesn't like jazz, loves Sidney Bechet": There was just something about his playing that was "very close to the French temperament" (Kurt Mohr). Familiar issues were sounded, including the varied and sometimes incompatible audiences he attracted: New Orleans jazz fans, who demanded the traditional repertoire, and music-hall goers, who wanted to hear him play familiar popular songs. These writers also believed that Bechet's reception as a New Orleans jazz musician had more to do with his city of birth than with his playing: His instrument, his compositions, and even his stylistic inclinations—all had reinvented tradition even before he left the States. None of the critics accepted that Bechet's playing had faded over time, though his output had been mixed. André Hodeir concluded:

> The two bogus figures that have been made of Sidney Bechet—the music-hall star and the champion-of-true-New-Orleans jazz—should not conceal from us the real Bechet. Let's hope that he will find a sufficient number of enthusiasts to encourage him to play the music that he likes more often and, in this way, to remain a true artiste [*un créateur authentique*].[59]

For Hodeir, then, neither populism nor re-creation truly described—contained— Bechet's style. The musician would not have disagreed. He complained of the "Dixieland musicianers" who, as well as trivializing the music, "tried to write [it] down and kind of freeze it"; "the music, it's got this itch to be going in it," he said. "[W]hen it loses that, there's not much left."[60] Still, the story he wanted to tell with his music went back "a long way."

TELLING HIS OWN STORY: THE LONG SONG

If his life and music had become a screen onto which were projected quite different sets of expectations and desires, it is little surprise that Bechet grew increasingly concerned, over his last few years, to wrest back some control of his representation. His attempts to shape his history—and his music's—are nowhere more apparent than in his extraordinary autobiography, *Treat It Gentle*. This book is rightly celebrated as one of the most evocative depictions we have of a "jazz life," and it has been well mined. A degree of caution is required, however, given the book's convoluted journey to publication, as well as Bechet's own capacity to fictionalize. The autobiography was finally published posthumously in 1960, by which time at least three collaborators had been involved with it.[61]

Despite all the interventions—I hope not due to them—the voice that speaks from Bechet's biography is a powerful one, resonant with an oral storytelling tradition. This is the case in particular of the opening chapter—with good reason, as it has turned out. In a long, rambling tale, Bechet locates the source of his musical gift, as well as of the whole jazz tradition, in his slave grandfather, Omar. Omar's story is extraordinary and not easily reduced to a plot. Deferring for the moment its music and poetry, however, its essential events are these: An admired musician and dancer, Omar falls in love with a young slave girl, Marie, whom he sees in Congo Square. Her master is jealous and shoots Omar, who loses an arm. Falsely accused of raping the master's daughter, he hides out in the bayou with a voodoo woman and runaway slaves. A manhunt follows; eventually Omar is betrayed and killed by a fellow slave, leaving Marie pregnant with Bechet's father.

The story, told over thirty pages, was not a mere stretching of the truth. According to John Chilton's research, Bechet's real grandfather, Jean Becher (Beschet, Beshé, Bechet, born ca. 1802) was a carpenter and a free man. Jean married Marie Gabrielle and Bechet's father, a cobbler genuinely called Omar (Omer, Homer), was born ca. 1855.[62] What is more, the musician's tale was well known in African American folklore as the legend of Bras Coupé, the one-armed man; it had even been published in multiple versions, notably (as a story-within-a-story) in George Washington Cable's *Les Grandissimes* (1880).[63] It is possible that Bechet had been told it as a child and believed it was truly about his grandfather. More likely, I think, is that Bechet understood its mythic power and was happy to appropriate it for his purposes—not because he thought he would be believed but because he wished to share the story's poetic insights.

In a recent essay, literary scholar Bryan Wagner has traced the checkered history of Bras Coupé, a real outlaw of the 1830s. His notoriety, Wagner finds, was the ironic outcome of fearmongering by the New Orleans police, eager to justify their contested weapons and powers. After he lost first his arm and then his life at the hands of the police, Bras Coupé became a folk hero among African Americans. The scene in Congo Square, which is Bechet's starting-off point, was actually a late addition to the story, notably in Cable's version (where it appears at the end). Yet Bras Coupé is central to the description of music and dancing in Congo Square in Herbert Asbury's *French Quarter* (1936), and this is the source, Wagner demonstrates, of accounts of the music's primal scene in early jazz histories—though there they appear minus Bras Coupé himself. "What does it mean," Wagner asks, "to find as the absence at the origin of jazz historiography, a slave maimed by the police?" *Treat It Gentle*'s "unstated yet unmistakable intention," he argues, "is to write Bras-Coupé back into the history of jazz."[64]

This must be overstating the matter on the level of intention, but it does capture the effect. Bechet's book—which at one point was called *Where Did It [Jazz] Come From?*[65]—repeatedly insists on the racial violence that he considers intrinsic to jazz's history: not for him any dewy-eyed imaginings of the Old South. What is striking, however—and where his version of the legend differs from many—is that it moves toward a point of reconciliation. Though Bechet portrays the slaveowner who shoots Omar as a brutal man, he also finds him tormented, and the shock of Omar's death elicits a remorse that sees Marie allowed to bring up Bechet's father in the master's house, with his support and kindness:

> That girl, Marie, she had a child. And my grandfather being dead, she had no name for it...the master and his wife told her to take their name, Bechet...And after that they let her alone...She had a name from each side of her memory to give this child. Omar Bechet, he was my father.[66]

Thus, Marie bears a child who represents the hope of a new beginning and of reconciliation between warring groups. In the published account, Omar junior's birth directly precedes the Emancipation, which is for Bechet what unlocked the music's potential: "That one day the music had progressed all the way up to the point where it is today, all the way up from what it had been in the beginning to the place where it could be itself."[67]

In Bechet's poetic narrative, then, jazz is born at the intersection of black and white communities, between African and European languages, and at the moment when desperation turns to hope. What is more, by reintroducing Bras Coupé to Congo Square as his "grandfather," Bechet lays claim to jazz history in a rather literal sense—suggesting that the transition from the old traditions to the new style took place through the body of his family member: "It was Omar started the song. Or maybe he didn't start it exactly....But it was Omar began the melody of it, the new thing." Bechet continues to explain how, of all the musicians he has encountered around the world, "if they was any good, it was Omar's song they were singing"— before adding, more circumspectly, "They all had an Omar, somebody like an Omar, somebody that was *their* Omar."[68]

Thus, Bechet has it both ways at once. It is clear that Omar is a symbolic figure, representing the generation who would create the earliest sounds of jazz. At the same time, Bechet insists on the direct familial connection that connects a good "musicianer" to his ancestors and locates himself in the central thread of that tradition. The story is at once general and personal, history and myth, true and not true, remembered and created, believed and performed. Logically nonsensical, his words—connecting the arrival of jazz with the coming of Emancipation—are intuitively correct and rhetorically persuasive: "Maybe that's not easy to understand. White people, they don't have the memory that needs to understand it. But that's what the music is…a lost thing finding itself…That's where the music was that day [of Emancipation]."[69]

Composing History: Memories and Memorials

Memory is a topic that has generated some interest in jazz studies recently. In his *Race Music* (2004), Guthrie Ramsey considers how music helped to sustain community and tradition at the local level, across generations of his own family in working-class Chicago.[70] In *Monk's Music* (2008), by contrast, Gabriel Solis investigates how the legacy of Thelonious Monk has been negotiated and inscribed by younger musicians who have played his compositions and learned from his idiosyncratic piano style.[71] My interest here is rather different: I am concerned, on the one hand, with how Bechet himself sought to write—and play—his way into the very foundation of jazz's history and, on the other, with how his "rememories" (to borrow a term from Toni Morrison) helped to reinforce a rather rose-tinted view of France's historical relationship to jazz.

In a flawed but powerful reading, Nicholas Gebhardt describes Bechet's autobiography as a "remytholigization," which, by assigning an origin myth to jazz, attempts to relocate its social meaning in the space between slavery and freedom; Bechet's task, in words as in music, is to explain the logic of the one condition (indentured servitude) in the terms of the other (free-market capitalism). This renders it an impossible act and makes Bechet's position, as a keeper of the tradition serving entertainment to the market, intractable. But jazz must keep trying to capture the change in black consciousness brought about—slowly rather than suddenly—in the transition between social and economic systems at which its history is located. (Where Gebhardt's reading of jazz performance differs from many is that he describes it not as a process of individual self-expression within the constrictions of the group but rather as a collective act made within social constrictions.)[72]

In a more fundamental way, Bechet's text and music reveal to Gebhardt the "master-slave" dynamic of American society (after the Civil War as much as before it). Dissecting jazz-historical accounts of the music's roots in the intersection of African and European practices, Gebhardt observes how they elide the Middle Passage (the way in which African and European practices came together in the first place). He—like Bechet, in his way—insists upon it:

> [T]he history of black American music is itself symptomatic of a fundamental
> and irresolvable antagonism between white and black, between master and slave,

and finally between Africa and Europe; and this antagonism, as such, is the inexplicable and irreducible fact of the jazz act that few wish, or even bother, to explain.[73]

Thus, Bechet's remythologization of jazz paradoxically requires moments in its prehistory to be understood, retrospectively, in terms of what they came to mean. As Bras Coupé's story was not that of a slave meaninglessly killed but rather one who died fighting for a prefigured freedom, so Bechet's description of jazz's emergence in the context of racial violence paradoxically holds a utopian vision for the future.

Even as he insists on accounting for music in terms of its production rather than its reception,[74] however, Gebhardt gives little sense of what this evolving black consciousness—failing better every time to resolve impossible contradictions—might actually sound like. Bechet is rarely more precise, but he does give a few pointers. In a parallel that is surely too neat to take at face value, he repeatedly sought in *Treat It Gentle* to position his move to France late in life as reuniting jazz's diverse elements, as Omar Bechet had first brought them together. Here is the most creative example:

> I felt when I settled in France that I was nearer to Africa, and I suppose too that being there is nearer to all my family and brings back something I remember of Omar and my father too. So I started to record some lovely Creole tunes that I remembered from when I was young and *some I made myself out of the same remembering.*[75]

This intriguing statement could, of course, represent an attempt to justify decisions made for commercial reasons (as Panassié might have suggested), but so effectively does it sum up Bechet's concerns in the book that it has a ring of truth—or at least the familiarity of a well-rehearsed story. Certainly, jazz scholar David Ake has sought to reposition Bechet in the specific context of French Creole culture in New Orleans. By playing the blues, he argues, Bechet was committing a political act: "playing...into being" a "blacker" identity by aligning himself with his African rather than his European heritage.[76] If this is the case, I wonder whether we might not hear Bechet's "French" recordings as attempts to play—or play back—into being a self-consciously creolized identity, one that by this time had much more to do with Paris than it did with New Orleans.

Striking in particular in the preceding quotation is Bechet's description of remembering as a generative, as well as a regenerative, act. An example might lie in his famous composition "Petite fleur." In form, it's a thirty-two-bar song: AABA. The first section feels rather earthbound, Bechet's bluesy melody competing with stabbed chords from an ensemble that seems to owe more to the Old World than to the New. In the second section, by contrast, Bechet reaches for the skies, the ensemble supporting him from beneath with sustained harmonies. The first time through the chorus, the effect is heightened when Bechet cuts off the second A after only two bars; he soars straight onto B, which is elongated to fourteen bars and accompanied by rapturous runs in the piano, as well as the sustained chords; by sequence, Bechet slowly eases us back down to the ground. (Only later is the B section heard at its "proper" length.)

In an evocative discussion of "remembering" in music, Bechet explained how sometimes "a high note comes through…[that's] got to rush itself right off…your horn because it's so excited.…All the music I play is from what was finding itself in my grandfather's time.…It's like the Mississippi. It's got its own story. There's something it wants to tell."[77] Granting, for the moment, Bechet's wish to relinquish agency, is this the soaring high note that rushes off his horn—ahead of time—in "Petite fleur" (and in other such moments that those familiar with Bechet's music will immediately recognize)? It is not an improvised gesture but a studied one whose trace in memory far outlasts its immediate visceral impact; what follows is of an emotional expansiveness that was quite unknown to the first section.

It is in such ways, I suggest, that Bechet's music of the 1950s may be not so much nostalgic for the past as it is still imagining the future: Where in "Les oignons" his bluesy playing scarcely gets off the ground, here he appears to break through the clouds above to a better place. If that place is France, it is not the France Bechet lived in, even with the fame he had latterly garnered, but rather an imagined France, viewed from afar: a location of which a shackled slave, an immobile sharecropper, or even a humble Creole cobbler like Bechet's father might dream; the place to which, if not this time, then next time, jazz might finally break through.

Meanwhile, French reactions would have brought him back down to earth with a jolt. Far from speaking of future freedoms, Bechet's music increasingly elicited a wistful longing in his adopted country for times past. Before Bechet came to Paris, one writer observed in 1957 "he was already our cousin from the country [de province]."[78] Another thought Bechet could "revive with his instrument the poetry of the blacks of Mississippi, that which floats over the bayous, the cotton or sugar-cane plantations, and even the 'show-boats' moored along the swampy rivers of America's former Old France."[79]

Such colonial nostalgia—at once affectionate and paternalistic—continued even after Bechet's death in 1959. Some of this was purely sentimental: Bechet's love of children, his appeal across barriers of age and race, his happy life in Paris (that he had, for years, divided his time between two ménages—his wife's and his child's mother's—was, of course, discreetly ignored). As well as eulogizing the musician as a "vedette française" (French star) and "Français de nom et de cœur" (French in name and heart), however, there were some imaginative renditions of his past.[80] According to one writer, Bechet was born "a little Creole with French blood mixed with his black blood," grandson to a man who "had been adopted by Monsieur Bechet, a French settler on whose plantations, of corn and cotton, the family worked."[81] Nonetheless, for this "jovial patriarch escaped from *Uncle Tom's Cabin*," France was the best country "because he had complete freedom": "Between segregation and exile, he chose exile."[82] Such was the people's attachment to him that his passing was "almost a national bereavement."[83]

"Between the French and Bechet," one last writer thought, "it was love at first sight: he settled in Paris like a native, even buying a beret."[84] Although the relationship was, as I have shown, a rockier one than this suggests, there is no doubt that Bechet died a well-loved celebrity in France at the end of the most successful decade of his career. Nevertheless, it is in the end the gap between Bechet's self-representation (albeit self-serving, albeit mediated) and representations of him in the French press that is the most telling. The sheer power of his music meant that Bechet could never be fully contained by the Uncle Tom caricatures he sometimes condescended to play, and his autobiography is always fighting against his location in a romanticized past—reliving instead the suffering, which could only fleetingly be overcome. To believe some in his adopted country, however, Bechet had, in 1919, escaped American racism to reclaim his historic birthright as a son of Greater France, in whose metropolis he had died a hero, some forty years on. This ignored not only the abortive nature of those early visits and the happenstance of Bechet's much later return but also the often intense debates about art and about race that jazz had generated in the interim. The gap between his perspective and theirs may also, therefore, allow some light to shine on the historiography of jazz in France.

In retrospect, the rediscovery of Ansermet's text in 1938 was a signal event, although it had to wait a decade before its symbolic importance was fully realized. Nevertheless, it was surely this perspicuous article, much more than the few lines penned by Jean Cocteau and others in the teens and twenties, that informed Charles Delaunay's claim as early as 1940 that the French avant-garde had recognized the "originality and promise" of jazz "*more than 10 years before*" the Americans.[85] Soon even American authors such as Rudi Blesh in his *Shining Trumpets* (1946) were calling France "the first country to accord intellectual recognition to jazz."[86] And Boris Vian reproached the Americans for "not tackling the challenge of jazz in the same way as they treated the challenge of the bomb."[87]

Meanwhile, Bechet began to find jazz history as it was evolving to be too static in its perception of the music:

> I began to think there's a whole lot of people, all they've been hearing is how ragtime got started in New Orleans, and as far as they know it just stopped there. They get to think in a memory kind of way all about this Jazz; but these people don't seem to know it's more than a memory thing. They don't seem to know it's happening right there where they're listening to it, just as much as it ever did in memory.[88]

One way to understand Bechet's French recordings, then, may be as an attempt to remake New Orleans jazz from the ground up rather than merely to reproduce its ossified sound. Taking French folksongs (real or imagined) and adding his own bluesy sound, Bechet was in effect restaging in fifties' France the hybridization of musics to which turn-of-the-century Louisiana had borne witness. If in one sense Bechet told the French what they wanted to hear, at the same time his presence—and his music—were productive of impossible memories: He "played them into being," to borrow David Ake's evocative phrase. Still, Bechet's most attentive audience may yet have been those crazed teenagers who heard the music of a man more than three times their age not as a reconstruction of the past but rather as an anticipation of the popular music of the future. That, of course, is to speak with the benefit of hindsight, but I think we can say this much of Bechet's "French jazz" of the

1950s: What seems at first a music out of time and out of place turns out to be peculiarly closely *of* its time and place—a music in which nostalgia for the past combines with a commitment to the moment and the knowledge that remembering, too, is an act conducted in the present tense.

NOTES

1. "Sidney Bechet," *Tintin: Le journal des jeunes de 7 à 77 ans* 11(580) (Dec. 3, 1959): 1, 4–7. In this chapter the translations are mine unless otherwise noted.

2. "Sidney Bechet," 7. Truncated but perfectly correct in the comic strip, this famous passage reads in full as follows: "Il y a au *Southern Syncopated Orchestra* un extraordinaire virtuose clarinettiste qui est, paraît-il, le premier de sa race à avoir *composé sur la clarinette des blues* d'une forme achevée. J'en ai entendu deux qu'il avait longuement élaborés, puis joués à ses compagnons pour qu'ils en puissent faire l'accompagnement. Extrêmement différents, ils étaient aussi admirables l'un que l'autre pour la richesse d'invention, la force d'accent, la hardiesse dans la nouveauté et l'imprévu" ("Sur un orchestre nègre," *La revue romande* [Oct. 5, 1919], repr. in Ernest Ansermet, *Écrits sur la musique* [Neuchâtel: Éditions de la Baconnière, 1971], 171–78, here 177 [emphasis in original]).

3. Ralph de Toledano, ed., "Bechet and Jazz Visit Europe, 1919" [Ansermet's "Sur un orchestre nègre," trans. Walter Schaap] in his *Frontiers of Jazz* (New York: Oliver Durrell, 1947), 115–22, here 115.

4. Ansermet, *Écrits sur la musique*, 175.

5. Ansermet, *Écrits sur la musique*, 176.

6. Ansermet, *Écrits sur la musique*, 178.

7. The first translator, Walter Schaap, rendered "front étoit" not as "low brow" but as "narrow forehead," which I do not think captures its implication. Similarly, his final phrase, "the highway the whole world will swing along tomorrow," was a poetic translation (of "la grande route où le monde s'engouffrera demain") that perhaps overplays the positive in Ansermet's prediction (de Toledano, *Frontiers of Jazz*, 122).

8. See Ted Gioia, "Jazz and the Primitivist Myth," in his *The Imperfect Art: Reflections on Jazz and Modern Culture* (New York: Oxford University Press, 1988), 51–71 (also repr. in *Musical Quarterly* 73 [1989]: 130–43). Gioia dates the rise of the myth to the early French jazz critics but does not address Ansermet.

9. *Jazz Notes* (Australia) (April–May 1948), cited in John Chilton, *Sidney Bechet: The Wizard of Jazz* (New York: Oxford University Press, 1987; repr., New York: Da Capo, 1996), 207.

10. Ansermet, cited in Raymond Mouly, *Sidney Bechet, notre ami* (Paris: La Table Ronde, 1959), 41–42. For a similar explanation, see Ernest Ansermet and J.-Claude Piguet, *Entretiens sur la musique*, 2d ed. (Neuchâtel: Éditions de la Baconnière, 1983 [first published 1963]), 41–43.

11. Ernest Ansermet, *Les fondements de la musique dans la conscience humaine*, ed. J.-C. Piguet, 2d ed. (Neuchâtel: Éditions de la Baconnière, 1987 [first published 1961, 2 vols.]). The ambiguity of the French word *conscience* (meaning both "consciousness" and "conscience") aptly encapsulates the character of the book, which is at once scientific (or scientistic) and theological or moral; it is unfortunately lost in translation.

12. Houston Stewart Chamberlain, *La genèse du XIXme siècle*, trans. Robert Godet, 2 vols. (Paris: Librairie Payot, 1913) (includes a long and rather circumspect "Préface de la version française" by Godet, vii–lxvi). Playing his cards close to his chest, Ansermet cites Houston Stewart Chamberlain and Oswald Spengler only once each (402, 574–75), in both cases to disagree with them, though their effect on HIS thinking was obviously profound. For more on this, see Jean-Jacques Langendorf, "Pourquoi une approche phénoménologique de la musique par Ernest Ansermet?" in his *Euterpe et Athéna: Cinq études sur Ernest Ansermet* (Geneva: Georg Editeur, 1998), 123–39, particularly 125–29. For an overview see J.-Claude Piguet, *La pensée d'Ernest Ansermet* (Lausanne: Éditions Payot, 1983). There are also strong parallels with various strains of anthropological thought, particularly that fostered in the United States by Lewis Henry Morgan and his students, although in this case the connection appears to be indirect. See Adam Kuper's influential account, now revised, *The Reinvention of Primitive Society: Transformations of a Myth*, 2d ed. (New York: Routledge, 2005); and Steven Conn, *History's Shadow: Native Americans and Historical Consciousness in the Nineteenth Century* (Chicago: University of Chicago Press, 2004), which usefully attends to archeological, as well as anthropological, thought.

13. Ansermet and Piguet, *Entretiens sur la musique*, 115–16. The preceding pages, 109–16, are a straightforward (if bizarre) exposition of Ansermet's three musical ages, only the last of which is "historical."

14. Ernest Ansermet, "Sur un orchestre nègre" (with parallel English translation by Walter E. Schaap), *Jazz Hot* 28 (November–December 1938), 4–9.

15. For a valiant attempt to do so, however, see Guy Demole, *Sidney Bechet: His Musical Activities from 1907 to 1959*, 3d ed. (Geneva: privately published, 2006); I am extremely grateful to the author for sending me his invaluable chronicle. The best of several biographies of Bechet, in French and English, remains Chilton, *Sidney Bechet*. Unless otherwise stated, these two volumes are the source of the basic information in this chapter.

16. Georges Claretie, "Un matin à Montmartre," *Le figaro* (Jan. 3, 1929).

17. Sidney Bechet, *Treat It Gentle: An Autobiography* (New York: Twayne, 1960; repr., New York: Da Capo, 1978), 155–56.

18. Hugues Panassié, *Le jazz hot* (Paris: Éditions Corrêa, 1934), 137; Robert Goffin, *Aux frontières du jazz* (Paris: Éditions du Sagittaire, 1932), 193.

19. Witness Charles Delaunay, recalling the period, in 1949: "Pour la clarté des faits, rappelons que c'est peu avant la dernière guerre mondiale que certains critiques de jazz commencèrent à 'découvrir' quels avaient été les véritables créateurs du jazz.…Ce n'est qu'en 1938 qu'on découvrait le génie de Sidney Bechet et qu'à sa suite on mobilisait à nouveau dans les studios d'enregistrement les derniers survivants de la Nouvelle-Orléans" ("Le cas Claude Luter: Comment se pose le problème," *Jazz Hot* 30 (February 1949), 6–7, here 6).

20. Chilton, *Sidney Bechet*, 113.

21. Chilton, *Sidney Bechet*, 205–206.

22. Walter Schaap, who was working on Delaunay's behalf, explained the circumstances in a letter to John Chilton dated June 12, 1985, reproduced in Chilton, *Sidney Bechet*, 213–14.

23. On the history of the hot club movement and the Panassié/Delaunay dynamic, see Tournès, *New Orleans sur Seine*, particularly 91–117; 141–94.

24. See, for example, Bernard Gendron, *Between Montmartre and the Mudd Club: Popular Music and the Avant-garde* (Chicago: University of Chicago Press, 2002): chapter 6, "Moldy Figs and Modernists," and chapter 7, "Bebop under Fire," 121–57. More comprehensive

discussions of American jazz criticism may be found in John Gennari, *Blowin' Hot and Cool: Jazz and Its Critics* (Chicago: University of Chicago Press, 2006), and Bruce Boyd Raeburn, *New Orleans Style and the Writing of American Jazz History* (Ann Arbor: University of Michigan Press, 2009).

25. Chilton, *Sidney Bechet*, 22.

26. "Le festival de Pleyel: Les impressions de Johnny 'Scat' James," *La revue du jazz* 6 (June–July 1949), 188 (ellipses in original).

27. André Hodeir, "Le festival 1949," *Jazz Hot* 34 (June 1949), 7, 9, here 7.

28. Boris Vian, "Retour sur...le festival du jazz," *Spectacles* 8 (June 1, 1949), repr. in Vian, *Œuvres*, 15 vols., vol. 8, *Jazz 3*, ed. Claude Rameil, 97–99 (Paris: Fayard, 2001). See also Vian, "Réflexions en l'air," *Combat* (June 10, 1949), repr. in *Œuvres*, vol. 7, *Jazz 2*, ed. Claude Rameil, 171–73 (Paris: Fayard, 2000).

29. Boris Vian, "Ne crachez pas la musique noire," *Radio* 49(238) (May 13, 1949), repr. in Vian, *Œuvres*, vol. 8, 109–11, here 110.

30. Tournès, *New Orleans sur Seine*, 289.

31. Mouly, *Sidney Bechet*, 10.

32. J. P., "À l'Alhambra: Sydney [*sic*] Bechet: Musique d'abord," *Franc-tireur* (Jan. 23, 1956), in Bibliothèque Nationale, Département des Arts du Spectacle, Collection Rondel (henceforth, Rondel), "Alhambra, 1951–1960," vol. 2 (8°Sw80).

33. *Esquire* (July 1958), cited in Chilton, *Sidney Bechet*, 284.

34. On Bechet's possible encounter with Bolden, see Chilton, *Sidney Bechet*, 5.

35. Gérard Pochonet, "Les disques: Vogue, Bechet-Luter," *Jazz Hot* 40 (January 1950), 16.

36. *Jazz Hot* (editorial), "Armstrong et Béchet [*sic*] en France," *Jazz Hot* 37 (October 1949), 1.

37. André Hodeir, "Popularité de Louis Armstrong," *Jazz Hot* 38 (November 1949), 1. One more tune Bechet recorded for the first time in 1949 and adopted into his "French" repertoire was the old Maurice Yvain song "Mon homme": another canny choice. While jazz singers, notably Billie Holiday, had long made it their own (as "My Man"), in France it was indelibly associated with the music-hall star Mistinguett. Frank Tenot noted that "Besides its own virtues, this side ['Mon homme'] may provide the opportunity for many uninitiated listeners to learn to appreciate the improvisation process in jazz. Bechet remains in this way the best of the popularizers of this music—but a popularizer without populism [*vulgarisateur sans vulgarité*]" (Frank Tenot, "Les disques: Vogue, Sidney Bechet," *Jazz Hot* 40 (January 1950), 16).

38. G. Joly, "À l'Olympia: Mouloudji et Sidney Bechet," *L'aurore* (Sept. 4, 1954), in Rondel, "Olympia, 1954–1960," vol. 2 (8°Sw106).

39. Jean Bouret, "Les variétés: Music-hall Saint-Germain-des-Prés," *Franc-tireur* (Sept. 4, 1954), in Rondel, "Olympia, 1954–1960," vol. 2.

40. Unidentified editorial in *Pourquoi pas?* (Belgium), cited in Boris Vian, "Revue de presse," *Jazz Hot* 96 (February 1955), repr. in Vian, *Œuvres*, vol. 6, *Jazz 1*, ed. Claude Rameil, 455–56 (Paris: Fayard, 1999).

41. Tournès, *New Orleans sur Seine*, Annexe IV, 465–67. The figures I cite here are attendances, not unique attendees, and include music-hall shows featuring jazz, as well as concerts. Tournès focuses his discussion (333–34) on concert audiences alone; hence, his interpretation reads slightly differently from mine, though the statistics are all his.

42. *Le figaro* (July 17, 1958), cited in Tournès, *New Orleans sur Seine*, 337.

43. *Le figaro* (Mar. 12, 1956), cited in Tournès, *New Orleans sur Seine*, 364.

44. Chilton, *Sidney Bechet*, 236.

45. Tournès, *New Orleans sur Seine*, 285–90.

46. *Paris-match*, cited without date in Tournès, *New Orleans sur Seine*, 365, which account I draw on here.

47. Anon., "Sidney Bechet millionaire," *Jazz Hot* 104 (November 1955), 38.

48. Hugues Panassié, "Les disques: Bechet," *Le bulletin du Hot Club de France* (henceforth, *BHCF*) 1 (October 1950), 12.

49. Hugues Panassié, "Les disques: Bechet," *BHCF* 1 (October 1950), 12; Panassié, "Les disques: Bechet-Luter," *BHCF* 6 (March 1951), 8.

50. Hugues Panassié, "Les livres: *La rage de vivre*," *BHCF* 1 (October 1950), 13.

51. Hugues Panassié, "Mezz et Luter au Vieux Colombier," *BHCF* 12 (November 1951), 5.

52. Hugues Panassié, "Les disques parus en France: Milton 'Mezz' Mezzrow–Claude Luter," *BHCF* 14 (January 1952), 13.

53. Hugues Panassié, "Les disques parus en France: Bechet-Luter," *BHCF* 18 (May 1952), 9.

54. Hugues Panassié, "Livres: *Les maîtres de jazz*, de Lucien Malson," *BHCF* 26 (March 1953), 25.

55. *La revue du jazz*, "2e série, no. 1" (July 1952), 2.

56. Charles Delaunay, "Autrefois les amateurs…," *La revue du jazz* (July 1952), 2–4, here 4.

57. "Quelques lettres peu connues: Une lettre de Sidney Bechet," *La revue du jazz* (July 1952), 14. Panassié responded briefly in "Revue de la presse," *BHCF* 20 (August–September 1952), 22; and "Mise en point au sujet de Big Bill et Bechet," *BHCF* 21 (October 1952), 17.

58. André Clergeat, André Hodeir, Kurt Mohr, Michel de Villers, and René Urtreger, "Le cas Sidney Bechet," *Jazz Hot* 101 (July–August 1955), 9–10, here 9.

59. Hodeir, "Le cas Sidney Bechet," 10.

60. Bechet, *Treat It Gentle*, 95–96; see also 114–15.

61. American poet John Ciardi, who first met Bechet in Paris in 1950, provides the most complete explanation. According to him, the document he received from Bechet turned out to have been compiled from taped interviews and monologues by Joan Reid (née Williams), whom Bechet called his "secretary." In preparation for publication, Ciardi removed Reid's own intrusions and filled in details, particularly of later years, from further interviews with Bechet. At this point, Reid insisted the work was hers and threatened to sue the prospective publisher, Twayne, who shelved the project (John Ciardi, "Writing *Treat It Gentle*: A Letter to Vince Clemente, September 22, 1985," in *John Ciardi: Measure of the Man*, ed. Vince Clemente (Fayetteville: University of Arkansas Press, 1987), 82–83). Years later, however, British writer Desmond Flower procured Ciardi's manuscript from Twayne and conducted his own interviews with Bechet, a process that was not complete when the musician died. The extent of Flower's intervention, like Reid's, is unclear, but Ciardi himself insisted at the time of the threatened suit that "In the finished manuscript *no word of [Reid's] appears: not one*. It's all Sidney's talk and," he continues tellingly, "talk I have put into his mouth" (Ciardi, letter to Jack Steinberg, Apr. 16, 1952, John Ciardi Papers, Library of Congress, cited in Edward M. Cifelli, *John Ciardi: A Biography* [Fayetteville: University of Arkansas Press, 1997], 154). Nevertheless, both Ciardi and later Flower stated that Bechet had approved their completed texts, albeit with the caveat by the time of Flower's version that he wanted to add more detail about the later years (Ciardi, "Writing"; Flower, "Foreword" in Bechet, *Treat It Gentle*).

62. Chilton, *Sidney Bechet*, 1.

63. George Washington Cable, *The Grandissimes: A Story of Creole Life* (New York: Scribner's, 1880).

64. Bryan Wagner, "Disarmed and Dangerous: The Strange Career of Bras-Coupé," *Representations* 92 (Fall 2005): 117–51, here 137. A version of this article also appears in Wagner's *Disturbing the Peace: Black Culture and the Police Power after Slavery*, 58–115 (Cambridge, Mass.: Harvard University Press, 2009).

65. *Melody Maker* (Oct. 13, 1951), cited in Chilton, *Sidney Bechet*, 291.

66. Bechet, *Treat It Gentle*, 46–47. Similarly, "those people there, the man and his wife, they were trying to make it up to her. It was almost like they were trying to tell her without putting it into words that they wanted her to come over to them and do their forgetting. Time changes a man, and that master he acted a very different way after all that trouble. It was like some part of the evil had been washed away out of him by all that had happened; and the evil had left a kind of sorrow in its place, a gentler thing" (49).

67. Bechet, *Treat It Gentle*, 48.

68. Bechet, *Treat It Gentle*, 202.

69. Bechet, *Treat It Gentle*, 48.

70. Guthrie P. Ramsey, Jr., *Race Music: Black Cultures from Bebop to Hip-hop* (Berkeley: University of California Press, 2003).

71. Gabriel Solis, *Monk's Music: Thelonious Monk and Jazz History in the Making* (Berkeley: University of California Press, 2008).

72. Nicholas Gebhardt, "Sidney Bechet: The Virtuosity of Construction," in his *Going for Jazz: Musical Practices and American Ideology* (Chicago: University of Chicago Press, 2001), 33–76.

73. Gebhardt, *Going for Jazz*, 67.

74. Gebhardt, *Going for Jazz*, 6.

75. Bechet, *Treat It Gentle*, 194–95 (my italics).

76. David Ake, " 'Blue Horizon': Creole Culture and Early New Orleans Jazz," in his *Jazz Cultures* (Berkeley: University of California Press, 2002), 10–41, here 36. See also the review by Gabriel Solis in *Ethnomusicology* 47 (2003): 392–95, which is circumspect about Ake's account of the racial context.

77. Bechet, *Treat It Gentle*, 46.

78. Christian Mégret, "De tout un peu," *Paris-variétés* (Mar. 13, 1957), in Rondel, "Bobino music-hall, 1933–1960," vol. 7 (8°Sw84).

79. Serge, "En écoutant Sidney Bechet," *Les nouvelles littéraires* (Mar. 14, 1957), in Rondel, "Bobino music-hall, 1933–1960," vol. 7.

80. François Millet, "Jazz: Sidney Bechet, vedette française," *L'express* (May 21, 1959); Lucien Malson, "Mort d'un grand jazzman," *Arts* (May 20, 1959), both in Rondel, "Bechet (Sidney): Articles biographiques et critiques le concernant publiés de 1949 à 1959" (8°Sw1232).

81. Robert Chaix, " 'Nuit silencieuse' pour Sidney Bechet," *Ici Paris* (May 20, 1959), in Rondel, "Bechet (Sidney)."

82. Raphaël Valensi, unidentified clipping; Robert Chazal, "Mort à 63 ans, le jour de son anniversaire, le grand saxophoniste Sidney Bechet," *France-soir* (May 15, 1959); Alain Guerin, "Sidney Bechet: Le chant interrompu," all in Rondel, "Bechet (Sidney)."

83. Millet, "Jazz: Sidney Bechet, vedette française."

84. "Sidney Bechet à l'agonie," *Tribune de Genève* (May 14, 1959), in Rondel, "Bechet (Sidney)."

85. Charles Delaunay, "Delaunay in Trenches, Writes 'Jazz Not American,' " *Downbeat* (May 1, 1940), 6, 19 (emphasis in original); also repr. as "From Somewhere in France," in *Keeping Time: Readings in Jazz History*, ed. Robert Walser, 129–32 (New York: Oxford University Press, 1999). Compare Walter E. Schaap in the American edition of Delaunay's

discography: "[A]lthough a distinctly American art form, [jazz] achieved intellectual recognition only when endorsed by European critics, who did the work our own writers should have done, but lamentably failed to do, some ten years earlier" (Schaap, "Foreword," in Charles Delaunay, *Hot Discography* (New York: Commodore Music Shop, 1940 [first published: Paris: Jazz Hot, 1938])).

86. Rudi Blesh, *Shining Trumpets* (New York: Knopf, 1946), 8.

87. Boris Vian, "Le jazz et sa critique" (unpublished, n.d.), *Œuvres*, vol. 8, 355–61, here 359.

88. Bechet, *Treat It Gentle*, 2.

PART II

CULTURAL EXPERIENCE: PRACTICES, APPROPRIATIONS, AND EVALUATIONS

CHAPTER 13

··

AN EVENING AT THE OPERA IN SEVENTEENTH-CENTURY VENICE

··

EDWARD MUIR

WHAT was it like to attend the very first operas, composed and performed in the early seventeenth century and made popular in the commercial theaters of Venice?[1] The audience at those events did not have the benefit of an operatic performance culture, which had become so pervasive by the eighteenth century that violating the conventions of *opera seria* could lead to riot. Opera evolved out of the theatrical and musical culture of the Italian Renaissance, which meant that those first operas did not seem as strange as they would have had ancient Greek music actually been rediscovered, but they must have been a little unsettling to witness, more like watching a New Orleans Mardi Gras parade than going to the Met for yet another evening with Tosca. And the experience was sexy, far more so than in any other form of entertainment. Women sang erotic songs on stage at a time when in England, for example, boys played female roles. Castrati challenged assumptions about gender and sexuality. Transvestite characters were common. The plots of early operas, which were habitually set in the distant world of pagan antiquity, sometimes included courtesan characters, women whose emotional and sexual lives were on display before an audience that also included numerous "public" women.

What opera soon became was not quite what its inventors had imagined. At the end of the sixteenth century the *Camerata* theorists and musicians in Florence invented a form of musical drama now called opera for performance in the court of the Grand Duke of Tuscany. The theorists wanted to reintroduce ancient Greek tragedy, which they believed had been entirely sung, but since none of them had a clue about how ancient Greek music sounded, they created something more indebted to the aristocratic theater of the Renaissance than to the ancients. The musical dramas performed in Florence, Rome, and Mantua between 1590 and 1608 ignored the Aristotelian rules for tragedy in favor of the tropes of the pastoral play, which concerned the amorous adventures of gods, nymphs, and shepherds. The first operatic composers—Peri, Caccini, Cavalieri, and Monteverdi—relied on the musical experiments of the late sixteenth century, including the polyphonic madrigal for the recitation of poetry, and the dramatists adapted the costuming, stagecraft, and spectacle machinery that had been developed for court drama. Opera began as a theoretical proposition that was impossible to realize. What these first operas did achieve was the invention of *recitativo*, the method for half-singing long poetic passages and the capacity to produce dramas with music that were much longer and more complicated than any previous musical genre. Despite these formal achievements, however, these early operas were ponderous courtly spectacles that might have faded into history like pastoral drama itself were it not for the musicianship of Claudio Monteverdi, whose *Orfeo*, produced in Mantua in 1607, managed to create a musical style of dramatic recitation that far transcended any of the other early operas.[2]

It was only in 1637, with the opening of the Teatro San Cassiano in Venice, that opera theaters that catered to a paying public created the lively art opera has remained for the past four hundred years.[3] Finding out what happened in Venice in the years before 1637, therefore, provides clues to the lure of those first evenings at the opera, when ecstatic audiences demanded more singing, more spectacle, more new productions.

The complexity of early opera placed unprecedented demands on composers and dramatists. Producing *Orfeo* and the following year his second opera, *Arianna*, along with his other duties as court composer in Mantua wore Monteverdi out, and gravely ill he retired to his father's house in Cremona. To escape overwork in Mantua, he accepted a position in 1613 as chapel master in Venice, to compose not operas but church music for the Basilica of San Marco. In Venice Monteverdi found that the light duties of the choirmaster allowed him to accept patronage from other religious institutions and aristocratic families. Venice provided a great variety of opportunities for patronage in comparison to Mantua, where everything depended on the tastes of the prince and his court. When Monteverdi arrived in Venice, the position of the choirmaster of San Marco might have been the best job for a composer in Italy outside of papal Rome, but unlike Rome, where tastes changed with the succession of cardinals, popes, and their nephews, the institutional continuity of the republic of Venice guaranteed stable patronage for a composer, and San Marco probably had one of the best companies of singers and instrumentalists in Europe. Monteverdi inherited a distinguished musical tradition at San Marco, which began with the appointment of Adrian Willaert in 1527, who was followed by Cipriano de Rore, Gioseffo Zarlino, Claudio Merulo, and the most important of all, Andrea Gabrieli and his nephew Giovanni.[4] Variety, stability, and talent made Venice a highly attractive musical center. In Venice the musical establishment was in place for the development of commercial opera, but the experienced opera composer Monteverdi did not bring the genre with him. He composed his great Venetian operas late in his life, only after others had reinvigorated the form for Venetian theaters.[5]

Music was everywhere in sixteenth- and seventeenth-century Venice. Ducal processions were staged every year at the rate of almost one per week. The participants in each of these processions, which consisted of all of the important office-holders, foreign ambassadors, and ecclesiastics, marched around the Piazza San Marco and sometimes to other parts of the city. Shawm and trumpet players accompanied these processions, and after the officials entered the basilica the choir and brass players performed. In addition to these official occasions, the confraternities, especially the six Scuole Grandi, sponsored processions and other musical events in the neighborhoods of their confraternal houses. The great mendicant churches of SS. Giovanni e Paolo and the Frari, both of which had a choir, organist, and music master, formed satellites to the musical center at San Marco. Many of the smaller churches commissioned works for the annual feast day of their patron saint.[6] These ubiquitous public musical performances supported a large number of professional musicians, created a demand for new music, and trained listeners' ears to appreciate musical innovations.

Not all music was public or religious. One of the significant innovations of the sixteenth century was the spread of private performances in the salons of patrician palaces, where the secular madrigal became the dominant form. The madrigal borrowed from the language theories of Pietro Bembo, who gave linguistic meaning to sound. Based on Petrarch's poetics, Bembo's ideas insisted on moderation as a universal stylistic principle. However:

> Petrarch's continual undercutting of verbal utterance through oxymoron and paradox symbolized even more importantly the reserve on which Venetians claimed to insist in other domains. Coupled with its intricate plays of verbal-psychic wit, this poetics, not surprisingly, entranced a society bound by civic habit to discreet emotional display and simultaneously absorbed in a stylized self-presentation.[7]

The madrigal sung in the privacy of a palace became an emotional solace for the members of the patrician class, who were obligated to live according to a rigid code of decorum. It is difficult to know who sang those madrigals, but certainly many of the singers were highly trained courtesans who entertained their clients with improvised songs accompanied by a lute or spinet. Whether dominated by a courtesan or a patrician wife or daughter, the Venetian salons of the sixteenth century became important experimental spaces in which a taste for the female voice was cultivated. The musical expression of female sexuality and the evocative power of the female voice would become signal elements in the culture of opera in the following century.[8]

Fascination with the erotically charged female voices in private salons found echoes in the "disembodied" female singers in convents. After the Council of Trent attempted to enclose nuns away from the temptations of the public, the sisters became invisible but remained audible, not just in Venice but throughout Italy. For security reasons convents for women were walled and built in cities, which meant that nuns may not be seen but could still be heard by neighbors, passers-by, and those who attended dramatic performances, office hours, and Masses in convents. Music became the most significant cultural production of the convents. Like their secular sisters in salons, nuns in the sixteenth century began to prefer the solo singer. Convents competed to find the soloists with the most angelic and powerful voices, which could be projected through the grilled window of the organ loft or over the wall of the inner chapel to be heard above the secular musicians who accompanied the nuns from outside the inner recesses of the convent.[9] Singing nuns created a taste for the diva's voice generations before she first appeared on an opera stage.

Opera, unlike Athena, did not leap forth fully armed from the heads of church musicians but evolved out of the Bacchanalian culture of carnival. There is a certain irony here because it was the public nature of the Venetian opera houses that made true privacy possible, especially in contrast to princely courts, in which the prince was the ultimate patron, acknowledged by everyone, and where performances took place in a small court theater for a few honored courtiers, ambassadors, and guests. In public theaters patrons could disguise their true identities or at least avoid full responsibility for what appeared on stage. They were the *incogniti* (the unknowns), as the most prominent academy that backed early opera was so aptly named. The carnival seasons of the 1630s and 1640s in Venice offered a singular opportunity for "unknowns" to indulge in theatrical experimentation on an unprecedented scale. Because it was the carnival season, the audience members were themselves masked, and thus unknown patrons staged the first operas for the unknowns in the audience.

The carnival mask was both an instrument and a metaphor for assumed anonymity. Both opera theaters and gambling casinos were open only between All Saints Day and Christmas, as well as during the long carnival season and the Ascension season in late spring. The law required all entrants to theaters and casinos to be masked.[10] Noble women developed the habit of arriving at the theater in masks but took them off once they took their places in their boxes. In the late eighteenth century a law required Venetian noblewomen to wear masks continuously in the opera theaters to distinguish them from prostitutes, who were appearing without masks and displaying themselves in the front of opera boxes.

The mask, however, was fraught with ambiguities. It first appeared in the early Renaissance as a carnivalesque form of license. Maskers turned the world upside down by pretending to be something they were not. In Venice, however, the mask evolved into a sign of patrician status. Its form was regulated by law: It should be a white half-face mask that reached just below the nose. Venetians considered it "a sober, dignified, and most of all conservative marker of roles." The mask hid individual identity as it heralded class identity, but it also made deceit possible. Anyone could put on a mask and appear to be a noble. Nevertheless, it is evident from the behavior in the casinos that people usually had an idea of who was behind the mask even if it were bad form to acknowledge it. Masking provided a fictional identity but risked the big lie of the cheat at the gaming tables or the little lie of the courtesan who masqueraded as a noble lady. Masking also allowed foreign ambassadors, who were prohibited by law from contact with Venetian senators, to trade diplomatic secrets through discreet encounters at the opera house.[11] The ambiguities of the mask were magnified by the social atmosphere of the opera house, which was the place to be seen. Audience members were notoriously inattentive to what happened on stage. They ate, drank, gambled, chatted, fought, made love, and occasionally listened to a favorite singer. As James H. Johnson has put it about Paris of the *ancien régime*, opera was a social duty: "[A]ttending the opera was more a social event than [an] aesthetic encounter."[12] A social event it may have been, but the social experience at the opera house was paradoxical. Attendees, who were almost all patricians and aristocratic tourists or diplomats, pretended not to know one another when they perfectly well did. They were acting a role as much as anyone on the stage, and thus the separation of stage and audience was artificial. They were all actors, the box as much a stage as the proscenium, every courtesan as much a prima donna as the soprano.

The history of early opera belongs as much to the history of drama as to that of music. *Opera lirica* was poetry dressed in music, "la poesia vestita di Musica."[13] The primacy of poetry over music meant that the librettist dominated the production and that libretti were frequently published at the time, whereas the music seems to have been virtually interchangeable from one opera to another. Most of the scores are lost, perhaps because they were considered ephemera but also because there was a great deal of improvisation in the performances. The composer-conductor provided the orchestra with only the most rudimentary score. Orchestration and the realization of harmonies took place on the spot, determined in part by the available instrumentalists. At least some of the singers could not read music but learned their parts by ear, and given their interactive relationship with the audience they were prone to virtuosic improvisation not just in the permissible ornamentations and cadenzas but also wherever they could get away with it and whenever the audience demanded it.

The spontaneous character of those early operatic performances owed a great deal to Venetian drama, which evolved during the sixteenth century as a carnival entertainment. Ribald and often satirical comedies were formalized in *commedia dell'arte*, which structured plays around standardized characters with improvised plots and gags. The connection between *commedia dell'arte* and opera was direct. By the time opera became the vogue in the mid-seventeenth century, the term *comico* still referred to anyone who performed on stage. The members of a *commedia dell'arte* troupe had to be able to act and dance, sing, or play an instrument. In early operas the large battle scenes and the intermezzi became the responsibility of the *commedia dell'arte* troupes, who gave the operatic singers a rest. In fact, the first commercial opera, *Andromeda*, performed at San Cassiano in 1637, could just as easily be considered a particularly elaborate *commedia*, which was the term still commonly applied at the time to an opera libretto.[14]

The history of Venetian theater betrays a recurrent dialectic between the licentious behavior of the *commedia* troupes (both professional and those run by patrician youth) on the one hand and an impulse for social control by the elderly patrician officeholders on the other. As early as 1508 the Council of Ten prohibited unauthorized theatrical performances for carnival and weddings, especially those that employed comedians and buffoons in masks who engaged in mime and exaggerated elocution.[15] From the mid-fifteenth to the late-sixteenth century, carnival theatrical entertainments and those for special occasions, such as the visits of princes and ambassadors, triumphal entries, and weddings, tended to be organized and financed by the Compagnie della Calza, which were festive clubs of young patricians known for their hedonism and for pushing the limits of their elders' tolerance.[16] The Compagnie protected their members through a code of silence: The statutes of at least three of the Compagnie have a provision that states, "each member must keep secret the affairs of the Company."[17] Comedy was play, but it was serious and sometimes politically dangerous play.

The Council of Ten's 1508 licensing requirement for comic theater was never abrogated but only selectively enforced. Official displeasure, however, tended to drive *commedie* out of the public piazzetta and neighborhood *campi*, where they had been performed on temporary outdoor stages, into private courtyards that could be closed off and transformed into temporary theaters. By circa 1580 patrician entrepreneurs had constructed two commercial theaters in Venice for performances by *commedia dell'arte* troupes. The inclusion in these theaters of boxes rented out to the public made them prototypes for the *teatro all'italiana*, the Italian opera house form that spread across Europe after the success of opera in seventeenth-century Venice. Both theaters were in the parish of San Cassiano, near the red-light district, one owned by the Michiel family and the other by the Tron, who in 1637 built the first opera theater in San Cassiano. The distinguishing feature of these theaters, especially in comparison to the arena seating plan of the *Teatro Olimpico* in Vicenza, was the inclusion of several floors of boxes that provided elevated, separated, and private spaces from which paying customers could watch performances. The shape and constricted space of these courtyard theaters seems to have dictated the theater box model over the arena arrangement of the outdoor bleachers in Venice and indoors in Vicenza. These theater boxes created a quasi-private space in a place of public access. These dark little spaces certainly provided opportunities for illicit relationships.[18] In 1581 the Florentine ambassador to Venice wrote in a letter that "it is maintained that the Jesuit priests have complained a great deal that in the boxes that have been erected in these two places many wicked acts take place creating scandal."[19] From the moment of its invention the Venetian theater box became a stage for the imagination and a metaphor for the libertine life. Courtesans frequented these theaters, and opera later borrowed from courtesan culture and even celebrated courtesans on stage.[20]

At first the Jesuits and their allies on the Council of Ten argued against the theaters on the grounds of public safety: The danger from fire in or collapse of the wooden structures was too great. In 1580, the Ten required that no comedy be presented "until first there be sworn statements from architects and specialists, who will be sent by the heads of this council diligently to inspect the places where the performances will be given, that they are strong and secure, so that no ruin may happen there."[21] In 1581 the Ten passed a decree that permitted young patricians to stage comedies but banned professional actors. The following carnival season, a minority of the Ten attempted to pass a decree to open up the scandalous boxes "so that everyone who passes by can see inside these boxes, and thus they must stay open for all these fifteen days." An additional decree that failed to pass attempted to light up all of the dark corners by ordering "that lamps be placed in all the corridors before the performances of the comedies and kept lit until they are over and everyone has left the place where they are performed."[22] The restrictions the Council of Ten placed on the two theaters for comedy escalated. The theaters closed, and in 1585 the Ten ordered them torn down.

Nevertheless, the archetypal Italian opera house evolved out of the temporary *commedia dell'arte* theaters in Venice. Operatic culture probably owed no little part of its success to the form of the commercial opera theater. Writing about the Teatro San Carlo built in Naples in 1737, Martha Feldman identifies how the space of the early Italian theaters helped form the operatic experience:

> Given such an arrangement, any view of the stage is forever fragmented. Good sightlines are hard to come by, and many boxes yield no real view of the stage unless the spectator pulls a chair up to the rail or cranes her neck. From many boxes, viewing the stage continuously requires an ongoing, strenuous effort no matter where one is seated, and nothing is easier than eyeing others across the hall or turning inward to fidget with garments, whisper to friends, stretch out in the back, or fondle a lover.[23]

Indeed, assignations with lovers behind the curtain of an opera box became a cliché. There are reports of operagoers who hated the music but loved the intimate, private space of the opera box. Going to the opera had a strong voyeuristic element as the audience watched for who was with whom and which curtains were closed while the singers carried on.

Writing in 1607, Antonio Persio, whose patron was Zaccaria Contarini, the head of the Ten when it ordered the dismantling of the theaters in 1585, credited the Jesuit fathers with agitating successfully for the destruction of the *commedia* theaters. Persio's account appeared in a manuscript written in defense of the papal cause during the Venetian Interdict of 1606–1607. Persio criticized the Venetians for their addiction to avarice and luxuria. His two examples of Venetian luxuria were the theaters and the plunging necklines of Venetian noblewomen. In his account the Jesuits had corrected the Venetians by having their theaters destroyed and the breasts of their women covered.[24] However, the interdict crisis put an end to the direct influence of the Jesuits. Exiled from Venetian territory in 1607, they were not allowed to return for half a century. The banishment of the Society of Jesus eliminated the most vociferous antitheater lobby, opening the way for the return of public *commedia* theaters. The Tron reconstructed their theater at San Cassiano, and it was in a rebuilt version of this famous theater that the first commercial performance of an opera took place during the carnival of 1637.

When it came to public morality, the ruling nobility disagreed over the influence of the Jesuits, who wanted to clean up Venetian public life. Even in 1652, during the War of Candia, when Venice desperately needed military support from the papacy, some fifty-three senators voted against allowing the Jesuits to return.[25]

Early opera in Venice was closely associated with the libertine Accademia degli Incogniti, which was founded by Giovanni Francesco Loredan and active from 1630 to 1660.[26] The members of the Incogniti included nearly every important Venetian intellectual of the mid-seventeenth century and many prominent foreigners. Besides writing opera librettos, they published novels, moral and religious tracts, and philosophical essays.[27] In 1640 the Incogniti inspired the construction of a brand-new building, the Teatro Novissimo, the fourth opera house to open in Venice. The Novissimo was committed to producing only heroic operas with music rather than anything overtly like the reviled *commedie*, and although it presented only six operas during its short life span of five years, these established a distinctive Venetian operatic tradition. The Novissimo brought together professional musicians from Rome with the learned Venetian academicians, who had articulated a theory of opera and produced the libretti for the new productions. Although several of the Incogniti had been active in opera from the earliest productions in Venice, at the Novissimo the Incogniti worked as a group. In 1641 they produced the first operatic hit, *La finta pazza* [The Fake Mad Woman], which set a standard for spectacular production, including machines, stage sets, costumes, and singing. With a libretto by the Incognito Giulio Strozzi, music by Francesco Sacrati, and stage sets by Giacomo Torelli (the engineer to the doge) and starring the prima donna Anna Renzi in the title role, *La finta pazza* generated tremendous audience appeal, especially because of the spectacular machines and sets. It also favored local Venetian tastes with its evocation of the myth of the Trojan origins of Venice and references to the contemporary Turkish wars.[28]

At the Novissimo the Incogniti succeeded in realizing in practice what had been until then a largely theoretical justification for attaching music to drama. The Incogniti had debated the classical precedents for sung drama. It is unclear how much they knew about the sixteenth-century Florentine theorists of opera, but the Incogniti drew up their own arguments, which pointed to the various uses of music in ancient drama and to the ways in which their dramas were similar to or different from those of the ancients.[29] Unlike the Florentines, the Venetians argued that in the end it did not really matter what the ancients had done. The Incogniti defended musical drama because it appealed to contemporary tastes. As the Incognito Gian Francesco Busenello, the librettist for Monteverdi's masterpiece *L'incoronazione di Poppea*, put it, "And may those who enjoy enslaving themselves to the ancient rules find their fulfillment in baying at the full moon."[30]

What were those contemporary tastes? The early operas probably represent a commercial and an artistic response to the decline in the comic performances' appeal to the patriciate. Crude comedies lowered the social quality of theater audiences, which by Cristoforo Ivanovich's report included "the vulgar." Some patricians proclaimed their desire for more noble entertainments.[31] The opportunity for profits and the enthusiasm of aristocratic patrons led theater owners to produce operas rather than *commedia dell'arte*. Most operas were historical with many plots derived from Tacitus, which allowed librettists to explore forbidden topics such as political assassinations. Special stage effects—tempests, earthquakes, volcanoes, battles—were essential. And as always sex sells. Seventeenth-century Venetian operagoers were fascinated with prostitutes and female sexuality, manifest most explicitly in the stories of Poppea and Messalina.[32] The risqué nature of these plots raises the question of who was sitting in all those opera boxes? Certainly there were very few married couples. Venetian opera matured at the moment when the practice of restricted marriage for patrician men and forced monachization for patrician women left most upper-class people out of the marriage market. Venice had become the world of the "single self," of persons who defined their social status and their sexuality outside of the bonds of marriage.[33] Unmarried men entered the thriving "sexual economy," which sustained numerous courtesans and many informal relationships and required a network of social welfare institutions for retired prostitutes and cast-off mistresses.[34] Opera became a commentary on restricted marriage by bringing into question the relationships between lust and love, sex and marriage, personal fulfillment and stoic suffering.

The masked inhabitants of the opera boxes were victims of one of the most rigid marital regimes known to the history of demography. Since at least 1422 the Venetian patriciate had attempted to impose on its members a rigorous endogamy that prevented noblemen from marrying women from outside the class.[35] The consequence of Venetian marriage practices, therefore, was the systematic production of patrician bachelors and patrician nuns.[36] By the middle of the sixteenth century the combination of dowry inflation, which discouraged many patrician fathers from the expense of marrying off their daughters, and price inflation, which eroded patrician patrimonies, expanded the practice of restricted marriage, whereby families limited the number of children allowed to marry in order to prevent the dispersal of the patrimony. There was both a financial and a political logic to marriage restriction. In the absence of primogeniture laws, inheritance had to be shared among all legitimate male and female offspring in each generation, and a partible inheritance became a diminished inheritance. For those seeking political alliances, a potential groom whose brothers remained unmarried would not be distracted by other affinal connections and could give his full support to his own in-laws, especially when it came to election to lucrative offices.[37] The officially unmarried brothers entered the sexual economy of Venice on their own terms through liaisons with male lovers, mistresses, prostitutes, or courtesans, or they married lower-class women secretly.

The same pressures that forced brothers to become bachelors drove sisters to become nuns, whether they had a vocation or not. Throughout Italy between 1550 and 1650 the mushrooming monachization rates meant that aristocratic women everywhere were more likely to become nuns than wives. In Venice the rise was particularly dramatic: In 1581 nearly 54 percent of patrician women were nuns, but by the 1640s the figure had risen to 82 percent.[38] In Milan between 1600 and 1650 nearly 75 percent of patrician women failed to marry and about 48 percent became nuns.[39] Even when blocked from marrying women of their own class, patrician men had access to the sexual economy or could marry secretly, but unmarried patrician women were denied access to both.[40] Their fertility and their lives were squandered. Involuntary nuns were condemned to the hell of convent imprisonment, unpurged of their sensual desires despite their chaste marriage to Christ.[41]

The results were a tragic wastage of humanity—unbridled sexual exploitation of lower-class women by noblemen; frustrated, angry nuns deprived of life and pleasure; and the demographic suicide of the Venetian ruling class. Matters reached a breaking point in 1646 and again in 1669, when the Venetian patriciate had to sell itself, offering titles of nobility for the price of one hundred thousand ducats in order to provide enough new men to fill political offices and to finance the Turkish wars.[42] The endogamous strategy the patriciate had devised in the fifteenth century to prevent pollution from below had bled it of life by the seventeenth and made class pollution the only alternative for survival.

During its first forty years opera became the paramount art form for this aristocratic society of the unmarried. By 1678, nine theaters had been adapted or built for opera, and the essential elements were in place that included competition among opera houses; librettists, composers, singers, and set designers jumping from theater to theater; hits and busts; the cult of the diva; extensive publicity campaigns; season-ticket holders; sold-out performances; claques for specific singers; and tourists who came to Venice just to hear operas during the carnival season. Opera soon suffered from the Sisyphean consequences of success because each season operagoers demanded new surprises and novelties. In 1650, a scant thirteen years after the first opera production in Venice, Pietro Paolo Bissari complained:

> The city of Venice, having enjoyed approximately fifty *opera regie* in only a few years, of which few cities have seen the like, and those only with difficulty, at a wedding or on some other solemn occasion of their princes, has rendered the authors sterile and nauseated the listeners, it having become difficult to come up with things not already seen, or to make them appear more effective, with greater spectacle and display, than they ever seemed before.[43]

With success Venetian opera became more specialized and professional. To keep up with demand, Venetian theaters had to rely on outside talent, and as a result Venetian opera became less Venetian and more a stop on the burgeoning opera circuit as singers and composers moved from court to court, town to town. The rise of public opera theaters in Venice, moreover, was just one manifestation of the European-wide transformation toward the commercialization of entertainment during the late sixteenth and seventeenth centuries. In Venice itself, the famous bridge battles, once a ritualized manifestation of popular culture and working-class rivalries, had by the early seventeenth century come to be managed by patrician fight fans, who gambled on the outcome and tried to influence it by hiring the best combatants. In the bridge battles one can trace the nascent commercialization of boxing.[44] In late sixteenth- and early seventeenth-century Madrid and London, public theaters supported playwrights such as Cervantes and Shakespeare, competed among themselves for audiences, thrived on novelty and scandal, and struggled with the vicissitudes of commercial success and failure. In all of these examples, the commercialization of entertainment survived through a hybrid system in which impresarios risked their capital and artists their talent and time to produce entertainments that still required patrons who owned the theaters or intervened financially to bail out productions.

Unlike in princely courts, in Venice opera was a business. Productions had to appeal to the ticket-buying public, or they would close.[45]

Through success opera soon became "normal" entertainment and in so doing began to lose its innovative spirit and to conform to the tried and true conventions that yielded predictable profits and provided theatergoers an occasion for social encounters, clandestine or otherwise. The notorious conclusion of the Incognito librettist Giovanni Francesco Busenello's *L'incoronazione di Poppea*, first produced in the 1642–1643 season, in which the Emperor Nero crowns the prostitute Poppea after repudiating his legitimate wife, was openly libertine.[46] A decade and a half later, the Accademia degli Imperturbabili, which rented the Teatro San Aponal in 1657 and whose members produced at least two librettos, offered a far less ambitious and scandalous theory of opera than had the Incogniti. The Imperturbabili proposed a program safer and more modest, "to pass, in honest and virtuous recreation, the most dangerous days of the year [i.e., carnival]."[47]

The desire to avoid scandal revealed a fundamental tension in early opera, which was a free-spirited form of drama utterly at odds with the ethos of the Catholic Reformation. The Jesuits articulated both the value and the dangers of drama. They partook of the same humanist influences as the theorists of opera, but their views evolved in an entirely different direction toward the creation of a distinctive Jesuit theater, a kind of antiopera.[48] In the Jesuit theater, pedagogues perfected their students' Latin eloquence through the recitation of "dialogues."[49] These simple dialogues were enormously successful, and they evolved into full-fledged plays that became an integral part of the academic calendar of the Jesuit colleges. In addition, the Jesuits conceived of acting as a form of methodical prayer, an imitation of Christ in which God's providential plan was represented not only for the guidance of Christians but also for the conversion of heathens.[50] Pastoral theater became a prop for Jesuit prestige, as important as missions and the colleges themselves, and in some cosmopolitan centers such as Lisbon Jesuits dominated the urban stage.[51] During the early seventeenth century Jesuit theater was a major force for inculcating the values of post-Tridentine Catholicism, virtually everywhere except for Venice. It is no accident that commercial opera first thrived in the most important Catholic city without a Jesuit presence.

The rules of the Jesuit colleges proclaimed that "tragedies and comedies must be in Latin, and they must be very few. Their subjects should be religious and edifying, and there should be no interludes that are not in Latin and in good taste. No female characters or costumes may be used."[52] In fact, no female spectators were even to be allowed into the performances. On no issue did the Jesuit theater and Venetian musical theater differ more than on the role of women on stage. Just as Venetian opera can be understood as a celebration of female eroticism and as encouraging the mixing of men and women in the audience, Jesuit dramatic theory was a harsh warning about the dangers of women in the theater. Among religious, the Jesuits were not alone in their cultivation of the theater as a form of pious expression. Italian nuns had a thriving dramatic tradition that included spiritual comedies, but gender segregation also prevailed at their productions. All the actors were women, and as a rule the audience members were exclusively other nuns and secular women. The presence of laymen and priests was the exception to the rule.[53]

In contrast, during carnival going back at least to the early sixteenth century, women and men mingled in the audiences for the comedies. Women started to appear on stage alongside male actors. Isabella Andreini (born 1562) of Padua attracted a considerable public following without apparent shame, becoming the first female "star" of the theater.[54] Nevertheless, the prejudice against women on stage persisted. For Christian moralists justification for the prejudice could be found in the writings of Salvanius, a disciple of Augustine. Salvanius argued that audiences were as complicit in sin as actors because of the audience's desire to identify with dramatic characters: "The indecencies of the spectacles involve actors and audience in substantially the same guilt."[55] English Puritans asserted that play acting is inherently evil because the actor substituted a contrived self for the "absolute identity" given by God. To pretend to be someone other than what God has ordained was to deny the divine will. The Puritans' attack on theater paralleled their critique of the liturgy. True worship must translate the inner spiritual state of the worshiper and should not be mediated by ritual scripts, formulas, or prescribed gestures. In addition, there were moral dangers in open displays of female seduction and of transvestitism that "symbolized irrational forces threatening chaos," forces that must be resisted at all costs.[56] The Puritan complaint about the insincerity of actors did not have much purchase in Catholic Italy, but Italian critics shared concerns about the moral dangers of women on stage.

The scourge of Italian theater was the Jesuit Gian Domenico Ottonelli. Ottonelli was a "guerrilla engaged in combat against the theater and especially against the role of women in it."[57] The first evidence of Ottonelli has him closing down a comedy performance in Catania in 1635 because of the appearance of a single obscene gesture. Obsessed with the presumed sexual promiscuity of actresses, Ottonelli employed a network of spies who attended performances and relied on the confessional to provide him with information. Noting that lecherous nobles had not infrequently raped famous actresses, the Jesuit demanded that women be excluded from the stage not for their own protection but because they were infernal Amazons, dressed up to look like someone other than who they were. The seduction of a woman's eyes especially troubled him, and he cited Aristotle as the source of the view that women's pupils contained poison. Aware that women had been banned from the stage in England, he considered the English solution of dressing boys up for the female parts but backed off because of the dangers of pederasty. In the end the most he would allow would be the sound of a woman's voice from offstage. Ottonelli had some successes in driving women and obscene comedies from the stages of Palermo, Naples, and Florence but little success in the Rome of the Barberini and none in Venice.

At the core of the Jesuit conception of theater was the *imitatio Christi*, the adoption of the outward role of an exemplary character as a way of inculcating inward spirituality. The Jesuit approach was theologically the opposite of the Calvinist-Puritan critique. For the Jesuits the words of the script were quasi-liturgical, becoming efficacious for the actor and for the audience by their mere repetition. The Jesuits emphasized the absolute power and meaning of words as the medium of persuasion, self-discovery, divine praise, and prayer. The actor became the mouthpiece of God.

Seventeenth-century Venetian opera, however, tended in the opposite direction, to dissociate meaning and voice. As one early eighteenth-century critic put it, "what is left in the theaters is only pure voice, stripped of any poetic eloquence and of any philosophical feeling."[58] Mauro Calcagno has analyzed the asynchronicity between the semiotics of music and language as they " 'slide' for a moment over each other," creating what is dramatically engaging about Venetian opera—the "oscillation between associating and dissociating music and verbal meaning."[59] He notes that, in the works of the Incognito thinkers, the aesthetic justification for the asynchronicity between music and text derived from the recurring tropes of nothingness and the singing of the nightingale, the ancient signifier of song sung for its own sake. These tropes came to be associated with the pure voice of a woman singing long melismatic passages utterly disconnected from the text of the libretto, a practice that led to the musical, lyrical, and emotional excesses so characteristic of early opera. The Incognito trope of nothingness was celebrated in the discourse *The Glories of Nothing*, written by Marin Dall'Angelo and published in a collection of discourses delivered at meetings of the Incogniti.[60] The trope revealed a certain discontent with the limits of Renaissance modes of expression and disorientation about the capacity of the arts to imitate nature.[61] The profound rhetorical skepticism of the Incogniti eroded confidence in artistic norms and rules and led the librettists and composers of opera to seek artistic forms free of constraints, enabling them to privilege creativity, spontaneity, and emotional expression over the representational burdens of language. As Calcagno asks, "why bother to musically reflect the meaning of words if they signify nothing?" The answer was found in opera: "Distrust of the meaning of language is compensated by trust in the power of voice."[62] At the moment of pure song, sung by a seductive female voice, by definition a woman uncontrolled and uncontrollable, a woman without a tether to meaning but only to the emotion of the moment, a pure, divine *pazza*, Venetian opera came into its own. The Renaissance project in rhetoric and musical theory to create an art that imitated nature through a principle of verisimilitude fell apart in the Incognito discourses and libretti, which depicted the world as not without meaning so much as divorced from nature, as divorced as Venetian sexual life was from monogamous marriage. Song helped reorient the emotional disorientation produced by a culture of extreme social restrictions.

In a certain sense the opera stage modeled the opera box.[63] The relationship between singers and the audience, of course, could hardly be a simple one or even a single one. The processes of artistic novelty and suggestibility were too indirect for anything so straightforward, and the traditions of carnival celebrations encouraged a considerable degree of give and take between performers and the audience. The artistic dynamic eschewed audience identification with a dramatic character for something far beyond make-believe. In opera, language evanesced in favor of pure voice so that audience members experienced life on a different plane.[64] The modeling between box and stage, I suggest, became so powerful in Venice because the actual experience of social and sexual life at the time was itself so completely divorced from the language of Christian morality.

In 1657 the Jesuits returned to Venice. During the Thirty Years' War (1618–1648) Venice lost its most lucrative markets in Germany, and the Cretan War (1645–1669) created a terrible financial drain on the public coffers.[65] Venice needed papal support against the Turks, and the price was an invitation to the Jesuits to reestablish the Society within the Venetian dominion. The consequences for the operatic stage were soon felt as a more conservative cultural atmosphere made impresarios cautious. The patrician families associated with the Jesuits gained the upper hand in the Senate, and prominent families such as the Grimani, who had staged *L'incoronazione di Poppea* in their theater, became concerned about how patronage of the arts might mar their public image. The abrupt cancellation of Francesco Cavalli's *Eliogabalo*, scheduled for the 1667–1668 season at the Grimani theater, seems to have been a direct consequence of the revived Jesuit influence in Venice.[66] No longer a great naval power, Venice was now becoming a stop on the itinerary of courtesan-seeking, opera-going tourists, a city that finally had to admit it needed the support of the pope more than it needed the books of the Incogniti, who had stopped meeting after the death of Loredan in 1661.[67]

The academies, comic theater, and commercial opera were, in fact, just a subset of a new literary economy during the seventeenth century, which centered on Venice but also connected the lagoon city to the broader intellectual and political developments of Europe. The new literary economy produced a tremendous variety of printed works including newssheets—the prototype for modern newspapers—pamphlets that popularized many new trends, novellas, poems, and librettos. One Venetian printer, Girolamo Albrizzi, turned out many different kinds of books—tourists' yearbooks, almanacs, and newssheets—printing anything that could bring him a profit. Within this new literary economy, opera found a market.[68]

Commercial theaters, pleasure-seeking tourists, and an expanded print culture came together in seventeenth-century Venice to make possible the experience of an evening at the opera. That experience was only in part a musical one, and it was a different one for many of those who attended. There were those who went to see and be seen, those who sought the privacy of the opera box for clandestine encounters with lovers or diplomatic informants, those who were ardent devotees of particular singers, and those who just wanted to be part of the scene. Contemporary evidence suggests that the drama, its poetic libretto, the sets, the spectacles, the intermezzi, and spying on and chatting with the rest of the audience made going to the opera an unprecedented and alluring entertainment. Despite all that, however, the ultimate and lasting charm of the opera was in the singing, which entranced because of the capacity of the human voice to engage the human emotions. Seventeenth-century opera was neither a displaced form of ritual borrowed from the church and liturgical procession nor quite the same as the modern operatic experience, with its veneration of composers and audience familiarity with the libretto and music of the standard repertoire. Going to the opera was an event, an event more exciting perhaps than most other mundane ones but more a part of life than an escape from it.

NOTES

1. This chapter develops some of the themes I first explored in "Why Venice?: Venetian Society and the Success of Early Opera," *Journal of Interdisciplinary History* 36 (2006): 331–54, and *The Culture Wars of the Late Renaissance: Skeptics, Libertines, and Opera* (Cambridge, Mass.: Harvard University Press, 2007; Italian translation, Bari: Laterza, 2008). I am also inspired by the concept of soundscapes as developed by Bruce R. Smith, *The Acoustic World of Early Modern England: Attending to the O-factor* (Chicago: University of Chicago Press, 1999), and the idea of music as an institutionalized discourse in Giles Hooper, *The Discourse of Musicology* (Aldershot: Ashgate, 2006).

2. Joachim Steinheuer, "Orfeo (1607)," in *The Cambridge Companion to Monteverdi*, ed. John Whenham and Richard Wistreich, 119–40 (New York: Cambridge University Press, 2007).

3. Ellen Rosand, *Opera in Seventeenth-century Venice* (Los Angeles: University of California Press, 1991), 1.

4. Iain Fenlon, "Music in Monteverdi's Venice," in Whenham and Wistreich, *Cambridge Companion to Monteverdi*, 163–78. See especially pp. 163–66.

5. Ellen Rosand, *Monteverdi's Last Operas: A Venetian Trilogy* (Los Angeles: University of California Press, 2007).

6. Fenlon, "Music in Monteverdi's Venice," 166–76. Iain Fenlon, *The Ceremonial City: History, Memory, and Myth in Renaissance Venice* (New Haven: Yale University Press, 2007); Edward Muir, *Civic Ritual in Renaissance Venice* (Princeton: Princeton University Press, 1981).

7. Martha Feldman, *City Culture and the Madrigal at Venice* (Los Angeles: University of California Press, 1995), xxix. On the relationship between book culture and musical knowledge in sixteenth-century Venice, see Cristle Collins Judd, *Reading Renaissance Music Theory: Hearing with the Eyes* (New York: Cambridge University Press, 2000), 181–88.

8. The most extensive study of the significance of the female voice in Venice is Wendy Heller, *Emblems of Eloquence: Opera and Women's Voices in Seventeenth-century Venice* (Los Angeles: University of California Press, 2003).

9. Although he does not treat Venice, I follow here the work of Craig A. Monson for Bologna and other north Italian cities. *The Crannied Wall: Women, Religion, and the Arts in Early Modern Europe*, ed. Craig A. Monson (Ann Arbor: University of Michigan Press, 1992), especially articles by Monson and Robert Kendrick, 191–233; Craig A. Monson, *Disembodied Voices: Music and Culture in an Early Modern Italian Convent* (Los Angeles: University of California Press, 1995).

10. Eleanor Selfridge-Field, *Song and Season: Science, Culture, and Theatrical Time in Early Modern Venice* (Stanford: Stanford University Press, 2007), 93.

11. James H. Johnson, "Deceit and Sincerity in Early Modern Venice," *Eighteenth-century Studies* 38 (2005): 399–415, quote on 406; Beth L. Glixon and Jonathan E. Glixon, *Inventing the Business of Opera: The Impresario and His World in Seventeenth-century Venice* (New York: Oxford University Press, 2006), 314; Martha Feldman, *Opera and Sovereignty: Transforming Myths in Eighteenth-century Italy* (Chicago: University of Chicago Press,

2007), 142–44, 179. On the instability of early modern identities and the vexed problem of defining sincerity, John Jeffries Martin, *Myths of Renaissance Individualism* (New York: Palgrave Macmillan, 2004).

12. James H. Johnson, *Listening in Paris: A Cultural History* (Los Angeles: University of California Press, 1995), 10.

13. Carmelo Alberti, "L'invenzione del teatro," in *Storia di Venezia dalle origini alla caduta della Serenissima*, vol. 7, *La Venezia barocca*, ed. Gino Benzoni and Gaetano Cozzi, 726 (Rome: Istituto della Enciclopedia italiana, 1997).

14. Selfridge-Field, *Song and Season*, 90–93.

15. Archivio di Stato, Venice [ASV], Consiglio dei Dieci, Misti, reg. 32, c. 55v, published in Alberti, "L'invenzione del teatro," 706–707.

16. Lionello Venturi, "Le compagnie della calza (sec. XV–XVII)," *Nuovo Archivio Veneto*, n.s. 16 (1908), 2: 161–221; 17 (1909), 1: 140–233. Matteo Casini is preparing a more up-to-date study of the Compagnie.

17. Quoted in Alberti, "L'invenzione," 746n2.

18. Eugene J. Johnson, "The Short, Lascivious Lives of Two Venetian Theaters, 1580–85," *Renaissance Quarterly* 55 (2002): 946.

19. Quoted in Johnson, "Short, Lascivious Lives," 938n11. Translation is mine.

20. Jonathan E. Glixon and Beth L. Glixon, "Oil and Opera Don't Mix: The Biography of S. Aponal, a Seventeenth-Century Venetian Opera Theater," in *Music in the Theater, Church, and Villa: Essays in Honor of Robert Lamar Weaver and Norma Wright Weaver*, ed. Susan Parisi, 137 (Warren, Mich.: Harmonie Park, 2000). On the relationship between courtesan culture and opera, Heller, *Emblems of Eloquence*, 13–17.

21. Quoted and translated in Johnson, "Short Lascivious Lives," 942.

22. Quoted and translated in Johnson, "Short Lascivious Lives," 948, 949.

23. Feldman, *Opera and Sovereignty*, 2.

24. Johnson, "Short Lascivious Lives," 938–39, 955–56.

25. Gaetano Cozzi, "Dalla riscoperta della pace all'inestinguibile sogno di dominio," in *Storia di Venezia dalle origini alla caduta della Serenissima*, vol. 7, *La Venezia barocca*, ed. Gino Benzoni and Gaetano Cozzi, 49 (Rome: Istituto della Enciclopedia italiana, 1997).

26. Gino Benzoni, "Le accademie," in *Storia della cultura Veneta*, ed. Girolamo Arnaldi and Manlo Pastore Stocchi, vol. 4, part 1, *Il Seicento*, 135 (Vicenza: N. Pozza, 1983). On the sixteenth-century academies, see David S. Chambers, "The Earlier 'Academies' in Italy"; Lina Bolzoni, " 'Rendere visibile il sapere': L'accademia veneziana fra modernità e utopia"; and Iain Fenlon, "Zarlino and the Accademia Venetiana," 1–14, 61–78, 79–90, respectively in *Italian Academies of the Sixteenth Century*, ed. D. S. Chambers and F. Quiviger, Warburg Institute Colloquia, general ed. W. F. Ryan (London: Warburg Institute, 1995).

27. Rosand, *Opera in Seventeenth-century Venice*, 37.

28. Rosand, *Opera in Seventeenth-century Venice*, 88–109.

29. On opera between its theoretical invention in Florence and the first commercial production in Venice in 1637, Paolo Fabbri, "Diffusione dell'Opera," in *Musica in Scena: Storia dello spettacolo musicale*, ed. Alberto Basso, vol. 1, *Il teatro musicale dalle origini al primo Settecento*, 106–107 (Turin: UTET, 1995).

30. Quoted and translated in Rosand, *Opera in Seventeenth-century Venice*, 42.

31. Alberti, "L'invenzione," 719.

32. Heller, *Emblems of Eloquence*. Cf. her " 'O delle donne miserabil sesso': Tarabotti, Ottavia, and *L'incoronazione di Poppea*," *Il saggiatore musicale* 7 (2000): 5–46; "Tacitus Incognito: Opera as History in *L'incoronazione di Poppea*," *Journal of American*

Musicological Society 52 (1999): 39–96; and "Poppea's Legacy: The Julio-Claudians on the Venetian Stage," *Journal of Interdisciplinary History* 36 (2006): 379–99.

33. Virginia Cox, "The Single Self: Feminist Thought and the Marriage Market in Early Modern Venice," *Renaissance Quarterly* 48 (1995): 513–76.

34. Laura Jane McGough, " 'Raised from the Devil's Jaws': A Convent for Repentant Prostitutes in Venice, 1530–1670," PhD diss., Northwestern University, 1997. Also see her, *The Disease That Came to Stay: Gender, Sexuality and the French Disease in Early Modern Venice* (New York: Palgrave Macmillan, 2011). Cf. Monica Chojnacka, *Working Women of Early Modern Venice* (Baltimore: Johns Hopkins University Press, 2001).

35. Stanley Chojnacki, *Women and Men in Renaissance Venice: Twelve Essays on Patrician Society* (Baltimore: Johns Hopkins University Press, 2000), 56, 63–65.

36. Patricia Labalme, "Sodomy and Venetian Justice in the Renaissance," *Legal History Review* 52 (1984): 217–54; Guido Ruggiero, *The Boundaries of Eros: Sex Crime and Sexuality in Renaissance Venice* (New York: Oxford University Press, 1985), 109–45; Guido Ruggiero, *Binding Passions: Tales of Magic, Marriage, and Power at the End of the Renaissance* (New York: Oxford University Press, 1993), 175–76, 256–58; Michael Rocke, "Gender and Sexual Culture in Renaissance Italy," in *Gender and Society in Renaissance Italy*, ed. Judith C. Brown and Robert C. Davis, 150–70 (New York: Longman, 1998); Julius Kirshner, "Family and Marriage: A Socio-legal Perspective," in *Italy in the Age of the Renaissance 1300–1550*, ed. John M. Najemy, 82–102 (New York: Oxford University Press, 2004).

37. James C. Davis, *A Venetian Family and Its Fortune, 1500–1900* (Philadelphia: American Philosophical Society, 1975), 93–106; Chojnacki, *Women and Men in Renaissance Venice*, 244–56. For a self-conscious discussion of restricted marriage by aristocrats in Friuli, see Edward Muir, "The Double Binds of Manly Revenge," in *Gender Rhetorics: Postures of Dominance and Submission in Human History*, ed. Richard C. Trexler, 65–82 (Binghamton: Medieval and Renaissance Texts and Studies, 1994).

38. Jutta Gisela Sperling, who collected these data, admits "this figure is too high to be realistic, but it indicates a clear trend." *Convents and the Body Politic in Late Renaissance Venice* (Chicago: University of Chicago Press, 1999), 28, table 2, note g. Cf. Federica Ambrosini, "Toward a Social History of Women in Venice: From the Renaissance to the Enlightenment," in *Venice Reconsidered: The History and Civilization of an Italian City-state, 1297–1797*, ed. John Martin and Dennis Romano, 423–24 (Baltimore: Johns Hopkins University Press, 2000).

39. Dante E. Zanetti, *La demografia del patriziato Milanese nei secoli XVII, XVIII, XIX* (Pavia: Università di Pavia, 1972), 83–85.

40. Sperling, *Convents*, 18–26.

41. Arcangela Tarabotti, *Paternal Tyranny*, ed. and trans. Letizia Panizza (Chicago: University of Chicago Press, 2004).

42. James C. Davis, *The Decline of the Venetian Nobility as a Ruling Class* (Baltimore: Johns Hopkins University Press, 1962), and Volker Hunecki, *Der venezianische Adel am Ende der Republik (1646–1797): Demographie, Familie, Haushalt* (Tübingen: Niemeyer, 1995), 357–358, 383. Italian trans. Benedetta Heinemann Campana, *Il patriziato veneziano alla fine della Repubblica, 1646–1797: Demografia, familia, ménage* (Rome: Jouvence, 1997).

43. Quoted and translated in Rosand, *Opera in Seventeenth-century Venice*, 155.

44. Robert C. Davis, *The War of the Fists: Popular Culture and Public Violence in Late Renaissance Venice* (New York: Oxford University Press, 1994).

45. Giovanni Morelli and Thomas R. Walker, "Tre controversie intorno al San Cassiano," in *Venezia e il melodrama nel Seicento*, ed. Maria Teresa Muraro, 103 (Florence: Olschki, 1976). Cf. Glixon and Glixon, *Inventing the Business of Opera*.

46. There is a considerable debate about how to interpret the apparent immorality of *Poppea*. For a discussion see my *Culture Wars of the Late Renaissance*, 111–17.

47. Glixon and Glixon, "Oil and Opera," 138.

48. There were, however, Jesuit operas. David Irving, "Jesuit Opera," *Early Music* 33 (2005): 358–59, and René Fulop-Miller, *Jesuit Opera and Jesuit Ballet* (Whitefish, Mont.: Kessinger, 2006).

49. G. M. Pachtler, S.J., *Ratio studiorum et institutiones scholasticae Societatis Jesu per Germaniam olim vigentes* (Berlin, 1887–1894), 3: 472, as translated in William H. McCabe, S.J., *An Introduction to the Jesuit Theater*, ed. Louis J. Oldani, S.J., 11–12 (St. Louis: Institute of Jesuit Sources, 1983).

50. Marc Fumaroli, "The Fertility and the Shortcomings of Renaissance Rhetoric: The Jesuit Case," in *The Jesuits: Cultures, Sciences, and the Arts, 1540–1773*, ed. John W. O'Malley, S.J.; Gauvin Alexander Bailey; Steven J. Harris; and T. Frank Kennedy, S.J., 96 (Toronto: University of Toronto Press, 1999).

51. Liam M. Brockey, "Jesuit Pastoral Theater on an Urban Stage: Lisbon, 1588–1593," *Journal of Early Modern History* 9 (2005): 3–50.

52. Pachtler, *Ratio studiorum*, 2: 272, trans. McCabe, *Introduction*, 14.

53. Elissa B. Weaver, *Convent Theatre in Early Modern Italy: Spiritual Fun and Learning for Women* (New York: Cambridge University Press, 2002).

54. Richard Andrews, "Isabella Andreini and Others: Women on Stage in the Late Cinquecento," in *Women in Italian Renaissance Culture and Society*, ed. Letizia Panizza, 316–33 (Oxford: European Humanities Research Centre, 2000).

55. Salvianus, *On the Government of God*, trans. Eva M. Sanford (New York: Columbia University Press, 1930), 163. Cf. Jonas Barish, *The Antitheatrical Prejudice* (Los Angeles: University of California Press, 1981), 80.

56. Barish, *Antitheatrical Prejudice*, 115.

57. Joseph Connors, "Chi era Ottonelli?" in *Pietro da Cortona*, ed. Christoph Luitpold Frommel and Sebastian Schütze, 21–27 (Milan: Electa, 1998). Gian Domenico Ottonelli's work is *Della Christiana moderatione del teatro* (Florence, 1655).

58. Gian Vincenzo Gravina, "Della tragedia" (Naples, 1715), in *Scritti critici e teorici*, ed. Amedeo Quondam, 507 (Bari: Laterza, 1973), quoted and trans. in Mauro Calcagno, "Signifying Nothing: On the Aesthetics of Pure Voice in Early Venetian Opera," *Journal of Musicology* 20 (2003): 461.

59. Calcagno, "Signifying Nothing," 463.

60. Giovan Francesco Loredan, *Discorsi academici de' Signori Incogniti* (Venice, 1635), 267–87.

61. Cf. the argument that the disorientation of the arts signaled the end of the Renaissance in William J. Bouwsma, *The Waning of the Renaissance, 1550–1640* (New Haven: Yale University Press, 2000), especially 129–42.

62. Calcagno, "Signifying Nothing," 472–73.

63. Glixon and Glixon make a similar point about the opera box in *Inventing the Business of Opera*, 19.

64. Feldman, *Opera and Sovereignty*, 14.

65. Domenico Sella, "Crisis and Transformation in Venetian Trade," in *Crisis and Change in the Venetian Economy in the Sixteenth and Seventeenth Centuries*, ed. Brian S. Pullan, 88–105 (London: Methuen, 1968).

66. Mauro Calcagno, "Censoring *Eliogabalo* in Seventeenth-century Venice," *Journal of Interdisciplinary History* 36 (2006): 355–77.

67. However, on the survival of skeptical, libertine, and heterodox ideas in Venice in the late seventeenth and eighteenth centuries, see Federico Barbierato, "La bottega del cappellaio: Libri proibiti, libertinismo e suggestioni massoniche nel '700 Veneto," *Studi veneziani* 44 (2002): 327–61; Federico Barbierato, "Dissenso religioso, discussione politica e mercato dell'informazione a Venezia fra Seicento e Settecento," *Società e storia* 102 (2003): 709–57; and Federico Barbierato, "Luterani, Calvinisti e libertini: Dissidenza religiosa a Venezia nel secondo Seicento," *Studi storici* 46 (2005): 797–844.

68. Brendan Dooley, *The Social History of Skepticism: Experience and Doubt in Early Modern Culture* (Baltimore: Johns Hopkins University Press, 1999). On the function of Venetian information networks, Peter Burke, "Early Modern Venice as a Center of Information and Communication," in *Venice Reconsidered: The History and Civilization of an Italian City-state, 1297–1797*, ed. John Martin and Dennis Romano, 389–419 (Baltimore: Johns Hopkins University Press, 2000).

CHAPTER 14

JOSQUIN DES PREZ, RENAISSANCE HISTORIOGRAPHY, AND THE CULTURES OF PRINT

KATE VAN ORDEN

SOME years ago I was invited to participate in a conference devoted to the works of Josquin des Prez.[1] It is hardly an exaggeration to say that Josquin (d. 1521) has traditionally occupied a position in the historiography of Renaissance music analogous to that of Ludwig van Beethoven for Romantic music. One of the first musicians whose creative personality was a matter of interest—and in his own time—he has been described as a genius who refused to compose on request, an individualist representative of the new spirit of humanism, and an artist whose innovations defined the next musical era.[2] Yet unlike Beethoven's life and works, the basic outlines of Josquin's biography and oeuvre are disturbingly unclear. Indeed, only recently his birthdate was dramatically revised from ca. 1440 to ca. 1450 or even as late as 1455, and in compiling the works list for the *New Josquin Edition (NJE)*, editors have cut a huge number of pieces from his canon owing to the insecurity with which pieces can be attributed to him.[3] Whereas Beethoven scholars can pore over the composer's sketchbooks in an attempt to understand his creative process and Beethoven himself conveniently circumscribed his own canon of "serious" works by assigning them opus numbers when they were issued in print ("lighter" works were left unnumbered), Josquin scholars have paltry material evidence on which to base any history of the composer's life and chronology of his works. A graffito in the Sistine Chapel—"Josquinj"—might have been scratched in the plaster by des Prez, but if it is by him, it is our only trace of his handwriting.[4] Even his whereabouts have been remarkably difficult to establish, sending scholars to the archives to troll through letters, notary documents, lists of singers employed by Italian chapels, and records of ecclesiastical benefices in an attempt to locate him in the service of a particular patron or institution at a given time.[5] Letters to Isabella d'Este and Francesco II Gonzaga acknowledging the delivery of four hunting dogs by one "Juschino our servant" are crucial pieces of evidence that seem to sight Josquin in the service of Ascanio Sforza in early 1499, for instance, but we have no idea just what the nature of his employment might have been, let alone why he might have been entrusted with the transport of precious hounds.[6] About the years just before that, all of this very much at the height of his career, virtually nothing is known.[7]

Thus, Josquin studies are source poor, both for archival materials and for musical manuscripts produced by or with the oversight of the composer, which makes Josquin an excellent example of how musicologists who work in this period are often forced to extremes to recover even the tiniest shreds of historical evidence. All the more surprising, then, was my discovery that printed sources had been relatively neglected in studies of Josquin. As a historian of the sixteenth-century chanson, most of my research invariably concentrates on print since few manuscript chansonniers survive from the period after 1540. Josquin had been dead for some twenty years by that time, but he had still come up in my work since one principal source of his chansons was printed in 1545 and another in 1550. My research for the conference paper I mentioned above began with those two prints and a simple investigation: I went back to the proceedings of the international Josquin conference that had been held in New York in 1971 to see what had been written about those posthumously printed chansonniers. What I discovered—quite by accident—cast into sharp relief a set of scholarly attitudes toward print that I had sensed but never been able to articulate. This, then, is a dual story: One strain concerns the unique place of Josquin's chansons in the culture of print (the topic of that original essay), and the other concerns the shifting fate of print in the historiography of Renaissance music. I use the term Renaissance quite deliberately here to denote the Burckhardtian conception of the period as one in which a new self-consciousness on the part of individuals spurred the greatest intellectuals to high artistic achievement in a celebration of the human spirit.[8] Burckhardt's work initiated an intractable fixation on great men and their masterworks that in turn pushed music historiography in the twentieth century toward cults of genius and uniqueness and a notion of authorship and authority that ultimately set the stage for a number of biases to develop against print.

A decade ago, as I sat looking through the index of the 1971 Josquin conference proceedings, one word jumped out at me: MANUSCRIPTS.[9] The editors found it necessary to use capital letters for this entry, a special typographical emphasis bestowed upon no other subject, not even "Josquin," the composer to whom the volume was dedicated. Needless to say—though I did hopefully leaf forward a few pages to check—there was no capitalized entry for PRINTS. There was, in fact, no entry for prints at all.[10] While the entry for MANUSCRIPTS occupied seven and a half columns and permitted the reader easy access to a long list of handwritten sources, prints were not indexed, not even Tielman Susato's *Septiesme livre* (1545), the earliest source of five (or six) of Josquin's chansons, or Pierre Attaingnant's *Trente sixiesme livre* (1550), the *only* source of three of Josquin's chansons (see table 14.1, listing sixteenth-century printed sources of Josquin's chansons, and table 14.2, listing the chansons by Josquin for which the earliest source is a print). Telling by its very absence in this seminal publication, PRINT marked out what had become a negative property in Josquin scholarship, a sort of tabloid source material that was too unreliable to be useful to the modern editor or scholar.

Table 14.1. Sixteenth-Century Printed Sources of Josquin's Chansons

RISM/Heartz #	Publisher	Short Title	No. of Chansons
1501[1]	Petrucci	Odhecaton A	7
1502[2]	Petrucci	Canti B	3
1504[3]	Petrucci	Canti C	6
1508[1]	Petrucci	Motetti a cinque	1
1520[3]	Antico	Motetti novi e chanzoni franciose	1[1]
ca. 1526	N. del Judici	Messa motteti ca[n]zonni	1
[ca.1528][6]	Attaingnant	Trente et quatre chansons musicales	1
Heartz 5 (1529)	Attaingnant	Trete et quatre chansons musicales	1[2]
Heartz 41 (1533)	Attaingnant	Chansons musicales a quatre parties	1[3]
1535[11]	Egenolff	Reutterliedlin	1
[ca. 1535][14]	Egenolff	[Lieder zu 3 & 4 Stimmen]	8[4]
1536[1]	Antico	La couronne et fleur des chansons a troys	6
1537[1]	Formschneider	Novum et insigne opus musicum	1[5]
1540[7]	Kriesstein	Selectissimae…familiarissimae cantiones	5
1544[13]	Susato	Cinquiesme livre des chansons à 5–6	1
1545[15]	Susato	Septiesme livre des chansons…Josquin	24
1549[29]	Susato	Unziesme livre contenant…à 4	1
Heartz 162 (1550)	Attaingnant	Trente sixiesme livre…Josquin	30
[1551	Du Chemin	Les joyeulx refreins de la ville et de la cour	5][6]
[1553	Du Chemin	Le Premier (–Tiers) livre…du prince des musiciens Jossequin de Prez	?][7]
1560	Le Roy&Ballard	Livre de meslanges	8
1572[2]	Le Roy&Ballard	Mellange de chansons	8
1578[15]	Le Roy&Ballard	Second livre de chansons a trois	4
1578[16]	Le Roy&Ballard	Tiers livre de chansons a trois	1

My thanks to Philippe Vendrix, who sent me corroborating data from the *Catalogue de la chanson polyphonique française de la Renaissance*, assembled by the "Ricercar" program under his direction at the Centre d'Études Supérieures de la Renaissance in Tours. In this table I count the chansons attributed to Josquin in the source itself unless otherwise noted. On the numerous lost sources that may contain Josquin's chansons, see Bonnie F. Blackburn, "Josquin's Chansons: Ignored and Lost Sources."

1. No attribution in the source.
2. No attribution in the source.
3. "Mille regretz" here attributed to "J. lemaire."
4. See Nanie Bridgman, "Christian Egenolff, Imprimeur de musique," *Annales musicologiques* 3 (1955): 77–177, and Martin Staehelin, "Petruccis Canti B in deutschen Musikdrucken des 16 Jahrhunderts," in *Gestalt und Entstehung musikalischer Quelle im 15. und 16. Jahrhundert*, ed. Martin Staehelin (Wiesbaden: Harrassowitz, 1998), 125–31. There are no attributions in the print.
5. A Latin contrafact of "Nymphes, nappés."
6. See François Lesure and Geneviève Thibault, "Bibliographie des éditions musicales publiées par Nicolas du Chemin (1549–1576)," *Annales musicologiques* 1 (1953): 269–373, catalogue number 25.
7. Ibid., no. 31.

Table 14.2. Josquin Chansons for which the Earliest Source is a Print

RISM/Heartz # of Earliest Source	Incipit	No. of Parts	Remarks
1502[1]	De tous biens playne	3	only source/s print
1501[1]	Fortuna d'un gran tempo	3	
1536[1]	La belle se siet	3	only source/s print
1504[3]	La Bernardina	3	
1501[1]	La plus des plus	3	
1501[1] or MunBS3154	O venus bant	3	
1536[1]	Si j'eusse Marion	3	only source/s print
1504[3]	A l'eure que je vous p.x.	4	only source/s print
1502[2]	Baisez moy	4	
1501[1] or SegC s.s.	Bergerette savoysienne	4	
[c.1528][6]	Cueurs desolez par toute nation	4	
1501[1]	De tous biens playne	4	
1504[3] or FlorC 2439	Fors seulement	4	
1504[3]	Je sey bien dire	4	only source/s print
1502[2]	L'homme armé	4	
Heartz 41 (1533)	Mille regretz	4	
Heartz 162 (1550)	Plus n'estes ma maistresse	4	only source/s print
1504[3]	Vive le roy	4	only source/s print
c. 1526	Cueur langoreulx	5	only source/s print
Heartz 162 (1550)	Cueurs desolez par toute nation	5	only source/s print
1545[15]	En non saichant	5	only source/s print[2]
Heartz 162 (1550)	L'amye a tous/Je ne vis oncques	5	only source/s print
1540[7]	Mi lares vous tousjours	5	only source/s print
1540[7]	N'esse point ung grant desplaisir	5	

(Continued)

Table 14.2. Continued

RISM/Heartz # of Earliest Source	Incipit	No. of Parts	Remarks
1508[1]	Nymphes des bois/Requiem	5	
1540[7]	Allegez moy	6	only source/s print
1502[2]	Baisez-moy	6	
1540[7]	J'ay bien cause de lamenter	6	
1537[1]	Nymphes, nappés	6	
1545[15]	Pour souhaitter	6	only source/s print
1545[15]	Regretz sans fin	6	only source/s print
1545[15] or Bol R142[3]	Tenez moy en vos bras	6	
1545[15]	Vous l'arez, s'il vous plaist	6	only source/s print
1545[15]	Vous ne l'aurez pas	6	only source/s print

1. For the chansons *a 3* and *a 4*, this table is based on the *New Josquin Edition* volumes no. 27 (*Secular Works for Three Voices*, ed. Jaap van Benthem and Howard Mayer Brown [Utrecht, 1987]) and *NJE* no. 28 (*Secular Works for Four Voices*, ed. David Fallows [Utrecht, 2005]). For the chansons *a 5* and *a 6* I take as a base the projected works list published in the *Proceedings of the International Josquin Symposium, Utrecht 1986* [Utrecht: Vereniging voor Nederlandse Muziekgeschiedenis, 1991], 216–217), and use the analysis of Lawrence F. Bernstein, "Chansons for Five and Six Voices" in *The Josquin Companion*, 393–422; see especially his table 13.1, pp. 394–95. Along with Bernstein (ibid., 409–10), I question the inclusion of "Mala se nea" and "Si vous n'avez" in the *NJE* and so have left them out of this appendix.
2. A contrafactum of the piece can be found in Leipzig Universitätsbibliothek MS Thom. 49/50, dated 1558.
3. On Bologna R142 see Bonnie F. Blackburn, "Josquin's Chansons: Ignored and Lost Sources," 50–53.

To some extent, the interest in manuscript studies was, in the early 1970s, fairly new, and it represented an important counter to the overreliance of earlier scholars on prints as source material. Foremost among them was Helmuth Osthoff, whose extremely influential study, *Josquin Desprez*, had been completed only in 1965; Osthoff's was the first book-length study of the composer and his music, one flawed for its neglect of manuscript sources, the evidence of which severely complicates the attributions accepted sometimes blindly from prints, not to mention readings of the music itself.[11] Edgar Sparks's contribution to the 1971 conference, for instance, pitted itself against Osthoff's claims of authenticity for six motets edited by Sigismund Salblinger and printed in Augsburg in 1545 (three of which are unica).[12] Sparks's argument was essentially stylistic (as was Osthoff's), but the unreliability of Salblinger's prints and of printed sources in general was a strong line in his attack. "We owe a great debt to Salblinger for printing such magnificent works as 'Absalon fili mi' and 'Responde mihi,'" Sparks wrote, "but we cannot fail to notice that his versions are marred by errors of the crudest sort.... The fact that such errors are perpetuated in later prints indicates how little care went into some sixteenth-century editions. It seems that the music was neither rehearsed nor proofread carefully."[13] Clemens Stephan and Johannes Ott—two more important printers of Josquin's music—came under the gun as well.[14] Arguably, such correctives were well needed. They were also a sign of the times, for it was during the 1960s that scholars began to

deepen our control over manuscript sources of polyphony more generally. The phenomenal attention to manuscripts at that time resulted in hundreds of disserta-
tions, articles, facsimiles, and editions, not to mention the collaborative production
of the *Census-Catalogue of Manuscript Sources of Polyphonic Music, 1400–1550*.[15] Yet
ultimately this enthusiasm for manuscript study, which may have begun in the spirit
of revolution, established its own scholarly regime under which print was considered
with suspicion.

Of course, there is good print and there is bad print. If Josquin scholars after
Osthoff shunned the books produced by Susato, Attaingnant, and others, those of
Ottaviano Petrucci managed to retain the luster they had always been accorded.
Petrucci honored Josquin in his prints in a way that reinforced modern ideas of the
composer's greatness, favoring Josquin with the first single-composer prints ever
assembled and naming him in the titles, thus highlighting his authorial status.
Moreover, by choosing Josquin's cyclic Masses for his series of three Josquin prints,
Petrucci favored sacred music over secular—a choice consonant with modern
notions of the masterwork—even though he probably aimed less to monumental-
ize Josquin with his Mass prints than he did to target the connoisseurs and cathe-
drals that could pay the price he had to charge for his product.[16] Best yet, Petrucci's
prints date from the composer's lifetime; the first two books of Masses (1502 and
1505) were produced in Venice at a time when Josquin seems to have been working
in nearby Ferrara, though there is no indication that Josquin was involved even
tangentially in their publication.[17] Small matter. Petrucci's exquisite and expensive
little books—books whose double-impression method of printing required pains-
taking exactitude—appeared on the cusp of the age of printed music in such a way
that modern editors found it easier to overlook the bad associations that ultimately
accrued to print. These were luxury prints, typographical novelties, and they seem
to have been collectors' items even in their own time, judging from the finely bound
secondhand copies purchased by Johann Georg von Werdenstein in the latter half
of the sixteenth century.[18] In the eighteenth century, Padre Giambattista Martini,
who knew of Petrucci's books as the first prints of polyphonic music, sought for
years to add them to his remarkable library before finally acquiring his copies of
Petrucci's *Misse* of Josquin and *Odhecaton*.[19] In addition, in the twentieth century,
Albert Smijers, editor of the first modern edition of Josquin's works, chose Petrucci
as the basis for the *Josquin Werken*, perhaps finding in Petrucci a soul mate with the
same goal of producing clean editions of the master's work.[20] While Smijers's edition may have inclined subsequent scholars to look kindly on Petrucci, in the
decades following the completion of the *Josquin Werken* (finished only in 1969),
many of Petrucci's readings were discovered to be inferior when compared to contemporary manuscripts, particularly those from the papal chapel, where Josquin
had been a singer.[21] Petrucci's famous prints, too, began to foster scholarly
anxiety.[22]

Music historians have not been alone in their vexation with print. Modern editors of Shakespeare, for example, have long agonized over the absence of manuscript sources and relied instead—and sometimes bitterly—on the "bad" quarto

editions of individual plays and the renowned folio edition printed in London by William Jaggard and Edward Blount in 1623, seven years after the playwright's death. Print is an obstacle to the truth when the truth is conceived in terms of an edition of the Bard's works representing his final intentions. The sources of the printed editions, particularly of second and third editions, have simply passed through too many hands to be relied upon with confidence. Copyists, compilers, and typesetters made inevitable errors; the abbreviations used in early printed books cannot always be deciphered; and earlier editors introduced serious variants. Indeed, Shakespeare scholars received a nasty shock when it was discovered that the version of *King Lear* known to us today is, in fact, a composite version of the play made in the eighteenth century by editors who cobbled it together from several radically different sources.[23] Shakespeareans learned to live with the proliferation of "Lears" while the old king of Britain wrestled with a textual multiple-personality disorder.

Such discoveries only seem to verify the unreliability of printed sources and the inaccessibility of an authoritative original in them. For textual critics who wish to focus on the production and interpretation of an ideal redaction of the text—on the text itself—print poses myriad problems. Moreover, such scholarly suspicions echo the complaints of some sixteenth-century authors. After all, Orlande de Lassus complained that he could hardly recognize his own work in some of its printed redactions, which no doubt led him to seek to control the publication of his music through an extraordinary series of royal and imperial privileges.[24]

Nonetheless, the scholar of the sixteenth-century chanson cannot avoid print, for as intensely as they complicate our understanding of this repertoire, printed sources are often the only ones we have. This is clearly the case for chansons attributed to Josquin: At least thirty of them have prints as their earliest remaining source, and of those thirty, half are transmitted only in printed sources (see table 14.2). In general, printed sources for the chansons easily rival manuscript sources in sheer number, and while this statistic alone would seem to elevate print at least to the status of an unavoidable necessity in any study of Josquin's chansons, I have come to wonder whether another "solution" has not won out: that Josquin's chansons have come to be studied less often owing to the "problem" of their transmission.[25] Compounding this misfortune is the nature of the chanson genre itself, which by the 1540s had become highly commercialized through the efforts of Attaingnant, Susato, and other printers. Most of Josquin's chansons came out as numbers in two popular series (the seventh book in Susato's series of fourteen *livres de chansons* and the last book in Attaingnant's series of thirty-six *livres*). These chansonniers were produced for a market in which music had become a genuine commodity. Thus, while Petrucci's prints were arguably luxury items, the same was not as true of the music printed by Susato and Attaingnant, who were real businessmen at a time when music printing had become a real business. By this time, some genres of print had become genuinely "vulgar" and printing *vulgarizing*, a technology by which the exclusive lost its uniqueness, authors lost control of their works, and the common tastes of a *grand public* shaped the cultural objects it consumed.[26] Without pressing the point too far, it is worth asking whether or not Josquin scholars picked up some of the anxieties of composers who published during the first age of commercial music printing, when dedications begged patrons to protect their works as they sallied forth in print and composers referred to their printed compositions as children cast out alone into the world, mistrusted the ways circulating their works in print might devalue them, and seem to have cared less about the forms in which their "lighter" works were printed.[27]

To turn away from the chansonniers of Susato and Attaingnant reaffirms that Josquin had nothing to do with commercial printing and its musical marketplace, thereby preserving a glorified notion of the master that raised him above the madding crowd, a place where many composers attempted to remain and many scholars attempted to keep them. However, as I hope to show, there are advantages to writing a history of Josquin that embraces printing and dirties our image of him with the ink of the press. It will never shore up the generally weak source traditions for his chansons, but it does open up the possibility of discussing his songs in a new way.

In place of a history of Josquin as an actual historical persona, we might instead attempt a history of the figure of Josquin, a figure that came into being largely after his death, in print, and upon which many inferences about his persona are based. Such a history would align with work by historians of the book, who have shown how print configured the authors of texts in such a way that the printed book seemed to become the text that it contained, allowing the author's name to achieve a new relevance attached to it. Roger Chartier, by examining the role of print in the formation of the "author," has questioned the applicability of modern notions of authorship to early books and manuscripts in ways that can, I believe, benefit a reception history of Josquin and his music in the sixteenth century.[28]

The case of Josquin is complicated by the fact that the "figuring" of the composer occurred posthumously and—as students of Heinrich Glarean's *Dodekachordon* well know—in the context of humanistic impulses that sought to make the texts of this "ancient" *auctoritas* widely available.[29] To further complicate matters, rather than concentrating on the Josquin received through prints of his Masses—a repertory stabilized in his lifetime through innumerable manuscript copies and by Petrucci's prints—in this chapter I concentrate on the reception of his chansons not only because this is the repertory I regularly work with but also because the vernacular culture in which the chanson was enmeshed felt the impact of high-volume printing most profoundly. Though the complex polyphonic style of Josquin's chansons would seem to make them unsuited to print culture and its mass commercialization of light genres such as the so-called Parisian chanson, Josquin's chansons achieved a unique success in print, a success all the more striking in light of the value placed on the new and readily consumable in the culture of print into which they issued. I propose that we might search through prints of Josquin's chansons not for the composer himself but for the typological figure of Josquin created by the printers Pierre Attaingnant, Tielman Susato, and Le Roy and Ballard, who managed to parlay the antiquated and difficult chansons of a dead composer into a commodity that consumers thought they had to have.[30] Focusing on Josquin's chansons in this way strikes at the heart of two issues neglected in Josquin scholarship: the importance of print culture in the formation, reception, and transmission of the composer's oeuvre and the importance of Josquin to the related topic of vernacular (as opposed to Latinate) humanism.

Josquin's chansons surely constituted a repertory of *musica reservata* par excellence before 1545 not merely because few of them could be purchased in print but also because chansons for five and six voices had never been the norm for the genre.[31] Of the chansons that will be included in the *New Josquin Edition*, more than one-third are for five or six voices.[32] When these expansive textures are compared to the scorings of his contemporaries, Josquin's predilection for them is clearly extraordinary. As Howard Mayer Brown has observed, even Josquin's motets for six voices were unusually large given contemporary standards; thus, all the more exceptional are his thirty-some chansons for five and six voices, most of which include canons.[33] These were the chansons for which Josquin would become famous in sixteenth-century prints.

If manuscript repertoires tended toward chansons for three or four voices, certainly the repertoires of the first music printers followed this tendency to an even greater extent: Petrucci's *Harmonice musices Odhecaton A, Canti B,* and *Canti C* contain only a few chansons for five or six voices; Pierre Attaingnant, who brought out almost one hundred editions of chansons between 1528 and 1553, printed four-voice chansons almost exclusively, and Jacques Moderne issued only four chansons for more than four voices during his entire career printing music in Lyons.[34] Others who dabbled in printing chansons before 1545 also stuck to those small forces. Indeed, judging from reprints of their contents, Andrea Antico's most successful chanson prints were those for three voices (1520^6 and 1536^1), and Antoine Gardane, too, specialized at this time in chansons for two, three, or four voices rather than larger ones.[35] In short, early printed chansons were overwhelmingly a four-voice repertoire, and by these standards, Josquin's larger chansons might not have appealed to the consumers being served by the smaller-voiced settings issued by Attaingnant and other printers. Had they been given manuscripts full of larger chansons, they might not have been very interested in printing them.

Then again, music printing got under way in the Low Countries only in the 1540s, and this is when we see a change in the printed repertoire, perhaps owing to local tastes and the resources of the first music printer there, the sackbut player, composer, and merchant-bookseller Tielman Susato, who first set up shop in Antwerp in 1542. Susato's catalogue differs dramatically from those of other printers of chansons in several ways that are well illustrated by the first chanson series he put out between 1543 and 1550 (see table 14.3):[36]

In title, Susato's first print, the *Vingt et six chansons musicales,* follows the model of Attaingnant, who, like Petrucci before him, assembled chansons in anthologies that named the number of songs they contained on the title page. However, in two respects, Susato broke new ground in this very first book: It contained only five-voice chansons, and it had a dedication (to Mary, the queen of Hungary, whose court resided in Brussels). Far more imposing than any chanson print to date, the

Table 14.3. Susato's *Livre* Series of Chanson Prints

RISM	Title	No. of Partbooks	Composer Named in Title
[1543]¹⁵	Vingt et six chansons musicales à 5	4*	
1543¹⁶	Premier livre des chansons à 4	4	
1544^Susato	Premier livre des chansons à 2 ou à 3	3	Tielman Susato
1544¹⁰	Second livre des chansons à 4	4	
[1544]¹¹	Tiers livre des chansons à 4	4	Thomas Crecquillon
1544¹²	Quatriesme livre des chansons à 4	4	
1544¹³	Cinquiesme livre des chansons à 5 et à 6	5*	Nicolas Gombert
1545¹⁴	Sixiesme livre des chansons à 5 et à 6	5*	
1545¹⁵	Septiesme livre des chansons à 5 et à 6	5*	Josquin
1545¹⁶	Huitiesme livre des chansons à 4	4	
1545^Manchicourt	Neufiesme livre des chansons à 4	4*	Pierre Manchicourt
1545¹⁷	Dixiesme livre contenant la Bataille	4	Clément Janequin, Philippe Verdelot
1549²⁹	Unziesme livre contenant…chansons amoureuses à 4	4	Crecquillon, Clemens non Papa
1550¹³	Douziesme livre contenant…chansons amoureuses à 5	5*	
1550¹⁴	Treziesme livre contenant…chansons nouvelles à 6 et à 8	5*	
1555¹⁹	Quatoirsiesme livre des chansons à 4	4	Lassus

* Dedication to a potential patron.

Vingt et six chansons musicales looked much more like a Mass or motet print with its engraving of Mary, its lengthy dedication to her, and its unusual two-tone printing for the last song in the tenor partbook, a piece Susato composed for the return of Charles V from Tunisia based on a puzzle canon solvable only by those who knew the precise date and time of the emperor's entry into Brussels.[37] The paratextual material, celebratory tone, five-voice texture, and insiders' canon (not to mention the eight other pieces that also have canons in this print) all represent significant departures from the conventions for chanson anthologies established by Attaingnant and Moderne.[38] Other such prints quickly followed: the fifth, sixth, seventh, twelfth, and thirteenth books featured chansons for five to eight voices, their larger textures necessitating the first chanson anthologies printed in five partbooks. In their material form alone, Susato's large sets of partbooks presented the chanson as something special, a wholly different kind of secular print that was presumably meant to compete with the manuscript chansonniers still being produced at a healthy rate in the Low Countries.[39]

In Susato's hands, the chanson—and more specifically, the chanson in the material form of print—became the medium for figurations of the composer that it had not known before—not in print and perhaps not in manuscript, either. Susato's prints drew the chanson into a unique social economy dominated by authors: Whereas the chanson had formerly been characterized in print by collectivity (the anthology) and a relatively high degree of anonymity,[40] Susato's lavish prints inscribed the genre with names in an unprecedented way, appealing to both the names or titles of patrons (the queen of Hungary, Nicholas Nicolai, and Philippe Nigri, the latter two both imperial councilors) and the names of composers (Josquin, Crecquillon, Gombert). Susato used composers' names as brand-name capital, putting out single-author prints with the composer's name on the title page (virtually unprecedented for the chanson) and liberally sprinkling the titles of other anthologies with composers' names for good measure. It may have been the importation of Italian madrigals into Flanders that inspired Susato in these directions, for in vernacular repertoires such practices of naming developed first in madrigal prints, or it may have been that the Netherlandish chanson for five or six voices appealed to its northern consumers through systems of connoisseurship that attached importance to authors early on. By that time, the prestige associated with Josquin's name appears to have entered a new phase: Ott had included prefaces praising Josquin in his motet prints of 1537 and 1538, and so many pieces appear to have been newly attributed to Josquin that Georg Forster, in the preface to *Selectissimarum mutetarum…tomus primus* (Nuremberg, 1540), was led to quip: "I recall a certain great man saying that now Josquin is dead he is writing more compositions than when he was still alive."[41] In 1547, Glarean's *Dodekachordon* further secured Josquin's place in subsequent music histories with extensive examples of Josquin's music, anecdotes, and lavish praise of his greatness.

Within this particular set of conditions, Susato issued his commemorative Josquin edition in 1545. *Le septiesme livre* contained twenty-three of the composer's chansons for five and six voices, that is, two-thirds of what we reckon today to be his full corpus of chansons for those forces. In the first instance, then, we can see in Susato's print an attempt to publish the beginnings of Josquin's *oeuvres complètes*, gathering his scattered lyric together into a book even while issuing that book as part of an ongoing series of anthologies (technically it is an anthology because it includes three epitaphs by other composers). The title page of the *Septiesme livre* would have appealed first to collectors of the *Livre* series by following its preestablished typographical formula (see figure 14.1). But it employs a style that appears quite arbitrary to the modern eye, for it is only on the verso of that page that we find the composer's name in large letters. IOSQVIN DES PRES is not on the front of the book, where we expect him/it to be (he is turning into his name here), since the conventions of the series do not allow for it. Instead, IOSQVIN DES PRES monumentalizes the composer in another space, one at odds with modern practices, in which the author's name appears prominently on the title page rather than with the table of contents (see figure 14.2). Although it is obviously quite large with a purpose, size is not the only important feature of the name, for by extending the Q beyond its usual boundaries with a special piece of type, the individual characters of IOSQVIN DES PRES meld into a typographical unit resembling a signature.

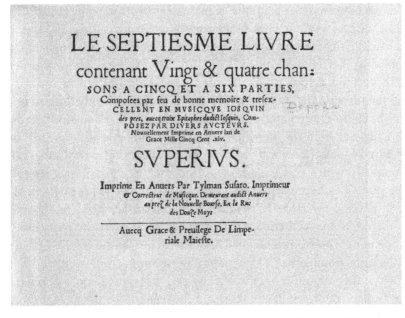

Figure 14.1. *Le septiesme livre* (Antwerp: Susato, 1545), title page of Superius partbook (recto)

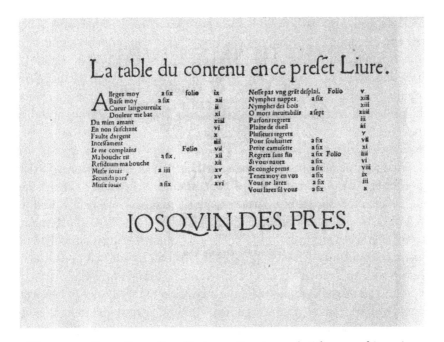

Figure 14.2. *Le septiesme livre* (Antwerp: Susato, 1545), title page of Superius partbook (verso)

Placed at the bottom of the page, the "signature" mirrors the imperial privilege just behind it, "authorizing" the book in a second way through a sleight of type.[42] Thus materialized in the form of a signed oeuvre, Josquin can be eulogized in Latin *déplorations* by Jheronimus Vinders, Benedictus Appenzeller, and Nicolas Gombert. IOSQVIN becomes an object—in the most literal sense—of praise.

The tail on the Q, with its scriptlike curve, evokes not only the author's hand but also the culture of civility that made writing itself a mark of good breeding and virtue. It suggests both the imprint of Josquin's hand—his name pressed into the page by a quill—and the edification that came with learning to read and write script more generally, which was a mark of distinction.[43] Such desires to represent the hand in print—a desire written into the tail of the Q—led printers in the next decade to develop *caractères de civilité* or civility typefaces, which looked like the gothic characters of northern script.[44] Authorship, even at the most mechanical level of penning a book, truly implied authority. Thus, in the cursive Q that breaks out of the usual boundaries of typography, we see in micro how manuscripts held their own in the cultural economy of texts even as printed books developed new ways to configure authorship and represent the hand of the scribe or author.

Although it is impossible to know the answer, it seems important to stop and ask how Susato acquired these songs, five (or six) of which appear here for the very first time, twenty-four years after Josquin's death. In the tenor partbook, Susato says that he looked for a long time to find music worthy of dedication to his friend Lazarus Doucher, suggesting that the pieces had not been easily come by; their rarity is further stressed in Susato's remark that he is printing them so that "everyone would be able to keep them in perpetual memory."[45] Clearly Susato had access to manuscripts now lost, as Bonnie J. Blackburn concluded in her 1976 article on ignored and lost sources of Josquin's chansons.[46] It is also probably significant that the three *epitaphes* were all written by composers who were adults in 1521 and could well have composed them at the time of Josquin's death. Indeed, Nicolas Gombert was reputedly a student of Josquin's.[47] All of this means that those chansons, too, could have languished in manuscript for decades before being brought to light by Susato.

Nonetheless, there is no way to verify the reliability of Susato's source or sources, and it remains impossible to ascertain the authenticity of the chansons, particularly of those for six voices, which have few concordances.[48] Lawrence F. Bernstein has argued convincingly for striking "Ma bouche rit" *a 6* from the canon, and Joshua Rifkin and he would both eliminate "En non saichant" (*a 5*);[49] Osthoff questioned the six-voice "Allegez moy" on the basis of its sexy lyrics, finding it difficult to believe that Josquin would—as Bernstein phrased it—"squander such compositional procedures on a poem as trivial as that of *Allegez moy*," though Jaap van Benthem and (less certainly) Bernstein would retain the ascription to the "Prince of Musicians."[50] One could elaborate at length the arguments for and against including these works in the canon, piece by piece. However, the point of my raising the question of authenticity is not to defend them. In fact, all are slated to appear in the *NJE*, and it is this that is quite to the point. For better or for worse, Susato's print made available a canon of five- and six-voice chansons believed to be by Josquin, and it was received as such both by modern scholars such as Smijers and Osthoff and by musicians and printers in the sixteenth century. It remains to be seen whether the *NJE* will shake the very few chansons from the *Septiesme livre* that should certainly be cut.

Susato's monument to Josquin eventually inspired Attaingnant to break with all of his own conventions and issue a very similar print, the *Trente sixiesme livre contenant xxx. chansons Tres Musicales, A Quatre Cinq & Six parties, En cinq livres, Dont le cinquiesme livre contient les cinquiesmes & sixiesmes parties, Le tout de la composition de feu Josquin des prez* (Heartz 162 [1550]). Attaingnant's publication is a carefully corrected reedition of Susato's *Septiesme livre* minus the *déplorations* and with the addition of seven other chansons.[51] It was the only publication of any sort Attaingnant ever printed in a set of five partbooks (all the more notable because by that time Attaingnant had moved to an all-in-one- or all-in-two-volume format for chanson prints); it was also one of the very few single-author chanson prints he ever issued.[52] Moreover, judging from the fact that Susato's imperial privileges generally pertained for three or four years, it appears that Attaingnant reprinted these pieces as soon as possible.[53] If it seems self-evident from our distance that prints of Josquin's chansons were marketable, we must stop and ask ourselves, then why not sooner? Only around 1550 was the Parisian music business ready for a print of this nature, an expensive single-author print of big chansons by Josquin des Prez. Clearly with this print Attaingnant acknowledged a French market for five-voice chansons of the Netherlandish sort that Susato had been printing for six to seven years, but it is the turn away from the anthology that I find even more striking. With Attaingnant's *Trente sixiesme livre*, chansons printed in Paris took one more step away from the anthology and began to align with the new emphasis on the Author and his Book, which had already been evident in prints of sacred music and was becoming increasingly important in literary circles in France.

As Josquin's chansons made the transition from manuscript culture to the print culture delineated by Susato's chanson series, we witness the first significant formation of Josquin's authorial persona in vernacular prints.[54] We can see the shift in the new practices of naming that arose in the print shop, practices tied to the way printers marketed music. Whereas consumers of manuscripts could order books tailor made and choose the repertory to be copied, the purchaser of print was forced to buy *prêt-à-porter* collections. Owing perhaps to this personal quality, manuscript chansonniers were almost always anthologies rather than books of a single composer's songs; they were compendia—usually with extra folios of blank staves for later additions—that gathered together works according to the output of a given institution, the taste of the music lover, or the repertory at hand in a given library or location at a given time. Not only did they therefore less often collect the works of a single composer, but manuscripts also often failed to say the obvious and to name the composers of chansons that were already known to be by the composer in the circles where the manuscript was to be used. The chansonnier Vienna 18746 offers a fine example. Copied in 1523 by Petrus Alamire, it includes chansons by Josquin,

Pierre de la Rue, and others. Since La Rue served the Habsburg court and Josquin's music was well known there, we can presume that Alamire—familiar with the Habsburg musical establishments—would have had no trouble identifying the composers whose works he copied. Yet only four chansons in the manuscript bear attributions.[55] As Honey Meconi explains, Alamire attributed only those chansons over which there might be some confusion of authorship: Vienna 18746 contains two settings of "D'un aultre amer" and six settings of "Fors seulement," and it is in connection with these multiple settings of the same text that most of the attributions arise.[56] This particular practice carried over into the first printed chanson-niers, where we find Petrucci including attributions in the tables of contents to the *Odhecaton A*, *Canti B*, and *Canti C* for chanson texts, of which there are multiple settings.

As printing caused works to travel in ever-widening circles from the places where the music was written and performed, attributions became essential. Petrucci knew this and included attributions in his page headers, for example. Yet the kind of naming that we find in Susato's prints is of a new order for the chanson and more highly conditioned by a material economy in which, by midcentury, authors literally began to make names for themselves in print. The contrasting careers of the French court poets Mellin de Saint-Gelais and Pierre de Ronsard illustrate this turn of events quite nicely, for while Saint-Gelais (d. 1558) never bothered to issue a print of his complete works and instead allowed his poetry to circulate in manuscript among courtiers and *lettrés*, Ronsard (d. 1585), who succeeded Saint-Gelais at court, took care to publish his work and even to conceive his poetry in "books" designed for the press. Prints of Saint-Gelais' poetry were not of his own making but were put together for financial gain by editors who seem to have had no contact with the poet at all.[57] Ronsard, on the contrary, oversaw the publication of six editions of his *Oeuvres* during his lifetime, and as early as 1552 books of his poetry included engravings of him crowned with the wreath of the poet laureate (a symbol bound to associate him with Petrarch) and clad in the breastplate of an ancient Roman warrior.[58] He had turned himself into a marketable object.

During the 1550s, lyric poetry became a prime vehicle for a career both in print and at court, a trend spurred on by the increasing importance of Petrarch's *Canzoniere* as a model for printed books of verse in France and one obviously connected to the spread of Bembist poetics through the imitative fury enabled by the high-volume publishing industry in Venice.[59] Like the Petrarchan madrigals printed in Venice, the chanson, too, became a significant medium of vernacular humanism as Ronsard and the other poets of the Pléiade attempted to recover ancient lyric practices and reinvent them in French. Yet, while the French poet could "tune his lute to the sound of the Greek and Roman lyre" by imitating the works of ancient masters (Horace, Virgil, Ovid, and even Petrarch),[60] the French composer lacked ancient models. It was in the context of this dearth of exemplary ancient chansons—a lacuna likely felt more strongly by poets and theorists than by composers—that the canonization of Josquin as an ancient French *auctoritas* and of his chansons as models of an *ars perfecta* took place. Here we should recall that although Glarean preferred Masses and motets to illustrate his text, he did praise Josquin as a musical Virgil in his *Dodekachordon*, a book that, significantly, included a biography of the composer placing him in the service of King Louis XII of France and presenting him as a French composer. Three years later Attaingnant brought to light the most complete edition of Josquin's chansons to date (the *Trente sixiesme livre*), a collection that hinted at the cultural wealth of the French nation and its traditional excellence in vernacular lyric.[61]

The publishing of this "French" Josquin was carried on by Attaingnant's successors as Royal Printers of Music, the firm of Adrian Le Roy and Robert Ballard.[62] In 1560 they issued a massive chanson anthology that placed Josquin squarely at the center of a history of the French chanson: It included eight of his five- and six-voice songs and a preface naming him as the *fons et origo* of the sixteenth-century chanson. The full title of the collection was *Livre de meslanges, Contenant six vingtz chansons, des plus rares, et plus industrieuses qui Se trouvent, soit des autheurs antiques, soit des plus memorables de nostre temps: composées à cinque, six, sept, & huit parties, en six volumes…1560*. Rare, industrious, antique, memorable: All of these epithets endow the book with meanings unusual for a chanson anthology, where titles usually stressed newness and sheer quantity ("Vingt et huit chansons nouvelles"). In the *Livre de meslanges*, by contrast, Le Roy and Ballard announce the singularity and artfulness of these songs ("des plus rares, et plus industrieuses") and crown them as the best chansons of all times ("soit des autheurs antiques, soit des plus memorables de nostre temps"). Canonizing a corpus of chansons both old and new, the print juxtaposes the work of Josquin—chief among the *autheurs antiques*—with that of the youngest generation of composers, offering its readers a historical anthology of French vernacular song. In its 1572 reedition under the title *Mellange de chansons tant des vieux autheurs que des modernes*, the collection further accentuated the play between the classical models offered by Josquin's songs and the most recent developments in lyric art by including the latest chansons of Claude Le Jeune and large-scale settings of poems by Ronsard and Jean-Antoine de Baïf.[63] It is striking in this regard that the collection includes none of the four-voice chansons that had been the absolute staple of the repertoire since printing got under way in France, which has the effect of heightening the chronological divide between old and new since it misses chansons by Clément Janequin, Pierre Sandrin, and their generation, with but one chanson by Claudin de Sermisy.

In physical format, the *Livre de meslanges* elevated the chanson to the level of the motet, for its generous oblong quarto pages were of a size that Le Roy and Ballard usually reserved for motet prints.[64] In the way it thus "sacralized" the secular through allusions to the motet, the print might be likened to the pairing of motets and Petrarchan madrigals in Adrian Willaert's *Musica nova*, published the previous year in Venice. Moreover, like the *Musica nova*, the *Livre de meslanges* was issued in six partbooks, a first for Le Roy and Ballard in any genre; it was also extraordinarily long, with 115 chansons disposed on sixty folios (in the superius partbook).

In keeping with such magnificent ambitions, the print was dedicated to François II in a preface written by none other than Pierre de Ronsard. Ronsard begins by reiterating almost every classical commonplace about music (the harmony of the spheres, the effects of the modes on the soul, the ability of music to instill virtue), illustrating his remarks with the stories of Ulysses, Alexander and Timothy, Agamemnon, Orpheus, Arion, Achilles' education with Chiron, and a reminder that the young king's father, Henry II, "honored, loved, and prized Music." Having thus firmly established the age-old value of music, Ronsard finally turns to the contents of the book itself, using the classical history he has just elaborated to explain its unusual emphasis on old chansons:

> Your Majesty should not marvel if this *livre de meslanges*…is composed of the oldest songs that can today be found, because the music of the ancients [*anciens*] has always been esteemed the most divine, the more so since it was composed in a happier age, less contaminated by the vices which reign in this last age of iron. …When some excellent worker in this art reveals himself, [Sire,] you should guard him with care, as being something so excellent that it rarely appears. Of such men have arisen within six or seven score years Josquin Desprez, a native of Hainaut, and his disciples Mouton, Willaert, Richafort, Janequin, Maillard, Claudin, Moulu, Certon, and Arcadelt, who in the perfection of this art does not yield to the ancients.[65]

Ronsard paints a picture of a distant and untroubled Golden Age, in which life was mythically unspoiled by vice. The notion of a lost "siècle plus heureux" was not uncommon in France at the time and understandable in view of the intense social and political crises brought about by the Reformation, the wars with the Habsburgs, and the recent accidental death of Henry II in a jousting tournament. By 1572, when the 1560 *Livre de meslanges* was reworked and reissued as the *Mellanges de chansons*, the age of François I and Henry II must have seemed all the more idyllic, for by then the Wars of Religion had raged for a decade. Indeed, civil strife reached a gruesome climax in the St. Bartholomew's Day massacres in August of that year. Without comment, a portrait of Henry II was included in the 1572 *Mellanges de chansons*, where it stood as a tacit emblem of his firmer reign. So, too, was music from that distant time accorded pacific effects: Ronsard charges music from that "happier century" with the power to harmonize and please.

Set up here as an "ancient" lyric *autheur* or *auctoritas*, Josquin heads a gallery of French chanson composers whose works are both inspired by and rival those of the ancients. And just as the Pléiade poets looked to Horace and Petrarch as models, Ronsard's preface suggests Josquin as a modern-day classic worthy of imitation. Josquin's status has been underscored in the music itself: Four chansons by Adrian Willaert setting the texts of well-known chansons by Josquin are grouped together on folios 9–12 in the print, where they allude to Willaert's "student-teacher" relationship with the master and recall Josquin's melodies and those tunes on which Josquin based his own settings.[66]

Ronsard's preface was not the only panegyric to place Josquin at the head of a venerable school of chanson composers: The language of progress, retrospection, and increasingly self-conscious historicism reached its high pitch in this sonnet by J. Mégnier, which prefaced the *Continuation du Mellange d'Orlande de Lassus* (Paris: Le Roy and Ballard, 1586):

Le bon père Josquin de la Musique informe
Ebaucha le premier le dur & rude corps:
Le grave doux Willaert secondant ses efforts
Cét oeuvre commencé plus doctement reforme:
　L'inventif Cyprian, pour se rendre conforme
Au travail de ces deux qui seuls estoyent alors,
L'enrichit d'ornemens par ses nouveaux accords,
Donnant a cétte piece une notable forme:
　Orlande a ce labeur avec eux s'estant joinct
A poli puis apres l'ouvrage de tout poinct,
De sorte qu'apres luy, n'y faut plus la main mettre.
　Josquin aura la Palme ayant esté premier:
Willaert le Myrte aura: Cyprian le Laurier:
Orlande emportera les trois comme le maistre.

　[Good father Josquin was first to sketch out
From shapeless Music the hard and crude form;
Grave, soft Willaert, supporting his efforts,
Reformed with great skill this work thus begun.
　Inventive Cipriano, to conform
To what both these once matchless men had done,
Embellished it richly by his new chords,
Giving notable form to this great task.
　Orlando, having joined in this labor,
Then polished their whole work so thoroughly
That, after him, not one thing should be touched.
　Having been first, Josquin will have the palm;
Willaert will be next, Cipriano third;
Master Orlando wins all three prizes.][68]

Music is handed off from one generation to the next as a diamond in the rough that reaches its state of polished perfection in the hands of Lassus. Josquin is awarded the palm of triumph, Willaert the myrtle symbolizing Venusian beauty, and Cipriano de Rore the laurel wreath, but Lassus wins all three for having cultivated and combined the styles of his three great "French" forebears to create a unified whole. By this late date, Le Roy and Ballard had exhausted their desire to reprint the works of Josquin—one specifically announced in the 1567 renewal of their privilege to print the works of "Lassus, Josquin, Mouton, Richafort, Gascongne, Jaquet, Maillard, Gombert, Arcadellt et Goudimel"—and favored instead the works of Lassus.[69] As we see in Mégnier's verse, Josquin continued to exert influence as a point of cultural orientation, though now he played the "good father" rather than the heroic role some earlier authors had accorded him.[70]

　Historical projects like that of the 1560 *Livre de meslanges* and the 1572 *Mellanges de chansons* were partially driven by the political goal of writing a French nation into being with histories, epics (such as Ronsard's *La franciade*), and books that collected and organized the cultural wealth of the nation, books produced, after all, by the king's printers. In contrast to these prints of state building, however, another series from Le Roy and Ballard featured Josquin in a gentler way, one that might better be characterized as nostalgic. For whereas the canons and rich polyphonic texture of Josquin's five- and six-voice settings marked them as relatively exclusive, his three-voice chansons were much more accessible. Though his *chansons rustiques* certainly had courtly pedigrees, the monophonic chansons they set came from the city and its bourgeois and seem to have circulated quite widely.[71] In the *Second* and *Tiers livre de chansons a trois* printed in 1578, Le Roy and Ballard gathered, edited, and issued "rare and ancient" chansons in the philological spirit of a vernacular humanism that was more inclusive than the textual elitism of the 1560 *Livre de mes-langes*. The form is similar—in the *Second* and *Tiers livre*, *chansons rustiques* by Josquin and his generation represent an ancient past[72]—but the message must have been altered by the content, for the melodies of the bourgeois theater, of city play-acting societies, and of street songs threaded through the polyphony surely reminded listeners of a less "classical," by-gone time.[73] Chansons such as Josquin's "Mon mari m'a diffamée" must have reminded some middle-class listeners of *sotties* and farces seen during their Parisian childhoods, the extremely unpetrarchan texts calling up a host of stock characters such as the *mal-mariée* of this song, wayward girls named "Marie," and misbehaving monks. At the same time, chansons such as "En l'ombre d'ung buissonet au matinet" and "En l'ombre d'ung buissonet tout au loing" may have encouraged listeners to construe Josquin in more Virgilian tones, as a writer of eclogues cast in the archaic language of sinuous melodic lines, quirky text underlay, and two-voice canons long since discarded by composers of polyphony.[74]

For the most part, though, the "siècle plus heureux" represented by Josquin's chansons was a time marked by exclusivity, the luxury good of five- and six-voice part writing, and—before 1545—the manuscript. This was a "happier century" not only for the purchasers of sixteenth-century books who wished to own the best chansons, both old and new, and perhaps to reflect upon a politically stable time but also for students of Josquin's chansons. It was a time less complicated by the "iron age" of moveable type and the mass production of cultural objects that color our understanding of Josquin's secular corpus. Yet no matter how severely print complicates our relationship with Josquin's chansons, his very importance in Renaissance studies is owed in large part to Petrucci, Antico, Susato, Salblinger, and others who published his music in multiple, printed editions. The Josquin rediscovered by historians Charles Burney and August Wilhelm Ambros, both of whom used sixteenth-century prints and copies of Glarean as their sources, was a version of the composer figured only after his death and shaped within the cultures of print.[75] Jessie Ann Owens has rightly observed that "the invention of music printing meant that Josquin had a historiographical fate far different from that of either Dufay or Machaut."[76] Indeed, had Ambros known much of fourteenth-century music, which at the time of writing his *Geschichte der Musik* in the 1860s still lay undeciphered in manuscripts scattered across Europe, he might have set the beginning of the Renaissance in accordance with the dates adopted by art and literary historians rather than (roughly) with the birthdate of Josquin.[77] Not only did the prints in the British Library and the Österreichische Nationalbibliothek in this way contribute decisively to the conception of our field as it stands today, print still conditions many of the tacit assumptions framing the study of Renaissance music, from our sense of Josquin's greatness to our predilections for his Masses as examples of that greatness. Prints are not the transparent, reliable sources they once were believed to be; they bring to light their own history of the period and its players, one enriched by complexities of the material cultures and social technologies of the time and one responsible for carrying "Josquin" and his music down to us.

NOTES

1. International Conference: New Directions in Josquin Scholarship, organized by Rob C. Wegman and held at Princeton University, Oct. 29–31, 1999. I would like to thank the conference participants, as well as Bonnie J. Blackburn, Anthony Newcomb, and Joshua Rifkin for their helpful reactions to earlier drafts of this chapter as it evolved from the paper I presented there.

2. See Paula Higgins, "The Apotheosis of Josquin des Prez and Other Mythologies of Musical Genius," *Journal of the American Musicological Society* 57 (2005): 443–510.

3. The most significant discoveries concerning Josquin's biography are given in David Fallows, "Josquin and Milan," *Plainsong and Medieval Music* 5 (1996): 69–80; Pamela F. Starr, "Josquin, Rome, and a Case of Mistaken Identity," *Journal of Musicology* 15 (1997): 43–65; Lora Matthews and Paul Merkley, "Iudochus de Picardia and Jossequin Lebloitte dit Desprez: The Names of the Singer(s)," *Journal of Musicology* 16 (1998): 200–26; and Adalbert Roth, "Judocus de Kessalia and Judocus de Pratis," *Recercare* 12 (2000): 23–51. For recent syntheses see Richard Sherr, "Chronology of Josquin's Life and Career," in *The Josquin Companion*, ed. Sherr (New York: Oxford University Press, 2000), 11–20, and David Fallows, *Josquin* (Tours: Centre d'Études Supérieures de la Renaissance and Turnhout: Brepols, 2009).

Ramifications of the new biography are neatly outlined by Jesse Rodin in "'When in Rome': What Josquin Learned in the Sistine Chapel," *Journal of the American Musicological Society* 61 (2008): 307–72, at 307–13, and the article as a whole places Josquin's work in stylistic context and illustrates how it may have been subject to outside influences in a way that is quite novel given the former tendency to view the composer's work as sui generis. On the works list and its decimation in the *New Josquin Edition* (*Josquin des Prez: New Edition of the Collected Works*, editorial board: Willem Elders, chairman, Lawrence F. Bernstein, Martin Just, Jeremy Noble, Herbert Kellman, advisory members [Amsterdam: Koninklijke Vereniging voor Nederlandse Muziekgeschiedenis, 1987–]), see Higgins, "Apotheosis," 465–67.

4. A photo of the graffito is reproduced as the frontispiece to Sherr, *Josquin Companion*. For more on the graffito see Klaus Pietschmann, "Ein Graffito von Josquin Desprez auf der Cantoria der Sixtinischen Kapelle," *Musikforschung* 52 (1999): 204–207, and

Klaus Pietschmann, "Die Sangergraffiti auf de Cantoria der Sixtinischen Kapelle zwischen Selbstglorifizierung und memorialer Frömmigkeit," *Analecta musicologica* 33 (2004): 81–99.

5. An up-to-date list of documents pertaining to Josquin's biography is given as appendix A in Fallows, *Josquin*, 353–82.

6. For more on the letters see William F. Prizer, "Music at the Court of the Sforza: The Birth and Death of a Musical Center," *Musica Disciplina* 43 (1989): 141–93; Lora Matthews and Paul Merkley, *Music and Patronage in the Sforza Court* (Turnhout: Brepols, 1999), 454–56; and Fallows, *Josquin*, 203–204, 367.

7. On this period in Josquin's life, see Fallows, "France: 1494–1503," in *Josquin*, 193–233.

8. Jacob Burckhardt, *The Civilization of the Renaissance in Italy*, trans. Samuel George Chetwynd Middlemore (S.l.: s.n., 1878). For an overview of music historiography of this period, see the essays by Gary Tomlinson and James Haar in *European Music, 1520–1640*, ed. James Haar (Rochester, N.Y.: Boydell, 2006), chapters 1 and 2, respectively.

9. *Josquin des Prez, Proceedings of the International Josquin Festival-Conference, New York, 1971*, ed. Edward E. Lowinsky, with Bonnie J. Blackburn (London: Oxford University Press, 1976), 770–74.

10. The index to David Fallow's magisterial new biography, *Josquin*, repeats this pattern, with a long entry for "manuscripts" but none for "prints."

11. Helmuth Osthoff, *Josquin Desprez*, 2 vols. (Tutzing: Schneider, 1962–1965).

12. Edgar Sparks, "Problems of Authenticity in Josquin's Motets," in *Josquin des Prez...New York, 1971*, 345–59. The collections are RISM 1545^3, *Cantiones septem, sex, et quinque vocum* (Augsburg: Kriesstein), and RISM 1545^2, *Concentus octo, sex, quinque, et quatuor vocum* (Augsburg: Ulhard).

13. Sparks, "Problems of Authenticity," 349n14. Sparks's mention of *Absalon fili mi* is ironic given the motet's subsequent expulsion from Josquin's canon. See Joshua Rifkin, "Problems of Authorship in Josquin: Some Impolitic Observations with a Postscript on *Absalon, fili mi*" in *Proceedings of the International Josquin Symposium, Utrecht 1986*, ed. Willem Elders, with Frits de Haen (Utrecht: Vereniging voor Nederlandse Muziekgeschiedenis, 1991), 45–52 and Jaap van Benthem, "Lazarus versus Absalon: About Fiction and Fact in the Netherlands Motet," *Tijdschift van de Vereniging voor Nederlandse Muziekgeschiedenis* 39 (1989): 54–82.

14. Sparks, "Problems of Authenticity," 349n14.

15. *Census-Catalogue of Manuscript Sources of Polyphonic Music 1400–1550*, comp. University of Illinois Musicological Archives for Renaissance Manuscript Studies, ed. Herbert Kellman (vol. 1 with Charles Hamm), 5 vols. (Neuhausen-Stuttgart: American Institute of Musicology, 1979–1988).

16. On the cyclic Mass as a modern construction formulated by the music historian August Wilhelm Ambros under the influence of Burckhardt, see Andrew Kirkman, "The Invention of the Cyclic Mass," *Journal of the American Musicological Society* 54 (2001): 1–47.

17. On the Petrucci prints see Stanley Boorman, *Ottaviano Petrucci: A Catalogue Raisonné* (New York: Oxford University Press, 2006), 274–78. Josquin's *Misse* were printed seven months before the composer arrived in Ferrara in late April 1503, and Boorman believes the prints were part of pro-Josquin propaganda at a time when the dispute was raging over whether to hire Josquin or Heinrich Isaac for the post of *maestro di cappella* there. On the one side, we have a letter to Ercole d'Este, dated August 14, 1502, claiming that Alfonso d'Este and the singers all favored Josquin; shortly thereafter, on September 2, Ercole received another letter, this one from his agent, Gian de Artiganova, who argued in favor of Isaac: "It is true that Josquin composes better, but he composes when he wants to

and not when one wants him to, and he is asking 200 ducats in salary while Isaac will come for 120—but Your Lordship will decide." For the letters, see Lewis Lockwood, *Music in Renaissance Ferrara 1400–1505: The Creation of a Musical Center in the Fifteenth Century*, 2d ed. (New York: Oxford University Press, 2009), 227.

Though neither establishes a significant connection between Josquin and Petrucci (in fact, before their discovery, it was easier to imagine a direct connection between Josquin and Petrucci), Bonnie J. Blackburn has identified two important likely sources of Petrucci's music. One was Petrus Castellanus, Petrucci's editor, *maestro di cappella* at SS Giovanni e Paolo in Venice and a collector of music. See Bonnie J. Blackburn, "Petrucci's Venetian Editor: Petrus Castellanus and His Musical Garden," *Musica Disciplina* 49 (1995): 15–45. The other source was Girolamo Donato, the Venetian ambassador of Lorenzo de' Medici, a music lover and dedicatee of the *Odhecaton*. Donato likely heard Josquin's music and quite possibly met the composer. See Bonnie J. Blackburn, "A Lost Isaac Manuscript," in *Musica Franca: Essays in Honor of Frank A. D'Accone*, ed. Irene Alm, Alyson McLamore, and Colleen Reardon, Festschrift Series no. 18 (Stuyvesant, N.Y.: Pendragon, 1996), 19–44.

18. See Richard Charteris, *Johann Georg von Werdenstein (1542–1608): A Major Collector of Early Music Prints* (Sterling Heights, Mich.: Harmonie Park, 2006), 80–81.

19. On the provenance of Martini's Petrucci prints, see Anne Schnoebelen, "The Growth of Padre Martini's Library as Revealed in His Correspondence," *Music and Letters* 57 (1977): 379–97, at 380 and 388.

20. *Werken van Josquin des Prez*, ed. Albert Smijers, 55 vols. (Amsterdam: Vereniging voor Nederlandse Muziekgeschiedenis, 1921–1969). Smijers followed the order of Petrucci's prints for most of the Mass volumes of the *Werken* and many of Petrucci's readings. For the chanson volumes, the basic order of pieces follows Susato's *Septiesme livre* of 1545. On the authority accorded to Petrucci by modern editors see Birgit Lodes, "Musikdruck als Medienrevolution? Das 'Ereignis' Petrucci," in *Vom Preis des Fortschritts: Gewinn und Verlust in der Musikgeschichte*, ed. Andreas Haug and Andreas Dorschel (Vienna: Universal Edition, 2008), 161–94, at 164–65.

21. See especially James Haar, "Josquin in Rome: Some Evidence from the Masses," in *Papal Music and Musicians in Late Medieval and Renaissance Rome*, ed. Richard Sherr (New York: Oxford University Press, 1998), 213–23.

22. In 1971, with the *Josquin Werken* only just completed, scholars were already calling for a new edition of Josquin's works. See the report of a symposium on the subject, "Problems in Editing the Music of Josquin des Prez: A Critique of the First Edition and Proposals for the Second Edition," in *Josquin des Prez... New York, 1971*, 723–54, esp. the contribution of Louis Lockwood, who questions the authority of Petrucci's prints and clearly favors manuscript sources (733–37).

23. For a positive reaction to this "problem" in Shakespeare studies, see Margreta de Grazia and Peter Stallybrass, "The Materiality of the Shakespearean Text," *Shakespeare Quarterly* 44 (1993): 255–83. See also Lukas Erne, *Shakespeare's Modern Collaborators* (New York: Continuum, 2008), chapter 4.

24. See James Haar, "Orlando di Lasso: Composer and Print Entrepreneur," in *Music and the Cultures of Print*, ed. Kate van Orden, with an afterword by Roger Chartier (New York: Garland, 2000), 125–62, at 141.

25. The work of Bonnie J. Blackburn is the most notable exception to this rule, particularly her "Josquin's Chansons: Ignored and Lost Sources," *Journal of the American Musicological Society* 29 (1976): 30–76.

26. See the study of chapbooks and the *bibliothèque bleue* in Roger Chartier, "Stratégies éditoriales et lectures populaires, 1530–1660," in *Histoire de l'édition française*,

vol. 1, *Le livre conquérant*, ed. Henri-Jean Martin and Roger Chartier (Paris: Promodis, 1982), 585–603, and Roger Chartier, "Communities of Readers," in *The Order of Books: Readers, Authors, and Libraries in Europe between the Fourteenth and Eighteenth Centuries*, trans. Lydia G. Cochrane (Stanford: Stanford University Press, 1994), 1–23.

27. Adrian Willaert offers a good example: His lighter madrigals came out in anthologies, but he reserved his larger madrigals and motets for the *Musica Nova*. See Martha Feldman, *City Culture and the Madrigal at Venice* (Berkeley: University of California Press, 1995), chapter 7. On dedications of music prints, see Tim Carter, "Printing the New Music," in van Orden, *Music and the Cultures of Print*, 3–37.

28. Roger Chartier, "Figures of the Author," in *Order of Books*, 25–59.

29. On Glarean see Cristle Collins Judd, *Reading Renaissance Music Theory: Hearing with the Eyes* (New York: Cambridge University Press, 2000), part 3, "The Polyphony of Heinrich Glarean's *Dodecachordon* (1547)."

30. My conception of the ways in which such a typological subject might be defined is indebted to the theories of Martha Feldman. See her "Authors and Anonyms: Recovering the Anonymous Subject in *Cinquecento* Vernacular Objects," in *Music and the Cultures of Print*, 163–99, and Feldman, *City Culture and the Madrigal at Venice*, esp. chapters 3, 7, and 8.

31. This is manifestly true for France but also true for the Low Countries. For instance, of the thirty-seven books of secular music printed by Susato between 1543 and 1561 (twenty-four of which contain only chansons), only eight are for five and/or six voices.

32. The provisional list of Josquin's works that will be included in the *New Josquin Edition* (as published in the *Proceedings of the International Josquin Symposium, Utrecht 1986*, 215–217) includes 21 chansons for five voices and 14 for six voices. In the volumes already completed, there are 36 chansons for three voices (*NJE 27, Secular Works for Three Voices*, ed. Jaap van Benthem and Howard Mayer Brown [Utrecht, 1987]) and 39 for four voices (*NJE 28, Secular Works for Four Voices*, ed. David Fallows [Utrecht, 2005]); it should be noted that all of these volumes include or will include a number of chansons of doubtful authenticity.

Given that Alexander Agricola (d. 1508) and Antoine Brumel (d. ca. 1515) primarily wrote three-voice chansons with a few for four voices and that Jacob Obrecht (d. 1505), Loyset Compère (d. 1518), and Johannes Ghiselin (fl. early sixteenth century) wrote chansons only for three and four voices (also true for Heinrich Isaac [d. 1517], with one exception *a 5*), we can see how unusual chansons for five and six voices were in the first decades of the sixteenth century. Jean Mouton (d. 1522), who wrote 21 chansons, composed 5 chansons for five voices and 1 for six voices, making his output at least a little more like that of Josquin, and of the 31 chansons composed by Pierre de la Rue (d. 1518), 4 are for five voices and 1 is for six. Noteworthy with regard to these composers is the fact that the principal sources for Mouton's larger-textured chansons are prints (1545^{14} and 1572^2)—a pattern consistent with the sources for Josquin's larger chansons. Moreover, 3 of La Rue's five-voice chansons were ascribed to Josquin in contemporary sources—a confusion that may witness an association between Josquin and these larger textures.

33. See Howard Mayer Brown, "Notes towards a Definition of Personal Style: Conflicting Attributions and the Six-part Motets of Josquin and Mouton," in *Proceedings of the International Josquin Symposium, Utrecht 1986*, 185–207.

34. On Attaingnant see Daniel Heartz, *Pierre Attaingnant, Royal Printer of Music* (Berkeley: University of California Press, 1969); Attaingnant published one print for two voices, one for two and three voices, three for three voices, and one notable exception for four, five, and six voices, the *Trente sixiesme livre…de feu Josquin des prez* of 1550. On Moderne see Samuel F. Pogue, *Jacques Moderne: Lyons Music Printer of the Sixteenth*

Century (Geneva: Droz, 1969); Moderne's most important chanson series, *Le paragon des chansons*, came out between ca. 1538 and 1543.

35. On chansons for two and three voices, see Daniel Heartz, "'Aupres de Vous': Claudin's Chanson and the Commerce of Publishers' Arrangements," *Journal of the American Musicological Society* 24 (1971): 193–225. On Gardane see Mary S. Lewis, *Antonio Gardano, Venetian Music Printer, 1538–1569: A Descriptive Bibliography and Historical Study*. Vol. 1, *1538–49* (New York: Garland, 1988), in which Gardane's chanson prints before 1550 are given as 1538[19] *a 4*, 1539[21] *a 2*, 1541[14] *a 2*, 1543[Buus] *a 6*, 1543[23] *a 3*, and 1545[Janequin] *a 4*. Tielman Susato, too, composed and printed some very successful chanson arrangements for two and three voices. On this smaller repertory, see my "Tielman Susato and the Cultures of Print" in *Tielman Susato and Instrumental Music in the Renaissance*, ed. Keith Polk (Stuyvesant, N.Y.: Pendragon, 2005), 143–63.

36. On Susato's output, see Kristine K. Forney, "Tielman Susato, Sixteenth-Century Music Printer: An Archival and Typographical Investigation," PhD diss., University of Kentucky, 1978, and Ute Meissner, *Der Antwerpener Notendrucker Tylman Susato: Eine bibliographische Studie zur niederländischen Chansonpublikation in der ersten Hälfte des 16 Jahrhunderts*, 2 vols., Berliner Studien zur Musikwissenschaft no. 11 (Berlin: Merseburger, 1967). A facsimile of the entire chanson series is available as Tielman Susato, *Premier [-le quatoirsiesme] livre de chansons* [Brussels: Éditions Culture et Civilization, 1970–1972].

37. See Kristine K. Forney, *Chansons Published by Tielman Susato*, vol. 30 of *The Sixteenth-Century Chanson*, ed. Jane A. Bernstein, 30 vols. (New York: Garland, 1994), xv, 211–17.

38. Attaingnant never dedicated chanson prints or included prefaces in them. Indeed, Attaingnant's entire catalogue includes only three dedications (Heartz, nos. 33, 85, 104), and only one is from the printer, that included in his monumental folio print of Masses from 1532 (Heartz no. 33).

39. For some sense of the range of music manuscripts being produced, the records of binding orders processed by Christopher Plantin are a valuable resource. They can be consulted at the Plantin-Moretus Museum in Antwerp; an example of the entries can be found in Kristine K. Forney, "A Gift of Madrigals and Chansons: The Winchester Part Books and the Courtship of Elizabeth I by Erik XIV of Sweden," *Journal of Musicology* 17 (1999): 50–75, at 54–55. As for surviving manuscripts, the Winchester Partbooks are an excellent example, as are the Stonyhurst Manuscript and Bologna Q26, but as the Plantin-Moretus catalogues show, many less beautifully bound music books are now lost to us today.

40. For example, sixty-eight of the chansons in *Canti C* are anonymous; two-thirds of the chansons in Attaingnant's *Trete et quatre chansons musicales* (Heartz 5 [1529]) are anonymous, and Attaingnant began his career with a number of chanson prints that contained no attributions at all (Heartz nos. 2, 5–10).

41. The Ott prints are *Novum et insigne opus musicum* (Nuremberg, 1537) and *Secundus tomus novi operis musici* (Nuremberg, 1538[3]); the text of the Forster is "Memini summum quendam virum dicere, Josquinum iam vita defunctum, plures cantilenas aedere, quam dum vita superstes esset," fol. 2r. For a list of references to Josquin up to 1777 see Fallows, *Josquin*, 383–409.

42. Interestingly enough, one reaction of authors to unauthorized prints of their works was to sign the title pages by hand as a guarantee of the book's authenticity. For examples from seventeenth-century England see Adrian Johns, *The Nature of the Book: Print and Knowledge in the Making* (Chicago: University of Chicago Press, 1995), 182. Susato, it should be noted, does use this elongated capital Q in other prints of the series.

43. On manners and writing, see Jacques Revel, "The Uses of Civility," in *Passions of the Renaissance*, ed. Roger Chartier and trans. Arthur Goldhammer, vol. 3 of *A History of Private Life*, general eds. Philippe Ariès and Georges Duby (Cambridge, Mass.: Belknap/ Harvard University Press, 1989), 167–205.

44. Civility type was designed, cut, and first employed by Robert Granjon in Lyon in 1557 and quickly adopted by Flemish printers, especially Christopher Plantin, Guillaume Silvius, and Aimé Tavernier. Granjon's stated aim was to provide the French with a typographical equivalent of their native script in a very self-conscious rejection of Italian typefaces—italics and roman letters. See Harry Graham Carter and H. D. L. Vervliet, *Civilité Types* (Oxford: Oxford University Press, 1966). Granjon's invention thus postdates Susato's *Septiesme livre* by more than a decade, but I refer to civility types here rather than italics to draw attention to the local script in Susato's Flanders.

45. "[C]est le present livre de chansons a cincq & six parties, composees par feu de bonne memoire Iosquin des Pres, en son temps tresexcellent & supereminent au scavoir musical, & ay voulu commancer a imprimer icelles oeuvres, affin que d'icelles chascung puisse avoir perpetuelle memoire, comme bien il a merite" (*Le septiesme livre* [Antwerp: Susato, 1545], fol. 1 verso, tenor partbook).

46. On Susato's possible sources see Blackburn, "Josquin's Chansons: Ignored and Lost Sources," 54–55. She concludes that Susato must have had recourse to a manuscript now missing since the only existent manuscript from the Netherlands that contains a notable number of concordances (6) is Vienna 18746, a manuscript copied and signed by Petrus Alamire in 1523 but then sent to Raimund Fugger the Elder in Germany.

47. According to Hermann Finck, as related in his *Practica musica* (Wittenberg,1556), facsimile ed. (Bologna: Forni Editore, 1969), fol. Aii.

48. See Fallows, *Josquin*, 337–38.

49. See Lawrence F. Bernstein, "'Ma bouche rit et mon cueur pleure': A Chanson a 5 Attributed to Josquin des Prez," *Journal of Musicology* 12 (1994): 253–86, and Joshua Rifkin, "Josquin's Chansons for Five Voices: Problems of Authenticity and Style" (paper presented at the Colloquium on European Secular Music of the Sixteenth Century, Rutgers University, 1984, and, in expanded form, at the International Josquin Symposium, Utrecht, 1986). The paper has not been published, but a summary can be found in Bernstein, "Chansons for Five and Six Voices," in Sherr, *Josquin Companion*, 393–422, at 414 ff. I thank Professor Rifkin for sharing his work with me in typescript.

50. See Osthoff, *Josquin*, vol. 2, 179, 181, 217ff., and Osthoff's analysis in Bernstein, "Chansons for Five and Six Voices," 410–13. Also see Jaap van Benthem, "Zur Struktur und Authentizität der Chansons à 5 & 6 von Josquin des Prez," *Tijdschrift voor Nederlandse Muziek* 21 (1968–1970): 170–88, at 171–76 and n. 11. Bernstein's chapter gives a thorough review of the literature dealing with the authenticity of the larger-voiced chansons (409–22). The "Prince of Musicians" phrase is well liked by Bernstein, who uses it, among other places, in Bernstein, "Chansons for Five and Six Voces," 393. For a fresh take on the problem of false ascriptions and a heartening acknowledgement that only by living with some doubt can we discuss Josquin's music, see Fallows, *Josquin*, 324–26.

51. For a comparison of the Susato and Attaingnant prints, a discussion of the emendations made by Attaingnant's editor (possibly Claude Gervaise), and a study of Attaingnant's possible sources for the chansons not printed by Susato, see Blackburn, "Josquin's Chansons: Ignored and Lost Sources," 55–64. Of the seven new chansons included by Attaingnant, only two can be confirmed as authentic.

52. The other single-author prints were six editions of chansons by Clément Janequin (Heartz 4, 40, 73, 75, 90, 155) and one by Gervaise (Heartz 166). Attaingnant had similarly

broken with his own conventions for printing motets in anthologies with a series of single-author prints in a large format by Claudin de Sermisy, Pierre Certon, and Johannes Lupi, all from 1542 (Heartz 103–105).

53. On Susato's privileges, see Meissner, *Der Antwerpener Notendrucker*, vol. 1, 46.

54. It is worth noting here that while Petrucci's Mass prints do name Josquin in the title, the titles themselves appear only on the Superius partbook and are very short, as in the third book: "Missarum Josquin. Liber Tertius." The other partbooks lack a proper title page altogether.

55. See Herbert Kellman, "Josquin and the Courts of the Netherlands and France: The Evidence of the Sources," in *Josquin des Prez... New York, 1971*, 181–216, esp. 184, 214, and Jaap van Benthem, "Einige wiedererkannte Josquin-Chansons im Codex 18746 der Österreichischen Nationalbibliothek," *Tijdschrift van de Vereniging voor Nederlandse Muziekgeschiedenis* 22 (1971): 18–42.

56. See Lawrence F. Bernstein, "Chansons Attributed to Both Josquin des Prez and Pierre de la Rue: A Problem in Establishing Authenticity," in *Proceedings of the International Josquin Symposium, Utrecht 1986*, 125–52, and Meconi's remarks in the discussion following the paper presentation, 154.

57. The first edition of his "complete works," *Saingelais, OEuvres de luy tant en composition que translation ou allusion aux Auteurs Grecs et Latins* (Lyon: Pierre de Tours, 1547), is, despite the claims of its title, actually an anthology of contemporary verse, and the poems attributed to Saint-Gelais—which constitute a mere fraction of those he wrote before 1547—include many spurious ones.

58. On Saint-Gelais and the circulation of his poetry orally and in manuscript, see my "Female Complaintes: Laments of Venus, Queens, and City Women in Late Sixteenth-Century France," *Renaissance Quarterly* 54 (2001): 801–45, at 807–16; on Ronsard's portrait, see my "Vernacular Culture and the Chanson in Paris, 1570–1580," PhD diss., University of Chicago, 1996), 119–21, and Chartier, *Order of Books*, plate following p. 52 and the discussion of Petrarch, 54–57.

59. See especially Feldman, *City Culture and the Madrigal at Venice*.

60. Joachim Du Bellay, *La deffence et illustration de la langue françoyse*, ed. Henri Chamard (Paris: Société des Textes Français Modernes, 1970), 112–13.

61. See Jessie Ann Owens, "Renaissance Historiography and the Definition of 'Renaissance,'" *Music Library Association Notes* 47 (1990): 305–30. She discusses the construction of Josquin as a classical authority, citing Glarean (308) and several other Italian and German writers.

62. As early as 1555 Le Roy and Ballard had issued a print of Josquin's motets, *Josquini Pratensis Musici Praestantissimi, Moduli, ex sacris literis delecti... liber primus*, presumably the first book in a series, although subsequent volumes are unknown. On this print and Josquin's legacy more generally, see Fallows, *Josquin*, 349–50. The other major music printer in Paris in the years after Attaingnant, Nicolas Du Chemin, also apparently brought out a print of Josquin's music. According to F. J. Fétis and Jacques Charles Brunet, in 1553 Du Chemin printed three volumes of chansons by Josquin, though no copies survive. See Blackburn, "Josquin's Chansons: Ignored and Lost Sources," 66.

63. For a fuller study of the historicizing aspect of the 1560 *Livre de meslanges* and the 1572 *Mellange de chansons* see my "Imitation and *La musique des anciens* in Le Roy & Ballard's 1572 *Mellange de chansons*," *Revue de Musicologie* 80 (1994): 5–37.

64. Chanson prints from Le Roy and Ballard were usually approximately 90 × 130 mm, whereas the *Livre de meslanges* measures 173 × 230 mm.

65. Ronsard's preface was also included in the *Mellange de chansons* (Paris: Le Roy and Ballard, 1572) with slightly different wording (Jacques Arcadelt is replaced as the contemporary master of the chanson by Lassus). Both versions are reproduced in facsimile in *Le Roy & Ballard's 1572 Mellange de chansons*, ed. Charles Jacobs (University Park: Pennsylvania State University Press, 1982), 12–14. The translation provided here is the one given by Gary Tomlinson in the "Renaissance" section of W. Oliver Strunk, *Source Readings in Music History*, rev. ed., ed. Leo Treitler (New York: Norton, 1998), 302–303. An edition of the 1572 preface is included in Ronsard, *Oeuvres complètes*, ed. Jean Céard, Daniel Ménager, and Michel Simonin, 2 vols. (Paris, Gallimard, 1994), vol. 2, 1171–74.

66. They are "Douleur me bat," "Faulte d'argent," "Petite camusette," and "Vous ne l'aurez pas." Josquin's settings of all of these texts had been included in Susato's 1545[15] and Attaingnant's Heartz 162 (1550). Of them, only Josquin's "Faulte d'argent" is included in the 1560 *Livre de meslanges*.

67. Reprinted in Horst Leuchtmann, *Orlando di Lasso: Sein Leben*, 2 vols. (Wiesbaden: Breitkopf and Härtel, 1976), vol. 1, 288.

68. I am grateful to my colleague Davitt Moroney for providing me with this sensitive translation.

69. On the 1567 privilege see François Lesure and Geneviève Thibault, *Bibliographie des éditions d'Adrian le Roy et Robert Ballard, 1551–1598* (Paris: Heugel, 1955), 12.

70. On contemporary characterizations of Josquin's role in music history, see Owens, "Renaissance Historiography," 308–13.

71. Louise Litterick also judges the three-voice settings based on monophonic melodies to be more strictly French and to have originated in the context of the court around 1500. See her "Chansons for Three and Four Voices" in Sherr, *Josquin Companion*, 335–91, at 358–70.

72. The composers represented in these prints include Antoine de Févin, Mathieu Gascongne, Hesdin, Jean Richafort, Mouton, and Willaert.

73. The chansons attributed to Josquin in these prints are "En l'ombre d'ung buissonet au matinet," "En l'ombre d'ung buissonet tout au loing," "Mon mari m'a diffamée," "Sy j'ay perdu mon amy," and "Petite camusette." On the *chanson rustique* see Howard Mayer Brown, *Music in the French Secular Theater, 1400–1550*, 2 vols. (Cambridge, Mass.: Harvard University Press, 1963), vol. 1, 105–39, and Lawrence F. Bernstein, *La couronne et fleur des chansons a troys*, 2 vols. (New York: Broude Trust, 1984). For a general discussion of the three-voice series and nostalgia, see my "Vernacular Culture and the Chanson in Paris," 214–38, from which this analysis is drawn.

74. There is certainly healthy evidence to support such a supposition, including Ronsard's poetry for the court in this genre, the bucolic tone of most of the *chansonettes mesurées* being penned by Jean-Antoine de Baïf in these years (think of his *Le Printans*), and Claude Le Jeune's settings of pastoral texts from the old *chanson rustique* repertory, which coincide with his involvement in the lyric experiments of Baïf's Academy.

75. See Don Harrán, "Burney and Ambros as Editors of Josquin's Music," in *Josquin des Prez…New York, 1971*, 148–77, esp. the appendix listing their sources, 169–77.

76. Owens, "Renaissance Historiography," 326.

77. Owens, "Renaissance Historiography," 328, and Kirkman, "Invention of the Cyclic Mass," 31–36.

....

CHAPTER 15

FROM "THE VOICE OF THE MARÉCHAL" TO MUSIQUE CONCRÈTE: PIERRE SCHAEFFER AND THE CASE FOR CULTURAL HISTORY

....

JANE F. FULCHER

As pointed out in this volume's introduction, traditionally a major goal of cultural history, whether it is practiced in the context of history or musicology, has been to penetrate experience—understanding, meaning, and communication—through a study of both the art and cultural practice. While more recently historians have recognized the dual necessity of comprehending not only context but also the language and hermeneutics of symbolic forms, musicologists are now more cognizant of material and social aspects of the construction and transmission of meaning.[1]

In sum, musicologists and historians have grown aware of how a text or a discourse is refracted through the modes of communication characteristic of each art and then inflected further through changing contexts, as well as material inscriptions and social framing.[2] Both fields are similarly more alert to the varied manners in which groups and individuals not only understand but also appropriate or contest specific symbols, shared cultural representations, or symbolic systems in the larger field of social power.

A prime example of the necessity of such continuing exchange of insights is the research on Pierre Schaeffer, which has been fractured into separate narratives and concomitantly into divergent understandings of his development, his artistic oeuvre, and its significance. Historians know Schaeffer as the engineer in Vichy radio who founded a conservative cultural venture called "Jeune France," the innovations or artistic quality of which were slight, and after which he was embraced by French technocratic postwar culture. Musicologists know a different side of Schaeffer—the pioneer in electroacoustic music, the inventor, as well as theorist, of *musique concrète*, whose background in the wartime period is insignificant and whose innovations lie within the context of the European postwar musical avant-garde.[3]

Both narratives occlude perception of Schaeffer's growth, not just subjective but also artistic, as well as the coherence of his trajectory, thereby veiling important insights into the sources of the new culture planted during Vichy, including the conceptual and aesthetic seeds of musique concrète. Accordingly, I focus on Schaeffer's own experience, understanding, and creative journey throughout these years, employing more recent insights into the culture of Vichy France and examining the works that he either fostered or created, as well as how they communicated and then engendered a still resonant aesthetic form. I begin with Schaeffer's spiritually and philosophically driven quest to develop a new culture of communication with the youth of Vichy France, where he learned how the emerging vehicle of the radio, which dissociates sound from its source and transforms the message, either masking or revealing meaning. From here I move on to his endeavor in Jeune France to explore further how the medium of transmission may expand the sense of a work of art and how a new technology or a new aural and visual culture transforms artistic traditions, to Vichy's increasing consternation.

This in turn leads me to Schaeffer's own growing political perception and hence resistance while at the Vichy-sponsored Studio d'Essai and his attempt now to explore a new radiophonic *domaine sonore*, which could break conceptual frames in order to foster a new awareness. Finally, I hope to demonstrate that for Schaeffer it was then but one more step to the conceptualization of a new aesthetic form that would carry the rich potential not just to enunciate his own experience but also to provoke deep reflection on artistic language, on authenticity, and on "the real."

The reality of Vichy's claims is indeed our point of departure: Ever since the revelations of Robert Paxton, the real political fragmentation and full extent of French complicity—state collaboration with the Nazis—have been established and shattered postwar myths. Contrary to Pétain's later claims, his new regime was no shield against the occupation forces but rather in fact a means for groups devoid of political power in the Third Republic to implement their previously thwarted social programs.[4] Vichy's purported nationalism and intent to serve as a buffer against the Germans were indeed more political rhetoric than reality, and so too, as we now recognize, was its claim to pursue a unilateral French traditionalism and conservative moral order.[5]

However, even though one faction promoted traditionalism, as well as regionalism, and another promoted technological innovation and central planning, all averred paradoxically that in spite of its concessions to the German enemy Vichy served French national interests. For it claimed to pursue a "national revolution," the contours of which were vague, aside from exclusions and the quest for institutions to effect a new morality—the values of "travaille, famille, patrie" and of social hierarchy, corporate organization, and state authority.[6] Accordingly, numerous projects for institutions, as Paxton puts it, "swarmed" around Vichy in July of 1940, and many of these were centered on French youth in order to achieve moral reform and to train France's future leaders. Here Vichy's "Janus face," which looked simultaneously to past and future, its ideological pluralism and complex, unstable ends naturally engendered a wide range of youth programs within both traditional and newer channels, creating a dynamism it eventually could not control.[7]

Originally, Pierre Schaeffer, like so many, projected his idealistic youthful vision onto Vichy in its first politically nebulous stage, when all seemed possible in the "new France," which would restore communal values after the venal, morally vacuous, and defeated Third Republic. In the eyes of the Catholic Left, from which he came, Vichy's quest to replace capitalism, parliamentary democracy, individualism, and secularization with a more organic, traditionalist, or elite-led alternative—thus ending the class struggle—seemed to mirror its own ideals.[8] To grasp Schaeffer's position one needs to consider the recent research of historians of France, for it has focused on Schaeffer's background in the French Catholic culture of the 1930s; it is not about the Schaeffer that historians of music know but is of key importance if we are to explain his successive projects and evolving goals.

Schaeffer was not originally simply an engineer turned artist but rather (as he ruefully described himself) the son of two musicians—a violinist and a singer and only a "polytechnicien par erreur." His path had slowly emerged, for his interests were always mixed, especially with his secondary studies, which included mathematics and philosophy at the lycée level and music at the Conservatoire de Nancy, where both his parents were professors. His father, as he clarified, not only taught violin but also played in various municipal orchestras and at the theater, while his mother taught the traditional repertoire of singers; after listening to all the lessons that his parents gave at home, as Schaeffer avowed, he ended up hating music.[9]

Perhaps, then, it was not only to escape this stifling atmosphere but also to differentiate himself from his parents and to discover a new world that he attended the elite École Polytechnique between 1929 and 1932 and then the École Supérieur d'Électricité et des Télécommunications. However, while a student he continued to pursue artistic interests through Catholic scouting groups and eventually joined an elite unit called the Routiers, or Rover Scouts, whose importance during his youth he later described in telling detail. As his coherent world was disappearing in the 1930s Schaeffer recorded it in a series of poetic essays that were published in the *Revue des jeunes* in 1934 and thereafter in a book about his scouting troop's inspiring leader, Clotaire Nicole, who died young, at only twenty-two. As Schaeffer pointed out, they all felt a certain "déformation polytechnicien," or too narrowly enclosed in subjects such as math, and it was Nicole who inspired them to seek a "culture plus complète," a goal that would long endure for Schaeffer, particularly during Vichy.[10]

Schaeffer's book *Clotaire Nicole* was produced by a new publishing house, Le Seuil, whose intellectual orientation was nonconformist (i.e., associated with French youth who were seeking a new spiritual path, one that abjured the political solutions of the established Left and Right). Schaeffer himself explained that although he was not disinterested, he still held himself apart from politics, musing that it was perhaps because he was more sensitive to questions of universal values than to immediate objectives or to particular ideologies, a characteristic that he would continue to reflect in his career and work.[11] In addition, the nonconformist movement stressed individual responsibility or "the human person," as well as one's place among all beings, and hence one's connection to humanity throughout the world, regardless of race, religion, nation, or class.[12] Schaeffer's association with such philosophical-religious circles would prove important to his later formulation of Jeune France, which would draw not only on its intellectual and spiritual themes but also on personalities who had prominently espoused its goals.

Both Jeune France and Schaeffer's preceding project, "Radio Jeunesse," would also draw on his theatrical endeavors in the context of scouting circles and specifically in Léon Chancerel's "Comédiens-Routiers," a performance group that was established in 1929. In order to develop an authentic communal spirit it included intensive choral training that involved not only singing but also recitations pronounced in unison, with an accent on clear articulation, as well as on incisive rhythm. In addition, well before his own efforts as a playwright within the context of Jeune France, Schaeffer wrote a Catholic mystery play, his *Mystère des Rois Mages* (named after his troop), which was staged in 1934 with a cast of all scouts at Saint-Etienne du Mont.[13]

It was with this distinctive set of values and experiences that, after his demobilization in the infantry in the summer of 1940, Schaeffer, at twenty-nine, was drawn to Vichy, attracted by the ferment of new ideas concerning cultural renewal and the formation of France's precious youth. As Schaeffer himself put it in his memoirs, he was allured by the sense of new beginnings and of professional opportunities: Clearly, for an ambitious young engineer of his background, Vichy's stress on youth and on communications appeared to provide an ideal career opening.[14] Sensing, like Messiaen, that he was part of a new French generation, he believed that France's youth could now find a space for expression that would enable them to pursue their own battles and dreams within the context of a political situation that remained unclear. Schaeffer was thus pulled into this exciting world of possibility, as were so many in Vichy's ideologically ambiguous stage, when the quest appeared to be for a better future, achieved in part through a reorganization of French society.[15]

Vichy was a cauldron of ideas, particularly concerning youth movements, and Schaeffer asserted himself quickly, now devising a plan and seeking out other former scouts, similarly drawn in by Vichy's technocrats, who considered youth and technology to be a natural pairing. Particularly helpful here was another engineer who had also been involved in Catholic scouting and youth movements, Georges Lamirand, who now held the key position of secrétaire général à la jeunesse. Both Lamirand and Schaeffer were well aware that Vichy's plan to form a new community of French youth depended largely on developing innovative means of communication: France's physical fragmentation demanded a new information culture, as well as novel forms of circulation or diffusion.[16]

Schaeffer perceived not only this but also that new communal networks could be established through new technologies, creating an "aural France" of French youth, one that could help combat moral decay, attributed by many to the effects of contemporary visual media, particularly newspapers and the movies.[17] Sound, devoid of the visual element, could both awaken and communicate powerfully, the medium of transmission here refracting the new message in crucial ways, hence further shaping the perception and understanding of French youth. Schaeffer thus sought an innovative sound culture, as well as new modes of presentation, in order to diffuse an ideological message in which at first he thought he believed, for it promised both a moral regeneration and a space for bold technological experimentation.

The result was his "Radio Jeunesse," which he developed in August of 1940, here inserting himself into a significant gap, especially in light of the sonorous experimentation being undertaken by Radio Paris, a Nazi-run station. Those whom he recruited included Maurice Martenot, who had been summoned to Vichy by Alfred Cortot, now the high commissioner of the Beaux-Arts; having learned that Martenot was out of work, Cortot proposed that he employ his méthode Martenot to teach music to the children of refugees who had come south to escape the occupied sector. The program in which they became involved was broadcast every day at noon, and its goal was to impart information and words of hope to France's now widely scattered youth.[18]

Even with propaganda Schaeffer's new team was creative, conceiving a series of eight broadcasts, "La réponse des jeunes au message du maréchal," a purported response by French youth to Pétain's speech on October 11, 1940, which addressed them specifically. However, Pétain's message was not read by the aged maréchal himself but was inspirationally declaimed by the great pianist Alfred Cortot, who because of his position now played a central role in the bureaucracy of the Beaux-Arts.[19] But particularly innovative was the style of delivery that Schaeffer's close circle of collaborators—Pierre Barbier, Albert Ollivier, and Maurice Jacquemont—devised, in effect to represent the response of France's youth. It was delivered collectively by scout performers as in previous Catholic scouting theatricals, but in order to address the entire community of French youth they were reinforced by members of Vichy's youth corps, the "Compagnons de France."[20]

However, in diffusing propaganda through such new modes of presentation and technology Schaeffer was already encountering an inherent tension that would only be augmented with time and would finally lead to a major aesthetic and subjective reassessment. As he later caustically put it, he was soon chafing at the task of merely imparting a noble tone to the "non-pensées," or vacuities of the maréchal, their platitudinous nature becoming all too evident as he sought effectively to broadcast them to French youth. Indeed, as his collaborator Claude Roy pointed out, the group that was working with Schaeffer was, in the course of its experience with these broadcasts, gradually becoming increasingly wary, and some in fact were "anti-Pétainiste."[21]

However, while those around him were defining their own values with alacrity, Schaeffer remained largely apolitical, absorbed in his realization that the medium of transmission transforms both the content and our perception as it separates sound from its original source and hence imbues it with a different meaning. He also now perceived that if the radio could veil certain messages as it bypasses the information revealed in image and in gesture, thus transforming a political discourse into something that is deceitful, it could also open up new meanings in other kinds of texts. Schaeffer thus went on to explore new modes of diffusing other sorts of texts, including the artistic, still believing idealistically that his project served the interests of French youth, as conceived benevolently by Vichy or as part of a larger cultural regeneration.[22]

His artistic impulse was now gradually growing stronger as he realized how new technologies could interact not only with emerging information cultures but also with established artistic traditions—that texts could be made dynamic within contemporary aural and visual cultures. Hence, his experience in Catholic scout theater, as well as his new circle of collaborators and important contacts within the Catholic branch at Vichy, at this point propelled him to conceive a more daring and ambitious cultural venture. According to André Clavé (his colleague), a further goal of the new association was not only to bring together French youth in the arts, thus providing them with work, but also to occupy and to train other young Frenchmen who were now grouped in Vichy's youth camps. Hence, the name "Jeune France," which Schaeffer borrowed (with permission after the fact) from the group of four musicians—Messiaen, Jolivet, Baudrier, and Daniel-Lesur, all of whom became valuable and active collaborators in his adventurous artistic project.[23]

Significantly, the original concert society, Jeune France, which had been established in 1936, also consisted of fellow Catholics with a predominantly "spiritualist" or nonconformist orientation. Daniel-Lesur had gone on to join Schaeffer in Vichy Radio; Olivier Messiaen would be recruited upon his release from a German prison camp; André Jolivet quickly became active in the association, as did the lesser-known composer Yves Baudrier.[24] However, this new venture would be centered on creative interaction and on community achieved through theater, as well as through other modes of performance, in addition to stressing decentralization of both France's patrimony and its new art, from the elite to the more popular. For Schaffer, drawing on his own recent experience, now fully realized that a work's meaning is inflected by the way in which one comes to know it—that the forms that carry discourse and the mode of presentation all help to shape the sense of a text. Aware of the power of transmitted sound and of the potential that theater and performance offer, he now sought other communicative possibilities not only by opening up new meanings in canonic texts but also by searching for new modes of creative expression.

Despite the official Vichy sponsorship and because of the division of France into two zones, as well as the fissures within Vichy itself, there was in fact little oversight, which made Jeune France a realm of relative artistic autonomy. This would eventuate in the very kind of dynamism and experimentation that Jean-Pierre

Rioux has distinguished as "la culture sous Vichy," as opposed to "la culture de Vichy"—one that could creatively adapt and utilize Vichy's shifting and ambiguous programs.[25] Among the musicians brought in, as noted earlier, were Olivier Messaien, who needed employment following his release from a German prison camp, as well as Maurice Martenot, the pedagogue and inventor of the electronic instrument that continued to fascinate Messiaen. Although he began in an administrative position, Messiaen also enthusiastically participated in the association's artistic projects as, again, did the other members of the original Jeune France: Daniel-Lesur, Jolivet, and Baudrier.[26]

In the south the association's musical activities centered around the teaching *maîtrise* (or workshop) in Lyon, under the direction of Maurice Martenot, whose pedagogical expertise was decidedly a substantial asset in training French youth between the ages of about eighteen and twenty-five to teach the arts to nonprofessionals and yet to do so always on the most exacting level.[27] The *maîtrises* themselves were organized around "ateliers," or studios, and one for orchestral musicians included a symphony orchestra—the Orchestre Symphonique de France—which also helped to provide employment for those orchestral musicians who had fled Paris, prominently including Jews, despite Vichy's reprehensible racial laws. Not only by hiring Jews in the orchestra but by other means as well, Martenot and Schaeffer protected them, helping many to dissemble their identities and hiding some forty-five Jewish families in the convent that served as Jeune France's base in Lyon.[28]

The humanist component of Jeune France was always strong, and perhaps the most prominent spiritualist and philosopher in Schaeffer's group was its "cultural advisor," Emmanuel Mounier, a leading figure in the nonconformist movement and the founder, as well as editor, of its central journal, *Esprit*. In all of his involvements Mounier stressed the importance of recognizing the element of transcendence and mystery within humankind—not that of Nazism or other totalitarian systems but that associated with people's sense of liberty, implying a respect for higher, or non-political, values.[29] What, then, did Mounier bring to Jeune France? Perhaps it was a quality that the anthropologist Jonathan Lear has termed *radical hope*—a vision that it "directed toward a future goodness" that transcends the current ability to understand precisely what it is. For it is in essence a creative response to disaster, one that draws upon the shared resources or traditions of a community in order to arrive at a new understanding of its own greater ends.[30]

Schaeffer's belief in Mounier's goals and in "the popular," which he maintained connected art to life and bound generations, as well as social strata, influenced the character of the *maîtrises* and brought youth together without distinction as to political orientation or class. To achieve this end Jeune France also renovated the established scouting model of evenings together around the campfire by mixing communal singing and folk dances with readings from great French writers such as Paul Claudel and the ideologically polyvalent Charles Péguy.[31] Just as in Radio Jeunesse it was the mode of presentation of such traditions—the context, framing, and juxtaposition—that inherently altered the ostensible message in order to further the organization's more comprehensive, progressive goals.

Hence, the key for Jeune France, especially in the south, where large public gatherings were permitted, was performance, conceived as a manner of uniting not only the artist but also isolated individuals with a broader culture, thus opening up new vistas and furthering a shared artistic heritage.[32] In presenting the classic theatrical repertoire, Schaeffer's "curation" of great works would thus always be creative, as he explored new sonorous and visual worlds through the agency of an emerging French technology. For him, this was a means not only to engage new communities but also to connect nascent networks of French youth in the service of goals that he still naively believed coincided with those of Vichy and of Pétain.

In the north, where French propaganda and manifestations of nationalism were strictly proscribed, Schaeffer could not stress the communal element, and hence the emphasis was on research, creation, and innovation, including an uncompromising reflection of the idea of popular culture.[33] In the south, where the Catholic and national figure of Jeanne d'Arc could be celebrated, Jeune France presented Claudel and Honegger's stylistically innovative oratorio, *Jeanne d'Arc au bucher*, beginning in Lyon on July 4, 1941. However, Jeune France again employed the politically multivalent figure of Jeanne d'Arc in the context of a new theatrical work, in which Schaeffer, Barbier, Messiaen, and Baudrier, in addition to others, participated. The work, *Portique pour une fille de France*, was initiated also as a result of Vichy's promotion of the festival of the saint in early May in the unoccupied zone and on an extremely lavish scale.[34]

Within the context of this ambitious celebration Schaeffer's team continued with temerity to explore not only the articulation of art and life but also the semiotic role that new visual techniques, as well as aural technologies, could play. Here we may also witness the emergence of Schaeffer's own seminal realization of how new artistic genres or aesthetic formations may result from such technological innovations by awakening individuals while forging new communal networks. Perhaps the most remarkable aspect of this work is not just its juxtaposition of aesthetic models but also its use of emerging technical resources, together with space—both visual and aural— and in a manner different from either traditional Catholic or fascist theater.[35]

Invoking the model of ancient Greece, if implicitly in order to expand the work's message, a so-called messenger placed on a podium behind a central microphone is surrounded on each side by *choryphés*, or choral spokespersons, each group with its own microphones and surrounded by the chorus, massed in a huge semicircle. However, the mixture of genres and styles is made even more explicit in the costumes employed, some of which are clearly medieval in design despite the ancient choral model and the sophisticated new sound technology.[36] Moreover, to make the work even more contemporary, the messenger's text implicitly suggests parallels with the current situation, the English characters sounding very much like the German occupants—hence a potential embarrassment for Vichy, which was now also a dependent or "client" government with a strong faction sympathetic to German fascism. Just as striking is another implicit reference, here specifically to the tradition of Republican civic theater, one cultivated by figures such as Romain Rolland at the turn of the century and more recently by the French Popular Front.

The composer Gustave Charpentier had mastered this model in the late nineteenth century within the context of civic fêtes and then incorporated it into his opera *Louise* (1900) with the satiric intent of a carnivalesque reversal of established social norms.[37]

In fact, in *Portique* one finds a telling parallel to the spectacle scene in *Louise*, the "Couronnement de la muse du peuple," and especially to Charpentier's "entrée" of the "petits miséreux," said to symbolize the future and who are referred to by the crowd with ironic naiveté as "divine beggars" and "young gods." Schaeffer and Barbier's text includes an "Entrée des gosses en pitieux état," the children entering in rows and, with pointed irony, singing "La victoire en chantant." The scene proceeds with a group of little girls who sing the old French chanson that Debussy had employed ironically in the "Rondes du printemps" of his orchestral *Images* of 1909, "Nous n'irons plus au bois."[38] This, however, was not the only aspect of *Portique* that flouted Vichy's nationalist propaganda: The third part of Schaeffer and Barbier's spectacle includes a ballet referred to as "une sorte de divertissement chorégraphique," in which the king and his court make their entry and then are followed by Jeanne herself. Such stress on "divertissement," or entertainment, as opposed to pure edification would soon be overtly condemned by those Vichy officials who were growing increasingly wary of the association's actual goals.

Nor were they reassured by the work's other aspects, for we may indeed imagine the kind of music (now lost) employed in the scene that takes place in Reims, written by Leo Preger, Yves Baudrier, and Olivier Messiaen. In Jeanne's final "Passion" her poignant parting words again alternate with music, and strikingly her text is in French, while that of the figures who persecute her speak in a "foreign" language— here, of course, it is Latin. We know from a work list of 1944 that Messiaen wrote the "Te Deum," as well as the "Impropères" or "Improperia," associated with the veneration of the cross in the Good Friday liturgy. Messiaen's contributions were for chorus and according to his own notations involved not only a large chorus but in addition a small mixed chorus, a capella.[39] Messiaen's next choral work, the *Trois petites liturgies de la Présence Divine* (1943), is probably an indication of his direction in this period since his development was always fairly consistent, and hence the style might well have included a series of vertical parallel chords, carefully spaced in emulation of Claude Debussy. These might also have alternated with more rhythmically incisive and texturally complex sections, often with a high level of dissonance and a carefully controlled use of range in order to help build the tension, as perhaps influenced by both Stravinsky and Poulenc. It may indeed have been the experience of writing his sections in *Portique*, those in which spoken text and chorus are intricately combined, that influenced not only the techniques of declamation employed in the *Trois petites liturgies* but also those in Messiaen's *Harawi* (1945), which similarly utilizes a provocative juxtaposition of languages.[40]

Attracting audiences of more than 130,000, it was performed outdoors and simultaneously, but with different mise-en-scène, in Lyon, in Marseille (using a large bicycle arena), and in another huge arena in Toulouse, thus creating a virtually unified new French community. This was, in fact, a creative means to explore or negotiate new communal bonds within a still nebulous national cultural space in the process of invention or indeed contestation and through a genre that transcends the common and reductive label of "pageant."[41] It was rather much closer to celebration, which is associated with the liminal or the socially transformative, and characterized by a "surplus of signifiers" or a "sensory overload" created by a profusion of images and the intermingling of cultural categories. The semiotics of such "ludic" spectacles are therefore "open, unorthodox, fragmented," and unique; hence, they may elude any social controls and transcend all established ideological formations.[42] This is precisely what was beginning to happen in *Portique pour une fille de France*, a work that was meant to serve a socially reflexive function and to illustrate that tradition did not have to be inert, while exploring new aesthetic formations.

Although Schaeffer was not yet an active resistant, others involved in the organization already were, including Jean-Marie Soutou, who helped to hide Jewish families using Jeune France facilities in Lyon, and André Clavé, who was eventually denounced and then deported to Buchenwald. Other resistants included Jean-Marie Serreau, who, together with his friend Joseph Rovan of the group "Amitiés chrétiennes," helped to hide Jewish children, also using Jeune France's facilities. Even if some members, such as Schaeffer, would join the Resistance only later, as he reflected in a postwar interview, in effect, by the beginning of 1942 they were all resistants, if not yet politically, for they now had no intention of diffusing Vichy's cultural propaganda.[43]

Vichy was eventually to perceive Jeune France's divergence from Pétain's stated doctrines and goals, and it then condemned works like *Portique pour une fille de France* as nothing more than mere "divertissements." Such semiotic instability, as the regime soon realized, was inherently inimical to its political propaganda; moreover, it recognized that such spectacles or celebrations articulated with its didactic and hortatory ceremonies in ideologically disconcerting ways. Furthermore, in increasing opposition to Vichy's ideal of achieving homogeneity or conformity through its programs for French youth, Schaeffer was evidently attempting not to foreclose but to enlarge both meanings and identity, influenced by his own personalist orientation. He acknowledged that it was through his experience in Jeune France and with such creative projects that he realized, by following their dynamic or logic, that he had crossed from the legal into the illegal realm.[44]

The results were becoming all too evident, and denunciations of both Schaeffer and his collaborators poured in, some sent by those Vichy loyalists whom Jeune France had been obliged to make members. One of the many accusations was that Jeune France had no interest in furthering Pétain's values or those of the Révolution Nationale but rather through its projects promoted left-wing, nonconformist ideals. Another recurring charge at this point was that Jeune France, despite the mandatory articles in its statutes, included Jews, as well as a half-Jew who was, in addition, known to be a communist. The many mounting charges also included the accusation that the organization was rooted in "elements," or aesthetic and social ideals, as well as figures who had been associated with the Popular Front, prominently including Louis Aragon.[45]

In November of 1941 Schaeffer was apprised of these serious charges, explicitly warned about the poor state of his records, and informed of the consternation over his lack of participation in the propaganda of the Révolution Nationale.[46] He responded assertively the following month: In a letter dated December 1, 1941, he enumerated all of the accomplishments of Jeune France despite the presence of entrenched adversaries at Vichy and remarked with acerbity on the paradox of the situation in which he now found himself: The government had given him money and its authority and yet no clear directives, leaving him free to pursue a "rénovation nationale," but of course as he understood it, and while attempting to mediate Vichy's opposing factions.[47]

Despite his impassioned self-defense, Schaeffer was fired or removed from Jeune France in January 1942, and by March the organization itself had been dissolved on Vichy's orders. This time his eyes were opened, and according to Schaeffer his "disgrace" with Jeune France and the disillusionment to which it led provoked a clear break in both his personal and his artistic logic.[48] Now he saw not only that the regime and its program were not all that he had at first thought but also that in order for him to remain true to his convictions his tactics would have to become subtler and indeed surreptitious.

The immediate result was a period of deep introspection in which Schaeffer sought a new personal center while pondering how best to react: Was it better to go underground and join the Resistance, risking all, or to remain right under Vichy's eyes, insidiously undermining its cultural discourse from within? Schaeffer's final decision at this point was to take full advantage of his contacts and of all he had learned both at Radio Jeunesse and in Jeune France in order most effectively to subvert Vichy's message. For his position, like that of Mounier, who also initially pushed the regime's limits (before he was imprisoned), was to conceive of courage in an Aristotelian sense—as consisting of a mean between the extremes of mere rashness and of cowardice.[49] Indeed, once more he would succeed in harnessing the potential of a Vichy program centered around communication and technology, but now he would direct it toward new cultural, ideological, and personal ends. For he decided eventually to return to Vichy radio and with an even more innovative and sophisticated project in mind; however, this was preceded by withdrawal and a sustained theoretical reflection.

Now with his personal objectives taking precedence, Schaeffer retreated to Marseille both to assess and write and remained there until the fall, not yet realizing the new directions in which his recent experience would lead him. It was here that he would reflect theoretically on the distinctive register of communication that results from the electrical transmission of sound, or how the means of reproduction may elicit new meanings in texts. Schaeffer dictated his treatise, "L'esthétique et la technique des arts-relais," to his secretary in the course of 1942–1943, beginning it in Marseille and later finishing it upon his return to Paris, while at the same renegotiating his own subjective and cultural moorings.[50] This would lead him ineluctably to new reflections not only on the definition of music but also on "la peception sonore," or how the conditions of electroacoustics impose themselves on the sonorous message.

In his treatise, Schaeffer discusses the radio metaphorically as a kind of "écriture sonore" in which objects or "things" become a language that is capable of expression almost like words. Just as the image is, in effect, a kind of language for the eyes, *bruitage*, or consciously planned noise making, is thus concomitantly another sort of language for the ears. Schaeffer then incisively observes that one knows what it is to "speak," but one may always be surprised when either an image or a sound can say something "other," or in a different manner.[51] Most revealingly of all, given his recent experience, Schaeffer explains that we cannot see or hear only what we want—instead we are like people who possess the dictionary of language yet discover that the real meanings they encounter are different. On the radio, one not only hears the slightest rustling or breath but also attempts, quite naturally, to construe precisely what it signifies; such, as he concludes, are the immense possibilities, as well as the weaknesses, of the language of "things."

In sum, for Schaeffer both the cinema and the radio possess a unique power over the concrete or the real: They both evoke magically, expressing through their own registers that which cannot be said through verbal language. We can, he concludes, move forward from being creatures who are subjugated by verbal language only if we re-create the real world by employing the "arts-relais," but on their own terms—not forcing them to be more specific.[52] Clearly, Schaeffer as a man was concerned with redefining his own subjectivity or position with regard to collective meanings, while as an artist he reconsidered the boundaries of music or of expressive articulation and how art may become an agent of one's interior survival. In the midst of Vichy France and in the wake of his own experience, then, Schaeffer was also reconsidering authentic art, conceiving it now as perhaps most fundamentally a reflection on reality, on human beings, and on autonomy. He realized that realities are, in part, the significations that one imparts to actions, to images, or to sounds; this is the way in which they acquire a personal sense, and not through established meanings, which can lie.

Already, a new horizon of creativity was emerging from Schaeffer's rumination on the semantics of sound systems and the ways in which they may affect human awareness, imagination, communication, and our relation to collective meaning. What fundamentally concerned Schaeffer at this stage was the new range of communicative possibilities that could emerge, and this would eventually lead him to a more extensive consideration of what constitutes a work and indeed the creative act. Schaeffer soon recognized a context in which he could apply his new theoretical insights, and again it was within the framework of a Vichy-sponsored project that he, even more consciously, would divert to his own personal, creative, and ideological ends. This was a workshop in recorded sound that took place in Beaune (in Bourgogne) in the fall of 1942 and where he had the added advantage of working with the renowned theater director Jacques Copeau.[53]

The context for this endeavor was a continuing concern in France since the 1920s with performing drama on the radio and hence considering it as a sort of "invisible theater." This kind of theater demanded that the audience develop new capacities of perception, and rather than compensating for the absence of the physical, those producing it sought to develop a different kind of presence. The goal of Schaeffer's workshop in Beaune, however, was to conduct research, as well as to help young technicians and artists gain experience, with Maurice Martenot and others selecting the actors, the directors, and the sound engineers. Here Schaeffer avidly explored the radio approached as a new mode of artistic expression, analyzing how the strengths and weaknesses of either a work or an interpretation are made more evident through its radiophonic transmission.[54]

Once more the texts included Péguy, as well as Homer and Proust, and again his concern was how to open up new meanings not only through the use of framing or juxtaposition with other texts but also through the control of amplification and sound quality. This also necessitated experimentation with a new kind of diction, one stripped of all the artifices of theater and rather employing that purely interior attitude recommended by Copeau, while at the same time respecting the techniques and demands of the medium. In addition, Schaeffer sought to elicit new meanings, but more subtly this time—here through the use of pure sound, including the effects not only of delivery but also of amplification, which, ironically, on the surface met with official approbation.[55]

As a result of his success and given Vichy's momentum and desire for effective propaganda through culture, Schaeffer was then charged, in late 1942, with creating a studio for experimental broadcasts in Paris. His "Studio d'Essai" addressed the current issues while recording a series of innovative programs (not all of them were intended for public diffusion) at a time when such endeavors remained relatively new. It was thus essentially a laboratory—not part of the normal French broadcast production, and although the questions that it addressed were not new, Schaeffer focused more closely on the aesthetic dimension.[56] Hence, as he had in Beaune, he experimented with the reading of great texts, ranging from classics such as Homer to more recent French figures, again including the still ideologically contested Péguy.

Once more his aim was to explore means of reinscribing and thus reinvesting canonic texts in such a manner that they could elude propagandistic appropriation and serve a new reflexive function. To this end Schaeffer experimented further with background noises and with placing multiple microphones at various distances, thus developing the notion of a *plan sonore* and carefully regulating the reverberation of sounds. Indeed, he and his team were aware of the incipient use and potential of the tape recorder: Journals such as *Radio national* had pointed out that the Germans were far ahead in this domain, possessing the equipment that the French still lacked. However, even without it (until 1950) Schaeffer realized that one could still employ the microphone in new ways, as he had in Jeune France, now adapting it so as, in effect, to help fabricate the sound.[57]

Beyond such experimentation the achievements of Schaeffer's studio led to more concrete results: On July 3, 1943, the French national radio presented an afternoon of artistic broadcasts prepared by his creative team. The effects of such manipulations of texts become clear when we examine these broadcasts, which fortunately have been preserved and now reissued on a set of CDs that trace the evolution of Schaeffer's studio.[58] In addition to the subtle yet striking innovations that are here evident, the Studio d'Essai went further, organizing itself around the exploration of the *domaine sonore* irrespective of genre and thus planting seeds that would fully flower later in postwar or Gaullist France. For Schaeffer was already reconsidering the question of "ownership" and the mutability of an artistic text, as well as the issue of the relation of individual to collective or established significations in the process of constructing meaning. He was also now ruminating on a concept that would later absorb him—*haute fidelité*, or how the transfer of a sonorous object into a space of restitution is accompanied not only by constraints, distortion, and dynamic changes but also by transformation of the perceptual field.[59] Concomitantly, it was here, too, that he initially became interested in *simulacres*—traces of real events or experiences removed from their usual contexts and then recomposed in a new assemblage for a substantially different end.

Yet even more was emerging within Schaeffer the person and the creator as he reflected on the implications of his activities and where they might eventually lead him in his personal artistic endeavors. As he explained, it was in the course of his experimentation with "things" that the sounds became both animate and transcendent: They began to "speak" as if they carried a message from another world.[60] He thus began further to consider how one might hear sounds in a different sense, forcing us to search for new personal referents as they are removed from older, established cultural contexts. Like the resistant Surrealist poets whom he would soon be recording, Schaeffer was concerned not just with the ways in which we think about reality but also with how to trigger constructive mental activity despite the obstacles imposed by language.

Not coincidentally, it was during this period that Schaeffer officially entered the French Resistance—in the latter part of 1943, while still involved with the Studio d'Essai, which was funded by the Vichy government.[61] One goal of the Resistance radio programs that were now being planned was to help build courage and resolution in order to face an inevitable and violent insurrection. The programs prepared thus centered on the works of Resistance poets and writers such as Aragon, Eluard, Desnos, and Jean-Paul Sartre, as well as those of musicians whom the Resistance protected or admired, including the Jewish composers Arnold Schoenberg, Darius Milhaud, and Paul Dukas.[62]

Significantly, the poets that were recorded were those who were Surrealists, as well as resistants, and whose aesthetic would play a crucial role for Schaeffer in his eventual transition to his postwar endeavors. From them he learned not only how to explore the construction of new perceptual frames but also how to elicit new meanings through the use of "structural dislocations," or semantic incompatibilities and ambiguities. Predictably, under the fascicizing new secrétaire d'état à la propagande, Philippe Henriot, who was appointed in January 1944 and was interested in only the most blatant propaganda, Schaeffer was once again fired, this time from his position at his own Studio d'Essai.[63]

Schaeffer, however, continued to explore how a new language, even one composed purely of sounds, can extend the very contours of one's thought, realizing
that if we break our older referential frames, we are thus forced constructively to
build new ones. His explorations, however, would be limited and then interrupted
by the liberation and its immediate aftermath; when Paris was finally liberated,
he was inevitably diverted, now placed second in command at the national radio,
after Jean Guignebert, who was appointed by de Gaulle's supporters. Moreover,
ironically, despite Schaeffer's firm resistance (at first internally and then more formally), he was called before an official purge commission as a result of his involvements, first with Vichy radio and then with Jeune France, both of which were
Vichy-sponsored programs.[64]

The Studio d'Essai was now closed, if temporarily, and when it reopened a year
later, in 1946, it was placed under the direction not of Schaeffer, its founder, but
rather the Resistance poet Paul Tardieu. In addition, it now audibly changed
direction, ostensibly in an effort at cultural de-Nazification, for the emphasis here
became the dissemination of jazz, while Schaeffer was sent briefly by the new French
government to work in the United States.[65] However, his creativity did not abate but
reached the next stage in 1948, when he was invited back by Tardieu, now to develop
the "Club d'Essai"—once more a kind of laboratory that was devoted to creative
and collective work on sound research. Again employing or adapting a government
program to his own end, Schaeffer began even farther-reaching explorations into
how the significations that are ascribed to specific sounds may be detached from
their culturally or experientially defined meanings and associations.[66]

It was within the context of these interests and reflections that the concept of
musique concrète emerged, as Schaeffer experimented first with recorded sounds,
then with the creation of new ones, and finally with the manipulation of his own
recordings. According to Schaeffer, his original intention was simply to "faire parler
les bruits," or to manipulate a "décor sonore dramatique"—that which commonly
served as background on radio programs of dramatic works; however, he soon
found himself increasingly approaching music. For while accumulating sounds that
carried significations, they ended up, as Schaeffer put it, by effacing themselves as
such—no longer evoking a decor but rather themselves "speaking," as well as con-
stituting their own suggestive *chaines sonores*. Undoubtedly aware of the early futur-
ist "bruiteurs," possibly through Martenot, he similarly rejected the previously
restricted world of sound and sought like the Futurists to organize it, including the
use of noise, however without their bellicosity and overt provocation.[67]

Schaeffer later explained that at this stage, since he had originally begun by
working with objects, he thus conceived a "Symphonie de bruits," one that eventually became for him a "Symphonie de psaumes."[68] Initially, upon his return to Paris
he had gone to *service de bruitage* of the French national radio, which stocked
various devices for producing suggestive sounds ranging from coconuts to horns of
all kinds. However, in this case he was not in search of the means to illustrate a text
within a specific dramatic context, and hence independently of John Cage (whose
work he came to know slightly later) he began to experiment with the objects

he found, even creating a *piano à bruits*, then moving on to an organ, already demolished, which he struck percussively with mallets.[69]

However, all of this in the end led him back to the recording booth and to the turntable, where he manipulated not the objects themselves but their effect when placed under the microphone, which rendered not only the sound but also its entire range of secondary sonorities. Here he could modify the attack, as well as alter the volume, and then record all of this, thus in effect creating his own instrument, which he preferred to early electronic devices. Such manipulation of the concrete, according to Schaeffer, in fact recalled his parents' music since it allowed him to remain in direct contact with the "sonorous material," or with the object producing the sound.[70]

These experiments eventually led to his work with Pierre Henry, their *Symphonie pour un homme seul*, a title intended to carry a double sense—referring both to their solitary experimentation and to their sense of isolation. As Schaeffer went on to explain, with palpable reference to his own beliefs and experience, "Man alone can find his symphony within himself, not only in conceiving his music abstractly but being himself his own instrument."[71] He elaborated more specifically that a human being possesses much more than twelve notes conceived in terms of *solfège*—for example, humans can cry, whistle, laugh, and moan. Again with clear reference to his wartime experience, Schaeffer also pointed out that one's heart beats, one's breath accelerates, one pronounces words and calls out to others, who respond, but nothing echoes a solitary cry more poignantly than the clamor of crowds.

Schaeffer put all of this awareness to use in his first large collaborative work with Henry, whom he encountered at an opportune moment, just as he was in the process of conceiving of his "symphonie." While auditioning young composers to come to his studio and collaborate, he was impressed not only by Henry's skill and breadth of knowledge but also by his aesthetic imagination, which was, perhaps not by coincidence, close to Schaeffer's own. For Henry had just spent three years in Messiaen's class and under his tutelage had experienced a revelation: Messiaen, he proclaimed, opened up a world of "gleaming mysticism, with its sparks, its stars, waters and mountains…a musical pantheism that pushed one to dream, to drift."[72] Henry was thus primed for collaboration with another inveterate spiritualist and personalist, this time Schaeffer, who brought with him the weight of both his recent and his early experience—philosophical, personal, technical, and artistic.

Henry's collaboration helped to transform the work, and after many revisions they arrived at a final plan that was far less explicitly programmatic, or conventionally dramatic, than Schaeffer's initial sketches. In the definitive version they decided to oppose the idea of the exterior, or of a physical space, with that of the personal, the interior, or of a psychological climate, still so resonant for many in post-Vichy France. As Schaeffer explained, those listeners who were inclined to the dramatic could thus search for their own imaginative scenario, while others could appreciate it more abstractly, for his goal was to capture the entire range of expression that was possible through radiophonic means, those broader than either the musical or the mechanical.[73]

The balance between the suggestive and the abstract is subtle, as we hear in the opening "Marche," the first of fourteen movements, some originally carrying generic titles such as "Quatuor" and "Chorale," with others marked by terms such as *batterie* (percussion) or *cris*. Schaeffer and Henry's *Symphonie* thus employs not only human but also other kinds of sounds, both pitched and nonpitched; in addition to vocal fragments, shouting, humming, and whistling there are footsteps, raps on doors, and a kind of "prepared piano."[74] Throughout the work the realistic character of the sounds disappears after having been only fleetingly suggested, thus revealing a world of latent meaning and inviting reflection on human experience and signification. Schaeffer and Henry thus explored the very border of the human and the appearance of the human, or the illusion of humanity and of meaning as, indeed, Schaeffer himself had done with Pétain's transmitted voice.

Also as in radio broadcasts, the form is conceived as a series of sequences articulating with one another, the opening "Marche" imposing the work's "decor" and the following "Quatuor," as Schaeffer put it, "exposing a swarming universe of human life with voices which create their own music."[75] In the ninth sequence and again with particular resonance for those who shared France's wartime experience under both Vichy and the Germans, the voices gradually become distinct and pronounce an intelligible yet highly charged and ambiguous word with the context—*absolument*. But perhaps the best example of the entire range of effects that the composers here employed, some dating back to the early Studio d'Essai, is the harrowing and haunting tenth sequence, simply titled, abstractly, "Intermezzo."

Schaeffer continued to work with and train young artists, inviting them to participate in his later "Groupe de recherches de musique concrète," with those flocking to his studio including not only a young Frenchman, Pierre Boulez, but also a young German, Karlheinz Stockhausen. The latter, ostensibly influenced by Schaeffer, would in 1956 produce his own powerful testament to wartime experience and to the implications of the new artistic form—his electronic composition "Gesang der Junglinge."[76] Here he similarly experiments with the resonance of the human voice when manipulated and while pronouncing a text, in this case the Bible, detached from its manifest content, yet still poignantly evoking both humanity and spirituality.

The implications of this new artistic form, imagined in wartime France, palpably endured for decades; thirty years later Steve Reich, who similarly considers music as part of life and of "process," evoked Schaeffer's work in his own, a suggestion of trains transporting Jews to their death. The wrenching second movement of his masterful *Different Trains* of 1986, for recorded voices of Holocaust survivors and string quartet, inevitably recalls Schaeffer's *Étude de chemins de fers*, which also relentlessly tears the listener away from any fixed orientation or established subject position.

Schaeffer's legacy has unquestionably lived on, becoming a central component of what we now call "experimental music," often associated largely with American postwar composers and primarily with John Cage. However, these tendencies all emerged gradually in Schaeffer: Throughout his career he was continually in search of new communicative possibilities and of ways to make the familiar say new things, and after exploring both theater and the radio he finally arrived at a new mode of artistic expression. His goal consistently was to engage the articulation of art with life and aesthetically to engage new communities, while at the same time forming a more total, more aware, or more autonomous person.

It would, in conclusion, be a historiographic error to ignore the aesthetic seeds of postwar musical developments in Vichy France, as it would be for historians of modern France to overlook this important line of French cultural continuity. Figures such as Pierre Schaeffer deftly harnessed the momentum established by Vichy and diverted it to their own loftier ends—those often associated with spiritualism and with a subtle if ever-mounting resistance. The full fruit of this dynamic ripened after the war: His former colleague, Roger Leenhardt, went on to explore the very grammar of film making, like Schaeffer's seeking to make art a part of life in a "living realism" that in cinema became associated with the "new wave." In theater the innovations and experimentation of Jeune France members continued to bear fruit, particularly in the case of figures like Jean Vilar, who in 1947 founded the still flourishing Avignon Festival.[77]

Still, all of this in the end leads us back to Schaeffer, through whom we may perhaps best make the case for pursuing a cultural history by crossing over disciplines and recognizing the coherence of life and of experience—of understanding the construction of meaning and communication. His career and work, as we have seen, cannot be divided into segments or even fields, nor can they be divorced from their contexts; it is only through perceiving this that we may grasp the significance, the sources, and the depth of Schaeffer's still vibrant art.

NOTES

1. See, for example, Carl E. Schorske, *Fin-de-Siècle Vienna: Politics and Culture* (New York: Knopf, 1979), and musicologist Kate van Orden's *Music, Discipline, and Arms in Early Modern France* (Chicago: University of Chicago Press, 2005).

2. This is discussed, within a historical context, by Roger Chartier in his *Publishing Drama in Early Modern Europe*. The Panizzi Lectures (London: British Library, 1998), especially in chapter 3, "The Stage and the Page," 51–73. Also see Jane F. Fulcher, "The Concert as Political Propaganda in France and the Control of Performative Context," *Musical Quarterly* 82(1) (Spring 1998): 41–67.

3. I am very grateful to Philip Nord both for talking with me and for sending me a copy of his excellent article "Pierre Schaeffer and Jeune France: Cultural Politics in the Vichy Years," *French Historical Studies* 30(4) (Fall 2007): 685–709, which I consulted extensively while writing my own and have frequently cited here. I am also grateful to another historian, Jonathyne Briggs, for sending me a draft of his very interesting article on Schaeffer, technocracy, and composition in France, with a focus on 1948. Because I read it in an unpublished version, I have not cited it in this chapter but do want here to acknowledge and draw attention to his work in the field.

In musicological studies see, for example, see Hans Heinz Stuckenschmidt's classic, *Twentieth-century Music* (New York: McGraw-Hill, 1969), 176–77. For a more recent example see Anthony Pople, "New Beginnings: The International Avant-Garde, 1945–62," in *The Cambridge History of Twentieth-century Music*, ed. Nicholas Cook and Anthony Pople, 343 (New York: Cambridge University Press, 2004).

4. See Robert O. Paxton, *Vichy France: Old Guard, New Order* (New York: Columbia University Press, 1972), especially 7, 46, 249–59.

5. Paxton, *Vichy France*, 259–68. Also see Stanley Hoffmann's equally groundbreaking "Collaborationism in France during World War II," *Journal of Modern History* 30(3) (September 1968): 377–78. On the collaboration of Vichy and the Germans in a common repressive apparatus see Denis Peschanski, "Exclusion, persécution, répression," in *Vichy et les français*, ed. Jean-Pierre Azéma and Francis Bédarida, 208–10 (Paris: Fayard, 1992).

6. On the national revolution and its initial ideological conflicts or vagueness, see Marie Guillon, "La philosophie politique de la Révolution nationale," in *Vichy et les français*, 169–71.

7. See Paxton, *Vichy France*, 20 and 29, on Vichy's attempt to carry out a domestic revolution in institutions and values. On Vichy's dynamism and eventual loss of control see Henry Rousso, "Vichy: Politique, idéologie, et culture," in *La vie culturelle sous Vichy*, ed. Jean-Pierre Rioux, 19–39 (Brussels: Editions Complexe, 1990).

8. On the Catholic Left see Nord, "Pierre Schaeffer and Jeune France," 686, and on young Catholic radicals see Paxton, 24 and 272.

9. See the small untitled and undated pamphlet (with no author given) in the Bibliothèque Nationale de France, Département de la Musique in 8 Vm. Pièce 1646, as well as the larger pamphlet that this file contains, titled "Titres et travaux de Pierre Schaeffer" (1973). Also see Pierre Schaeffer, *L'avenir en recoulons* (Paris: Casterman, 1970), 66.

10. Schaeffer, *L'avenir en recoulons*, 68, 74, and 94. And see Pierre Schaeffer, *Clotaire Nicole 1910–1932* (Paris: Editions de la Revue des Jeunes, 1938), 5 and 176.

11. On the nonconformist movement see Jean-Louis Loubet del Bayle, *Les Non-conformistes des années 30: Une tentative de la renouvellement de la pensée politique française* (Paris: Seuil, 1969), esp. 16, 23, 29, and 40. On the range of their journals see Olivier Corpet, "La Revue," in *Histoire des droites en France*, ed. Jean-François Sirinelli, 188 (Paris: Gallimard, 1992). Also see Roger Leenhardt, *Les yeux ouvertes: Entretiens ave Jean La Couture* (Paris: Seuil, 1979), 93, and Schaeffer, *L'avenir en recoulons*, 30.

12. See Michel Winock, *Le siècle des intellectuels* (Paris: Seuil, 1997), 209–11, as well as his more specialized *Histoire politique de la revue Esprit, 1930–1950* (Paris: Seuil, 1975). Also see Tony Judt, *Past Imperfect: French Intellectuals 1944–1956* (Berkeley: University of California Press, 1992), 19.

13. Nord, "Pierre Schaeffer and Jeune France," 688. Also see Véronique Chabrol, "Jeune France: Une expérience de recherche et de décentralisation culturelle Nov. 1940–Mars 1942," Thèse du 3e cycle, 1974, Université de Paris III, 258. In addition, see Schaeffer, *L'avenir en recoulons*, 49.

14. See Pierre Schaeffer, *L'avenir en recoulons*, 49–50, and Jean Laurendeau, *Maurice Martenot, luthier de l'électronique* (Montreal: Dervy, 1990), 117.

15. Rousso, "Vichy: Politique, idéologie, et culture," 33–34.

16. Nord, "Pierre Schaeffer and Jeune France," 668–90, and on Schaeffer's other contacts at Vichy see Véronique Chabrol, "L'ambition de Jeune France," in *La vie culturelle sous Vichy*, 163.

17. See Nord, "Pierre Schaeffer and Jeune France," 689–90, and Bernard Comte, "Les organisations de jeunesse," in *Vichy et les français*, 414.

18. Leenhardt, *Les yeux ouvertes*, 119–20; Nord, "Pierre Schaeffer and Jeune France," 688; and Laurendeau, *Maurice Martenot*, 116.

19. Laurendeau, *Maurice Martenot*, 116–17; Nord, "Pierre Schaeffer and Jeune France," 688; and see Schaeffer's letter of Dec. 1, 1941, in the Paris Archives Nationales, Resistance files—F1A 3686 #3. On Alfred Cortot and his role in this period see Myriam Chimènes, "Alfred Cortot et la politique musicale du gouvernement de Vichy," in *La vie musicale sous Vichy* (Brussels: Editions Complexe, 2001), 35–52.

20. Nord, "Pierre Schaeffer and Jeune France," 688. On the technical problem of transmission levels due to the lack of adequate electrical power that such a technique also addressed see Hélène Eck, *La guerre des ondes: Histoire des radios de langue française pendant la Deuxième Guerre Mondiale* (Paris: Colin, 1985), 39.

21. See Leenhardt, *Les yeux ouvertes*, 122, and Pierre Schaeffer, *Les antennes de Jéricho* (Paris: Stock, 1978), 284. Also see Claude Roy, *Moi-je* (Paris: Gallimard, 1969), 366–69.

22. On the concept of how the material forms that carry discourse help to transform the message, see Roger Chartier, *On the Edge of the Cliff: History, Language, and Practices*, trans. Lydia G. Cochrane, 75 (Baltimore: Johns Hopkins University Press, 1997).

23. See Francine Gaillard-Risler, *André Clavé: Théatre et résistances. Utopies et réalités 1916–1981* (Paris: Association des Amis d'André Clavé, 1998), 58. Also see Schaeffer, *Les antennes de Jéricho*, 274, and Leenhardt, *Les yeux ouvertes*, 122.

24. On the original concert society Jeune France, see Jane F. Fulcher, *The Composer as Intellectual: Music and Ideology in France 1914–1940* (New York: Oxford University Press, 2005), 291–96.

25. See Jean-Pierre Rioux, "Ambivalences en rouge et bleu: Les pratiques culturelles des Français pendant les années noires," in *La vie culturelle sous Vichy*, 41–60.

26. On Messiaen's participation, along with his other former colleagues in the earlier Jeune France, see Peter Hill and Nigel Simeone, *Messiaen* (New Haven: Yale University Press, 2005), 104–09.

27. On the formation and structure of Jeune France see Chabrol, "L'ambition de Jeune France," 163–73. Also see Gaillard-Risler, *André Clavé*, 38 and 57–58; Leenhardt, *Les yeux ouvertes*, 122–23, and Nord, "Pierre Schaeffer and Jeune France," 693–95.

28. Laurendeau, *Maurice Martenot*, 118.

29. Nord, "Pierre Schaeffer and Jeune France," 685, and on Mounier's related involvement with the leadership training school at Uriage see Bernard Comte, "L'esprit d'Uriage: Pédagogie civique et humanisme révolutionnaire," in *La vie culturelle sous Vichy*, esp. 192–93.

30. See Charles Taylor's insightful review of Jonathan Lear's *Radical Hope: Ethics in the Face of Cultural Despair* (Cambridge, Mass.: Harvard University Press, 2006) in the *New York Review of Books* (Apr. 26, 2007), 6–8.

31. See Chabrol, "L'ambition de Jeune France," 164–65, and Schaeffer's letter of Dec. 1, 1941, in AN-F1A 3686 #3, as well as his brochure in the same file, "Jeune France: Principes, directions, esprit."

32. Nord, "Pierre Schaeffer and Jeune France," 694, and Chabrol, "L'ambition de Jeune France," 168–69. On the living vernacular tradition that Jeune France hoped to sponsor see Gaillard-Risler, *André Clavé*, 60. Their goal was not to return to the past but to create it anew in order to arrive at an authentic spiritual affirmation. See Leenhardt, *Les yeux ouvertes*, 121, and Schaeffer's brochure, "Jeune France: Principes, direction, esprit," in AN-F1A 3686 #3.

33. Chabrol, "L'ambition de Jeune France," 168. Jeune France was official only in the south but permitted or "tolerated" by the occupant in the north. See Gaillard-Risler, *André Clavé*, 58.

34. Chabrol, "L'ambition de Jeune France," 175–76, and Nord, "Pierre Schaeffer and Jeune France," 697.

35. On fascist conceptions of theater see Gunter Berghaus, ed., *Fascism and Theater: Comparative Studies in the Aesthetics and Politics of Performance in Europe 1925–1945* (Providence, R.I.: Berghan, 1995). On Vichy's conception of theater and its role see Pierre Bertin, "Le théatre," in *France 1941: La Révolution nationale constructive: Un bilan et un programme* [no editor listed] (Paris: Éditions Alsatia, 1941), 315–38.

36. The printed copy of *Portique pour une fille de France* exists on microfilm at the Bibliothèque Nationale de France. It is listed under the names Pierre Schaeffer and Pierre Barbier (Avec la composition musicale de Yves Baudrier, Léo Preger et Olivier Messiaen). Représenté à Lyon et Marseille en la fête de Sainte-Jeanne d'Arc le 11 mai 1941. Etienne Chiron, éditeur [no city listed]. A diagram of the placement of the groups involved is also provided in the printed copy.

37. On Charpentier's use of the tradition of Republican civic theater, see Jane F. Fulcher, *French Cultural Politics and Music from the Dreyfus Affair to the First World War* (New York: Oxford University Press, 1999), 89–92.

38. On Debussy's ironic use of this chanson in his orchestral *Images* see Fulcher, *French Cultural Politics and Music*, 187–88.

39. Hill and Simeone, *Messiaen*, 109.

40. On Messiaen's composition of the *Trois petites liturgies* see Hill and Simeone, *Messiaen*, 137–39.

41. See Chabrol, "L'ambition de Jeune France," 175, and Nord, "Pierre Schaeffer and Jeune France," 698.

42. See Frank Manning, "Spectacle," in *Folklore, Cultural Performance, and Popular Entertainments*, ed. Richard Bauman, 27–28 (New York: Oxford University Press, 1992).

43. See Claude Roy, *Moi-je*, 406–409, and Gaillard-Risler, *André Clavé*, 35.

44. See Schaeffer, *Les antennes de Jéricho*, 279ff. On the "foreclosure" of identity in youth, particularly in totalitarian states, see Maurice R. Stein and Arthur J. Vidich, "Identity and History: An Overview," in *Identity and Anxiety: Survival of the Person in Mass Society*, ed. Maurice R. Stein, Arthur J. Vidich, and David M. White, 19–20 (Glencoe, Ill.: Free Press, 1960).

45. See the letter from Jean de Fabrègues in AN-F1A 3686, as well as that of Robert Loustou (undated), who sent it on to Pierre Pucheu, the minister of the interior, as well as others contained in this file.

46. Nord, "Pierre Schaeffer and Jeune France," 701.

47. Schaeffer, letter of Dec. 1, 1941, in AN-F1A 3686.

48. Schaeffer, *Les antennes de Jéricho*, 279.

49. See Charles Taylor's review of Jonathan Lear's *Radical Hope*, 8.

50. Nord, "Pierre Schaeffer and Jeune France," 703, and Schaeffer, *Les antennes de Jéricho*, 280.

51. Pierre Schaeffer, extract from his "L'esthétique et technique des art-relais," in his *Dix ans d'essais radiophoniques du Studio au Club d'Essai* (Paris: Phonurgia Nova,1994), 75.

52. Schaeffer, extract from his "L'esthétique," 76–77.

53. Nord, "Pierre Schaeffer and Jeune France," 703. On the background to this venture see HeleneEck, "À la recherche d'un art radiophonique," in *La Vie culturelle sous Vichy* 280–81.

54. Laurendeau, *Maurice Martenot*, 120, and Eck, "À la recherche," 287.

55. Sophie Brunet, *Pierre Schaeffer* (Paris: La Revue Musicale, Éditions Richard-Messe, 1969), 27. Also see Eck, "À la recherche," 271.

56. Laurendeau, *Maurice Martenot*, 13. On the official creation of the Studio d'Essai de la Radiodiffusion on Jan. 19, 1943, see François Porcile, *Les conflits de la musique françaises 1940–1965* (Paris: Fayard, 2001), 102.

57. Eck, "À la recherche," 278.

402   CULTURAL EXPERIENCE: PRACTICES, APPROPRIATIONS, AND EVALUATIONS

58. Consult the CDs that accompany the booklet in Schaeffer's *Dix ans d'essais radiophoniques*.

59. On these concepts and their origins see the pamphlet in the Bibliothèque Nationale de France, Département de la Musique 8Vm. 1646, "Titres et travaux de Pierre Schaeffer."

60. See Brunet, *Pierre Schaeffer*, 28.

61. On such Surrealist techniques see Inez Hedges, *Languages of Revolt: Dada and Surrealist Literature and Film* (Durham: Duke University Press, 1983), 84 and 91. On Schaeffer's official entry into the Resistance see Nord, "Pierre Schaeffer and Jeune France," 704.

62. Nord, "Pierre Schaeffer and Jeune France," 703, and Laurendeau, *Maurice Martenot*, 121.

63. Porcile, *Les conflits de la musique française*, 102.

64. Nord, "Pierre Schaeffer and Jeune France," 706. On the arrests in the National Radio see Schaeffer, *Les antennes de Jéricho*, 375–79 and Porcile, *Les conflits de la musique française*, 104.

65. Nord, "Pierre Schaeffer and Jeune France," 706–707.

66. Porcile, *Les conflits de la musique française*, 105–106.

67. See Pierre Schaeffer, *La musique concrète* (Paris: Presses Universitaires de France, 1967), 18. On the early Futurists and music see Glenn Watkins, *Soundings: Music in the Twentieth Century* (New York: Schirmer, 1995), 235–39.

68. Pierre Schaeffer, *À la recherche d'une musique concrète* (Paris: Seuil, 1952), 12.

69. Schaeffer, *À la recherche*, 13. And see Porcile, *Les conflits de la musique française*, 63.

70. Schaeffer, *À la recherche*, 15.

71. Schaeffer, *À la recherche*, 55.

72. Porcile, *Les conflits de la musique française*, 104.

73. Porcile, *Les conflits de la musique française*, 55–56, 64, and 106.

74. On the original titles of the segments and on Schaeffer's knowledge of Cage's work see Schaeffer, *À la recherche*, 58, and Porcile, *Les conflits de la musique française*, 63.

75. Porcile, *Les conflits de la musique française*, 64.

76. On this now canonic electronic composition see Stuckenschmidt, *Twentieth-century Music*, 186.

77. Nord, "Pierre Schaeffer and Jeune France," 707–708. And see Chabrol, "L'ambition de Jeune France," 162, as well as Schaeffer, *L'avenir en recoulons*, 29.

CHAPTER 16

A MATTER OF STYLE: STATE SACRIFICIAL MUSIC AND CULTURAL-POLITICAL DISCOURSE IN SOUTHERN SONG CHINA (1127–1279)

JOSEPH S. C. LAM

The *yang* has animated the imperial palace;
The sun is spinning over the south;
The heavenly gate is grand;
Welcoming the deities who are coming.
The imperial altar radiates,
Lights of yellow and pearl colors.
Why do the deities come so enthusiastically?
Because my ancestors are virtuous.

"Welcoming the Deities" is a piece of twelfth-century Chinese *state sacrificial music* (*yayue*) that its practitioners considered most beautiful and perfect (*jinshan jin-mei*). Premiered on the winter solstice day of 1143, the piece was performed, inside an imperial altar complex, by a choir of thirty-two men singers and 174 men musicians playing twenty-one kinds of ancient and ritual musical instruments.[1] Featuring the *syllabic style*, which rigidly matched individual musical tones in the melody of the song to individual words in its lyrics, the song heralded solemn offerings to

Example 16.1. "Welcoming the Deities" from the State Sacrifice to Heaven, Earth, and the Founders, 1143. Xu Song, *Zongxing lishu* [A Compilation of the Rituals and Music of the Southern Song], in *Xuxiu siku quanshu* (1180s; Shanghai guji chubanshe, 1995), vol. 822, 15.8. (For a discussion of this musical source, see Joseph S. C. Lam, "Musical Relics and Cultural Expressions: State Sacrificial Song from the Southern Song Court [AD 1127–1279]," *Journal of Sung-Yuan Studies* 25 [1995]: 1–10.)

heaven, earth, the dynastic founders, and a bevy of deities. The music and the ritual expressed and prompted negotiations of many agendas, including the claim that the Southern Song (1127–1279), an empire of Han Chinese people and culture,[2] received from the Northern Song (960–1127) heaven's mandate to rule China. The Northern Song ended in 1127, when the Jurchens, an ethnic rival from the north, broke Kaifeng, the Northern Song capital, captured the last two emperors of the empire, namely Huizong (reigned 1100–1125) and Qinzong (reigned 1125–27),[3] and took them to the north as hostages. Huizong was the father of Gaozong (reigned 1127–1162),[4] the founder of the Southern Song. He had "Welcoming the Deities" created as the second of twenty-three ritual songs of a newly designed state sacrifice honoring heaven, earth, and the founders.[5]

To Gaozong and his court, the stylized and distinctive sounds of state sacrificial music were beautiful and perfect for many reasons. Performed with singing and instrumental playing on bell chimes (*bianzhong*), stone chimes (*bianqing*), and other ancient musical instruments,[6] the music sonically embodied Chinese court tradition of state sacrifices, each a grand and complex ceremonial that was performed over a period of several months as an extended sequence of ritual preparations, preliminary ceremonies, ceremonies proper, and concluding celebrations.[7] Heard as the sonic component of state and sacred rituals, state sacrificial music perfectly signified the Confucian and imperial ideology of civilized music: It cultivated people's virtues so that they would harmoniously live in orderly societies that benevolent rulers operated with ritual and music.[8]

As performed and experienced in 1143, the Southern Song state sacrifice to heaven, earth, and the founders and its ritual music constituted an imperial lesson on cultural, social, and political living in twelfth-century China. Worshipping heaven, the ultimate authority among Chinese deities, was to seek and/or to keep the mandate to rule China.[9] Honoring earth as heaven's counterpart was to pay homage to deities whose *yin* activities complemented heaven's *yang* operation. Honoring deified dynastic founders as heaven's companions was to glorify imperial ancestors who had bequeathed empires and cultural-political institutions and whose legacy legitimized current rulers. Glorifying imperial ancestors was deemed an exemplary act of filial piety, a fundamental principle of traditional Chinese living. The *Classic of Filial Piety* (*Xiaojing*) prescribes that emperors should rule by practicing filial piety.[10] When emperors acted filially by showing respect and obedience to their ancestors/superiors, they showed their subjects how to behave in a patrilineal and authoritative society. Benevolent emperors should guide their subjects by exemplary actions, earning the latter's respect and obedience; only as last resorts should rulers use physical force or punishment to discipline the ruled.

The cultural and political meanings of "Welcoming the Deities" were unmistakable to Southern Song Chinese. The historical messages are still intelligible to contemporary audiences, Chinese and non-Chinese, who are familiar with Confucian and imperial China and who understand the power of music and in particular ritual music. In fact, even if many twenty-first-century audiences find the song stylistically alien and musically unintelligible, some musicologists would find it a textbook illustration of music as both a contextual and an interactive art, one that enables its participants to musically express and negotiate their lives in historically, culturally, and biographically particularized times and places.

Approaching music as such an art, however, raises many musical questions. For example, one asks, how does music like "Welcoming the Deities" express sonic and nonsonic meanings and propel cultural-political negotiations? Cultural and contextual explanations of historical types of music often highlight nonsonic elements at the expense of the sonic ones. This tendency is particularly prominent in interpretations informed by anthropology, sociology, and cultural studies, views that attempt to remedy deficiencies of positivistic and structural analyses of music with broad observations about cultures and societies. The cultural and historical description of "Welcoming the Deities" presented earlier, for example, is illustrative. It explains the song with cultural and contextual references, but it hardly explains how its stylized and distinctive sounds express or promote Southern Song negotiations and interactions.

How did the song musically and sonically project or help negotiate Confucian and imperial ideals with its specific melodic and rhythmic phrases, distinctive tonal modes, and structural-formal patterns? To answer these questions as problems of Chinese music history and as general issues of music and discourse, I present a case study of "Welcoming the Deities." This chapter posits that musical negotiations of cultural and political agendas operate with the participants' recognition and manipulation of stylized and distinctive musical sounds. Only with such musical understanding and manipulation can the negotiators objectify music as a meaningful and valuable bargaining chip, use it to define sites and contexts in which they can strategically and interactively negotiate with other participants, and advance their personalized agendas. "Welcoming the Deities" would not function as a critical component of Southern Song cultural-political discourse unless its syllabic style was recognized as distinctive and meaningful.

To present this matter of style, I begin by briefly surveying the cultural and political realities of Southern Song China and its musical capital, Lin'an, where citizens purposefully produced and consumed various types of music. Then I introduce Southern Song state sacrificial music by showing the historical and cultural messages that it carried and that its producers and consumers manipulated and negotiated. To illustrate Southern Song people's personalized negotiations with state sacrificial music, I outline the performance history and reception of the latter, focusing on what took place between 1143 and 1163. Personalized and particularized engagement with the stylized and distinctive music is what renders it meaningful and indispensable in the cultural and political discourse of the time.

SOUTHERN SONG CHINA

As Southern Song began in 1127, its government in exile faced numerous cultural and political problems created by the shocking and shameful collapse of the Northern Song.[11] Kaifeng, a grand and musical city, was not supposed to be broken by the Jurchens, who had built, only twelve years ago, their nascent Jin dynasty (1115–1234). The kidnapping of two former emperors, who were paraded (the sending of the emperors was quite public—to humiliate them!)away to the north, torpedoed Han Chinese pride. The defection of many Northern Song scholar-officials to the Jin court made a mockery of Han and Confucian morality. Gaozong's ascension to power was serendipitous: After the fall of Kaifeng, he became the only available imperial prince who could lead a resistance force. Gaozong gathered support by vowing to restore the Song empire, a promise that he could not keep. Military, political, and cultural struggles between the Jin/Jurchens and the Southern Song/Han

Chinese continued until their destruction by the Mongols. The Jin dynasty ended in 1234, and the Southern Song, in 1279; the Southern Song and the Mongols began to engage one another militarily in 1227.

Controlling only the southern part of China, the Southern Song, nevertheless, managed to creatively and brilliantly restore a Han Chinese empire. When it ended in 1279, the Southern Song had achieved much in historical, cultural, and comparative terms. Neo-Confucianism developed into a state ideology that dominated imperial China until its end in 1911. Governmental emphasis on education produced generations of learned citizens who not only served the empire as officials but also helped develop its economy, technology, and expressive culture. Southern Song scholarship, *ci* poetry, landscape paintings, ceramics, printing, textiles, and naval navigation, for example, represented major achievements in Chinese history and culture. Southern Song, however, was also a frustrated and limited empire. Realizing their inability to recover the north, many Southern Song citizens intoxicated themselves with the pleasures that Lin'an offered. And many observed their world in earnest, trying to figure out why and how it would last or end.[12] In his *Memoirs of Wulin* (*Wulin jiushi*), for instance, Zhou Mi (1232–1298) proudly and nostalgically described Southern Song expressive practices, providing a wealth of details that can help twenty-first-century historians understand his negotiated world.

Musical Lin'an

Music was an integral component of life in the Southern Song capital, Lin'an. By the 1160s, the city had become a vibrant metropolis where at least half a million citizens purposefully and discerningly created, changed, and sustained various types of music.[13] Supported by developed networks of land and water routes and blessed with a comfortable subtropical climate and scenic sites like the beautiful West Lake, Lin'an was a land where people could live comfortably, leisurely, and artistically. Thus, since Gaozong chose Lin'an as the capital in 1138, its population quickly exploded. Waves of war refugees flooded into the city, not only bringing capital and skills to develop trades and industries but also generating social needs and tax revenues to build a new capital where cultural and political bargaining commonly took place (figure 16.1).

As Lin'an developed into an imperial capital, it created many sacred and secular venues where rulers and the ruled could critically participate in a variety of activities, many of which involved music extensively. In other words, in Lin'an, events, landscape, and soundscape referenced one another so that its citizens could define and negotiate all kinds of expressive acts and messages. In fact, the citizens of Lin'an could knowingly and musically negotiate their lives because music was present on many occasions, all of which had culturally and politically specific functions and

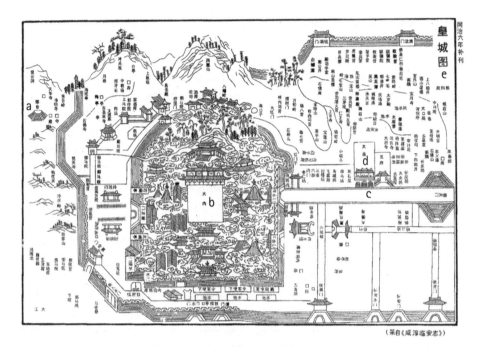

（采自《咸淳临安志》）

Figure 16.1. Overview of Lin'an: a. the suburban round mound altar; b. the palace; c. the imperial main street; d. the grand ancestral temple; e. the northern part of the city (not shown), where the temple of spectacular numina was located. *NanSong jingcheng Hangzhou*, ed. Zhou Feng (Hangzhou: Zhejiang renmin chubanshe), back matter, n.p. The map originally appears in a historical gazette, the *Xianchun Lin'an zhi* (Lin'an of the Xianchun reign [1265–1275]).

meanings. Coordinating different types of music with distinctive sites and situated performances, the citizens of Lin'an could promptly differentiate among musical genres and styles, tell what they signified, and relate how their objects and messages could be manipulated to advance particularized agendas.

This musical operation of the citizens of Lin'an becomes evident if one surveys the city's landscape and soundscape. As a capital, Lin'an was anchored in the south by the palace, where Southern Song emperors held court with all kinds of sacred and secular rituals and music. From there, Lin'an spread north along a central axis, namely the imperial main street (*yujie*), along which imperial and musical processions regularly wound their way, giving the residents a constant exposure to court music. For example, imperial processions traveling between the palace and the *temple of spectacular numina* (*jinglinggong*), in the northern corner of Lin'an, showcased grand processional music played by many drums, gongs, and wind instruments.[14] State sacrificial music performed inside the halls of the imperial temple floated beyond its walls and reached citizens who worked or lived nearby. Built throughout the city from the south to the north were city blocks of governmental and public facilities, as well as commercial establishments and private homes. The offices of the six ministries were, for example, built just north of the palace-city. They constituted an end point for many scholar-officials on their trips to and from the palace, and many were announced by some kind of processional music. Lin'an boasted a good number of Buddhist temples and Daoist shrines where the Southern Song elite, as well as commoners, prayed to their deities with ritual-specific chants, hymns, and other oral deliveries. Unique among these sacred sites and musical sounds was the Confucian temple (wenmiao), an integral part of the national university (taixue) complex in northern Lin'an. There scholars and officials ritually and musically honored Confucius twice a year, singing civilized songs in the syllabic style. In the other halls of the national university, students studied, socialized, and sang their poetic songs (shiyue). In the middle of Lin'an and in particular in the areas near the foothills of Fenghuang Mountain and Wu Mountain were many luxurious mansions. There the rich and the privileged entertained themselves and their guests with elaborate songs and dances performed by beautiful courtesans.

Most Lin'an citizens, however, enjoyed pleasurable sounds, sights, and social interactions in entertainment quarters (wazi), taverns (jiulou), music halls (geguan), and other commercial establishments found throughout the city.[15] Most entertainment quarters were located near city gates or bridges, where people could easily gather to conduct all kinds of transactions. The Northern Quarter (Beiwa), the entertainment area noted for its thirteen theaters, was, for example, built next to the People's Peace Bridge (Zhong'an Bridge) right in the middle of the city. Scattered throughout the capital were taverns and music halls where beautifully dressed courtesans would serve food and beverages, play music, and provide other entertainments to male, official, and/or rich clients. At many street bazaars and open spaces that lent themselves to casual gatherings, itinerant entertainers (luqiren) performed to the delight of their audiences. Performers who came from outside the capital probably played music from their hometowns or what they learned as they traveled. Floating on the West Lake were large and small pleasure boats on which the citizens enjoyed their moveable, musical feasts.

To successfully operate in this landscape and soundscape, the residents of Lin'an manipulated the objects, words, sights, and sounds of their world in their specific social and cultural roles. As emperors, imperial clansmen, officials, scholars, and educated and privileged citizens, elite men of the time authoritatively defined the style and function of state sacrificial music. They wrote expressive ritual lyrics for state sacrificial music, administratively controlled its grand performances in imperial temples and shrines, and politically and intellectually promulgated and preserved its practices through oral communications and written treatises. The elite, however, delegated actual performances of the music to court and lowly musicians recruited from among the commoners—the musicians performed as servants, if not human tools, for making music. In other words, if the elite controlled sacrificial music, it was not unknown and irrelevant to the commoners. In fact, this music was able to serve as both a powerful and an unmistakable expression of social power and identity because only the elite could compose and modify it with imperial sanction;

commoners could only perform the music as court servants or passively listen to its imperial sounds.

The musical commoners of Lin'an could, however, creatively shape many genres of music for secular enjoyment and entertainment. For example, even if elite poets wrote the lyrics of *ci* songs, their melodies and performances were largely entrusted to professional courtesans. Many female entertainers were professional musicians who had received rigorous training since childhood. Rich owners and managers of entertainment establishments spared no expense to hire the best available music masters to train novice courtesans to sing with clear voices and perform charming dances (*qingge miaowu*) that appealed to male and rich clients. Many clients were themselves music connoisseurs. As elite males of the time, however, they could not publicly perform music other than *qin* music, poetic songs, and other genres of civilized music. No elite men would perform processional or entertainment music that socially marginal professionals and commoners undertook to make their living.

In other words, while Southern elite and commoners played different musical roles in diverse sites, they were critically or casually acquainted with all types of music of their time. Even if a particular genre or style of music was nominally monopolized by a specific social group, it was experienced indirectly by all Lin'an citizens, elite or commoners. It was a musical sharing that simultaneously enforced and cut across hierarchical and social boundaries. This is why music made clearly defined but easily manipulable objects, sites, and processes for Lin'an citizens. It is a phenomenon that Zhou Mi vividly reported.[16]

Whenever the state sacrifice to heaven, earth, and the founders was performed, Zhou noted, its elaborate preparations and ceremonies transformed Lin'an into a ritual and musical landscape and soundscape that involved all of the citizens. The long process began with a formal announcement on New Year's Day that the state sacrifice would take place on the coming winter solstice. Then, during the summer months, preliminary preparations of the altar proper and other ritual sites began. One month prior to the performance on the winter solstice, public rehearsals and preparatory activities began taking place in different court offices and parts of the city. Two days prior to the performance, the emperor traveled to the temple of spectacular numina to inform his ancestors of his pending performance. After that ritual report, he would move to the grand ancestral temple in the southern part of the city, where he would spend the night and prepare himself for the ritual performance the next day. The emperor's trip between the palace and the temples was announced by court processional music; his arrival at or departure from the ritual sites was marked by processional and entertainment music. The citizens of Lin'an would watch the processions respectfully and with great interest. Following instructions from the authorities, they would neither climb up to high places to get a better view of the imperial entourage nor dress improperly so that their naked torsos or limbs would show.

By the time the emperor arrived at the grand ancestral temple, the route connecting the city to the round-mound altar complex in Lin'an's southern suburb had been physically transformed. Tightly guarded by soldiers and brilliantly illuminated by bonfires and torches, the route had been covered with a layer of sand spread smooth like a mat. Erected along the route were many temporary but elaborate tents, from which elite and privileged citizens would observe the passing of the imperial procession. Inside the tents they also entertained themselves and their guests with music and dancing. Outside the tents, merchants shuttled back and forth along the route, competing to sell their products and services; many would attract customers with musical calls. The festive activities along the ritual route would go on until the fifth night watch, when all of the lights were extinguished and a cleaning of the route began. At dawn, the emperor would leave the grand ancestral temple for the round-mound altar complex, traveling in his jade chariot and accompanied by a large entourage of guards, palace servants, musicians, and dancers. Escorted by auspicious, exotic elephants, the imperial entourage traveled in coordinated formations. Each group featured its own singers and instrumentalists performing processional or entertainment music. According to Zhou Mi, the entourage employed a total of 913 musicians.

When the emperor reached the round-mound altar compound, he would rest momentarily and then ritually prepare himself for the performance on the altar proper. When the specified hour for the ritual offering approached, the emperor, who had donned his ceremonial regalia, would ascend to the top level of the four-story altar proper. There he presented his offerings of silk, jade, and wine to the deities and deified ancestors amid state sacrificial music, which was played as either *elevated songs* (*dengge*) or *grand music* (*gongjia*). The elevated songs were performed on the altar proper by a choir of 8 men and 41 musicians in an orchestra that made use of 21 kinds of historical instruments; in the courtyard facing the altar proper, the grand music was performed by a choir of 32 men and 174 musicians playing in an orchestra that likewise used 21 kinds of musical instruments.[17] The elevated songs accompanied the emperor's offerings of silk, jade, the first wine, and all of the ritual actions that he personally performed on the altar proper. Grand music accompanied all the emperor's movements approaching and leaving the altar proper, the second and third offerings of wine, and all other transitional actions performed by the ritual staff. The alternations between elevated songs and grand music created unmistakable shifts of timbre, dynamics, and texture that sonically marked the unfolding of the state sacrifice.

By the time state sacrificial music was performed, Zhou Mi noted, tens of thousands of ritual observers had filled the inside and outside of the gigantic round-mound altar complex. As they silently listened to the stylized and distinctive sounds of the ritual music delivered by the breeze, they engaged with their rulers and deities. As Zhou claimed, they responded to the celestial tones played with bell chimes and stone chimes as music coming from the Ninth Heaven, the highest and most sacred part of the cosmos.

As the offering ceremony concluded, the emperor promptly left the altar proper and moved to a nearby audition hall, where he met his officials and accepted their congratulations for a successful ritual performance. Then he left for the palace amid processional music of drums and wind instruments. As soon as he passed through the south entrance of the palace city, he was greeted by performers playing entertainment music. He would then rest for a while and then appear on the observation terrace of the gate. There he would grant amnesty to a group of offenders whom officials had gathered for the occasion. On an auspicious day soon after the amnesty, the emperor would visit the temple of spectacular numina and the Daoist shrine of Taiyi. There he would ritually thank the imperial ancestors and Daoist deities for his successful performance of the state sacrifice. As he left the shrine, he would be greeted by joyous and entertaining sounds performed by court musicians, who would escort him back to the palace. That music and ritual procession publicly concluded the long sequence of musical and ritual activities of the state sacrifice to heaven, earth and the founders.

During the extended ritual period when Southern Song elite and commoners worked together as a musical community, they used different types and genres of sacred and secular music to mark their roles, positions, and the occasions. It was a cultural performance and a social-political negotiation that depended on the participants' thorough familiarity with the diverse types of music. It was an understanding that Southern Song labeling of musical genres and subgenres attests.

Zhou Mi's list of banquet music performed at imperial birthday celebrations, for example, illustrates how the Southern Song court categorized its ritual and entertainment music according to musical instruments and performance practices.[18] At these celebrations the first of three long sequences of toasts and musical entertainments, for instance, began with preludes played, in this order, with the oboe (*bili*), the flute (*di*), the mouth organ (*sheng*), and the steel chimes (*fangxiang*). The same sequence ended with an orchestral performance by all the musical instruments assembled for the banquets.

The elaborate use of diverse and distinctive musical sounds and instruments that Zhou has described was probably an imperial monopoly. Its aesthetics of manipulating stylized and distinctive music as meaningful sounds and expressions, however, applied to music performed outside the palace. Witness the music making at the lantern festival that both Lin'an elite and commoners celebrated on the fifteenth night after the lunar new year.[19] On that night, female palace musicians inside the royal residence would perform new compositions, and young palace eunuchs would dress up as commoners performing instrumental music and puppet shows. In addition, commoner musicians previously selected by city officials would be sent inside the palace to perform vernacular music. Outside the palace, Lin'an citizens entertained themselves with a variety of music and dances. Echoing performances inside the palace, numerous troupes of musicians and dancers would frolic throughout the city; their dances and flute and drum music would keep everyone's ears and eyes busy, Jiang Kui (1155–1221), the leading poet and composer of Southern Song noted.[20]

The citizens of Lin'an discerningly created and manipulated a diversity of vernacular music, all labeled specifically and revealingly. Zhou Mi's catalogue of such genres includes rhythmic and dramatic singing (*changzhuan*), simple singing (*xiaochang*), drums and clappers (*guban*), romantic ballads with lute accompaniment (*tanchang yinyuan*), capital songs (*jingci*), medley songs in different modes (*zhugongdiao*), short tunes (*chang xiaoling*), endless lute music (*bo buduan*), chanting and calling (*yinjiao*), and mouth organ ensembles (*hesheng*).[21]

Nei Deweng, another well-known observer of Lin'an life, gave similar labels to the music of the period, all reflecting sophisticated sensitivity to and understanding of musical sounds, styles, and performance practices.[22] Entertainment music and musicians of the time, Nei noted, were divided into thirteen branches, which included the following groups: oboes, hourglass drums, twirling dances, dramas, and comedies. The differences among the types were clearly noted. Small ensemble music, Nei explained, was performed with melodic instruments like flutes, oboes, mouth organs, fiddles (*xiqin*), and the steel chimes. The music of small ensembles sharply contrasted with the grand orchestral music because the latter featured the playing of big drums, hourglass drums, barrel drums (*jiegu*), shawns (*touguan*), lutes (*pipa*), and zithers (*zheng*). Small-ensemble music also differed from instrumental duets, trios, or other simple combinations of melody instruments like flutes and lutes with percussion instruments such as drums and clappers. Vocal genres were similarly differentiated; small and slow songs with clapper accompaniment contrasted with peddlers' songs, modal and ornamented songs with drum accompaniment, and rhythmic and dramatic song suites.

The Lin'an soundscape thus outlined has unfortunately vanished with the passing of time. The few extant musical scores and the relative abundance of textual descriptions of their distinctive timbres and performances nevertheless make it clear that Lin'an citizens would hardly confuse one music genre or style with another. For example, Zhang Kui's *ci* songs, which he composed for private performances by courtesans, with simple accompaniment by flutes and lutes cannot be stylistically more different from state sacrificial songs. His "Yangzhouman" [Song of Yangzhou] of 1176, for example, would have neither the metal and jade sounds of state sacrificial music nor its syllabic and angular melodic phrases sung by a male chorus. Its intimate expressions could hardly be performed loudly and rhythmically like martial or processional music.

> In this most famed city of the south of the Huai,
> At Bamboo–West Pavilion, a beautiful place,
> I unstrap the saddle for a brief halt at the first stage.
> Through ten miles in the spring wind,
> There is nothing but green shepherd's purse and wheat.
> Since Tartar horses left from spying on the Yangzi,
> Abandoned ponds and lofty trees
> Still detest talk of war.
> Gradually it becomes twilight,
> A clear horn blows out of the cold,
> In the empty city.
> Du Mu, the eminent connoisseur,
> Were he to return today, could not fail to be astonished.

Though his poem on the cardamom was skillful
And his dream at the blue mansion was lovely,
He would find it hard to express these deep feelings.
His Twenty-four Bridges still exist,
Waves stir at midstream—the cold moon makes no sounds.
I pity the peonies beside the bride,
For whom do they grow year after year?

Example 16.2. Jiang Kui's "Yangzhouman" [Song of Yangzhou]. (The music is a transcription from Song notation by Yang Yinliu and Yin Falu; see their *Song Jiang Baishi daoren chuangzuo gequ yanjiu* [A Study of the Creative Songs of Jiang Baishi of the Southern Song] [Beijing: Yinyue chubanshe, 1957], 49–50. The English translation of the lyrics is by Lin Shuen-fu, *The Transformation of the Chinese Lyrical Tradition*, 72–73.)

Ci and other popular songs performed by courtesans are noted for their exquisite expressions of intimate desires and emotions, which Lin'an citizens obviously cherished alongside their patriotism, ethnic pride, and other imperial and Confucian aspirations. Zhang Xiaoxiang (1132–1170), one of the most multitalented scholar-officials at Gaozong's court, for example, was simultaneously a dedicated lyricist of state sacrificial music and a poet of secular and romantic *ci* songs. His poem describing a zither-playing courtesan and her emotions reveals an unmistakable understanding of musical sounds, repertories, and meanings:

> Delicate fingers made up like red jade,
> Playing new tunes on the thirteen-stringed zither.
> Once plucked, the clear sounds of the instrument go up
>   through the clouds,
> Making the moonlit sky more blue.
> Quickly, the music chirps like bird songs,
> but holds expressions like Zhaojun's female lament.
> Don't play such meaningful sounds again;
> She is already leaning on the railing heavy with melancholy.[23]

STATE SACRIFICIAL MUSIC AND ITS DISCOURSE WITH THE SYLLABIC STYLE

Being musically informed and experienced, Lin'an citizens could shape their music, sacred or secular, in all the styles and genres that they knew or could imagine. Thus, we might well ask ourselves why the elite of the Southern Song chose the ascetic syllabic style for their state sacrificial music. The syllabic style, which obviously contrasted with all other musical sounds and styles of the time, could not have been the result of musical naïveté or lack of musical creativity.[24] The style was clearly a historical and cultural product and practice shaped not only by a court tradition of state sacrifices and state sacrificial music but by also Confucian music aesthetics as well.

The style and its use by the Southern Song elite also constituted a musical and creative discourse, one that the citizens of Lin'an could promptly engage for obvious reasons. The stylized sounds of Southern Song state sacrificial music played at imperial altars and inside shrines and with bell chimes, stone chimes, and other historical instruments were strategically distinctive. It ideologically emulated ancient music in the syllabic style; it featured vocal and instrumental sounds that contemporary musicians in Lin'an could hardly imitate with their limited and selective use of vocalists and popular musical instruments; its sonic asceticism was imperially guarded—unsanctioned imitations of state sacrificial music would be promptly censored. The citizens of Lin'an would hardly use the syllabic, angular, and short musical phrases of state sacrificial music to entertain themselves during private and public banquets or entertainment activities.

When Lin'an citizens listened to state sacrificial music in the syllabic style, they encountered a forceful sonic embodiment of the imperial and the Confucian. Unless the citizens were deaf or culturally and socially ignorant, they could not help but respond to the messages so forcefully delivered. And as soon as they responded, they found themselves locked in a musically defined site/situation that required them to either accept or reject the musical expressions of Confucian civility and Han ethnicity. Furthermore, when they negotiated their acceptance or rejection with other listeners right then and there, they not only interacted with one another but also activated webs of sonic and nonsonic references involving the music and its practices, launching a dynamic process of negotiation from contrasting roles and perspectives.

This process could continue long after the actual sounds of the music had ceased. How the performers and audience responded to and interpreted the music reflected who they were or wanted to be and affected the way they interrelated with other listeners. Imagine how a patriotic Southern Song general would react to "Welcoming the Deities"—he would not hear the music the way a political delegate representing the Jin empire would. Or imagine how a refugee from Kaifeng would compare what he heard with what he had experienced in the former capital. In other words, when Southern Song citizens compared, contrasted, and negotiated their personalized and diverse hearing of state sacrificial music with other listeners, they engaged in an interpretive and interactive discourse that allowed them to assert their social-political identities, agendas, and interrelationships. The nexus of the discourses was, needless to say, the distinctive syllabic style and the audience's recognition of it.

The discourse was dynamic because much depended on not only the social-political roles the audience played in their society but also how much they knew of their Han and non-Han culture and history. Commoners, especially those who were not familiar with Han and imperial practices codified by Confucian classics, would have simply submitted to the grandiosity of the music performance and its distinctive sonorities. Some might even have found ways to mimic the imperially controlled music as far as they were socially allowed to do so. Others might also have manipulated their experience with the music into some kind of social and cultural capital that could advance their needs.

Responses and manipulations by the Southern Song elite, especially those who were familiar with the Confucian classics and dynastic histories, would be more nuanced and complex. The more they knew about the music and its web of sonic and nonsonic references, the more they would have been able to connect and interpret, as well as to negotiate creatively and authoritatively. Upon hearing "Welcoming the Deities," for example, Southern Song elite would have promptly realized that the work emulated Zhou dynasty (1066BCE–221BCE) state sacrifices and state sacrificial music, verbal descriptions of which they studied well. They understood that the lyrics of "Welcoming the Deities" were written in the literary style and with the poetic-ritual vocabulary of Zhou court odes, preserved in the *Classic of Songs*. They would have remembered that heaven's mandate, the imperial ancestors' legacies, and the bell chimes and stone chimes were topics of classical songs that they had sung as students in the national university or other similar academies. For example, song number 271 from the *Classic of Songs* describes how King Cheng, a founder of the Zhou dynasty, strived to keep heaven's mandate and build his empire:[25]

> Heaven made its determinate appointment,
> Which [our] two sovereigns received.
> King Cheng did not dare to rest idly in it,
> But night and day enlarged its foundations by his deep and silent virtue.
> How did he continue and glorify [heaven's mandate]?
> Exerting all his heart,
> And so securing its tranquility?

Song number 280 describes how the Zhou court employed state sacrificial music to assert its legitimacy and authority:[26]

> Blind men, blind men,
> In the courtyard of Zhou.
>   They hung bells and chimes,
> On wooden frames with upright wedges and feather decorations.
> They lined up drums, large and small,
>   And tambourines, wooden-box resonator, and tiger-scraper.
> With panpipes and flutes, they made reverberating tunes;
> Solemn and harmonious, the music was.
> Our Zhou ancestors listened;
> And their heavenly guests came.
> The music ended, and we did not notice the passing of time.

The elite of the Southern Song who were familiar with their recent history would also have promptly seen how the syllabic style embodied recent theories and attempts to revive ancient and civilized music, such as those advocated by Hu Yuan (993–1059), Yang Jie (fl. 1080s), Zhu Xi (1130–1200), and other cultural and political leaders. Southern Song audiences who had studied musical instruments would have known what they individually signified. Cosmological association between sounds and non-sounds and between musical instruments and cultural myths are copiously registered in encyclopedic music treatises of the time, such as the *Music Treatise* (*Yueshu*) that Chen Yang presented to the court in 1104.[27] In his treatise, Chen argued that among the cosmic manifestations of *yin* elements, such as the female and the westerly direction, there was nothing more purely *yin* than gold/metal; as bell chimes were cast with gold/metal, they made the most *yin* sounds and expressions. Among the cosmic manifestations of *yang* elements, such as the male and the northerly direction, there was nothing more *yang* than jade, Chen declared, and that was why the jade sounds of the stone chimes could represent and activate the *yang* elements.

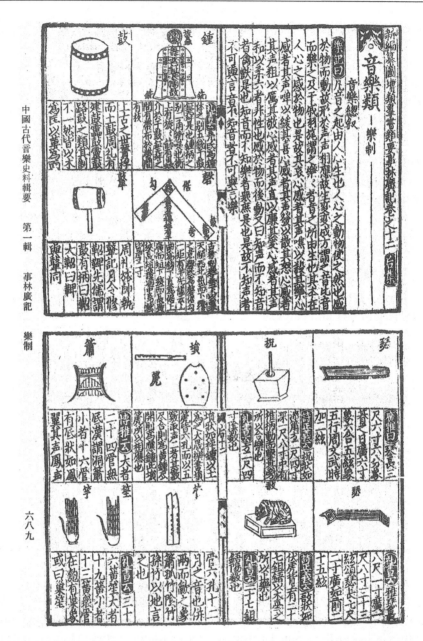

Figure 16.2. Musical instruments, as illustrated in a Southern Song encyclopedia. Chen Yuanjing, *Shilin guangji* (a comprehensive record of the forest of affairs; ca. 1270), in *Zhongguo gudai yinyue shiliao jiyao* (a compendium of sources of historical Chinese music) (Beijing: Zhonghua shuji, 1962), *houji* 12.7. From top to bottom and from left to right the musical instruments are drum, single bell, handheld drum, single stone chime, panpipe, flute and ocarina, wooden crate, *qin* [string zither], two kinds of mouth organs, oboes, wooden tiger scraper, and twenty-five-string zithers.

To echo with heaven's employment of the *yin* and *yang* in the human world, Chen noted, the court played metal and jade instruments to make music that honored heaven and the deified ancestors. Listening to "Welcoming the Deities" with reference to Chen's or other similar prescriptions, the Southern Song elite would have believed that the music harmoniously activated the *yin* and *yang* elements in their world (figure 16.2).

Associating, interpreting, and negotiating musical sounds with reference to historical facts and cultural myths constitutes dialectic, a process that allows individual Southern Song scholars to debate and assert their individual elite male voices. A case in point is Zhu Xi's discussion of the *Twelve Ritual Songs* as an exemplar of the syllabic style.[28] Zhu, the dean of neo-Confucianism, openly questioned the authenticity of the songs as music from eighth-century China. To register his skepticism and to stimulate further discussions, Zhu recorded the notation of the songs and raised three points. First, the musical source of the twelve ritual songs and their functions were unclear; second, ancient singers did not always sing syllabically; third, the use of octaves in the songs was historically suspect. Zhu's second point is historically verifiable as there are many records that ancient Chinese singers embellished their performances with ornamental tones and repeated notes.

Zhu was not historically noted as a musical gentleman, a fact that can serve as a yardstick of the Southern Song elite's musical familiarity with the syllabic style. If Zhu Xi, one could argue, understood so much about the style, musically informed and talented scholar-officials of the time would have had no difficulty noticing all kinds of unique stylistic details in state sacrificial music and comprehending their significance. Indeed, with analytical listening, one could promptly grasp the cerebral but functional musical creativity the style embodies. By noticing the shifts in modal tones and orchestral timbres in these musical performances, for example, one could closely follow the ritual progression of the state sacrifices. In addition, should one realize that modal changes in the music followed classical prescriptions, one would have promptly perceived how Gaozong had manipulated a glorified past to authenticate his struggling present. "Welcoming the Deities," for example, follows model prescriptions registered in the *Ritual of Zhou (Zhouli)*,[29] a seminal document on Zhou dynasty state sacrifices and state sacrificial music; it declares that music for welcoming heavenly deities should feature the mode of *jiazhong* ($<e^b>$) as *gong* ($<do>$) in its first variation; the mode of *huangzhong* ($<c>$) as *jue* ($<mi>$) in its second variation; the mode of *taicou* ($<d>$) as *zhi* ($<sol>$) in its third variation; and the *guxien* ($<e>$) as *yu* ($<la>$) in its fourth variation.[30] Gaozong's subscription to Zhou modal prescriptions connected him with an idealized and authenticated past.

If the modal variations in "Welcoming the Deities" are literal variations, they are nothing more than pedantic exercises. The four modal variations of the song are, however, not literal transpositions; each shows some structural and modal adjustments. Pitches have been altered to fit the limited range of a minor tenth (*c* to e^b), which is available on bell chimes and stone chimes. The use of the lower $<c^\#>$ in the first measure of the fourth variation is, for example, an octave displacement; it changes the original contour of the melody. Further analysis would show that each of the variations manifests consistent structural and modal attributes, such as cadencing on designated finals (e.g., the *gong* tone in the *jiazhong* [<e^b>] as *gong* mode).

The melodic phrases in the variations do not integrate into long, smooth tunes. The effect is deliberate and reflects classical notions of melodic shapes and vocal contours. As specified by the *Record of Music* (*Yueji*),[31] there are seven types of melodic contours: (1) going up straight (*juzhong ju*); (2) shaped like a hook (*juzhong gou*); (3) smooth like a string of pearls (*duan ru guanzhu*); (4) falling down fast (*xiaru zhui*); (5) folded and twisted (*quruzhe*); (6) starting from high and going down (*shangrukang*); and (7) stopping like a hibernating tree (*zhiru gaomu*). The first variation of "Welcoming the Deities" evokes the following (in order of occurrence): measure 1, folded and twisted; measure 2, starting from high up; measure 3, shaped like a hook; measure 4, folded and twisted; measure 5, folded and twisted; measure 6, shaped like a hook; measure 7, going up straight; and measure 8, smooth like a string of pearls or stopping like a hibernating tree.

SOUTHERN SONG STATE SACRIFICIAL MUSIC AS PERSONAL DISCOURSE

If the aforementioned stylistic features of "Welcoming the Deities" embodied imperial and Confucian messages, they could be strategically manipulated. In fact, every time state sacrificial music was performed, it acquired and projected newly contextualized or recontextualized meanings, a dynamic process that can be illustrated with a short review of Southern Song state sacrificial music history. As Gaozong ascended to the Song throne in 1127, he knew that performances of state sacrificial music honoring heaven, earth, and the founders would not only sonically mark the legitimacy of his emperorship but also project a sense of stability to his government in exile—growing up a prince and a music connoisseur, he knew how to enjoy and manipulate music, sacred or secular.[32] He chose not to have state sacrificial music performed in the first year of his long reign. Explaining his decision, he issued an edict to his court that any musical performance during that difficult time would only negatively affect his efforts to protect and provide for the empire. In the following year, 1128, however, he ordered a simplified performance.

It was still war time, and Gaozong's government in exile was in Yangzhou, where no round-mound altar had been built. Bell chimes, stone chimes, and other ancient musical instruments needed for a proper performance were also missing. Thus, Gaozong had a temporary altar built and sanctioned the use of military drums and gongs to accompany the singing of his state sacrificial songs. The music performed and heard there and then was, needless to say, atypical. Listening and responding to the music, Gaozong and the other audience members found themselves framed in an atypical soundscape in which they had to plan for their survival. If some accepted

Gaozong as their legitimate ruler and military leader, they also realized that their political and military future was precarious at best. As the music evoked personal and collective memories of the Northern Song and its grand performances of ritual and music,[33] it sharply contrasted the resplendent past with the tragic present. Touching their historically and biographically contextualized hearts, the music propelled the participants to confront the reality at hand. If many became more determined to fight against the Jurchens, some probably saw the situation as hopeless and wondered whether submission to the Jurchens was more practical. Was Gaozong one of the defeatists?

Fifteen years passed before Gaozong was able to have a proper performance of the state sacrifice to heaven, earth, and the founders. Premiered in 1143, the new ceremonial included twenty-three new ritual songs, the second of which was "Welcoming the Deities." Gaozong's new state sacrifice and ritual music marked a critical military-political turning point. In 1141, Gaozong signed a lasting peace treaty with the Jurchens. In the fifteen years between 1128 and 1143, Gaozong's officials engaged in many rounds of debates and made numerous revisions of court ritual and music. These included prescribing musical modes for specific types of court processional music and standardizing the numbers and types of musical instruments to be used in the ceremonials.[34] To prepare for the performance in 1143, a new round-mound altar was built in the south suburb of Lin'an, and liturgical and musical programs were comprehensively designed. When the state sacrifice took place, it constituted a grand political statement: A new and stable government was finally in place. Any witness of the ritual and musical performance, especially those who witnessed it up close, would sonically encounter Gaozong's claim of legitimacy and normalcy for his empire. Anyone who had experienced the atypical performance in 1128 knew how much progress (or return to Han civility) the Southern Song court had achieved. Needless to say, not all who attended agreed with Gaozong's rosy projection.

Many scholar-officials loyal to Gaozong responded by writing literary poems and essays to commemorate the event and to congratulate the emperor. Some would, however, urge the emperor to do more by proposing further revisions.[35] In fact, many adjustments, simple or substantive, followed. In 1144, the court adjusted the pitches of the stone chimes used for state sacrificial music and redesigned dance props to match classical prescriptions. In 1146, the court had the grand and single bell (*jingzhong*) cast and installed in the center courtyard of the round-mound altar complex. If the grand bell rendered the ritual sounds performed there and then more unique, it further underlined the cultural ideologies and political agendas being negotiated.[36] The clear and far-reaching sound of the bell, which was tuned to *huangzhong* (<c>), the primordial tone of the twelve standard pitches, signified the progenitor of music, which correlated with heaven, the progenitor of all animate and inanimate entities in the cosmos. When the grand bell was struck to announce the beginning of the ritual performance at the round-mound altar complex, the Southern Song court believed, its sonorous and far-reaching sounds would activate cosmic *qi* (ether) and escort heaven and other deities to the ritual compound to receive the offerings that Gaozong had prepared. The deities' presence at the altar and acceptance of the offerings signified their approval of Gaozong and his Southern Song empire.

That political agenda was inscribed on the grand bell as a set consisting of a commemorative prelude and a poem written by Qin Kui (1090–1155), the most prominent official of the time. It declared that by having the bell cast, Gaozong had found a way to communicate with the deities and leave an everlasting legacy to his descendents.[37] Gaozong clearly wanted to project himself as an effective and benevolent emperor, a fact that his poem at the 1149 performance of the state sacrifice attests. In translation, the poem declares the following:[38]

> Respectfully I visited the pure round-mound altar to perform the state
>   sacrifice to heaven, earth, and founders.
> My able ministers diligently assisted me, and their sincerity showed.
> Just before the performance, low and dense clouds covered the sky and
>   I worried;
> Then I looked up and found the sky clear as the clouds had drifted away.
> Qi returned to the sacrificial offerings prepared by many ritual staff,
>   signifying the deities' acceptance;
> Then the altar was filled with happiness—banners of the thousands of
>   officers fluttered, and their horses neighed vigorously.
> The brilliant and grand deities clearly heard our appeal.
> United by the same aspirations, we rely on their grace to run the empire.

Gaozong's poem highlighted natural and supernatural signs and communications; it hardly described ritual and musical details that his scholar-officials comprehensively detailed in their commemorative poems and essays. Zhou Linzhi (1118–1164), a literary-ritual-musical expert of Gaozong's court, for example, responded to the ritual and the music performance in 1149 or 1152 as follows:[39] Activated by musical sounds, the cosmic qi circled around the grand imperial altar; the exquisite tunes played by the grand orchestra welcomed and honored the deities, who descended to the ritual site; the sonorous sounds of the music playing on bell chimes, stone chimes, and other ancient musical instruments accompanied the emperor's ritual actions; he requested and received supernatural grace to implement his mandate to rule China and develop the empire.

More than a literary report of what the author witnessed, Zhou's poem also strategically negotiated his relationship with the emperor. A critical phrase in his poem brings music, filial piety, and court practices of worshipping deified founders together to make a powerful argument. Literarily incandescent and persuasive—stylistic elements and effects that cannot be translated here, the phrase literally says: "Filial performance of the music efficaciously reaches the deities and deified imperial ancestors." By describing Gaozong's music as "filial," Zhou asserted that Gaozong was a filial and thus benevolent ruler whose ritual actions guided his people and earned the gods' protection of the empire. By projecting Gaozong as an exemplary ruler, Zhou justified and projected his loyalty to the ruler.

By the end of Gaozong's reign in 1163, state sacrifices and state sacrificial music had become comprehensively established Southern Song institutions. This does not mean that they ceased to express and catalyze particularized negotiations. In 1161, Jin attacked Southern Song, and the military action ended with a new peace treaty signed in 1164. In the process, Gaozong retired and passed the throne to his adopted son, Xiaozong (1127–1194; reigned 1163–1189). Gaozong, however, became a retired emperor who nevertheless actively influenced court politics until his death in 1187. Relieved from overseeing daily operations of the empire, Gaozong found time and energy to entertain himself with many imperial banquets and grand musical entertainments. His retirement home, the Palace of Virtues and Longevity (Deshou gong), thus became a center of Southern Song court and secular music.

Such music was a luxury that Xiaozong could not afford. To please the retired but still powerful Gaozong, Xiaozong provided whatever his adoptive father wanted. Xiaozong's exercise of filial piety was costly, and it consumed much of his ritualmusical resources and energy. In the late 1160s, he faced a financially strapped postwar empire; to make ends meet, he had state sacrificial music performed with fewer musicians and fewer rehearsals. The result was, one can imagine, a change in the sonic qualities of the music and musical performance. Informed Lin'an citizens of the time would have had little difficulty hearing Xiaozong's ritual and music as a politically and financially strapped emperor's economy voice. Its "reduced" sounds would, however, have rendered his father's musical tunes grander and more imperial.

In 1189, Xiaozong passed the Southern Song throne to his son, Guangzong (1147–1200; reigned 1189–1194). His reign was wrecked by his family problems and by a political dispute over the choice of his crown prince apparent. Besides granting a court appeal to repair musical instruments and to increase rehearsal time, Guangzong left few imprints on the musical and political discourse of his time. His empress, however, made a move that underscored what liminal time and site state sacrifices and state sacrificial music could generate. In 1191, she had Guangzong's favorite imperial concubine killed when he left the palace to officiate at a preparatory ceremony in the grand ancestral temple. When Guangzong received news of his favorite concubine's sudden death, he was stunned, but as a son of heaven, he could not rush back to the palace. He had to move on to the round-mound altar complex and present offerings to the deities amid "heavenly" sounds of bell chimes and stone chimes. His performance was cut short by a storm that blew out all of the torches and other lights at the ritual site, rendering it a disaster area, a fact that invited all manner of interpretations. After the incident, Guangzong became mentally unstable. In 1194, he refused to officiate at the state funeral for his deceased father, Xiaozong, and was forced to abdicate to his son, Ningzong (1168–1224; reigned 1194–1224).

Ningzong ruled Southern Song for thirty years (1194–1224), a reign that was marked by an ill-planned attempt to fight the Jurchens (1206–1207). The effort ended with another humiliating peace treaty. Before the military action, Ningzong and his court attempted to invigorate the declining empire with a new version of state sacrifice to heaven, earth, and the founders.[40] Ningzong's successor was Lizong

(1205–1264; reigned 1225–1264), a negligent emperor who performed the state sacrifice to heaven, earth, and the founders only once during his reign of thiry-nine years. Under his watch, the Southern Song empire further deteriorated. The last Southern Song emperor was Duzong (1240–1274; reigned 1264–1274), who marked the beginning of his reign with a performance of the state sacrifice to heaven, earth, and the founders in 1266. Its elaborate performance and distinctive sounds created only sonic illusions. In 1279, the Southern Song dynasty formally ended with the Mongols' invasion of Han China.

Concluding Remarks

Duzong's 1266 performance nevertheless made a great impression on his subjects. Zhou Mi wrote a cycle of twenty poems to commemorate the event, projecting his Han and patriotic dreams.[41] Poem number five of the cycle specifically alluded to the elevated songs performed for the state sacrifice:

> Harmonious *qi* came at midnight, chasing coldness away and bringing
>   warmth;
> Stars in the sky made auspicious signs, brightly illuminating the altar.
> Thousands of officials attended in their full official regalia, holding their
>   jade permits and smelling the fragrance of sacrificial offerings;
> Quietly, they listened to the state sacrificial music, a performance of six
>   elevated songs.

Zhou referred to the elevated songs because they were stylistically distinctive and contrasted with other music performed during the ritual period: the processional music that accompanied the emperor's entourage, musical calls of the security guards checking the ritual sites, sonorous and far-reaching sounds of the grand bell, festive performances of entertainment music at the conclusion of the ceremonial, and so forth. Like other Lin'an citizens, Zhou heard the different types of music, recognized their stylized and distinctive sounds, and understood and manipulated their messages to negotiate an imperial and social agenda of the time: revive the dying empire! The beginning of Duzong's new reign, they wanted to believe, would give them a chance to reinvigorate and defend themselves against the invading Mongols. The syllabic tones of Duzong's state sacrificial music sounded their hope but gave them no military help.

When Zhou Mi, Wu Zimu, and other Southern Song historians nostalgically described Southern Song state sacrificial music in Yuan China (1279–1368), praising its sounds as the most beautiful and perfect expressions of their Confucian and imperial world, they manipulated their musical memories to lament the "barbaric" life that they led under Mongol rule. As they expressed their grief, they reiterated questions that they had debated for decades. Why did the Southern

Song fail to reclaim the north? Why did their civilized world collapse? Did they indulge too much with festive, entertaining music? There was and is no easy answer. There is, however, no denying that music was both an expression and a catalyst of cultural and political living in Southern Song China. With a simple quatrain, Lin Sheng (1163–1189) poetically encapsulated the observations and arguments of many Southern Song citizens with regard to music and their cultural-political repotiations:[42]

> Hills beyond hills, and mansions beyond mansions,
> Singing and dancing by the West Lake—when will they ever end?
> The warm breeze envelops revelers till they are drunk,
> Simply taking Hangzhou as the capital Bianzhou!

NOTES

Written for music and general readers, this chapter presents a minimum of historical and cultural facts about Song China and its historical sources and cites current studies in English when available. For a general history of Song China, see John King Fairbank and Merle Goldman, *China: A New History*, enlarged ed. (Cambridge, Mass.: Belknap, 1998), 88–127. For a comprehensive reference on Song historical documents, see Etienne Balazs, *A Sung Bibliography* (Hong Kong: Chinese University of Hong Kong, 1978).

1. *Songshi* [*Song History*], ed. Tuo Tuo (1345; Beijing: Zhonghua shuju, 1977), 130.3031.

2. China was and still is a multiethnic nation, with Han Chinese as the majority group.

3. This chapter refers to Song emperors by their posthumous titles, a traditional practice. Huizong's (1082–1135) personal name is Zhao Ji, and Qinzong's (1100–1161), Zhao Huan.

4. Gaozong (Zhao Gou, 1107–1187) was Huizong's ninth son.

5. The most commonly used Chinese nomenclature for the ceremonial is *jiaoji* (suburban sacrifice), which does not specifically name the deities that received the ritual honors. To underscore the identities of the main deities the Southern Song ritual honored, the ritual is labeled as a "state sacrifice to heaven, earth, and the founders." The ritual also honored a pantheon of secondary deities and deified figures as "companions" of heaven, earth, and the founders. The two dynastic founders honored were the first and second emperors of the Northern Song: Taizu (Zhao Kuangyin, 927–976; reigned 960–975) and Taizong (Zhao Kuangyi, 939–997; reigned 976–997). If the 35 songs performed during the two preparatory ceremonies of the ritual are counted, the state sacrifice includes a total of 58 ritual songs.

6. For a general introduction to Chinese musical instruments, see Alan Thrasher, *Chinese Musical Instruments* (New York: Oxford University Press, 2000).

7. For English descriptions of Chinese state sacrifices, see Howard J. Wechsler, *Offerings of Jade and Silk: Ritual and Symbol in the Legitimation of the T'ang Dynasty* (New Haven: Yale University Press, 1985), and Joseph S. C. Lam, *State Sacrifices and Music in Ming*

China (A.D. 1368–1644): Creativity, Orthodoxy, and Expressiveness (Albany: State University of New York Press, 1998).

8. For an English summary of Confucian theories of music, see Joseph S. C. Lam, "Musical Confucianism: The Case of 'Jikong yuewu' " in *On Sacred Grounds: Culture, Society, Politics, and the Formation of the Cult of Confucius*, ed. Thomas Wilson, 134–72, and in particular 145–48 (Cambridge, Mass.: Harvard University Press, 2002).

9. For a brief but standard discussion of heaven and its mandate, see Fung Yu-lan, *A History of Chinese Philosophy*, vol. 1, first paperback printing (Princeton: Princeton University Press, 1983), 30–31.

10. *Xiaojing*, in *Baihua shisanjing fu yuanwen* [*The Thirteen Classics in Contemporary Prose*, with original text], ed. Qian Bocheng, vol. 3, 2693–2701 (Beijing: Xinhua shudian, 1996).

11. For a standard reference on Southern Song political and cultural history, see James T. C. Liu, *China Turning Inward: Intellectual-political Changes in the Early Twelfth Century* (Cambridge, Mass.: Harvard University Press, 1988). See also He Zhongli and Xu Jijun, *NanSong shigao* (a draft history of the Southern Song) (Hangzhou: Hangzhou daxue chubanshe, 1999).

12. For a social and intellectual history of Southern Song China, see Linda A. Walton, *Academies and Society in Southern Sung China* (Honolulu: University of Hawai'i Press, 1999). For a standard reference on Southern Song *ci* poetry, see Shuen-fu Lin, *The Transformation of the Chinese Lyrical Tradition* (Princeton: Princeton University Press, 1978).

13. There is no definitive figure for the population of Lin'an, which clearly expanded during the course of the Southern Song empire. Half a million is a relatively conservative figure for the 1160s; by some accounts, the population of Lin'an exceeded a million by the 1260s. See Lin Zhengqiu, "Jingshi ju simin, renkou guan quanguo" [People Gathered in the Capital; Its Population Size Was Number One in the Empire], in *Nansong jingcheng Hangzhou* [*Hangzhou, the Southern Song Capital*], ed. Zhou Feng, 90–97 (Hangzhou: Zhejiang renmin chubanshe, 1997).

14. The map in figure 16.1 shows only the southern part of the city.

15. Zhou Mi, *Wulin jiushi* (Hangzhou: Zhejian renmin bubanshe, 1984), 92–95. For a study on cultural living in Song China, see Stephen West, "Playing with Food: Performance, Food, and the Aesthetics of Artificiality in the Sung and Yuan," *Harvard Journal of Asiatic Studies* 57(1) (1997): 67–106.

16. Zhou, *Wulin jiushi*, 6–10.

17. *Songshi*, 130.3031. The types of musical instruments used to accompany elevated songs or grand music appeared to be stable over the course of the empire. The exact number of singers or musicians playing specific types of musical instruments changed in different periods of the empire.

18. Zhou, *Wulin jiushi*, 13–17.

19. Zhou, *Wulin jiushi*, 29–32, and Wu Zimu, *Menglianglu* [Records of the Millet Dream], in *Dongjing menghua lu, wai sizhong* [Memoir of the Eastern Capital and Four Other Historical Resources] (ca. 1279; Beijing: Zhonghua shuju, 1962), 128–328.

20. For a musicological study of Jiang Kui, see Joseph S. C. Lam, "Writing Music Biographies of Historical Asian Musicians: The Case of Jiang Kui (A.D. 1155–1221), *World of Music* 43(1) (2001): 69–95.

21. Zhou, *Wulin jiushi*, 105–14.

22. Nei Deweng, *Ducheng jisheng* [A Record of Noteworthy Affairs in the Old Capital], in *Dongjing menghua lu, wai sizhong*, 89–110.

23. Zhang Xiaoxiang, *Yuhu jushi wenji* [*Collected Works of Zhang Xiaoxiang*], in *Sibu congkan* (Shanghai: Shangwu,1929), 34.340.

24. Between the 1950s and the late 1980s, musicologists in socialist China tended to discuss state sacrificial music in the syllabic style as music that lacked creativity and expression.

25. The translation of the song is from James Legge's *Chinese Classics*, available at http://etext.virginia.edu/chinese/shijing/AnoShih.html (accessed October 2010).

26. The English translation of the song is based on Cheng Junying's interpretation; see his *Shijing yizhu* [*The Classic of Songs*, translated and annotated] (Shanghai: Guji chubanshe, 1985), 634.

27. Chen Yang, *Yueshu*, *Siku quanshu* edition (1101; Taipei: Shangwu, 1979), 113.12b.

28. *Songshi*, 142.3340–41. See also Rulan Chao Pian, *Sonq Dynasty Musical Sources and Their Interpretation* (Cambridge, Mass.: Harvard University Press, 1967), 9–10, and 154–73, and Laurence Picken, "Twelve Ritual Melodies of the T'ang Dynasty," *Studia Memoriae Bela Bartok Sacra* (Budapest: Aedes Academiae Scientiarium Hungariae, 1956): 147–173.

29. Lin Yin annotated, *Zhouli jinzhu jinyi* [*The Rites of Zhou*, annotated and translated into contemporary Chinese] (Taipei: Taiwan shangwu yinshuju, 1972), 232.

30. In broad musical and conceptual terms, the Chinese twelve standard pitches (*shier lulü*) are comparable to the twelve Western pitches within an octave: *huangzhong* (<c>), *dalü* (<c#/d^b>), *taicou* (<d>), *jiazhong* (<d#/e^b>), *guxian* (<e>), *zhonglü* (<f>), *ruibin* (<f#/g^b>), *linzhong* (<g>), *yize* (<g#/a^b>), *nanlü* (<a>), *wuyi* (<a#/b^b>), and *yingzhong* (<b>). The Chinese labels for the heptatonic notes within an octave are also comparable to their Western counterparts: *gong* (*do*), *shang* (*re*), *jue* (*mi*), *bianzhi* (*fa*), *zhi* (*sol*), *yu* (*la*), and *biangong* (*ti*).

31. "Shiyi bian" [Music Master Yi], in *Baihua shisanjing fu yuanwen* [*The Thirteen Classics in Contemporary Prose*, with original text], ed. Qian Bocheng (Beijing: Xinhua shudian, 1996), vol. 1, 1267.

32. See Wang Zengyu, *Song Gaozong* (Changchun: Jilin wenshi chubanshe, 1996); see in particular 241–53.

33. For a discussion of Huizong's music, see Joseph S. C. Lam, "Huizong's *Dashengyue*: A Musical Performance of Emperorship and Officialdom," in *Huizong and the Culture of Northern Song China*, ed. Patricia Ebrey and Maggie Brickford, 395–452 (Cambridge, Mass.: Harvard University Press, 2006).

34. *Songshi*, 130.3030–3031.

35. *Songshi*, 130.3032.

36. *Zongxing lishu*, 13.2b–4b; *Songshi*, 130.3033.

37. *Songshi*, 130.3034. For an insightful study of Qin's biography, see Charles Hartman, "The Making of a Villain: Ch'in Kuei and *Tao-hsüeh*," *Harvard Journal of Asiatic Studies* 58(1) (June 1998): 59–146.

38. *Quan Songshi* [*A Comprehensive Collection of Song Poetry*], comp. Beijing daxue guwenxian yanjiusuo (Beijing: Beijing daxue chubanshe, 1998), vol. 35, 1982.22214.

39. Zhou Linzhi, "Jiaosi qingcheng," in *Quan Songshi*, vol. 38, 2087.23539–40.

40. *Songshi*, 132.3077–81. In 1197 or 1203 they produced and performed a new version with twenty-nine new ritual songs.

41. Zhou Mi, "Nanjiao qingcheng kouhao ershi shou, bing xu" [Twenty Chants for Commemorating a Successful Ritual Performance at the Round Mound Altar, with preface], in *Quan Songshi*, vol. 67, 3558.42522–24.

42. Trans. Lin Shuen-fu, "North and South: The Twelfth and Thirteen Centuries" In *Cambridge History of Chinese Literature, Volume 1: to 1375*, ed., Kang-I Sun Chang and Stephen Owen, 536. (Cambridge & New York: Cambridge University Press, 2010).

CHAPTER 17

ERNANI HATS: ITALIAN OPERA AS A REPERTOIRE OF POLITICAL SYMBOLS DURING THE RISORGIMENTO

CARLOTTA SORBA

1. OPERA, RISORGIMENTO, AND CULTURAL HISTORY

In 1954, film director Luchino Visconti had his first color movie, *Senso*, start with an operatic sequence that has since become iconic in the history of cinema. The encounter between the two main characters, patriotic aristocrat Livia Serpieri and the young Austrian lieutenant Franz Mahler takes place in the Fenice theater in Venice, where, during a performance of *Il Trovatore*, an anti-Austrian patriotic protest breaks out. Toward the end of the cabaletta "Di quella pira l'orrendo fuoco" [Of that pyre the horrid fire], when Manrico unsheathes his sword and shouts with the chorus, "All'armi, all'armi!" [To arms!], flyers with the colors of the Italian flag start falling from the loggione, while the patriots pin tricolor flowers and rosettes on their chests. The parallel between opera (especially Verdi's) and the Risorgimento, magisterially reenacted by the great Italian film director, was treated for a long time as a self-evident assumption that did not need to be filled with meanings, events, or specific references. It was embedded within a celebratory discourse on the unification process before the latter became the object of a thorough survey.

Only in the 1990s did this stereotyped image begin to be analyzed in the context of a more general effort to deconstruct the myth of the Risorgimento. Both historians and musicologists began asking questions about what political role the opera might have played in the Italian unification process and specifically in what ways it might have contributed to it. Historians began analyzing the different phases and modalities of what had been a pedagogical and celebratory construction of the myth of the Risorgimento, which was inscribed within a more complex process of cultural nation building.[1] On the other hand, some musicologists and sociologists went on to take apart and then reassemble the various pieces that made up the political mythology that had developed around the figure of Verdi as father of the nation, which had been so central to previous studies.[2] On both sides there was an attempt to unmask the construction of a public discourse centered around the Risorgimento as it had been shaped in the postunification era, with the aim of identifying the directions, shapes, and pace of its development. Can we include among the main outcomes the definite rejection of the image put forward by Visconti, which we should try to regard both as the product of postunification political "imagination" and as a skillful marketing operation around Verdi's iconic figure? Even if we assume that both elements have played a key role, thus helping to nurture a complex mythology especially around Giuseppe Verdi, they do not fully explain what kind of relationship arose between the Risorgimento movement and the world of the theater in the decades that preceded unification.

However, besides this timely and admirable work of deconstruction of the myth itself, within a historiographical context completely free of political rhetoric and more sensitive to the input from the international debate, there has been a renewed interest in the Risorgimento as a nationalist movement. This line of investigation, which has placed much attention on the emergence of the movement, on the dynamics of both the construction and expansion of national-patriotic discourses, and on its organizational, as well as symbolic, aspects, has strongly favored a cultural approach.[3] It is in this context that the role of music—and especially of opera—has found a new dimension in Risorgimento studies as new emphasis has been placed on its impact on the construction of a narrative stream that has strongly contributed to the definition of the very image of the nation. Although the debate as to the nature of the relationship between Verdi and politics has at times heated up among musicologists[4], more recent studies have led to a significant shift in the main questions and perspectives from which new investigations should move, simultaneously benefiting from the new approaches to the study of music that have been proposed internationally.

The main strands of investigation can be roughly traced along the following directions: (a) the opera house as a key place of sociability in Italy in the first half of the nineteenth century, while regarding the operatic system as a cultural circuit that quickly gained a national profile; (b) a zealous examination of the reception of texts and their margin of autonomy from the production process; (c) opera as a genre that played an active role in the construction and spreading of nationalist narratives, both on a discursive level (the narration of the country's history of oppression drew from the genre of melodrama, further developing its main constitutive elements[5]) and in the symbolic practices that emerged as the Risorgimento movement advanced. An important point of convergence between these last two perspectives can be identified in the key issue of the relationship between the public and the stage, which was then characterized by a constant interchange between reality and representation. Before the disciplining process became effective in the last decades of the century, the theater remained an open place that brought together a relatively uncontrolled audience and a stage, where the interpreter retained a certain leeway with respect to the original text. This space was usually outward looking, echoing strongly beyond the stage and fueling a public discourse that both preceded and followed theater performances in the towns. As we learn from contemporary newspaper accounts, in every lane, square, and coffeehouse, people talked about the opera being staged at the local theater.

If seen through these lenses, the relationship between romantic opera and the events that marked the Risorgimento period does not appear as linear and as one dimensional as in the traditional authorial approach, which tended instead toward tracing the composer's political intentionality. Nevertheless, it is by no means less pervasive or consistent. A variety of elements lead us to think both that opera was closely linked to the events that characterized the Risorgimento period in different and at times contradictory ways and that by looking at these connections it might be possible to shed light on key aspects of both the political and the cultural processes involved. Ultimately, one could say that the very development of the Italian national-patriotic movement was marked by melodramatic romantic opera, a theatrical genre that reached extraordinary popularity at the time since it addressed a broader public than either novels or poetry in spite of the complex and erudite language of the librettos.

Italian opera held a very peculiar status within a cultural market characterized by a poor level of literacy, as well as by the country's political and territorial fragmentation. Few contemporary Italian intellectuals seemed to fully understand its impact, while the majority continued to look contemptuously on the operatic genre as nothing more than a pastime. A few views from the period, however, offer illuminating observations that help us identify its role within the wider picture of early nineteenth-century cultural production. To begin with, let us consider the famous pamphlet *Filosofia della musica*, written in 1836 by Giuseppe Mazzini, who stated that in Italy the opera served a civic and political function attributed elsewhere to prose theater. According to the Genoese political agitator, opera should carry the people's hopes for a new "Italian art," which should merge "Byron's power" and "Schiller's active faith."[6] Ten years later, in 1846, critic Carlo Tenca, insider in and expert on the publishing industry, put forward an accurate critique of the poor conditions the Italian literary production faced at the time, moving from a comparison with opera, from which the literary world should learn. His words are harsh but free from academic prejudice and well informed about the international context. It is worthwhile analyzing a few passages.

According to Tenca, the main difference between the two worlds was the relationship with the public, or rather the ability that music theater had to create, attract, and move its audiences. Italian literati and literary critics should do the same:

> [P]lunge into the new, immense vortex of today's public, explore its inclinations, bring out that which secretly and indistinctly stirs at its core, and then shape it, direct it toward an end....It is difficult to explore the passions and inclinations of our society; however, we cannot entirely condemn the mob that, full of contempt for the world of letters which does not speak to it, tumultuously throws itself into the music theaters in search of easy excitement and the free effusion of joy and pain. In this harangue it sits jubilant, drawing pleasure from its triumphs and experiencing the fullness of life; here art embraces the whole sphere of sentiments, while a full harmony springs naturally between the artist and the mob.

One should not be surprised, he concludes, if "the multitude predilects this art before which it can throb and be moved to its own taste....Until literature is able to rise to the grandeur of public performances, music and dance will continue to attract universal attention.[7]"

Today we know that the difference between the world of literature and the world of music was partly structural: Unlike the publishing world, the opera industry could, as early as the first half of the century, count on a huge number of theaters spread quite uniformly across the entire peninsula, as well as on the rapid circulation of operas, thanks to a well-organized network of impresarios.[8]

Thus, a cultural history of the operatic world that takes into account not only its texts but also its practices and organization will shed light on key aspects of both the society and the culture of that period. The aim is to take into account not just the intricate ways in which the opera house contributed to the spreading of patriotic discourse in a context of strict censorship and tight police control or only the use that political activists, who were often at the heart of the demonstrations, consciously made of them[9] but also a more complex, two-way exchange between what was at the time the most popular Italian theatrical genre and the Risorgimento movement. Hence, contemporary political events often get blurred and reflected in the reception of operatic plots, while theatrical performances end up informing the political language, gestures, and behaviors of the time. While it is apparent that nationalism does not express itself only through narrative and artistic forms (which have indeed received a great deal of attention in recent years), it is also true that these function as privileged channels, thanks to their extraordinary performative power. They can be seen as a "mirrors held up to nature (or rather to society and culture), active mirrors (...), mirrors that probed and analyzed the axioms and assumptions of the social structure, isolated the building blocks of the culture, and sometimes used them to construct novel edifices."[10]

It seems that in this context of renewed investigation a new cultural history of politics is presently converging with a musicology that has become more sensitive to the inputs of semiotics. This common direction consists in the effort to devote enough attention to all aspects, both verbal and nonverbal, both musical and non-musical, that are at play in each case, as well as to a possible interaction among them. For instance, historians have recently demonstrated that both objects and gestures have their own expressive, communicative, and performative power in relation to political action and that they can offer a different kind of information with respect to verbal communication.[11] In this regard, moving from Lynn Hunt's approach to the study of the French Revolution, the aim is to try to understand the "embodied" practices of political action, on which a great deal of work still needs to be done. At the same time, from a musicological perspective opera is being increasingly regarded as a syncretic genre in which different textual levels interact with one another, while the visual element is acquiring greater importance next to verbal and musical textuality.[12] It is along these lines and in an attempt to integrate both perspectives that the rest of this chapter moves.

2. 1848: A Theatrical Revolution?

A very special connection arose in Europe in the early nineteenth century between politics and the theater, following the radical changes that took place in the realm of communication during the French Revolution. As a result of the theater's strong presence in the urban landscapes of the period, as well as of the widespread custom in the towns, right across the social spectrum, to attend theatrical performances, the theater audience became a collective political actor in many European countries—not just in Italy. Thus, the theater and its surroundings turned into a favored setting for uprisings and demonstrations characterized by a conscious transposition of the spectacular workings of the stage into political action. It happened in Georgian England during the famous 1809 riots at Covent Garden, in Spain during the Napoleonic wars, in the French provinces in the 1820s, and in Belgium during the 1830 revolution.[13] In such cases, the theater became an arena for social and political conflicts, a privileged scenario of sociopolitical dissent. Combining different modes of expression (narrative, musical, and performative) with a special interaction between various social actors,[14] the stage turned into a unique place where the political discourse could emerge. What is more, this connection seemed to act at an even deeper level. Sharp forms of theatricality informed collective behaviors in a time when the public sphere still found in both censorship and police control strict limitations to its free development. It is in this kind of context, where the small niches of freedom are so highly unstable as to appear and disappear very quickly, that the theater ends up turning into a fast-growing and often controversial repository of practices, gestures, plots, and roles for the political culture of the time, particularly for its more radical elements.[15] In the 1820s and 1830s, whether in the case of Saint-Simonism in France, Chartism in England, or Mazzinianism in Italy, the theater served not only as a key instrument of political awakening but also as a benchmark for the creation of new communicative practices, where the role of visual and gestural tools was anything but marginal.[16]

The Italian case should therefore be considered within the wider European context much more than it has been so far; on the other hand, it preserves its own specificity, such as the centrality of the music theater. Here, the interrelation between theater and politics becomes fully visible in the most highly conflictive stages of the Risorgimento process and especially in the triennium 1846–1849, when a set of key events took place, including the election of a new—and allegedly liberal—pope, the beginning of a series of patriotic demonstrations, the outbreak of the Milanese and Venetian uprisings, and, finally, the war against Austria.[17] Many of the protagonists of the 1848 Italian Revolution, as well as many of the foreigners who were present and wrote their own accounts. In describing these events, many of the protagonists of the 1848 Italian Revolution, as well as many foreigners who were present and wrote their own accounts, resorted to theatrical metaphors that are clearly regarded as the most appropriate way of accounting for what happened. There are many examples relating to very different situations and publics. Carlo Leoni, historian and patriot from Padua, is among those to whom the revolutionary days appeared like a real performance. He writes in his memoir that "the glorious events that have recently occurred in Italy seem, in their splendid appearance, a true theatrical performance. The democratic scenes of Venice, Rome and Turin are so warm and full of affection that they by far surpass those of the Middle Ages."[18] When describing the effervescent Italian situation to other American sympathizers, writer and journalist Margaret Fuller, who was the *New York Tribune* European correspondent, stresses many a time the extraordinary spectacle of those events, which she often perceives as if they were taking place on the stage.[19] In the *Revue des deux mondes*, patriot Cristina di Belgioioso describes what had happened a few months earlier in Venice, again resorting to theatrical images. The outbreak, which had initially appeared to her as a comedy, had unexpectedly turned into tragedy, so much so that its leaders "seemed to be acting in one of those mysterious dramas of which Venice had so often been the setting."[20] Even when she recounts her triumphant entry into Milan at the head of the Neapolitan volunteers shortly after the glorious "five days," the patriot cannot help but notice how truly spectacular it all was, as she is surrounded by acclaiming crowds and by "several hundred handkerchiefs" waving from the windows and balconies in what was a "warming sight of portentous effect."[21] However, this very excess of theatricality had indeed upset some of her more moderate interlocutors, such as Gabrio Casati, president of the provisional government of Milan, who felt compelled to "perform a scene" as he harangued the troops. For Giuseppe Massari, follower of neo-Guelph Gioberti, the Neapolitan volunteers' arrival in Milan had given "rise to one of those theatrical performances that are always inappropriate, but which on certain solemn occasions are intolerably scandalous."[22]

So far, we have been talking about metaphors that describe the political conflict and its practices in terms of mise-en-scène and are used both in a positive sense (the great revolutionary spectacle) and in order to underline its limits. In either case, the aim is to give shape to the account of events. However, in the picture that we can draw today, there are also more specifically theatrical elements. Such was the use among patriots of real stage costumes, historic costumes that marked the unique atmosphere of those days, evoking the almost obsessive preoccupation with the republican dress that had characterized the French Revolution.[23] One of the most vivid accounts—even if written after some time—is that by Milanese Giovanni Visconti Venosta. In his memoir, he described the situation in Milan after the city had been liberated from Austrian domination (March 23, 1848) as a theatrical scene in which it was not at all surprising if one bumped into people dressed up as medieval knights or bandits, while theatrical costume houses were stormed by even the most moderate characters, who grabbed jerkins, helmets, boots, skullcaps, and broadswords.

"They are gone! They are gone!" he wrote, talking about the former oppressors:

> And everyone felt the need to celebrate, such was the excitement that it looked like a delirium; people were moved by an urge to expand, to fraternize, to partake;…with ancient armor on their chests, wearing plumed hats or morions and yellow leather boots, armor and stage costumes. These strange displays of *patriotic garb* would last, alas, for much longer; even to some serious men it had not seemed strange, in those first few days, to dress in such a manner. Not even [the] secretary-general of the provisional government, Cesare Correnti, seemed to find it surprising since in those very days I saw him also wearing the traditional Lombard velvet dress, with the tricolor sash over his shoulder and a saber on one side.[24]

At a time of extraordinary collective elation, he continued, one could witness both tragic and funny things, yet all of them looked serious, with no exception. One felt the same degree of admiration for the wounded being carried on stretchers, as well as for the gallants "wearing shining armor, colored scarves, and plumed hats, carrying ancient broadswords and strolling like singers on the stage."[25] Finally, in Turin, where there had been no fighting, things had not been very different. Another patriot, Giuseppe Torelli, admitted to visiting five or six armories, where he randomly grabbed a number of sharp weapons that made him move awkwardly, making him look like the proud character of *Chiara di Rosemberg*, an opera by Luigi Ricci quite popular at the time.[26]

Traces of such theatricalities can also be found in Austrian accounts. One example is Count Hubner's memoir, written much later but copied directly from the diary that he had kept during those days. The Austrian official, who had arrived in Milan in early March on an exploratory mission to which he had been assigned by Metternich himself, stated that he was unexpectedly caught in the middle of the insurrection. He received a visit by two gentlemen armed to the teeth who had received orders to take him before the head of the provisional government: "Those gentlemen," he wrote, "like all their fellow combatants, were wearing very picturesque, fantastic costumes, which had apparently been borrowed from the theater wardrobe."[27] As he was taken to the government palace, he noticed what was happening in the streets. He mentioned the barricades, the colorful crowds, the gentlemen wearing velvet jerkins who seemed to have just left a masked ball, others wearing *Ernani* hats, and many shouting as he passed by them, "Death to the Germans!," gesturing as if they were performing in a pantomime. Physical and visual means were mutually reinforced in an atmosphere of collective euphoria combined with a proud display of theatricality.

It is striking that in 1848 the act of reading events in a theatrical key had spread well beyond the Italian context. One of the best-known examples is Alexis de Tocqueville's account of the tumultuous Paris riots of February 1848. He stated that the insurgents seemed to be staging the revolution fought by their fathers, which obviously none of them had witnessed directly. In 1850, when it was all over, he wrote the following from Italy:

> [W]e tried without success to warm ourselves at the heart of our fathers' passions; their gestures and attitudes as seen on the stage were imitated... Though I foresaw the terrible end to the piece well enough, I could not take the actors very seriously; the whole thing seemed a vile tragedy played by a provincial troupe.[28]

In Tocqueville, as in Marx (see the opening sentences of Marx's *Eighteenth Brumaire*: "Hegel remarks somewhere that all facts and personages of great importance in world history occur, as it were, twice. He forgot to add: the first time as tragedy, the second as farce"), the reference to the theater was the expression of an extremely critical view of events, as well as an attempt to control and attach meaning to memories after the failure of the revolutionary experience. For obviously different reasons, such theatricality was there to underscore its explicit fictional leeway, its coldness, and its distance from reality. Even Tocqueville, however, beyond metaphors, stresses the bizarre nature of the disguises. He tells us how from Armand Marrast's flowery imagination the idea arose of having the members of the National Constituent Assembly dress like the members of the Convention in 1793, wearing the white robe with wide cuffs, which characterized the theatrical character of Robespierre. Once again, one has the impression that an actual displacement from the stage to reality was occurring. This process—which, as we will see, was bidirectional—appeared natural only to those involved in it. It could have been one of those cases of convergence between "social dramas" and the theater described by anthropologist Victor Turner, who wrote extensively on the idea of "cultural performance," that is, those situations in which both argumentation and mise-en-scène, both plots and roles are inspired or influenced by the theater stage.[29] Thus, one should not be surprised at the way in which a contemporary Italian periodical explains the almost total paralysis of the opera season in the spring of 1848, when the theaters were either shut or were used to spread the accounts of the battles. Now that "we are surrounded by so many Attilas"—wrote a journalist for *Teatri, arte, e letteratura*, clearly referring to Verdi's opera, which was so popular at the time—"why should one go and see Attila on the stage?"[30]

3. Hats, Feathers, and Costumes

During the months preceding the March revolutionary uprisings, some papers devoted their attention to the historic-patriotic disguises that had appeared during the first demonstrations in 1846, spurred by Pope Pius IX's reformist attitude. The costumes evoked the figure of the armed knight or more generally of the combatant, at a time when the call to arms was becoming one of the main binding forces of the patriotic rhetoric. However, instead of appearing overtly belligerent, they rather suggested the image of the "knight-conspirator," whose *figurini* (costume sketch) resorted to elements of historic fashion, among which were the unfailingly present cloak, feathered hat, and the blouse that fit tightly at the waist. It is not easy to reconstruct the exact development of these clothing styles, whose traces are very sparsely scattered throughout the literature; what we do know, however, is that one of the most popular elements among the patriots was the *Ernani* hat, which alluded to the protagonist of one of the most popular of Verdi's operas. It was generally made of red felt with a truncated cone-shaped crown fastened by a buckle and a long feather on one side, like that worn by the proud bandit created by Victor Hugo's plume and freely set to music by Verdi. Similar headgear was seen during the patriotic celebrations that took place between 1846 and 1847 in Tuscany, Liguria, and Emilia-Romagna. Here, particularly in the papal legations, Verdi's opera also became the object of a creative nationalist reception by means of variations applied to the text by the interpreters, who inserted allusions to contemporary political events such as the amnesty the pope had granted to political prisoners.[31] The two events were probably meant to reinforce each other. In the dense, emulative cycle of those first demonstrations, the "Puritan hats" also appeared, this time with reference to one of the most highly political operas by Vincenzo Bellini, written by Carlo Pepoli during his exile in Paris. Finally, the "Calabrese hat" was also quite popular. This was not meant to allude to any theatrical image but rather to the Bandiera brothers' unlucky exploit—the two young patriots killed in Calabria in 1844. Their cult, which immediately entered the Mazzinian patriotic pantheon, went together with an operatic reference to the chorus "Chi per la patria muor vissuto è assai" [He who dies for his country has lived long enough] from an opera by Mercadante, apparently sung by the two patriots before they were executed. As in the case of *Ernani*, the image was that of a bandit who concealed a noble knight (figure 17.1).

During the course of 1848, the *Ernani* hat became a key element of the famous "Italian dress"—possibly of Piedmontese origin—whose *figurini* were published in February 1848 by *Il mondo illustrato*, one of the first illustrated periodicals to appear in Italy. The article describes it as "a modern make with an old feeling to it," that is, a contemporary design that drew on past styles (figure 17.2). The columnist adds that many more were seen at a ball held at the Philharmonic Academy in Turin, which from a mundane event had turned into an occasion for patriotic demonstrations—as was often the case in those days of great collective excitement. The men wore a velvet redingote fastened either by a belt or with a scarf tied on

Figure 17.1. *Foggia d'abito per tutti gli italiani* [Style of Dress for All Italians] (pamphlet, Florence: Tipografia del Vulcano, 1847).

one side, on which patriotic slogans had been written; the women, on the other hand, had on a velvet Amazon gown, sometimes worn on top of a silk chemise with long tricolor stripes. Everybody indistinctly wore the usual *Ernani* or Calabrese feathered hat. The journalist who recounted the event could attribute such a style of disguise only to the exceptional atmosphere of those days: "In previous years," he stated, "it would have been a masquerade. Today it is the symbol of a sentiment, it is like a test of the kind of fashion we would like all Italians to embrace."[32] And in some ways that was indeed the case since the so-called Italian dress (of which the

Figure 17.2. Italian clothing (*Il mondo illustrato*, February 1848).

hat was the most distinctive element) quickly became the most popular type of "demonstrative dress," very common in the celebrations and in the processions that preceded or accompanied the revolutionary uprisings and, later, the war (figure 17.3). The traceable examples are not limited to a small elite group of patriots, probably from the aristocracy, like those who attended the Turin ball. According to Alberto Mario, a famous Mazzinian patriot, at least four hundred students who took part in the anti-Austrian protests that broke out in Padua in February 1848 were dressed *all'italiana*. On that same occasion, black feathers were distributed among the townspeople—and worn not just by a circle of the most prominent activists—who pinned them on their hats so as to make their support of the cause more easily identifiable (figure 17.4).[33]

Hence, a tendency toward the dramatization and visual representation of the conflict marks the 1848 events, which look almost like tableaux ready to be immortalized in a painting (indeed, the historic paintings of the period tend to express the same theatricality, while they do not hide their own connections with melodramatic atmospheres, as is apparent in Francesco Hayez's works). What is striking about the protests of those days is the widespread need, at times fulfilled, to affirm one's identity as a patriot by resorting to a kind of stage costume as an unmistakable mark of recognition and as part of a system of signs endowed with a very strong allusive

Figure 17.3. *Ritratto di Luigia Battistotti Sassi in costume patriottico* [Portrait of Luigia Battistotti Sassi Wearing a Patriotic Outfit] (lithograph, Museo del Risorgimento, Ferrara).

power. Characterized by a high degree of secrecy since its inception, the Italian national-patriotic movement drew heavily on symbolic language and ritual practices, as did most early nineteenth-century opposition movements. Such tendency, however, really came to the fore only in the triennium 1846–1849, when both censorship measures and police control became weaker or even nonexistent. This gave rise to the brief but explosive proliferation of practices of patriotic ritual self-representation, which merged with the political language that was used in an extensive proselytizing mission. This process of visualization of the conflict was as short lived as it was extensive and conspicuous, clearly not just through clothes and hats but also by means of the more usual symbolic array, typical of revolutionary celebrations, of

Figure 17.4. *Manifestazioni popolari a Torino per la concessione dello Statuto albertino 1848* [Popular Demonstrations for the Granting of the Albertine Statute in Turin 1848] (watercolor on cardboard by Achille Dovera, Museo del Risorgimento, Genoa).

flags, rosettes, handkerchiefs, and numerous kinds of sashes. Such tendency to translate events into a visual challenge to the authorities would be described a few years later as one of the most distinctive characteristics of those days (figure 17.5):

> One day news would arrive from Rome about one of the pope's liberal initiatives, and the ladies would immediately show up at the theater in white-and-yellow garments. Then the news came about the Neapolitan Constitution, and in the blink of an eye all the men started wearing Calabrese hats. The police banned hats, and three days later everybody was wearing velvet cotton clothes from the Vaprio factory. What did this mean? Not much, but the police were getting worried, and that was a good reason for doing it. Nobody knew who gave these instructions or who directed these demonstrations, nor did anyone attempt to find out.[34]

As young Neapolitan patriot Alessandro Poerio traveled northward in the ranks of General Pepe's army to support the war that was being fought in Lombardy-Venetia, he wrote letters filled with references to tricolor banners and Italian clothing styles. He wrote from Ancona: "Everybody holds the tricolor ribbon or cross; everywhere tricolor flags with no coat of arms or insignia are waving in the most crowded places." In Venice, the piazza was full of national guards, "of young men dressed *alla Italiana*, with tight velvet garments and feathered hats, and of jubilant crowds, all waving tricolor ribbons, rosettes, or crosses."[35] These types of visual suggestions responded to a variety of situations, which is why they were effective. While

Figure 17.5. *Sulle barricate milanesi* [On the Barricades in Milan], ca. 1849 (Bertarelli Collection, Milan).

on a subjective level they confirmed one's self-perception as a patriot, as well as one's participation in the collective patriotic spirit, from the outside they both guaranteed the demonstrators' high visibility and served as a challenge to the Austrian authorities. Moreover, they worked perfectly beyond the national borders by allowing the supporters of the Italian cause to be easily identifiable outside of their own country. We know, for instance, that within the large Italian community of Pera, once a Genoese colony in the Ottoman Empire that would later become a district of Istanbul, the male patriots were easily recognizable because of their strange hats and long moustaches. Charles MacFarlane, an English gentleman and Tory sympathizer who in 1848 published a memoir of his journey through the Mediterranean and in particular along the Italian peninsula, informs us of such practices without hiding his contempt. He stated that he often witnessed them in the coffeehouses and in even greater number as he traveled throughout Italy, where "political opinions were also strongly pronounced in hats. The Liberals sported hats of all manner of shapes."[36] In Ancona, for instance, he described a crowd of characters, most of whom were "fiercely mustachioed and long-bearded men, nearly all wearing the uniform of the national guard or fantastic military caps…to denote that they were citizen-soldiers."[37]

Besides, the communicative and imitative potential of such practices was both known and feared by the Austrian authorities, who as early as February 1848 had banned them altogether. "Lately" (reads a notice from the general direction of the police force in Milan) "some have started to adopt the custom of wearing these so-called Calabrese, Puritan, or *Ernani* hats. Since their use cannot be tolerated, it is absolutely prohibited; offenders shall be arrested immediately."[38] In the 1850s, the ban would be extended to other states, including the papal states, thus unveiling the authorities' obsession with visual contagion apart from a clear awareness of the possibility that this might produce an imitative reaction among the common people. "It is prohibited to use those hats of a reddish colour so-called Ernani," wrote the police chief of Perugia in February 1850. "Those who are found wearing or selling hats or tricolor objects for the first time shall be subjected to the payment of a fine of five scudi; repeat offenders shall be held in custody and the fine shall be doubled."[39]

4. Opera *Figurini*

But why *Ernani*, and to what extent is such a strong emphasis on visual elements linked with the music theater? Verdi's opera had gained enormous popularity over the years following the Venetian premiere in 1844. Marcello Conati, who has gathered all of the data relating to its stagings, maintains that *Ernani* turned into a fashion phenomenon, which my analysis further confirms. In 1846, it was undoubtedly the most frequently performed opera in Italy, counting sixty-five stagings in as many theaters, followed at great distance, with thirty-one stagings each by "classic" operas such as *Il barbiere di Siviglia* (the first true repertory opera in the Italian music theater tradition) or more recent texts such as Verdi's *I due Foscari* and Donizetti's *Linda di Chamounix*.[40] Contemporary newspaper accounts allow us to follow with a good degree of accuracy the rapid growth of the opera's popularity.

Following the first Venetian performances in 1844, we learn that everywhere "in the lobbies, in the streets, in the halls, in the witty gatherings" people were singing the new arias and that "only a few scores have made a stronger and more vivid impression than this sweet-sounding Ernani.... [E]very single night the theatre was flooded by the crowds."[41] A few years and many stagings later, the *Ricoglitore fiorentino* informs us in a long and sarcastic piece about *Ernani*, "the most popular opera by the immensely popular Maestro Verdi," that people had finally had enough:

> I am only whispering it, I am getting tired of this *Ernani*. You go to the Pergola theatre, and they are singing *Ernani*; you go to the Piazza Vecchia, and they are performing *Ernani*; so, you go to the prose theatre just to find some peace, but there you go again: between one act and the next, the orchestra unfailingly starts strumming notes from *Ernani*...because this opera has been adapted for whichever instrument, from the ophicleide to the piccolo, from the contrabass to the viola.[42]

However, the most significant testimony of the opera's extraordinary popularity is perhaps to be found in the words written by the Neapolitan censor, who in

1845 banned the opera without any possibility of appeal since, he stated, it was so popular and so frequently heard (without ever having been performed in Naples, however) that it would have been impossible to censor some of the most sensitive parts without immediately stirring up protests.[43] It is possible that the opera's extraordinary popularity further brought out its allusive elements, centered especially around the conspiracy against the emperor and his subsequent pardon. It might also have enhanced the strong impact made upon the public by those interpretative variations that were projected onto the political context and which marked the numerous productions staged during the triennium, constantly adjusting to the political situation. At first the various allusions appeared at the end of the first act, when the emperor grants his forgiveness to the conspirators, evoking the magnanimity of the new pope, who soon after his election had granted amnesty to political prisoners. Later, after the pope denied his support for the patriotic war at the end of April 1848, interpretative variations to the text were applied to the conspirators' chorus. This time they embraced and, according to the stage directions, "at the highest point of excitement draw their swords and burst into singing": "Si ridesti il leon di Castiglia" [Let the lion of Castile reawaken], a choral passage full of belligerent vigor, which on a nationalist reading could be interpreted as either Saint Mark's lion (i.e., the Republic of Venice) or the lion of Caprera (i.e., Garibaldi).

All this can help us imagine how in those days, unlike today, the association between the figure of the bandit Ernani and the image of the conspirator was quite immediate, granting a unique communicative effectiveness to the political significance of the feathered hat. On the other hand, it is likely that the incorporation of elements of theatrical origin into dressing habits was also influenced by the affirmation of a practice that was becoming common in those same years and to which Verdi strongly contributed: the tendency to preserve and codify both the scenery and the costumes. With regard to the scenography, Mercedes Viale Ferrero attributes the turning point in this direction to the 1846 production of *Attila*. The set designs by scenographer Giuseppe Bertoja, a recurrent figure in Verdian staging, were reproduced in color lithographs in the magazine *L'Italia musicale*, becoming a model to which later productions would strictly adhere.[44] As for the costumes, some studies have already confirmed the existence of a distribution system organized by the theatrical agencies, which included most theatrical costumiers in the field, like Pietro Rovaglia in Milan. This network also extended to several European capitals, further confirming the highly international character of the various channels of the operatic system.[45] Apparently the first Verdian figurini to have appeared in the specialized periodicals were those for *Macbeth*, which were published in the *Gazzetta musicale di Milano* in the autumn of 1847, and, a few months later, those for *I masnadieri*, published by *L'Italia musicale*. The fact that in the same year Verdi went on his first European trip, traveling to London and Paris—where the publication of theatrical figurini was a common practice dating back to the *Petite galerie dramatique, ou recueil des différents costumes d'acteurs*, first published in 1800—can hardly be considered a coincidence.

Verdi strongly embraced the French directions regarding the total control and preservation of the mise-en-scène. So, in those years a tendency affirmed itself to preserve the array of visual elements by means of which the spectators would learn to recognize and participate in the Verdian sets even when these were adapted for the puppet theaters. Few traces of the figurini from the first sets dating back to the 1840s are left in the theater archives. We have, for instance, the pencil drawings from the 1844 staging of *Ernani* in Parma, where the main character appears almost completely wrapped up in his cloak with the famous feathered hat in his hand (figure 17.6). What seems interesting to note is that in the early nineteenth century, when the world was experiencing the first real outburst of the image market thanks to a series of extraordinary technological novelties—from lithography to the daguerreotype—theatrical performances also started to spread and be reproduced, favoring a wider consumption and often enhancing their own symbolic value. A direct correspondence between the costume drawings and the representation of

Figure 17.6. Figurini for *Ernani*, Parma 1844 (Archivio Storico del Teatro Regio, Parma).

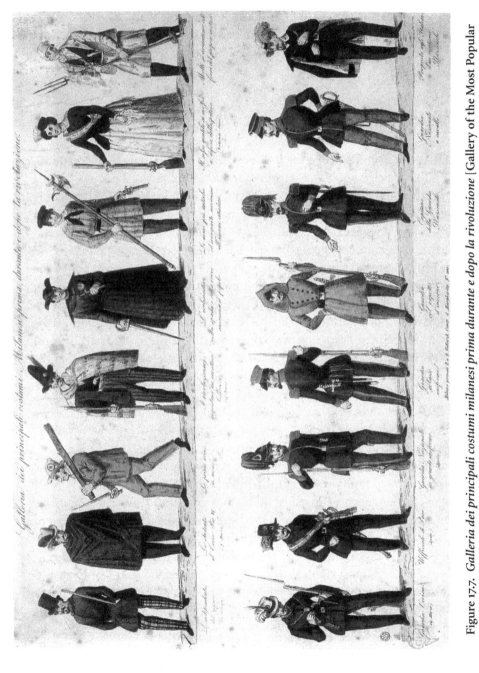

Figure 17.7. *Galleria dei principali costumi milanesi prima durante e dopo la rivoluzione* [Gallery of the Most Popular Milanese Outfits before, during, and after the Revolution], Milan 1849 (color lithograph, Bertarelli Collection, Milan).

the revolution that had just taken place can be found in Milan in a beautiful color lithograph whose title borrows from the French work mentioned earlier, adapting it to the political context (figure 17.7). In the *Galleria dei principali constumi milanesi prima durante e dopo la rivoluzione*, the various characters who played a role during the "five days of Milan" are introduced like actors on the stage. Needless to say, among the most recurrent elements are the cloak and the feathered hat.

5. Patriotic Gestures

The highly symbolic influence of the 1848 events was due not only to the predominance of the visual element but also to an exaggeration of physical gestures aiming at a reiterated expression of emotions. This brings us back to the level of the performance and to those theories of gesture as a natural sign of emotions and as an expression of the language of the soul, which had been widely circulated at the end of the eighteenth century. Johann Jacob Engel's epistolary treatise published in Germany in 1785, which was immediately translated across Europe, was one of the main works that theorized and spread the idea of gesture as a fundamental element in the communication process both on the stage and in everyday life. Engel's work also marked a kind of transition in the dramatic arts from the "description" to the "expression" of feelings—as was already the case with music, considered by most contemporary theorists as the least naturalistic and the most expressive of all the arts.[46] It is hard to define more accurately the ways in which these kinds of arguments slowly and imperceptibly permeate social practices and sensibilities. Nevertheless, one cannot help but notice the constant interferences between the two levels when looking at the explosion of emotional gesturing that characterized the Italian *quarantotto* and which reminds us once again of the stage.

Let us consider, in the first place, the plastic expression of "fraternity" among the patriots, which was as omnipresent as the tricolor flag and the feathered hat. One of the most frequent sequences in patriotic dramas consists in the act of tearfully embracing and kissing, not a spontaneous reaction but rather a kind of ritual act of mutual recognition performed through collective excitement, which was extremely common in the atmosphere of "poetic elation" during the triennium.[47] Another ritual that acquired an almost codified structure both before and during the war was that of the collective oaths to the national cause—with drawn swords where possible—as a public dramatization of the birth of a new political community. Many episodes of this kind are reported in the press and recorded in memoirs, as when the patriots, in unison, swore to devote their lives to the "holy Italian cause," solemnly cursing those who dared to betray it. In addition to the patriotic mise-en-scènes we find the processions and pilgrimages recalling a particular episode in Italian history, usually taken from the Middle Ages. The best-known and most recurrent example within the national-patriotic cult regards the fight put up by the Lombard communes against Emperor Barbarossa's attempted invasion. Since the late 1820s, this historic event had been charged with a highly allusive power in both prose and poetry as an example of an age-old destiny of oppression and, above all, of the possibility of freedom from foreign domination. The Turinese press described a procession winding through the streets in February 1848 to celebrate the granting of the Albertine statute for representative government. Among the lit torches, the *carroccio* [war chariot] advanced triumphantly, drawn by three oxen and accompanied by trumpeters and soldiers in steel armor carrying medieval-looking weapons such as clubs, poles, and visors. All of this symbolized the ancient Lombard League, an alliance among the communes, which, with papal support, had triumphed over the imperial army at Legnano in 1176 and represented the possibility of national resurgence.[48]

While both the procession and the traditional oath, as well as the use of the "civic national costume," have illustrious precedents in the republican revolutionary tradition of the late eighteenth century, they were brought back to life by the Italian movement of 1848, taking on specific politically charged shapes. Once again, they quickly resonated in the theater through a process of mutual influence, where the street performances were fictionalized on the stage. In what is yet another reversal between reality and performance, the carroccio symbolizing the Lombard League and set up for the Turin celebrations would triumphantly accompany the victorious knights in the last scene of *La battaglia di Legnano*, the only explicitly patriotic opera written by Verdi and staged in Rome in 1849 during the Mazzinian Republic. Both the stage directions and the text of the libretto, with the chorus singing "Giuriam d'Italia por fine ai danni, cacciando oltr'Alpe i suoi tiranni" [Let us swear to put an end to Italy's agony by chasing the tyrants back over the Alps], include the most famous passages from the kind of patriotic dramaturgy that had rapidly imposed itself since 1846: the fraternal embrace between the conspirators, the crossing of the swords, and the collective oath, which included a preventive condemnation of the possible traitors ("Il vil suo nome infamia suoni / ad ogni gente, ad ogni età" [Let his vile name sound like infamy to every people in every age]). Needless to say, the opera was immediately and extraordinarily successful. The various oaths contained in other operas (from *Ernani* to *La disfida di Barletta*, written by Ferdinand Karl Lickl) would also be met with thunderous applause, and the spectators would call for an encore.

In conclusion, it is quite apparent that as the revolutionary triennium 1846–1849 approached, the distinction between text and subtext, between the stage and reality, became more and more blurred in a framework of strong convergence between life and the theater. For the first time since the Jacobin triennium, examples of street politics characterized by an emotionally charged visual and gestural language are also to be found in Italy. It is in romantic opera—the most successful theatrical genre—that they are best reflected and represented. Symbolic and ritual mechanisms such as those described earlier are some of the key components of a sort of apprenticeship toward the creation of a national "imagined community" that finds both in the performance and in a consciously exaggerated theatricality an important opportunity not so much to imitate reality but rather to carry out an illusionistic amplification of it. To perform—writes Victor Turner—means to carry out a more or less complex process rather than to execute a single action.[49] In our case, the crowds that from Tuscany to Emilia-Romagna, from Genoa to Padua, gave rise to protests filled with melodramatic theatricality or the patriots dressed *all'italiana* and wearing *Ernani* hats as they embraced and swore to be faithful to the Italian cause were demonstrating national unity, thus experiencing it and bringing it to life at the same time.

However, this was only a brief, though intense, moment of high politicization, which would be followed by the failure of the revolutionary experience and the beginning of a new political phase in which the divisions within the national-patriotic front would greatly deepen. Many of those who would later identify with a moderate political orientation had, during the 1850s, already started to look at that experience much more critically than before, distancing themselves from it and making fun of the historic-patriotic performances by disparagingly calling them *quarantottate*—nothing but a farce. The political judgment is what eventually prevailed in light of a mainly moderate attitude that at times also informed theatrical criticism. Ten years later in Turin, on the eve of a new war against Austria that would eventually bring national unification, an opera like *La battaglia di Legnano* received a much colder reaction than it had at its Roman premiere. However, things had changed by then. About the 1848 revolution, the Piedmontese newspaper *L'Opinione* wrote the following:

> It was enough to put Italy on the stage, or the Lombard League with its carroccio, [to] talk about freedom, or the *patria*, [to] shout 'Death to the tyrants' to the oppressors to cause a storm of applause…Such was the milieu in those days, which luckily has now greatly changed. Today more than in words people believe in facts…in politics as well as at the theatre.[50]

What would then become of the *Ernani* hat? Even though Garibaldian Giuseppe Bandi wrote in his memoir that a "fashion of dressing in the *Ernani* style" was still common among the volunteers of the Expedition of the Thousand (May–September 1860), Garibaldi's followers in fact became identified with a different style of clothing, such as the famous red shirt. The references to the feathered hat that can be found in the literary production of the period tell us a different story: from originally being a symbol of political conspiracy, the *Ernani* hat turned into a frivolous fashion accessory in the postunification era. Writer Luigi Capuana has Giacinta wear it, the young heroine from the homonymic naturalistic novel he dedicated in 1879 to his master, Émile Zola.

NOTES

1. See the collection of essays *Il mito del Risorgimento nell'Italia unita*, "Il Risorgimento," 1–2 (1995); A. R. Ascoli and K. M. von Henneberg, eds., *Making and*

Remaking Italy: The Cultivation of National Identity around the Risorgimento (New York: Berg, 2001); *Pédagogie et liturgie nationale dans l'Italie post unitaire*, special issue of *Mélanges de l'École Française de Rome* 109 (1997); Massimo Baioni, *La "religione della patria": Musei e istituti del culto risorgimentale (1884–1918)* (Treviso: Pagus, 1994).

2. Birgit Pauls, *Giuseppe Verdi und das Risorgimento: Ein politischer Mythos in Prozess der Nationenebildung* (Berlin: Akademie, 1996); Roger Parker, *"Arpa d'or dei fatidici vati": The Verdian Patriotic Chorus in the 1840s* (Parma: Istituto nazionale di studi verdiani, 1997). See also John Rosselli, *The Life of Verdi* (New York: Cambridge University Press, 2000).

3. For a recent critical discussion of this research strand, see "Alberto Banti's Interpretation of Risorgimento Nationalism: A Debate," *Nation and Nationalism* 15(3) (2009). An outcome of this line of investigation is the volume edited by Alberto M. Banti and Paul Ginsborg, *Storia d'Italia, Annali 22: Il Risorgimento* (Torino: Einaudi, 2007).

4. Within this deconstructive approach a heated controversy has emerged among musicologists about the relationship between Verdi and politics. The two opposing positions are clearly summarized in the following essays: Roger Parker and Mary Ann Smart, "Verdi, 2001, and Us," *Studi verdiani* 18 (2004): 295–312; George Martin, "Verdi, Politics, and 'Va pensiero': The Scholars Squabble," *Opera Quarterly* 23(1) (2005): 109–32.

5. See Peter Brooks, *The Melodramatic Imagination* (New Haven: Yale University Press, 1976). A terminological clarification is necessary at this point. Since the seventeenth century, the Italian term *melodramma* has referred to opera as a theatrical genre in which the words are set to music. At the beginning of the nineteenth century, the French term *mélodrame* and the English term *melodrama* started to designate a popular theatrical genre derived from pantomime that proposed a new mixture of acting, music, and gestures. This is where the adjective *melodramatic* comes from, denoting emotional amplification and expressive exaggeration. As shown, for instance, by Emilio Sala (*L'opera senza canto: Il mélo romantico e l'invenzione della colonna sonora* [Venice: Marsilio 1995]) in the first half of the nineteenth century, Italian romantic opera was deeply influenced by the "melodramatic imagination" and its narrative structure, as proposed by Peter Brooks.

6. Giuseppe Mazzini, *Filosofia della musica*, ed. Marcello De Angelis (Florence: Guaraldi, 1977), 71.

7. Carlo Tenca, "Delle condizioni della odierna letteratura," *Rivista europea* 2 (1846): 206–27.

8. Carlotta Sorba, *Teatri: L'Italia del melodramma nell'età del Risorgimento* (Bologna: Il Mulino, 2001); John Rosselli, *Opera Industry in Italy from Cimarosa to Verdi: The Role of the Impresario* (New York: Cambridge University Press, 1984).

9. Peter Stamatov, "Interpretative Activism and the Political Usages of Verdi's Operas in the 1840s," *American Sociological Review* 67(3) (2002): 345–66; Carlotta Sorba, "*Comunicare con il popolo:* Novel, Drama, and Music in Mazzini's Work," in *Giuseppe Mazzini and the Globalisation of Democratic Nationalism 1830–1920*, ed. C. A. Bayly and Eugenio F. Biagini (New York: Oxford University Press for the British Academy, 2008), 75–92.

10. Victor Turner, *From ritual to theatre: the Human seriousness of play* (New York, 1982), 104.

11. Leora Auslander, "Beyond Words," *American Historical Journal* 110(4) (2005): 1015–45; Lynn Hunt, "Relire l'histoire du politique," in *La révolution à l'oeuvre: Perspectives actuelles dans l'histoire de la révolution française* (Rennes: Presses Universitaires de Rennes, 2005), 117–24.

12. See, for instance, Marco Beghelli, *La retorica del rituale nel melodramma ottocentesco* (Parma: Istituto nazionale di studi verdiani, 2003).

13. Marc Baer, *Theatre and Disorder in Late Georgian London* (Oxford: Clarendon, 1992); Sheril Kroen, *Politics and Theater: The Crisis of Legitimacy in Restoration France 1815–1830* (Berkeley: University of California Press, 2000); Alain Corbin, "L'agitation dans les théatres de province sous la Réstauration," in M. Bertrand, ed., *Popular Tradition and Learned Culture in France from XVI to XX Century* (Stanford: Anma Libri, 1985), 93–114.

14. Guy Debord states that "[t]he spectacle is not a collection of images; it is a social relation between people that is mediated by images" (*Society of the Spectacle* [London: Rebel, 1983], 7).

15. James Epstein and David Karr, "Playing at Revolution: British Jacobin Performance," *Journal of Modern History* 79(3) (2007): 495–530.

16. See James Epstein, "Understanding the Cap of Liberty: Symbolic Practice and Social Conflict in Early Nineteenth-century England," *Past and Present* 122 (February 1989): 75–118.

17. Lucy Riall, *The Italian Risorgimento: State, Society, and National Unification* (London: Routledge, 1994).

18. Carlo Leoni, *Cronaca segreta de' miei tempi* (Quarto d'Altino: Rebellato, 1976), 224.

19. Margaret Fuller, *Un'americana a Roma 1847–1849* (Pordenone: Studio Tesi, 1986).

20. Cristina di Belgioioso, "La rivoluzione e la repubblica di Venezia," *Revue des deux mondes* (Dec. 1, 1848).

21. Cristina di Belgioioso, "La guerra di Lombardia, l'assedio, e la capitolazione di Milano," *Revue des deux mondes* (Oct. 1, 1848).

22. Quoted in *La Patria* (Apr. 10, 1848).

23. Lynn Hunt, *Politics, Culture, and Class in the French Revolution* (Berkeley: University of California Press, 1984); Richard Wrigley, *The Politics of Appearances: Representations of Dress in Revolutionary France* (New York: Berg, 2002).

24. Giovanni Visconti Venosta, *Ricordi di gioventù: Cose vedute o sapute 1847–1860* (Milan: Cogliati, 1904), 112–14.

25. Venosta, *Ricordi di gioventù*, 96.

26. Giuseppe Torelli, *Ricordi politici* (Milano, 1873). *Chiara da Rosemberg* is an opera by Luigi Ricci, performed successfully for the first time at the Teatro alla Scala in 1831.

27. Le compte de Hubner, *Une année de ma vie 1848–49* (Paris: Hachette, 1891), 94–95.

28. Alexis de Tocqueville, *Recollections: The French Revolution of 1848*, ed. J. P. Mayer and A. P. Kerr (New Brunswick, N.J.: Transactions, 1987): 53; Rebecca Spang, "First Performances: Staging Memories of the French February Revolution," in Axel Körner, ed., *1848: A European Revolution? International Ideas and National Memories of 1848* (New York: Palgrave Macmillan, 2000), 164–84.

29. Turner, *From Ritual to Theatre*, 90.

30. *Teatri, arte, e letteratura* (25 May 1848).

31. On the staging of *Ernani*, see Carlotta Sorba, "Il Risorgimento in musica: L'opera lirica nei teatri del '48," in Alberto M. Banti and Roberto Bizzocchi, eds., *Immagini della nazione nell'Italia del Risorgimento*, 133–56 (Rome: Carocci, 2002).

32. "Resoconto del ballo all'Accademia Filarmonica," *Il mondo illustrato: Giornale Universale* 2(9) (Mar. 4, 1848): 144.

33. Alberto Mario, *Scritti scelti e curati da Giosuè Carducci*, vol. 1 (Bologna, 1884).

34. R. Bonfadini, *Mezzo secolo di patriottismo* (Milan: Treves, 1886), 233.

35. *Alessandro Poerio a Venezia: Lettere e documenti del 1848 illustrati da Vittorio Imbrani* (Naples: Morano, 1884).

36. Charles MacFarlane, *A Glance at Revolutionised Italy* (London: Smith, Elder, and Co. Cornhill, 1849), 18.

37. MacFarlane, *Glance at Revolutionised Italy*, 282.

38. The facsimile of this document is reproduced in Cesare Spellanzon, *Storia del Risorgimento e dell'unità d'Italia*, vol. 3 (Milan: Rizzoli, 1938), 620.

39. Quoted in *Le canzonette che fecero l'Italia*. A selection with commentary by Emilio Jona (Milan: Longanesi, 1962), 13.

40. Marcello Conati, "Observations on the Early Reviews of Verdi's *Ernani*," in *Ernani Yesterday and Today*. Bollettino dell'Istituto nazionale di studi verdiani 10 (Parma, 1989), 211–79.

41. Quoted in the *Gazzetta privilegiata di Venezia* (Mar. 30, 1844).

42. The article first appeared in the *Ricoglitore fiorentino* (October 1846) and was later republished in *Il messaggero bolognese* 4(32) (Nov. 4, 1846).

43. Marco Spada, "*Ernani* e la censura napoletana," *Studi verdiani* 5 (1989): 11–34.

44. Mercedes Viale Ferrero, "The Sets for the First *Ernani*: Notes on Verdian Scenography," in *Ernani Yesterday and Today*, 198–210.

45. Robert Cohen and Marcello Conati, "Un élément inexploré de la mise en scène du XIX siècle: Les 'figurinis' italiens des opéras de Verdi," *Opera e libretto* 1 (1990): 281-297; on the special attention not only Verdi but also the most important opera houses of the period devoted to the historical authenticity and material accuracy of the costumes, see Giacomo Agosti and Pier Luigi Ciapparelli, "La Commissione artistica dell'Accademia di Brera e gli allestimenti verdiani alla Scala alla metà dell'Ottocento," in *La realizzazione scenica dello spettacolo verdiano*, ed. Pierluigi Petrobelli and Fabrizio Della Seta, 215–29 (Parma: Istituto nazionale di studi verdiani, 1986).

46. For an analysis of Engel's treatise and its impact, see J. Veltruski, "Engel's Ideas for a Theory of Acting," *Drama Review* (December 1980): 71–80.

47. Alessio Petrizzo, "Spazi dell'immaginario: Festa e discorso nazionale in Toscana tra 1847 e 1848," *Storia d'Italia, Annali 22, Il Risorgimento*, 527–28.

48. Angelo Brofferio, *Storia del Piemonte*, vol. 1 (Turin: Pompeo Magnaghi, 1849).

49. Turner, *From Ritual to Theatre*, 18.

50. Quoted in *L'Opinione* (Apr. 4, 1859).

CHAPTER 18

MODALITIES OF NATIONAL IDENTITY: SIBELIUS BUILDS A FIRST SYMPHONY

JAMES HEPOKOSKI

The language in which we are speaking is his before it is mine. How different are the words *home*, *Christ*, *ale*, *master*, on his lips and on mine! I cannot speak or write these words without unrest of spirit. His language, so familiar and so foreign, will always be for me an acquired speech. I have not made or accepted its words. My voice holds them at bay. My soul frets in the shadow of his language.

—James Joyce, *A Portrait of the Artist as a Young Man*

IN Finland the 1890s were years of passionate national awakening, language-culture strife, and crystallizing self-definition. For most of the century the country had existed as an autonomous grand duchy of tsarist Russia, with Swedish (the language of Finland's rulers before 1809) as the official language of government, education, and most of the arts. As the century proceeded, however, a fervent Finnish-language movement among a circle of intellectuals and ethnographers was gaining legitimacy and cultural *éclat*. This ever-expanding circle was devoted to a preservationist recovery and stabilization of the strikingly different language of the majority of Finns, particularly those outside the major cities. A disputatiously partisan controversy over language, Finnish versus Swedish, merged readily not only with compelling issues of self-identity and ethnic assertion but also with an often ambiguous politics of resistance to an often harsh Russian rule. (A declaration of independence would not occur until late 1917, in the immediate wake of the Bolshevik revolution.) All of this was coming to a boil in the accelerated urban modernization of the 1890s, when writers, artists, intellectuals, and musicians rose to the fore to spearhead what would come to be regarded as a golden age of Finnish-language nationalist art.[1]

During this time the young Jean Sibelius was beginning his career as a composer. Originally a Swedish-speaking Finn from Tavastehus (the town's Swedish name, now more commonly known by its Finnish equivalent, Hämeenlinna) and educated musically also in Helsingfors (Helsinki), Berlin, and Vienna, he was steeping himself in things Finnish and taking on the task of devising an individualized, nationalist style that was also powered by a brashly flaunted, new-generation musical modernism. Toward that end and in resonance with the highly charged currents in his country he sought to forge a politically engaged music, a site of national memory and identity. By the last years of the decade this music was to be directed toward a twofold audience. On the one hand, such a work as the seemingly abstract First Symphony of 1899 was addressed within the country, to Finns, as a proclamatory act of national pride, the sort of product that anthropologist Michael Herzfeld has characterized as a signifier of "cultural intimacy" within an ethnic group or a mode of strategically engineered "self-recognition" or "practical essentialism."[2] On the other hand, the symphony was also to be addressed to a diverse spectrum of non-Finns in the larger, European marketplace of artistic authority in a career-building bid for personal and cultural acknowledgment, longed-for artistic prestige, and national legitimacy. The conflicting interests at play in any such state of affairs are complex, not easily untangled.

I wish to suggest a few aspects of this broader situation as it pertains to one of Sibelius's primary first-period cultural projects—that of symphonically constructing the impression of a core Finnishness evocative of a preindustrial Karelianist culture. This was the culture whose collected narrative fragments, woven together and published in the Finnish folk epic *Kalevala*, were taken to embody one of the most reliable touchstones of a primitivist, rugged authenticity of difference.[3] While my remarks focus on specific details of Sibelius's music and career, my immediate interest is to use them as an illustration of trends also to be found around that time in other ethnic areas concerned with matters of musical and cultural legitimacy. Of particular interest is the way that those trends played out in the realm of an institutionalized art music (the production and distribution of symphonies, chamber music, tone poems, operas, and the like) whose prestige norms and criteria for assessment had been forged far outside of those more remote areas themselves. In short, much of what I deal with in the case of Sibelius is transferable to those other European composers of the period who also foregrounded folkloric elements in their music. In what follows I am proposing a methodological model generalizable to the study of other art-music inflections of nationalism in nineteenth- and early twentieth-century music.

FOLK RECITATION AND SYMPHONY: THE CHASM

We might start with the elementary observation that there is a vast gap in sound and *Sitz im Leben* [function within a life situation]—a historical chasm or rupture—between the Finnish-revered originary culture (the posited authentic source, runic recitation patterns from the eastern and southeastern regions of Karelia and Ingria, most of which today are parts of Russia) and elite-urban European art. Figure 18.1 sketches the situation at hand, while examples 18.1 and 18.2 suggest the stark differences between the two worlds in question. In example 18.1 I have transcribed the initial six statement-and-response cycles heard on the 1905 wax-cylinder recording of oral-culture Kalevalaic recitation ("Tulen synty" [The Birth of Fire]) delivered by the rune singer Pedri (Petri) Shemeikka at the request of field ethnographer and composer Armas Launis, whose later-published studies of this and other folk repertories would come to be foundational.[4] This was the same Shemeikka whom Sibelius, much impressed, had met, heard, and transcribed in Korpiselkä (Karelia) thirteen years earlier, in the summer of 1892.[5]

Shemeikka's melodic recitation pattern is only one variant of hundreds of similar, highly recognizable formulas typically heard in Karelian folk communities of that day for the telling of extended, textually unstable fragments of traditional but disconnected tales from the *Kalevala*. (The F-minor signature and transcription locate only the pitches heard in the recording. Needless to say, within the originary culture this notation, much less a four-flatted F minor, had no role to play.) The primitive-voice quality and unlettered, coarse-grained character of that world—the raw stuff of ethnographic research—is impossible to convey in any rough transcription. For this reason it is instructive (indeed, essential) to consult modern transfers of early recordings of the practice. Shemeikka's 1905 cylinder is among the earliest, and extracts of it are also available on the Internet.[6] Equally vital to its initial context is the pagan-sacred aspect of ritually resuscitating once again the community memory of a seemingly timeless text. This *Kalevala* fragment was being ceremonially reanimated here, as it had been among generations of ancestors. For our purposes, though, as well as Sibelius's (capturing the intervallic sound and mood of the repeated formula), the verbal details of the folk fragment being delivered are not crucial features. (As Anneli Asplund has noted, Shemeikka's text consists of "a series of charms used to heal burns or put out fires"; "The old man of the air blasts out his lightning. The fire from it penetrates the earth and reaches down as far as Manala, the underworld. Iron stallions are born.")[7]

The six hypnotically reiterative two-bar rounds in example 1 (in this notational translation, 6 × 2 measures) occupy only the first thirty-three seconds of the recording. Ten similar back-and-forth recitations complete its total length of 1 minute 28 seconds, even as we realize that these sixteen recorded lines represent only a small slice of what would have been a much more extended recitation in actual practice—that obsessive, quasi-infinite sameness of the circular delivery, considered by the leaders of the Finnish-language movement from the mid-and late-nineteenth century onward to embody an elemental, premodern Finnishness or cultural essence.

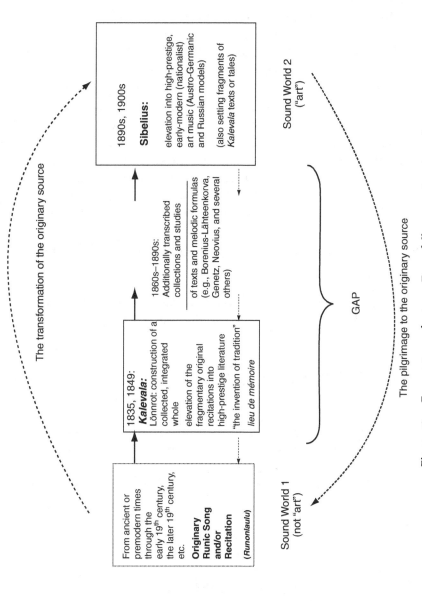

Figure 18.1. Encounter and return: From folk-source to art music.

The implied quintuple meter is also authentic and typical: I have notationally rendered it here as 15/8—instead of the more usual 5/4 transcriptions of Kalevalaic formulas, in which the first three beats of each measure are written as eighth notes—to reflect the slight rhythmic inflection in Shemeikka's delivery. Similarly characteristic is the modal flavor, bounded mostly by a single minor pentachord, with the first trochaic tetrameter line ending on 2̂ (mm. 1, 3, 5, 7, 9, 11), and the complementary second—here a text-line repetition—on 1̂ (mm. 2, 4, 6, 8, 10, 12). In this instance Shemeikka occasionally expanded the modal pentachord—notated here as bounded by the fifth F-C—by dipping down to a step below it, to the subtonic E flat, as in mm. 1, 3, and 7), in what was obviously one standardized way of delivering the first line (m. 1) of a complementary pair. Such moves onto adjacently neighboring pitches to the governing pentachord are not uncommon, although it is perhaps more typical for a Kalevalaic formula to remain within the pentachord proper.[8]

Nothing could be more central to my point than the utter difference of example 18.1 (and the multitude of oral-culture recitations similar to it) in real sound and cultural implication from the urban art-music world embraced by such Sibelian works such as the First Symphony. Represented on the right side of figure 18.1 is the composer's larger-project elevating of the archetypal modal-recitation style, marked above all by minor-mode, reiterative statement and response, into the high-prestige, art-music culture of the First Symphony. As an illustration of this, example 18.2

Example 18.1. Runic Recitation: Transcription of the Opening of Petri Shemeikka's Recording of "Tulen synty" ("The Birth of Fire", 1905)

* ennustuksella ?

Example 18.2. Sibelius, Symphony no. 1 in E Minor, op. 39/i, mm. 103–48

reproduces a familiar folkloric passage from the first movement's exposition: the initial forty-six bars of the secondary-theme zone (much of S-space), mm. 103–48. From one perspective this music is to be heard as fulfilling a standard formal role within late-nineteenth-century sonata-form practice. But within that sophisticated enterprise it seeks also to manufacture assertions of national identity and difference: heartfelt insistences upon a highly marked cultural ethos, minimally encoded declarations of "practical-essentialistic" solidarity. Ultimately, the glowing

Example 18.2.1. Continued

connotations of this enchantment of presence are political and ideological, something to be felt and shared in a generalized way as the music passes by, comes forth, and recedes in linear time. It is worth our trouble to stop the music—to throw it onto the examination table—to observe how Sibelius staged these effects.

Here the secondary-theme strategy was to unfurl an enhanced ethnic disclosure in two distinct stages: (1) a preparatory backward drift in conceptual time—a

Example 18.2.2. Continued

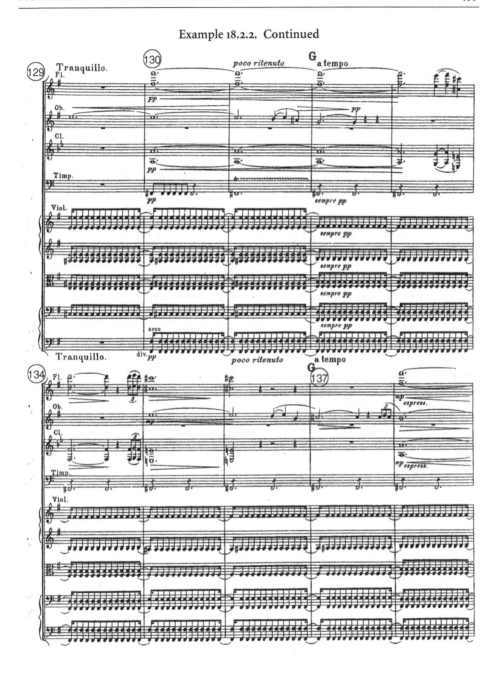

collective-memory corridor leading the participatory listener back toward evocations of a presumably mysterious or magical antiquity, followed by (2) "contact" with the presumed root-source proper ("There it is!"), suggesting that the generating past or at least a decipherable simulacrum of it has been successfully accessed and recovered, made audible once again through the deictic potentialities of modern symphonic art. The initial secondary-theme module (m. 108, led into with introductory, modal-chord oscillations in mm. 100–107) can be heard within the

Example 18.2.3. Continued

language context of standard symphonic practice as seeking to suggest a now-deep(er) reaching into the mysterious, cradle-rocking folk-soul of the Finnish past. That module is also the vehicle by means of which an even more foundational, harder-to-recover, and yet truer past can be activated and enabled to appear (m. 130). Throughout, Sibelius's mission was one of monumentalization: both to dramatize the appearance of any such folk-inflected music and massively to inflate its expressive significance through the grand gestures and colors accessible through the symphonic idiom. Let us consider each of the two spaces in turn.

Merged into by m. 103 (the process had started in m. 100), the first phase, the corridor, establishes a space of maximal difference from the music that has preceded it (much of which, as we shall see, had also been shot through with Finnish identifiers). Toward that end, the composer sought to arrest the choppy, forward-charging plunge of the primary theme and transition in order suddenly (pre-cinematically) to dissolve into a starkly contrasting, more immobile space: the opening up of a wide-angle, sonic tableau. Tonal-diatonic and chromatic-modern practices now give way to static modal oscillation. This coloristic harmony suggests an entry into a different expressive world, the premodern otherness of the invariant national soul, now called upon to occupy the secondary-theme zone of the exposition. The music around letter E (m. 108) is harmonically articulated through the tonic-subdominant oscillations of a static C-sharp dorian in harp and strings. The letter-E theme in the flutes is a transformation of the double-pentachord module from the introduction, mm. 17–20, another Finnish identifier that is discussed toward the end of this chapter.

But this light-staccato passage—recasting the clarinet introduction—turns out to be only the initiatory module within a multimodular S-space. The "off-tonic" C-sharp dorian has not yet settled on the proper (or at least eventual) pitch level for secondary-theme space. Once the modal past is touched around letter E, its persistent staccato chattering unlocks a second, deeper stage of fantasy revelation, which begins at m. 130, two bars before G (anticipated in the oboe in m. 129). We have been brought to a place of access, and the past can now flow into it. This is the moment of contact, the purer allusion to ritualized Kalevalaic recitation: the back-and-forth statement-and-response patterns of semantically parallel paired lines. In this portion of the secondary-thematic zone, now slipping onto the proper modal key, B minor (though over a pedal dominant), we are invited to experience an intimation of the real thing, an epiphany from the mythically reconstructed Finnish past, self-consciously staged as a commemoration of ancient times now being accommodated to the new-world promptings of the urban-modern symphony.

Consider the woodwind melodic material in mm. 130–46. Here Sibelius presents us with a second static sound-image: a B-aeolian or natural-minor melody (though harmonized with the ♯$\hat{7}$ of the harmonic minor scale) hovering over a pulsing dominant pedal that, in the richly textured backdrop strings, supports oscillations between a dominant-seventh chord and its neighboring $\frac{6}{4}$ position. What we experience is a back-and-forth shifting of harmonic colors evoking a recurring Kalevalaic-recitation cycle of timeless alternation, to which we have now gained access. In the interlocked exchanges between the flutes/clarinets and the oboe it is easy to perceive the allusion to the ancient practice of interlinear, semantic parallelism between successions of paired lines, in this case even preserving the characteristic endings of the flutes' and clarinets' statement on $\hat{2}$ (mm. 135–36 and 141–42) and the oboe's response on $\hat{1}$ (mm. 138–39 and 144–45).

Within this modern context, that summoned, epiphanic moment can be drawn forth only fleetingly before it recedes, like a revered but ephemeral vision, to rejoin

(m. 146) an already initiated variant of the earlier chattering, although now over the attained F-sharp pedal, transformed into V of B minor (which eventually resolves, peremptorily, almost as a gratuitous nod toward European-art obligation, onto the B-tonic at m. 166, the point of essential expositional closure [EEC]). It is as if, in the center of that secondary-theme space, a privileged curtain has been opened, one in which a more fully revealed, authentic Kalevalaic past is momentarily made more directly available through the prestige power of art music's claims, as well as being honorifically memorialized as part of the fixed letter of a symphony.

In such passages the composer asks his listeners to identify a self-evidently symphonic passage with the mood and spirit of premodern runic recitation, an identification offered here as a quasi-intuitive connection, a deep-rooted cultural affinity.[9] But the gap in sound and intention between these two sound-worlds is huge. In figure 18.1 the dotted arrow at the bottom, leading leftward to the originary source, suggests the pointing involved in Sibelius's 1899 musical allusion—a pointing under urban-modern conditions to what was being mythologized as a far-distant, once-timeless, and heroic past, though one now slipping ever further away, foreordained by the relentless rationality of an ever-advancing modernity to melt into extinction: a conceptual pilgrimage to a posited germinal source, to what was once a primeval totality of shared-community, face-to-face relations.[10] The complementary dotted arrow at the top suggests its subsequent appropriation, modernist transformation, and careerist elevation into the high-prestige, technological world of the late-century, urban-European symphony, thus completing a trajectory of departure and return: over the yawning chasm into a purportedly truth-telling past and back again on different terms.

National Negotiations: Recovering a Vanishing Past and the Drive for Recognition

In 1899 what made this conceptual journey possible was a preceding series of literary and musical collections fueled by political, folkloric, and preservationist concerns, each of which sought to transcribe the fluidity and fragmentariness of the recited originals into the fixity of print and musical notation. Any such selection and arrangement of texts, along with their translation into the modality of written script, substantially altered much that had been fundamental within the nonfixed, mutable runic sources. Elias Lönnrot's selection, editing, integration, and topical arrangement of scattered oral fragments into the 1835 and 1849 versions of the *Kalevala*—along with material of his own devising—constitute a classic exemplar of what Eric Hobsbawm famously called "the invention of tradition" among nineteenth-century cultures and nations seeking politically to engineer commemorations of a now-idealized past.[11] This was a monument to Finland's folk past, a high-prestige, now-literary place for present and future generations to visit within what was now, ever more clearly with each decade, an urban-modernizing age (an age of progress in the building of a "modern nation") on its way, eventually, to erasing the remaining traces and traditions of peasant or folk cultures, whose backward residues remained stubbornly only as fading glimmers within retreating geographical peripheries.

The *Kalevala* was a historicist project of recovery and preservation that operated on different social-class terms from those that had produced the original recitations in the first place. And yet Lönnrot's book of legends and heroes would soon be mythicized as immortalizing a unique, shared place of origin. To borrow the more general terms of Anthony D. Smith, historian of nationalism(s), the *Kalevala* provided Finns with a tangible "sacred center" serving as a "ready-made ethnic base" and treasure-house of age-old communal traditions for those Finnish-language speakers who wished to accept it as a spiritual home and the essential site that made possible their community's "rediscovery of the 'inner self' that is one of the chief ends of ethnic historicism."[12] As Smith put it in 1991, now addressing this specific situation:

> Here was the ideal self-definition and exemplar for a regenerated Finland in its heroic struggle against Swedish cultural and Russian political domination at the end of the nineteenth century. The recovery of an ancient but apparently "lost" period of Finnish history and culture restored to Finns ["the Finnish intelligentsia and later...the people"] that sense of community and dignity necessary for a small and relatively poor and despised society struggling to reassert its place through a "high" culture.[13]

In subsequent decades, additional poetry transcriptions and cultural and linguistic studies (such as those by the folklorist Arvid Genetz, who was also one of young Sibelius's teachers in Tavastehus/Hämeenlinna)[14] and music transcriptions of the hundreds of variants within the recitation-formula families (especially those in 1877 and following years by Axel August Borenius-Lähteenkorva, along with performance reports by such figures as Adolf Neovius) provided further stages in the production of these now-stable monuments to the past.[15] Sibelius's personal encounters in late 1891 with the Ingrian rune singer Larin Paraske—cited affirmatively in all biographical accounts—provides an additional binding ingredient in the legitimation myth of this generational laying-on-of-hands. In the early 1890s the high-art master-to-be came face to face, for the first time, with what those in his nationalist circle of artists and intellectuals were asserting to be the real thing and touched the core of what he had come to regard as an enduring, culture-defining truth that could continue to persist as the cornerstone of a now-awakening national soul.

Sibelius's personal encounters aside—there were a few others, including the important 1892 Karelian visit in Korpiselkä with Shemeikka[16]—what we see in figure 18.1 is a succession of negotiations (the smaller back-and-forth arrows in the center) bridging the gap between an eroding past and an advancing present that is grasping to preserve it, if only as a translated memory trace circulating within a different mode of communication. In the First Symphony and elsewhere Sibelius regularly wrote passages that point over the gap. Within Finland they were addressed, presumably, to his "in-the-know" listeners' cultural regard for the originary source-style, now musically reprocessed and theatricalized into a present-day, urban-modernist discourse. In such situations concerns of identity and uniqueness of origin are also animated by complex and conflicting impulses of loss. Even while there is no wish to restore the social conditions of a vanishing, premodern past, the point of any such "cultural nationalism" (to use John Hutchinson's term) is to ensure that a cherished past not be forgotten—or, more to the point, to teach and encourage chosen populations to revere and remember that selectively crafted past in an ineradicable age of progressive modernism. It is to be remembered both as an exalted "founding myth" and as a source of high-minded "moral regeneration of the historic community," a process capable of uniting a people "by returning to the creative life-principle of the nation," thus fulfilling a presumed "national destiny."[17]

Even though the details of the Finnish case are particularly salient, involving the conscious and labored construction of a full-blown folk epic, this mode of intellectualized, artistic preservation was hardly unique to Finland. It was a nineteenth- (and twentieth-) century nationalist phenomenon common to many other cultures as well. This deeply rooted drive to uncover and preserve seemingly lost or rapidly vanishing ethnic traditions has been much examined and interpreted in a number of different ways. There is a double consciousness at work here: a melancholic indulgence in one's irreversible exile from the idealized past of one's ethnic predecessors coupled with a keen embrace of technological advancement for one's nation and its full entry into the modernizing world.

The dual-aspect phenomenon is a familiar one. In a 2001 study of nostalgia, for instance ("*nostos*—return home, and *algia*—longing...a longing for a home that no longer exists or has never existed...a romance with one's own fantasy"), Svetlana Boym identified this familiar tendency as "reflective nostalgia" (as opposed to a more activist "restorative nostalgia," which seeks politically to reinstate the past). "Nostalgia, like progress, is dependent on the modern conception of unrepeatable and irreversible time." Reflective nostalgia blends together such "long-distance" factors as "anxiety about the vanishing past," "the meditation on history and passage of time," "individual and cultural memory," and the "savor[ing of] details and memorial signs, perpetually deferring homecoming itself."[18] While politically embracing an increasingly disenchanted, technological world rushing toward an international and hopefully prosperous future, the cultural imperative is repeatedly and sentimentally to recall and thereby retain a disappearing folk-world that might, through the alchemy of art, become momentarily re-enchantable.

The historical situation also resonates aptly with Pierre Nora's similarly recent, sharply intensified concept of the *lieu de mémoire*, or site of (cultural) memory:

> *Lieux de mémoire* exist because there are no longer any *milieux de mémoire*, settings in which memory is a real part of everyday experience....*Lieux de*

mémoire are fundamentally vestiges, the ultimate embodiments of a commemorative consciousness that survives in a history which, having renounced memory, cries out for it....These bastions buttress our identities, but if what they defended were not threatened, there would be no need for them....Moments of history are plucked out of the flow of history, then returned to it—no longer quite alive but not yet entirely dead, like shells left on the shore when the sea of living memory has receded....These *lieux* have washed up from a sea of memory in which we no longer dwell.[19]

From a slightly different perspective, Sibelius's 1899 symphonic transformation involved a related set of negotiations (figure 18.2). Here the local composer—represented by the rectangular box on the left—confronts the world of urban-European elite class and status, motivated by the drive for recognition among artistic representatives of what Milan Kundera calls "small nations" (or at least outlying nations distant from the radiating power-centers of aesthetic style, consecratory languages, and conferrals of legitimacy).[20] If one resides in such a cultural periphery, the initial problem is one of being noticed at all within a potentially humiliating game of insider and outsider, a deadly serious contest whose status-positions are defined on elusive and protean concepts of self and other, membership and non-membership, inclusion and exclusion. To be noticed as existing it was necessary to participate in the genre-game of the greater power, and one had to play it well and engagingly, drawing attention to oneself through the ratification power of its high-prestige luster.

Figure 18.2 illustrates some of the negotiations in play within figure 18.1's rightmost box (its Sibelius box). The central point in this small-nation quest for recogni-

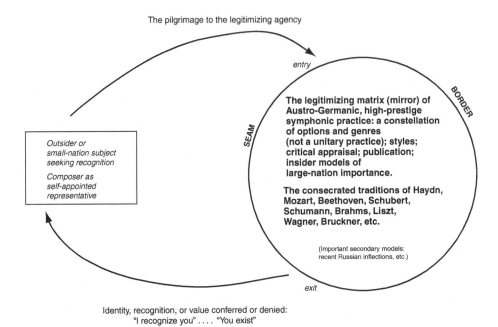

Figure 18.2. Outsider discourse in quest of legitimation.

tion is the obligatory embedding of that pursuit within a matrix of the large nation's discourse. In this case Sibelius's symphony sought inclusion within the high-prestige discourse norms of the late-nineteenth-century Austro-Germanic symphony (the large circle at the right) with its own well-policed fields of expectations and traditions, including stringent criteria for assessment and limits on permissible degrees of variability and experiment. This decision was made shortly after his breakthrough contract with Leipzig's Breitkopf & Härtel in 1898, along with some initial performances of his music in Germany and, most of all, in preparation for the Helsinki Philharmonic's large-scale northern-European tour in summer 1900.[21] Sibelius was now making a bid to emerge from the parochially local sphere hoping to compete in earnest for the prestige of recognition in the larger-European arena. Yet, following the insider-authenticity demands of figure 18.1, he was also obliged to build an idiosyncratic, Finnish-inflected symphony that, paradoxically, was also to serve as his principal attraction and mark of distinctiveness in larger-European markets. To be sure, for Sibelius in the 1890s, the situation was somewhat more complicated. Recent Russian compositions—such as those of Tchaikovsky and Borodin—were also important nationalist models for some of his harmonic, modal, and orchestrational strategies. Nonetheless, those nearby practices were themselves negotiations between Russian constructions of self and nation and the more fundamental Austro-Germanic discourse within which they were enabled. For all of these composers the symphony was a genre to be approached as the repository of a venerated "truth language," a high-prestige musical vehicle equipped with the power to consecrate small-nation cultural legitimacy simply by taking serious notice of it ("I recognize you; you exist").[22]

The process illustrated in figure 18.2, then, is a negotiation between insider small-nation interests and outsider large-nation consecratory power—very much to the essence of the First Symphony. Here the pilgrimage is to the legitimizing agency of expected symphonic practice. In figure 18.1 the balancing pilgrimage—backward in time—had been to the legitimizing or supposedly truth-telling folk source. In short, we have two different pilgrimages: two complementary moves seeking to gain access to utterly different modes of truth language. It is not without interest to observe that for the Swedish-speaking Sibelius, both truth languages (the Karelian runic recitation of the *Kalevala* myths, delivered in various dialects of Finnish, and the Austro-Germanic high-art language of music) were learned languages. In the period 1888–1893 the young Sibelius was urgently trying to absorb and master them both—to bring them together—but both were external to the cultural and linguistic place from which he had started. In short, both were educationally approached.

The large circle with a bold outline in figure 18.2 is also meant to imply the seam or protective border surrounding the consecrated traditions—an initial hurdle (or default of exclusion) separating Sibelius away as an outsider, yet enticing him to enter and prove his worth if he could meet the established terms of the enclosed practice. The hoped-for result was the manufacturing of an esteemed product, a "classic," to be reheard again and again in the formal rites of concert programming and performance: the ritual repetition of a national, now-unchangeable *lieu de mémoire*, a ceremony of spiritual identity mediated through the prestige of established symphonic tradition and inviting silent contemplation and reverential self-identification from the earnest listener.

From an only slightly adjusted perspective, the process in figure 18.2 resonates productively with the traditional belief that to have the right to exist—to matter at all, or at least to feel assured that one matters—is to be confirmed in that right, and thus legitimized, by outside observers that are culturally granted the power the bestow it. Some interpretations would go further to insist that this longing for external recognition lies at the heart of personal and cultural identity formation. On the recent terms, for instance, of Jacques Lacan and Slavoj Žižek, nothing less than one's personal awareness of one's existence is predicated on the fantasy of believing oneself to be the object of the Other's desire—being gazed upon by the Other (as in a mirror), thereby being able to assure oneself that one is worthy of that Other's longing gaze.[23] Within musical nationalism, broadly considered, one such mirror mechanism of self-legitimation can be the external genre of the symphony as a self-created fantasy projection—one that imagines that the authority-bearing language of a valorizing Other is looking back at you (as an object of desire), accepting you, and reassuring you that you are who you wish yourself to be. Thus, within figure 18.2, Sibelius could be interpreted as crossing the bold-border seam to manufacture a symphony, predicated largely in "their" language, that serves to look back both at himself as a unique creator and at his own nationally awakening culture, a fantasy-gaze of the Other, a reflecting fantasy, mirror-like, that offers to an insider, small-nation culture an image of how it longs to be seen by outside others with the power to consecrate: "I *do* recognize you. You *do* exist."

STRATEGIC TRIANGULATION: MUSICAL NEGOTIATIONS AMONG TRUTH LANGUAGES

The figure 18.2 situation is complicated further in that by the 1890s the Austro-Germanic constellation of symphonic traditions had split into opposing factions: a traditionalist base (Brahms and much conservatory practice) confronted by a schismatic and politicized modernism (the chromaticism, coloristic orchestration, and poetically generated formal deformations viewed as progressive in a post-Lisztian, post-Wagnerian world). This brings us to figure 18.3, a more complete way of conceptualizing Sibelius's symphonic choices as ongoing acts of negotiation. I refer to this as Sibelius's strategic triangulation among three negotiated sites, each of which points toward different modes of authenticity and truth-language claims.

Sibelius's symphonic music interweaves differing harmonic and tonal practices on multiple levels, the local, the intermediate, and the long-range. Perhaps too crudely, we might construe the melodic or harmonic components of the three nodes as (from

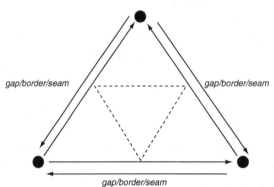

Austro-Germanic Tonal-Symphonic Tradition:
Classical Truth Language

gap/border/seam   *gap/border/seam*

gap/border/seam

Originary *Kalevala* Culture

Recitation formulas

Fundamental folk-source

Center of a potentially recoverable
cultural/national identity, not to be denied
or abandoned: "who you are"

Truth-claim resides in the conviction of a
primordial, uncompromised authencity

Post-Lisztian / Post-Wagnerian
Early Modernism

Chromaticism

Formal deformation, etc.

Truth-claim resides in its progressive
strides (realistic or metaphysical) beyond
the merely formal academicism of
traditional art music

Thus: a reinvigorated musical truth
adequate to modern times

Figure 18.3. Strategic triangulation: Three negotiated sites of authenticity/truth/identity.

the top, moving clockwise): first, the *diatonic-traditional* (the "classical" tonal-symphonic tradition); second, the *chromatic-progressive* (the harmonic-practice markers of the emerging, new-generational early modernism); and third, the *modal-antique* (the originary *Kalevala* folk-culture, ideologically mythicized as a wellspring of cultural identity and difference). Sibelius's music typically shuttles among these constellated nodes, in a process of regular negotiation among them, juxtaposing and overlaying them for structural and expressive purposes deemed appropriate to the symphonic moment at hand. This is why any single analytical system, such as Schenkerian analysis, which is adequate only to hierarchical voice-leading procedures within only one node of the triangulation—the traditional practice at the top—is reductive and inadequate. Sibelius's many forays into a more fully chromatic modernism at the lower right, for instance—replete with Tristan chord and diminished-seventh-chord arrivals, real-transposition sequences, octatonic- and hexatonic-system deployments—call for a complementary dialogue with such alternative analytical methods as neo-Riemannianism or transformation theory. Our analytical styles should be flexible and triangulated, not locked into a unitary practice.

But of course more than harmony is in play. Each musical site (each node of the triangle) participates in a wider musical nexus of ideological traditions, genres, and implications. Figure 18.3 suggests how Sibelius's music (like the First Symphony) may be considered from a broader cultural perspective—not as a reified object but as an ongoing process of negotiated motion, a performative display of multiple dialogues and exchanges. Such a work as the First Symphony dwells not on any one of the three black-dot nodes of this triangle but rather in the interstices or corridors that connect them, the back-and-forth motion-vectors that constitute its sides—navigating in, around, and through the connective passageways. In turn this suggests that the dotted-line triangle in the center is a more precise suggestion of the real triangulation at work—a triangulation not among merely the black-dot nodes as static categories but rather among the corridor gaps, seams, and borders, a strategic triangulation among negotiated processes.[24] Correspondingly, we might be advised to direct our own interpretive gazes toward the larger totality of the triangulated discourse network as a whole, the instabilities and gaps of the pulsating thing-in-motion.

For the listener or analyst the question is how we might appropriately enter into this thing-in-motion, which can appear different to each of us depending on our own cultural and intellectual positions, on how closely we individually identify with the cultural interests advocated by each of the three power-nodes of the triangle. Under such circumstances it becomes tempting to read ourselves and our own agendas into Sibelius's work and thereby to project onto it our own evaluations. Committed patriots, for instance, might be drawn fervently to the "spiritual-solidarity" thrust of the lower-left node—to the resonances of its ardent national inflection, to the inner pull of its claims on behalf of a presumably authentic expression of singularity and indelible difference in contact with the supposedly stable and eternal taproot of the true Finnish self ("Yes! It *is* truly *I*—it is *we*—who are recognized and constructed by this music!").

By contrast, academic analysis and criticism, invested overwhelmingly in reaffirming the prestige of established Austro-Germanic practice as the primary criterion of value, has often been discomforted by some of the nationalistic elements of the triangulation (the lower-left node), has often regarded them as parochial limitations, aesthetic embarrassments, or outright deficiencies. Against such dismissals the only counter within the academic system is a frankly recuperative strategy on traditionalist terms, an attempt to demonstrate the "real" value of Sibelius to the skeptic by arguing that the composer does indeed deserve to pass officially sanctioned analytical muster through the production of orthodox legitimizing procedures: intense Schenkerian graphs, motivic developing-variation charts, formal-process overviews, and so on.

From time to time it is invigorating to step back from all of this—to step back from the urge to reduce one's own view to that of any one of the three power-nodes and their agendas—and instead to grasp the larger totality of the triangulated discourse network as a whole, the instabilities and gaps of the pulsating thing-in-motion. And behind it all, the entire set of processes, at the turn of the century, was being placed in the service of the historical construction of a national identity. But all such identities are problematic: the blank void at the triangle's center, longing to be nourished with real content. The empty center: an appeal for recognition that welds an insider discourse of imagined communal kinship and solidarity for Finns to an exotic outsider discourse for others.

Building a First Symphony: Music as Nationalist Ideology

Figure 18.4 completes our overview by illustrating a familiar teleological plan—an archetypal musical plot—favored as an interior trajectory within individual pieces by many later-nineteenth-century nationalist composers. Here the musical linearity opens itself to political interpretation, inviting listeners to imagine the overcoming of external obstacles through struggle or resistance. When we consider a set of first performances of a work—that toward which the composer obviously prepares it—it is crucial to observe that the whole process, of necessity, is literally to be unfolded in the present—the present, that is, of those initial performances and audiences. At least initially, the work seeks to speak to that world as it stands at that moment. Thus a reasonable assumption is that the presented span of the symphonic discourse, from start to finish, is temporally focalized (to use Gérard Genette's term) in the here and now—in the case of Sibelius's First Symphony, from the point of view of Finnish audiences at the turn of the century.[25] (I set aside here the conceptual problems of performances in later decades or other places, ones that do not share Finland's preoccupations of that era.) Under those conditions the work's contents are to be perceived from a specific point of view, that of the participants' present-day situation, the audience's now-time. From this stable vantage point, a sonically iridescent temporal fulcrum, it becomes possible, while still holding confidently to the anchor of the present, the point of focalization, to survey musical allusions to the past (and thus to perceive them as past) as well as anticipated projections into an as-yet-unrealized future.

Once this has been grasped, it becomes clear why a composer might stage the whole discourse of a nationalist work to drive toward an ecstatically affirmative outcome at the end. When this happens, such a *telos* proclaims that the music has successfully completed a representational trajectory from "then" to "now," a historical journey from obscurity to recognition ("Here we are! We have arrived!"). What is metaphorically represented in such cases is the long-awaited emergence into history of a nation and with it the promise of its projection into a confident, modern future. (Smetana's *Vltava*, Tchaikovsky's Second Symphony and *1812* Overture, Dvořák's Eighth Symphony, Sibelius's *Finlandia*, and numerous other works provide familiar realizations.)[26] Under the terms of this standardized plot format, music-time (the linear progress of the piece from moment to moment, its aesthetic time-axis) is readily homologous to historical time—moving toward "us," so to speak, moving from the fantasy of our past to the fantasy of our urban-modern present. The forward-vectored musical unfolding of the piece—within a symphony the four-movement whole—is to be construed as an analogue of a culture's image of its own chronological history, the forging of a national soul, a musical enactment of proud awakening and assertion. Structure and process march inexorably toward the staging of a culminating, heroic self-realization, achieved at the climactic end of the

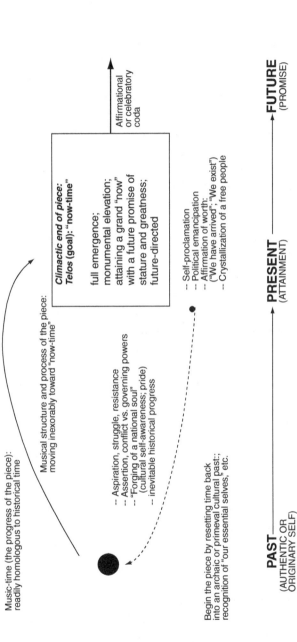

Music-time (the progress of the piece):
readily homologous to historical time

Musical structure and process of the piece:
moving inexorably toward "now-time"

Climactic end of piece:
Telos (goal): "now-time"

full emergence;
monumental elevation;
attaining a grand "now"
with a future promise of
stature and greatness;
future-directed

-- Aspiration, struggle, resistance
-- Assertion, conflict vs. governing powers
-- "Forging of a national soul"
     (cultural self-awareness; pride)
-- inevitable historical progress

-- Self-proclamation
-- Political emancipation
-- Affirmation of worth:
   ("We have arrived"; "We exist")
-- Crystallization of a free people

Affirmational
or celebratory
coda

Begin the piece by resetting time back
into an archaic or primeval cultural past;
recognition of "our essential selves," etc.

PAST
(AUTHENTIC OR
ORIGINARY SELF)

PRESENT
(ATTAINMENT)

FUTURE
(PROMISE)

Figure 18.4. One Characteristic Symphonic-Nationalist Plot: Self-Realization of a People; Emergence into History and the Future.

piece (as the arched upper arrow suggests)—a grand, liberated "now," a *telos* emancipated into historical reality in the finale and striding confidently, often in a major-mode, triumphant coda, into a bright future. The expressive carrier for all of this is that of the metaphor of the symphony—"their" prestige genre—conquered and completed and thus earned through struggle as "our" prestige genre as well, a sign of self-proclaimed, sophisticated accomplishment.

Sibelians will recognize the plot as precisely that of the D-major Second Symphony of 1901–02—another touchstone realization. But the E-minor First Symphony of 1899, its Karelianist counterpart and predecessor, denies its listeners the generic affirmative *telos* at the end. However unmistakably its internal struggles toward musical and cultural emancipation were staged, the First Symphony ends catastrophically in a ruthlessly smothering E minor. Especially in those politically strained times for Finland, the First Symphony's connotation was one of an over-whelming injustice still enforced from outside—the lid still on—while fierce resentment and unstoppable resistance continue to boil below, awaiting their day. This negative variant of the stereotypical plot may be unique. The First is perhaps the only overtly nationalistic, late-nineteenth-century symphony that projects a narrative of failure purposely kept from attaining the normatively positive *telos*. Instead, it lionizes the grimly persistent, clenched fist of resistance. It loses this first four-movement battle but resolutely gears up for the next one. In the Second Symphony the same plot would be revisited and brought to the more traditionally victorious, utopian outcome. The First and Second Symphonies are intercon-nected, companion works, negative and positive, opposite faces of the same narra-tive coin.[27]

Along the bottom of figure 18.4 we see that this standard nationalist plot car-ries the music from a presumed source-past, with which it must connect at the opening, through musical and historical time to a proclaimed present (attaining the point of temporal focalization as *telos*), and finally into what is usually a pro-jection into the future at the end. This means that the composer typically begins such a piece by resetting time back into an archaic or primeval cultural past, grasp-ing and transforming a presumed ancient source of folk authenticity (as in figure 18.1), a procedure that invites the insiders' recognition of "our essential selves." Hence the backward-moving dotted-line arrow, with the large black dot suggesting the opening measures of the piece, which is often an introduction or folk-soul preface before the main structure of the work gets underway. We are confronted with a temporal paradox in the opening bars of such a work. As the music moves forward in chronological, linear time, insider-listeners are asked to drift backward into the past, to recognize and secure an initial contact with a preindustrial folk source that they believe, as a binding myth, that they share as enduring features in the modernizing present.[28]

The opening of the First Symphony provides us with an illustration of this—and of figures 18.1 through 18.3 as well. The relevant music is shown in example 18.3, and at least for the purposes of this chapter I set aside the important issues both of the slow introduction's possible indebtedness to prestigious models in

Example 18.3. Sibelius, Symphony no. 1 in E Minor, op. 39/i, mm. 1–58

Tchaikovsky and others—which deepens crucial questions of intertextuality and modeling in obvious ways—and of the recently published evidence that during the earlier stages of labor on the symphony's composition Sibelius might not always have planned for there to be an introduction at all. (With regard to this latter issue, at least from the 1899 public premiere of the original work onward, the First Symphony seems always to have been performed—and then published—with a slow introduction.)[29]

The first sounds that we hear are those of the introductory Andante, ma non troppo preceding the onset of the Allegro energico sonata-form proper. In this

Example 18.3.1. Continued

preparatory musical "frame" we are presented with a solitary instrumental voice (the solo clarinet) exploring still-empty space in allusively modal formulations.[30] The initial melody is governed largely by the modal-minor, "Finnish" pentachord (the central folk element that Sibelius had emphasized three years earlier in a lecture on Finnish-nationalist aesthetics given in 1896 at what was then the Imperial

Example 18.3.2. Continued

Alexander University of Finland in Helsingfors/Helsinki).[31] All of this is to suggest a drifting back into a seamlessly whole folk-past (a Kalevalaic-recitation world of cultural memory—perhaps also imbued, as Ilmari Krohn suggested in 1945, with the melancholy flavor of a primordial Karelian singer of *itkukvirsiä*, or laments).[32] That distant and mystified past is now being grasped and brought—negotiated— over a substantial gap of time and sonority into the modern symphonic world of urban high-prestige art.

Apart from the sprouting of the modal pentachords at different pitch levels, several other signifiers are evocative here. The *alla breve* barlines are notationally present but barely perceived aurally: The clarinet solo is played, cadenza-like, in the largely free, nonrationalized space of a remote, lonely timelessness. Even the notational image of the clarinet on the page, isolated with the timpani on the otherwise empty staves of a full orchestral score, visually conveys this idealized solitariness, the faraway, Karelian voice translated from outside into the clarinet timbre and advancing toward the modern orchestra and its demands. For the audience participating in this performance ritual, the analogue is the visual presence of the large but silent orchestra—the consecratory group—assembled onto the stage, waiting to take up its own modern, high-art duties when given the go-ahead. The process is initiated by an almost-inaudible B-natural, *pianissimo* timpani roll in mm. 1–16. Here the fantasy curtain of the past is drawn open, a backdrop sound impulse dying away, *morendo*, in m. 16, leaving the clarinet even more isolated—a national voice, a historicized myth of authenticity, soon to be brought into engagement and put at risk in the urban-modern symphony to follow.

While the Finnish-pentachord signifiers of the introduction are self-explanatory, one might call attention to mm. 17–20 and its double-pentachord formation around e natural: a minor pentachord both below and above the axis of e natural (though the entire modular complex in mm. 17–20 may also be construed locally as A dorian if we regard the lowest pitch as the final). The appearance here of the double pentachord as an evocation of primeval Finnishness is no accident. Sibelius had noted the possibility of just such a complementary lower pentachord in his 1896 folk- and art-music lecture as a typically Finnish configuration that, properly treated by the modern composer, would imply a modal harmonization.[33]

Measures 1–21 play themselves out in melodic shapes bounded by the E-minor, B-minor, and A-minor modal pentachords. As the introductory solo voice is brought closer to the symphonic process proper, mm. 21–29 return to the opening melodic figure, now outlining the G-minor pentachord and in the process completing an extended series of descending fifths that had begun back in m. 1.[34] Measures 25–29 call for a triple *pianissimo* with a dissolving fade-out, *morendo*—an initial premise whose purer isolation recedes into near inaudibility even as the primeval world toward which it had pointed is now suddenly thrown into the world of the modern symphony with the Picardy-third effect of the G-B tremolo dyad at the Allegro energico—where the gears finally clench. A border is crossed; a seam negotiated; a conceptual line stepped over. The shimmering G-B-natural dyad is the sudden flipping of a switch, an alarm, an electrifying call to action.

The composer thus seeks to create the impression of launching a translated, Kalevalaic voice of the mythicized past into the contemporary-European symphonic process—a call to self-realization, now put onto the one-way tracks of the modern four-movement symphony. The potential metaphors multiply in different registers of connotation. First, the vector of musical-linear time suggests that of historical time toward a desired present still far down the road. Second, the much-noted E-minor/G-major conflict at the heart of the first movement, along with its high-pressure orchestral eruptions, suggests the staging of a technical struggle between the archaic and the symphonic materials, a recovered ancient self, politically and culturally under threat of erasure, plunging and navigating bar by bar through the sea of alien norms rigorously demanded by the modern symphonic process. Third, the symphonic unfolding suggests an image of the stormy, flamboyant Sibelius himself as careerist, seeking to conquer the resistant genre of the symphony phrase by phrase with explosive determination. Fourth, the E-minor/G-major conflict and symphonic process are also understandable as tonal metaphors of emancipatory struggle in the then-enveloping context of Finnish-Russian politics (and so on, surely in additional metaphorical registers as well). Throughout it all, Sibelius takes pains to ensure that his constructed Finnish musical identifiers remain expositionally omnipresent: outlines of the Finnish pentachord, along with frequent returns to what I have called the $\hat{3}$ - $\hat{2}$ - $\hat{1}$ "Finnish ideogram" and that recurring $\hat{5}$-#$\hat{5}$-$\hat{6}$ or $\hat{6}$-♭$\hat{6}$-$\hat{5}$ motion over a pedal bass, so typical of Sibelius's music of this period, the mechanism, borrowed from Russian practice, that here generates the G-major/E-minor conflict.[35]

The primary theme beginning in m. 33 is not unrelated to the Ur-melody of the introduction—an initial long note released into a more mobile descent. But its impact here is more aggressively clipped, more unsettled. Still, the primary theme at m. 33 can be read as a deformation of the originally relaxed or timeless clarinet theme, whose initial melodic identity is thrown into strain under different conditions, an ancient self subjected to the stress of modern times. Notice, for instance, that the Kalevalaic statement-response pattern (the telltale parallelism of Finnish epic recitation) is readily discernible (m. 33, violin 1, is freely imitated by violas and cellos, m. 34; the second statement, m. 37, is freely imitated below in m. 38), but now that signifier is rendered deformational, its parallelisms telescoped, its contours and rhythmic flow distorted under the high pressure of the Allegro-energico duties of a symphony proper. Two statements, two responses— and immediately after the third statement begins (m. 41), Sibelius interrupts it, explodes it into conflict in m. 42.

What we can hear in such music—and in the subsequent, secondary-theme music reproduced in example 18.2 earlier in this chapter—are differing registers of negotiation over the gap between the dissolving past and the then-politicized urban-modern, internationally enticed present, or, more precisely, registers of performative negotiation among at least three different worlds of musical sound: that of a presumed originary past as a source of self-recognition, that of traditional Austro-Germanic symphonic practice (here inflected in the direction of the antique), and that of the new-generational liberated norms of modern-urban chromatic and formal practice. Like other nationalistic works by other national composers, what we encounter is a strategic triangulation among different modes of musical sound, each of which bears its own ideological claims of authenticity, power, and truth-telling. The strongest analyses of—or commentaries on—such works will be those that keep the tense uncertainties and problematics of these gaps, borders, negotiations, and triangulations uppermost in mind.

NOTES

An earlier version of this chapter appeared in *Musurgia* 14 (2007): 27–47.

1. One of the most useful introductions to these cultural issues, as well as to the artistic and musical tone of Finland at this time—central to any consideration of nationalism in this area—may be found in Glenda Dawn Goss, *Jean Sibelius and Finland's Awakening* (Chicago: University of Chicago Press, 2009).

2. Michael Herzfeld, *Cultural Intimacy: Social Poetics in the Nation-State*, 2d ed. (New York: Routledge, 2005). Herzfeld associates the concept of cultural intimacy not merely with self-recognition per se but rather with the phenomenon of "rueful self-recognition," or "the recognition of those aspects of a cultural identity that are considered a source of external embarrassment but that nevertheless provide insiders with their assurance of common sociality" (3). "These are self-stereotypes that insiders express ostensibly at their own collective expense" (3), and they play out in the grip of a persistent tension between the affectionate embrace of traits of cultural embarrassment and prideful self-assertion. The result, on these terms, is the strategic production and acceptance of a "practical essentialism" (26–33) for the sake of self-preservation: a willing self-stereotyping played out on various levels of social grouping from the local to the national. The whole, in Herzfeld's terms, is predicated on a complex, processual phenomenon of "social poetics" (26).

3. For some relatively recent English-language overviews of the specific quest for a sense of Finnishness via Karelianism with specific respect to music (along with additional bibliography), see William A. Wilson, "Sibelius, the *Kalevala*, and Karelianism," in Glenda Dawn Goss, ed., *The Sibelius Companion* (New York: Greenwood, 1996), 43–60; Goss, "A Backdrop for Young Sibelius: The Intellectual Genesis of the *Kullervo* Symphony," *19th-Century Music* 27 (2003), 48–73; Goss, *Jean Sibelius and Finland's Awakening*; and Matti Huttunen, "The National Composer and the Idea of Finnishness: Sibelius and the Formation of Finnish Musical Style," in *The Cambridge Companion to Sibelius*, ed. Daniel M. Grimley, 7–21 (New York: Cambridge University Press, 2004).

4. See, for example, Armas Launis, "Über Art, Entstehung, und Verbreitung der Estnisch-Finnischen Runenmelodien" (diss., Alexander Universität, Helsingfors, 1910; printed by the Finnischen Literatur Gesellschaft, 1910) (rpt., rev., same title, Helsinki: Société Finno-Ougrienne, 1913), esp. iii–vii on previously transcribed sources and collections. Also invaluable is Launis's related collection of transcriptions, *Suomen Kansan Sävelmiä*, Neljas Jakso, ser. 4, *Runosävelmiä*: II, *Karjalan Runosävelmät* (Helsinki: Suomalainen Kirjallisuuden Seura, 1930), which provides hundreds of recitation melodies identified by location, the date of the original transcription or collection, and the original collector.

5. Sibelius described his July or August encounter with Shemeikka—and with other Karelian folk idioms—in a brief written report dated Nov. 11, 1892. This document was recently published in a French translation (by Anja Fantapié) as Sibelius, "Compte rendu du voyage d'étude du signataire en Carélie à l'été 1892," *Musurgia* 14 (2007): 179–80. (Some details of it are cited in n. 16, this chapter.) See also Veijo Murtomäki's discussion in "Sibelius and Finnish-Karelian Folk Music," *Finnish Music Quarterly* 3 (2005): 32–37. As Murtomäki notes, in tableau 1 of the original music for *Karelia* (1893), "A Karelian Home: News of War" [Karjalan koti; Sanoma sodasta], Sibelius harmonized a 5/4 melody (for two runic singers) that he had transcribed from his 1892 encounter with Shemeikka. A larger version of Murtomäki's essay, with the differing title "The Influence of Karelian *Runo* Singing and *Kantele* Playing on Sibelius's Music," will appear in Timothy L.

Jackson, ed., *Sibelius in the Old and New World: Aspects of His Music, Its Interpretation and Reception* (New York: Lang, 2010). A monumental statue of Shemeikka as one of the most authentic singers of the *Kalevala* was erected in the Karelian town of Sortavala (then Finland, now Russia) in 1935 and can be viewed at http://heninen.net/sortavala/karta/patsas/english.htm.

6. *The Kalevala Heritage: Archive Recordings of Ancient Finnish Songs*, Ondine, ODE 849-2 (1995). Extracts from this 1905 recording (and others) may be heard at http://www.amazon.com/Kalevala-Heritage-Archive-Recordings-Ancient/dp/B000003781. One should of course also realize that the recording situation (Armas's necessary placing of Shemeikka directly in front of the large recording horn, the commercial product of a modernist and foreign technology) was also a factor in the sound that has come down to us on the cylinder.

7. From the notes to *The Kalevala Heritage*, 28. Shemeikka's version of the "Tulen synty" text is not the same as that collected and included by Elias Lönnröt in the "official" *Kalevala*, Runo 47 [Poem 47]—which was also the text set by Sibelius in his own work, *Tulen synty*, op. 32, for baritone, male chorus, and orchestra (1902, rev. 1910). A roughly similar but still differing set of charms, and so on, may be found in the *Kalevala*, Runo 48: 301–66.

8. In addition, his tonic-pitch upbeat to m. 1, vocalized but untexted, is also idiosyncratic, giving the impression of an initial push into the text. Also notable is Shemeikka's decision to repeat the text of each line (the text of m. 1 is repeated in the m. 2 complement and so on). More often, the statement and the response consist of two different, interrelated lines of text. Discussions of Kalevalaic recitation formulas are not difficult to locate, but for quick overviews in *The New Grove Dictionary of Music and Musicians*, 2d ed., ed. Stanley Sadie. (London: Macmillan, 2001), see Ilkka Kolehmainen, "Finland: [II] Traditional Music," 8: 862–65; and James Hepokoski, "Sibelius, Jean," 23: 321–22.

9. On the claim of a Finnish "spontaneous," intuitive response—not a literal or studied response—to the spirit of the *Kalevala* as conveyed in the music of Sibelius from the 1890s, see Huttunen, "The National Composer and the Idea of Finnishness" (n. 3 this chapter), esp. 4–5.

10. The concept is not without resonances with what, some three decades later, the anti-rationalist Heidegger, in *Being and Time*, would identify as a striving for *Eigentlichkeit* [authenticity] within *Dasein*. The critical rejection of such claims is perhaps found most vehemently in Theodor W. Adorno, *The Jargon of Authenticity*, trans. Knut Tarnowski and Frederic Will (Evanston, Ill.: Northwestern University Press, 1973). Cf. Max Paddison, *Adorno's Aesthetics of Music* (New York Cambridge: Cambridge University Press, 1993), 54: "This notion of 'community' is ideological, according to Adorno, because to project a conception of the idealized community of the pre-industrial world on to modern industrialized society serves to conceal and mystify the true character of human relations in the modern world." Such a belief in invariance and the eternal in one's past is ideological, in Adorno's view, since it ignores the historicity of the construction of such a myth. Herzfeld (see n. 2) has an entirely different view of this.

11. Eric Hobsbawm, "Introduction: Inventing Traditions," in Hobsbawm and Terence Ranger, eds., *The Invention of Tradition*, 1–14 (Cambridge: Cambridge University Press, 1983).

12. Anthony D. Smith, *National Identity* (Reno: University of Nevada Press, 1991), for example, 16–18, 67, 93 ("rescue," 18; "[Social spaces that] also provide individuals with

'sacred centres,' objects of spiritual and historical pilgrimage, that reveal the uniqueness of their nation's 'moral geography,' " 16; "ready-made ethnic base," 67; "rediscovery of the 'inner self,' " 93. Cf. also the more recent Anthony D. Smith, *The Cultural Foundations of Nations: Hierarchy, Covenant, and Republic* (Malden, Mass.: Blackwell, 2008), which lays out essentially the same points.

13. Smith, *National Identity*, 67. Cf. Ernest Gellner's well-known, more tartly cynical view of modern nationalism in general—one that Smith contests here and there—in *Nations and Nationalism* (Ithaca: Cornell University Press, 1983). Gellner argues (e.g., 55–57) that most modern nationalisms (those of the nineteenth and twentieth centuries) were essentially enthusiasms promoted by elite groups of intellectuals—top-down, not bottom-up movements:

> It is nationalism which engenders nations, and not the other way round. Admittedly, nationalism uses the pre-existing, historically inherited proliferation of cultures or cultural wealth, though it uses them very selectively, and it most often transforms them radically....The cultural shreds and patches used by nationalism are often arbitrary historical inventions. Any old shred and patch would have served as well....The basic deception and self-deception practised by nationalism is this: nationalism is, essentially, the general imposition of a high culture on society, where previously low cultures had taken up the lives of the majority, and in some cases of the totality, of the population....But this is the very opposite of what nationalism affirms and what nationalists fervently believe. Nationalism usually conquers in the name of a putative folk culture. Its symbolism is drawn from the healthy, pristine, vigorous life of the peasants, of the *Volk*, the *narod*.

14. Murtomäki, "Sibelius and Finnish-Karelian Folk Music," 32.

15. Murtomäki, "Sibelius and Finnish-Karelian Folk Music," 32, reports that Borenius was "the first systematic collector of Finnish-Karelian folk melodies...[and his] catch was till 1895 almost 800 tunes." One might also note that in Launis's extensive collection of recitation melodies, *Suomen Kansan Sävelmiä;*, Neljas Jakso, ser. 4, *Runosävelmiä: II, Karjalan Runosävelmät* (see n. 4 this chapter), he observed noted the following on p. i of the "Vorwort": "Der bedeutendste Teil der in dieser Publikation vereinigten Melodien ist von Inspektor A. Lähteenkorva (Borenius) zusammengebracht worden. Ohne seine langjährige, emsige Arbeit in dem bezüglich seiner Melodien recht wenig erforschten Gebiet von Russisch-Karelien wäre die Kenntnis von unserem Runengesang in mancher Hinsicht mangelhaft."

16. In Sibelius's late-1892 report of his visit to Karelia (see n. 5 this chapter), apart from his single transcription of "the oldest melody that he heard" from Sheimekka (which he also regarded as the "source" of all the others), he transcribed three other melodies from other performers: two more *Kalevala* melodies and one lament. He also reported having heard dozens of variants of laments, *Kalevala* recitations, and kantele melodies. The next few years would find him continuing his explorations of the folk idiom and folksong transcription in still other ways: folksong arrangements, 1895 transcriptions for the *Kalevala*, and so on. (See also the discussion in Murtomäki, "Sibelius and Finnish-Karelian Folk Music," 34).

17. John Hutchinson, *The Dynamics of Cultural Nationalism* (New York: HarperCollins, 1987), excerpted as "Cultural Nationalism and Moral Regeneration" in John Hutchinson and Anthony D. Smith, eds., *Nationalism* (New York: Oxford University Press 1994), 122–31 (quotations from 123–24). A persistent question among scholars of

nationalism is whether it is inevitably a negative, even reactionary or antimodernist force in history, as, for example, Gellner and others have suggested. (See n. 13 this chapter.) Opposing this view, Hutchinson distinguishes between a potentially negative "political nationalism" and what he regards as a more constructive, if moralizing, "cultural nationalism of historians and artists," which typically played "a much more positive role in the modernization process" (127–28). It was Hutchinson's view that particularly appealed to Daniel M. Grimley in his recent study of Norwegian nationalism, *Grieg: Music, Landscape, and Norwegian Identity* (Rochester, N.Y.: Boydell, 2006).

18. Svetlana Boym, *The Future of Nostalgia* (New York: Basic Books, 2001), xiii, 13, 19, 41, 49–51.

19. Pierre Nora, "General Introduction: Between Memory and History," in Nora, director and ed., *Realms of Memory: Rethinking the French Past*, trans. Arthur Goldhammer, Engl. ed. Lawrence D. Kritzman (New York: Columbia University Press, 1998), 3 vols., vol. 1, 1–20 (quotations from 1, 6, 7). An earlier (and more frequently cited) translation of a somewhat different version of Nora's essay appeared as "Between Memory and History: *Les lieux de mémoire*," trans. Marc Roudebush, *Representations* 26 (Spring 1989): 7–25.

20. Milan Kundera, "*Die Weltliteratur*," in *Le Rideau* (Paris: Gallimard, 2005), 43–74 (e.g., 45, 47: "les petites nations"). The essay is also available in English, trans. Linda Asher, in Kundera, *The Curtain* (New York: HarperCollins, 2006), 29–56.

21. Note, however, that the First Symphony was initially published in Helsinki by Fazer and Westerlund, though (as mentioned in the 2001 *New Grove* article on Sibelius, vol. 23, 327), "again with links to Breitkopf (who acquired the rights to this music in 1905)."

22. The concept of "truth language" is borrowed and adapted from Benedict Anderson, *Imagined Communities: Reflections on the Origin and Spread of Nationalism*, rev. ed. (New York: Verso, 1991), for example, 12–19 and 36. Anderson writes here of the prestige and importance of the sacred truth languages of the past—for example, "Church Latin, Qur'anic Arabic, or Examination Chinese" (14)—which were initially considered to be "emanations of reality, not randomly fabricated representations of it" (14). The process of the print-culture dissemination of sacred (or "truth") ideas in more local vernaculars—in effect the breaking up of the once-invincible authority and exclusiveness of the original truth languages—is a central feature of the modernity of the past several centuries and is of course implicated in the "imagined communities" of nationalism. Within mid- and late-nineteenth-century musical culture in western Europe, the "language" of Austro-Germanic musical syntax and genres was making similar, virtually exclusionary claims about its appropriateness in approaching the seriousness of metaphysical or transcendental truth.

The concept of "the power to consecrate" is central to the art sociology of Pierre Bourdieu, elaborated, for example, in the essays "The Field of Cultural Production," "The Production of Belief," and "The Market of Symbolic Goods," in Bourdieu, *The Field of Cultural Production*, ed. Randal Johnson, 29–73, 74–111 (esp. 76–81), 112–41 (esp. 120–25) (New York: Columbia University Press, 1993), and Bourdieu, *The Rules of Art: Genesis and Structure of the Literary Field*, trans. Susan Emanuel (Stanford: Stanford University Press, 1996), 121–23, 159–61, 166–73, 223–27.

23. See, for example, "The Seven Veils of Fantasy," in Žižek, *The Plague of Fantasies* (New York: Verso, 1997), 3–44 (esp. 8–10).

24. While the concept of negotiated or "performative" identity (or "hybridity") along borders or seams is hardly unique to any writer (it is a commonplace among postcolonial theorists), the present discussion is most immediately in dialogue with ideas set forth in Homi K. Bhabha, *The Location of Culture* (New York: Routledge, 1994; rpt., 2005).

25. Gérard Genette, *Narrative Discourse: An Essay in Method*, trans. Jane E. Lewin (Ithaca: Cornell University Press, 1980), 189–94.

26. I have also discussed this much-adopted nationalist plot in "Beethoven Reception: The Symphonic Tradition," in *The Cambridge History of Nineteenth-century Music*, ed. Jim Samson, 442–43 (Cambridge: Cambridge University Press, 2002).

27. As if to make this point as clearly as possible, Sibelius brings the final bars of the Second Symphony's second movement back, with explicit echoes, to the conclusion of the First's finale—only now to break free of the shackles in the Second's subsequent two movements.

28. The paradox of simultaneously forward and backward motion on two different conceptual levels—one kind of narrative anachrony—has been influentially explored in Genette, *Narrative Discourse*, especially in ch. 1, "Order," 33–85, in which anachrony is defined as "all forms of discordance between the two temporal orders of story and narrative" (40). More specifically, the motion back to (or specific allusion to) an earlier, culture-grounding time might be understood as one type of analepsis (or flashback), in which the reference is secured at the outset as an essential token of national authenticity or generative contact with a culturally validating, timeless truth language.

29. My concern in this chapter is with the final, published version of the symphony—the one that has been publicly presented to audiences since its earliest appearances. The story of its genesis and sketching, however, is an engaging one indeed. By far the most thorough introduction to the compositional and publication history of the First Symphony appears at the beginning of its new critical edition: Timo Virtanen, "Introduction," in *Jean Sibelius, Symphonie no. 1 in E Minor, op. 39*, ed. Timo Virtanen, ser. 1 (Orchestral Works), vol. 2 of *Jean Sibelius: Complete Works* (Paris: Breitkopf and & Härtel, 2008), ix–xviii. In that comprehensive introduction Virtanen lays out evidence, at least partially locatable in sketches and the other manuscript documents (x–xi), that the slow introduction might not have been part of Sibelius's original conception of the work—that at an early stage the composer might have considered starting the symphony directly with music similar to the current Allegro energico. It is difficult to reconstruct these pre-premiere plans with absolute certainty, though, and newspaper reviews of the Apr. 26, 1899, Helsinki premiere of the symphony's original version did take note of the opening clarinet solo (see x–xi). As Virtanen also notes, Sibelius revised the work further in early 1900 in preparation for the trip of "the Helsinki Philharmonic Orchestra...to the Paris World Exhibition" shortly thereafter. Still, "even if the work 'took its final form' during the Spring of 1900, it does not mean that Sibelius did not make further, possibly minor, revisions later" (xi). The work was eventually published by Germany's Breitkopf & Härtel "during the summer of 1902" (xiv).

30. Virtanen, "Introduction" (xii), notes that there is at least a possibility (but in my view a remote one) that in the still pre-publication version performed in Helsinki in July 1900, shortly before the Paris tour, Sibelius might have experimented with "giv[ing] the solo of the first movement introduction to the English horn" since that instrument was mentioned (perhaps inaccurately?) in a local *Hufvudstadsbladet* review by Alarik Uggla. While it is difficult to assess the accuracy of this newspaper remark, if at any point Sibelius had directed the opening solo to be played by an English horn, it might well have conjured up—at least in his mind—such earlier works such as the *Kalevala*-based *The Swan of Tuonela*, not to mention precedents in Berlioz (e.g., *Symphonie fantastique*), Wagner (*Tristan und Isolde*), and many others.

31. The lecture (in Swedish) was titled "Some Reflections on Folk Music and Its Influence on the Development of Art Music." A French translation by Anja Fantapié has recently been published as "Quelques considérations sur la musique populaire et son influence sur l'art des sons," *Musurgia* 14 (2007), 181–88. See also the summary, for example, in Murtomäki, "Sibelius and Finnish-Karelian Folk Music," 35–36, or in my own *New Grove* entry, "Sibelius," 23: 324.

32. See, for example, Erik Tawaststjerna, *Sibelius*, vol. 1, *1865–1905*, trans. Robert Layton (Berkeley: University of California Press, 1976), 211. Cf. the Finnish-language 2d ed. of vol. 1 of Tawaststjerna's *Jean Sibelius* (Helsinki: Otava, 1989), 309–10, which reiterates the point with reference to the descending "sigh motif" that dominates the theme's "mood...not far from the Karelian world." (The reference in Tawaststjerna's Finnish volume is to Ilmari Krohn, *Die Stimmungsgehalt der Symphonien von Jean Sibelius*, vol. 1 (Helsinki, 1945), 37. The singer of laments was traditionally a woman, an *itkijänainen* (as translated in the Finnish edition of Tawaststjerna, *Jean Sibelius*, vol. 2, 144).

33. "Quelques considérations" (see n. 31 this chapter), 185–86.

34. The descent of fifths: B (m. 1), E (7, 10, 18, 20), A (17), D (21), G (29)—as if the originary signifier falls by fifths into the symphony proper.

35. Several of these analytical issues and terms are examined in my essay "Sibelius," in *The Nineteenth-century Symphony*, ed. D. Kern Holoman, 417–49 (New York: Schirmer, 1997). Richard Taruskin has investigated the sinuous, inner-voice $\hat{5}$-$\sharp\hat{5}$-$\hat{6}$ motion and its converse as a characteristically nineteenth-century Russian-"orientalist" device in Glinka, Balakirev, Borodin, Rimsky-Korsakov, Tchaikovsky, and related composers. Taruskin reads the gesture topically, as usually suggesting a voluptuous escape into an exotic "*nega*, a prime attribute of the Orient as imagined by Russians.... [It] is usually translated as 'sweet bliss,' but it really connotes a gratified desire, a tender lassitude.... In opera and song, *nega* often simply denotes S-E-X *à la russe*, desired or achieved." See Taruskin, " 'Entoiling the Falconet': Russian Musical Orientalism in Context," in *The Exotic in Western Music*, ed. Jonathan Bellman, 194–217 (Boston: Northeastern University Press, 1998) (quotation on 202). Much of this discussion is carried over into Taruskin, *The Oxford History of Western Music* (New York: Oxford University Press, 2005), vol. 3, 392–405.

While Taruskin's connotations are often apt within certain strains of Russian music, it is perhaps preferable to read the gesture proper (which may also be found in Schumann, as in no. 17, "Wie aus der Ferne," of the *Davidsbündlertänze*, op. 6) as suggesting a delicious slippage away from the tonal clarity of normative Western harmonic practice, a drifting off into another, dreamlike realm, of which the explicitness of a languorous orientalist eroticism *à la russe* was only one potential analogue. Sibelius makes frequent use of this Russian device in the 1890s and early 1900s, though rarely, if ever, as a signifier connoting sexuality. Rather, he reconstrued it in his own way, more likely regarding the harmonically exotic move as a coloristic, often sternly asserted "northern" identifier—thus implicitly nodding also toward Russian practice—a harmonic hue that, when deployed as a primary harmonic tint, as here, could give the impression of an escape from the sharp tonal focus of European-academic harmonic traditions.

CHAPTER 19

....

BEETHOVEN, NAPOLEON, AND POLITICAL ROMANTICISM

....

LEON PLANTINGA

On March 4, 1809, Beethoven wrote to his principal publisher at the time, Breitkopf and Härtel of Leipzig, to settle some final details about the publication of the sixth and seventh symphonies and the Piano-cello Sonata, op. 69. He also mentioned the possibility of a visit to Leipzig in the near future, provided, he said, that the "present threatening storm clouds do not gather."[1]

The storm clouds worrying Beethoven contained the threat of renewed war with France. The French Empire under Napoleon was approaching its broadest reach, encompassing most of the Italian and Spanish peninsulas, the Low Countries, and the German states between the Rhine and the Elbe.[2] Napoleon's relatives now ruled great stretches of these lands: He had given the newly created kingdom of Westphalia to his youngest brother, Jérôme; the kingdom of Spain went to his eldest brother, Joseph, and the kingdom of Naples to a brother-in-law, Joachim Murat. But now, in the spring of 1809, as Napoleon's attention was distracted by a revolt in Spain, it seemed to the Austrians, under their rather hapless Habsburg emperor Franz I, a propitious moment to attack their old enemy, the one who had inflicted defeat and humiliation on Austria in 1797, 1800, and 1805.[3] On April 9 Beethoven's storm clouds became a reality: Austria declared war on France, and, under the somewhat reluctant Generalissimus Archduke Carl its army marched against French troops and their German allies to the west in Bavaria.[4]

After losing a terrible battle at Ebelsberg, some ninety miles west of Vienna, the Austrians contented themselves with a more or less orderly retreat, which was to lead inevitably to the gates of the Imperial city. On May 4, the day after the defeat at

Ebelsberg, with the French forces still about eighty miles distant, the imperial family at Vienna saw the handwriting on the wall, packed their bags (just as they had done upon the French invasion of 1805), and repaired to safer places to the east. Their entourage was heavy laden with valuables such as jewelry and art collections, and— bitter memories of 1805 still fresh in their minds—they carried with them the plates used for printing Viennese currency.

Among these highly placed refugees was the twenty-year-old Archduke Rudolph, brother of the emperor and Beethoven's most valued patron, recently become his student. At this time, it is clear, Beethoven had done extensive work on the first movement of the *Lebewohl* Piano Sonata op. 81a in E-flat. Now, on the very day of the archduke's departure, as something of an afterthought, it seems, he sketched the beginning of the Adagio introduction and added a dated dedication and farewell to the archduke, thus uniting the sonata with its famous program.[5]

Just one month and a day after the Austrian declaration of war, Napoleon slept in the Austrian imperial palace at Schönbrunn, just outside the city walls of Vienna. He demanded surrender of the city on May 11 and spent that day positioning his artillery, concentrating the principal breeching batteries on the southwestern point near the Kärntner Tor, a position once occupied by the Turks in the great siege of 1683. Having received no reply from inside the city, at 9 o'clock in the evening Napoleon ordered the bombardment to begin. (Residents complained that the attack occurred just as the coffeehouses had closed for the evening, so that many people were caught defenseless in the streets.) According to an official report, twenty civilians were killed, thirty-one buildings destroyed by fire, and sixty-six damaged.[6]

Beethoven had recently moved into an apartment in the Walfischgasse, literally a stone's throw from the principal French gun emplacements. According to the well-known account of his student Ferdinand Ries, Beethoven fled to the apartment of his brother Caspar Carl (with whom he was often—and currently—on the outs). Caspar Carl lived in the Rauhensteingasse, just south of Saint Stephen's and consid-erably farther from the French guns; here Beethoven sought shelter in the cellar, using pillows to shield his sensitive ears from the explosions.

The principal Austrian forces had retreated to the north and east, hoping to meet the French on open ground more favorable to the Austrians' tactical special-ties. This left the defense of the city in the hands of a small garrison of local troops augmented by armed civilian volunteers, the Studentencorps (among them the young Franz Grillparzer) and the Künstlercorps (who, it was said, carried weapons taken from the property rooms of the theaters). The day after the bombardment saw these ill-assorted defenders in full retreat across the Danube to the north. Napoleon's soldiers accordingly entered Vienna and, accustomed to living off the land, engaged in widespread looting. A drummer in the French army recalled that their strongholds in the city resembled a "street fair," where the soldiers displayed their pillaged merchandise.[7] Still, though there was no formal capitulation, the hab-its of eighteenth-century warfare prevailed, and a semblance of normality was quickly restored. By the evening of May 13, two days after the bombardment, there were performances in some theaters—with French soldiers joining the Viennese audiences—and the coffeehouses were again crowded with customers.

Meanwhile, Napoleon's forces occupied the Danube island of Lobau, from which they launched an offensive against Austrian troops on the far side of the river. A series of horrific encounters culminated in the battle at Wagram, which sent the Austrians in full retreat northward to Bohemia. There, on July 11, an armistice was signed in the village of Znaim. So, just as in all their previous encounters with Napoleon—in 1797, 1800, and 1805—the Austrians suffered total defeat. The battle at Wagram is reckoned by military historians to have been the biggest and costliest in human life since the invention of gunpowder. The two sides suffered about sixty thousand dead, and for many months the hospitals in Vienna were filled to over-flowing with the wounded.[8] Military ceremonies and parades put on by the French, intended to reconcile the Viennese to their new situation, got a chilly reception; citizens, it was said, did not bother to look out their windows to view the fireworks displays the French provided for their benefit.

What were Beethoven's reactions to these momentous events? How did they impinge upon his career as a composer? And what role did the overwhelming presence of Napoleon and his conquests play in the composer's political and philosophical outlook? Like most residents of Vienna, Beethoven was of course much distressed by the events of 1809. (Among the others were Joseph Haydn, who died there in the midst of the tumult on May 31; Muzio Clementi, who had come to Vienna on business, only to be trapped there by the war; and the twelve-year-old Franz Schubert, newly enrolled at the Kaiserlich-Königliches Stadtkonvict when a French shell came through the roof of the school). On July 26, two weeks after the signing of the armistice, Beethoven wrote the following to Breitkopf and Härtel:

> During this time we have been suffering concentrated misery. Let me tell you that
> since May 4th I have produced very little coherent work... The basis for my
> livelihood, recently established, rests on shaky foundations. Even in this short
> time the promises made to me have not been entirely fulfilled. From Prince
> Kinsky, one of my patrons, I have not received a penny—and this at a time when
> one needs it most... What a destructive, desolate life I see around me, nothing
> but drums and cannons and human suffering of every sort.[9]

The "basis for his livelihood," to which Beethoven refers, was a contract made the previous February with three of his patrons, the Princes Lobkowitz and Kinsky and the Archduke Rudolph, whereby Beethoven was granted an annual annuity of four thousand florins simply to continue living and working in Vienna. This singular arrangement was itself a by-product of those tumultuous Napoleonic times: The youngest Bonaparte brother, Jérôme, now ruler of the hastily assembled kingdom of Westphalia, centered in Kassel, had offered Beethoven the position of Kapellmeister, and in January 1809 Beethoven (with what degree of sincerity is not clear) announced his decision to accept.[10] His hand was stayed, apparently, only at the last moment by this extraordinary offer. Thus Beethoven had a very particular reason to regret the departure of the archduke on May 4, memorialized in the *Lebewohl* Sonata, for with him went the composer's best hope of collecting his annuity. Kinsky had already left for Prague in February without, as Beethoven complained, leaving him a penny; Kinsky fell off his horse to his death the following year, still without having paid. Lobkowitz, after making one payment, had departed in March; soon thereafter his gambling addiction plunged him into bankruptcy.

During this troubling spring Beethoven was working in *Landsberg 5*, one of a large number of sketchbooks now located at the Staatsbibliothek Preußischer Kulturbesitz in Berlin. Beethoven used this book for approximately the first eight months of 1809. Its first large section (i.e., of the volume in its original form) is devoted almost exclusively to sketches for the second and third movements of the Fifth Piano Concerto and the first movement of the *Lebewohl* Sonata. All this work seems in every way systematic and purposeful; the music takes shape approximately in the order it will finally assume, and work on individual sections usually continues until they have attained something like final form.[11] The sketches for the first movement of op. 81a proceed apace on pages 42–45, with the opening Adagio and verbal drafts for the dedication to the archduke coming last—suggesting, as has been mentioned, that this sonata was well under way before it came to memorialize Rudolph's journey.[12]

But then comes a remarkable change. For the next two dozen pages or so, the entries become miscellaneous and scrappy. There are apparent beginnings for piano sonatas; there are keyboard exercises and fleeting sketches of pieces whose genre must remain in doubt. And there are passages copied from Fux, Mizler, Kirnberger, and Albrechtsberger, perhaps with an eye to resumed lessons for the archduke. But there are virtually no sketches for pieces that Beethoven ever finished. One exception is the beginning of an overture in E-flat that eventually became (now in C major) the *Namensfeier* overture of 1815.) These pages offer a vivid corroboration of Beethoven's complaint that after May 4—that is, the day of the archduke's departure and the writing of the dedication of op. 81a—he was unable to do sustained work. It was only in late summer that Beethoven seems to have recovered his bearings: After two false starts with ideas for piano concertos in A minor and D minor, he got to work on the String Quartet, op. 74, the third big piece in E-flat of that year, finishing it in the fall.

Landsberg 5 shows signs of an intersection of things political with Beethoven's work as a composer preceding the invasion. Early in March of 1809, before the declaration of war, when he was hard at work on the third movement of the Fifth Piano Concerto, Beethoven paused to make rather extensive sketches for a vocal composition closely bound up with the political climate of the city. (The draft of an angry letter on page 19 of the manuscript to the Countess Erdödy, with whom he was having a quarrel about a servant, allows us to be reasonably sure of the date.[13])

That early spring in Vienna was a time of near-hysterical patriotic fervor as the government of Franz I took measures to whip up enthusiasm for renewed war against Napoleon. Franz I and Empress Maria Ludovica led parades on horseback to the wild plaudits of huge crowds. The poet Karoline Pichler mentions in her memoirs an event in the Redoutensaal of the Hofburg on Easter Sunday, at which a chorus of thousands sang military songs with texts by Heinrich von Collin and music by Joseph Weigl.[14]

Beethoven moved to make his own contribution to the festivities. The vocal composition for which he interrupted his work on the Fifth Piano Concerto in early March was a setting of one of those *Wehrmannslieder* of Heinrich von Collin (the author of the heroic drama *Coriolan*, for which Beethoven had composed an overture two years previously). The poem in question is a set of dismal patriotic verses titled "Österreich über alles."[15] The first stanza, the only one for which Beethoven supplied music, goes like this:

Wenn es nur will,	If only it has the will,
Ist immer Österreich über alles!	Austria is always above all else!
Wehrmänner ruft nun frohen Schalles:	Soldiers now raise the joyful shout:
Es will, es will!	It has the will, it has!
Hoch Österreich!	Here's to Austria!

In *Landsberg 5* the first nine staves of page 19 are filled with sketches for this composition. Moreover, a new source has recently come to light, a separate leaf formerly unavailable in private hands, acquired by the library of the Gesellschaft der Musikfreunde, Vienna, in 1993. This leaf is entirely filled with further sketches for "Österreich über alles"; example 1 is my transcription of the first five staves.

Example 19.1. From GdM

Both sources show the beginnings of a composition for several voices, with much singing in a high register. The voices were to be accompanied by instruments; cues for violins and flutes suggest that an orchestra was to be involved. Both sources show mainly a beginning: All the words Beethoven scribbled down come from the poem's first stanza, and both sources seem to indicate a stanza in D major followed by an instrumental interlude moving in the flat direction, perhaps to B-flat or, particularly in the *Landsberg* sketches, to C minor. While we have no way of knowing just what was to follow, some pattern of strophic variation that Beethoven came to favor in later years seems a likely candidate.

But it came to naught. We cannot be sure why Beethoven abandoned this project (and we might differ about how much we regret the loss). Perhaps the composition became superfluous when the Austrian defeats in Bavaria turned patriotic fervor to despair, or perhaps other factors, such as withdrawal of a commission, may have discouraged performance of this distinctly occasional music. But a larger question is this: Why did he set about to compose this poem—this breathless paean to the glory of Austria and its hoped-for defeat of Napoleon—in the first place? Only two months earlier Beethoven had said he was about to enter the service of a Bonaparte at Kassel. Five years previously he had proposed to dedicate the *Eroica* Symphony to Napoleon (or simply to name it for him). Upon hearing that Napoleon had himself declared emperor, according to Ries's famous report, he removed that name from the score with an iconic exclamation of disillusionment about the liberator-turned-dictator ("Now he will trample all human rights under foot and only pander to his own ambitions; he will place himself above everyone else and become a tyrant!"[16]). A copy of the score from a couple of months later shows the erased name of Bonaparte but also the name reinstated in Beethoven's hand; in a letter from the same time Beethoven wrote to Breitkopf and Härtel that "the name of the symphony is really Bonaparte."[17] Moreover, as late as 1810 he apparently considered dedicating his C-major Mass to the French emperor.[18]

On the other hand, Beethoven had set Austrian patriotic military poems as early as 1796 and 1797 during campaigns against Napoleon on the Italian peninsula; in 1802, angry at Bonaparte's recently concluded concordat with the pope, he scoffed at the publisher Hoffmeister's invitation to celebrate the French revolution and Napoleon with a sonata.[19] Then, in 1813 he joined in the general jubilation over Napoleon's defeat at Victoria with his noisy *Battle* Symphony, *Wellingtons Sieg*. How are we to explain this mass of contradictions in Beethoven's view of the most momentous events of his adult life?

Beethoven was hardly alone among Europeans in being unable to make up his mind about Napoleon, his conquests, and what this had to do with the principles underlying the French Revolution. People of a generally liberal persuasion throughout the continent had contradictory feelings about the matter. Was Napoleon a liberator bearing gifts of equality and freedom born of the Enlightenment and the French Revolution, or was he an imperialist pure and simple, bent only upon brute conquest and dynastic power? In *The Prelude* Wordsworth remembered his first impressions of the revolution in these famous lines:

> Bliss was it in that dawn to be alive,
> But to be young was very heaven!

Under Napoleon, he lamented,

> But now, become oppressors in their turn,
> Frenchmen had changed a war of self-defence
> For one of conquest, losing sight of all
> Which they had struggled for...[20]

Franz Grillparzer recalled that, even as an eighteen-year-old taking part in the futile defense of Vienna's walls in 1809, he was of two minds about Napoleon: "I felt no less enmity toward the French than my father. But nonetheless, Napoleon attracted me with a magical force...I still see him, hands folded behind his back, standing there like iron, overseeing his passing troops with the impassive gaze of the master...He enchanted me as a snake does a bird.[21]

Napoleon offered all of Europe an inviting symbol for heroism, for the larger-than-life, self-made person at the center of world events who, in the initial view of many, set about to sweep away age-old injustices—a vision that seemed especially alluring to the young, the young Beethoven not excepted. But of course, there was also no denying the destruction and misery that Napoleonic imperialism eventually visited upon the continent, a misery Beethoven experienced repeatedly in person. The composer's shifting reactions to the phenomenon of Napoleon seem to resemble Grillparzer's more than Wordsworth's: He shows not enthusiasm followed by disillusion but a perplexing mixture of the two.

Many writers on Beethoven have struggled with the hero-despot polarity in the composer's reaction to Napoleon and its relation to the larger pattern of his social and political views. Certain patterns—something approaching a majority opinion—emerge in what they have concluded. Adolph Bernhard Marx declared in 1875, "For Beethoven, Napoleon was *the hero*, who, like any other of these world-shaking heroes—whether named Alexander, Dionysus, or Napoleon—embraces the world with his Idea and his will."[22]

Similarly Paul Bekker saw Napoleon as a generalized symbol of the heroic for the younger Beethoven: "Had Beethoven been born a few decades earlier, he would perhaps have seized upon a historical model, like Goethe in Götz [von Berchlingen], or an imagined social construct such as Schiller's *Räuber*."[23] According to Arnold Schmitz, Beethoven saw the General and Consul Napoleon as an ideal embodiment of heroism quite separate from the real-life political figure. Carl Dahlhaus has called attention to a persistent conflict of loyalties for Beethoven, never resolved, between his persistent republicanism—which early on he associated with France and Napoleon, and later with the freedoms of the English—and his patriotism for Austria: "The decisive factor in the former was idealistic, and in the latter it was pragmatic."[24]

After a meticulous recounting of Beethoven's recorded references to Napoleon and their puzzling contradictions, Maynard Solomon offers an assessment with a Freudian coloration:

> Striving to free himself from his lifelong pattern of submission to authority figures, Beethoven was drawn to the conqueror who had confounded the venerable leaders of Europe and set himself in their place. If homage is on the surface, the underlying themes are patricide and fratricide, mingled with the survivor's sense of triumph.[25]

More recently, Louis Lockwood writes that "Beethoven's lifelong attitude toward Napoleon oscillated between admiration and dislike, between approval and revulsion." Furthermore, the proposed dedication of the *Eroica* to Napoleon, as he suggests, may be seen in the light of Beethoven's long-standing (and probably unrealistic) hope for an appointment in Paris, "reflecting his characteristic way of blending personal idealism with practical calculation."[26]

Thus, many of those who have given thought to the matter have concluded that Napoleon existed in two different spheres or on two different levels—variously construed—in the composer's thought. He was a hero in the abstract, a role that other historical figures could have filled equally well, as opposed to that real-life, increasingly despotic conqueror. The hero, existing only in an ideal realm, was tied to Beethoven's liberal, republican—or, in Schmitz's formulation, Josephine—political instincts; the real-life conqueror of Austria who made Beethoven's life miserable was quite a different matter. Yet another factor, quite straightforward and removed from political ideals of any kind, surely played a role in Beethoven's ambivalence. In Vienna of 1809, simple prudence would urge disapproval of the wrecker of the city's peace and prosperity. Still, as Lockwood points out, even at that time the composer could also imagine certain pragmatic advantages in aligning himself with the French. Partly by instinct and partly by calculation, Beethoven remained ambivalent.

Stephen Rumph's *Beethoven after Napoleon: Political Romanticism in the Late Works* (2004) urges a very different view of this matter, one with far-reaching implications not only for Beethoven's social or political views, but also for the very nature of his later music. Because Rumph's position differs vividly from the usual ones and comes decked out in an imposing panoply of historical and philosophical references, it may be useful to consider it in some detail. His basic argument goes something like this: In his earlier years Beethoven had subscribed enthusiastically to enlightenment-like, Josephine views of politics and culture, views dominated by the new critical philosophy of Kant, which he had learned about as a young man in intellectual circles in Bonn. To those of such a persuasion, the Napoleonic reordering of Europe seemed, at least potentially, to offer the promise of a better future. At this time, according to Rumph, Beethoven became a "cosmopolitan composer writing heroic works with a distinctly French flavor."[27]

The composer's later career saw him at the opposite extreme, Rumph says, as a supporter of the reactionary politics of the Restoration and the Metternich system, in sympathy with the conservative, German nationalist, mystical/religious outlook of "political romanticism" as espoused by Adam Müller, Zacharias Werner, and the Schlegel brothers, and supported, according to Rumph, by a very large further cast of characters, including Fichte, Kleist, and even E. T. A. Hoffmann.[28] These people, he says, not only deplored the French Revolution and Napoleon's upending of Europe but also opposed every stripe of enlightened liberalism or contractual theories of government—particularly anything associated with either modernity or with the French. Beethoven's sympathies turned in this direction, and he became "a patriotic German writing propaganda pieces against Napoleon."[29]

Rumph's central argument shuttles smoothly between two hypotheses: First, Beethoven had become something of a political and religious conservative, and, second, this new ideological perspective provides a key to our understanding of the later works. To support his first hypothesis Rumph gives us rather a full exposition of "political romanticism" but cites almost nothing from Beethoven's own words—a commodity we have in great abundance in the years after 1809—to align the composer with this movement. Instead, he supports his thesis almost exclusively with appeals to (and interpretations of) the texts Beethoven set to music and—in something of an inversion of his second hypothesis—to characteristics of the music itself. Moving in a near-perfect circle, the ideas explain the music, and the music reveals the ideas.

During the year 1809, says Rumph, "Beethoven pioneered virtually every important element that would go into creating his late style."[30] These elements of style—each of them, he says, consonant with Beethoven's emerging conservative ideology—are historicism, counterpoint, lyricism, and written-out cadenzas. In respect to the first two, historicism and counterpoint, yes, it is true that Beethoven at this time began to show a heightened interest in historical models: He asked Breitkopf and Härtel to send him earlier music ranging from J. S. Bach to Haydn for informal performance and study, and, as we have seen, he copied passages from earlier contrapuntal treatises into *Landsberg 5*.[31] In the coming years, contrapuntal and fugal writing were to become a prominent feature of the late music.

But does this have anything to do with political or religious conservatism? In the early 1780s Mozart, too, became fascinated with the music of Bach and Handel: A new obsession with fugue in these years seems to have exerted a lasting influence upon his style. Muzio Clementi did much the same at about the same time. And the finales of Haydn's String Quartets op. 20 from a decade earlier seem to reflect a similar impulse. All three of these composers turned to older music for stylistic enrichment at particular points in their careers, and few of us would argue that they were moved by a burst of political or religious conservatism. Rumph gives us no reason to think Beethoven's case is any different.[32]

Rumph speaks of a pervasive lyricism in much of Beethoven's music after 1809, giving us along the way some sensitive commentary on the Harp Quartet, op. 74. This lyricism, he says, "offered Beethoven a way beyond the monumental style of French neoclassicism"—as if that is all the preceding years had to offer. How is this lyricism different in substance and significance from the lyrical music he composed during the so-called heroic period: in the first movements, say, of the Piano Sonata op. 28, the Fourth Piano Concerto, and the Violin Concerto? Moreover, what does this, in any case, have to do with conservative politics or religion? The only reasonably explicit connection Rumph offers points to the program for the *Lebewohl* Sonata: "[T]he homecoming of the archduke, forced into exile by Napoleon, can be understood as the restoration of legitimate power to Austria."[33] Yet the finale of the sonata, marked *vivacissamente*, is surely anything but lyrical. Furthermore, there were more compelling reasons than political ones for Beethoven to welcome the archduke—his meal ticket—back to the city.

In 1809 Beethoven wrote out cadenzas for his Fifth Piano Concerto and provided cadenzas for all his earlier concertos as well. This, Rumph says, shows the composer's interest in "control" and—in a dizzying conceptual leap—suggests that Beethoven also favored governmental and societal control. It would be more plausible, surely, to explain the written-out cadenzas of the *Emperor* Concerto in 1809 by observing that this was the year in which Beethoven stopped playing his concertos in public, thus depriving himself of his usual way of showing audiences how the cadenzas should go. It is very likely that he wrote out the other cadenzas for the use of his student, the archduke, feeling perhaps that it was he (rather than the entire citizenry of Austria) who needed controlling.

It is probably for good reason that Beethoven's own words play so small a role in Rumph's argument about Beethoven's politics: In the extant sources—the letters, the *Tagebuch* of 1812–1818, and the conversation books (beginning in 1818)—Beethoven scarcely ventures a single clear political opinion. Telling evidence of a certain political indifference, surely, is this: In the two-thousand-odd extant Beethoven letters dated after 1809 there is not a single reference to Prince Metternich, the principal architect and guide of the restoration state—an omission hardly attributable to the silence of discretion if the composer in fact approved of Metternich's political order. The letters contain, here and there, vague political insinuations, always in an ironic mode. An example is the mildly manic letter of April 1815 to Johann Nepomuk Kanka in Prague. It was written during "the hundred days," in which Napoleon escaped from his exile on the island of Elba, landed on the French Mediterranean coast, gathered a following within the French army, and retook Paris without resistance as Louis XVIII (on the throne for less than a year) fled to Belgium. Beethoven asked Kanka, "So how could I serve you with my art? Tell me, would you have the soliloquy of a fled king sung for you, or perhaps the perjured oath of a usurper?"[34]

Since Beethoven normally spoke his side of the exchanges recorded in the conversation books, they offer little direct evidence of his political sympathies. Still, it is fair to note, Beethoven's interlocutors in the conversation books have much to say about things political. His intimate friend, the librettist and editor Karl Joseph Bernard, for example, wrote the following in January of 1820:

> If Napoleon should return now, he could expect a much better reception in Europe. He understood the Zeitgeist and knew how to take charge. Our descendents will value him more than we did. As a German I was his biggest enemy, but these times have reconciled me... The children of the Revolution demanded such an iron personality. Everywhere he overthrew the feudal system and defended justice and law.

In April of the same year he added, "All of Europe has gone to the dogs. We should hire Napoleon for ten years. Germany has to support 38 courts and about a million princes and princesses."[35] We may perhaps detect Bernard's influence in Beethoven's own cryptic remark from some four years later, as reported by Czerny: "In 1824 I went on one occasion with Beethoven to a coffeehouse in Baden. There were several newspapers on the table. In one of them I read an announcement of Walter Scott's biography of Napoleon. 'Napoleon,' he said. 'I could not tolerate him before. Now I think quite differently.' "[36] Now that Europe's redesigner was safely isolated on the far-away island of Saint Helena, Beethoven seemingly found it easier to focus on the abstract Napoleon, the common man again become hero of common humankind.

The other central feature of "political romanticism" was its religious component: a renewed fealty to traditional Catholicism, especially its more mystical side, colored with a nostalgia for the solidity and centrality of the church in the Middle Ages. Arnold Schmitz gives us a useful account of the religious climate Beethoven found in early nineteenth-century Vienna. A loose "Catholic enlightenment" prevailed that in varying ways mingled elements of traditional Christianity with prevailing currents of rationalism—a rapprochement in vogue since the time of Joseph II. Even churchmen saw religion more as a set of moral principles than established dogma; guides to human thought and behavior could include Plato, Socrates, and Hippocrates, as well as the Holy Scriptures; human reason was generally to be trusted as a guide to understanding the world about us. This was a time when the secular religion of Freemasonry, though prohibited by the government of Emperor Franz II for its liberal politics, continued to flourish underground.[37]

In 1808 one Clemens M. Hofbauer arrived in Vienna and organized a campaign through his order, the Redemptorists, also known as Liguorians, to rescue traditional religious belief and practice from the pollution of fashionable secular rationalism. Though not himself of a literary turn of mind, he quickly attracted a circle of like-minded younger Viennese writers. Most prominent of these was the poet Zacharias Werner from Königsberg, a former Freemason who converted to Catholicism in 1810, entered the priesthood, and, beginning about 1814, attracted large crowds with his preaching. Werner was joined by another recent convert, Friedrich Schlegel, who at the turn of the century in Jena had been a leader in formulating the distinctly secular German variety of early romantic literary doctrine. After converting to Catholicism in 1808, he settled in Vienna and dedicated himself to a mystical and medievalist strain of religious belief.

At the same time Schlegel embraced a conservative political activism that included service in the Vienna chancellery in 1809. From a distance in Dresden, Adam Müller, who served in the Austrian diplomatic service, articulated the political component of "political romanticism" in a series of lectures in 1808 and 1809, published as *Die Elemente der Staatskunst*.[38] Here he argued for an "organic unity" of society and state that would take precedence over any individual interests and rejected Adam Smith's materialist notion of national wealth in favor of a somewhat diffuse idea of "spiritual capital."

What, then, did Beethoven and his circle think of this politico-religious movement? In 1813 and 1814 Beethoven seems to have composed a patriotic *Kriegslied* text by Werner, for which the music is lost.[39] Furthermore, among the dozens of opera librettos he considered over the years was apparently a "romantic, Indian" text of Friedrich Schlegel's.[40] But the many references to the "political romantics" scattered through the conversation books are uniformly ironic and derisive. In late December 1819, Bernard remarked that "Schlegel does nothing but eat, drink, and read the Bible." Three months later, Joseph Blöchinger, head of the school to which Beethoven entrusted his nephew Carl, reported, "Father Hofbauer is dead. The leader of this new papal sect, the so-called Liguorians, he was a miserable fanatic dogmatist who referred to Adam Müller as the greatest of theologians." And with high-spirited sarcasm Beethoven himself wrote to Tobias Haslinger in a letter of 1821, "Sing the Epistles of St. Paul every day, and on Sundays go to Father Werner, who will show you a little book that will send you straight to heaven."[41]

If Beethoven disdained Werner's brand of mystical Catholicism, in times of stress he was often given to expressions of religious sentiment—to fragmentary and strikingly diverse thoughts about God and the human condition that veered from classical stoicism to various Eastern mysticisms, with hints of modern varieties of Deism and pantheism. In his essay "The Quest for Faith" Maynard Solomon provides an able summary of the tortuous course of Beethoven's religious musings. During the onset of his deafness, around the turn of the century, and especially during the unsettled and musically unproductive years of the *Tagebuch* (1812–1818), Beethoven sometimes appealed to (or cursed) a personal deity, urged upon himself stoic resignation learned from Plutarch, and yearned after the ascetic withdrawal of Vedic Hinduism; nevertheless, he entered into his diary the occasional encomium to reason, such as "The frailties of nature are given by nature herself and sovereign Reason shall seek to guide and diminish them through her strength."[42]

During this period he read and thickly annotated his copy of the inspirational essays of the Lutheran pastor Christian Sturm, one for every day of the year, collected under the title *Betrachtungen über die Werke Gottes im Reiche der Natur.*[43] Sturm (who saw no frailties whatever in nature) marveled at the intricacy and order of the natural world, "the starry sky, the earth enameled with flowers, the melodious songs of the birds, the various landscapes and prospects, every one delightful." While we may detect a certain pantheistic tinge in some of Sturm's exultations, in the end he urges an orthodox theist response to natural wonders: We should "study the book of nature continually; to learn in it the truths which may remind us of the immense greatness of the Creator."[44] In a similar vein Beethoven wrote on a sketch leaf in 1815, "Almighty in the forest. I am happy, blissful in the forest: every tree speaks through you O God! What splendor: In such a woodland scene, on the heights there is calm, calm in which to serve Him."[45]

Beethoven's own words, in short, reveal no consistent set of political or religious beliefs. Like many Europeans he vacillated in his estimate of Napoleon and said almost nothing specific, so far as we know, on any other political subject. And in post-Enlightenment Europe he was hardly alone in his restless search for and periodic interest in alternatives to institutional Christian faith—to which, at times, he was also apparently drawn. The texts Beethoven chose to set—particularly when there was no commission involved—often seem to reflect his current enthusiasms, and there is no reason to doubt his sincere interest in a particular text at any given moment. His patriotic songs of 1796–1797 and *Österreich über alles* of 1809 probably record a surge of genuine enthusiasm for Austrian resistance to the real-life Napoleon (as opposed to that other, idealized Napoleon to whom he had proposed to dedicate the *Eroica*). The two monumental works into which Beethoven nearly simultaneously poured his immense creative energies in the early 1820s, the *Missa solemnis* and the Ninth Symphony, embraced the central liturgical act of institutional Christianity—as well as that peculiar mix of secular Josephine Enlightenment, Deism, and egalitarianism (with Masonic overtones) he had absorbed during his youth in Bonn and now revisited in the young Schiller's rather giddy poem. Beethoven apparently saw no contradiction; religious thought for him was a malleable thing, none of whose particular forms excluded the others.

Nonetheless, one principle Beethoven held to consistently: In his responses to the stirring events in the world around him and in the (very closely related) conduct of his professional life, he could be counted upon to act with a good bit of straightforward rational self-interest. That early enthusiasm for Napoleon, as has been suggested, was surely related to Beethoven's persistent thoughts during that period about making his career in France. A preoccupation with things French began shortly after 1800. In a curious remark to Franz Anton Hoffmeister in January 1801, Beethoven made a (for him) surprising suggestion: There ought to be a *Magazin der Kunst* to which "the artist need only bring his artworks to take what he needed." As Solomon has suggested, this apparently shows Beethoven's sudden attraction to current French utopian and socialist views.[46] When Cherubini, a major figure in Parisian musical circles, presented his postrevolutionary operas in Vienna in 1802–1803, Beethoven, little given to praising other composers' work, joined in the city's enthusiastic response (he later told Cherubini that he "valued his operas above all others").[47] In 1804 he abandoned work on Schikaneder's libretto *Vestas Feuer* in favor of the very French "rescue opera" *Leonora*; in the midst of work on that opera the following year, he took time to compose the Triple Concerto, op. 56, a work whose generic affiliations with the popular French *symphonie concertante* seem rather clear.[48]

In that letter of 1800 to the publisher Hoffmeister, Beethoven makes a veiled reference—veiled because of the delicate political situation in Vienna—to a projected trip (or move) to Paris: While sending him his Piano Concerto, op. 19, he is holding back his better concertos, he says, until "I myself have made a trip." In autumn 1803 two letters from Beethoven's student Ferdinand Ries to Nikolaus Simrock in Bonn are much more explicit: "Beethoven will remain here at the most 1½ years. Then he will go to Paris, which makes me extremely sorry," and "Beethoven is to receive the libretto for his opera soon. After that he plans to leave."[49]

A couple of months later Ries reported that Beethoven wished to postpone publication of the *Eroica*, with its (at that time) clear Napoleonic connections, to "reserve it for his trip." Early the following year, in a letter to Joseph Sonnleithner, at the time busy translating *Leonore* for him, Beethoven wrote, "I have received another letter about my journey, and this one has made my decision to travel irrevocable."[50] The dedication, at this time, of the Sonata for Piano and Violin, op. 47, to the Parisian violinist Rodolphe Kreutzer (whom Beethoven had met only once, years earlier) surely reflects an interest in cultivating contacts in the French capital. Beethoven's thoughts about France and things French, including France's first consul (later emperor), seem to have been inextricably intertwined with his own prospects for a life and career in Paris.

For that other proposed move, the one to Kassel in 1809, the lines between ideology and practicality are even more sharply drawn. Napoleon had projected the Kingdom of Westphalia, with his brother Jérôme at the helm, as the very model of the new world order: "[E]very trace of serfdom, or of a feudal hierarchy between the sovereign and the lowest class of his subjects, shall be done away with."[51] In the letter to Breitkopf and Härtel wherein Beethoven announced his intention of accepting Jérôme's appointment, he says nothing about any ideological virtues of the new regime in Kassel; he speaks only of a prospective freedom to do his work and—of perhaps equal importance—the honor to be accorded him as an artist.[52] We cannot be sure whether Beethoven ever really intended to make this risky move, but the threat was sufficient to move his Viennese patrons to action; the annuity agreement of March 1809 ensured that Beethoven would remain in the city with a comfortable yearly income.

The wording of the agreement included a hope that Beethoven's benefactors might one day be relieved of their obligation: The annuity was to be paid "until he receives an appointment that pays him the equivalent of the above-mentioned sum."[53] Beethoven assumed, rightly, no doubt, that this obscure talk had to do with an appointment at the Vienna imperial court. In a letter to his friend Ignaz von Gleichenstein he offered a clarification: "As to the Imperial Services, well, I think the point must be dealt with tactfully—and certainly not so as to suggest that I am asking for the title of Imperial Kapellmeister . . . I think that this point might be best expressed by saying that it is my most ardent desire to enter the service of the Emperor."[54] Beethoven, of course, referred to that other emperor, the unfortunate Franz I of Austria. So in the early months of 1809 Beethoven proposed first to attach himself to the emerging Napoleonic new order and then to the tottering remains of the old. The overriding issue here was the promotion of his career and his own material welfare.

Beethoven was a master of survival in a world of dizzying change. He was able to negotiate the contradictions of an artist's life played out in the new musical market economy together with remnants of the old patronage system. To succeed as a freelance composer in Vienna at this time was still a near impossibility. Beethoven did so brilliantly through astute dealings with his publishers while also extracting maximum benefit from his aristocratic admirers. Napoleon's meteoric rise was for him an inspiration, a possible opportunity, but also, most immediately, a threat. The inspiration remained something abstract. Both the opportunity and the threat had to do with his musical career, and for Beethoven this, rather than any ideal or ideology, was what mattered most.

NOTES

1. "Wenn sich nicht Die jezigen Drohenden Gewitter-Wolken zusammen ziehen." Ludwig van Beethoven, *Briefwechsel Gesamtausgabe*, ed. Sieghard Brandenburg (Munich: Henle, 1996), vol. 2, 45.

2. In July 1807 the terms of the peace treaty of Tilsit ceded to French control vast tracts of Prussia's territory west of the Elbe.

3. The literature on the Napoleonic wars is, of course, immense. A microscopic examination of the events of 1809 (only the first volume has appeared) is John H. Gill, *1809: Thunder of the Danube: Napoleon's Defeat of the Habsburgs* (London: Frontline, 2008). A more relaxed treatment of the subject is James R. Arnold, *Napoleon Conquers Austria: The 1809 Campaign for Vienna* (Westport, Conn.: Praeger, 1996).

4. Member states of the Confederation of the Rhine, a federation of German puppet states formed by Napoleon in 1805, contributed substantial numbers of troops—all under French command—to Napoleon's forces. The Habsburg army similarly included soldiers of several nationalities who spoke, variously, German, Czech, Flemish, Serbo-Croat, and Italian.

5. See the facsimile and transcription of the sketchbook he was using at the time: Ludwig van Beethoven, *Ein Skizzenbuch aus dem Jahre 1809 (Landsberg 5)*, Übertragung und Kommentar von Clemmens Brenneis (Bonn: Beethovenhaus, 1993), 44–45. The dedication reads as follows: Der Abschied am 4ten May, gewidmet und aus dem Herzen geschrieben S.[einer] K.[eiserlichen] H.[oheit].

6. See Alfred Plischnack, *"Vive l'empereur, weil's sein muß": Geschichte in Quellen und Zeitzeugenberichten* (Munich: Amalthea, 1999), 79.

7. Arnold, *Napoleon Conquers Austria*, 20.

8. Arnold, *Napoleon Conquers Austria*, 172.

9. Emily Anderson, ed., *The Letters of Beethoven* (London: Macmillan, 1961), vol. 1, 233–34; Beethoven, *Briefwechsel*, vol. 2, 71.

10. See the letter to Breitkopf and Härtel of Jan. 7, 1809, in Beethoven, *Briefwechsel*, vol. 2, 37, and Anderson, *Letters of Beethoven*, vol. 1, 211–12.

11. "Final form," that is, as was usual in the sketching process. Many elaborations were customarily left for the autograph stage.

12. Given this course of events, it seems remarkable that the introduction and the main part of the movement (Allegro) of this sonata are so closely unified. A descending stepwise melodic gesture dominates the thematic matter of the Allegro. In the introduction this becomes the familiar "horn thirds" pattern, to which Beethoven adds the text "Lebewohl." Yet that version of the pattern also appears in the coda of the Allegro, plainly sketched on p. 42 of *Landsberg 5*, apparently before the identification of this figure with "Lebewohl" on the following page. It seems likely that Beethoven had decided on this thematic material before the Archduke left on May 4 and simply adapted it to the programmatic need at hand. Nonetheless, the Allegro is something of a programmatic anomaly: A generally robust and cheerful movement intervenes between the "farewell" and the sorrowful "absence."

Horn thirds seem to have implied various things in the nineteenth century. An obvious connection with "departing" is the playing of the posthorn upon the arrival and departure of the mail coach. The posthorn is the logo of the Deutsche Post to the present day.

13. See Beethoven, *Briefwechsel*, vol. 2, 47–48.

14. See Plischnack, *"Vive l'empereur,"* 66.

15. This poem anticipates Hoffmann von Fallersleben's "Deutschland über alles" by about thirty years.

16. *Beethoven Remembered: The Biographical Notes of Franz Wegeler and Ferdinand Ries*, trans. Frederick Noonan (Arlington, Va.: Great Ocean, 1987), 68.

17. Letter of Aug. 26, 1804, in Beethoven, *Briefwechsel*, vol. 1, 219; and Anderson, *Letters of Beethoven*, vol. 1, 117. Napoleon was proclaimed emperor on May 28, 1804 (though not crowned at Notre Dame Cathedral until Dec. 2). Ries's visit to Beethoven must have occurred in early June of that year (though Ries, writing two decades later, mistakenly mentions the year as 1802). See *Beethoven Remembered*, 67. Maynard Solomon gives a good account of the title page and erasures in the surviving copy of the score, dated August 1804, now at the Gesellschaft der Musikfreunde, Vienna, in *Beethoven*, 2d, rev. ed. (New York: Schirmer, 1998), 174–75.

18. See Solomon, *Beethoven*, 182.

19. The songs are "Abschiedsgesang an Wiens Bürger," WoO 121, and "Kriegslied der Österreicher," WoO 122. For the letter to Hoffmeister see Beethoven, *Briefwechsel*, vol. 1, 105; Anderson, *Letters of Beethoven*, vol. 1, 73.

20. Wordsworth, *The Prelude*, Book Eleventh, ll. 107–108 and 206–209.

21. Translated from Franz Grillparzer, *Selbstbiographie*, ed. Arno Dusini, 53–54 (Vienna: Residenz, 1994).

22. A. B. Marx, *Musical Form in the Age of Beethoven*, ed. and trans. Scott Burnham (New York: Cambridge University Press, 1997), 158.

23. Translated from Paul Bekker, *Beethoven* (Berlin: Schuster and Loeffler, 1911), 165.

24. Translated from Arnold Schmitz, *Das romantische Beethovenbild* (Berlin: Dümmlers, 1927), 60; Carl Dahlhaus, *Ludwig van Beethoven*, trans. Mary Whittal (Oxford: Clarendon, 1991), 20.

25. Solomon, *Beethoven*, 183.

26. Lewis Lockwood, *Beethoven: The Music and the Life* (New York: Norton, 2003), 183–84.

27. Stephen Rumph, *Beethoven after Napoleon: Political Romanticism in the Late Works* (Los Angeles: University of California Press, 2004), 96.

28. The term *political romanticism* derives from the book *Politische Romantik* (1925) by the conservative political theorist (later a judicial official under the Nazi regime) Carl Schmitt. There is no room here to discuss Rumph's vastly inclusive category of "political romanticism," but here is a single example of the tortuous argument needed to implicate E. T. A. Hoffmann, usually thought to be mainly apolitical (see, e.g., Rüdiger Safranski, *E. T. A. Hoffmann: Das Leben eines skeptischen Phantasten* [Munich: Hanser, 1984], 174ff). In his famous review of Beethoven's Fifth Symphony Hoffmann was intent upon showing that this work shows a large-scale formal plan; thus, he repeatedly speaks of *das Ganze* (i.e., the whole of a movement or of the entire composition). Rumph pounces upon this word, wrenches it into an utterly foreign context, and writes: "No word better sums up romantic political theory, whose central axiom was the spiritual totality of the state…Hoffmann's celebrated thematic analysis suggests the clearest musical correlate to this totalizing Romantic doctrine" (*Beethoven after Napoleon*, 28).

29. Rumph, *Beethoven after Napoleon*, 96.

30. Rumph, *Beethoven after Napoleon*, 96.

31. See Beethoven, *Briefwechsel*, vol. 2, 72; Anderson, *Letters of Beethoven*, vol. 1, 235.

32. Rumph's broad general implication that conservatism in musical style betrays political conservatism surely requires demonstration (*Beethoven after Napoleon*, 99–100).

33. Rumph, *Beethoven after Napoleon*, 101.

34. Beethoven, *Briefwechsel*, vol. 3, 134; Anderson, *Letters of Beethoven*, vol. 2, 508. The "perjured oath" probably refers to Napoleon's breach of his renunciation of the emperor's throne, sworn the previous year.

35. *Ludwig van Beethovens Konversationshefte*, ed. Karl-Heinz Köhler and Dagmar Beck (Leipzig: VEB Deutscher Verlag für Musik, 1976), vol. 1, 209–10; vol. 2, 68–69.

36. Carl Czerny, *On the Proper Performance of All Beethoven's Works for the Piano*, ed. Paul Badura-Skoda (Vienna: Universal, 1970), 8. The conversation books show that Beethoven often discussed his difficulties with his nephew Karl with Bernard,, and relied on him extensively to advise him as to Karl's education.

37. Schmitz, *Das romantische Beethovenbild*, 82ff.

38. Berlin: Sander, 1809.

39. Cf. Beethoven, *Briefwechsel*, vol. 3, 26.

40. See *Konversationshefte*, vol. 2, 348.

41. *Konversationshefte*, vol. 1, 169, 352; Beethoven, *Briefwechsel*, vol. 4, 448; Anderson, *Letters of Beethoven*, vol. 2, 923–24. The editors of the *Briefwechsel* suggest that the "little book" in question is Werner's *Geistliche Übungen für drei Tage* [Italic] (1818).

42. Maynard Solomon, "The Quest for Faith," in *Beethoven Essays* (Cambridge, Mass.: Harvard University Press, 1988), 216–29; "Beethoven's *Tagebuch*" in the same volume, 287.

43. Beethoven's copy of this often-republished book, dated 1811, survives in the Staatsbibliothek Preußischer Kulturbesitz in Berlin. See Solomon, "Quest for Faith," 349.

44. *Beauties of Sturm, in Lessons on the Works of God, and of his Providence*, trans. Eliza Andrews (London: printed for James Scatchard et al., 1798)), 50–51.

45. Solomon, "Quest for Faith," 219.

46. See Solomon, "Beethoven's Magazin der Kunst," *in Beethoven Essays*, especially 196–204; also Beethoven, *Briefwechsel*, vol. 1, 64; and Anderson, *Letters of Beethoven*, vol. 1, 48.

47. See *Thayer's Life of Beethoven*, ed. Elliot Forbes (Princeton: Princeton University Press, 1964), vol. 2, 326–27, and Beethoven, *Briefwechsel*, vol. 5, 90; Anderson, *Letters of Beethoven*, vol. 3, 1016. There is an extensive literature claiming French influence upon Beethoven's music from shortly after this time. See, for example, Boris Schwarz, "Beethoven and the French Violin School," *Musical Quarterly* 47(1958): 431–47; and Michael Broyles, *Beethoven: The Emergence and Evolution of Beethoven's Heroic Style* (New York: Excelsior, 1987), 117ff.

48. See Leon Plantinga, *Beethoven's Concertos: History, Style, Performance* (New York: Norton, 1999), 182ff.

49. These letters are quoted in Erich H. Müller, "Beethoven und Simrock," in *N. Simrock Jahrbuch* 2 (1929): 23–24 and 27.

50. See Müller, "Beethoven und Simrock," 28, and Beethoven, *Briefwechsel*, vol. 1, 207; Anderson, *Letters of Beethoven*, vol. 1, 106–107.

51. Letter from Napoleon to his brother Jérôme, November 1807, quoted in George Rudé, *Revolutionary Europe, 1783–1815* (London, 1964), 257.

52. Beethoven, *Briefwechsel*, vol. 2, 37–38; Anderson, *Letters of Beethoven*, vol. 1, 211.

53. Alexander Wheelock Thayer, *Ludwig van Beethovens Leben*, ed. Hermann Dieters and Hugo Riemann, vol. 3, 125–26 (Leipzig: Breitkopf and Härtel, 1917).

54. Beethoven, *Briefwechsel*, vol. 2, 40; Anderson, *Letters of Beethoven*, vol. 1, 215.

CHAPTER 20

TRANSLATING HERDER TRANSLATING: CULTURAL TRANSLATION AND THE MAKING OF MODERNITY

PHILIP V. BOHLMAN

THE CULTURAL LIFE OF TRANSLATORS

The song that epigrammatically opens this exploration of the lives of translators would seem to stand innocently, if not eerily, alone, taken from the closing gesture of the first anthology of folk songs, Johann Gottfried Herder's *Stimmen der Völker in Liedern* and *Volkslieder*.[1] The printed version of "O sanctissima!" appeared at the end of Johann Gottfried Herder's life (1744–1803) or, more accurately, in 1807, four years after his death, when a new edition of his epoch-making folk-song volumes appeared with an entirely new appendix of songs from Herder's *Nachlaß*, the collections in his estate. It was in the posthumous edition that "O sanctissima!" appeared, designated as a "Sicilian Sailor's Song" and as a "Marian Song," which is to say, with the German title "An die Jungfrau Maria" (figure 20.1). In the somewhat plain printing, "O sanctissima!" seems innocuous to us today. It was, however, the only song with musical notation among the hundreds that filled the multiple volumes of folk-song anthologies edited and annotated by Herder in his lifetime. For this reason, it arrests our attention by suggesting that, at the end of his life, Herder was responding to the call for a new mode of representing the texts, for which he had coined the term *Volkslied* [folk song] in 1773. The other twenty-five songs added to the posthumous edition further suggest that change was afoot and that it had something to do with

Figure 20.1. "O Sanctissima!" Herder 1778–1779 (1975, 373–74).

representation, for, of the twenty-five, only three—with the titles "Ein Spruch," "Einige Sprüche," and "Der Fürstenstein"—come from German sources. Unifying the new songs were the differences of their languages. The melodies range from an Estonian song that begins the new section, through Tartar, Spanish, French, and Bohemian songs, to the German translations of French versions of eleven songs from Madagascar, which constitute a minianthology before the Peruvian song in an epilogue.[2]

With its text in Latin rather than a Sicilian dialect, "O sanctissima!" again seems at first glance innocuous in this deliberate expansion of the impulse toward representing folk song through world music that grew during Herder's life, taking shape as a new form of cultural history in the first decade of the nineteenth century. By including notation here, Herder was surely also domesticating the song, appropriating it more fully for Western consumption. Looking ahead only a decade, we would find our suspicion of appropriation confirmed by the appearance of "O sanctissima!", called simply "Siciliano," in Beethoven's 1817 folk-song settings of songs from "verschiedene Völker," the songs "without opus" 157. Beethoven probably received this song after George Thomson had encountered it in Herder's well-known publications, so that setting it in this way, Beethoven added one more layer of translation (figure 20.2).[3]

Before I follow this path of musical translation becoming cultural translation much farther, it might be helpful to return to oral tradition, indeed, to the many

Figure 20.2. Beethoven, "O sanctissima," WoO 157, no. 16.

versions and variants that were surely already converging in the first two decades of the nineteenth century, when print versions rerouted the time and place of folk song to unleash its multiple meanings for the cultural history of the following century. Of course, "O sanctissima!" is far better known as the German Christmas song "O, du fröhliche," and it is in this variant that Herder himself, as a German Lutheran pastor, would have sung it from his own oral tradition.[4] Herder's decision to use musical notation—this one time in his life—was an act of translation. It realizes the interplay between the familiar and the unfamiliar. It announces that "O sanctissima!" is different from "O, du fröhliche" in just about every way except the one that is the most paradoxical of all: The songs sound alike. By translating the song with musical notation, Herder rerouted the translation that occurred in oral tradition and fixed it for a historiographic process that has followed German song up to the present.

In contrast to the "O sanctissima!" at the end of Herder's life, it is the "Edward" ballad that serves as the translational icon at the beginning of his career. The print variants that follow Herder's translations of "Edward" from his critique of the ballad tradition, codified during the Scottish Enlightenment, are well known in their translations for nineteenth-century music history, if not the three settings in Schubert's D. 923, which retain texts, then the Brahms op. 10 d-minor *Ballade*, in which no words are found despite Brahms's own attribution to Herder (figure 20.3).

Eine altschottische Ballade, D.923, 11b

Dein Schwert, wie ists von Blut so rot?
Edward, Edward!
Dein Schwert, wie ists von Blut so rot
Und gehst so traurig da! – O!
Ich hab geschlagen meinen Geier tot!
Mutter, Mutter!
Ich hab geschlagen meinen Geier tot,
Und das, das geht mir nah! – O!

Figure 20.3. "Edward" in J. G. Herder's "Auszug aus einem Briefwechsel über Ossian und die Lieder alter Völker" (1773). In *Johann Gottfried Herder Werke*, vol. 2 (Frankfurt: Deutscher Klassiker Verlag), 461–62.

With the "Edward" ballad (Child's Ballad 13), Herder is not at all concerned with the melody but rather with the question of whether translatability is possible. He examined "Edward" for the first time in 1773, in his essay on Ossian, the fictional Scottish bard fabricated by James Macpherson, which he wrote in the same year he was coining the concept of *Volkslied*. In "Edward," the "music" is within, trapped in language, and the question arises as to whether Ossian can be rendered in German, as Michael Denis had attempted to do only a few years earlier in the German translation of the Ossian songs.[5] By publishing his own translation of "Edward" in 1773 and then refining it in later printings, not least among them in the *Volkslieder* volumes, Herder opened the spaces within the text for music to enter, to complete the process of translation that was already immanent. The Scottish ballad "Edward," passing through Herder to Schubert and Brahms, became German. In so doing, it also became modern.

These framing moments reveal something crucial about Herder's role in the cultural history of music, particularly in the post-Enlightenment period commonly called modernity. Historiographically, Herder identifies the self-reflective problems of representing music and its contexts through translation. Translation, in its multiple forms, transforms the musical object and affords it musical subject positions in history (e.g., nationalism, sacredness). The objects and subjects are, most critically, new, which is to say "modern." For Herder, in the course of his life as a cosmopolitan intellectual, polymath, polyglot, and inveterate translator, this would increasingly become troubling, for he became deeply disturbed by the limits of nation and empire and the ways translation pushed at these. Through translation, music had the potential to acquire a new measure—a translated subjectivity—of modernity.

ENCOUNTERING HERDER TRANSLATING

In the history of modern European thought, it is, quite simply, impossible to ignore the extraordinary significance of Johann Gottfried Herder. In his *New Grove* article on "Nationalism," Richard Taruskin states this significance for cultural nationalism and nineteenth-century Romanticism in unequivocal language:

> With its celebration of difference or uniqueness in counterpoise to the
> Enlightened pursuit of universality, Romanticism was nationalism's natural ally
> and its most powerful stimulant. The key figure in forging this nexus was the
> Prussian preacher Johann Gottfried Herder, and the key document Herder's
> *Abhandlung über den Ursprung der Sprache*. ("Treatise on the Origin of Language,"
> 1773)[6]

Michael Forster, the modern translator of Herder's philosophical works, is no less unequivocal in his discussion of Herder's influence on philosophy:

> Hegel's philosophy turns out to be an elaborate systematic extension of Herderian
> ideas (especially concerning God, the mind, and history); so too does

Schleiermacher's (concerning God, the mind, interpretation, translation, and art); Nietzsche is strongly influenced by Herder (concerning the mind, history, and morals); so too is Dilthey (in his theory of human sciences); J. S. Mill has important debts to Herder (in political philosophy); Goethe not only received his philosophical outlook from Herder but was also transformed from being merely a clever but conventional poet into a great artist mainly through the early impact on him of Herder's ideas.[7]

Theologians lay special claim to Herder's role as a nestor for modern exegetical and ethical studies, recognizing moreover the seminal role he played in the modern realization of basic texts in the Bible. It was Herder who established the order of the Gospels in the New Testament and was the first to analyze the interplay of musical and poetic structures in the Old Testament.

Herder's thought arose from and influenced a remarkable range of disciplines, so many, indeed, that it is impossible to know quite what to call him—pastor, poet, philosopher, or simply polymath? This question is complicated even more by reception history, by the historical moments of hagiography and demonization that lead Tilman Borsche to ask whether Herder reception should not be rejected and supplanted with new "chances for re-reading."[8] Rereading, or even reading, for that matter, is not so easy, as one discovers when looking for modern editions of Herder, even in 2003, the bicentenary of Herder's death: Herder, the foundational figure in so many fields, is not there to be read. How, we ask, is this possible?

This chapter proposes several simple answers to that question, albeit answers that, in their simplicity, lead—critically must lead—into domains that are not only complex but also ideologically charged for the ways they insist upon sets of rereadings of modernity that are reflexive and ethnographic acts of interpretation and the writing of cultural history. First, here are my simple answers: Herder's works are not present to be reread because they are not available in translation. Second, they are not available in translation because translating them is particularly difficult. Third, they are difficult to translate because Herder was himself a translator engaged in a *Lebenswerk* committed to translation. It is in this way that translators encounter each other to find a common practice toward cultural history.

As I approached Herder as a translator and set in motion a type of encounter between translators, the questions became increasingly complex. That complexity is evident in the ambiguous reflexivity of the question itself, Who is approaching whom *as a translator?* Herder has many translator's personae. Those of a writer on music and religion are already obvious, but what does it mean to be a writer on music, especially if one is writing libretti for cantatas and poetry for songs, as Herder so often did? Moreover, are writers on theology different if they assume a position in the pulpit on Sunday, as Herder did in Weimar? My own translator's personae are also multiple and complementary or contradictory in their own ways.[9] My motivations for translating Herder run from the pedagogical to the performative. Inseparable from this is my other translation work, as a friend and colleague who, basically for fun, supplies translations *sub rosa* to folk-music publishers and CD producers in Central Europe and who uses his own ensemble, the Jewish cabaret, New Budapest Orpheum Society, to translate Jewish popular and political music.[10]

Two translators encountering each other can communicate only when they find a common language, and surely translation theory itself is crucial to the formation of that language. Rather quickly we discover that translation is not about finding one word that is the equivalent of another but in a different language. Quite the contrary, the act of translation necessarily multiplies meaning, making it an interpretive act. Paul Ricoeur expresses this in his philosophical engagement with translation, arguing for two paradigms of translation, summarized thus by Richard Kearney: "There is, first, the *linguistic paradigm*, which refers to how words relate to meanings within language or between languages. And there is, second, the *ontological paradigm*, which refers to how translation occurs between one human self and another."[11] For Ricoeur the first paradigm arose from "the plurality and diversity of languages," while the second proposes that understanding itself depends on acts and processes of translation.[12] Developing these paradigms from his lifelong hermeneutic project on the inseparability of self from other,[13] Ricoeur regards translation as a series of what he would call "interpretive detours":

> The dilemma is the following: in a good translation, the two texts, source and target, must be matched with one another through a third non-existent text. Indeed, the problem is saying the same thing or claiming to say the same thing in two different ways.[14]

In *Faithful Renderings*, a cultural history of biblical exegesis as an act of translation, Naomi Seidman proposes yet another hermeneutic detour with implications for translating Herder.[15] Seidman addresses the political implications of translation as a space of encounter in Jewish-Christian dialogue and difference. The act of translating in Western religions engenders a fraught history of encounters that she regards as articulations—speech acts—of difference, not unlike Ricoeur's notion of foreignness, which emerges when self and other become inseparable through encounter. Translation, it follows, articulates narratives, which together reinscribe history through erasure.

History, too, as the temporal horizon within which translations emerge and acquire their meaning, is collapsed and neutralized in a discourse that imagines translation as the "recovery" of an original meaning or as a technique that aims at restaging the effect the source text has on its first readers. Translation, in these discourses, becomes the very erasure of time and difference from the scene of writing.[16]

Biblical translation, Seidman recalls, is one of the major acts of creating texts of history, especially modern history. The *Vulgate*, Luther, the "King James Version," Franz Rosenzweig, and Martin Buber—all took the past and retrieved its meanings in and for the present.

It is at this point, after a brief detour of my own, that I return to Herder, and it becomes clear that his otherness is not so different from my own. His otherness arises from a conviction that he could reveal music and poetry in biblical texts and theological interpretation. Such translational otherness becomes clear later when considering the *Songs of Solomon*, in which Herder acted as translator who transformed text through hermeneutics into various interpretations of modern history. My own translationalothernessresituatesme—historically,ethnographically,performatively—as an ethnomusicologist and a scholar of Jewish music who is attempting to wrest meaning from a modernity whose meanings begin to emerge with Herder and crescendo until a historical moment in the mid-twentieth century at which the dissonant relation between self and other collapses under the surfeit of common meanings of difference.

TRANSLATION AS AN ACT OF MODERNIZING

> Instead of a brief history of the noblest clarification of this
> love song, which is what I originally intended to write, let us
> speak of a humbler object, of several notable *translations* of
> the same. The German language possesses the great fortune
> to contain one of the oldest versions.[17]

As a translator, Johann Gottfried Herder stood on the threshold between the past and the present. Translation was rarely a transferral from one language to a temporarily parallel one—the French of the late eighteenth century to the German of the late eighteenth century—but rather a transformation of ideas from an earlier historical moment to the present. He was just as likely to use translation to breathe new life into a biblical text in Hebrew as he was to translate Middle High German into modern German or Renaissance Spanish into German. Translation created new subject positions from older linguistic objects. The shift from object to subjectivity was possible because translation was an act—a conscious act—of modernizing.

The act of modernizing relied on rhetorical and structural transformations. The rhetorical transformation was made possible, first, by establishing how linguistic structure was moored to historical moments and, second, by untethering linguistic structure so that it could find new and different historical moorings. This section opened epigrammatically with Herder's confessional about creating a translation of the biblical *Songs of Solomon* (*Shir ha-shirim*) by turning to the medieval realization of the songs by Minnesinger.[18] In so doing, he takes the rather bold step, for a Lutheran pastor, of emphasizing the qualities of secular love. Even the most orthodox exegetes would not deny the expression of secular—physical, sexual—love in *Shir ha-shirim*, but Herder turns to language, medieval German, to make his case, and in so doing he sets in motion a process of cultural history, for *Minnelieder* were to appear repeatedly in standard German folk-song anthologies for the next 150 years (e.g., *Der Zupfgeigenhansl*, the commonest songbook for the German youth group known as Wandervögel).[19] The second act of modernizing was for Herder the transformation of narrative meaning when myth crosses the threshold to history. It was history, of course, that contained the subject positions of modernity, the time boundedness of events linked teleologically by language.

A modern subjectivity resulted from the construction of a new text through translation, specifically through the creation of wholes from parts. Herder's own working methods and concepts of literary production were shaped and reshaped to enable him to create a multifaceted, if often enigmatic, language for transforming parts into wholes. He bound his ethnographic materials to the tools of translation carefully and deliberately so that he could create a language forged from transcription and translation, a language whose wholeness itself had been synthesized from fragments. For Herder the fragment would become precisely the tool he needed to expand the ontological scope of translation.

The fragment as aesthetic and narrative trope was by no means new in the mid-eighteenth century, when Herder studied in Königsberg and began his career as a pastor in Riga, Latvia.[20] Fundamental to an aesthetic of the classical was the conviction that the past was recoverable by gathering those fragments that survived and by imagining the ways in which they could be sutured together to provide some semblance of the present. The fragment assumed its meaning through a dialectic with wholeness. Friedrich Hölderlin, writing in 1801, would recognize the dynamic of that dialectic and thereby summarize the attraction to genre that had captivated his generation: "There is only one quarrel in the world, namely, which has greater meaning, the whole or the part?"[21]

If Herder's fascination with fragments was a response to his own era, it also owed a debt to Protestant theology. In his theological works, his concern for the fragment was expressed in a distinction between *spiritus* and *littera*, a distinction that dominated eighteenth-century Protestant thought. It is precisely this distinction, moreover, that appears again and again in the aesthetic works. It converges in three books from 1778, two of which are devoted to sculpture (*Plastik*)[22] and folk songs (*Stimmen der Völker in Liedern*) and a volume of translations of the *Songs of Solomon*.

Why did Herder regard the fragment as having such great narrative potential? First of all, the fragment is open ended. It can move around not just from the past to the present but also from one song to another. The ballad, so remarkably fertile for poets and musicians, was constituted of fragments, strophe, and motifs that moved from one ballad to another, crossing cultural and class borders, but shaping the narrative and national canon. Second, the use of fragments afforded hybridity and allowed genre to proliferate. We could take virtually any literary or musical genre of the late eighteenth and nineteenth centuries and describe the emergence of hybridity, with its power to convey modernity. The novel would be a prime example; so, too, would the epic. Third, the fragment contained what Novalis would call "the seeds" of narrativity and history.[23] Fragments define history, taken as they are from its incomplete contexts, and shape it in the future, creating context anew. By adding fragments again and again to his diverse and polymath writings, then, by translating and transforming the past, Herder imagined a nineteenth century that would accommodate the surfeit of fragments he was repositioning in the present. The songs that he obsessively published in translation increasingly came to fulfill the conditions of modernity, to narrate, even, the history of Herder's own present.

THE AGE OF MUSICAL TRANSLATION

Herder did, in fact, play a singular role in issuing in what I call the "age of musical translation." This age began in the closing decades of the eighteenth century and continued through the second decade of the nineteenth century. The critical change was, on its surface, the recognition that oral tradition was being lost and that some means had to be created to preserve it through translation. Translation itself followed several stages to define the age. First, collectors—anthologizers, ethnographers, and fabricators—gathered songs from oral tradition, motivated to do so by the anxiety of loss. Second, when published and printed, the songs underwent a process of standardization and contextualization. They appear, for example, with a standard orthography that translates oral to written tradition. Place affords one of the most powerful attributions of language. Third, melodic notation accrues to the songs, fixing them in written tradition but potentially returning them to oral tradition, for the melodies allow them to be sung off the page.

The pivotal period in the age of musical translation was roughly 1806 to 1808, not by chance the two years in which Achim von Arnim and Clemens Brentano published *Des Knaben Wunderhorn*.[24] It was during these years, moreover, that the posthumous edition (1807) of Herder's *Folk Songs* appeared. The turn toward translation was by no means limited to the German-language areas of central and eastern Europe. The turn leads us no less to Ireland and the contributions of Thomas Moore to the age of musical translation.

Thomas Moore (1779–1852) was the editor—or was he a collector, poet, composer?—of the *Irish Melodies*, which began appearing in 1808.[25] For those who know the *Irish Melodies* at all, Moore's publications have been experienced through the repertories they influenced (English and Irish domestic song in the nineteenth century) or in the translations into American popular song that began with antebellum minstrelsy in the 1820s and culminated with Stephen Foster. Like Herder's *Volkslieder* and Arnim and Brentano's *Des Knaben Wunderhorn* the *Irish Melodies* do not, in fact, have melodies attributable to Moore. They are, instead, texts from a wide variety of sources, variously transcribed from oral tradition or collected from diverse written sources. Their nationalism—and there can be no question that they make a case for Ireland as historically independent of England—results from the ways they cohere in published anthologies (figure 20.4).

In the midst of the age of musical translation, however, they would not fully enter written tradition and acquire the power to represent the absent modern nation

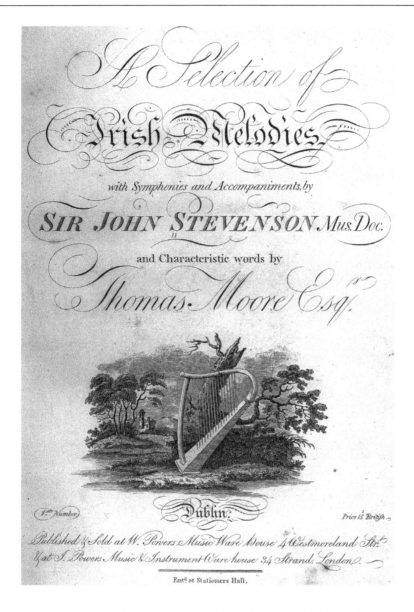

Figure 20.4. Title page of early edition of Moore's *Irish Melodies*.

of Ireland until melodies were assigned to them. Moore turned to others, particularly Edward Bunting, and attracted melodies and arrangements—from choral works to "symphonies"—that contained the underpinnings of nation, not least among them "harmonization" (figure 20.5).

As these fragments of music accrued to a melody, that is, to a text inscribed from oral tradition, the songs entered history and increasingly possessed the potential to narrate history. We witness these same stages of modernizing in other traditions that we can now label as "national." The stage following Herder's *Volkslieder* and Arnim and Brentano's *Des Knaben Wunderhorn* takes its most

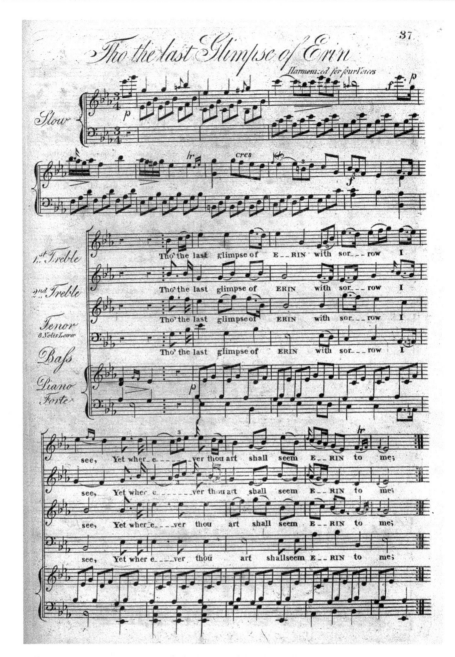

Figure 20.5. Thomas Moore, "Tho' the Last Glimpse of Erin," from *Irish Melodies*, vol. 1.

complete form in Groos and Klein's *Deutsche Lieder für Jung und Alt*, in which German songs appear in an anthology—of "German songs"—with melodies for the first time between 1816 and 1818. These "German songs" were to have appeared in yet another edition in 1823, this time with piano accompaniments and choral settings by Josef and Anton Gersbach, but in fact they never reached the printer.[26]

Standing on its threshold and providing it with the critical tools he forged as a translator, Herder inspired the age of musical translation. That age, in turn, inspired many who followed: Beethoven, Schubert, and Brahms, as well as countless inventors of modern, national tradition in the nineteenth and twentieth centuries who forged their own tools for translating the past into the modern soundscape of their nations.

HERDER TRANSLATOR 1: THE SONG AS HISTORICAL OBJECT AND LIVING SUBJECT

Dear Reader, should you wish to follow me with an open mind and without preconceived theory, then here is what I have come to decide after my transformation through this holy myrtle pasture! Everything depends upon which way you open your heart [to the *Songs of Solomon*], with the innocent eye of a dove or with the lewd glance of a rogue.[27]

Translating songs brought Johann Gottfried Herder to the brink of crisis in the mid-1770s. After a half-dozen years of more or less unsatisfying positions serving the aristocracy of the small lands of Germany, where he had arrived after leaving Riga in 1769, Herder found an established position as a church administrator in the principality of Saxony-Weimar and Eisenach. His peripatetic career had fruitfully afforded him multiple opportunities to reflect upon the fragments of the theological and humanistic sciences he was mustering. Among those fragments were songs of all sorts—folk songs, popular songs, biblical songs, and sentimental songs; songs fixed in literary traditions and those gathered from his journeys through the Baltic lands as an ethnographer and through Alsace-Lorraine as a literary companion of Goethe.

Herder's songbag was full to the brim, and we might imagine from a series of aborted efforts to publish them, notably a projected 1774 volume called *Alte Volkslieder*, which survives only as a preface with song fragments, that he had struggled with the appropriate repertories and formats for the songs.[28] We glimpse some of the dimensions of the struggle in the epigraph that begins this section, which itself survives as a fragment from yet another volume of songs, this one finding its way to manuscript in 1776. It was through translation that Herder resolved the crisis of giving meaning to song that he opened a path to and through the heart. To resound song, he would devise a new approach to translating, and that approach would leave an indelible imprint on the emergence of modern anthropology.[29]

By examining the collections of fragments and songs that so engaged Herder in the 1770s, one can discern the clear formulation of a theory of translation. Song is an object that we encounter in its strangeness, in its marking of an otherness that we do not understand, but translation transforms it in such a way that its subjectivity is revealed, so that we understand it as connected to us. Translation in this sense is a type of performative act that allows us to experience the song in new ways.

Translation thus transforms the song from an object of otherness to a vessel that shapes new and varied subject positions of selfness.

Historical Excursus: The Absent German Historical Narrative

Probably no approach to late Enlightenment cultural history is as familiar to modern readers as the transformation of song from object to subject position in the two volumes of folk songs whose contents appeared serially from 1778 to 1779.[30] It is necessary to comment on these only as a reminder that the *Voices of the People in Songs* and the *Folk Songs* were by no means anthologies of German folk songs, much less some sort of objective canon for nineteenth-century nationalists. Of 162 songs in the volumes, only 38 have German texts, and of these, 23 are art songs. The two volumes thus contain only 15 German folk songs. For Herder, the real goal of his two volumes of folk songs was to restore them to the human conditions from which they arose and to the cultures whose histories they narrated. Herder's introduction to volume two (1779) resonates as no less than a mandate for world music:

> Song loves the masses, it loves to take shape out of the common voice of the many: Song commands the ear of the listener and the chorus of voices and souls. Song never could have come into existence as the art of letters and syllables, as a portrait of images and colors for readers in their armchairs. More to the point, song would never have come to be what it is without all peoples of the world. Every culture and every language, especially the oldest, most nebulous ones of the Orient, produced traces for the masses from such origins, when it was necessary to lead them forward and take stock of them.[31]

To examine a different translational path here, I turn instead to a lesser-known volume of songs, also from 1778, the *Lieder der Liebe*, or *Love Songs*.[32] The *Lieder der Liebe* that this volume might originally have contained in more literally authentic versions were the biblical *Songs of Solomon*, the *Shir ha-shirim*. It was Herder's original goal to publish these in a new translation from the original Hebrew, which would produce a new version to resolve the problem that, as Herder expressed it, "no book in the Old Testament is as mishandled as the so-called *Hohelied Salomons*."[33] The "mishandling" of the *Songs of Solomon* had a long genealogy in the German theological tradition, one that inevitably ran through the Luther translation of the Bible. The problem Herder sought to resolve was that all previous translations seemed to justify themselves by claiming that they reflected "the way it is in the Bible," "es steht ja in der Bibel."[34] Herder sought to liberate an entirely different set of meanings, indeed, to breathe new life into the *Songs of Solomon* by realizing their fundamental sensuality through modern translation. We should not underestimate the meaning of this rethinking of biblical meaning.

Herder's translation of the *Songs of Solomon* was to be radical even for the late Enlightenment. After attempting with frustration to draw modern, sensual meaning from the Hebrew texts—and his Hebrew was impeccable—he turned to a set of texts he believed engaged the deeper meanings: a collection of forty-four medieval Minnesinger texts. The songs of the Minnesinger, which fill the third chapter[35] of the three-chapter book, provided deliberate evidence of the ways in which new subject positions could be established through translation. The title of the chapter is, in fact: "Von Übersezungen des Buches, insonderheit Einer in alten Minneliedern" [On Translating the Book, Especially One in Ancient Minnesongs]. Herder fully

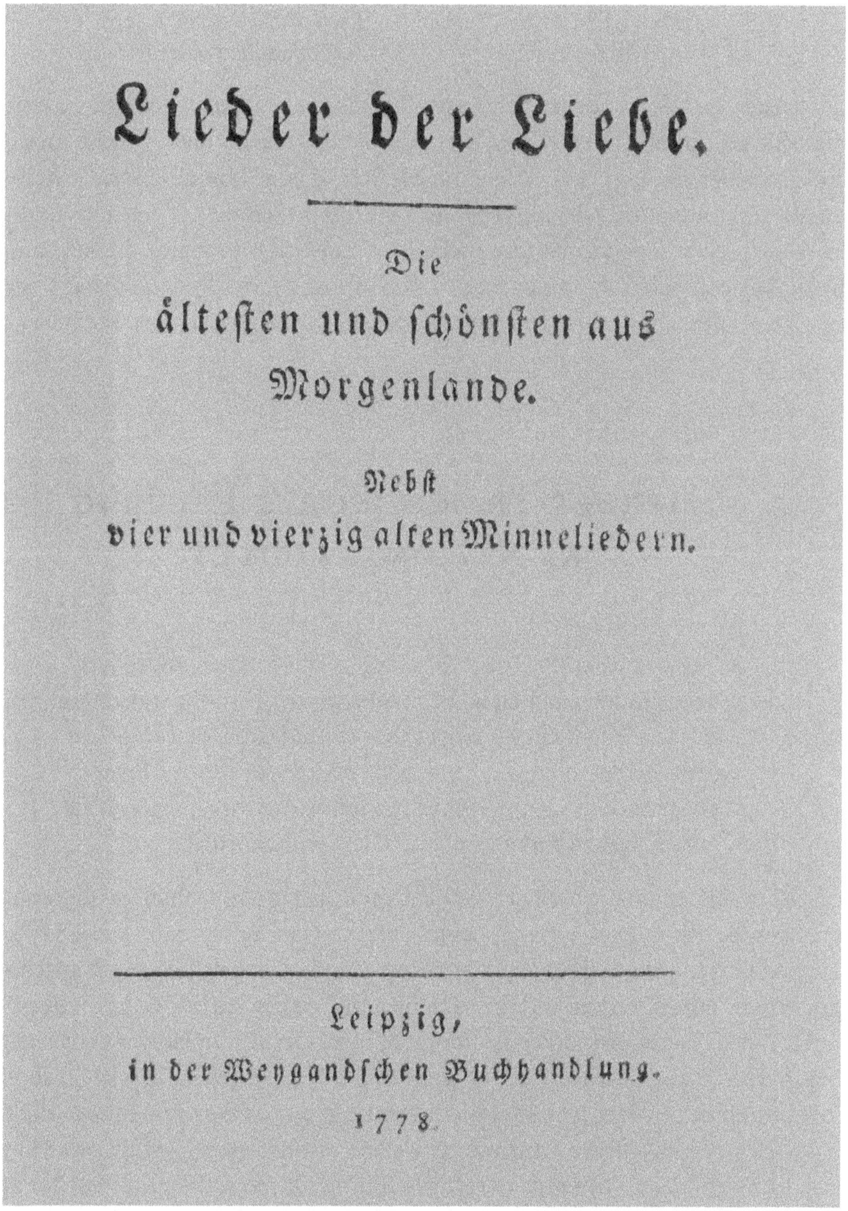

Lieder der Liebe.

Die
ältesten und schönsten aus
Morgenlande.

Nebst
vier und vierzig alten Minneliedern.

Leipzig,
in der Weygandschen Buchhandlung.
1778.

Figure 20.6. Title page of *Lieder der Liebe*.

recognized just how radical this new approach to translating the Bible really was because he allowed it to be published anonymously. Later editions, too, failed to refer to Herder as the author (see figure 20.6).

Herder's translation brilliantly reimagines the subject positions of those who populate the songs and those who read them. Speaking about the relation between lover and beloved, he wrote: "*You* and *he*, *I* and *we* are exchanged: Even from afar, he is near her, she can speak with him if she so wishes."[36] But her voice is different, as Herder leads into the song itself: "Her voice is silent; it allows itself to be heard in a completely different way":

Schwarz bin ich und doch lieblich,	I am black, but still lovely,
Ihr Töchter Jerusalem!	You daughters of Jerusalem!

Lieder der Liebe is not an anthology of the *Songs of Solomon* but rather a rich texture of poetic texts intoned by the "you, he, I, and we" that Herder always sets in motion. "Wie anders ist hier Alles!" ("How different is everything here!") rejoices Herder as he reflects on his own translation, which recedes into a text in which subject positions multiply and lend themselves to personal interpretation. Translation provides the key, indeed, for unlocking embodied meaning. Song is freed from its text. We, the readers, are drawn closer to God as the *Songs of Solomon* resonate in ways that transcend the Bible.

Herder Translator 2: The Epic as National Object

> "Ruy" means "Rodrigo." No singer of romances, moreover, needs to tell a tale in a *historical manner* from the outset, for it is the listeners themselves that should experience the romance as *romantic*. They hear. Whoeveer is not a lover of poesy should simply regard the following romances as little tales and read them as prose. They are historical.[37]

With this enigmatic passage, rendered more as a footnote than an epigraph, Herder qualifies the title page of his largest epic project, a translation of the Iberian epic, *El Cid*. Throughout his life, Herder was fascinated by epic precisely because it articulated the gap between the historical and the romantic. The epic was a bridge from the past to the future, and it therefore marked the moment of modernity. In Herder's concept the epic began with fragments that, through performance, could cohere as a larger form.[38]

The epic drew Herder to the Mediterranean and at the same time to the timeless past before modernity. He turned to the epic, nonetheless, not as a journey to the past but rather as an attempt to retrieve fragments from the past in order that they might lay claim to the future. In smaller experimental essays such as "Homer and

Ossian," he seeks the common ground between fragments and wholes, but it was with the *Cid* translation that his experiments yielded a type of historical truth that would be foundational for the conditions of modernity.[39]

Herder's work on *El Cid* is much better known in the German-language traditions than in the English, thus making a bit of context necessary. As a theologian and scholar of classics, Herder cultivated a deep familiarity with epics from the eastern Mediterranean. Whereas modern epic theory emphasizes the stichic structures of the epic, with its relatively fluid course of narrative structure, Herder turned his attention to the narrative fragments within the epic itself and to their potential to cohere as a modern text. Herder's *Cid*, then, was a collection of ballads, of Spanish *romances* whose formal logic was internal and distinctive in the anthology of seventy total tales within the epic history.

Herder drew his romances from a wide array of sources in both Spanish and French, and he shuffled them about in contrasting ways. He used the Spanish *romances*, in fact, didactically to learn the language, translating several each day to teach himself Spanish. The first thirteen were recycled from his massive aesthetic work, *Adrastea*.[40] His translation—nineteenth-century publications claimed that the epic was *besungen* by Herder, meaning something like "sung into existence"— came from both French and Spanish versions, more the former (*romances* 1–52) than the latter. The *romance*, too, could have different meanings and functions as a genre, fully a poetic androgyny in Herder's vision of the epic project as modern. For the new romantic generation, Herder believed the *Cid* should indeed be serious stuff, the Spanish national epic. It presaged and realized the modern struggle between Christianity and Islam in Europe.

From the perspective of cultural history we recognize that Herder's epic project was not about the nation as it had been but rather as it would become in the nineteenth century. It was in the nineteenth century, moreover, that the epic would assert itself as the musical and poetic genre of the nation and of nationalism. The epic contained the poetic language that allowed the nation to possess a history previously denied it. It was in the nineteenth century, of course, that the Serbian *Kosovo Cycle* was *besungen* by Vuk Stefanović Karadžić (1787–1864) and the *Nibelungen* epic was *besungen* by Richard Wagner. The nineteenth century became the era of epic history, and it did so with no small debt to Herder's *Cid* translation, which had made explicit the goal of collapsing the gap between the "historical" and the "romantic" around the moment of modernity.

At first glance it may seem an exaggeration to claim that Herder invented the "modern epic," should something like that properly exist. Herder himself would reject such a claim out of hand, for he knew his Homer far too well. What Herder did, however, was to reimagine the epic for the modern nation. Formally, he repositioned the epic between oral and written tradition. He reinscribed it as a new and different genre of performance whose narrative structure shifted from the stich to the strophe and whose creator shifted from the Homeric singer of tales to the *Romanzensänger* of Herder's *Cid*, or the folksinger whose ballads increasingly employed the conventions of High German to sing the modern German song into existence.

HERDER TRANSLATOR 3: MUSICAL SOUND AS COLONIAL OBJECT

A new subjectivity pervades the appendix to the 1807 posthumous edition of the *Volkslieder*, in which "O Sanctissima!" appeared. The joyous worship of the Sicilian sailors gives way to lament from another part of the world, from Madagascar, eleven songs that bring Herder's lifelong project of cultural history through song translation to a close with a final quatrain from Peru. Translation charted new territory for Herder as he entered a new century and a new era. The Madagascar songs—translations of translations, for they originally appeared in French—are dark records of colonial encounter. In varying forms ranging from verse to prose to antiphonal call-and-response, the voices of the people of Madagascar rise in lament and anger at the tragedy wrought by the French colonial forces and the missionaries who accompanied them. "Show no sadness for the white people," enjoins one king, "for death would be preferable."[41] Mothers mourn the loss of their children in battle. "Die, oh my son, die once, so that you will not have to die a thousand times."[42]

Herder's final song translations foreshadow the darkness that will fall from the age of musical translation he ushered in. We might imagine these songs as evidence of a postcolonial project *avant la lettre*, if indeed the literalness of translation was not open to question by Herder at every stage, and if, more darkly, the postcolonial cultural history chronicled through song—folk song, German song, the songs of all people—had not subjugated the subjectivity of so many in the centuries to come. Through translation we hear the laments of the people of Madagascar at the beginning of the nineteenth century. Translation, however, has no power to give voice to the people of German West Africa, that is, Namibia, who were subjected to genocide at the hands of German colonizers at the beginning of the twentieth century. Reflecting historically and also projecting into the future, we recognize the limits of translation, but we also recognize that Herder, too, perceived those limits. Reflecting becomes reflexive and in so doing brings us back to the reflexivity and self-reflexivity enacted by the title of this chapter.

POSTSCRIPT: ENCOUNTERING HERDER WHILE TRANSLATING THE HOLOCAUST

Over the course of the past few years, I have encountered Herder the translator as I translate his writings and translations. Moreover, I have increasingly encountered him in my various acts of translation to realize the music of the Holocaust, particularly the works for the theatrical stage of the concentration camps.[43] These are works that I translate for modern editions and perform throughout the world. In such translation projects, I again encounter Herder.

How, we may ask, does Herder belong to this moment of crisis in modernity and modernism? On one level, it has been impossible to lose sight of Herder because of the burden of modern German history that has accrued to his writings. He is and has been blamed for a nationalism run amok in the twentieth century.[44] As a translator of Herder and of the music of the Holocaust, I simply cannot separate the readings of Herder at the beginning and end of German modernity as if they did not exist. To paraphrase Paul Ricoeur, Herder's self has come to be a part of another.[45] In a different way, my translation of Herder's works on music and nationalism increasingly draw me closer to a Herder engaged in projects dedicated to translations that would produce religious and ethical understanding. Translation endows cultural history with moral responsibility. Translations, I believe, bring an entirely new level of criticism to the cultural history that unfolds as modernity. They presage its end no less than they mark its beginning.

The detours through Herder to translating in my own work—my acts of writing and performance—ultimately lead me back to the historiographic reflection that joins ethnomusicology and cultural history—and beyond to my own sense of personal and professional self. Upon my return journey through translation, I reencounter the reasons that I believe so powerfully in what we do as musical scholars and cultural historians—and why we do it. The cultural translation in which we engage—and we share this as scholars and musicians—has profound ethical meanings. Through translation the ethical dimensions of our encounters with others may realize an exhilarating sense of selfness. Perhaps more often, the mirrored encounter with otherness is disturbing and darkened by the levels of narrative that lie behind them. In the cultural history of music, I believe, cultural translation does not open a magic door to truth, to "music as it really is," freed as a movable signifier from lives as they are lived. Translating Herder translating, I find myself increasingly incapable of freeing myself from the significance of what I do as an ethnomusicologist and a historian. The detour forged by our ethical commitment to cultural translation is long, and the longer we journey, the fewer opportunities it offers for rest. The voice of the translator, nonetheless, assures us that it is the right path to take.

NOTES

Earlier versions of this chapter were presented at colloquia at the University of California–Berkeley, Cambridge University, and the University of Pennsylvania. I have benefited enormously from the discussions that followed those earlier presentations.

1. Johann Gottfried Herder, *Stimmen der Völker in Liedern* and *Volkslieder*. Figure 20.1 appears in the most widely circulating modern edition (Stuttgart: Reclam, 1975), 373–74. Together with Herder's first modest publication of folk songs, *Alte Volkslieder* (1774), the

two volumes of folk songs also appear in Herder's collected works: Johann Gottfried Herder, *Volkslieder, Übertragungen, Dichtungen.*

2. In the 1975 Reclam edition the 1807 "Anhang" appears on pages 369–98.

3. For a recording of this setting see *Complete Beethoven Edition*, vol. 17, *Volkslied-Bearbeitungen*, CD 4, tr. 17.

4. The oral tradition of the song is global even in the twenty-first century. In fact, few songs circulated more widely in German in fieldwork I have done in German-speaking communities in the American Midwest, in Eastern European *Sprachinseln*, or even in Israel.

5. Michael Denis, *Die Gedichte Ossians* (Vienna, 1768–69).

6. Richard Taruskin, "Nationalism," 691. Herder spent his early years in the Baltics and his final years in Weimar and was therefore never in Prussia.

7. Johann Gottfried Herder, *Herder: Philosophical Writings*, vii.

8. Tilman Borsche, ed., *Herder im Spiegel der Zeiten*. The reevaluation of Herder has also been necessitated by the misuse of his writings on nationalism during the era of German fascism and the Third Reich; see Jost Schneider, ed., *Herder im "Dritten Reich."*

9. I am currently preparing a volume of translation and commentary titled *Herder on Music and Nationalism* (Berkeley: University of California Press, in preparation).

10. See, for example, New Budapest Orpheum Society, *Jewish Cabaret in Exile.*

11. Richard Kearney, "Ricoeur's Philosophy of Translation," in Paul Ricoeur, *On Translation*, xii.

12. Ricoeur, *On Translation*, 11.

13. Paul Ricoeur, *Oneself as Another.*

14. Ricoeur, *On Translation*, 7.

15. Naomi Seidman, *Faithful Renderings.*

16. Seidman, *Faithful Renderings*, 2–3.

17. Statt einer kleinen Geschichte der vornehmsten Erklärungen dieses Liedes, die ich zu geben Willens war, laßt uns von einem neidloseren Gegenstande, einigen merkwürdigen *Übersezungen* desselben, reden. Die Deutsche Sprach hat das Glück, eine der ältesten sich erhalten zu haben. (Johann Gottfried Herder, *Lieder der Liebe*, 118; spelling and italics in the original)

18. Herder, *Lieder der Liebe.*

19. Hans Breuer, ed., *Der Zupfgeigenhansl.*

20. See, for example, Mary-Ann Constantine and Gerald Porter, *Fragments and Meaning in Traditional Song*, 21–49.

21. Letter dated March 1801 in Friedrich Hölderlin, *Sämtliche Werke*, vol. 6, 419.

22. Johann Gottfried Herder, *Plastik*. For a superb translation with extensive commentary, see Johann Gottfried Herder, *Sculpture.*

23. Novalis, *Schriften IV*, 241–42.

24. Achim von Arnim and Clemens Brentano, *Des Knaben Wunderhorn.*

25. Thomas Moore, *Irish Melodies.*

26. Lisa Feurzeig has completed, edited, and provided critical commentary to the unpublished manuscript, which is in Special Collections of the Regenstein Library at the University of Chicago. See Lisa Feurzeig, ed., *Deutsche Lieder für Jung und Alt.*

27. Willt [sic] du mir ohne Vorurteil und Hypothese folgen, Leser, hier ist meine Meinung, mein Wandeln in diesem heiligen Myrthenhaine! Nur kommt alles darauf an, mit was Herzen du in ihm wandelst, ob mit dem Taubenauge der Unschuld oder mit einem Blick voll Unzucht und Schalkheit. (quoted in Regine Otto, "Nachwort," in Johann Gottfried Herder, *Lieder der Liebe*, 168)

28. *Johann Gottfried Herder Werke*, vol. 3, 11–68.

29. See John H. Zammito, *Kant, Herder, and the Birth of Anthropology*.

30. Herder, *Stimmen der Völker*.

31. Gesang liebt Menge, die Zusammenstimmung vieler: er fodert das Ohr des Hörers und Chorus der Stimmen und Gemüther. Als Buchstaben- und Sylbenkunst, als ein Gemählde der Zusammensetzung und Farben für Leser auf dem Polster, wäre er gewiß nie entstanden, oder nie, was er unter allen Völkern ist, worden. Alle Welt und Sprache, insonderheit der älteste, graue Orient liefert von diesem Ursprunge Spuren die Menge, wenn es solche vorzuführen und aufzuzählen Noth wäre. (Herder, *Stimmen der Völker*, 167)

32. Herder, *Lieder der Liebe*.

33. Cited in Otto, "Nachwort," 168 (see note 27 this chapter).

34. Otto, "Nachwort," 168 (see note 27 this chapter).

35. Herder, *Lieder der Liebe*, 118–65.

36. Herder, *Lieder der Liebe*, 10.

37. Title page of Herder's translation of *Der Cid*. Johann Gottfried Herder, *Der Cid*, in *Johann Gottfried Herder Werke*, vol. 3, 545.

38. See, for example, his late aesthetic writings in *Kalligone* and "Homer und Ossian," both in *Johann Gottfried Herder Werke*, vol. 8.

39. Herder, "Homer und Ossian," in *Johann Gottfried Herder Werke*, vol. 8.

40. Johann Gottfried Herder, *Adrastea*, compiled as *Johann Gottfried Herder Werke*, vol. 10.

41. Herder, *Stimmen der Völker*, Anhang, 542.

42. Herder, *Stimmen der Völker*, Anhang, 550.

43. See, for example, Philip V. Bohlman, "On Colonialism and Its Aftermaths," and "The European Nation-State in History," in Philip V. Bohlman, *Music, Nationalism, and the Making of the New Europe*, chapter 2, 23–57.

44. Schneider, *Herder im "Dritten Reich."*

45. Ricoeur, *Oneself as Another*.

BIBLIOGRAPHY

Arnim, Achim von, and Clemens Brentano. 1806 and 1808. *Des Knaben Wunderhorn*. 2 vols. Heidelberg: Mohr und Zimmer.

Beethoven, Ludwig van. 1997. *Volkslied-Bearbeitungen*. Vol. 17, *Complete Beethoven Edition*. 7 CDs. Deutsche Grammophon 453 786–2.

Philip V., Bohlman 2007. "On Colonialism and Its Aftermaths." *SEM Newsletter* 41(1): 4–5.

———. 2011. *Focus: Music, Nationalismn and the Making of the New Europe*. 2nd ed. New York: Routledge.

Borsche, Tilman, ed. 2006. *Herder im Spiegel der Zeiten: Verwerfungen der Rezeptionsgeschichte und Chancen einer Relektüre*. Munich: Fink.

Breuer, Hans, ed. 1908. *Der Zupfgeigenhansl*. Leipzig: Hofmeister.

Constantine, Mary-Ann, and Gerald Porter. 2003. *Fragments and Meaning in Traditional Song: From the Blues to the Baltic*. London: British Academy.

Feurzeig, Lisa, ed. 2002. *Deutsche Lieder für Jung und Alt*. Middleton, Wisc.: A-R Editions. Recent Researches in the Oral Traditions of Music 7.

Herder, Johann Gottfried. 1773. *Von deutscher Art und Kunst: Einige fliegende Blätter.* Hamburg: Bode.

———. 1774. *Alte Volkslieder (Vorreden).* Planned first publication of a volume of folk songs, with contents for four books.

———. 1778a. *Der Cid: Geschichte des Don Ruy Diaz, Grafen von Bivar, nach Spanischen Romanzen.* In *Johann Gottfried Herder Werke,* vol. 3, 545–691. Frankfurt: Deutscher Klassiker Verlag, 1990.

———. 1778b. *Lieder der Liebe: Die ältesten und schönsten aus Morgenlande, nebst vier und vierzig alten Minneliedern.* Leipzig: Weygandsche Buchhandlung. Modern edition as single volume. Zurich: Manesse, 1992. With an afterword by Regine Otto.

———. 1778c. *Plastik: Einige Wahrnehmungen über Form und Gestalt aus Pygmalions Bildendem Traume.* Riga: Hartknoch.

———. 1778d. *Volkslieder, Übertragungen, Dichtungen,* in *Johann Gottfried Herder Werke,* vol. 3, 9–430. Frankfurt: Deutscher Klassiker Verlag, 1990.

———. 1778–1779. *Stimmen der Völker in Liedern* and *Volkslieder.* 2 vols. Leipzig: Weygandsche Buchhandlung.

———. 1801–1804. *Adrastea.* In *Johann Gottfried Herder Werke.* Vol. 10. Frankfurt: Deutscher Klassiker Verlag, 2000.

———. [1998a]. "Homer und Ossian." In *Johann Gottfried Herder Werke.* Vol. 8, 71–87. Frankfurt: Deutscher Klassiker Verlag.

———. [1998b]. *Kalligone: Vom Angenehmen und Schönen.* In *Johann Gottfried Herder Werke.* Vol. 8, 641–964. Frankfurt: Deutscher Klassiker Verlag.

———. 2002a. *Herder: Philosophical Writings.* Trans. Michael N. Forster. Cambridge Texts in the History of Philosophy. New York: Cambridge University Press.

——— 2002b. *Sculpture: Some Observations on Shape and Form from Pygmalion's Creative Dream,* trans. and ed. Jason Gaiger. Chicago: University of Chicago Press.

Hölderlin, Friedrich. 1943–1985. *Sämtliche Werke,* ed. F. Beissner and Adolf Beck. Stuttgart.

Moore, Thomas. 1808–1832. *Irish Melodies.* 10 vols. London: Various publishers.

New Budapest Orpheum Society. 2009. *Jewish Cabaret in Exile.* Chicago: Cedille Records. CDR 90000 110.

Novalis. 1975. *Schriften IV: Tagebücher, Briefwechsel, zeitgenössische Zeugnisse,* ed. Richard Samuel. Stuttgart.

Ricoeur, Paul. 1992. *Oneself as Another,* trans. Kathleen Blamey. Chicago: University of Chicago Press.

———. 2006. *On Translation,* trans. Eileen Brennan. Thinking in Action. New York: Routledge. Orig.: *Sur la traduction.* Paris: Bayard, 2004.

Schneider, Jost, ed. 1994. *Herder im "Dritten Reich."* Bielefeld: Aisthesis.

Seidman, Naomi. 2006. *Faithful Renderings.* Chicago: University of Chicago Press.

Taruskin, Richard. 2000. "Nationalism." In *The New Grove Dictionary of Music and Musicians,* 2d ed. Vol. 17, ed. Stanley Sadie, 689–706. London: Macmillan.

Zammito, John H. 2002. *Kant, Herder, and the Birth of Anthropology.* Chicago: University of Chicago Press.

CHAPTER 21

THE EYE OF THE NEEDLE: MUSIC AS HISTORY AFTER THE AGE OF RECORDING

LEON BOTSTEIN

I

The writing of music history holds an alluring promise. Through the close study of music and musical culture something distinct if not new might be added to our understanding of the past defined in the broadest of terms. However, to do so, inquiry into the history of music must be motivated by issues and questions that link musical culture to the conduct of life beyond the confines of music. Yet the enterprise of music history, despite scholars who are determined to break from the inherited patterns of self-referential, autopoetic historical reasoning, remains stubbornly dependent on the ongoing tradition of the criticism and normative judgment of music as an art.[1] What we study in music history and how we study it continue to be defined by aesthetic claims and commitments. Historians, in the choice of their subjects, rely on and indeed exploit a commonplace idea. The writing of history and biography in music is justified because it illuminates music judged as having lasting aesthetic merit. History, in some pseudo-Darwinian way, is understood as selecting for objective value. This axiom itself has never been properly scrutinized. Nonetheless, the audience for music history has been and remains made up of readers interested first and foremost in music as an active art form and experience (e.g., performers and listeners). Music is an arena in which subjective aesthetic taste reigns supreme. Preferences for particular music and not curiosity about history per se shape historical scholarship. The history of art, architecture, and literature, while also subject to the priorities set by criticism, appear to have moved a bit further away from the limits of criticism. Through the study of the history of these art forms, which is not driven wholly by normative judgments of past practice, the visual and the literary have contributed to general historical understanding far more than have accounts of the history of the musical in human experience.[2]

Consider, for example, the study of the symphony as a genre in the late eighteenth and early nineteenth centuries. It remains hostage to interest in Beethoven's exceptional achievement and a construct of a Viennese classical tradition (generated in the mid-nineteenth century) defined primarily by the extraordinary output of Mozart and Haydn.[3] When confronted with the works of Anton Eberl and Paul Wranitzky, despite evidence of an extensive contemporary performance history and positive critical reception, impatience with the presumed limited artistic merit of works by these composers results in a somewhat distorted framing of research and interpretation. It is in the problematic nature of music as a subject that many more of the nearly thirteen thousand known examples of eighteenth-century symphonies need to be played and listened to without Beethoven and Mozart in mind if scholarship on what the eighteenth-century symphony might tell us about the past is to be undertaken. In the end, ironically, that task would be justified not only by what we might learn about the eighteenth century. We might also rediscover works for the active concert repertoire. In addition, no doubt, some more light would inevitably be shed on the genius of the three great masters. However, in contrast to painting and literature, confronting musical works once successful and well regarded by musically literate patrons, critics, and performers but no longer in the repertoire is relatively hard and expensive, especially if live performance and not recorded music is considered essential to scholarship and any evaluation of its past significance for the literate public. Empathy for past musical practices and tastes that are no longer in demand as part of active music making remains hard to generate outside a limited scholarly community despite the historical significance of practices and tastes based, ironically, on a past commitment to aesthetic values now lost.[4]

In the history of music since the mid-eighteenth century, the continued dominance in the narrative of musical culture by "great" music and leading figures—composers whose works remain in the repertory of contemporary concert life—has conspired to block a fuller understanding of the history of musical life and its place and significance in culture and society. The history of reception and so-called canon formation does little more than document the process of aesthetic selection over time and verify the erosion of memory.[5] A persistent "great-composer" and "great-work" fetish distorts much scholarship that purports to understand music in the larger framework of history or history through music—writing that uses music as a defining constituent of the cultural past. In general music history appropriates and confirms generalizations and insights derived from the study of other phenomena—politics, art, architecture, literature, and philosophy—and locates them within music.

Music becomes not a primary source of historical understanding but a subsidiary, confirming phenomenon. The finest of such efforts, such as Jeffrey Kallberg's work on Chopin, has differentiated and expanded our understanding of canonic works and composers using interpretive strategies developed in other fields.[6] On the other hand, the limitations of this approach are evident in recent scholarship on Gustav Mahler and Richard Strauss. Work in that field continues to rely too heavily on constructs of fin-de-siècle culture and politics developed without close consideration of music. What music and the musical culture of that era might uniquely reveal has been obscured to the detriment of our understanding of the fin de siècle and, unfortunately, Mahler and Strauss.[7]

The suspicion remains, rightly so, that more could be achieved. Embedded in the fabric of music and music-making—significant activities in European life and culture before 1945—are aspects of the human experience whose expressions and impact are not wholly redundant with regard to what we can find by studying other arenas of human endeavor. The fabric of the musical life of the past cannot, however, be defined overwhelmingly by a retrospective selective bias in favor of either our own normative judgments or the so-called test of time or verdict of history.

The sustained popularity and subsequent disappearance from the opera repertory of much of the French nineteenth-century repertoire, beginning with works by Auber and Meyerbeer and ending with those by Reyer, Magnard, Chabrier, and other French Wagnerians, represents just one example of how aesthetic judgment and the understanding and writing of history may have been at cross-purposes. Works and composers once widely played and disseminated survive merely as asides and footnotes.[8] We simply no longer know music that once had a significant following. Some of it might once again delight audiences. In surveys of publishers' catalogues and advertisements in popular music journals, particularly before 1914, one encounters well-regarded but now unfamiliar composers and works within concert genres and amateur domestic music whose role in the formation of taste and definition of musical literacy has yet to be explored. This paradoxical opportunity applies as well to the history of music in the Soviet era of Russian history, from whose subsidized legacy only the music of Shostakovich and Prokofiev remains well known and closely studied.[9]

The justification of music history independent of the history of critical and commercial judgment ought to be based in part on the assumption and conceit that music, in the West, has been and remains meaningful and expressive in distinct ways beyond the range of the visual arts and forms of literature.[10] The privileging of music as a discrete and important form of life is not merely the consequence of late eighteenth- and early nineteenth-century philosophical prejudices. The suggestion of music as a basic constituent of social action has received support from anthropology, evolutionary biology, and neurobiology. If music and musicality are inherently human—hard wired, perhaps—and therefore universal, the study of music and music-making becomes essential to forming an adequate understanding of human behavior. This idea has inspired research in the social and economic character of musical life, bringing the approach to the history of music in modern Europe closer to methods once identified almost exclusively with ethnomusicology.[11]

Nonetheless, the central barrier to a more adequate and revealing history of music remains the construct of the past that is driven by normative aesthetic judgment. Music history demands more resistance. Reconstructing the musical culture of the past requires engaging historically significant music and musical practices that have been forgotten. On the positive side, although it is still defined by the context of normative criticism, the writing of biography has helped revive the music and reputation of unfairly neglected composers.[12] What is needed, however, is an equivalent in music to the history of design, decorative arts, and material culture. These rubrics offer powerful correctives to the conventional history of art and architecture, fields that, like music history, still negotiate against the claims of normative aesthetic judgment.

For the past several decades a methodological countertrend to this seemingly laudable strategy and point of view has actually taken hold. It is apparent in musicology's emulation of paths charted by literary studies. Close readings of well-known texts in search of counterintuitive meanings often purport to unlock historical, as well as aesthetic, insights. Novel analyses of great music can indeed suggest a revision of historical understanding through virtuosic forays into the art of textual criticism. The works of Richard Wagner have lent themselves best to this approach. Revisiting acknowledged masterpieces or a body of work by leading historical figures whose music still holds sway on the concert stage may be a useful historical strategy, but in the case of Wagner, close literary and philosophical commentary rather than insight into the music have made that idea plausible.

In the more recalcitrant arena of instrumental music, inspired concentration on canonic works and composers has yielded some exceptional results. Close scrutiny of Brahms's music has refined and complicated the character of late nineteenth-century political commitments, particularly liberalism and nationalism. In Reinhold Brinkmann's writings, comparisons to contemporary literature and painting (e.g., Menzel and Fontane) play a major role.[13] In Jonathan Bellman's persuasive account of Chopin's Polish Ballade, op. 38, now obscure dimensions of musical culture illuminate the structure and meaning of a single work, justifying Bellman's view that looking closely at a single "tree" can reveal the "forest."[14] The second ballade is shown to be a "nationalistic tale" representing the "martyrdom" of the Poles and their national "aspirations." Bellman does not actually revise what contemporaries perceived as the significance of Chopin's work. Where Kallberg used historical factors concerning sexuality and gender (e.g., the role of women as a dominant segment of nineteenth-century audiences) that have been left out of traditional interpretations of Chopin, Bellman confirms contemporary suspicions about the work's patriotic meaning by locating Chopin's sources in forgotten cultural practices and forms. He succeeds in defining the work's "program" precisely. Questions about the musical structure are answered by placing a canonic work in a musical historical context defined by once popular amateur program music for the piano, ballad poetry, and operatic conventions. However, one needs to know more about those forgotten phenomena whose significance is once again subordinated to an admirable illumination of a famous piece of music.

Klára Móricz's study of early twentieth-century Jewish Russian composers associated with the Society for Jewish Folk Music alongside music of Ernest Bloch and Arnold Schoenberg—probing their engagement with the Jewish question and issues of race, utopian politics, and national identity—utilizes music together with archival biographical materials to reconsider the framing of Jewish identity in modernity.[15] The impact of European anti-Semitism before 1933, the dynamics of exile, and a comparison of strategies within the project of modernism in the era of fascism and Nazism are her subjects.[16] Primarily in the case of Schoenberg, the insights challenge standard accounts of his character, his Zionism after 1933, and the intersection of music, utopian thought, and political ideology. Music functions as a primary instrument of revision in our understanding of how Jews in Europe reacted to the politics surrounding them in the first half of the twentieth century. Familiar and obscure musical texts are integral to Móricz's argument. In contrast to Chopin's opus 38, particularly in the case of Bloch, many of the works Móricz considers have little if any current sounding presence either in performance or recording.[17]

Much of the music cited even in passing by Bellman and Móricz, and, sadly, still mentioned at best marginally in the Mahler and Strauss literature, was once important but remains well outside of what is played and listened to today.[18] This suggests that a closer look at discontinuities and disappearances is needed, particularly with respect to what we play and listen to and how it fits into the past. Decoding the character and meaning of a piece of music deemed by posterity as exceptional in value as the object of history requires a close look at the unfamiliar. Neutrality, if not skepticism, regarding the reasons for our extreme familiarity with some works (e.g., opus 38) is required. Self-criticism regarding our responses demands an unraveling of the way we react to the historical but unknown in music. Do we use a proverbial tool kit that relies on the idea of family resemblances (e.g., it sounds like something I know) or on reflexes of unwitting habitual expectations, comparative judgment, and surprise (e.g., it is just not as good)? What does it mean to write about a now obscure work one has never heard live and knows only from having read a score, or a work that was never recorded or perhaps only in fragments?

Discontinuities in musical practice may be silent, but their silence exerts it own power. It points to the need to be cautious about the way we approach canonic works within the historical context and character of musical culture. Continuities in the content of the active repertoire may justify selective textual analysis and commentary and the application of methods of criticism developed in literary studies. However, the facile presumption that such continuity is descriptive of history or is sufficient to form a picture of the musical culture of the past distorts historical inquiry and encourages methods too dependent on aesthetic criticism.

How one avoids this dilemma seems contingent on details about the subject of historical inquiry: the local niche, the specific time and place. We need to be cautious about assuming some stability in the general habits of musical culture in listening, playing, and reading. Such habits appear, albeit deceptively, to be evolutionary in origin. Are traditions rooted in the past (e.g., music education, concert life) and within the history of music and music making in modern Europe and North America sufficiently stable to permit historical writing and research to rely on often tacit and camouflaged assumptions about so-called common practice? If one considers contemporary views about the state of music and the place of music in one's own time, then radical change and difference, not sameness, need to be taken into account as defining the vantage point of the contemporary scholar.

II

The scholarly and methodological trends of the past twenty years, including the appropriation of methods from literary criticism and the use of strategies from the sociology of knowledge and culture to break music's self-referential historical framework and link music to larger historical currents, reflect, implicitly and explicitly, three contemporary political and cultural obsessions in our own time. First and foremost is the conviction that the traditions of classical music are on the decline. There has been a perceived loss of audience since the end of World War II. Music in the concert and classical genres no longer seems to make a case for itself as significant in the larger realm of culture and politics.[19]

The contemporary writing of its history inevitably takes this issue into account. A polemical function can be detected even in the form of a need to conserve or preserve tradition in a moment in which the prospects of irrelevance and extinction seem real. The writing of history seeks to justify and explain, in a moment of perceived decline, the centrality of a cultural phenomenon once preeminent. If music history written before 1950 assumed a reading public for whom the importance of music seemed commonsensical, today's writers assume they face a skeptical and limited audience. Eras in the past when classical composers and musicians were actually important (consider the cases of Beethoven, Verdi, Wagner, Elgar, and Paderewski) take on a counterintuitive aspect for writer and reader alike. Nostalgia, whether based in fact or not, is cloaked in the elaborate deconstruction of a few select composers and works, often those of greatest reputation. We seek to protect the best from oblivion by challenging conventional readings and rendering the obvious problematic. Faced with extinction, writing on music mimics a clever subordination of historical scholarship to criticism that has proven invaluable to the sustaining of interest in the traditions of literature and painting. Why not then, in a period of insecurity, imitate art and literary criticism in music in order to secure a sense of meaning for a limited set of iconic works when the sense that classical musical culture in the larger public realm has vanished?[20]

There are ironies here. As the genre of sophisticated textual criticism of musical works grows (much of it imitative of literary scholarship directed at a limited readership), music journalism for the larger public is in rapid decline. Until 1945, in the United States the university infrastructure in musicology was weak in comparison to both art history and the study of literature. In contrast to the role that music journalism played outside the university, the place of music as a field of scholarship within the university was insignificant. In the sixty years after 1945, academic professionalism in music has flourished. It has encompassed and eclipsed independent, professional music journalism even in the popular press, creating a historical dis-continuity in the quality and extent of music journalism. The academic pursuit of music has marginalized music journalists and criticism in the press. The decline in journalistic criticism itself supports the notion of a shift of classical music tradi-tions to the margins of cultural significance.[21]

The second discontinuity in our time that affects the writing of music history is related to the first. We are witness to the abandonment and rejection of twentieth-century modernism in music. That disavowal masks a more general loss of interest in new, contemporary music that began in the mid-twentieth century. In no previous era of music within the classical tradition—since the early 1700s—has the enter-prise of writing and performing new music been so completely subordinated to the performance of music from the past. Modernism, which made its appearance between 1908 and 1930, initially had difficulty taking hold and attracting the alle-giance of an audience. That resistance, however, did not lessen with time. The larger part of modernist music written both before and after 1945 continues to be rejected by the majority of the concert-going public. It has failed to recruit an audience of its own. Over the course of the twentieth century, interest in the music written either before modernism or written explicitly in opposition to it has entirely overwhelmed self-consciously modern contemporary composition. The historical or the nearly nostalgic (in stylistic terms) now dominates. This has created an unprecedented imbalance between old and new music unknown before 1914. Classical concert music (not popular music) has been redefined not as exemplary of the present but as a medium in open defiance of a definition of the present as progressive, novel, or in evident contrast to the past.

The concert stage has assumed the function of a historical museum, in which most of what has been collected (as, unfortunately, is the case in the great encyclo-pedic museums) remains not on display but in storage. Since the 1960s (if not ear-lier) the successfully dynamic, progressive, and modern in new music can be found in popular commercial forms. These share only limited substantive connections to inherited classical traditions. The music historian now faces the past, knowing that its parallels in the present—in new music, in rituals (e.g., concerts), and in institu-tions (e.g., orchestras, opera companies, festivals, conservatories)—survive in only a highly atrophied manner. A paradoxical consequence of this circumstance is the fact that although even the audience for the historical in music appears to be dwin-dling and ageing, more and more young people the world over are choosing to study instruments designed to play classical music from the past.[22] They are doing so at extraordinarily high levels of proficiency, thereby raising the technical stan-dard of performance of an ever more-limited historical repertoire.

The third and perhaps most decisive discontinuity between the historical subject matter in music and the scholar working in the present can be located in the role of sound technology. Musicians and historians working today have been influenced by a pattern of technological change that has altered how we access, hear, remember, and think about music. Musicians, scholars, and listeners active now in the first decade of the twenty-first century came of age in a technological context in which recording assumed a commanding presence. Now they are witnessing that presence diminish and change. We are at the threshold of the demise of a specifically twentieth-century phenomenon, the golden age of so-called high-fidelity recording. Music's reliance on and romance with the sound document for more than half a century is coming to an end.

The perspective of contemporary musicians and historians has been unavoidably defined by a century of engagement with a once-novel and ultimately revolutionary means of music making and experience. At first, in its infancy in the early 1900s, recording was embraced as a technical marvel, a trick of progress that seemed to document sound and the audible faithfully and accurately in a manner parallel to photography's startling capacity to document sight and represent the visible. Enthusiasm for sound-recording technology was based on the idea that an experience that once could be remembered only in the imagination—the hearing of music—and whose recall could be amended and solidified by notation—could be not merely documented but also reproduced persuasively. Music played could be captured in a sounding artifact that preserved and re-created the acoustic and time-specific experience of sound. The preservation of musical performance offered expanded opportunities for listening and opened up the possibility of radically democratizing the experience of music. This generated an extension of musical culture well beyond the economic and social range made possible in the nineteenth century through publishing and instrument manufacture, particularly piano manufacturing. So astonishing were initial recordings that recorded sound (now heard as primitive in range and sound quality in terms of any purported representational realism) well before 1945 was heralded by many contemporaries as superior to the so-called original, the live sound of a voice or an instrument.[23]

By the interwar era the gramophone had succeeded in wiping out its immediate predecessor, the mechanical player piano, a transitional technology that preserved the presence of the piano's acoustic sound but eliminated the need for a performer. Recording's rise to prominence followed the spread of radio transmission. Music on the radio was initially created by the broadcast of concert performances that extended the concert experience into the home. That led, in turn, to the development of studios within radio stations devoted to the broadcast of live music. This was the age in which the BBC and the radio orchestras of Europe came into being. It was also the era of the NBC Orchestra and the legendary Toscanini broadcasts. For a whole generation, these new broadcast realities defined the access to and the sense of musical culture.[24]

The early embrace of recording (in contrast to radio broadcast) reflected an enthusiasm akin, as a species of manias and fads in history, to fashions in design and architecture that favored new technology over traditional means. Wood was rejected in favor of plastic in interior design (e.g., the replacement of stone tiles with Formica and linoleum in the 1950s), just as cotton and wool were supplanted by synthetics. The consequences of the musical public's initial romance with recorded and transmitted sound were quickly mirrored in architecture. The reverberant acoustics of Boston's Symphony Hall (1900) or the Musikverein in Vienna (1870) were rejected between 1930 and the mid-1980s in favor of a modern, dry, absorbent, and "clean" acoustic ideal designed to mimic the aesthetics of recorded sound in the construction of new public spaces for music such as Radio City Music Hall (1932) and the concert halls built in the 1950s and early 1960s.[25]

The 1950s and 1960s marked the apogee of the romance with recording. The 33⅓ long-playing vinyl record replaced the already-popular but fragile and limited 78 rpm disc. Advances in speakers and the electronics of sound reproduction all conspired to make the live performance an antique of sorts, an imperfect primitive and outmoded experience. Close repeated listening to the full range of classical music, including opera and orchestral music, became possible as an analogue to reading a book in the privacy of the home. Listening no longer was dependent on public space and a concert schedule but compatible with a limitless private experience that even for solo piano music did not require of the individual the capacity to play the instrument. For those who played instruments, there appeared even a "music-minus-one" phenomenon, where one could play a concerto at home with the recorded orchestral accompaniment.

At first, recording was an offshoot of live performance, a documentary outgrowth dependent on the allure, reputation, prestige and relative inaccessibility of live experiences in a music hall or a well-appointed privileged home with a music parlor or, by the 1920s, heard on the radio through broadcasts in real time.[26] This causal link gradually became reversed as recording technology improved the product and its distribution and reduced its cost. With Glenn Gould as its most articulate and celebrated apostle, a new ideology emerged after 1945 in which the recording became the ideal medium for communicating the art music of the past.[27] Recordings became the primary and driving force not only in the economics of music but also in the reception and perception of works of music and the career of performing artists. The studio and its output in recordings, not the concert stage, made reputations and set the standard of performance. Radio listening no longer was based on broadcasts of live performances either in a hall or studio but on the playing of recordings. Recordings, not performances or sheet music, became the dominant means by which audiences came to hear and learn music. Performers could now become famous first through recordings (consider the fame of Soviet artists in the West before they traveled abroad). Their reputations were then only confirmed by the live experience. Criticism of recordings and the qualities of sound reproduction overwhelmed the reportage of live concerts and dominated music journalism in the 1960s and 1970s.

Even more important were the ideological conceits generated by the advent of the ideal of a persuasive and accurate sonic documentation of music that set a standard to be emulated. The implication of modern sound reproduction was that it could provide a pure, complete, and presumably objective representation of a musical work. Furthermore, the optimum conditions of the recording studio—a species of silence with no apparent ambient sound disturbances, particularly those created by the performers themselves or a body of listeners—came to mirror the ideal preconditions for musical contemplation or listening on the part of the hearer. One could listen undistracted and (eventually with headphones) isolated from the world around one. The increased sophistication in the technique of editing redefined sufficient accuracy and made the encounter with random error and the inevitable inconsistencies in any live performance intolerable.

The possibility emerged of an apparently objective realization of a musical text now properly isolated from a presumed distracting or sullying surrounding environment of listeners. Insofar as listening to a work can be said to "complete" it, the act of listening was separated in time from the act of performance. Behind the real or proverbial glass window of the studio were engineers and producers whose presence at the time of recording was rendered subsequently irrelevant and invisible. They may not have been integral as listeners to the process of recording, but they determined the outcome through editing. The listener was redefined as a solo, anonymous consumer and user, separated from any community of listeners. Each individual determined independently how, where, and when to listen. The music was protected and immune from any intervention from listening, much like a piece of sculpture might be from being seen.

The context and conditions of hearing and judging music were altered. Criticism of a new work based on a live performance in an age before recording (even a performance in a home such as the first four-hand piano renditions of the last two Brahms symphonies) or reliant on published scores (as was common from the late eighteenth to the end of the nineteenth century) was supplanted by criticism based on multiple and often fragmented encounters with first time recordings. However, the discontinuity with past practice was greatest with respect to the historic repertoire. Music came to be known through the repeated playing of one or many recordings (consider the impact of the distribution of the first sets of all nine Beethoven symphonies, particularly Toscanini's).[28] Knowledge of the repertoire gained in this manner, when applied to the criticism of performance in concert or, rarely, in response to score texts (the reading of which became a dying art among nonprofessionals), had an influence on the way music was understood and judged, particularly in criticism. One could become quite familiar with a musical work without hearing anyone play it live or without even looking at a score, much less thinking about one. The ability to read music or play an instrument was no longer required for musical literacy.

The advent of mass-produced, high-quality recording exacerbated and accelerated the split between the activities of composition and performance, which began at the turn of the century. Before the 1920s, most performers also composed. Those who did not compose were nonetheless adept at improvisation since their training included composition.[29] It is ironic that, from its inception, sound transmission and reproduction inspired the notion that modern sound technology would influence composition by expanding the possibilities of usable sound and therefore the aesthetics of new music, which indeed it did.[30] At the same time, however, it also generated an intense reaction against the pride of place occupied by the virtuoso performer as interpreter bequeathed by the age of Liszt and Paganini. Precisely when the representational possibilities offered by modern recording and transmission began to be realized, composers, notably Schoenberg and Stravinsky, campaigned against the prominent role played in musical life by interpreters trained in the spirit of Wagner, Liszt, and von Bülow.

Interpretation as an art form akin to improvisation declined in prestige as the dependency on live performance weakened. Parallel to the rise of modernism emerged the idea of true fidelity to a composer's intentions and with it a belief that the interpreter needed to resist imposing self-important ideas not integral to the work. The intentions of the composer, whether gleaned from an authentic historic text or gained from a living composer's own rendition, could be documented accurately without the so-called arbitrary intervention of performers who were subject to the accusation that they were imposing their personality on a work without justification. The idea of recording as the ideal medium for the objective realization of the true nature of a piece of music gained momentum.

Recording implicitly advanced an objectivist, anti-Romantic aesthetics that derided ornamentation and expressive subjectivity as superficial. The epiphany of musical experience was transferred out of the shared space occupied by composer, performer, and listener at one time in one place, characteristic of live performance, to a presumed direct, private engagement by the individual with an error-free faithful realization of a work. The work was defined by a construct of the text as containing a complete set of instructions sufficient to render the substance of the composer's creation. The historic interplay between traditions of composition and performance was altered, elevating the composer's text as providing exclusive authority. Indeed, with the advent of recording came an increased emphasis by composers on including a detailed, complete, and exclusive set of instructions in the musical text, further limiting the influence of the performer. The notion of the performer as someone who realizes a work with individuality lost its value and allure as did the idea that a piece of music is something that invites a truly wide range of interpretation. The listener to the record became analogous to the reader of a book. The reader as interpreter required no intermediary.[31] Music was the record.

The irony was that recording technology did not help the popularity of new classical music, especially music that utilized novel sounds made possible by technology, except in popular genres. What recording did was to raise the technical standards of performance and expectations in the standard repertory with regard to the athletic skill expected at live performances. Accustomed to flawless renditions created in the studio, the performer now had to match—at a live performance—the clean accuracy of the record. Indeed, modern editing techniques forced a general improvement in the athletic dimension of music making in terms of standards of intonation, dexterity, accuracy, and consistency. The musician in the practice room had to compete with a studio-produced document. The priority of recording devolved into a preference for a completely antiseptic ambient context: no extraneous noises and often, in opera recordings, the elimination of acoustic distances reflective of the stage, eliminating any danger of problems of balance. The microphone leveled the playing field. Edited performances became standard references that inspired imitation in the concert hall. By the end of the twentieth century, this pattern had resulted in what some observers began to lament as an absence of originality and spontaneity in the character of live performances. Many connoisseurs preferred to stay home.

However, the most powerful consequence was the popularization of the notion that music written for three-dimensional spaces and performances in real time by performers with an audience present—particularly music requiring large forces (e.g., orchestral and operatic music)—could be represented properly by recordings. This assumption is clearly false as a basis for constructing the history of music written before the advent of modern recording. It is not at all clear how a Beethoven symphony, a Dvorak choral work, or a Strauss tone poem—much less any opera written for the stage—can be represented by a recording or understood, as a matter of history, on the basis of one. A recording is, at best, analogous to a photographic reproduction of a painting.

Furthermore, recording, already in the 78-rpm format, the first truly successful commercial format for classical music, helped define the subject matter of music history by codifying the repertoire. Recording underscored a fin-de-siècle conservative historicizing trend in the definition of the concert repertoire. The roots of a standard repertoire of historical works are evident in the extension of musical culture during the later nineteenth century. The impact of recording on the repertoire of music was to accelerate the formation of a historical canon by the very fact of its capacity to extend selectively the reach of music to a mass audience. In its earliest incarnations, recording offered a narrow range of repertoire, much of it in excerpts. Yet with each technological advance, an opening for repertoire expansion was created. New cheaper and more durable formats called for new content. In the 1950s the range of the repertoire expanded. Everything from the Bach cantatas and the Alban Berg Violin Concerto to complete opera recordings became available for the first time. Demand for the novel format led to the recording of more music.

By the 1960s, the long-playing record had spanned enough of the historical repertoire to become the basic tool for defining, transmitting, and hearing classical music. As a result, a new type of audience for live performances emerged. The text, so to speak, of the music being performed was defined not by amateur playing and singing or by sheet music but by recordings with which concertgoers were intimately familiar. So-called definitive recordings led to the circumstance by which knowledge of the music bypassed the printed notation of music. The judgments of interpretation became comparative: recordings of the same work were pitted against each other, not only against a live, unedited event. Perhaps the best examples of this pattern can be found in orchestral music and opera, where access to live performance remained limited and where new high-fidelity techniques rendered the recorded sound sufficiently impressive. The contemporary attachment to and understanding of Mahler and Bruckner owe more to high-fidelity recording than to the impact of live performances. Criteria of judgment, once dependent on the contents of a score, vanished to such an extent that music history and criticism were written by those who could not read a score. Music literacy was redefined even for scholars. Access to music sufficient to pass judgment and write about music was extended to those who could not imagine sounds implied by a musical text and were dependent on recordings alone.

In comparative historical terms, recording so greatly expanded the range and reach of music that it facilitated a type of rigid familiarity unknown before recording. That familiarity was the result of repeated hearings of the same recording at home. The role and even necessity of memory were diminished, eviscerating any lingering aura associated with live performance. Absent the text, sympathetic comprehension of the traditional possibilities of interpretation atrophied. Insofar as interpretation continued to thrive, it was standardized and defined by recordings. Even in live concerts, performance and interpretation turned into a dialogue with widely accessible recorded versions and the dominance of certain recordings of particular pieces in public opinion and the marketplace.

By the later twentieth century, therefore, credence was given to the notion that truly great live performers were phenomena of the past (e.g., Toscanini, Furtwängler, Caruso, Heifetz). This seemed plausible, given the subordination of live performance to recording after 1945. All succeeding generations of performers, with rare exceptions (among them, Gould) were defined as engaged in a species of nostalgic reproduction, imitators of personalities from a great age that had passed. Playing a historic work was understood as an act similar to what an artisan does when making an exact replica of an eighteenth-century table. A class of connoisseurs came into being who proudly preferred any historic or so-called standard recording to a live event or new recording.

Recording contributed to a historical process that preceded it, in which, particularly during the nineteenth century, shifting standards of musical literacy altered tastes. The deepening of a preference for the historical over the contemporary was the result of a strong allegiance to a familiar and honored past over music of the present. This preference was based in insecurity. As the audience for music expanded, it was increasingly unable to access new or unfamiliar music through the reading and playing of notated music. The contribution made by recording was first to create a canon of accessible recordings sufficient to define standards of taste and supplant the use of printed music and also to legitimate the idea that a work of music, in order to merit recording and therefore live performance as a consequence, had to achieve the elusive and limited status as a "masterpiece." In the mid-twentieth century, owing to recording, new or unfamiliar historic works were judged, by genre, against a few exemplary works (e.g., a Beethoven symphony or a Puccini opera).

The use of the criterion of masterpiece status became rampant in a manner not found within art and literary criticism, owing to the overwhelming dependence on recording and the disappearance of older traditions of musical literacy. Tolerance for anything less than a masterpiece disappeared. The same hierarchy of status was applied to recorded performances of familiar masterpieces. Consider CBS's marketing decision to define its classical recordings as a "Masterworks" series. If one wished to make an analogy with reading, one would have to imagine a context in which printed materials and reading skills vanished and only audio recordings survived, making John Gielgud's and Laurence Olivier's performances as Hamlet the basis for knowing and understanding the play by Shakespeare. A decline in literacy would limit potential readers' access and response to the new and unfamiliar in prose and poetry.

The digital revolution and the CD of the late twentieth century marked the last stage in the golden age of recording. Once again a new format opened up the possibility of creating a massive library of recordings once considered impractical and uneconomic. The new format resulted in an impressive output of new and rediscovered and reissued historical recordings. A few enterprising labels, such as Marco Polo, BIS, Naxos, and Chandos—including ones dedicated to new music and particular niches (New World, CRI, and Albany)—produced first recordings of new and rare repertoire.

However, with the advent of the computer and the iPod, the possibilities of storage and portability of large chunks of sound were transformed. The economic basis of recording collapsed. Yet the democratization of the technology permitted individuals, as well as companies, to continue what had begun with the CD format: the generation of a wide array of recordings produced easily and cheaply. Massive amounts of recorded material supplemented by video (e.g., on YouTube) are now available on the Internet. What has changed is more than the aggregate volume. It turns out that listeners prefer convenience and ease of access to quality of recorded sound. High fidelity in recording has retreated into a fetish of a very few. As a result the illusion that a recording is the "real" musical object and competes successfully with acoustic sound—an illusion harbored for decades—has begun to collapse.

The easy access to an impressive, startling, and unprecedented array of historic recordings, especially from before 1945, raises the complex but subsidiary question of their role as evidence of past performance practices.[32] There is much to be learned from recordings, especially those from the mid- and early twentieth century. One can detect older habits of playing, including the use of portamento, different types of vibrato, and rubato. Older styles of singing, constructs of tempo relations, and other markers of past interpretative practice can be gleaned from recordings. However, it is hazardous to infer too much from very early examples of recording. The emphasis on shorter works and fragments (which derived from the comparatively short durational capacity of early recording) and the limitations of recording conditions and technology cast doubt on the idea that what we now hear on recordings entirely represents what occurred in an age when concert hall practice still dominated.

Old recordings may not offer an accurate representation of how people used to play. The task facing historians who use recorded evidence is somewhat akin to that of the archeologist who is faced with fragments not necessarily of objects but of indirect pictorial documentations of artifacts and practices. Speculative reconstruction and inference are required in the task of imagining past cultural practice. Until the mid-twentieth century, the recording studio represented a novel, subsidiary and artificial venue for performers. A recorded document from an era when live performance and the distribution of printed music were the primary means of musical communication can be used only with considerable restraint and skepticism as the

basis for formulating general claims about habits of performance and their significance. That holds true as well for the piano rolls made by legendary pianists and
composers, Mahler among them.[33]

Now that access and convenience have trumped any attachment to sound quality, recording has lost its own short-lived aura and has become unremarkable and
commonplace. Profitability has vanished and with it the possibilities of the carefully
crafted studio recording. What now is produced are new documents of live performances and a very few studio products. By the middle of the first decade of the
twenty-first century the commercial market for recording disappeared in the wake
of the inexhaustible supply of downloadable recorded documents by artists both
renowned and obscure, including digitally remastered sound documents from the
nearly forgotten past of the first half of the twentieth century. Furthermore, direct
access to live performances through audio and video streaming and hundreds of
radio channels promises to expand the virtual library of recorded documents that
one can listen to on the computer.

Concurrent with this state of affairs another shift in acoustic fashion has taken hold.
With the decline in the allure of recorded sound, the dry, short reverberation-time
acoustics favored in the 1950s lost its appeal. The social habit of listening to music in a
dedicated sense at home with fine speakers has become a marginal phenomenon. With
the easy availability of sound documents we now face new habits of background listening (while doing something else, such as exercising or driving) to low-fidelity sound. It
is therefore not surprising that one can perceive a renewed taste for reverberant acoustics in large spaces for listening, concert halls, and opera houses. With that trend we are
witnessing renewed affection for the collective experience of listening to music with others in a public space and for the spectacle of watching people play and sing, the live
performance.

Performance in real time and space has returned to the center of musical culture. The audience wants to witness the theater and the unpredictability of performance. Individuality as expressed in live performance is again in demand even if it
takes on more of a visual than an aural aspect, as is evident from the theatricality of
gesture in performance favored by rising stars who are pianists, violinists, and conductors. Most major concert halls built since the late 1990s seek to deliver a rich
reverberant sound designed to highlight high-range overtones, sonic brilliance, and
a sensual directness. There are now many more individuals going to concerts and
operas, and, given the growth of high-level musical training around the world, more
people are playing concerts on any given day than will buy or listen to recordings of
classical music in a year. More people will devote the time required to listen to
works lasting more than ten minutes by going to a concert than will do so by putting on a recording and listening to it uninterrupted at home.

This is not to say that recorded documents have not fundamentally altered
how we think about music. Nonetheless, the interconnections between the musical text or score—using many types of notation—and performance and recording
(even a so-called live recording) will continue to be in flux. The ideologies associated with the heyday of studio recording are in retreat. We are entering a period

in which the role of performance is moving to a place oddly more comparable to the norm of the mid-nineteenth century. The live concert, after decades of being viewed as a ritual on the decline, even if sustained by an older audience, may, if reinvented, experience a renascence.[34] The historian needs to be aware that the habits of listening developed between World War II and 1990, when recording as an adequate representation of a musical work was in its ascendancy, are not only insufficient as a basis for historical analysis but also far from normative. Recording and access to sound documents will remain part of the way in which we study and learn about the history of music. However, their function will not be as surrogates for live performance or as sufficient representations of a musical work or its text. Recordings have become more like snapshots and slides—reference tools—subordinate in terms of appreciation, criticism, and historical analysis to notated texts and performances. For new music, noncanonic works and genres, and the historic repertoire (particularly that which has still not been recorded), which are essential to the writing of history, this shift constitutes a renewed imperative for live performance. The text—notated music—may remain the limited province of professionals and highly trained amateurs. No doubt there will come a time when unfamiliar scores of all kinds will be scanned to produce a computer-generated sonic realization. This then will become a welcome new means by which to study the music of the past for which there are neither live performances nor sound documents, for there will be no illusion of sufficiency.

III

The study of the influence of recording in music history has its parallel in art historical scholarship: the role of photography in documenting the history of art and its use in the evolution of painting. In the history of painting, photography was influential earlier than once suspected, just as recording influenced the history of composition in the twentieth century. For example, Ferdinand Georg Waldmüller used photography as a tool as early as the mid-nineteenth century.[35] Photographic reproductions of art works transformed the writing and dissemination of art history just as recording influenced performers, historians, and listeners. With the advent of computer-generated sound and programs that translate notation into sound and sound into notation, the process of composition during the last two decades has changed, just as the computer has altered the creative processes of artists and architects. As in art history, the role played by technological reproduction in music needs to be differentiated by music historians if a deeper understanding of the character and role of music in history is to be attained. The first step is a self-critical assessment of the influence of recording on the historian's methodological assumptions if only to demark past from present and challenge facile claims of continuity and common practice.

Consciousness of contrasts between the contemporary and the historical is particularly crucial for biography, a genre basic to music history. Consider the way in which composers and performers first hear and learn about music. György Kurtág describes his decisive encounter with classical music as child. He heard a radio broadcast of Schubert's Symphony no. 8 in B minor—the *Unfinished* Symphony. It inspired him to try to write a "Jewish symphony" in E minor with the title "Eternal Hope."[36] Contrast his experience with that of Ernest Bloch a half century earlier. The close study of the score of Wagner's *Siegfried* and a performance of *Die Meistersinger* led Bloch to formulate his ambition to write music that communicated a distinct Jewish national character.[37] Likewise, Mahler's influence on the young Anton von Webern came through live performance. Webern's memories were articulated in the diary accounts he kept, and they in turn led to close scrutiny of published scores.[38] Georges Enescu, like Mozart, returned home from performances and reconstructed what he remembered by writing out a score of what he had heard. This habit for Enescu extended, astonishingly, to performances of Wagner operas.[39]

Historians of musical culture before the spread of recording or the era of the radio (after World War I) must unravel the differentials between their own process of coming to terms with music and those of their subjects. What are the constituent elements of knowing something about a work or learning a piece of music in contemporary culture? How do they compare to past practices? This is especially relevant when music criticism is used as a key aspect of a historical argument. Between 1820 and 1848 criticism of Beethoven's music was based first on texts and only partially on first and early performances, whose character and conditions not only demanded renewed scrutiny but were inaccessible, relatively speaking, and frequently understood as highly flawed.[40] Depending on the genre, the critic's access to a work, often through publication, including a piano reduction, was dependent on a critic's own musical skills. Such factors tend to render the historical use of criticism of performances problematic. The varied patterns and levels of access demand a deeper inquiry into the biography of critics.

Still, the historical circumstances before the age of recording all stand in stark contrast to how we access music, much less prepare for a performance. The initial acoustic encounter with a work of music or its silent reading, once seminal, has been replaced by access to repetition; it has been indelibly altered by multiple recorded accounts and historical recordings. What is more, like the art historian, we can now juxtapose reproductions of the same work and others from the same historical period to an extent unfamiliar to anything experienced by the historical subjects themselves.

Yet the role of recording in music history poses special problems different from the role played by reproduction in art history. The photograph, the slide, and the printed reproduction have been standard tools as references to artworks defined as the "original" despite the many sophisticated deconstructions of that notion by artists and scholars. In commonsense terms, the original work of art can be defined and readily located. In music there is uncertainty as to what that might be. Is it the score? Or is it the work realized in a performance, in a specific space at a specific time, replete with the listener's reaction and memory? Does the work exist without being played and heard? Perhaps a recording is a sufficient answer?

One tentative shift perceptible over the past few years is the notion that the recording may not be a sufficient definition of a work. This is particularly acute in the cases of late romantic and early modernist orchestral music and opera. Mahler's symphonies, Strauss's operas, Stravinsky's *Rite of Spring*, and Varese's *Arcana* have all been well recorded. But are they merely sonic snapshots of the authentic subject or the musical equivalent of the "original"? Absent the acoustic sound in the space for which the sound was intended, one containing an audience—the very locus imagined by the composer—those works may be just implied by recordings. Any live rendition perhaps approximates more closely the character of the work, particularly vis-à-vis its reception history before 1945 than any fine edited recording. For some this may be a paradoxical premise that needs to be accounted for in reception history and aesthetic criticism.

The case of opera is even more complicated. Opera seems resistant to sufficient technological reproduction. For example, film and video versions (HD technology notwithstanding) eliminate the viewer's capacity to coordinate sight and sound individually and to select events and negotiate the constant simultaneity of elements essential to opera. The director is in charge, distorting the experience. The subject of historical research and commentary in opera must take performance, not only texts and sound documents, into account. Recorded documentation, visual and aural, amounts to a useful approximation. For opera written today, normative criticism that relies on recordings and video documents may be suggestive. Yet the utility of such commentary and its underlying sources as the basis of historical claims is slim. Our contemporary understanding of the link between words and music derived from the experience of opera performances, particularly ones that use supertitles, highlight the need take into account the impact of discontinuities in the modes of access. For skeptics of opera as a genre, such as Adorno, recording in its modern form was an ideal advance, resurrecting opera's aesthetic potential from its anachronistic character. But the opposite is the case for the historian.*

Technology has influenced as well the way in which we use language to describe and account for musical experiences. The impact of recording, as a historical phenomenon within musical culture, can be compared therefore with the role played by reading in the history of music. With the expansion of concert life and music publishing during the nineteenth century, a crucial and powerful element in the reception and evaluation of music came into play. That element was the act of reading. The use of language to describe and analyze a work of music gained significance as early as the second half of the eighteenth century. It was only after 1815, with the

---

* See Theodor W. Adorno, "Opera and the Long Playing Record" (1969), in *Essays on Music*, ed. Richard Leppert, trans. Susan H. Gillespie (Berkeley: University of California Press, 2002), 283–87.

development of an influential and widespread reading public, that music journalism and the appropriation of practices derived from literature began to wield influence. Information about particular music was often read before the music was heard or printed. The intersection between writing and reading about music and musical culture in the nineteenth century was complex and decisive. Therefore, composers frequently turned to writing. Some were able to help support themselves by writing criticism and even fiction. This distinguished tradition reaches back to Berlioz, Liszt, and Schumann and extends to Debussy and Prokofiev. The master of the use of prose to shape the character and perception of a yet-to-be-experienced musical event was certainly Wagner.

The reading public that was drawn into musical culture, like the public that acquired recordings, was far larger than the public that either had access to professional concert life or was sufficiently well educated to negotiate music actively by playing or writing it well enough to grasp the intricacies of notated compositional logic and musical thought. The journalism before 1848 contains more in the way of theoretical and analytical music language than journalism after 1848. After 1848 music criticism increasingly focused on the presumptive meaning and impact of the musical experience rendered in literary nonmusical technical language. The gradual shift of the music experience from a domestic and private sphere to a public encounter in a space akin to the theater during the nineteenth century ran parallel to a widening of the distances between spectator and composer and performer quite in contrast to the relationship between spectator and actor in the spoken theater. If in the early nineteenth century the spectator could duplicate or approximate the language used by the actor (i.e., reproduce the text), by the end of the century the listener could not do so in terms of music. The response to the concert experience required mediation through linguistic description and evaluation dependent on habits of reading about music. Language and literary analogues were used as vehicles of reception, just as the late twentieth-century audience relied on the experience of recording as the basis of response to live performance.[41]

A late but poignant example of the impact of reading on the listening comes, once again, from György Kurtág in response to a question about his attitude to the Ninth Symphony of Beethoven. Like Brahms, nearly a century earlier, Kurtág had not heard the Beethoven Ninth Symphony before late adolescence (Brahms was twenty-three when he first heard a live performance), but a close friend obtained what Kurtág called a "good recording." If in the case of the Bartok Violin Concerto the recording Kurtág first heard seemed thin by comparison to his own piano playing and his experience of sitting through live rehearsals with the same artists (Antal Doráti and Yehudi Menuhin), in the case of the Ninth Symphony Kurtág recalls, "I had read a lot about Beethoven's Ninth, but I was hugely disappointed when I first heard it because my picture of it from what I had read had led me to expect something quite different. On that basis, I had imagined a Ninth Symphony for myself and the reality was so totally different in comparison that I was simply unable to find my bearings in it."[42]

The further variable unique to music in history concerns the link between notation and sound. Notation, the written account of music, can generate a mental sound "picture" of a composition. As in language literacy, the open questions concern the character, even the completeness, of that picture and the comparability of understanding on the part of different listeners hearing or reading the same words. In music, historians face more uncertainty with respect to both the actual character of any performance vis-à-vis the text and the differentials in the impact of any performance on listeners. In music there seem to be wide contrasts in levels and types of literacy: what listeners can remember and readers of scores hear in their imagination when faced with the "same" text. What sounds are conjured in any single case by the reading of printed notation? Roger Sessions, who can be said to have possessed a high order of skill in reading music, once quipped late in life that any live performance of the Ninth Symphony would be inadequate to his own performance in his head reading the score. But what was that performance like? How did it sound in the imagination, and how was it shaped? Kurtág's anticipation of the Ninth was not based on a score but on literary accounts that led to expectations about a piece that seemed incongruous when the same person, influenced by reading, in this case a profoundly gifted young musician, encountered a sonic realization of the work.

What distinguishes a written text from a musical text from the vantage point of the historian are the explicit expectation of performance, the wide variations in performance and imagined sonorities, all contingent on the character of musical literacy past and present. There is a resultant uncertainty about references to a common text that ultimately can be "read" so differently by so many. The sound recording provides too easy a common ground for modern observers and in the end may offer an illusory solution; it may not constitute the same subject as the historical object of inquiry defined by text and any single performance.

The history of music, if it is to be written adequately and accurately, must confront not only the character of responses to musical events as evidenced by written accounts but also the underlying bases of those responses. This, in turn, necessitates a highly differentiated inquiry into the history of music literacy. This then requires the historian to look into the conditions of familiarity with music in relationship to reading, particularly after 1848. Any particular historical witness needs to be investigated, if not interrogated, by the historian with respect to the level and type of musical literacy, and the mode of access and response to the musical experience. For the twentieth century, these questions demand research into radio listening and the influence of recording. At the core, however, is the need to recover the full range of musical experiences within the past.

This demands the sort of scholarly and archival effort still most aptly described by Clifford Geertz as "thick description." In the enterprise of using music as a constituent of the formation of historical claims about the past, broadly defined as matters of political, cultural, intellectual, and social history, such detailed efforts are a rarity. Scholars infrequently penetrate below the most accessible historical documents from the arenas of biography and criticism in which the same, admittedly important, historical figures dominate. What music in the nineteenth century might actually tell us about issues such as national identity or the development of aesthetic values and cultural judgments that seem to suggest historical trends that apply to literature, art, and architecture has therefore yet to be uncovered

IV

What is clear, however, is that within music history the shifting character and context of musical perception, as well as the changing preconditions surrounding the attribution of meaning to musical experience, have influenced the way we construe what is historically significant in the history of music. If this history is to be written in a manner that influences a broader understanding of the past, tacit acceptance of normative assertions about value and importance must be replaced by the realization that important musical events in the past are not necessarily those that we wish to remember and that the works of importance in past eras are not necessarily those that contemporary performers choose to favor.

A particularly telling example has to do with musical culture during the Nazi era, a subject about which an enormous amount has been written. As Chris Walton has recently demonstrated, little consideration has been given to the life and music of Othmar Schoeck, in part on account of Schoeck's enthusiasm for the Nazis. His most revealing work, in terms of history, not in terms of subjective aesthetic value, remains an object of controversy: Schoeck's opera *Das Schloß Dürande*, op. 53, for which there is no recording and no real performance history after its premiere in Berlin in 1943. The politically obnoxious overtones of Schoeck's opera may legitimate a resistance to modern performance and revival. Yet the work must be closely looked at, as Walton has done, if we are to understand the complexity of how the Nazi regime influenced the world of music and, in turn, how cultural life was affected by politics and how a German-speaking composer of stature responded to the ideology and success of the Nazis. A close look at Schoeck helps, as Walton has demonstrated, to unravel and illuminate the tortured and many-sided history of Switzerland's role during the late 1930s and the war years. Understanding Schoeck and his music can advance the historical understanding of Switzerland,[43] but for that to occur his music must be performed and heard, including opus 53.

Another case of the distortion of the musical culture of the past (representing a lost opportunity for revision) derived from the recalcitrant power of normative aesthetic claims is the way key works once important and now forgotten are treated. Three examples suffice: Brahms's *Triumphlied*, Max Bruch's *Odysseus*, and Franz Schmidt's *Book of the Seven Seals*. In his recent monograph, *Music and Monumentality: Commemoration and Wonderment in Nineteenth-Century Germany*, on the place of music in German culture, Alexander Rehding focuses on the concept of monumentality. In it he suggests that Schmidt's work may not be a proper object of historical observation because its "place in the collective memory is highly doubtful." Brahms's *Triumphlied* and Beethoven's *Wellington's Victory* are likewise set aside by Rehding because "they have largely fallen out of favor" despite the stature of the composers and their own high opinion of these works. Whether one agrees with Rehding's view that these works are in some sense subordinate, the proper question remains, what once *was* the place of these works in history?[44]

In the case of Schmidt's 1937 oratorio, we choose at our own peril not to acknowledge that the work did enter collective memory in Austria immediately after the Anschluss. Performance history shows an enormous number of performances between 1937 and 1945. The work and its composer, rightly or wrongly, became associated with Nazi aesthetics. With the exception of periodic revivals in Austria after the war, which intentionally or unintentionally signaled a connection between the work and Austrofascism and Nazism—a history that many in the period immediately after 1945 wished to forget—the work was indeed largely forgotten (with the exception of a Salzburg performance by Dmitri Mitropoulos). Nonetheless, the oratorio and its reception remain crucial to the understanding of Austrian history and the significance of music in the 1930s and 1940s.[45] Furthermore, the temporary popularity of the work helped define collective memory. The final irony is that its success in doing so may derive from normative qualities of the work, political associations aside, that may enable its overdue return to the active concert repertory outside of Austria.

The two remaining examples concern the intersection between music and German nationalism after 1870. In Daniel-Beller McKenna's 2004 book, *Brahms and the German Spirit*, an entire chapter is devoted to Brahms's *Triumphlied*, which in Rehding's 2009 monograph plays no important role.[46] Beller-McKenna suggests a strident nationalist agenda on Brahms's part with which we may be uncomfortable and unaccustomed.[47] Beller-McKenna's admirable close reading may be insufficient precisely because it is not based on contact with the work in performance. The unmistakable compositional references to Handel and to the *Hallelujah* chorus in the *Messiah* may in a concert-hall context have suggested to the contemporary audience a link between Handel and England, aligning the new Germany in a quite pointed manner. That linkage could suggest that the musical model Brahms chose was designed explicitly to underscore the possibility, dear to the national liberals of post-1870 Germany, that the new German empire's politics, Bismarck notwithstanding, would veer from autocratic monarchic absolutism toward the English model, one of a constitutional monarchy with genuine parliamentary power.[48] Handel's dual identity and English allegiance offered the perfect foil for the liberal Brahms against Prussian conservatism.

The character of German nationalism shifted away decisively from any possible English trajectory with the death of Wilhelm I and the untimely death of his heir and son, Friedrich Wilhelm, who, through the influence of his wife, the daughter of Queen Victoria, was more disposed to the English and might have led Germany in a different direction. Perhaps the *Triumphlied* was a celebratory patriotic appeal against an antiliberal direction favored by Bismarck, who co-opted German liberals through his success in unifying Germany.

However, the nastiest side of German nationalism came to the fore in the reign of Wilhelm II. Brahms's use of Handel in 1870 differentiates his cultural definition of nationalism from that of Wagner in precisely the same period. The distinction between nationalisms could not have been greater. Insofar as Wagner came to define the character of German nationalism, it was because it buttressed the racialist chauvinism characteristic of Wilhelmine Germany. Wagner's centrality to the character of German nationalism at the turn of the century represented the defeat of a longstanding alternative nationalist sensibility eclipsed by the victory of 1870. But the vision shared by the liberals did not vanish, and is represented in music by the *Triumphlied*. The musical strategy on Brahms's part and the reception history of the work before 1900 may therefore provide novel insights into the post-1870 cultural and political contest over the character of the new German Reich.

This supposition is bolstered by Brahms's advocacy of Max Bruch's 1872 oratorio, *Odysseus*. Brahms performed the work at the last concert he conducted as director of the concerts of the Gesellschaft der Musikfreunde in Vienna in the 1874–1875 season. Brahms was notoriously critical of his contemporaries. Yet he found sufficient merit in Bruch's work to program it. Bruch wrote the oratorio explicitly for amateur choral participation in performance in the context of the new German Reich.[49] The work sought to put forward a cultural ideal drawn from classical antiquity in explicit contrast to Wagner. This is why Brahms chose to program it precisely at a time when Wagner's popularity was in the ascendency, particularly in Vienna.[50] Bruch's source was Homer, underscoring the revival in interest in Greek and Roman history in the 1870s. The underlying conceit was the idea that the new Germany might become the new neoclassical force, a new Athens as a world historical cultural and political power. Bruch's music was designed to inspire both sentimental pride and optimism regarding the formation of a homeland. Germany became the ideal of a community restored, evoked through the image of Odysseus's triumphant return and his defeat of the rival suitors. Bruch used the explicitly anti-Wagnerian form of the secular oratorio, a genre linked to Mendelssohn, to inspire an anti-Wagnerian cultural ideal. Odysseus in Bruch's characterization became an anti-Wotan, a powerful antidote.

Brahms's nationalist sentiments and intentions in the *Triumphlied* correspond to his advocacy of Bruch's oratorio. Bruch's work became a successful cultural icon of the *Gründerzeit*. It ultimately failed in its attempt to popularize an image of Germany competitive with the heroic grandeur and fantasy of the Wagnerian. Although popular in and characteristic of the 1870s and 1880s, by the early 1900s *Odysseus*'s aesthetic premises, as constituents of cultural politics, were in retreat. Yet, like the *Triumphlied*, it became part of the collective memory, as Mendelssohn's *Paulus* had been earlier in the century before its gradual disappearance from the repertoire. The disappearance of Bruch's *Odysseus* after 1918 suggests that it perhaps could have served as a source of a bad conscience as fascism and its aesthetics triumphed. The revival of both works even in Germany after 1945 has been hampered by a reductive account of German nationalism and the pursuit of a causal connection between the era of the 1870s and the rise of Hitler.

However, for the *Triumphlied* and *Odysseus*, given the monumental scale of these works, only an encounter with the works in concert can suggest ways to understand the differentiated character of their reception, particularly in light of their extensive performance history. What the works might have signified to their audiences may not be accessible from either scores or recordings. After all, it was through performance that these works sustained their publics.

Now that the great age of recording is over, the taste for live performance is on the rise, and a far more potent and inclusive technology is within our grasp, the writing of music history may be able to reclaim the past from the tyranny of criticism and judgment rooted in the twentieth-century romance with recording. To do so, however, a larger part of the musical culture of the past that has remained obscured to the detriment of the concert stage and our understanding of history must be restored in performance. In the meantime, historians must be particularly vigilant in separating their points of access and judgment regarding music from those that prevailed in the past.

NOTES

1. Leon Botstein, "Cinderella; or Music and the Human Sciences: Unfootnoted Musings from the Margins," *Current Musicology* 53 (1993): 124–34.

2. There is a simple reason for the ease in doing this in art and literature. Since the mid-nineteenth century, for nonspecialist historians—Jacob Burckhardt, for example, and theorists of history, such as Wilhelm Dilthey and Max Weber—assessing the visual and literary seemed plausible and possible. Understanding music in turn requires the acquisition of comparatively rarefied skills. Weber, for example, was just a typical enthusiastic listener.

3. See David Wyn Jones, *The Symphony in Beethoven's Vienna* (New York: Cambridge University Press, 2006), and Richard Will, *The Characteristic Symphony in the Age of Haydn and Beethoven* (New York: Cambridge University Press, 2002).

4. There is of course the case of so-called early music, where a community of devoted practitioners and listeners exists, in part committed to an explicitly premodern sound and aura. The preceding comments refer most directly to music after 1750, the era that has bequeathed the basic repertoire of instrumental concerts and opera. For that period, see a welcome addition to the literature of the largely unexplored and unheard that brings new material to the fore: John Koegel, *Music in German Immigrant Theater: New York City, 1840–1940* (Rochester: University of Rochester Press, 2009), and Jonathan D. Bellman's discussion of now obscure amateur piano music genres popular in Chopin's day in *Chopin's Polish Ballade: Op. 38 As Narrative of National Martyrdom* (New York: Oxford University Press, 2009).

5. See Lydia Goehr, *The Imaginary Museum of Musical Works: An Essay in the Philosophy of Music* (New York: Oxford University Press, 2007), and William Weber, *The Great Transformation of Musical Taste: Concert Programming from Haydn to Brahms* (New York: Cambridge University Press, 2008).

6. Jeffrey Kallberg, *Chopin at the Boundaries: Sex, History, and Musical Genre* (Cambridge, Mass.: Harvard University Press, 1996).

7. Consider the need to study closely the operetta traditions. A recent publication that is suggestive of the possibilities is, ironically, an annotated collection of caricatures about Strauss: Roswitha Schlöttere-Traimer, ed., *Richard Strauss: Sein Leben und Werk im Spiegel der zeitgenössischen Karikatur* (Mainz: Schott, 2009). In footnote 18 (this chapter) see also the list of Mahler and Strauss contemporaries whose music still awaits exploration.

8. A perfectly admirable example is Vincent Giroud's recent *French Opera: A Short History* (New Haven, Conn.: Yale University Press, 2010). For less conventional accounts, one is indebted to the writings of Stephen Huebner, in particular his *French Opera at the Fin de Siècle: Wagnerism, Nationalism, and Style* (New York: Oxford University Press, 1999), and Jane Fulcher, *The Nation's Image: French Grand Opera as Politics and Politicized Art* (New York: Cambridge University Press, 1987).

9. Consider the music of Scherbachov, Popov, B. Tchaikovsky, and B. Tischenko. See Boris Schwarz, *Music and Musical Life in Soviet Russia 1917–1970* (New York: Norton, 1972); Levon Hakobian, *Music of the Soviet Age 1917–1987* (Stockholm: Melos Music Literature, 1998); and *Sowjetische Musik: Im Licht der Perestroika*, ed. Hermann Danuser, Hannelore Gerlach, and Jürgen Köchel (Laaber: Laaber, 1990).

10. See Tim Blanning, *The Triumph of Music* (Cambridge, Mass.: Harvard University Press, 2008).

11. See Jann Pasler, *Composing the Citizen: Music as Public Utility in Third Republic France* (Berkeley: University of California Press, 2009), and the writings of Philip Bohlmann.

12. New well-documented biographies of Stanford, Pfitzner, Schoeck, D'Indy, Chausson, Schreker, Zemlinsky, and Carpenter have appeared in recent decades.

13. See Reinhold Brinkmann, *Late Idyll: The Second Symphony of Johannes Brahms*, trans. Peter Palmer (Cambridge, Mass.: Harvard University Press, 1997), and "Zeitgenossen: Johannes Brahms und die Maler Feuerbach, Böcklin, Klinger, und Menzel," in *Johannes Brahms: Internationalen Brahms-Kongress 1997*, ed. F. Krummacher and M. Struck, 71–96 (Munich: Henle, 1999), and Daniel Beller-McKenna, *Brahms and the German Spirit* (Cambridge, Mass.: Harvard University Press, 2004).

14. See Bellmann, *Chopin's Polish Ballade*, 160–70, 175.

15. See also the more extensive study on the Russian Jewish group in James Loeffler, *The Most Musical Nation: Jews, Culture, and Modernity in the Late Russian Empire* (New Haven: Yale University Press, 2010).

16. Klára Móricz, *Jewish Identities: Nationalism, Racism, and Utopianism in Twentieth-century Music* (Los Angeles: University of California Press, 2008).

17. The contrast is between *Schelomo*; *America, an Epic Rhapsody*; and the *Israel Symphony*, for example.

18. Consider the work of forgotten composers in the essay collections *Monographien Moderner Musiker*, 2 vols. (Leipzig: Kahnt Nachfolger, 1906), and Arthur Seidl, *Deutsche Musikbucherei: Neuzeitliche Tondichter* (Regensburg: Bosse, 1926): Wolf-Ferrari, Huber, Kistler, Thuille, Fried, Gast, A. Mendelssohn, Becker, Sommer, Reiter, Hausegger, Kaun, Schumann, Bungert, Andreae, Ansorge, Baussnern, Berger, Blech, Bossi, Bischoff, Burkard, Butting, Cornelius, Hegar, Kämpf, Kaminski, Klose, Koch, Lindner, Limbert, Mikorey, Nicodé, Reiter, Rosch, Rabl, Reznicek, Scheinpflug, von Schillings, Schoeck, Suter, Taubmann, S. Wagner, Weingartner, Wolf, Zilcher, and Zöllner.

19. An eloquent expression of this sentiment appears in Edward T. Cone's essay "The Missing Composer," written in the late 1980s but published posthumously in *Hearing and*

Knowing Music, ed. Robert P. Morgan (Princeton: Princeton University Press, 2009), 11–15. See also Leon Botstein, "Why Music Matters," *Musical Quarterly* 87(2) (Summer 2004): 177–87; Dawn Bennett, *Understanding the Classical Music Profession: The Past, the Present, and Strategies for the Future* (Burlington, Vt.: Ashgate, 2008); and Lawrence Kramer, *Why Classical Music Still Matters* (Los Angeles: University of California Press, 2007).

20. Leon Botstein, "Music of a Century: Museum Culture and the Politics of Subsidy," in *The Cambridge History of Twentieth-Century Music*, ed. Nicholas Cook and Anthony Pople, 40–68 (New York: Cambridge University Press, 2004).

21. There are exceptions to this general observation. Most notable is the case of Alex Ross, the critic at the *New Yorker*. See also his *The Rest Is Noise: Listening to the Twentieth Century* (New York: Farrar, Strauss, and Giroux, 2007).

22. See Heiner Gembris, "Entwicklungsperspektiven zwischen Publikumsschwund und Publikumsentwicklung," in *Das Konzert: Neue Aufführungskonzepte für eine klassische Form*, ed. Martin Tröndle, 61–79 (Bielefeld: Transcript, 2009).

23. There is a growing body of fine scholarship on the history of recording and its impact. See, for example, David Suisman, *Selling Sounds: The Commercial Revolution in American Music* (Cambridge, Mass.: Harvard University Press, 2009); Robert Philip, *Performing Music in the Age of Recording* (New Haven: Yale University Press, 2004); Colin Symes, *Setting the Record Straight* (Middletown, Conn.: Wesleyan University Press, 2004); Timothy Day, *A Century of Recorded Music: Listening to Musical History* (New Haven: Yale University Press, 2000); and William Howland Kenney, *Recorded Music in American Life: The Phonograph and Popular Memory 1890–1945* (New York: Oxford University Press, 1999).

24. See Joseph Horowitz, *Classical Music in America: A History of Its Rise and Fall* (New York: Norton, 2005).

25. See Emily Thompson, *The Soundscape of Modernity: Architectural Acoustics and the Culture of Listening in America, 1900–1933* (Cambridge, Mass.: MIT Press, 2004), and Eric F. Clarke, "The Impact of Recording on Listening," *Twentieth-Century Music* 4(1) (March 2007): 47–70.

26. An early example of such broadcasts can be found in Marcel Proust's listening to *Pelléas and Mélisande* by means of a telephone-based transmission. See William C. Carter, *Marcel Proust: A Life* (New Haven: Yale University Press, 2000), 497–98.

27. See Geoffrey Payzant, *Glenn Gould: Music and Mind* (Toronto: Van Nostrand Reinhold, 1978), and *The Glenn Gould Reader*, ed. Tim Page (New York: Knopf, 1984).

28. Joseph Horowitz, *Understanding Toscanini: How He Became an American Culture-God and Helped Create a New Audience for Old Music* (New York: Knopf, 1987).

29. Consider the great Czech pianist Rudolf Firkusny's debut recital in Warsaw in the 1920s after winning a prize at the Prague Conservatory. For an encore he turned to the members of the audience and asked them for their favorite tunes so that he could improvise on them.

30. This view was initially shared by Schoenberg and was realized in the electronic music movement of the 1950s and 1960s.

31. See the essay collection *Schriften zur Musikpsychologie und Musikästhetik: Der Hörer als Interpret*, ed. Helga de la Motte-Haber and Reinhard Kopiez (Frankfurt: Lang, 1995). To be fair, Glenn Gould, the defender of the studio recording, used it not to lessen the range of interpretation, but to experiment and enlarge it.

32. See Allan Evans, *Ignaz Friedman: Romantic Master Pianist* (Indianapolis: Indiana University Press, 2009); Kenneth Hamilton, *After the Golden Age* (New York: Oxford University Press, 2008); Jonathan Sterne, *The Audible Past: Cultural Origins of Sound Reproduction* (Durham, N.C.: Duke University Press, 2003); Timothy Day, *A Century of*

Recorded Music: Listening to Musical History (New Haven, Conn.: Yale University Press, 2000); Colin Symes, *Setting the Record Straight* (Middletown, Conn.: Wesleyan University Press, 2004); Robert Philip, *Early Recordings and Musical Style: Changing Tastes in Instrumental Performance 1900–1950* (New York: Cambridge University Press, 1992); Evan Eisenberg, *Explorations in Phonography: The Recording Angel* (New York: McGraw-Hill, 1987); and Roland Gelatt, *The Fabulous Phonograph 1877–1977* (New York: Collier, 1977).

33. See Henri-Louis de la Grange, *Gustav Mahler: A New Life Cut Short (1907–1911)*, vol. 4, 1619–35 (New York: Oxford University Press, 2008).

34. See the essays in Tröndle, *Das Konzert.*

35. Gunther Holler-Schuster, "Waldmüller und die Fotografische," in *Ferdinand Georg Waldmüller 1793–1865*, ed. Agnes Husslein-Arco and Henri Loyrette, 19ff (Vienna: Brandstätter, 2009).

36. Bálint András Varga, *György Kurtág: Three Interviews and Ligeti Homages*, vol. 67 of Eastman Studies in Music (Rochester, N.Y.: Boydell and Brewer, 2009), 4.

37. See his letters in Ernest Bloch, *Sa vie et sa pensée*, vol. 1, *Les années de galères, 1880–1916*, ed. Joseph Lewinski and Emmanuelle Dijon (Geneva: Slatkine, 1998).

38. See Hans Moldenhauer and Rosaleen Moldenhauer, *Anton von Webern: A Chronicle of His Life and Work* (New York: Knopf, 1979).

39. The manuscripts of these efforts are held in the Enescu archives in Bucharest.

40. Ian Bent, ed., *Music Analysis in the Nineteenth Century: Fugue, Form, and Style*, vol. 1 of *Cambridge Readings in the Literature of Music*, ed. John Stevens and Peter le Huray (New York: Cambridge University Press, 1994).

41. See *Music and the Cultures of Print*, ed. Kate van Orden (New York: Garland, 2000), and Irene Lawford-Hinrichsen, *Music Publishing and Patronage: C. F. Peters, 1800 to the Holocaust* (Kenton, England: Edition Press, 2000).

42. Varga, *György Kurtág*, 5, 29.

43. Chris Walton, *Othmar Schoeck: Life and Works* (Rochester: University of Rochester Press, 2009).

44. Alexander Rehding, *Music and Monumentality: Commemoration and Wonderment in Nineteenth-Century Germany* (New York: Oxford University Press, 2009), 35.

45. See Norbert Tschulik, *Franz Schmidt* (Vienna: Lafite, 1972).

46. Rehding, oddly enough, does not cite or use McKenna's book.

47. See Beller-McKenna's, *Brahms and the German Spirit*, 98–132.

48. Consider, for example, Max Weber's critical assessment of the national liberals after 1870.

49. See Christopher Fifield, *Max Bruch: His Life and Works* (New York: Braziller, 1988).

50. Leon Botstein, "Brahms and His Audience: The Later Viennese Years, 1857–1897," in *The Cambridge Companion to Brahms*, ed. Michael Musgrave, 51–78 (New York: Cambridge University Press, 1999). This argument regarding Bruch's *Odysseus* is bolstered by the temporary enthusiasm for August Bungert's massive *Die Odyssee* (1898–1903), part of a projected *Homer's World* theater work intended to rival Wagner's *Ring*.

CHAPTER 22

....

AFTERWORD: WHOSE CULTURE? WHOSE HISTORY? WHOSE MUSIC?

....

MICHAEL P. STEINBERG

1. ENCOUNTERS

....

The initial story is known well but not well enough.

In early 1999 preparations were under way for the eastern German city of Weimar to assume its place as that year's designated European cultural capital. It was the year of Johann Wolfgang von Goethe's 250th birthday, and Goethe remains Weimar's most celebrated ghost. The musical plans for the summer events remained unclear, however, and that gap prompted their principal impresario, Bernd Kaufmann, to visit Daniel Barenboim in Berlin to solicit his interest and participation. Barenboim would be conducting at the nearby Bayreuth Festival, so convenience was on Weimar's side.

The notion that a Goethe commemoration should place music into the context of civic and cosmopolitan responsibility led Barenboim to discuss the invitation with his friend Edward Said. Together, Said and Barenboim proposed the formation of a workshop that would bring together musicians from Israel, Palestine, and other countries of the Middle East. In naming the group, or rather the project, they invoked Goethe's gesture of poetic, generous orientalism as an emblem of unrealized, contemporary cross-cultural dialogue. Goethe had learned Arabic at the age of sixty and in his *West-Östlicher Divan* had put into a play a West-Eastern parity in a manner reminiscent of Montesquieu's experiment of the *Persian Letters* almost a century before. The ensemble quickly developed into a full orchestra. Within a few years, the West-Eastern Divan Orchestra had attained the status of a world-class orchestra, meeting for one month every summer in a conservatory setting and in that setting offering concerts and minitours. In 2003 the government of Spain and specifically the regional government of Andalucía awarded the orchestra a major subvention and a permanent summer institute in the town of Pilas, near Seville, guided by the example of medieval Andalucía and specifically the thirteenth-century court of Alfonso X of Castile as a successful meeting ground of Jews, Christians, and Muslims. The orchestra rotates a portion of its membership annually but remains 40 percent Israeli, 40 percent Arab, and 20 percent Spanish.

My own association with the West-Eastern Divan dates from late 2006. Invited to the United Nations to play a December concert in honor of the departing secretary general, Kofi Annan, the Divan had added a concert in Carnegie Hall and now sought a university setting in which to rehearse and to advance their parallel agenda of cultural and political dialogue and knowledge. This reunion proved particularly challenging following the summer of 2006, when the war in Lebanon prevented about fifteen of the musicians from participating in the summer program or from wanting to participate, or both. The abiding political fault lines within this fragile community not only divide it into two factions but multiply within the two factions as well.

On a Friday afternoon in September 2006 I received an urgent message from an unknown caller in Berlin, asking me to return the call to a cell phone as soon as possible. The caller turned out to be Tabaré Perlas, personal assistant to Daniel Barenboim and general manager of the West-Eastern Divan Orchestra. When I reached him, he asked me whether Brown University would be willing to host Mr. Barenboim, the ninety-seven musicians, and the twelve staff members of the West-Eastern Divan for four days in December, which was three months away. The orchestra would engage in various discussions with the university community and require daily rehearsal space and technical support, including the provision of large instruments such as tympani and harp. In return they would be glad to offer a concert, for which they would forego the substantial customary fee. I said yes. Then I added, "But please give me until Monday to get permission." To the daunting prospect of hosting this orchestra on campus for four days, my university responded with levels of generosity, goodwill, and hard work that continue to move me. The four-day visit proved a profound experience for the university and the city, and it has generated a long-lasting association.

The Divan's double agenda is at once musical and political. The musical agenda is clear. The political one is less so. The orchestra takes no political position, and its spokespersons disavow politics as its core mission, preferring to deploy Edward Said's category of a humanistic rather than a political intervention. Nonetheless, the creation of a sphere of exchange and dialogue among representatives of radically different and often opposed viewpoints is itself a mode of political work. The ninety-seven musicians form a musical entity, but before such an entity can come into being they form a kind of polis: in other words a highly contrived and deliberate social body based on difference, debate, and deliberate, indeed effortful, cooperation.

It is not a utopian project, nor does it frame musical performance as an oasis from the political world.

What, then, is the specific character of the musical agenda in relation to the political one? In the shadow of politics, does the music become a mere cipher, replaceable by, let's say, soccer (as the opening sequence of Paul Smaczny's superb documentary might suggest—a wonderful film with the felicitous title *Knowledge Is the Beginning*) or any other cooperative venture? Of what significance is the ironic reality of music as the ultimate *inarticulate* sonic, discursive practice in relation to a political challenge, where *articulation* is of the utmost importance?

Music and politics constitute the project's open question then. But other ramifications arise as well. To watch Daniel Barenboim rehearse this orchestra is to absorb a transformative pedagogical argument. That argument is first about the relationship between teacher and student, which in contemporary professional discourse is often assumed to be an interpersonal one and, as such, not unrelated to a conversation between analyst and analysand, with similar dynamics of transference and the like. This is not in itself wrong. However, in the context of instruction rather than therapy, it is secondary to the principle that this dialogical relationship is always focused principally on a third element: the text, the world, or both. In musical work, this simultaneous mutuality of devotion to an externality on the part of teacher and student is performed through the very literal and very metaphorical problem of technique. The whole world depends on how you hold the bow, how you shape a phrase. Moreover, because the phrase is Beethoven's and not yours or mine, technique controls the transmission of repertory and thus the relationship to the content and survival of what might be referred to as the musical canon.

And here the second dimension of pedagogical transformation occurs. What happens when young Israeli and Arab musicians play Beethoven? What happens when they are joined by several German musicians, one or two of whom happen to be members of the Berlin Philharmonic, moonlighting with the Divan out of sheer love of the project, sitting in remote positions as stand partners to the youngest members? But not so fast: In fact, it turns out that the concertmaster of the Berlin Philharmonic is a young Israeli alumnus of the Divan and its principal double bass player is a young Egyptian alumnus of the Divan. But this only reinforces my point. The pedagogical transformation I refer to here is one that affects us all, I submit, and it involves a seismic shift that has occurred in the last generation. The canon belongs to no one. Beethoven is a foreign "country" to young Germans as well. Paradoxically, alienation affords access and loosens the taboos of access. The vehicle of access is technique. Technique combined with affective commitment produces musicality or, stated more broadly, a sense of art. Moreover—and this assertion introduces the body of my argument here—this membrane of technique, what in German is called *Fingerspitzengefühl*, is metonymic of the relation of music to the world. The canon wars are diffused by the understanding that engagement and technical mastery proceed without the privilege of inheritance or the claim of ownership. Music is a thing of the world, and the love of and esteem for music become a kind of homage to the world.

This is my topic: the transformation of musical experience, both performance and listening, which results from the dislodging of the repertoire from patterns and assumptions of cultural continuity, ownership, familiarity, legacy, and tradition and which in turn produces the potential reclaiming of this repertoire through a principle of dialogic exchange. The result is the production of a certain intimacy—between player and music, between listener and music. The result as well is a newly grounded community of listening and taste.

Essential to the alchemy of the West-Eastern Divan and its cultural power is the friendship between Daniel Barenboim and Edward Said during the last decade of Said's life. That friendship received an impressive intellectual articulation in the collection of dialogues and essays called *Parallels and Paradoxes: Explorations in Music*, published in 2004, months after Said's death. The volume includes a short text by Barenboim called "In Memoriam," which I quote here as a kind of handle on the new paradigm for the arts and humanities that I believe this project has defined.

> Edward saw in music not just a combination of sounds, but he understood the fact that every musical masterpiece is, as it were, a conception of the world. And the difficulty lies in the fact that this conception of the world cannot be described in words—because were it possible to describe it in words, the music would be unnecessary. But he recognized that the fact that is indescribable doesn't mean it has no meaning.[1]

2. TRANSLATION

The culture of globalization often assumes that a connected world equals a completely translatable one. It remains the task of the humanities to interrogate this assumption, which also becomes a way of differentiating modes of exchange (which do not exclude monetary transactions) from their total commodification. We remain convinced that the simplest act of linguistic translation carries cultural and existential baggage along with it—baggage that is sometimes light, sometimes heavy, sometimes visible, sometimes hidden. Thus all translation is a dance between commensurability and incommensurability.

Walter Benjamin's classic 1921 essay, "The Task of the Translator," grounded this argument for literary theory and the growing field of translation studies. Written to accompany his own translations of Baudelaire's *Tableaux parisiens*, Benjamin's text opens with a famously austere passage about any text's disavowal of the experience of its reader or, for that matter, its listener: "No poem is intended for the reader, no picture for the beholder, no symphony for the listener."[2] The essay has also generated a famous and meaningful anecdote. Toward the end of the essay, Benjamin states that where a text pertains directly to realms of truth or dogma, it is fundamentally translatable: *ist er übersetzbar schlechthin*. In translating this passage into French,

Benjamin's distinguished reader and French translator, Maurice de Gandillac, apparently let his instinct get the better of him so that he translated the passage into its opposite. He wrote that in such cases the text is fundamentally *untranslatable*: *purement et simplement intraduisible*. All of this led the critic Paul de Man to suggest that, in some basic sense, the conditions of translatability and untranslatability are in fact the same.[3]

This paradox informs various translation contexts: from one spoken language to another—German to French, in this example, as well as from one discourse or medium to another—music or image to descriptive speech, for example. It might also inform the translatability/untranslatability from nondiscursive experiences to discursive or descriptive ones, such as from experiences of the body, including pain and pleasure, into descriptive or depictive language and metaphors. Elaine Scarry grounded her influential treatise on the politics of pain (*The Body in Pain*) in the proposition that one body's, one person's pain is unrepresentable and thus incomprehensible to another person. More recent philosophies of pain have strongly rejected this position, arguing that experience and sympathy can in fact produce comprehension of another's pain.[4] For anthropologists and other cultural analysts, the question becomes one of cultural translation, where Claude Lévi-Strauss and other structuralists look for maximum translatability and their critics look for maximum untranslatability.

The Divan's core repertory has been the Central European symphonic tradition, with which Daniel Barenboim is most closely associated. Barenboim has the habit of adding a fundamental challenge to each summer's reunion. This challenge can be an extension of the repertory by genre (opera, for example), level of difficulty (Schoenberg's Variations for Orchestra in 2007), quantity (all the Beethoven symphonies in 2010), or controversy (Wagner).

The Wagner case is particularly sensitive as the controversy it invokes is asymmetrical. The playing of Wagner remains a cultural taboo in Israel, part of a received national cosmology; introducing Wagner to the Divan thus gives the Israeli musicians an additional component of cultural and political negotiation that their Arab and Spanish colleagues do not automatically face. The first Wagner that Barenboim brought to the orchestra is the same excerpt that both he and Zubin Mehta have brought into Israel: the Prelude and Liebestod from *Tristan und Isolde*, in other words, Wagner's unpolitical sublime. But the challenge of 2008 was the complete first act of *Die Walküre*.

The issue is addressed in a superb recent book-length portrait of the Divan: Elena Cheah's *An Orchestra beyond Borders*. Cheah is an American cellist who since 2006 has played an important performing, as well as teaching and coaching, role with the Divan. Her book is a sequence of portraits of a well-chosen cross-section of the players and sections. Yuval Shapiro of the trumpet section has this to say about the Wagner controversy:

> The Israel Philharmonic was founded as the Palestine Symphony Orchestra in 1936, and they played Wagner regularly in the first two years. After Kristallnacht in 1938, they decided to ban Wagner from their repertoire; his music became taboo in

Israel. We have German trains, we have BMWs and Volkswagens, we have AEG and Bosch power tools; everything is okay except this composer who died in 1883. Most people in Israel only know Wagner from Bugs Bunny cartoons: you know, when Elmer Fudd sings "Kill the wabbit" to the melody of the "Ride of the Valkyries."[5]

The Wagner case suggests that the issue of received cultural antipathy is clearer than the one of received cultural sympathy. To put it another way, this asymmetrical negative received cosmology appears to have no positive analogue. This becomes the new cultural secret of the so-called classical repertoire, and its application is by no means limited to the special circumstances of the West-Eastern Divan.

What does Beethoven signify for young musicians of the early twenty-first century? Beyond the globalized sonic veneer of the brotherhood of man and bah-bah-bah-BAAH, Beethoven begins today as something foreign to everyone. This, I would submit, is the emancipatory leveling of the cultural playing field in the world of culture, arts, and humanities following the so-called culture wars of the 1980s.

The culture wars resulted from the conflicting university economies of limited faculty resources on the one hand and the globalization of the curriculum on the other. What to teach and whom to hire? The globalization was not only geographical but also multicultural—and multicultural in terms of "local" representation across gender, class, race, and other categories. So the stakes were clearly those of representation (in the political sense of the word). Nonetheless, the original debates were waged on assumptions of both cultural representation and cultural ownership. Thus, Toni Morrison was an African American woman writer (perhaps only until the Nobel Prize catapulted her to the equally problematic status of literary universality), and Beethoven was a dead white German male. Such classifications based on representation and ownership—also known as identity politics—did grave injustice to the complicated patterns of cultural translatability/untranslatability and incommensurability. (The most infamous remark of the moment was possibly also the most craven: Saul Bellow's challenge that someone produce the Tolstoy of the Zulus.)

The question is not the de-Germanization of Beethoven but rather the ways in which his Germanness (among many other abiding, specific contexts) does or does not signify. Beethoven does not carry the traumatic aura of Wagner in Israel or elsewhere despite the fact that the Nazis championed him and considered his *Egmont*, much more than Wagner's *Siegfried*, the musical correlative of the kind of heroism they wished to extol. Barenboim's Beethoven in fact reproduces in musical terms a strong Germanic formal and performance tradition, its descent from Furtwängler and Schenker clearly audible in its resulting structures, vertical/ horizontal relationships, and implied musical arguments. All the same, the sounds invoke their own contextual genealogies only to those who care to hear and to understand them in this way. Beethoven is simply no longer a received cultural idiom—for the bourgeoisie, for Germans, for anyone. Identity politics falls fundamentally out of the picture.

For the summer 2009 institute in Pilas and the subsequent European tour, the Divan learned and performed Beethoven's only opera, *Fidelio*. This was the orchestra's first complete opera. Barenboim chose to open the performances with the mammoth *Leonore* Overture no. 3 rather than with the conventional *Fidelio* Overture, as the orchestra had already performed it several times. Its harmonic sequence required, in turn, a switching of the conventional order of the first two scenes. Barenboim used a performing version he had developed with Edward Said for the Chicago Symphony, which casts the action as a flashback narrated by the heroine, Leonore. Waltraud Meier, who had sung the Chicago performances and had since become a stalwart of and major presence in the Divan community and performances, returned to sing the 2009 performances.

Ludwig van Beethoven's personal paradox is that of a Catholic bourgeois composer with aristocratic pretensions who writes revolutionary music—music revolutionary not only in formal terms—as in "the man who freed music"—but also as the music of the age of revolution and the rights of man. His biographers continue to sort out and debate this complicated map. *Fidelio* offers additional paradoxes. Its plot involves a woman's heroic rescue and liberation of her unjustly imprisoned husband, who has dared to speak out against tyranny. Its dramatic and circumstantial source—the rescue drama *Léonore, ou l'amour conjugal* by Brouilly—recalls and reproduces the true story of a man from Tours who was imprisoned by the Terror and not by the ancient regime.

Said's text highlights the opera's focus on human rights and political imprisonment. Leonore's opening narration makes it clear that the political happy ending of the story she is about to reenact was short lived:

> Arbitrary power was our bane. You could be arrested without reason, and also released; or you could be killed. Who were the other prisoners? And what happened to them after Don Fernando had them released with Florestan? We were so caught up with the triumph of the moment, so thankful for finding each other at last, that we scarcely thought of what was to happen next. And that trumpet call, that providential, or was it magical, clear note blasting through the prison walls all at once. Was it an illusion, or reality or the beginning of a totally new era as we thought at the time?

Said's text emphasizes the calls of political justice and secular humanism. His general emphasis on secularity resonates with the categories of rescue and rescue opera. An allegory of the contemporary Middle East is evident. Rescue is both a personal and a political act. As a political act it is also a secular act, and thus to be distinguished importantly from acts of redemption. The operatic passage from Beethoven (*Fidelio*) to Weber (*Der Freischütz*) to Wagner involves precisely the paradigm shift from rescue to redemption, from a politics of action to one of ideology. At least so I have thought.[6] My work with the Divan in 2009 led me to complicate this argument, an outcome produced both by the opera itself and by the existential buttons it pushed among the players.

My task during the week of rehearsals was to introduce the players to the plot, characters, and multiple contexts of the drama—historical, literary, political— through short summaries interspersed scene by scene with Barenboim's musical guidance through the score. Two graduate students participated as well, thus tripling the lines of individual conversation with Divan members, as well as preparing a PowerPoint presentation on the performance history of *Fidelio*.[7]

The opera's political and ethical foci were clear to everyone. As the implicit ethic of the Divan involves "listening to the other" rather than reproducing received paradigms of victimization of the self (individual or collective), I looked forward especially to a presentation/discussion of the dungeon scene in the second act.

At this juncture, the heroine Leonore (disguised as Fidelio) has gained access to the cell of her imprisoned husband, Florestan, whose murder by the prison warden, Pizarro, is imminent. Leonore is to assist the jailor, Rocco, in the task of digging Florestan's grave. The first half of the scene involves a melodrama (spoken dialogue punctuated by assertions in the orchestra) between Leonore and Rocco, followed by a sung duet. The duet is also in two parts and involves two different understandings of the nature of work—Rocco's static one and Leonore's evolving and transformative one. Here we might also invoke Hannah Arendt's distinction between labor and work, in other words between mechanical and creative exertion.[8] The first—Rocco's mode of labor—is mechanical in two senses: It involves mechanical work (grave digging, in this case) and also the assumption that all work by definition meets an ethical norm by virtue of bodily exertion and the completion of an assigned task. "Following orders" carries an automatic normative value. The duet's second part is generated by a kind of Kantian epiphany on Leonore's part, a moment that for many (including me) is the core moment of the opera. Losing focus on the digging (to Rocco's annoyance), Leonore gazes at the unconscious prisoner (whom she has not yet recognized) and asserts, "Wer Du auch seist, ich will Dich retten" [Whoever you may be, I will rescue you]. This depersonalization of the idea of justice is key to the stylistic and ethical/political momentum of Beethoven's music. It is the core ethic of the Divan.

The subsequent scene brings into relief the relation of a secular, ethical imperative to a sacred and Christian cosmology. Without doubt, Beethoven's opera and the texts of his librettists Sonnleithner and Treitschke combine the themes of justice and liberation with profound religiosity. God and divine justice are mentioned repeatedly, orienting the good and evil characters alike. However, the most evocative religious moment is generated implicitly.

When she recognizes her husband, Leonore persuades Rocco to give him a piece of bread and a sip of wine. That they should be carrying wine rather than water would appear to argue for a somewhat strained production of a sacred moment. The opera's dénouement—the moment of rescue—is thus preceded by a moment of implied communion and the imbibing of bread and wine, to which Beethoven composed a deeply stirring vocal trio. Here came my surprise. Though I had expected the discussion of the previous scene, of its speech-act discovery of depersonalized justice, to capture—more than any other scene—the collective attention of the players, it was in fact the religious implications of the scene's second part that did so. An orchestra can function like a class, exuding a kind of electricity at moments of mutual discovery.

I continue to think about this unexpected moment of recognition, as it has altered my own reception of both *Fidelio* and the dynamics of the Divan. Did this surfacing of a core Christian paradigm strike a chord of sameness or otherness (or both) among the players? Did a moment of religious solidarity supplant an ethic of political justice and thus provide some kind of recognition or relief—or both? In a community of Israelis, Arabs, and Spaniards, where some of the Arabs are Christian and some Muslim, did the Christian paradigm allow for a moment of identification? If so, was it an identification with a self? With an other? With neither—in other words, with an external zone of potential cultural mediation?

These questions remain unanswered for me. However, the next day a conversation reinforced the importance of the moment. I was approached by Bassam Mussad, a member of the trumpet section and in fact the other trumpet player (along with Yuval Shapiro) profiled in Elena Cheah's book. Bassam first described himself to me in words that echoed the published profile:

> I was born in Sudan, where my parents were working as Evangelical Protestant missionaries. They met while they were working there, but they are both Egyptian. We used to spend a few months a year in Egypt, but I lived and went to school in Sudan until I was nine years old. That was when we moved to Pasadena, California, where my father went to get his doctorate in Islamic studies.[9]

In the *Fidelio* performances, Bassam's great solo moment was the trumpet fanfare at the dénouement of the dungeon scene, announcing the arrival of the minister of state—the *politicus ex machina* whose appearance guarantees not only Leonore's and Florestan's survival but also the release of a multitude of fellow prisoners. Since the same trumpet fanfare appears as the implied dramatic dénouement of the Leonore Overture no. 3, Bassam had already played it a number of times. Struck by the previous day's discussion of the dungeon scene's Christian aura, Bassam now asked me whether the trumpet fanfare could be understood as an allegorical herald of Christ, whose arrival is prophesied to follow the sounding of the trumpet. I thought then, and continue to think, that such an understanding takes *Fidelio* much too far on the road from rescue to redemption. However, I found that I had absolutely no interest in discouraging Bassam's insight, especially if it were to give his performance more conviction, more meaning, and indeed more pleasure.

3. TECHNIQUE

In October 2002 Daniel Barenboim and Edward Said were jointly awarded the Principe de Asturias Prize, an annual award honoring achievements in the sciences, humanities, or public affairs. In his acceptance speech, Said offered "tribute to Daniel Barenboim, whose great musicianship has been offered as a gesture of the highest form of human solidarity to Palestinians and other Arabs."[10]

This noble statement appears to rest on a non sequitur. How can musicianship, a technical and untranslatable quality, produce human solidarity? Said goes on to close at least part of this gap:

> Strange though it may seem, it is culture generally and music in particular that provide an alternative model to identity conflict.... [T]here is what I might call the long-range politics of culture that provides a literally wider space for reflection, and ultimately for concord rather than endless tension and dissonance. Literature and music open up such a space because they are essentially arts not of antagonism principally but of collaboration, receptivity, recreation, and collective interpretation. No one writes or plays an instrument just to be read or listened to by oneself: there is always a reader and listener, and over time, the number increases.[11]

Said writes contra Benjamin here (recall the latter's "No poem is intended for the reader," etc.) The problem remains the incommensurability between literature and music and the abiding issue of the contentlessness of music. For this reason, Said rightly relies on the category of technique (musicianship). However, the passage does not attempt the work of translation from technique to human communication and solidarity. Its sentences appear to skip over several steps of the argument—those steps that will close—perhaps only engage—the paradox of technique as the marker at once of music's untranslatability and translatability.

Technique is, after all, the realm of the purely musical. Here is Elena Cheah's account of "the maestro at work":

> If the first violins were faster than the second violins in a certain passage, Barenboim took every aspect of musical expression into consideration while analyzing the problem. How much bow was each section using? Did they start with the bow on the string or above it? Did they understand where the summit of the phrase was? Did they understand where the harmony changed, altering the course of the progression? Did they make the crescendo in the right place and at the same rate as the rest of the orchestra? Did they know which voice was the most important during this passage? In many orchestras, professional or not, these questions were never asked. If at all, they came up at the first rehearsal, not the last. Throughout the dress rehearsal, he made us all listen to the music with his ears.[12]

The teaching of musicality is the teaching of listening, and listening is not a metaphor. Musical listening amounts not to a metaphor for other kinds of listening. Listening is listening.

4. MELANCHOLY

The Divan's 2009 summer tour ended with a performance of *Fidelio* as a Proms concert in the Royal Albert Hall, London, before an audience of some six thousand and an unlimited television audience via a BBC broadcast and an eventual film of the event. Following the performance and its ovations, Barenboim turned to the hall and asked for the public's indulgence while he addressed the orchestra, as he put it, "in the relative intimacy of the Royal Albert Hall." He thanked the players for their courage and participation in the Divan project in general and then, clearly addressing the widest public, reminded his listeners that "what you see before you is not normalization; it is an alternative."

The West-Eastern Divan is a melancholy project. This assertion has nothing to do with its mood, which is spirited, humorous, energized, inspired, and usually exhilarated (even, indeed especially, through exhaustion). Neither does it have to do with an understanding of melancholy as the result (pathological or not) of an experience of loss. Rather, and in keeping with some new scholarship on the character and importance of melancholia, the Divan as a project is melancholy in the same way that music itself is a fundamentally melancholy mode of art and knowledge. Melancholia in this sense can be understood as the recognition of the always-receding horizon of knowledge. Music, driven on by the desire to know, knows that it will not achieve this knowledge—of the world or of itself—and that it will end in silence, a kind of death, consoled only by the ephemeral memory of the effort that has been made.

The new cultural history of music strives to understand musical form and musical practice as modes of knowledge. Ours is also a melancholy knowledge because of the inarticulacy and untranslatability of the music in which we strive to hear and to know the world. That melancholy is overcome, if only momentarily, when acts of listening succeed in translating the untranslatable.

NOTES

1. Daniel Barenboim, "In Memoriam: Edward Said (1936–2003)," in Daniel Barenboim and Edward W. Said, *Parallels and Paradoxes: Explorations in Music and Society*, ed. Ara Guzelimian (New York: Vintage, 2004), x.

2. Walter Benjamin, "The Task of the Translator," in *Illuminations*, trans. Harry Zohn (New York: Schocken, 1969), 69.

3. Paul de Man, "Task of the Translator," in *The Resistance to Theory* (Minneapolis: University of Minnesota Press, 1986), 79–80.

4. Elaine Scarry, *The Body in Pain* (New York: Oxford University Press, 1985).

5. Elena Cheah, *An Orchestra beyond Borders* (London: Verso, 2009), 137.

6. Michael P. Steinberg, *Listening to Reason: Culture, Subjectivity, and Nineteenth-century Music* (Princeton: Princeton University Press, 2004), chapter 2, "Beethoven: Heroism and Abstraction," esp. 73–83.

7. Jonathan Gentry and Adam Sacks of the Brown University Department of History deserve thanks and credit for their work.

8. See Hannah Arendt, *The Human Condition* (Chicago: University of Chicago Press, 1958), esp. part 3 ("Labor") and part 4 ("Work"). The creativity of work produces what Arendt calls the permanence or durability of the world, as evident especially in works of art:

Nowhere else does the sheer durability of the world of things appear in such purity and clarity, nowhere else therefore does this thing-world reveal itself so spectacularly as the non-mortal home for mortal beings. It is as though worldly stability had become transparent in the permanence of art, so that a premonition of immortality, not the immortality of the soul or of life but of something immortal achieved by mortal hands, has become tangibly present, to shine and to be seen, to sound and to be heard, to speak and to be read. (Doubleday Anchor ed. [1959], 147)

Adam Sacks has observed that *The Human Condition* might be read as a sustained answer to and critique of Heidegger's thought, written as it was during the period of Arendt's and Heidegger's postwar rapprochement. This passage in particular can be understood as a counterargument to Heidegger's essay "The Origin of the Work of Art" and the latter's focus on artworks as cultural, national emblems. See "The Origin of the Work of Art," in Martin Heidegger, *Basic Writings*, ed. David Farrell Krell (New York: Harper Classics, 2008), and my discussion in Michael P. Steinberg, *Judaism Musical and Unmusical* (Chicago: University of Chicago Press, 2007), 86–94.

9. Cheah, *Orchestra beyond Borders*, 123.

10. The address appears as an appendix in Cheah, *Orchestra beyond Borders*, here at p. 276.

11. Ibid.

12. Cheah, *Orchestra beyond Borders*, 114.

INDEX

. . . .

Page numbers written in italics refer to illustrations.